THE RELATIONSHIP BETWEEN EUROPEAN COMMUNITY LAW AND NATIONAL LAW: THE CASES

VOLUME 2

This is the second volume of the only comprehensive collection of court decisions dealing exclusively with the "constitutional" relationship between European Community law and the national laws of the Member States. The first volume covered the period 1962 to 1993 and contained ninety decisions. This volume contains a further fifty-five decisions given between 1994 and 2001 by both the Community's Court of Justice (ten cases) and the courts of the fifteen Member States (forty-five cases). Major recurring topics of the decisions are the supremacy and direct effect of Community law, its impact on national sovereignty and constitutional rights, and the remedies available before national courts for its enforcement. All the texts are presented in English, having been translated wherever necessary. Each decision is preceded by a concise summary and key-word headings. The volume also includes a systematic introduction, digest of key-word headings, table of cases and detailed index.

ANDREW OPPENHEIMER is a Fellow of the Lauterpacht Research Centre for International Law and a Research Fellow in European Law at the University of Durham. He is Associate Editor (Civil Law Jurisdictions) of the *International Law Reports* and a member of the Editorial Board of the *International Environmental Law Reports*. He is a barrister and a legal translator and has carried out extensive research into European Community law at the Universities of Brussels, Cambridge and Durham.

THE RELATIONSHIP BETWEEN EUROPEAN COMMUNITY LAW AND NATIONAL LAW: THE CASES

VOLUME 2

Lauterpacht Research Centre for International Law
University of Cambridge

THE RELATIONSHIP BETWEEN EUROPEAN COMMUNITY LAW AND NATIONAL LAW: THE CASES

VOLUME 2

Edited
with an Introduction by

ANDREW OPPENHEIMER, MA (CANTAB), BARRISTER

Licencié spécial en droit européen de l'Institut d'Etudes Européennes
de l'Université Libre de Bruxelles
Fellow of the Lauterpacht Research Centre for International Law, University of Cambridge
Research Fellow in European Law, University of Durham

CAMBRIDGE
UNIVERSITY PRESS

PUBLISHED BY THE PRESS SYNDICATE OF THE UNIVERSITY OF CAMBRIDGE
The Pitt Building, Trumpington Street, Cambridge CB2 1RP, United Kingdom

CAMBRIDGE UNIVERSITY PRESS
The Edinburgh Building, Cambridge, CB2 2RU, UK
40 West 20th Street, New York, NY 10011-4211, USA
477 Williamstown Road, Port Melbourne, VIC 3207, Australia
Ruiz de Alarcón 13, 28014 Madrid, Spain
Dock House, The Waterfront, Cape Town 8001, South Africa

http://www.cambridge.org

First published 2003

Printed in the United Kingdom at the University Press, Cambridge

Typeface Baskerville Monotype 11/11.5 pt. *System* LaTeX 2ε [TB]

A catalogue record for this book is available from the British Library

ISBN 0 521 63098 3 hardback

To Sir Elihu Lauterpacht CBE QC

Mentor and friend for many years

CONTENTS

PREFACE

This is a companion volume to the first volume with the same title, which was published in 1994. It contains fifty-five cases devoted to the relationship between European Community law and the national laws of the Member States. As with the first volume, the decisions fall into two categories: those emanating from the national courts and reflecting the relationship as perceived from the standpoint of the individual Member States with their respective legal traditions; and those decided by the Court of Justice of the European Community in the course of its development of the principles governing the Community legal order.

The forty-five national cases in this volume represent most of the leading decisions rendered by the courts of all fifteen of the Member States on the subject, between 1994 and 2001. Forty-one of the decisions are printed with full-length texts, translated into English wherever necessary, with a further four decisions being covered in notes. The first volume contained some seventy national cases and covered the period from the inception of the Community until 1993.

The volume also contains ten of the leading decisions of the Court of Justice of the European Community rendered between 1994 and 2001, six of which have been reproduced in full, with a further four being covered in notes. One decision of the European Court of Human Rights is also included because of its bearing on Community law. The first volume contained some twenty leading decisions of the Court of Justice of the Community rendered between 1962 and 1993. Once again, due to limitations of space, only a small number of decisions of the Court of Justice could be included. Those selected have been chosen either because they are clearly of fundamental importance or because they contribute most to a proper understanding of the national decisions contained in the volume.

The decisions of the Court of Justice and the European Court of Human Rights are printed first, in chronological order. The decisions of the courts of the Member States follow, arranged according to countries, in chronological order within each country. The only exceptions are the decision of the Court of Justice in *Factortame* and the decision of the German Supreme Court in *Brasserie du Pêcheur* which, for ease of reference, are printed together with the *Factortame* proceedings before the courts of the United Kingdom.

With regard to editorial policy, reference should be made to the section on *Editorial Points* contained in the Preface to the first volume.

ACKNOWLEDGMENTS

Three people in particular have, as with the first volume, given considerable assistance to this project for which I am deeply grateful. Sir Elihu Lauterpacht CBE QC, Honorary Professor of International Law, University of Cambridge, and Christopher Greenwood QC, Professor of International Law, London School of Economics and Political Science, who are the joint editors of the *International Law Reports*, have both given much encouragement and also allowed me to take time off from my responsibilities, as Associate Editor of those *Reports*, in order to complete this project. Jean-Victor Louis, Professor at the Free University of Brussels, has again given much valuable advice, particularly in drawing my attention to additional cases. Professors Rosa Greaves and Colin Warbrick have also helped by providing a stimulating environment for research and teaching at the University of Durham.

The English translations of the decisions of the Danish Supreme Court in *Carlsen* v. *Rasmussen* were provided by the Danish Foreign Ministry. The English translation of the *Adria-Wien Pipeline* decision of the Austrian Constitutional Court is based upon a text printed in the *Human Rights Law Journal* published by N. P. Engel. The English translation of the *Brasserie du Pêcheur* decision of the German Supreme Court is reproduced from the *Common Market Law Reports*, published by Sweet & Maxwell.

The remaining translations and summaries are mainly my own responsibility, but I have received much valuable assistance from the following: Mr Tim Johnston translated most of the German and Italian decisions; Mr Emmanuel Maganaris translated the Greek decisions; Mr Andrew Muttitt translated most of the Spanish and Portuguese decisions; Justice Goran Schader translated the Swedish decision; and Mr Geoffrey Thomas translated some of the Austrian and German decisions.

Advice, clarifications or references to additional cases have been provided by: Professor Bruno De Witte, Mr Niilo Jääskinen, Professor Henry Schermers, Professor David Vaughan QC, Professor Joe Verhoeven, Counsellors at the Embassies of Austria and Germany, staff at the Research and Documentation Department and the Information Office of the Court of Justice in Luxembourg, and staff at the libraries of the Institute of Advanced Legal Studies of the University of London and the University of Durham.

The index was compiled by Mr John Jeffries. Mrs Diane Ilott checked the copy; Mr Adrian Lee read the proofs. I would like to thank the publishers, Cambridge University Press, for the care with which they have produced this volume and, in particular, Ms Finola O'Sullivan and Dr Jennie Rubio, for all their help.

To all those who have thus contributed to this truly European and therefore, at times, somewhat daunting undertaking(!), I offer my warmest thanks.

Finally, I would like to thank my wife Judy and our children for their love, understanding and support.

Law Department
University of Durham

ANDREW OPPENHEIMER

October 2002

TABLE OF CASES

(Cases are reported in full unless the word "note" appears after the page number of the report.)

COURT OF JUSTICE OF THE EUROPEAN COMMUNITY

EUROPEAN COURT OF HUMAN RIGHTS

COURTS OF THE MEMBER STATES

Austria

Belgium

DIGEST OF CASES

LIST OF MAIN HEADINGS

Supremacy

Community law and subsequent national law

—Consequences for contrary national law

Constitutions and Community law

DIGEST OF CASES

(This Digest does not include entries for cases which are covered only in Notes in the present Volume.)

Direct Effect *(cont.)*

having retroactive effect — Whether directive may be relied upon by individuals before national courts in relation to period prior to extension of time limit — Council Directive 77/388—Harmonization of "VAT"—France, *Conseil d'Etat*

Minister for the Budget v. *SA Jacques Dangeville; SA Cabinet Revert et Badelon* 207

Directives — Conditions for direct effect — Improper implementation of directive in national law—Whether directive may be relied upon by individuals before national courts—Council Directive 79/7 on equal treatment in social security matters—Ireland, High Court

Tate and Robinson v. *Minister for Social Welfare and Attorney General* 328

Directives — Conditions for direct effect — Failure of Member State to implement provisions of directive by specified time—Whether directive may be relied upon by individuals against other individuals or only against the State and its organs—Scope of legal effects of non-implemented directive which cannot be invoked by individuals—Council Directive 85/577—Consumer protection—Italy, Court of Cassation

Recreb Srl v. *Salustri (Case No 2369/96)* 381

Directives — Conditions for direct effect — Failure of Member State to implement provisions of directive by specified time—EC Treaty, Article 189—Whether directive may be relied upon by individuals before national courts — Whether provisions sufficiently precise and unconditional — Directive conferring margin of discretion on Member States — Council Directive 79/409 — Conservation of wild birds — Portugal, Supreme Administrative Court

League for Environmental Protection v. *Council of Ministers* 407

Directives — Conditions for direct effect — Failure of Member State to implement directive correctly — Whether directive may be relied upon by individuals before national courts—Bodies against which directive may be relied upon — Emanation of the State — Definition — Whether definition laid down by European Court of Justice conclusive—Council Directive 77/187 on Acquired Rights—United Kingdom, Court of Appeal

National Union of Teachers and Others v. *Governing Body of St Mary's Church of England (Aided) Junior School and Others* 457

Directives — Conditions for direct effect — Whether directive creating rights which may be relied upon by individuals before national courts—Whether content of rights identifiable on

legislature — Whether State regarded as single entity in respect of liability for breaches of international commitments irrespective of organ responsible — Article 215 of EC Treaty concerning non-contractual liability of Community institutions — Whether evidence of general principle that public authorities should make good damage caused in performance of their duties — Court of Justice of the European Community

Brasserie du Pêcheur SA v. *Federal Republic of Germany; R* v. *Secretary of State for Transport, ex parte Factortame Ltd and Others (Joined Cases C-46/93 and C-48/93)* 474

Remedies — Claim against Member State — Breach of Community law for which Member State responsible—Conditions for State liability — Whether governed by Community law or national law — Whether conditions in principle the same whether Member State or Community institution incurring liability — Requirement that breach of Community law be sufficiently serious—Test of whether Member State or Community institution has manifestly and gravely disregarded the limits of its discretion—Whether any requirement to prove fault—Deliberate adoption of legislation in breach of Community law—Test of whether national legislature clearly able to determine that legislation is contrary to Community law at the time of its adoption — Relevance of position already taken by Court of Justice and Commission — Court of Justice of the European Community; Germany, Federal Supreme Court; United Kingdom, House of Lords

Brasserie du Pêcheur SA v. *Federal Republic of Germany; R* v. *Secretary of State for Transport, ex parte Factortame Ltd and Others (Joined Cases C-46/93 and C-48/93)* 474

Remedies — Claim against Member State — Breach of Community law for which Member State responsible—Damages—Grounds for awarding damages—Loss suffered by individuals—Scope of right to reparation under Community law — Scope of applicability of national rules on liability — Requirement that conditions should be no less favourable than those applicable to similar domestic claims — Community rules governing claims brought before national courts against Member States — Requirement that reparation must be commensurate with loss or damage sustained — Requirement that loss of profits must be claimable — Requirement that exemplary or other special damages must be available if such damages could be awarded under domestic law — Requirement that reparation should also cover loss sustained prior to court judgment finding infringement of Community law — Court of Justice of the European Community; United Kingdom, House of Lords

Brasserie du Pêcheur SA v. *Federal Republic of Germany; R* v. *Secretary of State for Transport, ex parte Factortame Ltd and Others (Joined Cases C-46/93 and C-48/93)* 474

Enforcement in National Courts *(cont.)*

Legal Order in General (*cont.*)

States—Role of national courts in application of Community law—Luxembourg, Court of Appeal

Soares Teixeira v. *Le Foyer SA* 395

Special character — Effect on legal order of possible entry of Community into institutional system of European Convention on Human Rights — Whether accession of the Community to the Convention would entail a substantial change in the Community system for the protection of human rights, requiring amendment of EC Treaties — Court of Justice of the European Community

Re Accession of the European Community to the Convention for the Protection of Human Rights and Fundamental Freedoms (Opinion 2/94) 45

Special character — Nature of obligations undertaken by Member States — Existing treaty obligations — EC Treaty, Article 234 — Whether authorizing Member States to exercise rights in intra-Community relations under treaties concluded prior to the EC Treaty which conflict with Community obligations—European Convention on Establishment, 1955, Article 13 — Whether capable of constituting derogation from Article 48(4) of EC Treaty—Court of Justice of the European Community

Commission of the European Communities v. Grand Duchy of Luxembourg (Case C-473/93) 72

Special character — Community treaties forming part of legal order — Transfer of competences to Community institutions — Effect of European Convention on Human Rights on exercise of powers by Member States within the framework of Community legal order—Whether Member States remaining responsible within Convention system for consequences of Community action—European Court of Human Rights

Matthews v. *United Kingdom* 108

Special character — Contrast with regimes established by other international treaties—Effect of Community legal order on sovereignty of Member States—Whether Member States retaining status as fully independent States recognized with formal equality under public international law—Germany, Federal Constitutional Court

European Parliament Unequal Representation Case (Case No 2 BvR 635/95) 253

Special character — Nature of obligations undertaken by Member States under EC Treaty — Requirement of uniform application of Community law in Member States — Whether

National Constitutions

Powers *(cont.)*

Article 61 — Whether limiting scope of application of Article 48 of EC Treaty — Protocol to EC Treaty on Grand Duchy of Luxembourg, Article 2 — Scope of right of Grand Duchy to have its special demographic situation taken into account — EC rules on freedom of movement of workers — Scope of permissible derogations — Nationality requirement for employment in public service — EC Treaty, Article 48(4) — Court of Justice of the European Community

Commission of the European Communities v. *Grand Duchy of Luxembourg (Case C-473/93)* 72

Extension by treaty — Treaty on European Union, 1992 — Legal basis for extension of powers of European Community — Principle of conferred powers contained in EC Treaty — Definition — Whether Community institutions competent to determine their own powers — Article 235 of Treaty — Scope of application — Denmark, Supreme Court

Carlsen and Others v. *Rasmussen* 175

Extension by treaty — Treaty of Amsterdam, 1997 — Nature of obligations entered into by Member States — Introduction of measures concerning asylum, immigration and the crossing of internal borders of Member States—Provisions for taking such measures by qualified majority voting and the "co-decision" procedure, after a transitional period of five years — Whether requiring transfer of sovereign powers from Member States — France, Constitutional Council

Re Treaty of Amsterdam, 1997, amending the Treaty on European Union and the Treaties Establishing the European Communities (Decision No 97-394 DC) 219

Extension by treaty — Legal basis for powers of European Community — Principle of conferred powers contained in EC Treaty — Definition — Articles 100 and 235 of Treaty — Scope of application—Germany, Federal Constitutional Court

Television Broadcasting Directive Case (Case No 2 BvG 1/89) 232

Extension by treaty — Treaty on European Union, 1992 — Nature of obligations entered into by Member States — Provisions for implementation of third stage of EMU — Whether requiring further transfer of sovereign powers from Member States — Germany, Federal Constitutional Court

European Monetary Union Constitutionality Case (Cases Nos 2 BvR 1877/97 and 50/98) 258

Extension by treaty — Financial contributions by Member States — Replacement by Community's own resources — Treaty on European Union, 1992 — Protocol and Agreement on Social Policy — Exemption for United Kingdom — Ratification of treaty by United Kingdom — Whether constituting parliamentary approval for indirect contributions by United Kingdom to administrative costs associated with Agreement, through contribution to Community's own resources — Scope of duty of United Kingdom to contribute to Community budget — United Kingdom, Scottish Court of Session

Monckton v. *Lord Advocate* 655

Supremacy

Community law and subsequent national law — Consequences for contrary national law — Automatic inapplicability of conflicting national provisions — Whether national provisions thereby rendered non-existent or national courts simply under duty to disapply them — Court of Justice of the European Community

Ministero delle Finanze v. *IN. CO. GE.'90 Srl and Others (Joined Cases C-10/97 to C-22/97)* 85

Community law and subsequent national law — Consequences for contrary national law — Duty of national courts not to apply conflicting national provisions — Principle that uniformity and full effectiveness of Community law must be ensured — Whether national constitutional court entitled to wait to examine possible incompatibility of domestic provision with Community law until after review of provision for compatibility with the Constitution—Austria, Constitutional Court

Austrian Tourism Promotion Tax Case (Case No G 2/97) 137

Community law and subsequent national law — Consequences for contrary national law—Duty of national courts not to apply conflicting national provisions — Finland, Supreme Administrative Court

VAT Deduction Rights Case 193

Community law and subsequent national law — Consequences for contrary national law — Duty of national courts not to apply conflicting national provisions — Finding of European Court of Justice that national provisions violating Article 30 of EC Treaty — Whether national provisions automatically inapplicable — Rules restricting advertising of imported alcoholic products—France, Court of Cassation

United Distillers France v. *Agent Judiciaire du Trésor Public* 195

Community law and subsequent national law — Consequences for contrary national law — Duty of national courts not to apply national provision in conflict with

Supremacy (*cont.*)

general principle of Community law — Right of individuals to compensation for loss suffered as a result of breach of Community law by a Member State — Scope of right — Italy, Court of Cassation

President of Council of Ministers v. *Mariotti and Others (Case No 10617)* 371

Community law and subsequent national law — Consequences for contrary national law — Duty of national courts not to apply conflicting national provisions — Whether conflicting national provisions automatically inapplicable — Whether fundamental constitutional rights could take precedence over Community law — Italy, Court of Cassation

Talamucci v. *Minister of Health (Case No 1512)* 388

Community law and subsequent national law — Consequences for contrary national law — Duty of national courts not to apply national provision even if subsequently enacted—Luxembourg, Court of Appeal

Soares Teixeira v. *Le Foyer SA* 395

Community law and subsequent national law — Consequences for contrary national law — Whether ordinary courts under automatic duty not to apply conflicting national provisions — Whether Community law endowed with constitutional rank and force—Spain, Constitutional Court

Martinez Perez (Case No 45/96) 423

Community law and subsequent national law — Consequences for contrary national law — Duty of national courts not to apply national provisions—Principle that effectiveness of Community law must be ensured — Sweden, Supreme Administrative Court

Lassagard AB (Case No 219/1997) 428

Community law and subsequent national law — Consequences for contrary national law — Whether existing national provisions automatically inapplicable—Whether declaration that conflicting national provisions incompatible with Community law sufficient — Employment discrimination — EC Treaty, Article 119 — Equal Pay Directive 75/117 — Equal Treatment Directive 76/207 — United Kingdom, House of Lords

R v. *Secretary of State for Employment, ex parte Equal Opportunities Commission and Another* 437

Community law and subsequent national law — National administrative measure restricting right of free movement between

Supremacy (*cont.*)

TREATY ARTICLES

AMENDED NUMBERING

Amended numbering for the articles of the EC Treaty and the Treaty on European Union was introduced by the Treaty of Amsterdam and became applicable on 1 May 1999. Since almost all the decisions contained in this volume refer only to the old numbering it was decided to retain the old numbering throughout the body of the text. For ease of reference, the new numbering of those articles referred to in this volume is set out below:

Old numbering	*New numbering*
Treaty on European Union	
Article F	Article 6
European Community Treaty	
Article 3	Article 3
Article 3a	Article 4
Article 3b	Article 5
Article 3c	Article 6
Article 30	Article 28
Article 34	Article 29
Article 36	Article 30
Article 38	Article 32
Article 39	Article 33
Article 40	Article 34
Article 42	Article 36
Article 48	Article 39
Article 52	Article 43
Article 93	Article 88
Article 100	Article 94
Article 119	Article 141
Article 169	Article 226
Article 170	Article 227
Article 171	Article 228
Article 173	Article 230
Article 175	Article 232
Article 177	Article 234
Article 189	Article 249
Article 228	Article 300
Article 233	Article 306
Article 234	Article 307
Article 235	Article 308

ABBREVIATIONS

AC	Appeal Cases (Law Reports)
AJDA	Actualité Juridique Droit Administratif
All ER	All England Law Reports
BGBI	Bundesgesetzblatt
BGHZ	Entscheidungen des Bundesgerichtshofs (Zivilsachen)
Bull Civ	Bulletin des Décisions de la Cour de Cassation (Chambre Civile)
BVerfGE	Entscheidungen des Bundesverfassungsgerichts
CDE	Cahiers de Droit Européen
CJEC	Court of Justice of the European Community
CMLR	Common Market Law Reports
CML Rev	Common Market Law Review
EAEC	European Atomic Energy Community
EC	European Community
ECHR	European Convention on Human Rights; European Court of Human Rights
ECJ	See CJEC
ECR	European Court Reports
ECSC	European Coal and Steel Community
ECT	Treaty establishing the European Community
ECU	European Currency Unit
EEC	European Economic Community
EL Rev/EuLR	European Law Review
ESCB	European System of Central Banks
EuGRZ	Europäische Grundrechte Zeitschrift
EuR	Europarecht
EUT	Treaty on European Union
(IL)Foro It	Il Foro Italiano
GATT	General Agreement on Tariffs and Trade
GG	Grundgesetz
ICLQ	International and Comparative Law Quarterly
ICR	Industrial Court Reports
IR	Irish Reports
IRLR	Industrial Relations Law Reports
JBL	Juristiche Blätter
JT	Journal des Tribunaux
JZ	Juristenzeitung
NJW	Neue Juristische Wochenschrift
OJEC	Official Journal of the European Communities
Pas Lux	Pascrisie Luxembourgeoise
QB/QBD	Queen's Bench Division (Law Reports)
RDI	Rivista di Diritto Internazionale
Rec Lebon	Recueil des Décisions du Conseil d'Etat
REDI	Revista Espanola de Derecho Internacional
RFDA	Revue Française de Droit Administratif
RMC	Revue du Marché Commun

RTDE	Revue Trimestrielle de Droit Européen
SC	Session Cases (Law Reports)
SLT	Scots Law Times
UFR	Ugeskrift for Retsvaesen
WLR	Weekly Law Reports
ZaöRV	Zeitschrift für ausländisches öffentliches Recht und Völkerrecht

INTRODUCTION

This introduction is written as a supplement to the Introduction to the first volume of this work and should be read in conjunction with it. Its purpose is to present the principal points covered in the fifty-five cases contained in this book (covering the period 1994 to 2001) in the same systematic framework as the ninety cases contained in the first volume (covering the period 1962 to 1993). It is not intended as a detailed commentary on the individual cases.[1]

I.

The purpose of the two volumes of this book is to present the basic principles of the legal order of the European Community, as elaborated in the case-law of the European Court of Justice on the basis of the provisions of the EC Treaty, and to show how the Member States have responded to the development of those principles through the case-law of their national courts. As noted in the Introduction to the first volume (p. 2), the relationship between the European Court of Justice and national courts is best described as one of permanent dialogue.

This *judicial* dialogue has continued, during the eight-year period covered by this second volume, against a background of almost continuous *political* deliberations, in conferences and treaty negotiations, involving the governments of the Member States and aimed at amending the provisions of the existing treaties on a range of institutional matters. As soon as the Maastricht Treaty entered into force in November 1993, preparations began for a new inter-governmental conference, culminating in the Amsterdam Treaty which was signed in June 1997 and entered into force in May 1999 after the last ratification was lodged. That treaty opened the way for negotiations for the enlargement of the Community to begin. But certain key institutional reforms, required in the perspective of enlargement, were "left over". Preparations for a new inter-governmental conference began immediately, culminating in the Nice Treaty signed in February 2001. By June 2002 the parliaments of all the Member States except Ireland had adopted the Treaty. A "no" vote in a referendum of the Irish people was followed by a "yes" in a second referendum in October 2002, clearing the way for the final

[1] Commentaries on the national case-law of the various Member States are contained in a number of excellent recently published collections, including: O'Keefe (ed.), *Judicial Review in European Union Law, Liber Amicorum in Honour of Lord Slynn* (Kluwer Law Publishing, 2000); Slaughter, Sweet and Weiler (eds.), *The European Court and National Courts* (Hart Publishing, 1998); *Annual Reports on Monitoring the Application of Community Law* (published by the European Commission) (Report for 2000 published in August 2001); and the ongoing series of review articles on the application of EC Law in individual Member States published in the *Common Market Law Review* (particularly from 1998 onwards).

ratification of the Nice Treaty. Meanwhile negotiations with applicant countries have continued and a further inter-governmental conference, planned for 2004, is being prepared by the Convention on the Future of the European Union, established in December 2001.

The Court of Justice itself has, from time to time, become involved in the debates on proposed treaty amendments. For instance, in 1994 it was called upon by the Council of the European Community to submit an opinion on the possible accession of the Community to the European Convention on Human Rights (*Opinion 2/94*, 1996, p. 45). In 1995 it was asked to submit a report to the Inter-governmental Conference on the revision of the Treaty on European Union. In that report, the Court of Justice stressed that "the success of Community law in embedding itself so thoroughly in the legal life of the Member States is due to its having been perceived, interpreted and applied . . . by the courts and tribunals of all the Member States as a uniform body of rules upon which individuals may rely in their national courts".[2]

Nevertheless, controversy has continued to surround both the role of the Court of Justice in the development of the principles of the Community legal order and the attitude of the courts of the Member States to the status of Community law in national legal systems. That controversy relates, in particular, to the extent of the transfer of sovereignty from the Member States to the Community, the scope of fundamental rights protection within the Community and the relationship between national constitutional courts and the European Court of Justice.[3] These issues, as well as the so-called "unwritten constitutional principles" of supremacy, direct effect and State liability, provide the main subject matter of the judicial decisions contained in this volume.

II. SUPREMACY

The Principle

The three new Member States which joined the European Community in 1995 appear to have rapidly and readily recognized the supremacy of Community law. This was confirmed in Finland by the Supreme Administrative Court in the *VAT Deduction Rights Case* (1996, p. 193), in Sweden by the Supreme Administrative Court in *Lassagard* (1997, p. 428), and in Austria by the Constitutional Court in the *Austrian Tourism Promotion Tax Case* (1998, p. 137). Supremacy in these countries appears to

[2] *Report of the Court of Justice on Certain Aspects of the Application of the Treaty on European Union*, May 1995, p. 2.

[3] For detailed consideration of these matters see, *inter alia*, Slaughter, Sweet and Weiler, *The European Court and National Courts*, pt 2 and De Witte, Direct Effect, Supremacy and the Nature of the Community Legal Order, in Craig and De Burca, *The Evolution of EU Law* (Oxford University Press, 1999).

have been recognized on the basis of the jurisprudence of the European Court of Justice (*Costa* v. *ENEL*, 1964, Volume 1, p. 50) in the absence of specific constitutional provisions regulating the status of EC law in national law. The position is discussed in Notes concerning Austria (p. 144), Finland (p. 193) and Sweden (p. 435).

With regard to the old Member States, in Belgium the *Conseil d'Etat* in *Orfinger* (1996, p. 162) aligned itself with the position of the Court of Cassation in the *Le Ski Case* (1971, Volume 1, p. 245) and based recognition of the inherent supremacy of EC law on the settled jurisprudence of the European Court of Justice. The Luxembourg Court of Appeal took a similar position in the *Teixeira Case* (1997, p. 395). In Ireland too, supremacy is now routinely recognized by the Supreme Court without any need being felt to refer to any constitutional provision (see *Meagher*, 1993, p. 308 and *Nathan*, 1996, p. 352).[4] On the other hand, in France it appears that the courts continue to base recognition of supremacy on Article 55 of the Constitution[5] and the *Conseil d'Etat* expressly referred to this provision in *Association of Patients for Alternative Medicine* (1999, p. 229). In Greece, however, the Council of State has cast doubt on the scope of its acceptance of the principle of the supremacy of Community law in a series of decisions including *Diamantopoulos* (1997-8, p. 286) and *Katsarou* (1998, p. 300).[6]

The potential for conflict between the requirements of the principle of supremacy of Community law and national constitutional provisions continues to be a major issue in cases before national courts and this is examined in section V below.

Consequences for National Courts

In a significant number of important decisions since 1993, the consequences of the supremacy of Community law, where a conflict actually arose with the provisions of national law, have been elucidated by the courts. The European Court of Justice confirmed in *Ministero delle Finanze* v. *IN.CO.GE.'90* (1998, p. 85) that its *Simmenthal* judgment (1978, Volume 1, p. 73) required national courts immediately to disapply rules of national law incompatible with Community law, although this did not require the national courts to treat conflicting rules of national law as void *ab initio*, as if they had never existed.

The duty of national courts immediately to disapply conflicting national provisions in such circumstances has been upheld in decisions

[4] For discussion of these and other Irish judgments see Finlay and Hyland, Duties of Co-operation of National Courts and the Community Institutions under Article 10 EC, *Irish Journal of European Law* 2000, p. 267.

[5] See Dutheil de la Rochère, The Attitude of French Courts towards ECJ Caselaw, in O'Keefe, *Judicial Review in European Union Law*.

[6] For criticism of these decisions see articles by Maganaris: EL Rev 1998, p. 179; 1999, p. 426 and 2000, p. 200.

in France by the Court of Cassation in *United Distillers* (1995, p. 195), in Italy by the Court of Cassation in *Talamucci* (1998, p. 388) and in Luxembourg by the Court of Appeal in *Soares Teixeira* (1997, p. 395). In the United Kingdom, in the *Equal Opportunities Commission Case* (1994, p. 437) the English House of Lords held that judicial review proceedings were available in order to challenge provisions of national legislation as incompatible with Community law and the appropriate remedy was a declaration to that effect.[7] In Austria, however, it appears from the *Austrian Tourism Promotion Tax Case* (1998, p. 137) that the Constitutional Court considers that it is entitled to postpone examination of the possible incompatibility of national provisions with EC law until the conclusion of constitutional review proceedings. Such a position is incompatible with the *Simmenthal* judgment of the Court of Justice (Note, Volume 1 p. 73).

III. DIRECT EFFECT

The Principle

Acceptance of the principle of direct effect has not posed any discernible problems for the courts of the new Member States which joined the Community in 1995.[8] In both the new and the old Member States, direct effect of treaty provisions satisfying the conditions laid down by the Court of Justice has routinely been accepted by national courts as, for instance, by the Austrian Constitutional Court in the *Adria-Wien Pipeline Case* (1999, p. 146), the Luxembourg Court of Appeal in *Soares Teixeira* (1997, p. 395) and the Spanish Constitutional Court in the *Moroccan Seaman Case* (1995, p. 419).

Directives

The jurisprudence of the Court of Justice on the conditions for the direct effect of directives has continued to provoke interesting judgments in the national courts. In *Faccini Dori* (1994, p. 19) the Court of Justice confirmed and clarified the reasons for its refusal to grant so-called horizontal direct effect to non-implemented directives in relations between individuals. The importance of the issue was reflected in the fact that the Court invited all the Member States to submit their observations on the matter. The Court followed the view of nearly all the Member States

[7] For discussion of the significance of this decision for the enforcement of the principle of supremacy in British courts see Chalmers, The Application of Community Law in the United Kingdom, 1994-98, CML Rev 2000, p. 83 at pp. 87-9.

[8] See Bernitz, Sweden's Implementation and Application of European Law, CML Rev 2001, p. 903 at p. 927; Fisher and Lengauer, The Adaptation of the Austrian Legal System to EU Membership, CML Rev 2000, p. 763 at p. 774; Jaaskinen, The Application of Community Law in Finland, CML Rev 1999, p. 407 at p. 420.

as well as the European Commission, albeit against the view of several distinguished Advocates-General, and upheld the approach which it had followed since the *Marshall* judgment (1986, Volume 1, p. 136).[9] Nevertheless, the Italian Court of Cassation subsequently found an ingenious method (based on general principles of equity) to circumvent the lack of direct effect of the directive at issue in *Recreb* (1996, p. 381).[10]

The direct effect of directives in so-called vertical relations has been successfully relied upon by individuals against the State, in Austria before the Constitutional Court in the *Tyrolean Provincial Allocation Office Case* (1996, p. 135), in France before the *Conseil d'Etat* in *Revert et Badelon* (1996, p. 207), in Ireland before the High Court in *Tate and Robinson* (1995, p. 328) and in the United Kingdom before the English Court of Appeal in the *National Union of Teachers Case* (1996, p. 457). On the other hand, in Portugal the Supreme Administrative Court refused to allow a public interest group to rely on an environmental protection directive against the State in the *League for Environmental Protection Case* (1995, p. 407). In France, in *SA Lilly* the *Conseil d'Etat* held that it would be unconscionable to allow the State itself to rely on an unimplemented directive against individuals (1995, p. 198).

However, national courts have sometimes been reluctant to make a reference to the Court of Justice for a preliminary ruling even though the precise requirements of the directive might have been open to doubt (see, for instance, the judgment in the United Kingdom of the English House of Lords in the *Three Rivers District Council Case* (2000, p. 627)). This problem is discussed further below, at p. 15.

Interpretation of National Law

The lack of direct effect of directives in relations between individuals has continued to be ameliorated by the requirement (confirmed by the Court of Justice in *Faccini Dori* (1994, p. 19) that national courts when applying national law, whether adopted either before or after the directive in question, must interpret the law, as far as possible, in the light of the purpose and wording of the directive. Accordingly, it has been held that national legislation introduced to implement directives must be interpreted in accordance with the directive concerned: in Austria by the Constitutional Court in the *Natural Mineral Water Case* (1995, p. 133), in Belgium by the Court of Arbitration in the *Fédération Belge Case* (1997, p. 168) and in Italy by the Constitutional Court in *Messaggero Servizi* (1995, p. 378).

[9] For discussion of the issues see, *inter alia*, Arnull, *The European Union and its Court of Justice* (Oxford University Press, 1999), pp. 137 ff.

[10] See Adinolfi, The Judicial Application of Community Law in Italy (1981-97), CML Rev 1998, p. 1313 at pp. 1332-3.

IV. ENFORCEMENT IN NATIONAL COURTS

Fundamental to the development of the principles of direct effect and supremacy by the Court of Justice has been its insistence that there must be uniformity in both the interpretation (see *Van Gend en Loos*, 1963, Volume 1, p. 44) and application (see *Simmenthal*, 1978, Volume 1, p. 100) of Community law in all the Member States. By contrast, the rules governing procedures for the enforcement in the Member States of rights recognized by Community law and remedies for their infringement have continued to be characterized by a lack of uniformity and the Court of Justice has limited itself to the imposition and continuing refinement of a general requirement that remedies should satisfy the principle of effectiveness.[11]

This principle has led the Court of Justice to develop, *inter alia*, rules concerning the availability of judicial review (*Johnston*, 1986, Volume 1, Note, p. 460) and interim relief (*Factortame*, 1990, Volume 1, p. 823). Subsequently, the Court of Justice took the bold step of establishing the principle that Member States could be liable in damages to individuals for breaches of Community law for which they were responsible. The basis of this liability was that it was indispensable for the full effectiveness of Community law and consequently inherent in the EC Treaty (*Francovich*, 1991, Volume 1, p. 188). This judgment has been followed by a series of further judgments of the Court. First, the Court established the conditions under which Member States could incur liability and further explained the basis of that liability in the EC Treaty, applying it to the case of action by a national legislature in breach of Community treaty provisions (*Brasserie du Pêcheur* and *Factortame*, 1996, p. 474). Subsequently, the Court clarified the application of the conditions for establishing liability in a range of different situations, including the failure to transpose a directive into national law (*Dillenkofer*, 1996, Note, p. 588), the incorrect transposition of a directive into national law (*British Telecommunications*, 1996, Note, p. 588) and unlawful administrative action by the State (*Hedley Lomas*, 1996, Note, p. 588).[12]

The impact of these judgments of the Court of Justice in requiring modification of national laws, so as to provide for a damages remedy against the State in the appropriate circumstances, has already been considerable and continues.[13] Applying the conditions elaborated by the

[11] See, for instance, the excellent general accounts by Arnull, *The European Union and its Court of Justice*, chapter 5; Craig and De Burca, *EU Law* (Oxford University Press, 1998), chapter 5; and Tridimas, *The General Principles of EC Law* (Oxford University Press, 1998), chapter 8.

[12] For commentary on the above judgments see Casenote by Oliver, CML Rev 1997, p. 635 and Waelbroeck, Treaty Violations and Liability of Member States, in Heukels and McDonnell (eds.), *The Action for Damages in Community Law* (TMC Asser Institute, 1997), chapter 17. For a discussion of more recent developments in the case-law of the Court of Justice see Tridimas, Liability for Breach of Community Law: Growing Up and Mellowing Down?, CML Rev 2001, p. 301.

[13] See Van Gerven, Bridging the Unbridgeable: Community and National Tort Laws after *Francovich* and *Brasserie*, ICLQ 1996, p. 507; Barav, State Liability in Damages for Breach of

Court of Justice, the Supreme Court in Germany whilst recognizing that a claim in damages against the State would be possible, held that there was no liability to pay damages in the circumstances of the case (*Brasserie du Pêcheur*, 1996, p. 588) but the House of Lords in the United Kingdom held that damages were payable (*Factortame*, 1999, p. 596). In another case, *Three Rivers District Council*, the House of Lords rejected a claim for damages, holding that no breach of Community law had been established on the facts of that case (2000, p. 627).

In France, little adaptation was required to allow a remedy in damages against the State to be recognized for breach of Community law and this was confirmed by the Court of Cassation in *United Distillers* (1995, p. 195) and by the *Conseil d'Etat* in *Dangeville* (1996, p. 207). In Italy, the Court of Cassation initially only recognized a limited right for individuals to claim damages against the State for breach of Community law (*Mariotti*, 1995, p. 371) but subsequently the Court of Cassation appears to have expanded the scope of State liability so as to allow for full *Francovich*-type liability (1999, Note, p. 377).

These cases should be distinguished from decisions of national courts allowing individuals to recover adequate and effective compensation against the State under the terms of Community directives implemented in national laws and giving individuals the right to claim compensation in the event of infringement of their provisions, based on principles well established in the jurisprudence of the Court of Justice (*Von Colson*, 1984, Volume 1, Note, p. 187; *Marshall*, 1993, Volume 1, Note, p. 165).

V. NATIONAL CONSTITUTIONS[14]

The Constitutional Framework for Community Membership

The new Member States which joined the European Community in 1995 had recourse to varied constitutional devices to provide the legal basis for membership. In Austria membership was possible on the basis of Article 9(2) of the Constitution, which provides for the transfer of sovereign rights to international organizations. In addition, various constitutional amendments were approved, in particular Articles 23a to 23e, providing the framework for the exercise of executive and legislative powers in relation to the European Community and the European Union (see Note, p. 144). In Sweden, a specific constitutional amendment was enacted to Chapter 5, Article 10, of the Instrument of Government,

Community Law in the National Courts, in Heukels and McDonnell, *The Action for Damages in Community Law*, chapter 20; and Vaughan, Rights and Remedies in EC Law: A View from the Trenches, Durham University Law Lecture, November 2001.

[14] For an excellent survey of this subject see Wouters, National Constitutions and the European Union, *Legal Issues of Economic Integration* 2000, p. 25.

providing for the transfer of powers to the European Community (see Note, p. 435). In Finland it was possible to derogate from the Constitution without amending it, through the enactment of an Exception Act, and this procedure was followed (see Note, p. 193).

The constitutional framework for membership of the Community has continued to be the subject of important judicial proceedings before the courts of the old Member States, although there does not appear, as yet, to have been any case involving a fundamental constitutional challenge before the courts of the new Member States.

Judicial Decisions on the Maastricht, Amsterdam and other Community Treaties

In **Belgium**, individuals able to justify an interest or the courts are empowered by Article 107 of the Constitution to refer questions for preliminary rulings by the Court of Arbitration on the constitutionality of laws covered by certain provisions of the Constitution. In the *European School Case* (1994, p. 155), a landmark decision on the scope of its jurisdiction, the Court of Arbitration held that laws giving assent to international treaties (and consequently EC treaties) were also covered by this procedure. No rule of international law gave the power to States to conclude treaties which were contrary to their constitutions. Accordingly, any law giving assent to a treaty could be the subject of constitutional review. In this case the Court of Arbitration, at the instance of parents seeking to avoid the payment of school fees, reviewed a law giving assent to the Statute of the European School and concluded that it did not violate the constitutional right to free education.

In proceedings in **Denmark**, various private individuals sought a declaration against the Danish Prime Minister that the procedure followed for implementing amendments to the EC treaty introduced in the Maastricht Treaty was unconstitutional. According to Danish case-law, such proceedings could only be brought by persons able to establish a legal interest but the Supreme Court held in *Carlsen and Others* v. *Rasmussen* (1996-8, p. 174) that the proceedings were admissible because of the vital and general importance of Danish accession to the amended EC Treaty for the population as a whole. The applicants argued that Article 20(1) of the Danish Constitution authorized the transfer of powers to international organizations only "to such an extent as shall be authorized by statute" and that this condition had not been complied with. In a thorough and wide-ranging judgment on the merits, the Supreme Court (1998, p. 185) dismissed the application. In its judgment, in a manner somewhat comparable in significance to the judgment of the German Federal Constitutional Court in the *Maastricht Treaty Constitutionality Case* (Volume 1, 1993, p. 526), the Supreme Court carefully analysed the scope of the constitutional requirement for the specific attribution of powers and concluded, in particular, that neither the powers of the Community under Article 235 of the EC Treaty, nor the broad competence claimed by the Court of Justice in its case-law on the basis of Article 164 of the Treaty, violated this requirement.[15]

In **France**, pursuant to their powers under Article 54 of the Constitution, the President and Prime Minister jointly referred to the Constitutional Council the question of whether the authorization to ratify the Amsterdam Treaty of 1997, which amended the EC Treaty and the Treaty of European Union, contained any clauses contrary to the Constitution and could therefore only be ratified after a constitutional amendment. Examining the Amsterdam Treaty in the light of the principles contained in the Constitution, the Constitutional Council concluded in *Re Treaty of Amsterdam* (1997, p. 219) that, despite the insertion of Article 88 into the Constitution at the time of the ratification of the Maastricht Treaty, a further constitutional amendment was required to provide expressly for the transfer of certain additional powers necessitated by the Amsterdam Treaty.[16] The necessary constitutional amendments were subsequently enacted (Note, p. 225).

In **Germany** a constitutional complaint was lodged under Article 93 of the Basic Law against the manner in which seats in the European Parliament were allocated by the Treaty on the Accession of the new Member States in 1994. The complaint contested the approval by the *Bundestag* (Federal Parliament) of the Act of Accession. The Federal Constitutional Court, in the *European Parliament Unequal Representation Case* (1995, p. 253), declined to rule on the complaint, holding that it had no prospect of success. European Parliamentary elections could not be judged by the same constitutional criteria as those applicable to German parliamentary elections. Subsequently, four German university professors lodged constitutional complaints against the participation of Germany in the third stage of European monetary union. The Federal Constitutional Court had ruled in the *Maastricht Treaty Constitutionality Case* (1993, Volume 1, p. 526) that German participation in the monetary union was permitted by Articles 23 and 88(2) of the Basic Law. But the complainants argued that Germany had failed to ensure that the strict economic convergence criteria laid down in the Maastricht Treaty were applied, so that their democratic and property rights under Articles 38 and 14 of the Basic Law had been violated. Without ruling on whether the complaints were admissible, the Federal Constitutional Court in the *European Monetary Union Constitutionality Case* (1998, p. 258) dismissed the complaints as manifestly unfounded since

[15] For discussion of the significance of the judgment of the Danish Supreme Court see, *inter alia*, Hoegh, The Danish Maastricht Judgment, EL Rev 1999, p. 80; Rasmussen, Confrontation or Peaceful Co-existence, The Danish Maastricht Ratification Judgment, in O'Keefe, *Judicial Review in European Union Law*, p. 377.

[16] See Boyron, The French Constitution and the Treaty of Amsterdam, *Maastricht Journal of European and Comparative Law* 1999, p. 169 and Monthaan, Amending the Amended French Constitution, EL Rev 2000, p. 592.

the criteria at issue left scope for economic and political forecasting and assessment, which was the responsibility of the Federal Government and parliament, so that individuals had no right to obtain constitutional review.

In the **United Kingdom** a petition for judicial review in *Monckton* v. *Lord Advocate* to the Scottish Court of Session (1994, p. 655) sought a declaration that the payment of money out of the consolidated fund to defray administrative costs arising from the EC Agreement on Social Policy (annexed to the Maastricht Treaty, 1992) was unlawful because the Protocol on Social Policy provided for an "opt-out" for the United Kingdom from participation in the operation of the Agreement. The petition was dismissed on the ground that the administrative costs at issue comprised expenditure properly payable out of the Community budget, to which the United Kingdom was authorized to contribute by the European Communities Act 1972.

The Issue of Sovereignty

The extent to which membership of the European Community involves significant limitation of the sovereignty of the Member States has continued to provoke important pronouncements by the courts and a considerable amount of academic comment.[17] In its famous statement in *Costa* v. *ENEL* (1964, Volume 1, p. 67) the Court of Justice insisted that the transfer of powers from the Member States carried with it a permanent limitation of their sovereign rights. In its judgment in *Commission* v. *Luxembourg* (1996, p. 72) the Court of Justice recognized, however, that the preservation of the Member States' national identities was a legitimate aim respected by the Community legal order and acknowledged by Article F(1) (now 6(3)) of the Treaty on European Union. Nevertheless, such an interest, even where it was constitutionally protected, could not justify the reservation of certain educational posts to nationals contrary to the EC Treaty since respect for national identity could effectively be safeguarded in other ways.[18]

National courts, however, continue to insist that they retain the right of constitutional control over the scope of transfers of sovereign rights to the Community, in accordance with the constitutional principle of the limited specific attribution of powers: Germany, Constitutional Court, *Maastricht Treaty Constitutionality Case* (1993, Volume 1, pp. 556-7);

[17] See, for instance, De Witte, Sovereignty and European Integration, in Slaughter, Sweet and Weiler, *The European Court and National Courts*, p. 277 and Wouters, *Legal Issues of European Integration* 2000, pp. 37-40.

[18] For discussion of the significance of this judgment, see Wouters, *Legal Issues of European Integration* 2000, at pp. 40 and 54.

Denmark, Supreme Court, *Carlsen* v. *Rasmussen* (1998, p. 185); and France, Constitutional Council, *Re Organic Law Concerning Application of Article 88(3) of the Constitution* (1998, p. 228).

In France the Constitutional Council has confirmed in *Re Treaty of Amsterdam* (1997, p. 219) that whilst France may transfer competences to international organizations by agreement, any such agreement infringing the essential conditions for the exercise of national sovereignty requires constitutional revision prior to ratification. This was actually held to be the case in relation to several provisions of the Amsterdam Treaty concerning new areas of competence not covered by Article 88 of the Constitution. In Germany, on the other hand, the Constitutional Court in the *European Monetary Union Constitutionality Case* (1998, p. 258) held that a constitutional challenge to German participation in the third stage of monetary union was unfounded because the necessary authority had been provided in principle by constitutional amendment of Article 23 of the Basic Law, which expressly permitted sovereign rights to be transferred so as to enable German participation in the development of the European Union. The Treaty on European Union, which had been ratified by the German Parliament, laid down the detailed procedures for monetary union and their implementation did not require any additional transfer of sovereignty.

In Belgium, on the other hand, the *Conseil d'Etat* in *Orfinger* (1996, p. 162) (closely following the jurisprudence of the Court of Justice summarized in *Commission* v. *Luxembourg*, referred to above) stated that the application of Community law was not dependent upon constitutional amendment, in the event of a conflict with the Constitution, and was obligatory even in the absence of amendment and even so far as the interpretation of an EC Treaty provision by the Court of Justice was concerned. This approach may be compared with that of the Supreme Court of Denmark in *Carlsen* v. *Rasmussen* (1998, p. 185) which held that the Danish courts would be bound to rule that a Community measure or ruling of the Court of Justice was inapplicable if it exceeded the limits of the transfer of sovereignty brought about by the Act of Accession. In any event, powers could not be transferred to such an extent that Denmark could not be considered an independent State. It should be stressed, however, that none of the above-mentioned statements by national courts actually led them to override a Community measure or a judgment of the Court of Justice. They merely contemplated the possibility as an ultimate power.

Several national courts have also stated categorically that the Member States ultimately retain the right to renounce Community membership or to seek renegotiation of its conditions, particularly in the event of conflict with their national constitutions: compare Belgium, *Conseil d'Etat, Orfinger* (1996, p. 162); Italy, Court of Cassation, *Talamucci* (1998, p. 388) and United Kingdom, Divisional Court, *Rees-Mogg* (1993, Volume 1, p. 923).

The Issue of Democratic Legitimacy

The question of the source and extent of the democratic legitimacy of the European Community has increasingly been the subject of judicial discussion, provoked in particular by the judgment of the Federal Constitutional Court in Germany in the *Maastricht Treaty Constitutionality Case*. In that judgment, the Constitutional Court stressed that any further European unification should be underpinned by a corresponding enhancement of the democratic foundations of the institutions of the Community, as well as the continued operation of a vibrant democracy within the Member States, upon which the Community was built (1993, Volume 1, p. 575). In Denmark the Supreme Court in *Carlsen* v. *Rasmussen* implied a similar conclusion in stating that it was reasonable to assume that the Danish Parliament would have the task of considering whether participation by Denmark in further European integration should be conditional upon any additional democratic control (1998, p. 185).

In another judgment in Germany, in the *European Parliament Unequal Representation Case* (1995, p. 253), the Federal Constitutional Court rejected a complaint that the manner in which seats in the European Parliament were allocated to Germany violated constitutional principles. It was argued that Germany, according to its population size following reunification, should have received a higher allocation of seats. The Constitutional Court, however, dismissed the claim that the principle of equal voting rights contained in the Basic Law had been violated. At the current stage of European integration, the European Parliament served merely to provide additional political underpinning for the policies of the European Community. Exercise of the Community's sovereign powers derived legitimacy from the peoples of the democratic Member States, first and foremost via their national parliaments. Equality of voting rights, which ensured this legitimacy, was therefore guaranteed by the right to vote in national elections.

By contrast, however, the European Court of Human Rights in *Matthews* v. *United Kingdom* (1999, p. 108) appears to have adopted a more stringent approach, from the standpoint of the European Convention on Human Rights, in accepting jurisdiction and upholding a claim by a citizen of Gibraltar that her fundamental rights were violated by her exclusion, by agreement between the Member States, from the right to participate in elections to the European Parliament. The Court of Human Rights held that the exclusion of citizens of Gibraltar violated their right to freedom of expression in the choice of the legislature, enshrined in Article 3 of Protocol No 1 to the European Convention.

The European Parliament represented the principal form of democratic accountability in the European Community system, derived its domestic legitimation from direct elections by universal suffrage and, as such, was the European Community structure best reflecting "effective political democracy".

Judicial Decisions on Secondary Community Law

Scope of constitutional review and protection of fundamental rights by national courts

It was established by the Court of Justice in *Internationale Handelsgesellschaft* (1970, Volume 1, p. 419) that the effect of a Community measure within a Member State could not be affected by allegations that it ran counter to either fundamental national constitutional rights or national constitutional principles. Accordingly, in *Commission* v. *Luxembourg* (1996, p. 72) the Court of Justice rejected the argument that a constitutional reservation of certain civil service posts to nationals, being a "supreme rule" of national law, precluded the establishment of any breach of European Community treaty obligations. In other words, according to the Court of Justice, Community law cannot be subject to review by national courts for its compatibility with national constitutional law. But a number of national courts have found it difficult to accept this position.[19]

In Belgium the *Conseil d'Etat* expressly adopted the case-law of the Court of Justice in *Orfinger* (1996, p. 162). On the other hand, the Court of Arbitration (the Belgian court with jurisdiction in constitutional matters) was prepared to subject the arrangements for the establishment of European schools to constitutional review, although it held in *European School* v. *Hermans-Jacobs* (1994, p. 155) that in the event there had been no breach of constitutional principles.

In Denmark the Supreme Court in *Carlsen* v. *Rasmussen* (1998, p. 185) held that the power of constitutional review of the Danish courts meant that they could not be deprived of their right to examine whether a particular Community measure exceeded the limits of the transfer of sovereignty brought about by the Act of Accession.

In Greece the Sixth Chamber of the Council of State, in the *Katsarou Case* (1998, p. 300), went much further and actually took the position that the supremacy of Community law covered only ordinary national law and did not extend to constitutional provisions. The case was referred to the Plenary of the Council of State, which upheld the decision of the chamber on different grounds but implicitly gave precedence to a

[19] See, *inter alia*, Kumm, Who is the Final Arbiter of Constitutionality in Europe?, CML Rev 1999, p. 351 and Hoffmeister, Casenote on the EC Banana Regulation Decision of the Federal Constitutional Court, CML Rev 2001, pp. 791 and 801.

constitutional ban on the operation of foreign universities over a Community Directive on mutual recognition of qualifications.[20]

In Germany the Constitutional Court has confirmed its previously enunciated position (*Wünsche ("Solange II")*, 1986, Volume 1, p. 461) and held in the *Banana Market Organization Constitutionality Case* (2000, p. 270) that complaints alleging infringement of fundamental constitutional rights by secondary Community law are inadmissible unless they can clearly demonstrate that the development of Community law has now fallen below the standard of human rights protection required by the Basic Law. When no evidence was submitted to establish that this was the case, the complaints had to be dismissed as inadmissible.[21]

The Court of Cassation in Italy, reviewing the jurisprudence of the Italian Constitutional Court in this matter, has confirmed that the power of constitutional review of the Constitutional Court does not apply to secondary Community provisions since they are not part of the domestic legal order, but that the Constitutional Court has jurisdiction in relation to statutes implementing Community treaties whose application might violate fundamental constitutional rights (*Talamucci*, 1998, p. 388).[22]

In Spain the Constitutional Court has continued to take the position, confirmed in *Martinez Perez* (1996, p. 423), that a potential conflict between Community law and national law is an "infra-constitutional" matter to be resolved by the ordinary courts. Consequently, as the Constitutional Court confirmed in the *Data Protection Law Constitutionality Case* (2000, Note, p. 427), Community secondary legislation does not have the same status as constitutional law and cannot constitute a yardstick for constitutional review. The Constitutional Court has thereby so far avoided review of Community law from the standpoint of fundamental constitutional rights, although the possibility of such review does not appear to be completely excluded.

There have also been several national judicial decisions establishing the principle that the governments of Member States, in exercising their powers within the Community's legislative process, are also subject to scrutiny for compatibility of their actions with constitutional principles and fundamental rights. This was held to be the case by the Constitutional Court in Italy in *Umbrian and Marches Regions* v. *Italy* (1997, Note, p. 370). In Germany, in the *Television Broadcasting Directive Case* (1995, p. 232), the Federal Constitutional Court held that the Federal Government had violated the rights of the *Länder* (states) by the manner

[20] For critical comment see Maganaris, The Principle of Supremacy in Community Law—From Direct Challenge to Non-application, EL Rev 1999, p. 426.

[21] For further discussion see Hoffmeister, Casenote, CML Rev 2001, p. 791 and Peters, The Bananas Decision of the Federal Constitutional Court, *German Yearbook of International Law* 2000, p. 276.

[22] For a recent discussion of the position in Italy see Tesauro, Community Law and National Courts – An Italian Perspective, in O'Keefe, *Judicial Review in European Union Law*, p. 142.

in which it had exercised its powers in the European Council of Ministers in relation to national quota rules on broadcasting, without informing and seeking the prior agreement of the *Bundesrat* in the final stage of deliberations in the Council on a new EC Directive.[23]

It must therefore be concluded that there is a discernible pattern for national courts with constitutional review jurisdiction to be prepared, at least in principle, to treat the enforcement of Community law as subject to constitutional limitations and, in particular, to exercise their jurisdiction to review legislation implementing Community treaties for their compatibility with basic national constitutional principles and fundamental rights. It is true that the exercise of this jurisdiction by national constitutional courts does not appear so far to have led them actually to override secondary Community legislation. But whereas the principle of supremacy of Community law over ordinary national legislation is clearly established in almost all the Member States, its supremacy over national constitutional law remains very much a "live" issue. To this extent, supremacy is not yet fully accepted by national courts.[24]

There is also another aspect of the "supremacy issue" concerning not the hierarchy of law but the hierarchy of courts. Ordinary national courts have, on the whole, been prepared to enter into a dialogue with the Court of Justice by regularly having recourse to references for preliminary rulings under the procedure laid down by Article 177 (now 234) of the EC Treaty. This applies even to the highest courts of appeal such as the English House of Lords and the German Supreme Court. By contrast, however, national constitutional courts have been extremely reluctant to subordinate themselves to the jurisdiction of the Court of Justice by making references for preliminary rulings.

The Italian Constitutional Court has gone so far as to justify its refusal to make a reference to the Court of Justice on the basis that it is not a "court or tribunal of a Member State" within the meaning of Article 177 of the EC Treaty (*Messaggero Servizi*, 1995, p. 378). In Austria, however, the Constitutional Court has reached the opposite conclusion, taking the view that it was required by the terms of Article 177 to make a reference to the Court of Justice and thereby becoming the first full constitutional court to do so (*Adria-Wien Pipeline Case*, 1999, p. 146). Previously, the Court of Arbitration in Belgium became the first court with jurisdiction in constitutional matters to make a reference for a preliminary ruling to the Court of Justice in the *Fédération Belge Case* (1997, p. 168). It remains to be seen whether the constitutional courts of other Member States will follow suit.

[23] See Herdegen, After the TV Judgment of the German Constitutional Court, CML Rev 1995, p. 1369 and Wouters, *Legal Issues of Economic Integration* 2000, pp. 86 ff.

[24] For an excellent discussion of this issue see De Witte, in *The Evolution of EU Law*, pp. 119-205.

VI. HUMAN RIGHTS

The Protection of Fundamental Rights by the Court of Justice[25]

The development of its jurisprudence on the protection of fundamental rights by the Court of Justice is unquestionably one of its more important achievements. As noted in the previous section, the Court of Justice has ruled that the constitutional review of Community measures by national courts for compatibility with fundamental rights is unacceptable and this has provoked a conflict with a number of national constitutional courts. But, at the same time, the Court of Justice has held that fundamental rights are to be protected within the Community framework by the Court itself, inspired by the constitutional traditions common to the Member States (*Internationale Handelsgesellschaft*, 1970, Volume 1, p. 435) and on the basis of those rights contained in the European Convention on Human Rights, as general principles of Community law (*Johnston*, 1986, Volume 1, Note, p. 460). The jurisdiction of the Court of Justice in this respect is now codified as a result of the combined effect of Articles 6(2) and 46(d) of the Treaty on European Union, in so far as observance of fundamental rights by the *Community institutions* is concerned. But even though all the Member States are signatories of the Convention, the Court of Justice has confirmed that its jurisdiction to ensure the observance of fundamental rights by the *Member States*, in references made by national courts for a preliminary ruling, is limited to national legislation which falls within the scope of Community law (*Kremzow*, 1997, Note, p. 70).[26]

Since the Court of Justice protects rights enshrined in the European Convention as general principles of Community law, rather than as Convention rights *per se*, and reviews the acts of Member States only to the extent that they fall within the scope of Community law, the scope of the protection of fundamental rights by the Court of Justice is more limited than that afforded by a number of national constitutional courts and only rarely has the Court of Justice found a breach of fundamental rights.[27]

It has long been recognized that one way to strengthen the protection of fundamental rights within the Community legal order would be for the Community itself to accede to the European Convention on Human Rights. The question of whether the Community was empowered to

[25] For recent contributions to the debate on the scope of the jurisdiction of the Court of Justice in this area see, *inter alia*, Jacobs, Human Rights in the European Union: The Role of the Court of Justice, EL Rev 2001, p. 331; Lenaerts, Fundamental Rights in the European Union, EL Rev 2000, p. 575; and De Witte, The Past and Future Role of the European Court of Justice in the Protection of Human Rights, in Alston (ed.), *The EU and Human Rights* (Oxford University Press, 1999), p. 859.

[26] See Lenaerts, EL Rev 2000, p. 590, for a discussion of when national legislation should be regarded as falling within the scope of Community law.

[27] See De Witte in *The EU and Human Rights*, p. 869.

do so by the existing Community treaties was eventually referred to the Court of Justice by the Council of Ministers. In *Opinion 2/94* (1996, p. 45) the Court of Justice held that treaty amendment would be necessary before the Community could accede to the Convention since no treaty provision conferred any general power on Community institutions to enact rules on human rights or conclude international conventions in that field. Whilst respect for human rights was a condition for the lawfulness of Community acts, accession to the Convention would have entailed a substantial change in the Community system for protecting those rights.[28]

It appears that the assertion of jurisdiction by the European Court of Human Rights, in a recent case concerning the legality of action by Member States of the Community in the exercise of Community powers, was in part a response to *Opinion 2/94* of the Court of Justice.[29] In *Matthews* v. *United Kingdom* (1999, p. 108) the European Court of Human Rights held that, whilst acts of the European Community could not be directly challenged as such before that Court, because the Community was not a party to the European Convention, the responsibility of Member States to secure the observance of those fundamental rights contained in the Convention continued even after the transfer of competences to Community institutions. Consequently, the Member States could be held to account before the European Court of Human Rights.[30]

It is also appropriate to refer here to the adoption by "Solemn Proclamation" of the Charter of Fundamental Rights of the European Union in December 2000. The Charter, which was adopted by the Community institutions rather than the Member States, is not legally binding and it remains to be seen whether it will merely be regarded as a political document or will be taken into account by the Court of Justice or national courts as one of the human rights instruments from which they will draw inspiration when dealing with questions involving fundamental rights.[31] This latter position seems to have already been taken by the Constitutional Court in Spain in the *Data Protection Law Constitutionality Case* (2000, Note, p. 427). In a recent decision, the European Court of First Instance has referred to Article 47 of the Charter as "reaffirming" the right to an effective remedy based on the constitutional traditions common to the Member States and Articles 6 and 13 of the European Convention.[32]

[28] For critical commentary on this judgment see *Gaja*, Casenote, CML Rev 1996, p. 973 and Waelbroeck, Editorial, CDE 1996, p. 549.

[29] See Lenaerts and De Smijter, The Charter and the Role of the European Courts, *Maastricht Journal of European and Comparative Law* 2001, p. 90.

[30] For discussion of the issues raised by this decision see, *inter alia*, Lenaerts and De Smijter, *ibid.*, p. 92 and Oliver, Fundamental Rights in European Union Law, in O'Keefe, *Judicial Review in European Union Law*, p. 319.

[31] For discussion of this issue see, *inter alia*, De Witte, The Legal Status of the Charter, *Maastricht Journal of European and Comparative Law* 2001, p. 81 and White, Editorial, EL Rev 2001, p. 330.

[32] *Jégo-Quéré* v. *Commission*, Case T-177/01, judgment of 3 May 2002.

The Convention on the Future of the European Union established a number of working groups in May 2002, one of which was asked to consider the possibilities of both the incorporation of the Charter into the Community Treaties and the accession of the Community to the European Convention on Human Rights. Recommendations on both these possibilities are therefore likely to be placed before the intergovernmental conference in 2004.

Direct effect — Directives — Conditions for direct effect — Failure of Member State to implement provisions of directive by specified time — EC Treaty, Article 189 — Rationale for direct effect of directives — Whether directive may be relied upon against an individual or only against the State and its organs — Whether wording of Article 189 or nature of directives precluding so-called "horizontal" direct effect

Direct effect — Directives — Conditions for direct effect— Failure of Member State to implement provisions of directive by specified time—Whether provisions sufficiently unconditional and precise—Directive conferring margin of discretion on Member States—Provisions involving choice from range of options — Whether "minimum obligation" incumbent upon Member States can be adequately defined — Council Directive 85/577 — Approximation of rules concerning consumer protection in case of contracts negotiated away from business premises

Direct effect—Directives—Interpretation of national law— Duty of national courts to interpret national law consistently with provisions of directive — Scope of obligation — Applicability to national law predating the relevant directive

Enforcement in national courts—Remedies—Claim against Member State — Breach of Community law for which Member State responsible—Principle of State responsibility for harm caused to individuals by such breach — Basic conditions for liability imposed by Community law—The law of the European Community

FACCINI DORI *v.* RECREB SRL

(Case C-91/92)

Court of Justice of the European Community. 14 *July* 1994

(Due, *President*; Mancini, Moitinho de Almeida, Díez de Velasco and Edward, *Presidents of Chambers*; Kakouris, Joliet (*Rapporteur*), Schockweiler, Rodríguez Iglesias, Grévisse, Zuleeg, Kapteyn and Murray, *Judges*; Lenz, *Advocate-General*)

SUMMARY: *The facts*:—The plaintiff in the main action, Ms Faccini Dori, concluded a contract for an English language correspondence course with a private company called Interdiffusion Srl at Milan Central Railway Station, away from its business premises. Some days later she informed the company that she was cancelling her subscription. The company ignored this notification and assigned its rights to Recreb, which obtained an order from an Italian court for payment of the agreed sum. The plaintiff lodged an objection to the order with the same court, relying on a right of cancellation provided for in Council Directive 85/577 concerning consumer protection in respect of contracts negotiated away from business premises. At the relevant time, Italy had taken no steps to transpose the Directive into national law, although the period laid down for its implementation had expired. The national court was uncertain whether the Directive could be relied upon by the plaintiff in these circumstances. Accordingly, a reference was made for a preliminary ruling by the Court of Justice as to whether the relevant provisions of the Directive were sufficiently unconditional and precise to be capable of being relied upon by an individual and, if so, whether they could be relied upon by one individual against another individual or only against the State. Because of the importance of the issue, the Court of Justice wrote to all the Member States asking for their views.

Opinion of the Advocate-General:—The Advocate-General first examined the provisions of the Directive, concluding that only Articles 1(1) and 5 were sufficiently unconditional and precise to be capable of having direct effect. He then stated that the principle of vertical direct effect, which enabled an individual to rely on a provision of a directive after the expiry of its prescribed period for implementation, was of no assistance in this case since so-called "vertical" direct effect only enabled an individual to rely on a directive against the State and its institutions, not against another private individual. Nevertheless, there were other ways in which the Court of Justice had sought to maximize the judicial protection of individuals. It had recognized the obligation on all State institutions to apply Community law by interpreting national law so as to conform with the requirements of Community law. Furthermore, the Court of Justice recognized that shortcomings in the implementation of a directive could entail an obligation on the Member States to compensate a private individual where, as here, he benefited from its provisions.

The Advocate-General considered, however, that it was necessary to reconsider the lack of so-called "horizontal" direct effect of non-implemented directives. The position in accordance with the Court of Justice's consistent case-law was clear: a directive could not, of itself, impose obligations which could be relied upon against an individual. But the Advocate-General considered that this approach was unsatisfactory. Drawing support from statements in recent cases before the Court by Advocates-General Van Gerven and Jacobs, he argued that horizontal direct effect should now be recognized on the basis, in particular, of the principle of the prohibition of discrimination and arguments relating to equality in conditions of competition.

According to the Advocate-General, the principle of the uniform effective application of Community law required directives satisfying the conditions for direct effect to be given *erga omnes* effect, in the same manner as directly applicable Treaty provisions. He rejected the arguments of the Court of Justice against recognizing horizontal direct effect based on the wording of Article 189 of the Treaty and the nature of directives. However, he accepted that if directives were now recognized as having direct effect, on grounds of legal certainty it should only be for the future and not in relation to the past.

Held:—(1) Articles 1(1), 2 and 5 of Council Directive 85/577 were unconditional and sufficiently precise as regards determination of the persons for whose benefit they were adopted and the minimum period within which notice of cancellation should be given (pp. 40-1).

(2) The Court had consistently held, since its judgment in *Marshall*,[1] that a directive could not of itself impose obligations on an individual and could not therefore be relied upon as such against individuals. The Court's case-law on the possibility of relying on directives against State entities was based on the fact that, under Article 189, a directive was binding only in relation to "each Member State to which it is addressed". That case-law sought to prevent the State from taking advantage of its own failure to comply with Community law. It would be unacceptable if a State, when required by Community legislation to adopt certain rules intended to govern the State's relations with individuals, and to confer certain rights on individuals, were able to rely on its own failure to discharge its obligations so as to deprive individuals of the benefits of those rights (pp. 41-2).

(3) The effect of extending the case-law of the Court of Justice to the sphere of relations between individuals would be to recognize a power in the Community to enact obligations to individuals with immediate effect, whereas it had competence to do so only where it was empowered to adopt regulations. It followed that, in the absence of measures transposing the directive within the prescribed time-limit, consumers could not derive from the directive itself a right of cancellation as against traders with whom they had concluded a contract or enforce such a right in a national court (p. 42).

(4) It should also be borne in mind that Article 5 of the Treaty required the Member States to take all appropriate measures to achieve the result envisaged by directives and this duty was binding on all the authorities of the Member States, including the courts. Accordingly, as the Court had held (*Marleasing* judgment),[2] when applying provisions of national law, whether adopted before or after the directive, the national court was required to interpret them as far as possible in the light of the wording and purpose of the directive so as to achieve the result which it had in view and thereby comply with the third paragraph of Article 189 of the Treaty (p. 42).

(5) If the result prescribed by the directive could not be achieved by way of interpretation, it should also be borne in mind that Community law required Member States to make good damage caused to individuals through failure to transpose a directive, provided that three conditions were fulfilled: the purpose of the directive had to be to grant rights to individuals; it had to be possible to identify the content of those rights on the basis of the directive's provisions; and there had to be a causal link between the breach of the State's obligation and the damage suffered (*Francovich* judgment)[3] (pp. 42-3).

[1] Volume 1, p. 136. [2] Volume 1, p. 167. [3] Volume 1, p. 188.

The text of the judgment of the Court of Justice of the European Community commences at p. 38. The following is the text of the opinion of Advocate-General Lenz delivered on 9 February 1994:

[3328] A—*Introduction*

1. The request for a preliminary ruling from the Giudice Conciliatore (Judge-Conciliator), Florence, which is now before the Court raises questions concerning the interpretation and application of Council Directive 85/577/EEC to protect the consumer in respect of contracts negotiated away from business premises.[1] In the event that the question as to the applicability of the directive should be answered in the affirmative, the national court asks about the legal consequences of its application for the period between the date by which it should have been implemented (23 December 1987) and the date when it was actually transposed into Italian law (2 March 1992), as regards both relations between individuals and the State and as regards relations between individuals *inter se.* Whilst the question as to the effects of the directive in relations between the individual and the State is evidently hypothetical for the purposes of deciding the case before the national court, the question as to the effect of an unimplemented directive on relations between individuals *inter se* bears on the vexed issue of the horizontal direct effect of directives.

2. The dispute stems from a contract for an English-language correspondence course which was concluded near Milan Central Railway Station. The party in the main proceedings who lodged an objection to an order, Ms Dori, relied on the right of renunciation provided for in Article 5 of Directive 85/577 in order to release herself from the contract.

3. The national court does not expand further on either the facts or the substantive content of the directive, merely observing that "evidence of the conclusion of the contract off the premises of the undertaking providing the service and of the exercise of the right to renounce it" has been adduced.

4. The national court considers it necessary to consider Ms Dori's argument to the effect that Directive 85/577 should be recognized as being fully effective in the Italian State. It has doubts about whether this argument is right in view, among other things, of the wording of Article 189 of the EEC Treaty[2] **[3329]** and of the fact that there is no obligation to publish directives.[3] However, since the content of some directives is precise and substantively that of a regulation, the question arises as to whether in such a case a directive can acquire "legislative

[1] Council Directive 85/577/EEC of 20 December 1985, OJ 1985 L 372, p. 31.

[2] Since 1 November 1993, the EC Treaty as a result of the Treaty on European Union of 7 February 1992 (OJ 1992 C 224, p. 1).

[3] This has no longer been the case since 1 November 1993 as a result of Article 191 of the EC Treaty.

force" in excess of the inherent effects of directives. The national court refers to the Court's case-law and considers that the results are in some respects unsatisfactory, for example, where a measure is legislative in nature between some subjects and not in relation to others. It takes the view that a preliminary ruling is called for, on the ground that the "only sure factor is the uncertain effects of directives".

5. The questions referred to the Court for a preliminary ruling read as follows:

> Is Community Directive 85/577/EEC of 20 December 1985 to be regarded as sufficiently precise and detailed and, if so, was it capable, in the period between the expiry of the 24-month time-limit given to the Member States to comply with the directive and the date on which the Italian State did comply with it, of taking effect as between individuals and the Italian Member State and as between individuals themselves?

6. Initially, the parties to the main proceedings, the Commission and the German, Greek and Italian Governments took part in the proceedings. The Court put a question to all the Member States in which it asked them for their views on the question raised by the national court as to "whether the provisions of a directive which has not been transposed into national law within the time-limit set could be relied upon directly by an individual in a dispute with another individual", and this prompted the French Government also to submit written observations. Lastly, representatives of the Danish, German, Greek, French, Italian, Netherlands and British Governments took part in the oral procedure. All the representatives of the Governments of the Member States, with the exception of the representative of the Greek Government, argued, in common with the Commission, that the court's case-law to date should be maintained. The oral procedure revealed the complexity of this case, although, for the most part, the arguments for and against cover common ground. I shall be returning to the various arguments when I carry out the legal assessment.

B—*Discussion*

I. *The Precise and Unconditional Nature of Directive 85/577*

1. *Overall assessment of Directive 85/577*

7. The national court's first question asks whether the provisions of the directive are precise and unconditional, which is the *sine* **[3330]** *qua non* for direct applicability.[4] The national court has not targeted its

[4] Leading judgment of 5 April 1979 in Case 148/78 *Ratti* [1979] ECR 1629, paragraph 23; judgment in Case 8/81 in Case 8/81 *Becker* v. *Finanzamt Münster-Innenstadt* [1982] ECR 53, paragraph 25.

question at specific provisions of the directive, even though not all of them are potentially applicable in this case.

8. As regards the Member States' margin of discretion for the transposition of Directive 85/577 into national law, the starting premiss is that a Member State has various possibilities open to it in the context of its freedom to choose the "form and methods".[5] It may incorporate the provisions of the directive into an existing legislative code, adopt a separate law or refer in a separate law to provisions of the general civil law.

9. In addition, in several respects the content of Directive 85/577 leaves Member States with leeway to implement it in different ways. For instance, *Article 3* allows Member States to decide that the directive is to apply only to contracts exceeding a minimum amount. The last sentence of *Article 4*, which requires traders to give written notice of certain particulars, leaves the Member States a relatively broad discretion in so far as they are to lay down "appropriate consumer protection measures in cases where the information referred to in this Article is not supplied".

10. The consumer's right of renunciation laid down in *Article 5* is the central core of the directive and is to be carried out "in accordance with the procedure laid down by national law". That form of words warrants doubts as to whether this is a reference to the general civil law—such as the rule on the lodgement of declarations of intention—or to independent rules which are to be laid down in the implementing measure.

11. *Article 7* provides that the legal effects of renunciation are to be governed by national laws. The very terminology used, which in the German version employs first the term "Rücktritt" (withdrawal) and then the term "Widerruf" (revocation), shows that very different legal effects may be attached to the right of renunciation. According to the stage reached in the performance of the contract, very different legal effects can be envisaged as attaching to revocation, withdrawal or cancellation.

[3331] 12. Consequently, in several respects the directive leaves the Member States room to exercise their legislative discretion. However, for the purposes of the instant case, it might be sufficient to consider merely the interpretation and application of those provisions containing a *minimum guarantee*[6] for the consumers who are to be protected.

13. Although the national court has not brought the facts of case under any particular provision of the directive, it would appear that the application of Articles 1 and 5 is inescapable. Article 1 defines the scope of the directive *ratione materiae* and Article 5 creates the consumer's right of renunciation. Each of those articles should therefore satisfy the

[5] See Article 189 of the EEC Treaty.

[6] Judgment in Joined Cases C-6/90 and C-9/90 *Frankovich and Others* [1991] ECR I-5357, paragraph 20.

requirements of unconditionality and precision on which the Court's case-law makes the direct applicability of a provision of a directive depend.

2. *Article 1 of Directive 85/577*

14. Article 1(1) of Directive 85/577 reads as follows:

> This Directive shall apply to contracts under which a trader supplies goods or services to a consumer and which are concluded:
> — during an excursion organized by the trader away from his business premises,
>
> or
>
> — during a visit by a trader
> (i) to the consumer's home or to that of another consumer;
> (ii) to the consumer's place of work;
> where the visit does not take place at the express request of the consumer.

15. In itself, that paragraph is precise and unconditional, since it covers clearly defined **[3332]** operative facts, such as an excursion organized by a trader or a visit by a trader to the consumer's home or place of work. Moreover, Article 1(1) does not, in my view, afford any possibility of an extended interpretation since that would entail forgoing the application of those operative facts, which are essential ingredients.

16. Article 1(2), which extends the scope of the directive to cover certain contracts concluded during a trader's visit to a consumer, may be disregarded, as far as can be judged, for the purposes of deciding this case, since there is no evidence to suggest that the contract was concluded during a visit made to Ms Dori's home or place of work at her request.[7]

17. It can therefore be considered at this stage that Article 1(1) is sufficiently precise to qualify for direct applicability.

18. In contrast, the application of Article 1(3) and (4), each of which paragraphs covers "conditions similar to those described in paragraph 1 or paragraph 2", could prove awkward. It is open to question whether paragraphs 3 and 4 of Article 1 extend the scope *ratione materiae* of the directive by comparison with paragraphs 1 and 2 so as to include other consumer contracts not concluded on the trader's premises—on the highway or in public places, for instance—or whether they do not include within the scope of the directive circumventing transactions concluded in locations or fact situations covered by paragraphs 1 and 2.

19. That question could be of practical importance for the purposes of deciding this case, since—as has already been seen with regard to

[7] The contract was concluded "near Milan Central Railway Station", whereas Ms Dori lives in Monza.

paragraph 2—there is no evidence that the contested contract was concluded, as paragraph 1 requires, during an excursion organized by the trader or during a visit by the trader to Ms Dori's home or place of work.

20. It therefore turns on whether Article 1(3) and (4) may be interpreted so as also to bring contractual offers made in other locations or fact situations within the scope of the directive. Article 1(3) and (4) read as follows:

> (3) This Directive shall apply to contracts in respect of which an offer was made by the consumer under conditions similar to those described in paragraph 1 or paragraph 2 **[3333]** although the consumer was not bound by that offer before its acceptance by the trader.
>
> (4) This Directive shall also apply to offers made contractually by the consumer under conditions similar to those described in paragraph 1 or paragraph 2 where the consumer is bound by his offer.

21. All the parties who took part in the hearing were asked whether they considered that the directive was applicable to the main proceedings. Some answered in the negative, others in the affirmative. Consequently, the answer to the question is by no means obvious. If, in addition, account is taken of the fact that the directive has given rise to controversy in academic writings, it is, in my view, scarcely possible to consider that Article 1(3) and (4) exhibit the precision required in order for a provision of a directive to be directly applicable.

22. On the other hand, the Court is called upon to give a binding interpretation of the directive. Consequently, in replying to the national court's questions, it can provide that court with the criteria which it needs in order to decide the case.

23. The title of the directive suggests that it is intended to apply generally to contracts negotiated away from business premises. The preamble confirms this. The fourth recital in the preamble reads as follows:

> Whereas the special feature of contracts concluded away from the business premises of the trader is that as a rule it is the trader who initiates the contract negotiations, for which the consumer is unprepared or which he does not expect; whereas the consumer is often unable to compare the quality and price of the offer with other offers; whereas *this surprise element generally exists not only in contracts made at the doorstep but also in other forms of contract concluded by the trader away from his business premises*.[8]

24. The words "under conditions similar to those described in paragraph 1 or paragraph 2" could be construed, against the background of the other forms of contract "concluded by the trader away from his business premises" referred to in the preamble, as meaning that contracts negotiated in geographical and factual conditions differing from those mentioned in paragraph 1 should also be covered. On the other

[8] My emphasis.

hand, there is a substantial difference between paragraphs 3 and 4, on the one hand, and paragraphs 1 and 2, on the other, in so far as they take **[3334]** account of the contractual *offer*. Accordingly, I consider that the correct view is that paragraphs 3 and 4 extend the effects of the directive to cover possible circumventing transactions.

25. In the absence of a binding interpretation by the Court of Article 1(3) and (4), those provisions are not, in my view, sufficiently precise and unconditional to be capable of being directly applicable.

26. It is for the national court to apply the provisions to the facts of the main proceedings. The national court manifestly started out from the premiss that the facts of the case fall within the scope *ratione materiae* of the directive. The Court will not assess the relevance of a request for a preliminary ruling for the purposes of deciding the case. It is therefore for the national court to draw the necessary conclusions from the above considerations for the case before it.[9]

3. *Article 5 of Directive 85/577*

27. The applicability of the directive is of practical utility for the consumer only if he can rely on the right of renunciation provided for in Article 5 in order to release himself from a contract concluded away from the trader's premises. Ms Dori expressly relied on Article 5 of the directive in the main proceedings.

28. As I have already observed in my general remarks on the Member States' margin of discretion in transposing Directive 85/577 into national law,[10] Article 5(1) is worded so as to leave a discretion as to where in the national legal system and with what content the conditions for the exercise of the right of renunciation are to be governed. The Community legislator manifestly started from the premiss that the conditions for the exercise of right of renunciation may differ from one Member State to another, since it grants that renunciation is to be notified "in accordance with the procedure laid down by national law". In my view, that openness to variable implementation of the directive is not compatible with the directive's having direct applicability.

[3335] 29. The idea that the provision in question is sufficiently precise could be assumed at the most from the limited angle of the main proceedings, in which—as far as appears from the documents before the Court—the contract was not in any way performed. Notification of the exercise of the right of renunciation within seven days would then be the minimum requirement for triggering the legal consequence described in Article 5(2), namely:

> The giving of the notice shall have the effect of releasing the consumer from any obligations under the cancelled contract.

[9] Judgment in Case 14/86 *Pretore di Salo* v. *Persons unknown* [1987] ECR 2545, paragraph 11.

[10] See section 10.

The release of the consumer from his contractual obligations can therefore be construed as a *minimum guarantee*[11] for the consumer. To my mind, therefore, Article 5 of Directive 85/577 is eligible for direct applicability only subject to the reservations set out above.

II—*The Effects of a Directive which has not yet been Implemented*

1. *Relations between the individual and the State*

30. In the event that the question as to whether the directive is particularly precise is answered in the affirmative, the national court wishes to know whether the directive could have effects between the individual and the Italian State after the period for its implementation elapsed and before it was actually implemented. As the Court has consistently held,[12] an individual may, after the expiry of the period prescribed for implementation, rely directly against the Member State in default upon a provision of a directive which is in his favour, unconditional and precise. In such circumstances, the Member State may not take advantage of its conduct contrary to the Treaty.[13]

31. That effect attaching to directives, which may also be described as vertical direct effect, affords satisfactory protection for the legal interests of individuals only if the directive is intended and fit to have effects in such vertical legal relations. The directive will not be directly applicable where the obligation in question is incumbent, not on the State, but on a private individual.

32. However, that is precisely the case in the main proceedings. The obligation to release a party from the contract is incumbent, not on the State, but on the other party to the contract. The fact that the directive can be relied upon as against the State and all its institutions does not assist in resolving the actual issue in a dispute between private persons. **[3336]** The Court has evolved various approaches in its case-law in order to overcome this obstacle.

(a) *Broad meaning for the concept of the State*

33. With a view to setting broad limits to the direct applicability of directives, the concept of the State has to be understood in the broad sense. The broad definition covers local or regional authorities,[14] public authorities[15] and bodies coming under the State[16] even in the form of

[11] Judgment in *Francovich and Others*, cited above, paragraphs 20, 21 and 22.

[12] See, for instance, the judgments in *Ratti* and *Becker*, cited above.

[13] See the judgment in *Becker*, cited above, paragraph 24.

[14] Judgment in Case 103/88 *Fratelli Costanzo* v. *Comune di Milano* [1989] ECR 1839, paragraph 31.

[15] Judgments in *Becker*, cited above, in Case 152/84 *Marshall* v. *Southampton and South-West Hampshire Area Health Authority* [1986] ECR 723, in Case 222/84 *Johnston* v. *Chief Constable of the Royal Ulster Constabulary* [1986] ECR 1651, in *Costanzo*, cited above, and in Case C-221/88 *Busseni* [1990] ECR I-495.

[16] Judgment in Case 31/87 *Beentjes* v. *State of the Netherlands* [1988] ECR 4635.

nationalized undertakings.[17] It is above all the inclusion within the definition of the State of State-controlled undertakings which has given rise to criticism. It is doubtless the cases in which it was possible to rely on a directive against a nationalized undertaking in its capacity as an employer,[18] and not against a private person, to which the national court adverts when it states that "a legislative measure takes effect as between some individuals who are subject to a particular legal system and not others".[19]

34. In my estimation, the Court's case-law based on a broad definition of the State[20] is perfectly coherent. It covers not only holders of direct public power but also holders of indirect public power.[21] Nevertheless, the limit on extending the definition of the State has certainly been reached where an undertaking controlled by public bodies is linked to the State, whilst a change in the majority on the supervisory organs means that the same undertaking is a private undertaking.

(b) *Obligation on all State institutions to apply Community law by way of interpretation*

35. Another means of procuring the widest possible application of directives which, by default, have not yet been transposed into national law or have been insufficiently transposed consists of the obligation on all public authorities to take all appropriate measures within their jurisdiction, whether general or particular, to ensure fulfilment of the Member States' obligation arising from a **[3337]** directive.[22] That Community obligation on national institutions means, for example, that national courts are under a duty to interpret and apply their national law, to the entire extent of their discretion, in conformity with the requirements of Community law.[23]

36. The obligation to ensure the effectiveness of Community law by way of interpretation does not relate only to the legislation adopted in order to implement a directive,[24] but to the national legal system as a whole.[25] The public administration is also bound by an obligation to

[17] Judgment in Case C-188/89 *Foster and Others* [1990] ECR I-3313, paragraph 20.

[18] Judgment in *Foster*, cited above.

[19] See the national court's order, p. 11 of the original version.

[20] For the functional concept of the State, see the judgment in *Beentjes*, cited above.

[21] Purely incidentally, I would observe that in labour law it does not only make a difference as far as the effect of directives is concerned whether the contract of employment was concluded with an employer subject to public law or with a private employer.

[22] See the judgments in Case 14/83 *Von Colson and Kamann* v. *Land Nordrhein-Westfalen* [1984] ECR 1891, paragraph 26, in *Beentjes*, cited above, paragraph 39, in Case C-106/89 *Marleasing* [1990] ECR I-4135 and in Case C-373/90 *X* [1992] ECR I-131, paragraph 7.

[23] Judgment in *Von Colson and Kamann* v. *Land Nordrhein-Westfalen*, cited above, paragraphs 26 and 28.

[24] Judgment in Case 111/75 *Mazzalai* v. *Ferrovia del Renon* [1976] ECR 657, paragraphs 7/9 and 10/11.

[25] Judgments in *Von Colson and Kamman*, cited above, paragraph 26, and in *Marleasing*, cited above.

comply with directives which is comparable to that to which national courts are subject.[26]

37. There are, however, natural limits to the possibility of construing national law in conformity with Community law. They are discernible when the Court refers to the obligations incumbent, under Community law, on all public authorities to take appropriate measures "*within their jurisdiction*".[27] Consequently, the limits on the interpretation of the law also constitute limits on the power of the national courts to ensure the implementation of unimplemented directives in national law.

(c) *Entitlement to compensation from the State*

38. A third attempted solution designed to optimize the judicial protection of the individual in the event of a prior infringement by the Member State of its obligation to implement a directive within the prescribed period consists in granting a right to compensation on the basis of Community law.[28] In such case, an individual can bring an action against the State on account of the loss of a right or the absence of legal protection. The State is bound to compensate the private individual by reason of its liability under Community law.

Intermediate conclusion

39. *(aa)* Consequently, in so far as the national court's question relates to the effects of Directive 85/577 in relations between an individual and the Italian State in the period between the expiry of the period prescribed for the transposition of the directive into national law and its actual implementation, its attention should be drawn to the existence of the right to compensation on the basis of Community law.

[3338] 40. *(bb)* Another question—to which, in the final analysis, the Court also does not have to reply—concerns the extent to which the national court may determine the case in the context of its obligation (described in section II.1(b)) to interpret its national law in conformity with Community law.

41. The Commission provided information about Italian civil law both in its written observations and at the hearing, and mentioned two provisions which, in its view, are suitable for the implementation of the right of renunciation.

42. The Court may not rule on the application of national law. The burden imposed on individuals indirectly by the proposed interpretation was, admittedly, allowed by the Court in *Marleasing*.[29] As has been rightly objected, renunciation of the effects of the contract presupposes the existence of a right of renunciation. The Court is under a duty to rule on that condition where it is asked about the effects of the directive during

[26] Judgment in *Costanzo*, cited above.

[27] Judgments in *Von Colson and Kamann*, cited above, paragraph 26.

[28] Cf. judgment in *Francovich*, cited above.

[29] Cited above.

the interim period—between the end of the period for transposition and actual implementation—on relations between private individuals *inter se*. To refer in that context to the obligations arising for the national court under Community law and that court's exclusive jurisdiction to interpret national law would be to ignore the true issue.

2. *Horizontal applicability of directives*

43. The answer afforded by the Court's consistent case-law to question as to the effects of an unimplemented directive on legal relations between private persons—also known as horizontal effect—is straightforward and clear; a directive may not of itself impose obligations on an individual.[30]

44. The Court's justification for this is as follows: ". . . according to Article 189 of the EEC Treaty the binding nature of a directive, which constitutes the basis for the possibility of relying on the directive before a national court, exists only in relation to 'each Member State to which it is addressed'. It follows that a directive may not of itself impose obligations on an individual and that a provision of a directive may not be relied upon as such against such a person".[31]

45. Consequently, emphasis is clearly placed on the refusal to impose a burden on a private person. According to the wording of the Treaty, an obligation is imposed only on the Member States to which the directive is addressed.

[3339] 46. It would be possible to draw the line at this point and argue that the existing case-law should be maintained.

47. However, such an approach appears unsatisfactory to me. Following the judgments in *Foster*[32] and *Marleasing*,[33] calls have increasingly been heard in academic circles for directives to be given horizontal effect. Among the members of the Court, to date Advocate General Van Gerven[34] and, recently, Advocate General Jacobs[35] have spoken out in favour of the horizontal applicability of directives—albeit not in response to questions having a bearing on the determination of the cases then before the Court.[36]

48. Considerations favouring the horizontal effect of directives reflect a drive to do justice by the beneficiary of a provision which the

[30] Judgments in *Marshall*, cited above, paragraph 48, in Joined Cases 372 to 374/85 *Traen* [1987] ECR 2141, paragraph 24, in *Pretore di Salo* v. *Persons unknown*, cited above, paragraph 19, in *Busseni*, cited above, paragraph 23, and in *Marleasing*, cited above, paragraph 6.

[31] Judgment in *Marshall*, cited above, paragraph 48.

[32] Cited above. [33] Cited above.

[34] Section 12 of his Opinion of 26 January 1993 in Case C-271/91 (judgment of 2 August 1993) *Marshall* v. *Southampton and South-West Hampshire Area Health Authority* ("*Marshall II*"), [1993] ECR I-4367.

[35] Section 15 et seq. of his Opinion of 27 January 1994 in Case C-316/93 *Vaneetveld*, [1994] ECR I-763, at I-765.

[36] Judge Schockweiler has also spoken in favour of the horizontal effect of directives in his contribution *Effets des directives non transposées en droit national a l'égard des particuliers* to Mr Díez de Velasco's Festschrift "*Hacia un nuevo orden internacional y europeo*".

Community legislator intended to be binding and not to abandon his situation for an indefinite period to the whim of a Member State in default of its obligations.

49. At the time of the completion of the internal market—an area without internal frontiers[37]—when harmonizing provisions governing legal relations between private individuals are increasingly being adopted, it seems to me to be appropriate to reconsider the effect of directives. In the preamble to Directive 85/577, the Community legislator referred to the need to approximate legislation in completely unambiguous terms:

> Whereas any disparity between such legislation may directly affect the functioning of the common market; whereas it is therefore *necessary*[38] to approximate laws in this field.[39]

50. Foremost among the arguments in favour of directives having horizontal effect is that relating to equality of the conditions of competition. Moreover, in the absence of horizontal effect, persons in Member States which comply with Community law are frequently placed at a disadvantage.

51. The principle of the *prohibition of discrimination*, which ranks as a fundamental right, also militates in favour of directives **[3340]** being given horizontal effect, from several points of view. First, it is unsatisfactory that individuals should be subject to different rules, depending on whether they have comparable legal relations with a body connected with the State or with a private individual. Secondly, it is contrary to the requirements of an internal market for individuals to be subject to different laws in the various Member States even though harmonizing measures have been adopted by the Community.

52. If those disparities were to be maintained, it would go against the stated aim of the approximation of legislation. That finding cannot be refuted by arguing that it is in the nature of directives that there are bound to be different conditions as between Member States until such time as the directives are transposed into national law.[40] Such inequality should be allowed only during the period prescribed for implementation. It is one of the aims of directives that comparable conditions should prevail after that period has expired.

53. The discrimination argument has gained even more substance since the entry into force of the Maastricht Treaty and of citizenship of the Union, enshrined in the EC Treaty. According to the intention

[37] Since 1 January 1993, in accordance with Article 8a of the EEC Treaty, which has since become Article 7a of the EC Treaty.

[38] My emphasis.

[39] Second recital in the preamble to Directive 85/577.

[40] See section 8 of my Opinion of 10 October 1989 in Case C-38/89 *Blanguernon* [1990] ECR I-83, at I-87.

of the Contracting States,[41] the Treaty on European Union marks "a new stage in the process of European integration undertaken with the establishment of the European Communities". Articles 3a and 7a of the EC Treaty stress the importance of the internal market. Articles 2, 3 and 3a of the EC Treaty promote the placing of economic policy more on a common footing. Article 3(s) requires a contribution to be made to the strengthening of consumer protection. More detailed provisions in that regard are set out in Article 129a. The introduction of citizenship of the Union raises the expectation that citizens of the Union will enjoy equality, at least before Community law.

54. In the case of directives whose content is intended to have effects in relations between private persons and which embody provisions designed to protect the weaker party,[42] it is obvious that the failure to transpose a directive deprives it of *effet utile*. Following the expiry of the period for transposition, the application of protective provisions with precise and unconditional content should be possible. A provision of a directive, which the Community legislator intended to be binding, should be recognized as having substantive effect and the conduct of a Member State contrary to the Treaty should not be able to impede the assertion of legal positions which are in themselves complete.

[3341] 55. In order to come out in favour of the horizontal direct effect of directives, the starting point should be that the *rationale* and manner of effect are fundamentally different than in the case of directives having vertical direct effect. Whereas, on the traditional view of the direct applicability of directives, conduct contrary to Community law on the part of the Member State directly determines legal relations between the individual and the State, a third party who is a private person has no influence on the implementation of a directive.[43] The arguments and legal principles[44] put forward in support of the direct applicability of directives vis-à-vis the Member State to the effect that the Member State is not entitled to profit by its conduct contrary to Community law[45] apply no more in relations between private persons *inter se* than the reference to the nature of a sanction[46] of direct effect vis-à-vis the State.

56. The direct applicability of directives as between private persons would cease to be in the nature of an objection in the sense that the

[41] Expressed in the first recital in the preamble to the Treaty on European Union, cited in footnote 2.

[42] See, for example, Council Directive 80/987/EEC of 20 October 1980 on the approximation of the laws of the Member States relating to the protection of employees in the event of the insolvency of the employer (OJ 1980 L 283, p. 23; see in this regard the judgment in *Francovich and Others*, cited above) or Directive 85/577/EEC, which is the subject-matter of the present proceedings and of the judgment in Case C-361/89 *Di Pinto* [1991] ECR I-1189.

[43] Admittedly, even in the context of the existing case-law on the effect of directives, direct responsibility for the infringement of the Treaty is not necessary, as witness the broad interpretation given by the Court's case-law to the concept of the State; see section II.1(a), above.

[44] *Nemo auditur, venire contra factum proprium*, estoppel.

[45] Judgment in *Becker*, cited above, paragraph 24.

[46] See my Opinion in *Costanzo*, cited above, section 23.

favourable provision is "relied upon". The directly applicable provision of a directive would in contrast be given effects *erga omnes*. It would as a result be equated with the directly applicable provisions of the Treaty.[47] The provision of a directive producing horizontal effects would participate in the primacy of Community law, which would be desirable in the interests of the uniform, effective application of Community law.

57. Although horizontal direct effect of directives appears desirable for the reasons given above, substantial arguments exist against such a change in the case-law.

58. Reference is made regularly in those arguments to the *wording of Article 189 of the EEC Treaty* and to the *nature of directives*, which are binding only on Member States and then only as to the results to be achieved.

59. In my view, those arguments can be refuted. As regards in the first place the freedom given to the Member States as to the choice of the form and methods for implementing directives, that freedom is completely unaffected until the transitional period expires. Even after that, the Member States retain—also where individual provisions have direct effect—leeway wherever **[3342]** that is intended by the directive. Only a fraction of provisions of directives will lend themselves to horizontal applicability. For the rest, the Member States are not entitled to invoke, after the expiry of the period for transposition, freedoms which were conferred on them only for the purposes of the due implementation of the directive within the time-limit laid down.

60. The obligation for the Member State to achieve the results intended by the directive exists immediately that the directive takes effect. As far as the results intended to be achieved by a directive are concerned, the Member States do not normally have any discretion. Such results include, for example, making protective provisions binding by no later than the end of the period for implementation.[48] The binding nature of such rules is—as I have already observed—intended by the Community legislator and inherent in the nature of directives. Directives are not measures of lesser quality but are addressed, with a view to their implementation, to the Member States, which are under an obligation under the Treaty to transpose them into national law in full and in good time.

61. In my view, the nature of directives does not preclude their having horizontal effect. Neither would that eliminate the demarcation between regulations and directives, since directives cannot have direct effect until

[47] For example

—Article 12: judgment in Case 26/62 *Van Gend & Loos* [1963] ECR 1;
—Articles 53 and 37(2): judgment in Case 6/64 *Costa* v. *ENEL* [1964] ECR 585;
—Articles 9 and 13(2): judgment in Case 33/70 *SACE* v. *Ministry for Finance of the Italian Republic* [1970] ECR 1213;
—Article 48: judgment in Case 41/74 *Van Duyn* v. *Home Office* [1974] ECR 1337;
—Article 119: judgment in Case 43/75 *Defrenne* v. *Sabena* [1976] ECR 455.

[48] Judgments in Case 9/70 *Grad* v. *Finanzamt Traunstein* [1970] ECR 825, paragraphs 10 and 13, and in *SACE*, cited above, paragraph 11.

the period for transposition has elapsed and only in the case of clear and unconditional provisions.

62. Another argument put forward against horizontal applicability for directives relates to the *burden imposed on third parties on the ground that it is incompatible with the rule of law.* That argument cannot in fact be dismissed forthwith. It is questionable whether a private person whose conduct is lawful under the national legal system may have burdens imposed upon him under an unimplemented directive not addressed to him for which, moreover, he will have scarcely any remedy against the Member State in default.[49]

63. On grounds of legal certainty the horizontal effect of directives appears to me to be extremely problematic from the point of view of the third party suffering the burden. The fact that private individuals have had burdens imposed on them indirectly as a result of directly applicable directives—for example, owing to irregularities committed in a tender calling in question the legal situation of the other tenderers and, possibly, the contractor[50] or owing to the effect of such directives resulting from their interpretation in conformity with Community law in a dispute between companies subject to private **[3343]** law[51]—cannot eliminate the reservations evoked by horizontal effect on grounds of the rule of law.

64. The basic condition for a burden imposed on the citizen by legislative measures is their *constitutive publication* in an official organ.[52] That condition is not fulfilled by directives adopted on the basis of the EEC Treaty.[53] The usage of publishing directives in the *Official Journal of the European Communities* as measures whose publication is not a condition for their applicability does not remedy that situation. Publication in the *Official Journal of the European Communities* is purely declaratory and is not a condition for directives to take effect, which is sometimes clarified by a footnote indicating the date on which the directive was notified to the Member States,[54] since directives take effect by notification.[55] The fact that it is possible to take cognizance of a measure does not replace its constitutive publication.

65. In the case of directives adopted and to be adopted following the entry into force of the Maastricht Treaty on 1 November 1993, the situation is fundamentally different. Article 191 of the *EC Treaty* also requires directives to be published in the *Official Journal of the Community.*

[49] Asserting a claim for compensation will raise problems as regards the time of the damage, since if the Member State had transposed the directive in good time, the burden on the private individual would still have existed.

[50] Judgment in *Costanzo*, cited above.

[51] Judgment in *Marleasing*, cited above.

[52] Judgment in Case C-192/89 *Sevince* v. *Staatssecretaris van Justitie* [1990] ECR I-3461, paragraph 24.

[53] That objection cannot be raised against the direct applicability of provisions of the Treaty.

[54] For example, the footnote to Article 9 of Directive 85/577/EEC.

[55] See the second paragraph of Article 191 of the EEC Treaty.

An objection based on absence of publication could therefore no longer be raised against the horizontal effect of such recent directives.

66. For reasons of *legal certainty*, which is a fundamental right of the citizen on whom a burden is imposed, the public must be prepared as of now for the fact that directives will in future have to be recognized as having horizontal direct effect. For those reasons, too, one must be gratified at the aforementioned stands taken by members of the Court.[56]

67. The principle of *legitimate expectations* is invoked in favour of private individuals on whom a burden is imposed and against the horizontal effect of directives. Expectations deserving of protection certainly exist, in so far as a private individual does not have to reckon with the imposition of additional burdens provided that he acts lawfully within the context of his national legal system. On the other hand, once a directive has been published and the period for transposition has expired, the burden is foreseeable. I would ask whether the expectation that the national legislature will act contrary to Community law is worthy of protection.

68. An argument based on the *democratic principle* is put forward against the horizontal effect of directives. According to that **[3344]** argument, the democratic deficit, which is deplored in any event in the context of Community legislation, is increased where national parliaments are by-passed when directives are implemented.

69. As far as the alleged democratic deficit is concerned, I would observe, on the one hand, that the European Parliament's rights to collaborate in drawing up Community legislation have gradually been increased by the Single European Act and the Maastricht Treaty. On the other hand, it cannot be argued, I submit, that the national legislature is by-passed.

70. The national legislature has every freedom during the period for transposition to choose the form and means of transposing the directive into national law.[57] Even after the period for transposition has elapsed, the obligation[58] on the national legislature to transpose the directive continues to exist, as well as leeway to fulfil that obligation in one way or another to the extent permitted by the directive. Only provisions of directives or protective rules which are sufficiently precise to be asserted without being fleshed out in any way and therefore have to be taken over by the national legislature would have legal effects as between the addressees of the legislation in question within the national legal system. To my mind, fears that there will be a hiatus between the legal situation existing during the intermediate period preceding the transposition of the directive into national law and that existing thereafter are groundless,

[56] See section 47 and footnote 36, above.

[57] Judgment in *Grad*, cited above, paragraph 13.

[58] Judgment in Case 102/79 *Commission* v. *Belgium* [1980] ECR 1473, paragraph 12.

since the provisions suitable for horizontal applicability must also be found in the implementing measure.

71. The objection that recognition of the horizontal direct effect of directives would increase Member States' carelessness in transposing them does not convince me, since the national legislature remains responsible for their implementation in full. Recognition in principle of horizontal effect might possibly encourage Member States to effect transposition within the prescribed period in order to forestall horizontal application by the authorities and courts of the Community and the Member States. In my view, the arguments on the educative effect of horizontal applicability balance themselves out and hence do not tip the balance for or against.

72. Before concluding, I would further observe that, if directives are recognized as having horizontal effect, the necessary consequences should be drawn as regards *legal protection*. Thus they should be capable of **[3345]** being challenged—as regulations and decisions are—under the second paragraph of Article 173.[59]

73. In the final analysis, I consider that for reasons of legal certainty it is not possible to envisage directives having horizontal effect as regards the past. As far as the future is concerned, however, horizontal effect seems to me to be necessary, subject to the limits mentioned, in the interests of the uniform, effective application of Community law. In my view, the resulting burdens on private individuals are reasonable, since they do not exceed the constraints which would have been applied to them if the Member State concerned had acted in conformity with Community law. Lastly, it is the party relying on the unconditional and sufficiently precise provision of a directive who will have to bear the risk of the court proceedings.

C—*Conclusion*

74. In view of the foregoing provisions, I consider that the reply to the national court's questions should be as follows:

(1) Article 1(1) and Article 5 of Directive 85/577/EEC have the precision necessary for direct applicability in so far as it is possible to infer from them a minimum guarantee as to renunciation of the effects of a contract which has not yet been performed. For the rest, the directive leaves the Member States leeway in several respects as regards the measures for the transposition of the directive into national law.

(2) (a) On the basis of the case-law to date, an unimplemented directive can have effects vis-à-vis the State in so far as all public authorities, in particular, the courts, are under a duty to take all appropriate

[59] See my Opinion in Case 298/89 *Gibraltar* v. *Council* (judgment of 29 June 1993), [1993] ECR I-3605.

measures, whether general or particular, to ensure fulfilment of obligations arising from a directive.

[3346] (b) Shortcomings in the implementation of the directive may entail an obligation on the Member State to compensate a private individual who benefits from its provisions.

(3) In accordance with that which the Court has consistently held, an unimplemented directive cannot have direct effect in relations between private individuals. That case-law should be maintained on grounds of legal certainty as regards past situations.

(4) For the future it appears necessary that the law based on the EC Treaty should develop in the interests of the uniform, effective application of Community law so as to recognize the general applicability of precise, unconditional provisions in directives in order to respond to the legitimate expectations nurtured by citizens of the Union following the achievement of the internal market and the entry into force of the Treaty on European Union.

[The following is the text of the judgment of the Court of Justice of the European Community:]

[3349] JUDGMENT

1. By order of 24 January 1992, received at the Court on 18 March 1992, the Giudice Conciliatore di Firenze (Judge-Conciliator, Florence), Italy, referred to the Court for a preliminary ruling under Article 177 of the EEC Treaty a question on the interpretation of Council Directive 85/577/EEC, concerning protection of the consumer in respect of contracts negotiated away from business premises (OJ 1985 L 372, p. 31, hereinafter "the directive"), and on the possibility of relying on that directive in proceedings between a trader and a consumer.

[3350] 2. The question was raised in proceedings between Paola Faccini Dori, of Monza, Italy, and Recreb Srl ("Recreb").

3. It appears from the order for reference that on 19 January 1989, without having been previously approached by her, Interdiffusion Srl concluded a contract with Miss Faccini Dori at Milan Central Railway Station for an English language correspondence course. Thus the contract was concluded away from Interdiffusion's business premises.

4. Some days later, by registered letter of 23 January 1989, Miss Faccini Dori informed that company that she was cancelling her order. The company replied on 3 June 1989 that it had assigned its claim to Recreb. On 24 June 1989, Miss Faccini Dori wrote to Recreb confirming that she had cancelled her subscription to the course, indicating *inter alia* that she relied on the right of cancellation provided for by the directive.

5. As is apparent from its preamble, the directive is intended to improve consumer protection and eliminate discrepancies between

national laws providing such protection, which may affect the functioning of the common market. According to the fourth recital in the preamble, where contracts are concluded away from the business premises of the trader, it is as a rule the trader who initiates the negotiations, for which the consumer is wholly unprepared and is therefore often taken by surprise. In most cases, the consumer is not in a position to compare the quality and price of the offer with other offers. According to the same recital, that surprise element generally exists not only in contracts made on the doorstep but also in other forms of contract for which the trader takes the initiative away from his business premises. The purpose of the directive is thus, as indicated by the fifth recital in its **[3351]** preamble, to grant the consumer a right of cancellation for a period of at least seven days in order to enable him to assess the obligations arising under the contract.

6. On 30 June 1989, Recreb asked the Giudice Conciliatore di Firenze to order Miss Faccini Dori to pay it the agreed sum with interest and costs.

7. By order of 20 November 1989, the judge ordered Miss Faccini Dori to pay the sums in question. She lodged an objection to that order with the same judge. She again stated that she had withdrawn from the contract under the conditions laid down by the directive.

8. However, it is common ground that at the material time Italy had not taken any steps to transpose the directive into national law, although the period set for transposition had expired on 23 December 1987. It was not until the adoption of Decreto Legislativo No 50 of 15 January 1992 (GURI, ordinary supplement to No 27 of 3 February 1992, p. 24), which entered into force on 3 March 1992, that Italy transposed the directive.

9. The national court was uncertain whether, even though the directive had not been transposed at the material time, it could nevertheless apply its provisions.

[3352] 10. It therefore referred the following question to the Court for a preliminary ruling:

> Is Community Directive 85/577/EEC of 20 December 1985 to be regarded as sufficiently precise and detailed and, if so, was it capable, in the period between the expiry of the 24-month time-limit given to the Member States to comply with the directive and the date on which the Italian State did comply with it, of taking effect as between individuals and the Italian State and as between individuals themselves?

11. The directive requires the Member States to adopt certain rules intended to govern legal relations between traders and consumers. In view of the nature of the dispute, which is between a consumer and a trader, the question submitted by the national court raises two issues, which should be considered separately. The first is whether the provisions of the directive concerning the right of cancellation are unconditional

and sufficiently precise. The second is whether a directive which requires the Member States to adopt certain rules specifically intended to govern relations between private individuals may be relied on in proceedings between such persons in the absence of measures to transpose the directive into national law.

Whether the Provisions of the Directive concerning the Right of Cancellation are Unconditional and Sufficiently Precise

12. Article 1(1) of the directive provides that the directive is to apply to contracts concluded between a trader supplying goods and services and a consumer, either during an excursion organized by the trader away from his business premises or during a visit by him to the consumer's home or place of work, where the visit does not take place at the express request of the consumer.

[3353] 13. Article 2 states that "consumer" means a natural person who, in transactions covered by the directive, is acting for purposes which can be regarded as outside his trade or profession and that "trader" means a natural or legal person who, for the transaction in question, acts in his commercial or professional capacity.

14. Those provisions are sufficiently precise to enable the national court to determine upon whom, and for whose benefit, the obligations are imposed. No specific implementing measure is needed in that regard. The national court may confine itself to verifying whether the contract was concluded in the circumstances described by the directive and whether it was concluded between a trader and a consumer as defined by the directive.

15. In order to protect consumers who have concluded contracts in such circumstances, Article 4 of the directive provides that traders are to be required to give consumers written notice of their right of cancellation, together with the name and address of a person against whom that right may be exercised. It adds that, in the case of Article 1(1), that information must be given to the consumer at the time of conclusion of the contract. Finally, it provides that Member States are to ensure that their national legislation lays down appropriate consumer protection measures for cases where the information in question is not supplied.

16. Furthermore, pursuant to Article 5(1) of the directive, the consumer is to have the right to renounce the effects of his undertaking by sending notice within a period of not less than seven days from the time at which the trader informed him of his **[3354]** rights in accordance with the terms and conditions laid down by national law. Article 5(2) provides that the giving of such notice is to have the effect of releasing the consumer from any obligations under the contract.

17. Admittedly, Articles 4 and 5 allow the Member States some latitude regarding consumer protection when information is not provided

by the trader and in determining the time-limit and conditions for cancellation. That does not, however, affect the precise and unconditional nature of the provisions of the directive at issue in this case. The latitude allowed does not make it impossible to determine minimum rights. Article 5 provides that the cancellation must be notified within a period of not less than seven days after the time at which the consumer received the prescribed information from the trader. It is therefore possible to determine the minimum protection which must on any view be provided.

18. As regards the first issue therefore, the answer to be given to the national court must be that Article 1(1), Article 2 and Article 5 of the directive are unconditional and sufficiently precise as regards determination of the persons for whose benefit they were adopted and the minimum period within which notice of cancellation must be given.

[3355] *Whether the Provisions of the Directive concerning the Right of Cancellation may be Invoked in Proceedings between a Consumer and a Trader*

19. The second issue raised by the national court relates more particularly to the question whether, in the absence of measures transposing the directive within the prescribed time-limit, consumers may derive from the directive itself a right of cancellation against traders with whom they have concluded contracts and enforce that right before a national court.

20. As the Court has consistently held since its judgment in Case 152/84 *Marshall* v. *Southampton and South-West Hampshire Health Authority* [1986] ECR 723, paragraph 48, a directive cannot of itself impose obligations on an individual and cannot therefore be relied upon as such against an individual.

21. The national court observes that if the effects of unconditional and sufficiently precise but untransposed directives were to be limited to relations between State entities and individuals, this would mean that a legislative measure would operate as such only as between certain legal subjects, whereas, under Italian law as under the laws of all modern States founded on the rule of law, the State is subject to the law like any other person. If the directive could be relied on only as against the State, that would be tantamount to a penalty for failure to adopt legislative measures of transposition as if the relationship were a purely private one.

[3356] 22. It need merely be noted here that, as is clear from the judgment in *Marshall*, cited above (paragraphs 48 and 49), the case-law on the possibility of relying on directives against State entities is based on the fact that under Article 189 a directive is binding only in relation to "each Member State to which it is addressed". That case-law seeks to prevent "the State from taking advantage of its own failure to comply with Community law".

23. It would be unacceptable if a State, when required by the Community legislature to adopt certain rules intended to govern the State's relations—or those of State entities—with individuals and to confer certain rights on individuals, were able to rely on its own failure to discharge its obligations so as to deprive individuals of the benefits of those rights. Thus the Court has recognized that certain provisions of directives on conclusion of public works contracts and of directives on harmonization of turnover taxes may be relied on against the State (or State entities) (see the judgment in Case 103/88 *Fratelli Costanzo* v. *Comune di Milano* [1989] ECR 1839 and the judgment in Case 8/81 *Becker* v. *Finanzamt Münster-Innenstadt* [1982] ECR 53).

24. The effect of extending that case-law to the sphere of relations between individuals would be to recognize a power in the Community to enact obligations for individuals with immediate effect, whereas it has competence to do so only where it is empowered to adopt regulations.

25. It follows that, in the absence of measures transposing the directive within the prescribed time-limit, consumers cannot derive from the directive itself a right of cancellation as against traders with whom they have concluded a contract or enforce such a right in a national court.

[3357] 26. It must also be borne in mind that, as the Court has consistently held since its judgment in Case 14/83 *Von Colson and Kamann* v. *Land Nordrhein-Westfalen* [1984] ECR 1891, paragraph 26, the Member States' obligation arising from a directive to achieve the result envisaged by the directive and their duty under Article 5 of the Treaty to take all appropriate measures, whether general or particular, is binding on all the authorities of Member States, including, for matters within their jurisdiction, the courts. The judgments of the Court in Case C-106/89 *Marleasing* v. *La Comercial Internacional de Alimentación* [1990] ECR I-4135, paragraph 8, and Case C-334/92 *Wagner Miret* v. *Fondo de Garantía Salarial* [1993] ECR I-6911, paragraph 20, make it clear that, when applying national law, whether adopted before or after the directive, the national court that has to interpret that law must do so, as far as possible, in the light of the wording and the purpose of the directive so as to achieve the result it has in view and thereby comply with the third paragraph of Article 189 of the Treaty.

27. If the result prescribed by the directive cannot be achieved by way of interpretation, it should also be borne in mind that, in terms of the judgment in Joined Cases C-6/90 and C-9/90 *Francovich and Others* v. *Italy* [1991] ECR I-5357, paragraph 39, Community law requires the Member States to make good damage caused to individuals through failure to transpose a directive, provided that three conditions are fulfilled. First, the purpose of the directive must be to grant rights to individuals. Second, it must be possible to identify the content of those rights on the basis of the provisions of the directive. Finally, there must be a

causal link between the breach of the State's obligation and the damage suffered.

28. The directive on contracts negotiated away from business premises is undeniably intended to confer rights on individuals and it is equally certain that the minimum content of those rights can be identified by reference to the provisions of the directive alone (see paragraph 17 above).

[3358] 29. Where damage has been suffered and that damage is due to a breach by the State of its obligation, it is for the national court to uphold the right of aggrieved consumers to obtain reparation in accordance with national law on liability.

30. So, as regards the second issue raised by the national court, the answer must be that in the absence of measures transposing the directive within the prescribed time-limit consumers cannot derive from the directive itself a right of cancellation as against traders with whom they have concluded a contract or enforce such a right in a national court. However, when applying provisions of national law, whether adopted before or after the directive, the national court must interpret them as far as possible in the light of the wording and purpose of the directive.

Costs

31. The costs incurred by the Danish, German, Greek, French, Italian, Netherlands and United Kingdom Governments and the Commission of the European Communities, which have submitted observations to the Court, are not recoverable. Since these proceedings are, for the parties to the main proceedings, a step in the action pending before the national court, the decision on costs is a matter for that court.

[3359] On those grounds,

THE COURT,

in answer to the question referred to it by the Giudice Conciliatore di Firenze, by order of 24 January 1992, hereby rules:

> **Article 1(1), Article 2 and Article 5 of Council Directive 85/577/EEC of 20 December 1985, concerning protection of the consumer in respect of contracts negotiated away from business premises, are unconditional and sufficiently precise as regards determination of the persons for whose benefit they were adopted and the minimum period within which notice of cancellation must be given.**
>
> **In the absence of measures transposing Directive 85/577 within the prescribed time-limit, consumers cannot derive**

from the directive itself a right of cancellation as against traders with whom they have concluded a contract or enforce such a right in a national court. However, when applying provisions of national law, whether adopted before or after the directive, the national court must interpret them as far as possible in the light of the wording and purpose of the directive.

[Report: [1994] ECR I-3325]

Institutions — Council — Powers — Whether European Community empowered to accede to European Convention on Human Rights, 1950 — EC Treaty, 1957 — Whether containing any provisions conferring a general power on Community institutions to enact rules or conclude international conventions on human rights—Whether Article 235 of EC Treaty could provide legal basis for accession to Convention — Whether accession requiring amendment of EC Treaties

Human rights—Scope of protection within the Community—Whether respect for human rights constituting condition for lawfulness of Community acts—Significance of the European Convention on Human Rights within the Community legal order

Legal order in general—Special character—Effect on legal order of possible entry of Community into institutional system of European Convention on Human Rights—Whether accession of the Community to the Convention would entail a substantial change in the Community system for the protection of human rights, requiring amendment of EC Treaties

Institutions—Court of Justice—Powers—Jurisdiction—EC Treaty, Article 228(6)—Competence of Court to give opinions on the compatibility of proposed international agreements with provisions of the EC Treaty — Scope of competence — Whether reference for opinion concerning an envisaged agreement admissible even before negotiations have formally begun—The law of the European Community

Re ACCESSION OF THE EUROPEAN COMMUNITY TO THE CONVENTION FOR THE PROTECTION OF HUMAN RIGHTS AND FUNDAMENTAL FREEDOMS

(OPINION 2/94)

Court of Justice of the European Community. 28 *March* 1996

(Rodríguez Iglesias, *President*; Kakouris, Edward, Puissochet and Hirsch, *Presidents of Chambers*; Mancini, Schockweiler (*Rapporteur*), Moitinho de Almeida, Kapteyn, Gulmann, Murray, Jann, Ragnemalm,

Sevón and Wathelet, *Judges*; Lenz, Jacobs, La Pergola, Cosmas, Léger, Elmer, Fenelly and Ruiz-Jarabo Colomer, *Advocates-General*)[1]

SUMMARY: *The facts*:—The Council of the European Union sought the opinion of the Court of Justice of the European Community pursuant to Article 228(6)[2] of the Treaty establishing the European Community ("the Treaty") on whether the European Community could accede to the Convention for the Protection of Human Rights and Fundamental Freedoms, 1950 ("the Convention"). According to the Council, no decision could be taken on the principle of opening negotiations until the Court had considered whether such accession was compatible with the Treaty.

The Council, supported by the Commission, the Parliament and five Member States, argued that, while the text of the "agreement envisaged" within the meaning of Article 228(6) of the Treaty did not yet exist, the request for an opinion was nevertheless admissible. The Convention to which the Community would accede was known and the legal issues to which accession would give rise were sufficiently clear, even if there were various possible solutions with regard to Community participation in the bodies established under the Convention. Other Member States argued, however, that the request for an opinion was inadmissible, or at least premature.

The Community institutions and eight Member States contended that Article 235[3] of the EC Treaty constituted the legal basis for the envisaged accession, in the absence of specific provisions. They also contended that the accession, and in particular the submission of the Community to the legal system of the Convention, was compatible with Articles 164 and 219 of the Treaty. Five Member States argued against any application of Article 235. They also submitted that the accession was incompatible with Articles 164 and 219, in particular because it would call into question the autonomy of the Community legal order and the exclusive jurisdiction of the Court of Justice in matters of Community law.

Held:—The request for an opinion was admissible. In the present state of Community law, the Community had no competence to accede to the Convention.

(1) The purpose of the special procedure laid down by Article 228(6) of the Treaty was to ascertain, before the conclusion of an international agreement which would be binding on the Community, whether it was compatible with the Treaty. In this case, in order to assess the extent to which the lack of

[1] Under the procedure provided for in Article 228(6), the Court sits in private session and the opinions of the Advocates-General are not made public.

[2] Article 228(6) provides:

> The Council, the Commission or a Member State may obtain the opinion of the Court of Justice as to whether an agreement envisaged is compatible with the provisions of this Treaty. Where the opinion of the Court of Justice is adverse, the agreement may enter into force only in accordance with Article N of the Treaty on European Union.

[3] Article 235 provides:

> If action by the Community should prove necessary to attain, in the course of the operation of the common market, one of the objectives of the Community and this Treaty has not provided the necessary powers, the Council shall, acting unanimously on a proposal from the Commission, and after consulting the European Parliament, take the appropriate measures.

firm information regarding the terms of the envisaged agreement affected the admissibility of the request, two separate problems had to be distinguished: (i) the competence of the Community to conclude such an agreement; and (ii) the compatibility of the agreement with the provisions of the Treaty, in particular those relating to the jurisdiction of the Court of Justice (p. 67).

(2) So far as competence was concerned, it was in the interests of the Community institutions and States concerned to have this question clarified from the outset, even before the main points of the agreement were negotiated,[4] provided the purpose of the envisaged agreement was already known, which was clearly the case here. If the procedure under Article 228(6) was to be effective, it had to be possible to refer the question of competence to the Court not only as soon as negotiations had commenced but also before they had formally begun, provided they were clearly envisaged (pp. 67-8).

(3) The Court had been given no information regarding the arrangements by which the Community envisaged submitting to the judicial control machinery established by the Convention. Without information as to how the Community would give effect in practice to such submission to the jurisdiction of an international court, the Court of Justice was not in a position to give an opinion on the compatibility of Community accession to the Convention with the rules of the Treaty (p. 68).

(4) It followed from Article 3b of the Treaty that the Community had only those powers which had been conferred upon it. That principle of conferred powers had to be respected in both the internal action and the international action of the Community. The competence of the Community to enter into international commitments derived both from express provisions of the Treaty and by implication.[5] No Treaty provision, however, conferred on the Community institutions any general power (express or implied) to enact rules on human rights or to conclude international conventions in that field (pp. 68-9).

(5) Article 235 was designed to fill the gap where no specific Treaty provisions conferred on the Community institutions express or implied powers to act, if such power nonetheless appeared necessary to enable the Community to carry out its functions with a view to attaining one of the objectives laid down by the Treaty. Article 235 could not, however, be used as a basis for the adoption of provisions whose effect would, in substance, be to amend the Treaty (p. 69).

(6) The importance of respect for human rights had been emphasized in various declarations of the Member States and of the Community institutions. Reference was also made to respect for human rights in the Single European Act and the Treaty on European Union, especially Article F(2) which provided that the Union was to respect fundamental rights, as guaranteed in particular by the Convention. It was also well settled that fundamental rights formed an integral part of the general principles of law whose observance the Court ensured. Respect for human rights was therefore a condition of the lawfulness of Community acts. Accession to the Convention would, however, entail a substantial change in the present Community system for the protection of human rights in that it would bring about the entry of the Community into a distinct international institutional system as well as integration of the Convention into

[4] See Opinion 1/78, paragraph 35 [1979] ECR 2871 at 2909.

[5] See Opinion 2/91, paragraph 7 [1993] 3 CMLR 800 at 815-16.

the Community legal order. Such a modification of the system for the protection of human rights in the Community would be of constitutional significance and would therefore go beyond the scope of Article 235. It could be brought about only by way of Treaty amendment (pp. 69-70).

The following is the text of the opinion of the Court:

[1763] The Court of Justice has received a request for an Opinion, lodged at the Registry of the Court on 26 April 1994, from the Council of the European Union pursuant to Article 228(6) of the EC Treaty, which provides:

The Council, the Commission or a Member State may obtain the opinion of the Court of Justice as to whether an agreement envisaged is compatible with the provisions of this Treaty. Where the opinion of the Court of Justice is adverse, the agreement may enter into force only in accordance with Article N of the Treaty on European Union.

SUMMARY

I—*The Request for an Opinion*

1. The Council, represented by J.-C. Piris, Director-General of the Legal Service, J.-P. Jacqué, Director in the Legal Service, and A. Lo Monaco, of its Legal Service, acting as Agents, requests the Opinion of the Court on the following question:

Would the accession of the European Community to the Convention for the Protection of Human Rights and Fundamental Freedoms of 4 November 1950 (hereinafter "the Convention") be compatible with the Treaty establishing the European Community?

2. According to the Council, no decision on the principle of opening negotiations can be taken until the Court has considered whether the envisaged accession is compatible with the Treaty.

In its oral observations, the Council, whilst recognizing that the text of the envisaged agreement does not yet exist, submits that the request is admissible. The Council has not committed a misuse of procedure but is confronted by fundamental issues concerning legal and institutional order. Furthermore, the convention to which the Community would accede is known and the legal **[1764]** issues to which accession gives rise are sufficiently clear for the Court to be able to give an Opinion.

3. The Council, setting out the aim and objectives of the agreement envisaged, states its position on the scope of accession, Community participation in control bodies and the modifications which would have to be made to the Convention and the Protocols.

4. With regard to the scope of accession, the Council states that each Community will have to adhere to the Convention within the framework of its powers and within the limits of the scope of its law. Accession should cover the Convention and the Protocols which have come into force and been ratified by all the Member States of the Community. Such accession should not have any effect on the reservations entered by the Member States, parties to the Convention, which will continue to apply in the areas falling within national jurisdiction. The Community would agree to submit to the machinery for individual petitions and inter-State applications; actions between the Community and its Member States would, however, have to be excluded in recognition of the monopoly conferred in such matters by Article 219 of the EC Treaty on the Court of Justice.

5. With regard to Community participation in control bodies, in particular the future single Court of Human Rights, there are various possible solutions: no Community judge, appointment of a permanent judge with the same status as the other judges, or the appointment of a judge with special status, entitled to vote only in cases concerning Community law. That judge would not be a member of the Court of Justice at the same time. The procedure for appointing the judge would be governed by the Convention on the understanding that the appointment of candidates proposed by the Community would be an internal Community matter. Community participation in the Committee of Ministers would not be envisaged; the Committee would moreover no longer have any function in the future judicial framework.

6. It would be necessary to amend the Convention and the Protocols which are currently open to accession only by Member States of the Council of Europe. The Community does not propose to join the Council of Europe. It would similarly be necessary to modify the technical provisions providing for the Member States of the Council of Europe to intervene in the control machinery of the Convention. In the event of accession, the Community would be bound only within the limits of its powers. There would have to be machinery enabling the Community and the Member States to determine the division of competence before the Convention authorities.

7. In reviewing the conformity of accession with the Treaty, the Council considers the Community's competence to conclude the agreement envisaged and the compatibility of **[1765]** the system of courts under the Convention with Articles 164 and 219 of the Treaty.

8. The Council recognizes that the Treaty confers no specific powers on the Community in the field of human rights. Such rights are protected by way of general principles of Community law. The need for such protection, reaffirmed by the case-law, is now enshrined in Article F of the Treaty on European Union. The Council considers that the protection of human rights flows from a horizontal principle forming an integral part

of the Community's objectives. In the absence of a specific article, Article 235 of the EC Treaty would serve as the basis of accession, provided that the conditions of that article's application are fulfilled.

9. The Council also raises the question whether accession of the Community to the Convention, in particular to the system of courts, calls in question the exclusive jurisdiction conferred on the Court of Justice by Articles 164 and 219 of the Treaty and the autonomy of the Community legal order.

10. The Council emphasizes that judgments of the European Court of Human Rights have no direct effect: that court cannot repeal or amend a provision of national law but can only impose on a contracting party an obligation to bring about a certain result. The Court of Justice would, however, have to apply judgments of the Court of Human Rights in its own decisions. The requirement that in order for individual petitions to be admissible domestic remedies must first have been exhausted would mean that the Community's internal courts, in particular the Court of Justice, would rule on the compatibility of a Community act with the Convention. In Opinion 1/91 [1991] ECR I-6079, the Court accepted the Community's submission to judicial machinery created by an international agreement provided that the court simply interpreted and applied the agreement and did not challenge the autonomy of the Community legal order. The Council raises the question whether that statement applies only where the judgments of that court concern solely the international agreement or also where those judgments may cover the compatibility of Community law with the agreement.

II—*Procedure*

1. In accordance with Article 107(1) of the Rules of Procedure of the Court of Justice, the request for the Opinion was served on the Commission and the Member States. Written observations were submitted by the Belgian Government, represented by J. Devadder, Director of Administration at the Ministry of Foreign Affairs, Foreign Trade and Development, acting as Agent; the Danish Government, represented by L. **[1766]** Mikaelsen, Ambassador, and P. Biering, Head of Department, Legal Advisers at the Ministry of Foreign Affairs, acting as Agents; the German Government, represented by E. Röder, Ministerialrat at the Federal Ministry of Economic Affairs, and A. Dietrich, Regierungsdirektor at the Federal Ministry of Justice, acting as Agents; the Greek Government, represented by V. Rotis, Honorary President of the Council of State, S. Zissimopoulos, Legal Adviser to the Permanent Representation of the Greek Republic, and N. Dafniou, secretary to the Special Service for Community Legal Affairs of the Ministry of Foreign Affairs, acting as Agents; the Spanish Government, represented by A. Navarro González, Director-General for Community Legal and Institutional Coordination,

and Rosario Silva de Lapuerta, Abogado del Estado, of the Department of Community Legal Affairs, acting as Agents; the French Government, represented by E. Belliard, Deputy Director at the Legal Affairs Directorate of the Ministry of Foreign Affairs, C. de Salins, Head of Section in that directorate, and C. Chavance, Foreign Affairs Secretary in the same directorate, acting as Agents; the Netherlands Government, represented by A. Bos, Legal Adviser at the Ministry of Foreign Affairs, acting as Agent; the Portuguese Government, represented by L. Fernandes, Director of the Legal Service Directorate of the Directorate-General of Community Affairs of the Ministry of Foreign Affairs, and M. L. Duarte, Consultant in the same directorate, acting as Agents; the United Kingdom, represented by J. Collins, of the Treasury Solicitor's Department, acting as Agent, and S. Richards and D. Anderson, Barristers; and the Commission, represented by J. Amphoux, Principal Legal Adviser, J. Pipkorn, Legal Adviser, and R. Gosalbo-Bono, of the Legal Service, acting as Agents.

2. After the accession of the Republic of Austria, the Republic of Finland and the Kingdom of Sweden to the European Union, the request for an Opinion was also served on those Member States. Written observations were submitted by the Austrian Government, represented by K. Berchtold, university lecturer, acting as Agent, and by the Finnish Government, represented by H. Rotkirch, Head of Service at the Ministry of Foreign Affairs, acting as Agent.

3. At its request, the European Parliament, represented by G. Garzón Clariana, jurisconsult, and E. Perillo, of the Legal Service, acting as Agents, was granted leave to submit observations.

4. At the hearing on 7 November 1995 the Court heard the oral observations of the Belgian Government, represented by J. Devadder; the Danish Government, represented by L. Mikaelsen and P. Biering; the German Government, represented by A. Dietrich; the Greek Government, represented by A. Samoni-Rantou, Special Deputy Legal Adviser to the Special Service for Community Legal Affairs of the Ministry of Foreign Affairs, acting as Agent, and N. Dafniou; the Spanish Government, represented by R. Silva **[1767]** de Lapuerta; the French Government, represented by J.-F. Dobelle, Deputy Director in the Legal Affairs Directorate of the Ministry of Foreign Affairs, acting as Agent, and C. Chavance; Ireland, represented by D. Gleeson SC, acting as Agent, and M. Buckley; the Italian Government, represented by Professor U. Leanza, Head of the Department for Contentious Diplomatic Affairs, Treaties and Legislative Matters at the Ministry of Foreign Affairs, acting as Agent; the Netherlands Government, represented by M. Fiestra, Deputy Legal Adviser at the Ministry of Foreign Affairs, acting as Agent; the Portuguese Government, represented by L. Fernandes and M. L. Duarte; the Finnish Government, represented by H. Rotkirch; the Swedish Government, represented by L. Nordling, Adviser in the

Legal Directorate for European Affairs of the Ministry of Foreign Affairs; the United Kingdom, represented by J. E. Collins and by S. Richards and D. Anderson; the Council of the European Union, represented by J.-C. Piris, J.-P. Jacqué and A. Lo Monaco; the Commission, represented by J. Pipkorn and R. Gosalbo-Bono; and the European Parliament, represented by G. Garzón Clariana and E. Perillo.

III—*History of respect for human rights by the Community*

1. Neither the EC Treaty nor the ECSC or EAEC Treaties makes any specific reference to fundamental rights other than by resolving "to preserve and strengthen peace and liberty" in the last recital in the preamble.

2. The Court of Justice has upheld the protection of fundamental rights by way of general principles of Community law, referring to common constitutional traditions and to international instruments, in particular the Convention.

3. Drawing on that case-law, the Single European Act refers in its preamble to respect for the fundamental rights recognized in the constitutions and laws of the Member States, in the Convention and in the European Social Charter.

4. Article F(2) of the Treaty on European Union states that the Union "shall respect fundamental rights, as guaranteed by the European Convention . . . and as they result from the constitutional traditions common to the Member States, as general principles of Community law". The fifth indent of Article J.1(2) of that Treaty refers to respect for **[1768]** human rights and fundamental freedoms. Article K.2(1) of the Treaty contains an express reference to compliance with the Convention in cooperation in the fields of justice and home affairs.

5. Reference to respect for fundamental rights has also been made in political declarations by the Member States and Community institutions. These include the Joint Declaration by the European Parliament, the Council and the Commission on fundamental rights of 5 April 1977 (*Treaty Series* 1995, p. 877); the Joint Declaration by the European Parliament, the Council, the representatives of the Member States, meeting within the Council, and the Commission against racism and xenophobia of 11 June 1986 (*Treaty Series* 1995, p. 889); the Resolution of the Council and the representatives of the governments of the Member States, meeting within the Council, of 29 May 1990 on the fight against racism and xenophobia (OJ 1990 C 157, p. 1), the Resolution of the Council and of the Member States, meeting in the Council, on human rights, democracy and development of 28 November 1991 (*Bulletin of the European Communities*, No 11/1991, p. 130, point 2.3.1) and the Conclusions on the implementation of that resolution adopted by the Council and the Member States on 18 November 1992. Declarations by various

European Councils may also be mentioned, such as the Declaration by the Heads of State or Government of the Member States of the EC on the European identity of 14 December 1973 (*Bulletin of the European Communities*, No 12/1973, point 2501), the Declaration by the European Council on democracy of 8 April 1978, the Declaration by the European Council on the international role of the Community of 2 and 3 December 1988 (*Bulletin of the European Communities*, No 12/1988, point 1.1.10), the Declaration by the European Council on human rights of 29 June 1991 (*Bulletin of the European Communities*, No 6/1991, Annex V) and the Statement by the European Union on human rights of 11 December 1993 on the occasion of the 45th anniversary of the Universal Declaration of Human Rights (*Bulletin of the European Communities*, No 12/1993, point 1.4.12).

6. In a report of 4 February 1976, sent to the European Parliament and the Council, entitled "Protection of fundamental rights in the creation and development of Community law" (*Bulletin of the European Communities*, Supplement 5/76), the Commission ruled out the necessity of accession by the Community as such to the Convention.

7. Formal accession was first proposed by the Commission to the Council by the Memorandum on the accession of the European Communities to the Convention for the Protection of Human Rights and Fundamental Freedoms of 4 April 1979 (*Bulletin of the European Communities*, Supplement 2/79).

8. That proposal was renewed by the Commission's Communication on Community accession to the European Convention for **[1769]** the Protection of Human Rights and Fundamental Freedoms of 19 November 1990.

9. On 26 October 1993, the Commission published a working document entitled "Accession of the Community to the European Convention on Human Rights and the Community legal order", in which it considered in particular the questions as to the legal basis of accession and the monopoly of jurisdiction of the Court of Justice.

10. The European Parliament has on several occasions made statements in favour of accession, most recently by a resolution of 18 January 1994 on Community accession to the European Convention on Human Rights, adopted on the basis of a report of the Committee on Legal Affairs and Citizens' Rights (OJ 1994 C 44, p. 32).

IV—*Admissibility of the request for an Opinion*

1. *Ireland* and the *United Kingdom* argue that the request for an Opinion is not admissible. The *Danish*, *Finnish* and *Swedish Governments* also raise the question whether the request is premature.

In its oral observations, Ireland points out that there is no specific proposal for an agreement on accession on which the Court could give its opinion. The technical problems are numerous and a variety of solutions is conceivable. No option has yet been taken for determination by the parties who have to negotiate.

According to the United Kingdom, no agreement is "envisaged" within the meaning of Article 228(6) of the Treaty. The Court may be seised only after the draft agreement has been substantially negotiated. In Opinion 1/78 [1979] ECR 2871, the request was admittedly held to be admissible notwithstanding the fact that the negotiations were still to take place. However, at the time the request was made the agreement existed in **[1770]** draft; negotiations took place during the proceedings and the Court was informed of the most recent state of the texts before delivering its Opinion. In these proceedings, in contrast, there is no draft agreement and no negotiations are envisaged before the Opinion is delivered. The request for Opinion 1/78 was relevant since the legal basis of the agreement was at issue. In this case, there is consensus as to the only possible legal basis, namely Article 235 of the Treaty.

As well as the fundamental problems outlined by the Council, the United Kingdom refers to other difficulties. It raises the question of the scope of accession given the reservations made by the Member States, the power of the latter to derogate at any time from certain provisions of the Convention and the risk of a discrepancy between the obligations of the Member States and those of the Community, the problem of the Community's participation in the organs of the Convention, in particular in the future single court, the division of competence between the Community and the Member States, the difficulty of the Community's acceding to the Convention without first acceding to the Council of Europe, and the future of the ECSC and EAEC Treaties. Given the number and gravity of these problems, the United Kingdom submits that the Court could not at the present stage give an Opinion of value.

Article 235 of the Treaty, the only possible legal basis, requires a unanimous decision of the Council. The fact that there is no such unanimity emphasizes the hypothetical and unrealistic nature of the request for an Opinion. In the context of references for a preliminary ruling, the Court has always refused to rule on general or hypothetical questions.

The Danish Government notes that there is no negotiated draft agreement. Still less has any agreement been reached within the Council as to the opening of negotiations.

The Finnish Government points out that, according to Article 107(2) of the Rules of Procedure and the case-law of the Court, an Opinion may deal with the compatibility of the envisaged agreement with the Treaty and with the question of the powers of the Community. In the present case, the admissibility of the request for an Opinion depends on whether the agreement envisaged can be extracted from the documents annexed to the request or referred to therein with sufficient precision to enable the Court to deliver an Opinion. If so, the fact that the request may be premature would not prevent the Court from ruling generally and as a matter of principle.

In its oral observations the Swedish Government also points out that there is as yet no draft text in existence or even a Council decision to open negotiations. Even if the Court were to admit this request for an Opinion, once the legal and technical **[1771]** questions had been tackled during the negotiations, a subsequent request might be unavoidable.

2. The *Commission*, the *Parliament*, and the *Belgian*, *French*, *German*, *Italian* and *Portuguese Governments* submit that the request for an Opinion is admissible since it concerns an agreement envisaged within the meaning of Article 228(6) of the Treaty.

The Commission refers to the change in the wording of Article 228. The former text of the second subparagraph of Article 228(1) of the EEC Treaty, under which the Opinion of the Court of Justice could be obtained beforehand as to whether the agreement envisaged was compatible, followed on from the first subparagraph referring to the conclusion of agreements between the Community and third countries or an international organization. The new text of Article 228(6) of the EC Treaty refers only to an agreement envisaged with no mention of an Opinion before the conclusion of the agreement in question. In Opinion 1/78, the Court gave a broad interpretation to the concept of agreement envisaged; that case may be regarded as reinforced in the light of the new wording. As in the request for Opinion 1/78, the question before the Court relates to powers and there is no risk that the matter will come before it again during any negotiations.

The Parliament emphasizes that the purpose of Article 228 is, as is clear from Opinion 1/75 [1975] ECR 1355, to forestall disputes relating to the compatibility with the Treaty of international agreements. This case concerns the compatibility of the legal system established by the Convention with the Community legal order. The specific legal question is whether the Court's being subject to a judicial body outside the Community legal system is compatible with the Court's monopoly of jurisdiction. The Court accepted, in Opinion 1/78, cited above, that it is in the interests of all the States concerned, including non-member countries, for a question of powers to be settled as soon as negotiations are commenced.

The Belgian Government also refers to the precedent of Opinion 1/78 and the new wording of Article 228(6) of the Treaty. It stresses three points. The Member States have accepted that the compatibility of accession with Community law must be established before negotiations are opened. The Court has already acknowledged, in Opinion 1/78, cited above, and Opinion 1/92 [1992] ECR I-2821, that a request for an Opinion must be admitted provided that the subject-matter of the agreement envisaged is known and that the originator of the request has an interest in the outcome, even if the content of the agreement envisaged has not yet been defined in all detail. To require that the institution which makes the request for an Opinion entertains no doubt as to the compatibility of the agreement envisaged with Community law at the time the Court is seised would undermine the effectiveness of Article 228(6) of the Treaty.

[1772] In its oral observations the German Government submits that the request is admissible since, when it was made, discussions on accession had reached a stage where an Opinion appeared necessary and justified. The Convention which is to be acceded to as well as the adaptations which such accession requires are known. In accordance with what the Court held in Opinion 1/78, it is in the interests of all the Member States that the question of the power of the Community to accede to the Convention be settled before negotiations begin.

The French Government, in its oral observations, accepts that the Court does not have before it a draft agreement, that there are many uncertainties surrounding the negotiations and that for the moment there is no consensus within the Council on the expediency of accession. However, the Court should admit the request for an Opinion since the legal questions concerning the compatibility of accession with the Treaty are clear and their relevance cannot be disputed.

The Italian Government, in its observations, refers to Article 107(2) of the Rules of Procedure from which it is clear that a request for an Opinion may concern the compatibility with the provisions of the Treaty of the envisaged agreement or the power of the Community to enter into that agreement. If, as in the present case, the request concerned the Community's powers, the existence of a draft agreement already sufficiently defined would not be required. Even if the request also concerns the compatibility of accession with the substantive rules of the Treaty, the Court could not decline to give an Opinion since the Convention to be acceded to exists and its general aspects are known.

The Portuguese Government, in its oral observations, also points out that the result of the negotiations to be carried out and the terms of the Convention to which the Community proposes acceding are known.

V—*The legal basis of the envisaged accession*

1. The *Austrian Government*, after referring to the case-law relating to the external competence of the Community, submits that the exercise of all the Community's powers involves respect for fundamental rights. The guarantee of the rights protected by the Convention is based on the powers on the basis of which the Community institutions act in each field concerned. Such internal horizontal application of the rights guaranteed by the Convention is at the same time the basis of the Community's external competence to accede to the Convention.

[1773] 2. The *Commission*, the *Parliament* and the *Belgian*, *Danish*, *Finnish*, *German*, *Greek*, *Italian* and *Swedish Governments*, together with the *Austrian Government* as a subsidiary argument, submit that, in the absence of specific provisions, Article 235 of the Treaty is the legal basis for accession. The conditions for the application of Article 235, namely the necessity for action by the Community, the attainment of one of the objectives of the Community and the link with the operation of the common market, are fulfilled.

The Commission refers to its working document of 26 October 1993, cited above, in which it described respect for human rights as a transverse objective forming an integral part of the Community's objectives.

It is clear from the judgment in Case 43/75 *Defrenne* [1976] ECR 455 that the objectives, within the meaning of Article 235 of the Treaty, may be made clear in the preamble of the Treaty. The preamble to the Single European Act makes reference to respect for human rights and to the Convention.

The Parliament also considers that the protection of human rights is encompassed within the Community's objectives. The embodiment in the Treaty of citizenship of the Union is a new legal factor supporting that argument. By virtue of the combined provisions of the third indent of Article B of the Treaty on European Union and Article 8 of the EC Treaty, it is for the Community to ensure that the fundamental rights of a citizen of the Union are protected to the same extent as his rights as a national citizen with regard to State acts. The Parliament emphasizes the need for the Community, including the Court of Justice, to be subject to the same international judicial control as Member States and their courts of final appeal. According to the Parliament, the choice of Article 235 of the Treaty should be supplemented by reference to the second subparagraph of Article 228(3) of the Treaty, requiring, for the conclusion of certain international agreements, the assent of the Parliament. The need for such assent may be explained by reference to the *ratio legis* of that provision, which is to ensure that the Parliament is not required by an international agreement, in its role as co-legislator and by virtue of the Community's international obligations, to amend an act adopted following the codecision procedure.

The Austrian, Belgian, Finnish, German, Greek, Italian and Swedish Governments emphasize that the protection of human rights is a general horizontal principle which applies to the Community in the exercise of all its activities and that such protection is essential for the proper functioning of the common market.

According to those governments, the Court has realized that protection by way of general principles of Community law, drawing on common constitutional traditions and international instruments, in particular the Convention. The preamble to the Single **[1774]** European Act, the preamble to the Treaty on European Union and Articles F(2), J.1 and

K.2 of that Treaty enshrine respect for human rights and, in that context, the role of the Convention.

The Greek Government also refers to Article 130u(2) of the EC Treaty, which mentions the objective of respecting human rights in cooperation and development.

The Austrian Government submits that, to determine the objectives of the Community, reference should also be made to the preamble to the Treaty which refers to the preservation of peace and liberty; that objective encompasses the rights guaranteed by the Convention.

The Finnish Government considers that, at the present stage of the Community's development, the protection of human rights is a proper objective of the Community.

According to all those governments, accession to the Convention and external judicial control are necessary to protect individuals against disregard of the Convention by the Community institutions.

The Belgian Government stresses the need to avoid divergent interpretations in Community case-law and that of the organs of the Convention. It notes that the system of remedies in Community law, which excludes actions for annulment by an individual in respect of an act which is not of direct and individual concern to him, affords less protection than that of the Convention.

The Italian Government, in its oral observations, points out that all the Member States, acting within their powers, have voluntarily submitted to the international control machinery for the protection of human rights. The transfer of State powers to the Community requires that the Community be subject to the same international control in order to restore the balance originally desired by the Member States.

The Austrian Government refers to the need for a uniform interpretation of the Convention, to the continuing increase in the integration envisaged by the Treaty on European Union, an area in which the protection of human rights is particularly important, and the law governing Community officials.

The Finnish Government submits that accession is necessary from the point of view of strengthening the social aspect of the Treaty. The new bases of competence laid down **[1775]** in the Single European Act and the embodiment in the Treaty of the principle of subsidiarity have however restricted the scope of Article 235 of the Treaty. Whether that provision applies would depend on the structure and content of the accession agreement.

3. The *French*, *Portuguese* and *Spanish Governments* and *Ireland* and the *United Kingdom* assert that neither the EC Treaty nor the Treaty on European Union contains any provision allocating specific powers to the Community in the field of human rights capable of being the legal basis of the envisaged accession. Article F(2) of the Treaty on European Union simply gives constitutional status to the existing case-law in the

field of the protection of human rights and moreover envisages such protection only by way of general principles of Community law.

The French and Portuguese Governments add that Article J.1(2) of the Treaty on European Union, concerned with the common foreign and security policy, and Article K.2(1), concerned with justice and home affairs, which are moreover not within the jurisdiction of the Court of Justice, are in the nature of a programme and do not confer specific powers on the Community. The French Government also rules out Article 130u of the EC Treaty.

The Spanish, French and Portuguese Governments and Ireland and the United Kingdom also argue against any application of Article 235 of the Treaty. Respect for human rights is not among the objectives of the Community as set out in Articles 2 and 3 of the Treaty. The United Kingdom adds that reference to Article F(2) of the Treaty on European Union cannot justify recourse to Article 235.

Those governments deny that a legal vacuum or deficit in the protection of human rights requires the envisaged accession. The Court of Justice has substantially incorporated the Convention into the Community legal order and fully integrated it into the corpus of Community law. The French Government lists the fundamental rights enshrined by the Convention, protection of which has been upheld by the Court of Justice.

The Portuguese Government adds that the risk of divergent interpretations of the Convention by the Court of Justice and the European Court of Human Rights is theoretical and may be explained by the Community's specific objectives of economic and political integration. This government raises the possibility of the Court of Justice making a reference for a preliminary ruling to the European Court of Human Rights on the interpretation of the Convention.

[1776] According to the governments, Community law comprises a complete system of remedies for individuals. Accession is not necessary in the context of the operation of the common market.

4. The *Danish Government* sets out arguments for and against accession. It refers to the lacuna in the protection of human rights in the law governing Community officials while recognizing that that lacuna is not fundamental but procedural in nature. Respecting the Convention by a sort of self-limitation which the Court has developed differs from respecting it by virtue of an international obligation, even if the difference is theoretical. The advantage of accession would be essentially political, in that it would underline the importance attached to respect for human rights. Accession would also enable the Community to undertake its own defence if Community law were challenged before the organs provided for by the Convention. The Government notes that in general disputes concern a combination of Community and national rules, in which case the national rules are in principle disputed; in that situation, the

institutions, in particular the Commission, could assist the national government before the organs of the Convention.

Opposed to that political advantage are, says the Danish Government, practical and legal problems. Currently, accession is only possible for States; the position of the other Contracting Parties is not clear; accession by the Community would give rise to problems with regard to the derogations granted to the Member States and the reservations made by them; accession would probably not extend to the whole of the Convention; it would be necessary to establish machinery for determining the entity responsible for infringement of the Convention, given that *ex hypothesi* the disputed act would be national; the question would also arise as to representation of the Community in the Convention's control bodies, in particular in the future single Court. In the light of the gravity of those problems, the Danish Government proposes that an agreement be concluded between the Community and the Contracting Parties to the Convention enabling the Court of Justice to refer questions concerning human rights to the European Court of Human Rights for a preliminary ruling and authorizing the European Court of Human Rights to seek a preliminary ruling on Community law from the Court of Justice.

VI—*Compatibility of accession with Articles 164 and 219 of the Treaty*

1. The *Commission*, the *Parliament*, and the *Austrian*, *Belgian*, *Danish*, *German*, *Finnish*, *Greek*, *Italian* and *Swedish Governments* submit that the envisaged accession, in particular the submission of the Community to the legal system of the Convention, is not **[1777]** contrary to Articles 164 and 219 of the Treaty.

The Commission notes that, unlike in the case of the Agreement on the European Economic Area, the objectives of the Convention and the Treaty concur in the area of human rights. The Convention lays down classic international-law control machinery and the judgments of the European Court of Human Rights have no direct effect in the internal legal order. Admittedly, the Convention has the specific feature that individuals may petition. That however is simply one aspect of control, alongside the applications which may be made by the Contracting Parties; it would moreover be contradictory to accept that control machinery and to refuse individual petitions. The European Court of Human Rights would not rule on the question of the division of competence between the Community and the Member States, which is regulated solely by the Community legal order. Thus there should be no possibility of any action between the Community and the Member States.

Neither can it be asserted that the control machinery of the Convention, in that it extends to all Community powers, calls in question the autonomy of the Community legal order. The Convention imposes only minimum standards. The control machinery has no direct effect in the Community legal order. Since it has not been considered contrary to the constitutional principles of the Member States, that machinery could hardly be considered to be incompatible with the principles of Community law.

The Parliament refers to Opinion 1/91, cited above, in which the Court recognized that the Community had power to submit to decisions of an international court. The submission of the Community to a court competent in human rights matters is consistent with the development of the Community order which is no longer directed at the economic operator but at the citizen of the Union. External control in the field of human rights does not affect the autonomy of the Community legal order any more than it prejudices that of the Member States. The Parliament refers to its resolution of 18 January 1994, cited above, in which it noted the importance of being able to bring a direct action before an international court in examining the compatibility of a Community act with human rights and stressed that the envisaged accession is not such as to call in question the Court's competence in questions of Community law.

The Belgian Government considers that the Court is required to decide whether the fundamental rights integrated in the Community legal order, where they are drawn from the Convention, become Community law or retain their specific character. Whether or **[1778]** not the envisaged accession affects the autonomy of Community law will depend on the answer.

The Government notes first that the rights and freedoms of the Convention have their own status among the general principles of Community law. The Convention simply establishes a minimum threshold of protection and does not affect the development of that protection from other sources recognized by the Court, namely the Community legal order properly so called and the common constitutional traditions. When it refers to the Convention, the Court takes into consideration the interpretation given by the organs of the Convention, thus underlining the specific place of rights guaranteed by the Convention in the Community legal order. To that extent, the autonomy of the Community legal order, within the meaning of Opinions 1/91 and 2/92, cited above, is from now on simply relative.

The Belgian Government next argues that the agreement envisaged preserves the autonomy of the Community legal order. In accordance with the possibility provided in Article 62 of the Convention, any action between the Community and its Member States would be excluded, which would respect Article 219 of the Treaty. In order to avoid any external influence on the division of competence between the Community and the Member States, the latter could, in the event of an individual petition, adopt a position on the issue of who was liable for the alleged infringement; the machinery to be established would be based on

Annex IX to the United Nations Convention on the Law of the Sea of 10 December 1982.

The Belgian Government emphasizes, thirdly, that absolute autonomy of the Community legal order in the field of the rights and liberties guaranteed by the Convention is not desirable. The risk that the organs of the Convention will consider themselves competent to rule on the compatibility with the Convention, if not of Community acts, at least of national implementing acts, cannot be ruled out if the protection of human rights in the Community legal order is less than that of the Convention.

Even if the Court of Justice were to conclude that the criteria laid down in Opinions 1/91 and 1/92 relating to the autonomy of the Community legal order were applicable, the envisaged accession could proceed.

The Belgian Government notes the lack of any personal and functional link between the Court of Justice and the organs of the Convention. The European Court of Human Rights may simply require the relevant party to comply with its judgments without being able to annul or invalidate the national measure in dispute. With regard to the effect of **[1779]** the judgments of that Court, the Government distinguishes two cases. If the provision of the Convention is sufficiently precise and complete, it will be respected simply by recognizing that it is directly applicable. If the infringed provision is not directly applicable, it will be for the State to take the appropriate measures to remedy the infringement. In neither case would the autonomy of the Community legal order be called in question.

According to the Austrian, Danish, Finnish, German, Greek and Italian Governments, the Court accepted in Opinion 1/91, cited above, that the Community may submit to a court set up by an international agreement for the interpretation and application of that agreement provided that the autonomy of the Community legal order is not affected. The Court stressed in particular the need to respect the independence of the Community judicature and the monopoly of the Court of Justice in the interpretation of Community law.

The Danish Government emphasizes that in the Agreement on the European Economic Area the difficulty lay in the fact that that law was the same as Community law. In this case, the Community institutions, including the Court of Justice, would be taking into consideration the case-law of the organs of the Convention solely in respect of human rights. Without wishing definitively to settle the question, the Government stresses that the case-law of the Convention already influences that of the Court of Justice, which argues in favour of accession being compatible with the Treaty.

The German Government also asserts that the question of the division of competence between the Community and the Member States remains within the jurisdiction of the Court of Justice, since the European Court of Human Rights does not rule on the internal law of the Contracting Parties. The Court of Justice safeguards fundamental rights by reference both to the constitutional tradition of the Member States and to the Convention, and achieves greater protection than the Convention. It cannot therefore be argued that the autonomy of Community law is called in question because identical provisions are interpreted differently by virtue of their different objectives. The sole obligation which the Convention would impose on the Community, namely a minimum level of respect, is within the limits laid down in Opinion 1/91, cited above. The German Government also refers to the fact that there is no personal link between the two courts.

The Greek Government considers that any involvement of the European Court of Human Rights in the Community legal order would be limited to interpreting the rights guaranteed by the Convention. Respect for the autonomy of the Community legal order would not prohibit any external involvement, but would require the fundamental principles and the institutional **[1780]** balances of Community law to be protected. The participation of a judge from the Community who would not at the same time be a member of the Court of Justice should ensure that the European Court of Human Rights takes into consideration the specific features of Community law.

The Italian Government, in its oral observations, points out that the accession agreement will have to respect the criteria laid down by the Court in Opinions 1/91 and 1/92 as regards respect for the Community legal order. The Italian Government particularly emphasizes in this regard that judgments of the European Court of Human Rights do not have direct effect in the internal legal systems and cannot have the effect of declaring internal acts unlawful.

The Austrian Government emphasizes the difference from the Agreement on the European Economic Area. Accession would not create a normative package essentially comprising rules already part of the Community legal order and to be integrated into that order. The European Court of Human Rights would not have jurisdiction to rule on questions of Community law which would for this purpose be treated in the same way as the law of the States party to the Convention.

The Swedish Government considers that accession could be incompatible with Articles 164 and 219 of the Treaty only in the event of a risk of a failure to observe the binding character of judgments of the Court and therefore an undermining of the autonomy of the Community legal order. In order to avoid that risk, the Swedish Government suggests that it would be possible to exclude, by special agreement, disputes between Member States or between Member States and the Community from the settlement machinery of the Convention. It also puts forward the idea of references being made by the European Court of Human Rights to the Court of Justice on questions of Community law.

The Finnish Government does not rule out the possibility that the envisaged accession and the subordination of the Community institutions to the jurisdiction of the European Court of Human Rights may have effects on the interpretation by the Court of Justice of provisions of Community law to the extent that such provisions affect human rights. If the principles set out by the Court of Justice in Opinion 1/91 were applied, it would none the less be necessary to recognize that human rights, protected by way of general principles of Community law, were not within the economic and commercial framework of that law and accession would not prejudice its autonomy.

2. The *French*, *Portuguese* and *Spanish Governments* and *Ireland* and the *United Kingdom* argue that accession by the Community to the Convention is incompatible with the Treaty, in particular Articles 164 and 219. **[1781]** Referring to Opinions 1/91 and 1/92, the governments emphasize that the envisaged accession calls into question the autonomy of the Community legal order and the Court of Justice's monopoly of jurisdiction.

The Spanish Government cites Articles 24 and 25 of the Convention establishing inter-State and individual petitions, Article 45 conferring jurisdiction on the European Court of Human Rights over the interpretation and application of the Convention, Articles 32 and 46 conferring a binding character on the decisions of the organs of the Convention, Article 52 on the final nature of judgments of the European Court of Human Rights, Article 53 obliging the Contracting Parties to abide by judgments and Article 54 investing the Committee of Ministers with a duty to supervise execution of judgments. Article 62 of the Convention, submitting all disputes between Contracting Parties concerning the interpretation or application of the Convention to the means of settlement laid down therein, is incompatible with Article 219 of the Treaty; it would be necessary to provide for a reservation or special agreement to exclude disputes between the Member States *inter se* or with the Community. In contrast to the criteria laid down in Opinions 1/91 and 1/92, the organs of control of the Convention would not simply interpret it but would examine the legality of Community law in the light of the Convention, which would have an impact on the case-law of the Court of Justice.

The French Government asserts that the Community legal order has available an autonomous and specific judicial organization. No right of action in respect of an issue of human rights has been or could currently be instituted beyond the respect for the law conferred as a general principle on the Court.

It also considers the problem of the prior exhaustion of domestic remedies. In the Community system, actions open to individuals are limited and the Court of Justice is in the majority of cases seised by way of reference for a preliminary ruling. The question must arise whether the organs of the Convention would be moved to require the

Community to widen access to the preliminary-reference procedure or whether, conversely, they might not refuse to take account of that procedure in assessing the requirement that domestic remedies be exhausted. It would accordingly be easier to amend the second paragraph of Article 173 of the Treaty so as to enable individuals to challenge Community acts affecting their fundamental rights.

The French Government also emphasizes the risk of proceedings involving Community law being submitted to Convention organs consisting of nationals of States which are members of the Council of Europe but not of the Community. It similarly notes the difficulties of participation by Community judges in the control bodies of the Convention. In those circumstances, accession could occur only after amendment of the Treaty, including the Protocol on the Statute of the Court of Justice of the EC.

[1782] Ireland, in its oral observations, points out that accession by the Community to the Convention puts in question the exclusive jurisdiction of the Court, under Articles 164 and 219 of the Treaty, to settle any dispute relating to application and interpretation of the Treaty.

The Portuguese Government also stresses that the control bodies of the Convention are competent to apply and interpret provisions with a horizontal effect; that competence would inevitably interfere with the application and interpretation of Community law. Admittedly, Article 62 of the Convention would enable the inter-State action provided for in Article 24 of the Convention to be excluded in order to respect Article 219 of the Treaty. The *ratio legis* of that article cannot however be limited to proceedings between Member States but means that no method of judicial resolution of disputes other than that applied by the Court of Justice may interfere with the interpretation and application of the Treaty. The European Convention of Human Rights would be moved to interpret Community law and take decisions on the competence of the Community. It would be difficult to devise practicable machinery enabling the Community and the Member States to resolve questions of competence. To determine whether domestic remedies had been exhausted, the European Court of Human Rights could even rule on the jurisdiction of the Court of Justice; thus it would have to decide whether an individual could have brought an action for annulment against a Community act which directly and individually concerned him.

The Spanish Government and the United Kingdom also note the legal effects of decisions of the European Court of Human Rights and the future single court. They stress in particular that that Court is competent to grant just satisfaction to the injured party which may take the form of monetary compensation. In the event of accession, the Court of Justice would surrender, within the scope of application of the Convention, its ultimate authority as the interpreter of Community law. In contrast to the criteria laid down in Opinion 1/91, the European Court of Human Rights does not limit itself to the interpretation and application of an international agreement. It would be involved in the interpretation and application of Community law and would have to rule on the competence of the Community and the Member States.

3. The *Netherlands Government* simply notes the problems which must be considered before taking a decision on whether accession is appropriate, without taking a definite position. It refers in particular to the question whether relations between the Court of Justice and the organs of the Convention are compatible with Article 164 of the Treaty, the question of the respective obligations under the Community Treaties and the Convention of the Member States, parties to the Convention and members of the Community, and the problem of determining the responsibility of the Community and the Member States with regard to observance of the Convention.

[1783] OPINION OF THE COURT

Admissibility of the Request for an Opinion

1. Ireland and the United Kingdom, as well as the Danish and Swedish Governments, submit that the request for an Opinion is inadmissible or is, at any rate, premature. They argue that there is no agreement framed in sufficiently precise terms to enable the Court to examine the compatibility of accession with the Treaty. In the opinion of those Governments an agreement cannot be said to be envisaged at a stage where the Council has as yet not even adopted a decision in principle to open negotiations on the agreement.

2. Article 228(6) of the Treaty provides that the Council, the Commission or a Member State may obtain the opinion of the Court of Justice as to whether an agreement envisaged is compatible with the provisions of the Treaty.

3. As the Court has stated, most recently in paragraph 16 of Opinion 3/94 of 13 December 1995, the purpose of that provision is to forestall complications which would result from legal disputes concerning the compatibility with the Treaty of international agreements binding upon the Community.

4. The Court also stated in that Opinion (at paragraph 17) that a possible decision of the Court to the effect that such an agreement is, by reason either of its content or of the procedure adopted for its conclusion, incompatible with the provisions of the Treaty could not fail to provoke, not only in a Community context but also in that of international relations, serious difficulties and might give rise to adverse consequences for all interested parties, including third countries.

[1784] 5. In order to avoid such complications, the Treaty has established the special procedure of a prior reference to the Court of Justice for the purpose of ascertaining, before the conclusion of the agreement, whether the latter is compatible with the Treaty.

6. That procedure is a special procedure of collaboration between the Court of Justice on the one hand and the other Community institutions and the Member States on the other whereby, at a stage prior to conclusion of an agreement which is capable of giving rise to a dispute concerning the legality of a Community act which concludes, implements or applies it, the Court is called upon to ensure, in accordance with Article 164 of the Treaty, that in the interpretation and application of the Treaty the law is observed.

7. As regards the existence of a draft agreement, there can be no doubt that, in this particular case, no negotiations had been commenced nor had the precise terms of the agreement for accession of the Community to the Convention been determined when the request for an Opinion was lodged. Nor will they be so when the Opinion is delivered.

8. In order to assess the extent to which the lack of firm information regarding the terms of the agreement affects the admissibility of the request, the purposes of the request must be distinguished.

9. As is clear from the observations submitted by the Governments of the Member States and by the Community institutions, accession by the Community to the Convention presents two main problems: (i) the competence of the Community to conclude such an agreement and (ii) its compatibility with the provisions of the Treaty, in particular those relating to the jurisdiction of the Court.

10. As regards the question of competence, in paragraph 35 of Opinion 1/78 of 4 October 1979 ([1979] ECR 2871) the Court held that, where a question of competence has to be decided, it is in the interests of the Community institutions and **[1785]** of the States concerned, including non-member countries, to have that question clarified from the outset of negotiations and even before the main points of the agreement are negotiated.

11. The only condition which the Court referred to in that Opinion is that the purpose of the envisaged agreement be known before negotiations are commenced.

12. There can be no doubt that, as far as this request for an Opinion is concerned, the purpose of the envisaged agreement is known. Irrespective of the mechanism by which the Community might accede to the Convention, the general purpose and subject-matter of the Convention and the institutional significance of such accession for the Community are perfectly well known.

13. The admissibility of the request for an Opinion cannot be challenged on the ground that the Council has not yet adopted a decision to open negotiations and that no agreement is therefore envisaged within the meaning of Article 228(6) of the Treaty.

14. While it is true that no such decision has yet been taken, accession by the Community to the Convention has been the subject of various Commission studies and proposals and was on the Council's agenda at the time when the request for an Opinion was lodged. The fact that the Council has set the Article 228(6) procedure in motion presupposes that it envisaged the possibility of negotiating and concluding such an agreement. The request for an Opinion thus appears to be prompted by the Council's legitimate concern to know the exact extent of its powers before taking any decision on the opening of negotiations.

15. Furthermore, in so far as the request for an Opinion concerns the question of Community competence, its import is sufficiently clear and a formal Council decision to open negotiations was not indispensable in order further to define its purpose.

[1786] 16. Finally, if the Article 228(6) procedure is to be effective it must be possible for the question of competence to be referred to the Court not only as soon as negotiations are commenced (Opinion 1/78, paragraph 35) but also before negotiations have formally begun.

17. In those circumstances, the question of Community competence to proceed to accession having been raised as a preliminary issue within the Council, it is in the interests of the Community, the Member States and other States party to the Convention to have that question settled before negotiations begin.

18. It follows that the request for an Opinion is admissible in so far as it concerns the competence of the Community to conclude an agreement of the kind envisaged.

19. However, the same is not true as regards the question of the compatibility of the agreement with the Treaty.

20. In order fully to answer the question whether accession by the Community to the Convention would be compatible with the rules of the Treaty, in particular with Articles 164 and 219 relating to the jurisdiction of the Court, the Court must have sufficient information regarding the arrangements by which the Community envisages submitting to the present and future judicial control machinery established by the Convention.

21. As it is, the Court has been given no detailed information as to the solutions that are envisaged to give effect in practice to such submission of the Community to the jurisdiction of an international court.

22. It follows that the Court is not in a position to give its opinion on the compatibility of Community accession to the Convention with the rules of the Treaty.

[1787] *Competence of the Community to accede to the Convention*

23. It follows from Article 3b of the Treaty, which states that the Community is to act within the limits of the powers conferred upon it

by the Treaty and of the objectives assigned to it therein, that it has only those powers which have been conferred upon it.

24. That principle of conferred powers must be respected in both the internal action and the international action of the Community.

25. The Community acts ordinarily on the basis of specific powers which, as the Court has held, are not necessarily the express consequence of specific provisions of the Treaty but may also be implied from them.

26. Thus, in the field of international relations, at issue in this request for an Opinion, it is settled case-law that the competence of the Community to enter into international commitments may not only flow from express provisions of the Treaty but also be implied from those provisions. The Court has held, in particular, that, whenever Community law has created for the institutions of the Community powers within its internal system for the purpose of attaining a specific objective, the Community is empowered to enter into the international commitments necessary for attainment of that objective even in the absence of an express provision to that effect (see Opinion 2/91 of 19 March 1993 [1993] ECR I-1061, paragraph 7).

27. No Treaty provision confers on the Community institutions any general power to enact rules on human rights or to conclude international conventions in this field.

[1788] 28. In the absence of express or implied powers for this purpose, it is necessary to consider whether Article 235 of the Treaty may constitute a legal basis for accession.

29. Article 235 is designed to fill the gap where no specific provisions of the Treaty confer on the Community institutions express or implied powers to act, if such powers appear none the less to be necessary to enable the Community to carry out its functions with a view to attaining one of the objectives laid down by the Treaty.

30. That provision, being an integral part of an institutional system based on the principle of conferred powers, cannot serve as a basis for widening the scope of Community powers beyond the general framework created by the provisions of the Treaty as a whole and, in particular, by those that define the tasks and the activities of the Community. On any view, Article 235 cannot be used as a basis for the adoption of provisions whose effect would, in substance, be to amend the Treaty without following the procedure which it provides for that purpose.

31. It is in the light of those considerations that the question whether accession by the Community to the Convention may be based on Article 235 must be examined.

32. It should first be noted that the importance of respect for human rights has been emphasized in various declarations of the Member States and of the Community institutions (cited in point III.5 of the first part of this Opinion). Reference is also made to respect for human rights in the preamble to the Single European Act and in the

preamble to, and in Article F(2), the fifth indent of Article J.1(2) and Article K.2(1) of, the Treaty on European Union. Article F provides that the Union is to respect fundamental rights, as guaranteed, in particular, by the Convention. **[1789]** Article 130u(2) of the EU Treaty provides that Community policy in the area of development cooperation is to contribute to the objective of respecting human rights and fundamental freedoms.

33. Furthermore, it is well settled that fundamental rights form an integral part of the general principles of law whose observance the Court ensures. For that purpose, the Court draws inspiration from the constitutional traditions common to the Member States and from the guidelines supplied by international treaties for the protection of human rights on which the Member States have collaborated or of which they are signatories. In that regard, the Court has stated that the Convention has special significance (see, in particular, the judgment in Case C-260/89 *ERT* [1991] ECR I-2925, paragraph 41).

34. Respect for human rights is therefore a condition of the lawfulness of Community acts. Accession to the Convention would, however, entail a substantial change in the present Community system for the protection of human rights in that it would entail the entry of the Community into a distinct international institutional system as well as integration of all the provisions of the Convention into the Community legal order.

35. Such a modification of the system for the protection of human rights in the Community, with equally fundamental institutional implications for the Community and for the Member States, would be of constitutional significance and would therefore be such as to go beyond the scope of Article 235. It could be brought about only by way of Treaty amendment.

36. It must therefore be held that, as Community law now stands, the Community has no competence to accede to the Convention.

[1790] In conclusion,

THE COURT

gives the following opinion:

As Community law now stands, the Community has no competence to accede to the European Convention for the Protection of Human Rights and Fundamental Freedoms.

[Report: [1996] ECR I-1759]

NOTE.—In a subsequent judgment of 29 May 1997 in *Kremzow* v. *Austria* (Case C-299/95) the Court of Justice was again required to consider the scope of the protection of fundamental rights within the Community legal order. The applicant was claiming compensation from Austria for his conviction and sentence in criminal proceedings which had subsequently been held by the European Court of Human Rights to be in breach of Articles 5 and 6 of the European Convention on Human Rights. On a reference for a preliminary ruling under Article 177, the applicant sought a ruling from the Court of Justice that the decision of the European Court of Human Rights was binding on the national courts in Austria as a matter of Community law. The Court of Justice declined to exercise jurisdiction to give a ruling, holding that:

(1) As the Court had consistently held, fundamental rights formed an integral part of the general principles of Community law whose observance the Court ensured. For this purpose, the Court drew inspiration from the constitutional traditions common to the Member States and from the guidelines supplied by international treaties for the protection of human rights on which the Member States had collaborated or of which they were signatories. The Convention had special significance in this respect. It followed that measures were unacceptable in the Community if they were incompatible with observance of the human rights thus recognized and guaranteed.

(2) Where national legislation fell within the field of application of Community law the Court, in a reference for a preliminary ruling, was required to give the national court guidance as to the interpretation necessary to enable it to assess the compatibility of that legislation with the fundamental rights whose observance the Court ensured. However, the Court had no such jurisdiction with regard to national legislation lying outside the scope of Community law. The situation of the appellant in these proceedings was not connected in any way with any of the situations contemplated by the Treaty provisions on free movement of persons. Whilst any deprivation of liberty could impede the person concerned from exercising his right to free movement, a purely hypothetical prospect of exercising that right did not establish a sufficient connection with Community law to justify the application of Community provisions. Furthermore, the appellant had been sentenced for murder under provisions of national law which were not designed to secure compliance with rules of Community law [[1997] ECR I-2645].

Supremacy — Constitutions and Community law — Whether EC law taking precedence even over conflicting national constitutional provisions

Legal order in general — Special character — Nature of obligations undertaken by Member States—Existing treaty obligations—EC Treaty, Article 234—Whether authorizing Member States to exercise rights in intra-Community relations under treaties concluded prior to the EC Treaty which conflict with Community obligations — European Convention on Establishment, 1955, Article 13 — Whether capable of constituting derogation from Article 48(4) of EC Treaty

Powers — Derogations — Existing treaty obligations — EC Treaty, Article 233 — Scope of derogations permitted to members of Benelux Union from EC Treaty rules — Benelux Treaty, 1958, Article 61—Whether limiting scope of application of Article 48 of EC Treaty—Protocol to EC Treaty on Grand Duchy of Luxembourg, Article 2—Scope of right of Grand Duchy to have its special demographic situation taken into account—EC rules on freedom of movement of workers — Scope of permissible derogations — Nationality requirement for employment in public service—EC Treaty, Article 48(4)

Institutions — Court of Justice — Powers — Actions against Member States for failure to fulfil treaty obligations—EC Treaty, Articles 169-71 — Finding by Court of breach of Treaty by Member State — Whether Court empowered to grant period of grace for compliance with its judgments—The law of the European Community

COMMISSION OF THE EUROPEAN COMMUNITIES *v.* GRAND DUCHY OF LUXEMBOURG

(Case C-473/93)

Court of Justice of the European Community. 2 *July* 1996

(Rodríguez Iglesias, *President*; Kakouris, Edward, Puissochet and Hirsch, *Presidents of Chambers*; Mancini, Schockweiler, Moininho de Almeida, Kapteyn, Gulmann, Murray, Jann (*Rapporteur*), Ragnemalm, Sevón and Wathelet, *Judges*; Léger, *Advocate-General*)

SUMMARY: *The facts*:—The Commission of the European Communities brought an action under Article 169 of the EC Treaty for a declaration that, by maintaining a Luxembourg nationality requirement for employment in posts in the public sectors of research, teaching, health, inland transport, posts and telecommunications, as well as in water, gas and electricity distribution, the Grand Duchy of Luxembourg had failed to fulfil its obligations under Article 48 of the EC Treaty. In the various sectors in question, Luxembourg nationality was required by specific laws, subject to certain very limited exceptions, in accordance with the principle enshrined in Article 11 of the Luxembourg Constitution that only Luxembourg nationals could occupy civil and military posts. Article 48(4) of the EC Treaty provided that the rules on freedom of movement of workers within the European Community did not apply to "employment in the public service".

The Commission contended that, in all the areas with which its application was concerned, the functions involved in the posts subject to the nationality condition were generally too remote from the specific activities of the public service to be covered by the derogation provided for in Article 48(4) of the Treaty. Luxembourg nationality could not therefore be required for all posts in those areas. As for those posts specifically related to the public service, it was for the Luxembourg Government to demonstrate the existence of such a relationship. Luxembourg did not deny that the posts in question were generally restricted to its own nationals but invoked Article 11 of its Constitution[1] and three different treaty provisions[2] in support of its claim that the action should be dismissed.

In his submissions to the Court, Advocate-General Léger examined and rejected each of the pleas, concluding that the Commission's application should be granted and that the Court should rule that Luxembourg had failed to fulfil its obligations under Article 48 of the EC Treaty by maintaining in force the nationality requirements at issue.[3]

Held:—The nationality requirements constituted a violation by the Grand Duchy of Luxembourg of its obligations under Article 48 of the EC Treaty.

(1) A Member State which, in the public sectors of research, education, health, inland transport, posts and telecommunications, as well as water, gas and electricity distribution, did not restrict its nationality requirement for civil servants to posts involving direct or indirect participation in the exercise of powers conferred by public law or duties designed to safeguard the general interests of the State, failed to fulfil its obligations under Article 48 of the Treaty (pp. 83-4).

(2) Article 11(2) of the Luxembourg Constitution reserved employment in civil and military posts to Luxembourg nationals save where express legislative exception was made. It was argued that since this was a supreme rule of domestic law, this provision precluded the breach of obligations alleged by the Commission. However, according to the Court of Justice's settled case-law, recourse to provisions of the domestic legal systems of Member States to restrict the scope

[1] See p. 76 below. [2] See pp. 81-2 below.

[3] The submissions of the Advocate-General, which are not reproduced here because they were essentially reiterated and adopted in the grounds of the judgment of the Court, are printed in ECR [1996] I-3209-47.

of the provisions of Community law would have the effect of impairing the unity and efficacy of that law and consequently could not be accepted (p. 81).

(3) Article 13 of the European Convention on Establishment, 1955, permitted States to reserve for their own nationals the exercise of public functions. This Convention had been signed by most of the Member States, including Luxembourg. While Article 234(1) of the EC Treaty[4] allowed Member States to honour obligations owed to non-Member States under international agreements preceding the conclusion of the EC Treaty, it did not authorize them to exercise rights under such agreements in intra-Community relations. Even if Article 13 of the European Convention was to be given a broader interpretation than Article 48(4) of the Treaty, Luxembourg could not rely on the former provision in order to escape its Community obligations (p. 81).

(4) Article 61 of the Benelux Treaty, 1958, allowed States to continue to reserve the exercise of official posts and public functions to their own nationals. Article 233 of the EC Treaty[5] was intended to prevent the application of Community law from causing the disintegration of the Benelux Union or from hindering its development. It therefore enabled the three Member States concerned to apply, in derogation from Community rules, the rules in force within their Union in so far as it was further advanced than the Common Market. However, Community law went further than Article 61 of the Benelux Treaty, in granting nationals of other Member States access to all posts in the public service, except those involving exercise of powers conferred by public law. Article 61 of the Benelux Treaty could not therefore prevent the alleged breach of obligations from being found (pp. 81-2).

(5) Article 2 of the Protocol on Luxembourg provided that when framing the regulations on freedom of movement for workers provided for in Article 48(3) of the Treaty, the Commission should take account of the special demographic situation in Luxembourg. However, Article 2 merely allowed Luxembourg to request specific changes required by its special demographic situation, to be made upon enactment of the regulations for implementing freedom of movement for workers. The existence of that right could not authorize Luxembourg unilaterally to exclude workers from other Member States from entire areas of occupational activity (p. 82).

(6) Luxembourg had asked, in the event that it should be found in breach of its obligations, to be granted a long period of grace in order to comply with its Community obligations, bearing in mind that massive reforms at both the constitutional and the legislative level would be required. That request could not be granted since Article 171 of the EC Treaty did not confer any power on the Court to grant a period of time for compliance with its judgments (p. 83).

[4] Article 234(1) provides:

The rights and obligations arising from agreements concluded before the entry into force of this Treaty between one or more Member States on the one hand, and one or more third countries on the other, shall not be affected by the provisions of this Treaty.

[5] Article 233 provides:

The provisions of this Treaty shall not preclude the existence or completion of regional unions between Belgium and Luxembourg, or between Belgium, Luxembourg and the Netherlands, to the extent that the objectives of these regional unions are not attained by application of this Treaty.

The following is the text of the judgment of the Court:

[3249] JUDGMENT

1. By application lodged at the Court Registry on 17 December 1993, the Commission of the European Communities brought an action under Article 169 of the EC Treaty for a declaration that, by maintaining a nationality requirement in relation to workers who are nationals of other Member States as regards access to civil servants' or public employees' posts in the public sectors of research, teaching, health, inland transport, posts and telecommunications, and in the water, gas and electricity distribution services, the Grand Duchy of Luxembourg had failed to fulfil its obligations under Article 48 of the EEC Treaty and Articles 1 and 7 of Regulation (EEC) No 1612/68 of the Council of 15 October 1968 on freedom of movement for workers within the Community (OJ, English Special Edition, 1968 (II), p. 475).

[3250] 2. Article 48(1) to (3) of the EEC Treaty, which is now the EC Treaty, lays down the principle of the free movement of workers and the abolition of all discrimination based on nationality between workers of the Member States. Article 48(4) of the Treaty provides that the provisions of this article are not to apply to employment in the public service. According to the case-law of the Court, Article 48(4) covers posts which involve direct or indirect participation in the exercise of powers conferred by public law and duties designed to safeguard the general interests of the State or of other public authorities and thus presume on the part of those occupying them the existence of a special relationship of allegiance to the State and reciprocity of rights and duties which form the foundation of the bond of nationality. On the other hand, the Article 48(4) exception does not cover posts which, whilst coming under the State or other organizations governed by public law, still do not involve any association with tasks belonging to the public service properly so called (judgment in Case 149/79 *Commission* v. *Belgium* [1980] ECR 3881, paragraphs 10 and 11).

3. As regards Articles 1 and 7 of Regulation No 1612/68, these provisions lay down the rule of equal treatment in access to employment, on the one hand, and in its exercise, on the other.

4. Having found that, in certain Member States, a large number of posts regarded as belonging to the public service had no connection with the exercise of powers conferred by public law or with the safeguarding of the general interests of the State, the Commission decided in 1988 to implement a "strategy" on the basis of Communication 88/C 72/02: Freedom of movement of workers and access to employment in the public service of the Member States—Commission action in respect of the application of Article 48(4) of the EEC Treaty (OJ 1988 C 72, p. 2). In that communication, the Commission reminded the Member States to give

nationals of other Member States access to posts in bodies responsible for administering commercial services, such as public transport, supply of electricity and gas, airlines and shipping lines, posts and telecommunications, and in radio and television companies, public health care services, State education and research for non-military purposes conducted in public establishments. The Commission considered that the functions involved in posts falling in those areas would only in very rare cases be covered by the exception provided for in Article 48(4) of the Treaty.

[3251] 5. Pursuant to that strategy, on 5 January 1988 the Commission sent the Grand Duchy of Luxembourg a letter reminding it to take the measures needed for abolishing the nationality condition which that State applies to access to employment in the areas listed above. In a letter of 30 October 1990 the Grand Duchy replied that it did not envisage taking any special measures of the kind desired.

6. On 12 March 1991, the Commission sent the Luxembourg Government six formal letters concerning the areas of research, education, health, inland transport, posts and telecommunications and water, gas and electricity distribution. In those letters the Commission requested the Luxembourg Government to submit its observations within a period of six months.

7. On 4 May 1992 the Luxembourg Government replied that it was maintaining its previous position because the principle of free movement of workers was already widely applied in the areas in question.

8. On 14 July 1992, the Commission issued six reasoned opinions regarding the areas concerned, each giving the Luxembourg Government a period of four months in which to comply. When no reply was received to those opinions, the Commission brought this action.

9. According to the documents before the Court, in the Grand Duchy of Luxembourg the areas with which the Commission's application is concerned come within the public service. In all those areas, Luxembourg nationality is in principle required as a qualification for all the posts, whether they are occupied by established civil servants, servants with like status or employees serving under a contract of employment.

[3252] 10. This principle is laid down in the second paragraph of Article 11 of the Luxembourg Constitution, which provides that only Luxembourgers may occupy civil and military posts, in Article 3(a) of the Law of 27 January 1972 laying down the rules governing State employees, in Article 2(1)(a) of the amended Law of 16 April 1979 laying down the general regulations applicable to State officials, in Article 2(1)(a) of the Law of 24 December 1985 laying down the general regulations applicable to commune officials, in Article 3(a) of the Grand-Ducal Regulation of 26 May 1975 bringing the rules governing commune employees into line with those governing State employees, in Article 2(1) of the Staff Regulations of Luxembourg Railways, which provide, however, for derogations in the cases laid down by international agreements and where there are no candidates of Luxembourg nationality, subject to authorization from the Government.

11. The same condition is also laid down by Article 24 of the Law of 10 August 1992 on the conversion of the Posts and Telecommunications Office into the "Posts and Telecommunications Enterprise", which provides for the General Regulations applicable to civil servants and State employees to be applied to its servants, and by Article 2(b) of the Grand-Ducal Regulation of 11 August 1974 laying down the conditions for the admission, appointment and promotion of State paramedical staff.

12. Finally, it would appear from Articles 4 and 5 of the Law of 9 March 1987 on the organization of technological research and development in the public sector that nationals of other Member States may take up a post in research only if, by way of exception, the body, government department or public higher education establishment or university employing them does not require Luxembourg nationality.

13. By way of exception, this condition is not imposed on staff of the Luxembourg Hospital Centre, a public establishment having a management governed by private law, or on teaching staff at the Luxembourg University Centre.

[3253] 14. In all the cases in which the requirement of Luxembourg nationality is laid down, it is framed in general terms, without any distinction according to the nature of the duties entailed by, or the hierarchical level of, the posts in question.

15. The Commission contends that in all the areas with which its application is concerned the functions involved in the posts subject to the nationality condition are generally too remote from the specific activities of the public service for them to be covered virtually without exception by the derogation provided for in Article 48(4) of the Treaty. The Grand Duchy of Luxembourg could not therefore require Luxembourg nationality for all posts in those areas. As for the special posts having such a relation with the specific activities of the public service, it is for the defendant government to demonstrate the existence of such a relationship.

16. The Grand Duchy of Luxembourg does not deny that in Luxembourg posts in the areas in question are generally restricted to its own nationals. However, for a number of reasons it does not consider that it should be found to be in breach of its obligations.

Admissibility

17. First of all, the Grand Duchy of Luxembourg challenges the admissibility of the Commission's action on the ground that the Commission gave it a period of only four months in which to comply with the reasoned opinions. That period was manifestly insufficient to allow it to carry out the major reform demanded, which required it to overhaul its administrative system starting at its very roots.

[3254] 18. In response, the Commission maintains first of all that the period of four months given in the reasoned opinions was exceptionally long since the usual period allowed is only one or two months. The Commission goes on to point out that the entire pre-litigation procedure lasted more than 33 months, not to mention the fact that at the time when that procedure commenced the Grand Duchy of Luxembourg had long been aware of the Commission's intentions because of the strategy it had announced. Finally, the Grand Duchy never asked for the period to be extended but always insisted that it would not amend its legislation.

19. In view of those arguments, the Court must reiterate that the purpose of the pre-litigation procedure is to give the Member State concerned an opportunity, on the one hand, to comply with its obligations under Community law and, on the other, to avail itself of its right to defend itself against the objections raised by the Commission (judgment in Case 293/85 *Commission* v. *Belgium* [1988] ECR 305, p. 13).

20. In view of that dual purpose the Commission must allow Member States a reasonable period to reply to the letter of formal notice and to comply with a reasoned opinion, or, where appropriate, to prepare their defence. In order to determine whether the period allowed is reasonable, account must be taken of all the circumstances of the case (judgment in Case 293/85 *Commission* v. *Belgium*, cited above, paragraph 14).

21. In the present case, the period of four months laid down in the reasoned opinions was twice as long as the period normally allowed by the Commission.

22. Furthermore, the Grand Duchy of Luxembourg had been aware of the Commission's position since 18 March 1988 when it published Communication 88/C 72/02, mentioned above, which was therefore nearly three years before it received the letters, dated 12 March 1991, giving it formal notice, which in turn allowed it a period of six months.

[3255] 23. In the replies which it gave to the Commission the Grand Duchy of Luxembourg made it clear that it was not going to carry out any legislative reforms.

24. In those circumstances the four-month period imposed by the reasoned opinions cannot be regarded as unreasonable. The action is therefore admissible.

Substance

25. On the substance, the Grand Duchy of Luxembourg submits first of all that Article 48(4) of the Treaty must be interpreted in an "institutional" sense so that the exception which it lays down should cover all posts which under national law constitute public service posts, including those involving purely executory, technical or manual duties if they are performed for the State or for public authorities. Only nationals can be

depended on to show the special degree of integrity and trustworthiness which must be capable of being required of civil servants and public employees.

26. With regard to that argument, it suffices to refer to the Court's settled case-law according to which the concept of public service within the meaning of Article 48(4) of the Treaty requires uniform interpretation and application throughout the Community and cannot therefore be left entirely to the discretion of the Member States (see, in particular, the judgment in Case 152/73 *Sotgiu* [1974] ECR 153 and the judgment in Case 149/79 *Commission* v. *Belgium*, cited above, paragraphs 12 and 18).

27. So, in order to determine whether posts fall within the scope of Article 48(4) of the Treaty, it is necessary to consider whether or not the posts in question typify the specific activities of the public service in so far as it exercises powers conferred by **[3256]** public law and has responsibility for safeguarding the general interests of the State or of other public bodies. For that reason, the criterion for determining whether Article 48(4) of the Treaty is applicable must be functional and must take account of the nature of the tasks and responsibilities inherent in the post, in order to ensure that the effectiveness and scope of the provisions of the Treaty on freedom of movement of workers and equal treatment of nationals of all Member States is not restricted by interpretations of the concept of public service which are based on domestic law alone and which would obstruct application of Community rules (judgment in Case 307/84 *Commission* v. *France* [1986] ECR 1725, paragraph 12).

28. Secondly, the Grand Duchy of Luxembourg objects to the Commission's "global" approach, consisting in excluding entire areas from the Article 48(4) derogation in the absence of Community rules and without providing more details of the posts concerned. In its view, it is clear from the case-law of the Court (see, in particular, its judgment in Case 149/79 *Commission* v. *Belgium*, cited above) that the Commission must examine the posts concerned on a case-by-case basis instead of designating entire areas which are to be excluded in principle from the Article 48(4) derogation by putting the burden on Member States to prove the contrary in specific individual cases.

29. The Commission states in this regard that in Communication 88/C 72/02 it examined the posts in the various areas concerned in the light of the criteria laid down by the Court for the interpretation of Article 48(4) of the Treaty. That examination led it to conclude that those posts are too remote from the specific activities of the public service to be covered in general by the Article 48(4) exception. In those circumstances, it must be entitled in principle to exclude application of that provision in all the areas concerned by these proceedings without any preliminary post-by-post examination being necessary.

[3257] 30. The Commission also claims that it found that the activities performed in the areas in question either existed in the private sector, too, or could be performed in the public sector without being subject to a nationality condition.

31. The Court observes in this regard that, as the Luxembourg Government itself admits, the generality of posts in the areas of research, health, inland transport, posts and telecommunications and in the water, gas and electricity supply services are remote from the specific activities of the public service because they do not involve direct or indirect participation in the exercise of powers conferred by public law or duties designed to safeguard the general interests of the State or of other public authorities (see, in particular, as regards the area of health, the judgment in Case 307/84 *Commission* v. *France*, and, as regards research for civil purposes, the judgment in Case 225/85 *Commission* v. *Italy* [1987] ECR 2625).

32. As regards the area of education, the Luxembourg Government submits in particular that teachers must be Luxembourg nationals in order to transmit traditional values and that, in view of the size of the country and its specific demographic situation, the nationality requirement is therefore an essential condition for preserving Luxembourg's national identity. Its identity could not be preserved if the majority of teachers came from other States of the Community. In the case of primary and secondary school teachers, the Luxembourg Government points out that these teachers perform non-commercial functions which do actually entail safeguarding the general interests of the State.

33. As to that argument, the Court has already stated that the very strict conditions which posts must satisfy in order to come within the exception laid down in Article 48(4) of the Treaty are not fulfilled in the case of trainee teachers (judgment in Case 66/85 *Lawrie-Blum* [1986] ECR 2121, paragraph 28), in the case of foreign-language assistants (judgment in Case 33/88 *Allué and Coonan* [1989] ECR 1591, paragraph 9) or in the case of secondary school teachers (judgment in Case C-4/91 *Bleis* [1991] ECR I-5627, paragraph 7).

[3258] 34. For the same reasons, the same applies to primary school teachers.

35. This conclusion cannot be shaken by considerations relating to the preservation of national identity in a demographic situation as specific as that prevailing in the Grand Duchy of Luxembourg. Whilst the preservation of the Member States' national identities is a legitimate aim respected by the Community legal order (as is indeed acknowledged in Article F(1) of the Treaty on European Union), the interest pleaded by the Grand Duchy can, even in such particularly sensitive areas as education, still be effectively safeguarded otherwise than by a general exclusion of nationals from other Member States. As the Advocate General points out in paragraphs 132 to 141 of his Opinion, nationals of other Member States must, like Luxembourg nationals, still fulfil all the conditions

required for recruitment, in particular those relating to training, experience and language knowledge.

36. Consequently, the protection of national identity cannot justify exclusion of nationals of other Member States from all the posts in an area such as education, with the exception of those involving direct or indirect participation in the exercise of powers conferred by public law and duties designed to safeguard the general interests of the State or of other public authorities.

37. Thirdly, the Grand Duchy of Luxembourg refers to the second paragraph of Article 11 of its Constitution, according to which only Luxembourg nationals may occupy civil and military posts, save where a Law makes an exception in an individual case. Being a supreme rule of domestic law, that provision precludes the breach of obligations alleged by the Commission from being found.

[3259] 38. In reply to that argument it is sufficient to refer to the Court's settled case-law according to which recourse to provisions of the domestic legal systems to restrict the scope of the provisions of Community law would have the effect of impairing the unity and efficacy of that law and consequently cannot be accepted (see, in particular, the judgment in Case 11/70 *Internationale Handelsgesellschaft* [1970] ECR 1125, paragraph 3, and, regarding in particular Article 48(4) of the Treaty, the judgment in Case 149/79 *Commission* v. *Belgium*, cited above, paragraph 19).

39. Fourthly, the Grand Duchy of Luxembourg relies on Article 13 of the European Convention on Establishment of 13 December 1955, which provides: "Any Contracting Party may reserve for its own nationals the exercise of public functions or of occupations connected with national security or defence, or make the exercise of these occupations by aliens subject to special conditions." The Grand Duchy points out that this Convention has been signed by most of the Member States, including the Grand Duchy.

40. In that regard, the Court observes that it is settled case-law that, whilst the first paragraph of Article 234 of the Treaty allows Member States to honour obligations owed to non-Member States under international agreements preceding the Treaty, it does not authorize them to exercise rights under such agreements in intra-Community relations (see, in particular, the judgment in Case 10/61 *Commission* v. *Italy* [1962] ECR 1 and the judgment in Case C-158/91 *Levy* [1993] ECR I-4287, paragraph 12). Even if Article 13 of the European Convention on Establishment must be given a broader interpretation than Article 48(4) of the Treaty, the Grand Duchy of Luxembourg cannot therefore rely on the former provision in order to escape its Community obligations.

41. Fifthly, the Luxembourg Government refers to Article 61 of the Treaty instituting the Benelux Economic Union of 3 February 1958, according to which the Contracting Parties maintain the right to reserve the exercise of, *inter alia*, official posts, public functions or professions to

their own nationals. It argues that, since, as is clear from Article 233 of the EEC Treaty, that provision leaves room for the Benelux Treaty, Article 61 of that Treaty precludes Article 48(4) of the EEC Treaty from being interpreted in the way advocated by the Commission.

[3260] 42. As the Court held in its judgment in Case 105/83 *Pakvries* [1984] ECR 2101, paragraph 11, the aim of Article 233 of the Treaty is to prevent the application of Community law from causing the disintegration of the Benelux Union or from hindering its development. It therefore enables the three Member States concerned to apply, in derogation from the Community rules, the rules in force within their union in so far as that union is further advanced than the common market.

43. In so far as it grants nationals of other Member States access to all posts in the public service, except those involving exercise of powers conferred by public law, Community law goes further than Article 61 of the Benelux Treaty, on the assumption, however, that this provision must indeed be interpreted in the way suggested by the Grand Duchy of Luxembourg. Consequently, Article 61 of the Benelux Treaty cannot prevent the alleged breach of obligations from being found.

44. Finally, the Grand Duchy of Luxembourg draws attention to its special demographic situation. It states that its tiny population, the attraction which civil servants' and public employees' posts continue to have in this country, as well as the economic crisis may cause a massive influx of workers from other Member States who would monopolize the vacant posts so that the very future of the country could be put in question. That is why the States which signed the EEC Treaty on 25 March 1957 adopted the Protocol on the Grand Duchy of Luxembourg which, in Article 2, provides that: "When framing the regulations on freedom of movement for workers provided for in Article 48(3) of this Treaty, the Commission shall take account, as regards the Grand Duchy of Luxembourg, of the special demographic situation in that country". The Grand Duchy argues that this provision should also apply in this case.

45. In this regard, it is sufficient to state that Article 2 of that Protocol allowed the Grand Duchy of Luxembourg to request specific changes, required by its special demographic situation, to be made upon enactment of the regulations for implementing **[3261]** freedom of movement for workers. However, the existence of that right cannot authorize it unilaterally to exclude workers from other Member States from entire areas of occupational activity.

46. It follows from the foregoing considerations that the Grand Duchy of Luxembourg may not generally make all posts in the areas concerned subject to a nationality condition without exceeding the limits of the exception provided for by Article 48(4) of the Treaty.

47. The fact that some posts in those areas may, in certain circumstances, be covered by Article 48(4) of the Treaty cannot justify such

a general prohibition (see also the two judgments delivered on this same date in Case C-173/94 *Commission* v. *Belgium* and Case C-290/94 *Commission* v. *Greece*).

48. In those circumstances, in order to give full effect to the principles of freedom of movement for workers and equal treatment in access to employment, the Grand Duchy of Luxembourg was obliged to open the areas in question to nationals of other Member States by restricting application of the nationality condition to only those posts which actually involve direct or indirect participation in the exercise of powers conferred by public law and duties designed to safeguard the general interest of the State or of other public authorities.

49. As regards the basis of the action, it must be observed that Article 7 of Regulation No 1612/68 concerns conditions of exercise of employment and not access to it. However, only access by nationals of other Member States to employment is at issue in this case. No breach of obligations can therefore be found on the basis of Article 7 of Regulation No 1612/68.

[3262] 50. It must accordingly be declared that, in not restricting the requirement of Luxembourg nationality to access to civil servants' and public employees' posts involving direct or indirect participation in the exercise of powers conferred by public law and duties designed to safeguard the general interests of the State or of other public authorities in the public sectors of research, education, health, inland transport, posts and telecommunications, and in the water, gas and electricity distribution services, the Grand Duchy of Luxembourg has failed to fulfil its obligations under Article 48 of the Treaty and Article 1 of Regulation No 1612/68.

On the request for a period of grace

51. In the event that the Court should find that it is in breach of its obligations the Grand Duchy of Luxembourg asks that it be granted a long period of grace in order to comply with its Community obligations. It observes in this regard that any amendments to the rules and regulations in question could only be carried out through massive reforms, both at constitutional and legislative level, which will take considerable time.

52. That request cannot be granted. Article 171 of the EC Treaty does not confer any power on the Court to grant a period of time for compliance with its judgments.

Costs

53. Under Article 69(2) of the Rules of Procedure, the unsuccessful party is to be ordered to pay the costs. Since the Grand Duchy of Luxembourg has failed in its submissions it must be ordered to pay the costs.

[3263] On those grounds,

THE COURT,

hereby:

> **1. Declares that, in not restricting the requirement of Luxembourg nationality to access to civil servants' and public employees' posts involving direct or indirect participation in the exercise of powers conferred by public law and duties designed to safeguard the general interests of the State or of other public authorities in the public sectors of research, education, health, inland transport, posts and telecommunications, and in the water, gas and electricity distribution services, the Grand Duchy of Luxembourg has failed to fulfil its obligations under Article 48 of the EEC Treaty and Article 1 of Regulation (EEC) No 1612/68 of the Council of 15 October 1968 on freedom of movement for workers within the Community;**
>
> **2. Orders the Grand Duchy of Luxembourg to pay the costs.**

[Report: [1996] ECR I-3207]

Supremacy — Conflict between Community law and subsequent national law — Consequences for contrary national law — Automatic inapplicability of conflicting national provisions—Whether national provisions thereby rendered non-existent or national courts simply under duty to disapply them

Enforcement in national courts — Remedies — Claim against Member State—National charge levied contrary to Community law—Duty of national courts in principle to uphold claim for recovery of charge—Procedural conditions under national law—Whether such conditions subject to requirements of Community law—Council Directive 69/335 concerning indirect taxes on the raising of capital

Institutions—Court of Justice—Powers—Jurisdiction under Article 177 of EC Treaty—Dispute over classification of legal relationship affecting jurisdiction of national courts—Role of Court of Justice under preliminary reference procedure—Duty of national courts to ensure resolution of jurisdictional issue consistently with protection of individual rights—The law of the European Community

MINISTERO DELLE FINANZE *v.* IN. CO. GE.'90 SRL AND OTHERS

(Joined Cases C-10/97 to C-22/97)

Court of Justice of the European Community. 22 *October* 1998

(Rodríguez Iglesias, *President*; Kapteyn, Puissochet (*Rapporteur*), Hirsch and Jann, *Presidents of Chambers*; Mancini, Moitinho de Almeida, Gulmann, Murray, Edward, Ragnemalm, Sevón, Wathelet, Schintgen and Ioannou, *Judges*; Ruiz-Jarabo Colomer, *Advocate-General*)

SUMMARY: *The facts*:—An annual registration charge for companies, introduced in Italy in 1972, was held by the Court of Justice in 1993 to be prohibited by Council Directive 69/335 concerning indirect taxes on the raising of capital. Following that judgment, Italian law was amended so that the charge ceased to be payable annually. IN. CO. GE.'90 and other companies then sought to recover registration charges paid for previous years. Under Italian procedural rules a three-year limitation period applied to claims for the recovery of money paid by mistake if the claims were of a general civil rather than a specifically fiscal nature. The Ministry of Finance argued that the former was the case and the *Pretore* (Examining Magistrate) of Rome agreed. The *Pretore* considered that since, in accordance with the case-law of the Court of Justice, he was under a duty not to apply any provision of national law, even if adopted subsequently, which was contrary to Community law, without first requesting or awaiting its repeal, the non-application of the Italian law in question necessarily had the effect of rendering the contested charge non-existent, so that its repayment was a general civil matter. However, the *Pretore* stayed the proceedings and made a reference for a preliminary ruling on the point to the Court of Justice.

Opinion of the Advocate-General:—The Advocate-General, in his submissions to the Court of Justice, disagreed with the theory supported by the Commission that national provisions contrary to Community law were non-existent. He concluded that such a theory was a legal fiction not required by the case-law of the Court. Rather, the national court was obliged to disapply offending national provisions on the ground that they were invalid.

Held:—(1) It was for the legal system of each Member State to determine which court had jurisdiction to hear disputes involving individual rights derived from Community law. However, it was the Member States' responsibility to ensure that those rights were effectively protected in each case. Subject to that reservation, it was not for the Court of Justice to involve itself in the resolution of questions of jurisdiction to which the classification of particular legal situations based on Community law might give rise in the national judicial system (p. 103).

(2) The incompatibility with Community law of a subsequently adopted rule of national law did not have the effect of rendering the rule of national law non-existent. Faced with such a situation, a national court was obliged to disapply that rule, provided always that this obligation did not restrict the power of the competent national courts to apply, from among the various procedures available under national law, those which were appropriate for protecting the individual rights conferred by Community law (p. 104).

(3) The obligation on a national court to disapply national legislation introducing a charge contrary to Community law should lead that court, in principle, to uphold claims for repayment of the charge. Such repayment should be ensured in accordance with the provisions of its national law, on condition that those provisions were no less favourable than those governing similar domestic actions and did not render virtually impossible or excessively difficult the exercise of rights conferred by Community law (pp. 105-6).

The text of the judgment of the Court of Justice of the European Community commences at p. 100. The following is the text of the opinion of Advocate-General Ruiz-Jarabo Colomer delivered on 14 May 1998:

[6309] 1. In each of this series of joined cases the Pretore di Roma (Magistrate, Rome) has referred the same question concerning the consequences of the incompatibility with Community law of a national measure where that measure imposes a tax regarded as incompatible with Community law and the taxpayers have brought proceedings to recover the amounts thus paid.

Facts, Main Proceedings and Question Referred to the Court

2. The orders of reference contain very little information on the facts in the main proceedings. It may be inferred that for certain unspecified years each of the companies which are parties to the main proceedings paid an annual tax on government concessions in respect of its entry on the Business Register. The tax had been introduced by Decree of the President of the Republic No 641 of 26 October 1972 ("Decree No 641/1972") and the amount had been the subject of various statutory amendments.[1]

3. After the Court of Justice had delivered its judgment in *Ponente Carni and Cispadana Costruzioni*[2] (hereinafter "*Ponente Carni*") in answer to a number of questions on the interpretation of Directive 69/335/EEC of the Council of 17 July 1969 concerning indirect taxes on the raising of capital,[3] the Italian legislature abolished the annual tax and reduced the amount of the tax payable when a firm was initially entered on the Register to LIT 500,000.[4]

4. The Italian courts also declared that the annual tax was incompatible with Community law[5] and that, consequently, the sums paid by way of that tax were not due.

[6310] 5. The companies referred to above obtained a *decreto ingiuntivo*,[6] whereby the Italian tax authorities were ordered to reimburse the amounts which the companies had paid at the relevant time. The Ministero delle Finanze lodged a number of objections to the *decreto ingiuntivo* and claimed, in particular, that the Pretore had no jurisdiction to deal with the matter and that the action for reimbursement was void.

6. The Pretore, before reaching a decision on those objections, raised a matter of doubt the resolution of which requires a ruling by the Court of Justice: if the legal relationship between the tax authorities and the

[1] For a fuller account of the legislative history of the tax, reference is made to point 7 et seq. of my Opinion in Case C-231/96 *Edis* v. *Ministero delle Finanze* [1998] ECR I-4951, I-4954 (hereinafter "*Edis*").

[2] Joined Cases C-71/91 and C-178/91 [1993] ECR I-1915.

[3] OJ, English Special Edition 1969 (II), p. 412.

[4] Decree-Law No 331 of 30 August 1993, converted into Law No 427 of 29 October 1993.

[5] See, in that regard, judgments of the Court of Cassation (First Civil Section) of 23 November 1994, No 9900, and 23 February 1996, Nos 4468/96 and 3458/96, the latter delivered by the Combined Chambers (Sezioni Unite). Similarly, in the second recital in judgment No 56 of 1995, of 24 February 1995, the Constitutional Court, after noting the legislative vicissitudes of the tax, held in respect of the year in which it was abolished (1993): "Since the tax was unduly levied by the Italian State, contrary to Article 10 of Directive 69/335/EEC of 17 July 1969 as interpreted by the Court of Justice in its judgment of 20 April 1993 in Joined Cases C-71/91 and C-178/91, the amounts paid are recoverable on the basis of Community law, which is directly applicable in the Italian order".

[6] Article 633 of the Code of Civil Procedure provides that where certain conditions are met (where the debt is certain, liquidated and payable and supported by documentary evidence) the courts may issue a "decreto ingiuntivo" whereby the debtor is put on notice to pay the amount claimed forthwith, albeit on a provisional basis.

undertakings which paid the tax is of a fiscal nature the Pretore has no jurisdiction to deal with the matter, since it is not for him to determine "cases concerning levies and taxes". Similarly, the application of the rules which determine whether the actions are void or time-barred depends on whether the actions are classified in law as fiscal or as merely civil.

7. Consequently, and on the basis that the national law which established the tax is incompatible with Community Law, the Pretore has asked the Court of Justice whether that incompatibility requires that the law be disapplied in its entirety and whether it must also have an effect on the legal relationship between the tax authorities and the person who paid the tax forming the basis of the action for recovery.

8. The literal wording of the question referred to the Court is as follows:

> Does the incompatibility with Article 10 of Directive 69/335/EEC of the Council of 17 July 1969, as interpreted by the Court of Justice in its judgment of 20 April 1993 (in Joined Cases C-71/91 and C-178/91 *Ponente Carni and Cispadana Costruzioni* v. *Amministrazione delle Finanze dello Stato* [1993] ECR I-1915), of Article 3(XVIII) and (XIX) of Decree-Law No 853 of 19 December 1984, converted into Law No 17 of 17 February 1985, mean, on the basis of the criteria for integration of national law and Community law which that Court has laid down, that the said Article 3(XVIII) and (XIX) must be set aside in their entirety, and in particular does it mean that the national court must not take account of those internal provisions, even when classifying the legal relationship on the basis of which a national of a Member State calls on the finance administration to refund sums that were paid in contravention of the said Article 10 of Directive 69/335?

[6311] *First Part of the Question*

9. In reality the question poses two problems in turn, the first being wider in scope than the second. Although the national court asks the Court of Justice to rule on the relationship between the incompatibility of the internal provision with Community law and the disapplication of that provision, it subsequently concentrates on a specific aspect of that disapplication, namely its effect on the "classification" of a specific legal relationship.

10. The answer to the first part of the question has already been provided by the Court of Justice on numerous occasions: a national provision which is incompatible with Community law cannot be applied and, consequently, the national courts must refrain from applying it to the dispute before them.

11. The uniform application of Community law would not be guaranteed if Member States claimed that their own internal provisions

prevailed over the Community provisions, that is to say, if they were able to apply national law in preference to the Community provisions in the event of inconsistency between them.

12. Ever since the judgment of 9 March 1978[7] in the leading case of *Simmenthal*, that statement has been formulated in terms that leave no room for doubt. It should be pointed out that the questions referred in that case to the Court by the Pretore di Susa, like the question in the present case, concerned the repayment of certain charges of a public-law nature demanded by the Italian authorities pursuant to national provisions that were contrary to Community law (specifically a fee charged for the health inspection of imported beef).

13. It is now 20 years since the Pretore di Susa sought to ascertain what consequences flowed from the direct applicability of a provision of Community law in the event of its incompatibility with a subsequent legislative provision of a Member State. The Court's answer, which subsequently became almost a standard formulation in its case-law on the matter, was that a national court which is called upon, within the limits of its jurisdiction, to apply provisions of Community law is under a duty to give full effect to those provisions, if necessary refusing of its own motion to apply any conflicting provisions of national legislation, even if adopted subsequently, and that it is not necessary for the court to request or await the prior setting aside of such provisions by legislative or other constitutional procedures.

14. That principle of case-law, whose acceptance in the legal life of the Member States **[6312]** has not been exempt from controversy,[8] has been repeatedly confirmed by the Court of Justice.[9] It is unquestionably applicable to the tax at issue in the present case, as the highest Italian courts have in fact declared.[10] Furthermore, the principle is not disputed by any of the parties to the main proceedings.

15. The answer to the first part of the question must therefore confirm that a national court faced with a national provision which is incompatible with Community law must disapply that provision.

Second Part of the Question: the Consequences of Disapplying National Law in Relation to the Classification of Specific Legal Relationships

16. While the Court has shown resolution in maintaining the principle of the primacy of Community provisions, it has also shown prudence in

[7] Case 106/77 [1978] ECR 629.

[8] In the case of Italy, see A. Barav, "Cour constitutionnelle italienne et droit communautaire: le fantôme de Simmenthal", *Revue trimestrielle de droit européen*, 1985, pp. 313 to 341.

[9] For a recent example, see the judgment of 5 March 1998 in Case C-347/96 *Solred* v. *Administración General del Estado* [1998] ECR I-937, paragraph 30.

[10] See point 4 and footnote 5 above.

not reaching a decision on the underlying legal categories beyond the obligation to disapply the national provision which is inconsistent with the Community provision.

17. In fact, as I have just observed, the Court has confined itself to stating that such national provisions cannot be applied, as otherwise the very realisation of the European Community as a community subject to the rule of law would fail. However, it has—rightly in my view—refrained from determining the abstract, general concept, that is to say, the legal category into which the obligation to disapply falls.

18. The Court's case-law could, in theory, have had recourse to some of the legal categories well known in the general theory of law (such as, for example, "non-existence", "invalidity", "nullity", "ineffectiveness", "loss of force", "illegitimacy" or other similar categories) in order to identify the defect which affects national provisions where they are incompatible with the Community order.

19. However, the Court has carefully avoided employing such concepts in its decisions, no doubt because it is aware that the choice of any of those concepts—whose meaning, moreover, varies from one legal system to another—is more a matter for the individual legal systems. Within the limits of the solutions adopted by each of those systems, it will fall to the national courts, and specifically those on which, in each Member State, jurisdiction has been conferred to review the "lawfulness" of legislation, to rule on the matter.[11]

[6313] 20. In *Lück*[12] the Court of Justice gave an express ruling in that regard. The question referred to the Court was whether, owing to the primacy of a Community provision—in this case Article 95 of the EEC Treaty—the provisions of national law incompatible with it must (following the entry into force of paragraph 3 of Article 95) be regarded as void or merely inapplicable.

21. The answer in *Lück* was that although Article 95 of the Treaty has the effect of excluding the application of any national measure incompatible with it, it does not restrict the powers of the national courts to apply, from among the various procedures available under national law, those which are appropriate for the purpose of protecting the individual rights conferred by Community law. Consequently, the Court went on, "it is for the court making the reference to choose a solution from among those suggested in the question [referred for a preliminary ruling] and, indeed, any others".

22. For the purpose of protecting the primacy of Community law over incompatible national provisions the crucial point is that those provisions should not be applied in the national legal order: this ensures that

[11] This does not alter the fact that in the interests of legal certainty the national legislature should repeal the national law that is contrary to Community law.

[12] Case 34/67 [1968] ECR 245.

Community law is observed and also that it is uniformly applied in all the Member States.

(i) *The supposed "non-existence" of a national provision which is incompatible with Community law*

23. In its written observations[13] the Commission states that when the Court is confronted with a national provision which introduces a tax incompatible with Community law it must establish whether that provision "is to be regarded as non-existent *ex tunc*" or "inapplicable as regards the future because it has been declared incompatible with Community law". Elsewhere in its observations it merely refers, in these cases, to the "lack of legislative competence of the State" or the mere "non-existence of the tax obligation" as matters which in such cases should determine the answer to be given to the national court.

24. I shall begin by examining, under this heading, the problems raised by the proposition that a national provision incompatible with Community law should be declared "non-existent". In the next part I shall deal with the supposed lack of legislative competence of the State in the present case, since the referring court refers to that question when discussing the classification of the legal–fiscal relationship.

25. To my mind the Court should not abandon the prudent approach to which I **[6314]** have referred earlier in favour of a hazardous course of defining or selecting its own dogmatic categories in relation to these matters, or resolving the rather academic debate as to which of the abovementioned categories is applicable. Such a course of action is neither necessary—since by retaining the criterion of the inapplicability of the national provision the primacy of the Community provision is guaranteed—nor perhaps appropriate, having regard to the different conceptions which can be defended in this sphere.

26. It is certain, however, that a passage in paragraph 17 of the *Simmenthal* judgment could be construed—as in fact it was—in a sense opposite to the one I have just proposed. I am referring to the passage where the Court states:

Furthermore, in accordance with the principle of the precedence of Community law, the relationship between provisions of the Treaty and directly applicable measures of the institutions on the one hand and the national law of the Member States on the other is such that those provisions and measures not only by their entry into force render automatically inapplicable any conflicting provision of current national law but—in so far as they are an integral part of, and take precedence in, the legal order applicable in the territory of each of the Member

[13] In reality in paragraph 20 of its observations in Case C-231/96 *Edis*, to which the Commission refers in the present case.

States—also *preclude the valid adoption of new national legislative measures to the extent to which they would be incompatible with Community provisions.*[14]

27. One line of interpretation of this passage, which is supported by a minority of commentators, maintains that it is authority for the "non-existence" of a subsequent national provision which is incompatible with Community law. In its observations the Commission seems to agree with this point of view, since, after citing paragraph 17 of the *Simmenthal* judgment, it infers from that paragraph that the incompatibility with Community law of the national provision "means that the Member State has no power whatever to impose taxation" and, in paragraph 20 of its observations, asks whether the Court should declare the national provision non-existent.

28. While I acknowledge the force of that argument, I do not subscribe to it.

29. The Commission's stance on the choice between non-existence and derogation as the only categories applicable is to my mind, on the one hand, oversimplistic and, on the other, confused in that it fails to distinguish between the temporal and the substantive problems relating to each category.

30. It is possible—and to a certain extent frequent in some legal systems—to declare a national provision invalid and to endow that declaration with effects *ex tunc* without its amounting in law to a ruling that the provision is "non-existent".

31. Similarly, there is no good reason why, when a provision is set aside, it should not be **[6315]** set aside with retroactive effect. That would certainly imply an exception to the general rule that a declaration setting a provision aside takes effect for the future, but the legislature is also able to confer retroactive effect on its decisions which repeal existing measures. How the legal system regulates situations which came into existence by virtue of the provision set aside while it was *de facto* in force is another matter.

32. Therefore the temporal problems should not be confused with the particular nature and effects of the various competing legal categories. The problems are distinct and require a differentiated analysis.

33. That apart, the Commission's theory concerning the choice between non-existence and setting aside (in its view the only choice available to the Court) is to my mind oversimplistic. The Court has not considered it necessary to make a finding in that regard but has adopted a solution (non-application) which avoids the problems inherent in both categories.

34. In so far as the Commission refers to the supposed "non-existence" of a national provision contrary to Community law, I shall

[14] Emphasis added.

begin by stating that such a fiction—and it is beyond doubt a legal fiction, since the provision has existed and, in cases such as this, has in fact produced its effects over the years—is not even required by paragraph 17 of the *Simmenthal* judgment, which merely refers to the "valid adoption" of the national legislative measures which are incompatible with Community provisions. It is therefore more a question of invalidity than of non-existence.

35. I consider, on the other hand, that when it comes to analysing the effects which, under a national law which has been actually applied, are produced when it is subsequently declared incompatible with Community law, it makes no sense, in strictly legal terms, to speak of the "non-existence" of the law.

36. The declaration of "non-existence", as the legal system's response to or penalty for the exceptional gravity of the defects which affect a measure, is employed in some Member States to classify certain administrative measures. On parallel lines, the Court has accepted that a Community administrative measure which exhibits particularly serious and manifest defects could also be classified as "non-existent".[15]

[6316] 37. On the other hand, in those same national legal systems—that is, those in which the category of "non-existence" is available as a very exceptional sanction in the case of manifest defects of particular importance—it is not the custom to classify legislative provisions enacted by Parliament, published and in force as "non-existent", even where they have defects which render them invalid.

38. It is in this context that we encounter the phenomenon, well known in many legal orders, of the declaration of "illegality" (I use the word "illegality" in its wider sense, which encompasses all the various hypotheses, which differ according to the legal system concerned, in which a provision lacks binding force, usually because it conflicts with rules of law of a higher order). Where in such a case, following a declaration of unconstitutionality or similar procedure, a law is retrospectively declared to be defective to the point of being invalid, that does not mean that it is held to have been "non-existent".[16]

[15] See Case 15/85 *Consorzio Cooperative d'Abruzzo* v. *Commission* [1987] ECR 1005, paragraph 10. The distinction between "non-existence" and mere "invalidity" of a Community measure was analysed by the Court of Justice when it determined the Commission's appeal against the judgment of the Court of First Instance in Joined Cases T-79/89, T-84/89, T-85/89, T-86/89, T-89/89, T-91/89, T-92/89, T-94/89, T-96/89, T-98/89, T-102/89 and T-104/89 *BASF and Others* v. *Commission* [1992] ECR II-315. In its judgment in Case C-137/92 P *Commission* v. *BASF and Others* [1994] ECR I-2555 the Court of Justice set aside the judgment delivered at first instance on the ground that the declaration that Commission Decision 89/190/EEC was "non-existent" was unlawful. Instead the Court of Justice merely annulled the decision.

[16] It might in theory be accepted that this classification should be attributed to legislative measures whose promulgation or adoption was affected by particularly serious irregularities, as a result of which there would only be a "semblance" of a law, or a *de facto* law: such provisions would, in legal terms, be non-existent. This would apply, for example, where a law was adopted by only one Chamber in a State with a bicameral legislature, or published without the approval of the authority recognised as competent by the Constitution.

39. Nor, following the same parallelism as that referred to above, does one speak in Community law of the "non-existence" of a Community legislative provision because it contains elements which render it invalid. As I said earlier, declarations of that type are made in respect of administrative measures but not legislative provisions.[17]

40. Moreover, it is clear upon analysing the judgments in which the Court has specifically reviewed national legislative measures having a fiscal content for their compatibility with Community law that it is inappropriate to speak of "non-existence" in this case. Such a legal category would preclude judicial decisions which accept that certain effects of the national law subsist in spite of the fact that the law was contrary to the Community order.

41. I shall give two significant examples. The first is readily seen in the consistent case-law of the Court on repayment by the Member States of taxes collected but not owed. It has been accepted in that line of decisions that actions for recovery (where the taxes in question were demanded pursuant to a national **[6317]** provision that was contrary to Community law) might be subject to the five-year limitation period established by the national legislative measure, even where that measure precludes total or partial repayment of the taxes.[18]

42. This line of decisions implicitly makes the point that, despite being contrary to Community law, the national provision has existed and has produced effects in time which, taking into consideration situations which are legally "exhausted", are now not amenable to judicial review. The recognition of such effects would not be possible if it were necessary to regard the national law as wholly "non-existent".

43. The second example refers to certain rulings of the Court of Justice on the temporal aspects of a declaration that national tax measures are incompatible with Community law. As is well known, in certain cases the Court, for reasons of legal certainty, has restricted the temporal effects

[17] In Joined Cases 15/73 to 33/73, 52/73, 53/73, 57/73 to 109/73, 116/73, 117/73, 123/73, 132/73 and 135/73 to 137/73 *Kortner and Others* v. *Council, Commission and Parliament* [1974] ECR 177, the Court expressly stated that a Community provision (in this case Article 4(3) of Annex VII to the Staff Regulations of Officials of the European Communities) could not be termed "non-existent" merely because it contained elements of discrimination which had led to its being indirectly annulled in a previous judgment. The Opinion of Advocate General Trabucchi in that case reflects the same point of view as I support: ". . . In a system such as our Community law system, there appears to be no reason to depart from the criterion followed in the various national legal systems, according to which an act laying down regulations capable of implementation and which complies with the essential requirements as to procedure, form and competence as regards its introduction and publication, is an act which may be rendered invalid owing to some incompatibility of its contents with superior rules or principles, but which can never be repudiated as null and void."

[18] This problem, and also the recent judgment in Joined Cases C-114/95 and C-115/95 *Texaco* v. *Middlefart Havn and Others* [1997] ECR I-4263; Case C-90/94 *Haahr Petroleum* [1997] ECR I-4085; and Case C-188/95 *Fantask and Others* v. *Industriministeriet* [1997] ECR I-6783, are considered in my Opinions in the *Edis, SPAC* and *Ansaldo* cases.

of its own judgments,[19] which are not applicable to legal situations which are still amenable to judicial review.

44. That means accepting, albeit exceptionally, not only the existence but also even the applicability of the national law which is contrary to Community law. The use of this technique of limiting the temporal effects of judgments would be inconceivable if the national tax law incompatible with Community law were to be regarded as non-existent.

(ii) *The classification of the legal relationships in the main proceedings*

45. As the Italian, French and United Kingdom Governments maintain, the classification of the legal relationships existing between the parties to the main proceedings is a matter for the national court, not for the Court of Justice. It is for the national court to decide whether they are fiscal relationships or merely civil relationships and what the consequences of that fact are for the dispute.

46. The national court, however, expresses its doubts as to the impact that the declaration that a provision is incompatible with Community law may have on the legal classification of such relationships. In that perspective, **[6318]** the question is not inadmissible, since the Court of Justice can assist the national court in specifying the consequences of the fact that the national provision is inapplicable.

47. At the risk of stating the obvious, I shall state at the outset that where the *tax* authorities receive from a *taxable* person acting as such the amount of a *tax* remitted by way of payment of a previously quantified *tax* debt, it is difficult to deny that the legal relationship established has also been a fiscal relationship.

48. It is a separate matter where the legal premiss which served as the basis for the payment of the tax (that is, the provision governing it) is subsequently declared to suffer from a defect that renders it invalid. The defect in question, like the invalidity of the obligation itself, will no doubt produce certain legal effects (including, generally, reimbursement of the sum paid), but will not alter the fact that the relationship in the context of which payment was made was from its inception fiscal in nature.

49. At the hearing the Commission, which had already claimed in its written observations that the fiscal obligation deriving from a provision of this type was non-existent, maintained that argument at the hearing and in that regard referred to various decisions of the Court of Justice.[20]

[19] In my Opinion in the *Edis* case I consider the application of this position in relation to the normal temporal effectiveness of the rulings given on questions of interpretation.

[20] The Commission referred, in particular, to paragraph 28 of the judgment in Case C-228/90 *Simba and Others* v. *Ministero delle Finanze* [1992] ECR I-3713, which reads as follows: "where national courts consider a national law introducing a duty such as the national tax on consumption to be incompatible with provisions of Community law contained in agreements, conferring rights on individuals, the individuals concerned are not required to pay such a duty".

50. To my mind that argument calls for some qualification. It is true that the fact that a national tax provision is incompatible with Community law means that taxpayers are not obliged to pay the tax and that if they do they will be entitled to reimbursement. In the latter case, however, the fact that the tax obligation was not valid does not necessarily imply any particular classification of the previous legal relationship: it will be for the various national legal systems to determine that point. It may be the case that for reasons of legal certainty certain fiscal relationships, including those based on provisions which have been declared void, are not susceptible of being reclassified and have consolidated the corresponding legal situations, which are regarded as intangible in law.

51. This type of situation exists not only in national law but also in Community law. At the hearing the Commission referred, in support of its argument that a fiscal relationship deriving from a provision which has been declared void is non-existent, to an extract from the judgment of the Court of Justice in **[6319]** *FMC and Others*,[21] according to which the invalidity of a Community rule requiring payment of a specific financial contribution may be invoked by those concerned from its entry into force and not only from the date on which legal proceedings were brought in respect of that provision.[22] Immediately afterwards, however, the same judgment acknowledges that Community law does not preclude "the application of a period of limitation or prescription laid down by a rule of national law which restricts the period . . . in respect of which reimbursement of undue payments may be obtained . . .".[23] The Court thus acknowledges that the legal situations resulting from a Community provision which has been declared void may have become stable and be unassailable, notwithstanding the invalidity of the obligation on which they are based.

52. In the majority of Member States a declaration of invalidity of provisions which impose an obligation to pay a tax requires a judicial decision, either annexed to a declaration of unconstitutionality by the Constitutional Court or similar organ[24] in the case of a statute or by similar procedures, depending upon the place which the provision occupies in the hierarchy of norms, by the appropriate judicial organs.[25]

[21] Case C-212/94 [1996] ECR I-389.

[22] The extract was from paragraph 62, which states that the operators concerned could invoke the invalidity of an invalid Community regulation "not only subsequent to, but also prior to, the bringing of an action or the making of an equivalent complaint, in principle as from the date on which the provisions declared invalid by the Court entered into force".

[23] Paragraph 64.

[24] A declaration that a law having a fiscal content is unconstitutional does not necessarily entail its nullity, with the consequent effect *ex tunc*. In that regard, see the article by E. García de Enterría: "Un paso importante para el desarrollo de nuestra justicia constitucional: la doctrina prospectiva en la declaración de ineficacia de las leyes inconstitucionales", *Revista Español de Derecho Administrativo*, 1989, No 61, p. 5 et seq.

[25] In some Member States, as in Spain, the ordinary courts' power of review extends to decree-laws, for the purpose of determining whether the executive has exceeded the powers conferred on

53. Such a declaration that a provision is invalid may or may not, depending on the case, imply the reclassification of the legal situations which came into being by virtue of that provision; if it does so, the reclassification may affect only the situations which are still pending or even (more rarely) those which have already exhausted all their effects.

54. It is for the national legal systems to regulate all those matters and to specify, in the case of fiscal provisions, the legal effects of a declaration that they are inconsistent with a rule of law of a higher order. There is nothing to prevent the legislature, or the national court, from establishing that these effects include reclassifying the legal relationships which came into being by virtue of the provision, so that what was previously a fiscal relationship may subsequently be classified as a merely civil relationship.

[6320] 55. The referring court is aware that the Corte Suprema di Cassazione has already resolved the problem in Italy and held that the original relationship was of a fiscal nature and that, accordingly, the applicable rules are those which specifically regulate the reimbursement of taxes paid but not due. None the less, the national court further states that it does not find this judicial solution "persuasive" and insists that the non-application of the national fiscal provision that is contrary to Community law presumes "the total absence of any power of taxation vested in the State, having regard to (or, rather, because of an infringement of) the pre-existing Community legislation".

56. I have pointed out above how the Commission also expressly and repeatedly employs the expression "the total absence of any power of taxation vested in the State" to refer to the same phenomenon.

57. In my view that approach is not appropriate. As a matter of principle Member States retain the power to establish national taxes. In so far as indirect taxes on the raising of capital are concerned, they are required to comply with the terms of Directive 69/335, which deals with the harmonisation of national legislation concerning such taxes. That directive allows them, *inter alia*, to charge "duties paid by way of fees or dues", that is those which cover the cost of a specific service, as is the case of the registration of undertakings and company documents in a public register.

58. It may happen that in exercising the legislative power to establish and determine the form of such taxes (which, in the last analysis, is what is known as the power of taxation) a Member State infringes the directive, for example by imposing an annual tax for registration on the public register in an amount which bears no relation to the cost of the service and therefore in reality is not "paid by way of fees or dues". That was the case of the Italian tax in issue.

it by the legislature. In *Derecho Comunitario: sistema constitucional y administrativo de la Comunidad Europea* (Madrid, 1994, p. 476) R. Alonso García maintains that if the powers delegated by the national legislature allow the executive to implement rules contained in Community legislation the ordinary courts will have jurisdiction to review the relevant measures.

59. The fact that a Member State, when legislating on a tax which has been harmonised at Community level, infringes the harmonised rules does not mean that it thereby loses its power to tax. It simply means that the national provision that is contrary to the Community rule must yield to the primacy of the Community rule and therefore cannot be applied.

60. Therefore the "total absence of any power to legislate" must not be confused with the irregular or improper exercise of that power. The former concept implies that an institution—or, in this case, the State—is denied competence to regulate specific matters because the power to do so is reserved for other authorities.[26] The term "irregular exercise", on the other hand, means that the body in whom competence to legislate is vested misuses that competence and adopts a legislative **[6321]** provision which, owing to the primacy of the Community provision, must not be applied by the national courts.

61. Where a Member State, in using one of its own powers, such as the power to impose indirect taxes on company activities, infringes the harmonised Community rules in some way, it will not be able to claim that its own provisions should be applied—and will even have to repeal them—but that does not mean that it does not retain its own power or competence to introduce and regulate taxes.

62. For that reason I reject the approach proposed both in the order for reference and in the Commission's observations; and having done so, and having reiterated that the national court has jurisdiction to classify the legal relationships which exist between the parties to a dispute before it, I must conclude by stating that the application of the principle of the primacy of the Community provision has no direct impact on such a question.

63. Consequently, in those legal systems which so allow, the national court can reclassify such situations if the provision under which they came into being is subsequently declared contrary to a rule of law of a higher order. From the point of view of Community law, the principle that a national provision that is incompatible with Community law is not applicable neither requires nor precludes the reclassification of pre-existing legal relationships.

64. None the less, the principle of equivalence between actions brought with a view to securing reimbursement of amounts paid but not due, whether they be based on grounds of Community law or on grounds of national law, would preclude the application to this problem of solutions different from those which domestic law provides in the event of the infringement of national rules. In other words, if the reclassification of the previous legal relationship (which would no longer be a fiscal relationship but merely a civil relationship governed by the provisions

[26] Thus, for example, the Member States are not competent to introduce a customs tariff in their relations with non-member countries, since they have conferred power to adopt such a common measure on the Community.

of a civil law) were a necessary consequence of the incompatibility of a national tax provision with a rule of national law of a higher order—for example, a rule of constitutional law—the same consequence should apply where the provision in question is incompatible with Community law.[27]

65. It does not appear, however, in the light of the information before the Court, that this is the position in Italy. As I pointed out in my Opinion in *Edis* (points 58 to 64), the case-law of the Italian Corte di Cassazione[28] on the consequences of declarations of unconstitutionality of laws with a fiscal content, as **[6322]** regards the taxes already paid pursuant to that law, is as follows:

- Judgments of the Corte di Cassazione which declare to be unlawful provisions ranking as laws eliminate the latter from the legal order *ex tunc*, in the sense that they can no longer be applied to outstanding legal relationships; legal relationships which have run their course, that is to say those whose effects have been consolidated to such a point that they cannot be changed, are not affected by such pronouncements.
- Specifically, such judgments do not affect those tax relationships arising by operation of law which, for various reasons, must be regarded as having come to an end. Those reasons may include the existence of a previous judgment, or the fact that the tax assessment has become final (through not being challenged or through dismissal of a challenge), or the effluxion of prescription periods or time-limits laid down by the rules governing the tax.
- Therefore, payments of tax debts based on fiscal provisions held to be unconstitutional cannot be affected where the taxpayers allowed the legal relationship in question to consolidate itself.
- There is no basis for the view that, because of the retroactive effect of declarations of unconstitutionality, the tax obligation is non-existent *in radice* and, therefore, the general rule on charges improperly levied (Article 2033 of the Civil Code) would immediately take effect, so that the action could be brought without reference to the procedures for challenging tax assessments and regardless of the time-limits laid down by the tax provisions.
- In conclusion, there is no basis for the view that in such cases (even where it is contended that there was no valid tax relationship, either original or supervening) an action for recovery of the sums unduly paid provided for by the Civil Code would be available, rather than one covered by the specific rules for tax litigation, both substantive and procedural.

[27] The Commission referred to this question in its observations in the *Edis* case, and suggested that the question referred by the national court be reformulated. I refer to point 51 et seq. of my Opinion in that case.

[28] Judgments of 9 June 1989, No 2876, and 21 June 1996, No 5731.

66. I do not find, therefore, that in this matter the application of Italian law, as carried out by the supreme courts of that country, implies a difference in treatment between the consequences of a declaration that a tax law is incompatible with Community law and the consequences of a declaration that that law is unconstitutional, on purely domestic legal grounds.

[6323] *Conclusion*

67. I therefore propose that the Court should answer the question referred to it by the Pretore di Roma as follows:

A national court which is required, within the scope of its jurisdiction, to apply Community law is under an obligation to ensure that full effect is given to it by disapplying, if necessary, provisions of national law which are incompatible with it. Where those provisions have introduced a tax that is incompatible with the provisions of a directive and must therefore be disapplied, Community law neither precludes nor requires a particular classification or reclassification of pre-existing legal situations which came into being by virtue of the national provision.

[The following is the text of the judgment of the Court of Justice of the European Community:]

[6327] 1. By 13 orders of 17 December 1996, received at the Court on 16 January 1997, the Pretura Circondariale di Roma (District Magistrate's Court, Rome) referred to the Court for a preliminary ruling under Article 177 of the EC Treaty a question concerning the consequences arising under national law from the incompatibility of a domestic charge with Community law.

2. That question was raised in a series of disputes between the Ministry of Finance, on the one hand, and IN. CO. GE.'90 and 12 other limited-liability companies ("IN. CO. GE.'90 et al."), on the other, relating to the detailed rules governing repayment of the *tassa di concessione governativa* (administrative charge) for entering companies on the register of companies (hereinafter "the registration charge").

3. The registration charge was introduced by Decree No 641 of the President of the Republic of 26 October 1972 (GURI No 292 of 11 November 1972, Supplement No 3, hereinafter "Decree No 641/72"). In so far as it applies to the registration of documents recording the incorporation of companies, it has been the subject of successive amendments regarding its amount and periodicity.

4. The amount of the registration charge was first substantially increased by Decree-Law No 853 of 19 December 1984 (GURI No 347

of 19 December 1984), converted into law by Law No 17 of 17 February 1985 (GURI No 41*bis* of 17 February 1985), which also provided that from then on the charge would be payable not only upon **[6328]** registration of the instrument of incorporation but also on 30 June of each calendar year thereafter. The amount of the charge was then further altered in 1988 and 1989. In 1989 the amount came to LIT 12 million for public limited companies and partnerships limited by shares, LIT 3.5 million for private limited companies and LIT 500,000 for other companies.

5. In its judgment in Joined Cases C-71/91 and C-178/91 *Ponente Carni and Cispadana Costruzioni* v. *Amministrazione delle Finanze dello Stato* [1993] ECR I-1915, dealing with the registration charge, the Court held that Article 10 of Council Directive 69/335/EEC of 17 July 1969 concerning indirect taxes on the raising of capital (OJ, English Special Edition 1969 (II), p. 412) was to be interpreted as prohibiting, subject to the derogating provisions of Article 12, an annual charge due in respect of the registration of capital companies even though the product of that charge contributed to financing the department responsible for keeping the register of companies. The Court also held that Article 12 of Directive 69/335 was to be interpreted as meaning that duties paid by way of fees or dues referred to in Article 12(1)(e) might constitute payment collected by way of consideration for transactions required by law in the public interest such as, for example, the registration of capital companies. The amount of such duties, which might vary according to the legal form taken by the company, was to be calculated according to the cost of the transaction, which might be assessed on a flat-rate basis.

6. Following that judgment, the registration charge was reduced to LIT 500,000 for all companies by Decree-Law No 331 of 30 August 1993 (GURI No 203 of 30 August 1993), converted into law by Law No 427 of 29 October 1993 (GURI No 255 of 29 October 1993), and it ceased to be payable annually.

7. Pursuant to Article 633 et seq. of the Italian Code of Civil Procedure, IN. CO. GE.'90 et al. successfully applied to the Pretura di Roma for orders enjoining the Ministry of Finance to repay to them the sums which they had paid by way of the registration charge over previous years.

[6329] 8. The Ministry of Finance, however, challenged those injunctions by raising two objections alleging, first, that the Pretura di Roma lacked jurisdiction to hear disputes involving tax matters and, second, that the applicants' entitlement to repayment, which, it claimed, was limited to the amounts paid during the three-year period preceding lodgment of their claims, was barred by lapse of time in accordance with Article 13 of Decree No 641/72.

9. It appears from the order for reference that those objections must stand or fall together, in so far as they both hinge on the question whether the dispute is of a fiscal or civil nature. If the dispute is of a fiscal nature, the Pretura will lack jurisdiction to hear it and it will not therefore be open to it to consider the plea of time-bar. On the other hand, if the dispute is not of a fiscal nature but comes under the civil-law rules for recovery of amounts paid but not due, the national court will have to resolve the dispute and the three-year time-limit laid down in Article 13 of Decree No 641/72 will not be applicable.

10. The Pretura di Roma adds, in that connection, that in Judgment No 3458 of 23 February 1996, the Combined Chambers of the Corte Suprema di Cassazione (Supreme Court of Cassation) ruled that repayment of the registration charge falls within the scope of Article 13 of Decree No 641/72 since that provision applies to all charges paid but not due, irrespective of the reason for the undue payment.

11. The national court, however, does not share that view. It points out that, in accordance with the case-law of the Court, a national court is under a duty not to apply any provision of national law, even if adopted subsequently, which is contrary to Community law, without being obliged to request or await the repeal of that provision by legislative or any other constitutional means (Joined Cases C-13/91 and C-113/91 *Debus* [1992] ECR I-3617). In the present cases, the non-application in its entirety of the Italian law which introduced the registration charge necessarily has the effect of divesting of its fiscal nature the legal relationship established between the Ministry of Finance and the applicant companies when the contested amounts were paid. Since those amounts were levied by way of a charge which is non-existent, and thus in the absence of any fiscal debt owed to the State, their **[6330]** repayment falls within the general rules for recovery of amounts paid but not due, which is subject to a ten-year limitation period under the Civil Code.

12. It was in those circumstances that the Pretura di Roma stayed proceedings and referred the following question to the Court for a preliminary ruling:

Does the incompatibility with Article 10 of Council Directive 69/335/EEC of 17 July 1969, as interpreted by the Court of Justice in its judgment of 20 April 1993 (in Joined Cases C-71/91 and C-178/91 *Ponente Carni and Cispadana Costruzioni* v. *Amministrazione delle Finanze dello Stato* [1993] ECR I-1915), of Article 3(XVIII) and (XIX) of Decree-Law No 853 of 19 December 1984, converted into Law No 17 of 17 February 1985, mean, on the basis of the criteria for integration of national law and Community law which that Court has laid down, that the said paragraphs (XVIII) and (XIX) of Article 3 must be set aside in their entirety, and in particular does it mean that the national court must not take account of those internal provisions, even when classifying the legal relationship on the basis of which a national of a Member State calls on the finance administration to refund sums that were paid in contravention of the said Article 10 of Directive 69/335?

Jurisdiction

13. The United Kingdom Government submits that the Court lacks jurisdiction to reply to the question submitted by the Pretura di Roma in so far as that question concerns the interpretation of Italian law and not of Community law. It points out that it is for each Member State to designate the courts and tribunals having jurisdiction and to lay down the detailed procedural rules governing actions for safeguarding rights which individuals derive from the Community legal order (Case 33/76 *Rewe* v. *Landwirtschaftskammer für das Saarland* [1976] ECR 1989 and Case 45/76 *Comet* v. *Produktschap voor Siergewassen* [1976] ECR 2043).

[6331] 14. It should be noted in this regard that, according to a consistent line of cases decided by the Court, it is for each Member State to determine which court or tribunal has jurisdiction to hear disputes involving individual rights derived from Community law. However, it is the Member States' responsibility to ensure that those rights are effectively protected in each case. Subject to that reservation, it is not for the Court to involve itself in the resolution of questions of jurisdiction to which the classification of particular situations based on Community law may give rise in the national judicial system (Case 179/84 *Bozzetti* v. *Invernizzi* [1985] ECR 2301, paragraph 17; Case C-446/93 *SEIM* v. *Subdirector-Geral das Alfândegas* [1996] ECR I-73, paragraph 32; and Case C-54/96 *Dorsch Consult* v. *Bundesbaugesellschaft Berlin* [1997] ECR I-4961, paragraph 40).

15. However, the Court has power to explain to the national court points of Community law which may help to solve the problem of jurisdiction with which that court is faced (*Bozzetti*, paragraph 18, and *SEIM*, paragraph 33, both cited above). To that end, it may, if appropriate, extract the relevant points from the wording of the question submitted and the facts set forth by the national court (see, in particular, Case 54/80 *Procureur de la République* v. *Wilner* [1980] ECR 3673, paragraph 4).

16. It appears in this regard from the order for reference that the Pretura di Roma is uncertain as to the consequences arising under national law from the incompatibility of a domestic charge with Community law. The Pretura bases its opinion that the disputes pending before it are not of a fiscal nature but fall, under Italian law, within the general rules for recovery of amounts paid but not due on the fact that such incompatibility, inasmuch as its effect is to disapply the relevant national provisions in their entirety and deprive the charge in question of any existence in law, necessarily has the effect of divesting it of its fiscal nature.

17. It follows that the Court does have jurisdiction to reply to the question submitted.

[6332] *The Question Submitted*

18. The Commission points out that, in its judgment in Case 106/77 *Amministrazione delle Finanze dello Stato* v. *Simmenthal* [1978] ECR 629, the Court held, *inter alia*, that the provisions of the Treaty and the directly applicable measures of the institutions have the effect, in their relationship with the domestic law of the Member States, not only of rendering automatically inapplicable any conflicting provision of national law in force but also of precluding the valid adoption of new national legislative measures which would be incompatible with Community provisions. From this, the Commission infers that a Member State has no power whatever to adopt a fiscal provision that is incompatible with Community law, with the result that such a provision and the corresponding fiscal obligation must be treated as non-existent.

19. That interpretation cannot be accepted.

20. In *Simmenthal*, the issue facing the Court related in particular to the consequences of the direct applicability of a provision of Community law where that provision was incompatible with a subsequently adopted provision of national law. The Court had already stressed, in its previous decisions (see, in particular, Case 6/64 *Costa* v. *ENEL* [1964] ECR 585), that it was impossible for a Member State to accord precedence to a national rule over a conflicting rule of Community law, but did not draw any distinction between pre-existing and subsequently adopted national law. So, in *Simmenthal*, the Court held that every national court must, in a case within its jurisdiction, apply Community law in its entirety and protect rights which the latter confers on individuals, setting aside any provision of national law which may conflict with it, whether prior or subsequent to the Community rule (*Simmenthal*, paragraphs 21 and 24). That case-law has been reaffirmed on numerous occasions **[6333]** (see, in particular, *Debus*, cited above, paragraph 32; Case C-158/91 *Levy* [1993] ECR I-4287, paragraph 9; and Case C-347/96 *Solred* v. *Administración General del Estado* [1998] ECR I-937, paragraph 30).

21. It cannot therefore, contrary to the Commission's contention, be inferred from the judgment in *Simmenthal* that the incompatibility with Community law of a subsequently adopted rule of national law has the effect of rendering that rule of national law non-existent. Faced with such a situation, the national court is, however, obliged to disapply that rule, provided always that this obligation does not restrict the power of the competent national courts to apply, from among the various procedures available under national law, those which are appropriate for protecting the individual rights conferred by Community law (see Case 34/67 *Lück* v. *Hauptzollamt Köln-Rheinau* [1968] ECR 245).

22. It remains to be considered whether non-application, as the result of a judgment given by the Court, of national legislation which introduced a levy contrary to Community law has the result of depriving that levy retroactively of its character as a charge and thereby divesting of its fiscal nature the legal relationship established when that charge was levied between the national tax authority and the companies liable to pay it.

23. It is settled case-law that the interpretation which, in the exercise of the jurisdiction conferred upon it by Article 177 of the Treaty, the Court gives to a rule of Community law clarifies and defines where necessary the meaning and scope of that rule as it must be or ought to have been understood and applied from the time of its entry into force. It follows that the rule as so interpreted may, and must, be applied by the courts to legal relationships arising and established before the judgment ruling on the request for interpretation, provided that in other respects the conditions enabling an action relating to the application of that rule to be brought before the courts having jurisdiction are satisfied (see Case 61/79 *Amministrazione delle Finanze dello Stato* v. *Denkavit Italiana* [1980] ECR 1205, paragraph 16, and Case C-188/95 *Fantask and Others* v. *Industriministeriet* [1997] ECR I-6783, paragraph 37).

[6334] 24. Further, in terms of that case-law, entitlement to the recovery of sums levied in breach of Community law is a consequence of, and an adjunct to, the rights conferred on individuals by the relevant Community provisions as interpreted by the Court. A Member State is therefore in principle required to repay charges levied in breach of Community law (*Fantask and Others*, paragraph 38).

25. However, in the absence of Community rules governing the matter, such repayment may be claimed only if the substantive and formal conditions laid down by the various national laws are complied with, provided that such conditions are not less favourable than those governing similar domestic actions and do not render virtually impossible or excessively difficult the exercise of rights conferred by Community law (see, in particular, Case C-312/93 *Peterbroeck* v. *Belgian State* [1995] ECR I-4599, paragraph 12, and Case C-212/94 *FMC and Others* v. *Intervention Board for Agricultural Produce and Ministry of Agriculture, Fisheries and Food* [1996] ECR I-389, paragraph 71).

26. Thus, the obligation on the national court to ensure that a domestic charge levied in breach of Community law is refunded must, subject to compliance with the two conditions laid down by the Court in its case-law, be discharged in accordance with the provisions of its national law. It follows that the detailed rules for repayment which are to apply and the classification, for that purpose, of the legal relationship established when that charge was levied between the tax authorities of a Member State and particular companies in that State are matters which fall to be determined under national law.

27. Furthermore, as the Court has recently held, Community law does not in principle preclude the legislation of a Member State from laying down, alongside a limitation period applicable under the ordinary law to actions between private individuals for the recovery of sums paid but not due, special detailed rules governing claims and legal proceedings to challenge the imposition of charges and other levies (Case C-231/96 *Edis* v. *Ministero delle Finanze* [1998] ECR I-4951, paragraph 37, and Case C-260/96 *Ministero delle Finanze* v. *Spac* [1998] ECR I-4997, paragraph 21).

[6335] 28. The possibility thus recognised by the Court of applying those special detailed rules to the repayment of charges and other levies found to be contrary to Community law would be deprived of any effect if, as the Commission argues, the incompatibility between a domestic levy and Community law necessarily had the effect of depriving that levy of its character as a charge and divesting of its fiscal nature the legal relationship established, when the charge in question was levied, between the national tax authorities and the parties liable to pay it.

29. The answer to the question submitted must therefore be that the obligation on a national court to disapply national legislation introducing a charge contrary to Community law must lead that court, in principle, to uphold claims for repayment of that charge. Such repayment must be ensured in accordance with the provisions of its national law, on condition that those provisions are not less favourable than those governing similar domestic actions and do not render virtually impossible or excessively difficult the exercise of rights conferred by Community law. Any reclassification of the legal relationship established between the tax authorities of a Member State and certain companies in that State when a domestic charge subsequently found to be contrary to Community law was levied is therefore a matter for national law.

Costs

30. The costs incurred by the Italian, French and United Kingdom Governments and by the Commission, which have submitted observations to the Court, are not recoverable. Since these proceedings are, for the parties to the main proceedings, a step in the proceedings pending before the national court, the decision on costs is a matter for that court.

[6336] On those grounds,

THE COURT,

in answer to the question referred to it by the Pretura Circondariale di Roma by orders of 17 December 1996, hereby rules:

The obligation on a national court to disapply national legislation introducing a charge contrary to Community law must lead that court, in principle, to uphold claims for repayment of that charge. Such repayment must be ensured in accordance with the provisions of its national law, on condition that those provisions are not less favourable than those governing similar domestic actions and do not render virtually impossible or excessively difficult the exercise of rights conferred by Community law. Any reclassification of the legal relationship established between the tax authorities of a Member State and certain companies in that State when a domestic charge subsequently found to be contrary to Community law was levied is therefore a matter for national law.

[Report: [1998] ECR I-6307]

Human rights—Scope of protection within the Community—Whether respect for human rights constituting condition for lawfulness of Community acts—Significance of European Convention on Human Rights, 1950, within Community legal order — Article 1 of Convention — Responsibility of Member States of Community to secure Convention rights — Community itself not a party to the Convention — Whether Member States of Community nevertheless remaining responsible for securing protection of Convention rights after transfer of competences to Community institutions

Legal order in general — Special character — Community treaties forming part of legal order — Transfer of competences to Community institutions—Effect of European Convention on Human Rights on exercise of powers by Member States within the framework of Community legal order — Whether Member States remaining responsible within Convention system for consequences of Community action

Human rights—Scope of protection within the Community—European Convention on Human Rights, Protocol No 1, Article 3 — Right of everyone to participate in elections to "legislature" — Whether including direct elections to European Parliament—Fundamental importance of direct elections for ensuring democratic legitimation and thereby effective political democracy

Institutions — European Parliament — Legal nature — Whether forming part of institutional order of Member States—Whether constituting "legislature" under Article 3 of Protocol No 1 to European Convention on Human Rights — Significance of role of European Parliament in ensuring democratic political accountability within European Community — Direct elections to European Parliament—Council Decision on Direct Elections, 1976—Implementation by Member States—Scope of applicability to Gibraltar—The law of the European Convention on Human Rights

MATTHEWS *v.* UNITED KINGDOM

European Court of Human Rights. 18 *February* 1999

(Wildhaber, *President*; Palm, Ferrari Bravo, Jörundsson, Ress, Cabral Barreto, Costa, Fuhrmann, Jungwiert, Fischbach, Vajić, Hedigan, Thomassen, Tsatsa-Nikolovska, Panţîru and Traja, *Judges*; Freeland, *Judge* ad hoc)

SUMMARY: *The facts*:—Ms Matthews, a British citizen resident in Gibraltar, applied for registration as a voter in elections to the European Parliament. She was informed that her application could not be accepted because Gibraltar was not included in the franchise for those elections. The Act concerning the direct election of representatives to the European Parliament of 20 September 1976 applied only to the United Kingdom and not to its overseas and dependent territories such as Gibraltar. The EC Treaty itself applied to Gibraltar, by virtue of its Article 227. Although certain parts of the Treaty, covering, for instance, rules on free movement of goods and commercial policy, did not apply to Gibraltar, other important parts such as rules on free movement of persons and capital, the environment and consumer protection, were applicable to Gibraltar.

Ms Matthews claimed that the refusal to register her as a voter in the European elections violated Article 3 of Protocol No 1 to the European Convention on Human Rights, taken alone or in conjunction with Article 14 of the Convention. Article 3 of Protocol No 1 required parties to the Convention to undertake to hold free elections ensuring the free expression of opinion in the choice of the legislature. Accordingly, Ms Matthews lodged an application in April 1994 against the United Kingdom before the European Commission of Human Rights. The Commission concluded in October 1997 that there had been no violation of the provisions of the Convention. The case was referred to the European Court of Human Rights.

Held (by fifteen votes to two):—The exclusion of Gibraltar from European Parliamentary elections constituted a violation of Article 3 of Protocol No 1 to the European Convention.

(1) Article 1 of the Convention required the parties to secure to everyone within their jurisdiction the rights and freedoms contained in the Convention. The Convention had been extended to Gibraltar by a declaration of the United Kingdom in 1953 and Protocol No 1 accordingly also applied to Gibraltar. The question arising in this case was whether the United Kingdom was required to secure elections to the European Parliament notwithstanding the Community character of those elections and the nature of the European Parliament as a Community organ (p. 120).

(2) Acts of the European Community could not be challenged as such before the European Court of Human Rights because the European Community was not a party to the Convention. However, whilst the Convention did not exclude the transfer of competences to international organizations, the responsibility of the Member States to secure Convention rights continued even after such a transfer. The Council Decision on Direct Elections and the Treaty on European

Union, 1992, containing an extension of the powers of the European Parliament, were international instruments freely entered into by the United Kingdom, which formed part of the Community legal order. The United Kingdom was responsible, under Article 1 of the Convention and Article 3 of Protocol No. 1, for the consequences of those instruments (pp. 120-1).

(3) European Community legislation affected the population of Gibraltar in the same way as domestic legislation and, to this extent, there was no reason why the United Kingdom should not be required to secure the rights under Article 3 of Protocol No 1 in respect of European legislation. The United Kingdom was therefore responsible under Article 1 of the Convention for securing the rights guaranteed by Article 3 of Protocol No 1 in Gibraltar, regardless of whether the elections were European or purely domestic (p. 121).

(4) "Legislature" in Article 3 of Protocol No 1 did not necessarily mean the national parliament. European Community law sat alongside and indeed took precedence over domestic law in Gibraltar, in the same way as in other parts of the European Union, and to accept the contention that the European Parliament's sphere of activities fell outside the scope of the provision would risk undermining one of the fundamental tools by which "effective political democracy" could be maintained. No reason had been made out which could justify excluding the European Parliament from the ambit of the elections referred to in Article 3 of Protocol No 1 on the ground that it was a supranational representative organ (pp. 122-3).

(5) Bearing in mind the *sui generis* nature of the European Community, the European Parliament represented the principal form of democratic, political accountability in the European Community system. Whatever its limitations, it derived domestic legitimation from the direct elections by universal suffrage and had to be seen as that part of the European Community structure which best reflected concerns as to "effective political democracy". There were significant areas in which European Community activity had a direct impact on Gibraltar and the European Parliament was sufficiently involved in specific legislative processes, as well as in the general democratic supervision of the activities of the European Community, to constitute part of the "legislature" of Gibraltar (pp. 124-6).

(6) There was no indication of "local requirements" which could limit the application of the Convention. While States enjoyed a wide margin of appreciation in the choice of electoral system, the applicant in this case had been completely denied any opportunity to express her opinion in the choice of the members of the European Parliament and the very essence of her right to vote had therefore been denied (pp. 126-8).

The following is the text of the judgment of the Court:

PROCEDURE

1. The case was referred to the Court, as established under former Article 19 of the Convention,[1] by the European Commission of Human

[1] Since the entry into force of Protocol No 11, which amended Article 19, the Court has functioned on a permanent basis.

Rights ("the Commission") on 26 January 1998, within the three-month period laid down by former Articles 32(1) and 47 of the Convention. It originated in an application (No 24833/94) against the United Kingdom of Great Britain and Northern Ireland lodged with the Commission under former Article 25 by Ms Denise Matthews on 18 April 1994.

The Commission's request referred to former Articles 44 and 48 and to the declaration whereby the United Kingdom recognised the compulsory jurisdiction of the Court (former Article 46). The object of the request was to obtain a decision as to whether the facts of the case disclosed a breach by the respondent State of its obligations under Article 3 of Protocol No 1, taken alone or together with Article 14 of the Convention.

2. In response to the enquiry made in accordance with Rule 33(3)(d) of former Rules of Court A,[2] the applicant stated that she wished to take part in the proceedings and designated the lawyer who would represent her (former Rule 30).

3. As President of the Chamber which had originally been constituted (former Article 43 of the Convention and former Rule 21) in order to deal, in particular, with procedural matters that might arise before the entry into force of Protocol No 11, Mr R. Bernhardt, the President of the Court at the time, acting through the Registrar, consulted the Agent of the United Kingdom Government ("the Government"), the applicant's lawyer and the Delegate of the Commission on the organisation of the written procedure. Pursuant to the order made in consequence, the Registrar received the applicant's and the Government's memorials on 20 and 25 August 1998 respectively.

4. After the entry into force of Protocol No 11 on 1 November 1998 and in accordance with the provisions of Article 5(5) thereof, the case was referred to the Grand Chamber of the Court. The Grand Chamber included *ex officio* Sir Nicolas Bratza, the judge elected in respect of the United Kingdom (Article 27(2) of the Convention and Rule 24(4) of the Rules of Court), Mr L. Wildhaber, the President of the Court, Mrs E. Palm, Vice-President of the Court, and Mr G. Ress, Mr J.-P. Costa and Mr M. Fischbach, Vice-Presidents of Sections (Article 27(3) of the Convention and Rule 24(3) and (5)(a)). The other members appointed to complete the Grand Chamber were Mr L. Ferrari Bravo, Mr Gaukur Jörundsson, Mr I. Cabral Barreto, Mr W. Fuhrmann, Mr K. Jungwiert, Mrs N. Vajić, Mr J. Hedigan, Mrs W. Thomassen, Mrs M. Tsatsa-Nikolovska, Mr T. Panţîru and Mr K. Traja (Rule 24(3) and Rule 100(4)). Subsequently Sir Nicolas Bratza, who had taken part in the Commission's examination of the case, withdrew from sitting in the Grand Chamber (Rule 28). The Government accordingly appointed

2 *Note by the Registry*. Rules of Court A applied to all cases referred to the Court before the entry into force of Protocol No 9 (1 October 1994) and from then until 31 October 1998 only to cases concerning States not bound by that Protocol.

Sir John Freeland to sit as an *ad hoc* judge (Article 27(2) of the Convention and Rule 29(1)).

5. At the Court's invitation (Rule 99), the Commission delegated one of its members, Mr J.-C. Soyer, to take part in the proceedings before the Grand Chamber.

6. In accordance with the President's decision, a hearing took place in public in the Human Rights Building, Strasbourg, on 19 November 1998.

There appeared before the Court:

(a) *for the Government*

Mr M. EATON, Foreign and Commonwealth Office,	*Agent*,
Mr D. ANDERSON, Barrister-at-Law,	*Counsel*,
Ms D. COLLINS, Cabinet Office Legal Advisers,	
Ms C. POWER, Foreign and Commonwealth Office,	*Advisers*;

(b) *for the applicant*

Mr M. LLAMAS, Barrister-at-Law,	
Mr L. BAGLIETTO, Barrister,	
Mr F. PICARDO, Barrister,	*Counsel*,
Mr R. BENZAQUEN, Legislation Support Unit, Gibraltar,	*Adviser*;

(c) *for the Commission*

Mr J.-C. SOYER,	*Delegate*,
Ms M.-T. SCHOEPFER,	*Secretary to the Commission*.

The Court heard addresses by Mr Soyer, Mr Llamas and Mr Anderson.

THE FACTS

I. *The Circumstances of the Case*

7. On 12 April 1994 the applicant applied to the Electoral Registration Officer for Gibraltar to be registered as a voter at the elections to the European Parliament. The Electoral Registration Officer replied on 25 April 1994:

> The provisions of Annex II of the EC Act on Direct Elections of 1976 limit the franchise for European parliamentary elections to the United Kingdom [see paragraph 18 below]. This Act was agreed by all member States and has treaty status. This means that Gibraltar will not be included in the franchise for the European parliamentary elections.

II. *Relevant Law in Gibraltar*

A. *Gibraltar and the United Kingdom*

8. Gibraltar is a dependent territory of the United Kingdom. It forms part of Her Majesty the Queen's Dominions, but not part of the United Kingdom. The United Kingdom parliament has the ultimate authority to legislate for Gibraltar, but in practice exercises it rarely.

9. Executive authority in Gibraltar is vested in the Governor, who is the Queen's representative. Pursuant to a dispatch of 23 May 1969, certain "defined domestic matters" are allocated to the locally elected Chief Minister and his Ministers; other matters (external affairs, defence and internal security) are not "defined" and the Governor thus retains responsibility for them.

10. The Chief Minister and the Government of Gibraltar are responsible to the Gibraltar electorate via general elections to the House of Assembly. The House of Assembly is the domestic legislature in Gibraltar. It has the right to make laws for Gibraltar on "defined domestic matters", subject to, *inter alia*, a power in the Governor to refuse to assent to legislation.

B. *Gibraltar and the European Community*

11. The Treaty Establishing the European Community ("the EC Treaty") applies to Gibraltar by virtue of its Article 227(4), which provides that it applies to the European territories for whose external relations a member State is responsible. The United Kingdom acceded to the precursor to the EC Treaty, the Treaty Establishing the European Economic Community of 25 March 1957 ("the EEC Treaty"), by a Treaty of Accession of 22 January 1972.

12. Gibraltar is excluded from certain parts of the EC Treaty by virtue of the Treaty of Accession. In particular, Gibraltar does not form part of the customs territory of the Community, with the result that the provisions on free movement of goods do not apply; it is treated as a third country for the purposes of the common commercial policy; it is excluded from the common market in agriculture and trade in agricultural products and from the Community rules on value-added tax and other turnover taxes, and it makes no contribution to the Community budget. European Community ("EC") legislation concerning, *inter alia*, such matters as free movement of persons, services and capital, health, the environment and consumer protection applies in Gibraltar.

13. Relevant EC legislation becomes part of Gibraltar law in the same way as in other parts of the Union: regulations are directly applicable, and directives and other legal acts of the EC which call for domestic legislation are transposed by domestic primary or secondary legislation.

14. Although Gibraltar is not part of the United Kingdom in domestic terms, by virtue of a declaration made by the United Kingdom government at the time of the entry into force of the British Nationality Act 1981, the term "nationals" and derivatives used in the EC Treaty are to be understood as referring, *inter alia*, to British citizens and to British Dependent Territories citizens who acquire their citizenship from a connection with Gibraltar.

C. *The European Community and the European Parliament*

15. The powers of the European Community are divided amongst the institutions set up by the EC Treaty, including the European Parliament, the Council, the Commission ("the European Commission") and the Court of Justice.

16. Before 1 November 1993, the date of the entry into force of the Maastricht Treaty on European Union of 7 February 1992 ("the Maastricht Treaty"), Article 137 of the EEC Treaty referred to the "advisory and supervisory powers" of the European Parliament. Since 1 November 1993, the words "advisory and supervisory powers" have been removed and the role of the European Parliament has been expressed by Article 137 to be to "exercise the powers conferred upon it by [the] Treaty". The principal powers of the European Parliament under the EC Treaty may now be summarised as follows:

Article 138b provides that the European Parliament shall "participate in the process leading up to the adoption of Community acts by exercising its powers under the procedures laid down in Articles 189b and 189c and by giving its assent or delivering advisory opinions". Further, the second paragraph of Article 138b empowers the European Parliament to request the European Commission to submit any appropriate proposal on matters on which it considers that a Community act is required for the purpose of implementing the Treaty.

The reference in the first paragraph of Article 138b to "assent" refers to a procedure whereby the EC Treaty (for example, in Articles 8a(2) and 130d) provides for adoption of provisions by the Council on a proposal from the European Commission and after obtaining the assent of the European Parliament. The procedure is called the "assent procedure".

Article 144 provides for a motion of censure by the European Parliament over the European Commission whereby if a motion is carried by a two-thirds majority, representing a majority of the members, the members of the European Commission are required to resign as a body.

Article 158 provides that the European Parliament is to be consulted before the President of the European Commission is nominated, and the members of the European Commission, once nominated, are subject as a body to a vote of approval by the European Parliament.

The first paragraph of Article 189 provides:

In order to carry out their task and in accordance with the provisions of this Treaty, the European Parliament acting jointly with the Council, the Council and the Commission shall make regulations and issue directives, take decisions, make recommendations or deliver opinions.

Article 189b provides:

1. Where reference is made in the Treaty to this Article for the adoption of an act, the following procedure[3] shall apply.

2. The Commission shall submit a proposal to the European Parliament and the Council.

The Council, acting by a qualified majority after obtaining the opinion of the European Parliament, shall adopt a common position. The common position shall be communicated to the European Parliament. The Council shall inform the European Parliament fully of the reasons which led it to adopt its common position. The Commission shall inform the European Parliament fully of its position.

If, within three months of such communication, the European Parliament:

(a) approves the common position, the Council shall definitively adopt the act in question in accordance with that common position;

(b) has not taken a decision, the Council shall adopt the act in question in accordance with its common position;

(c) indicates, by an absolute majority of its component Members, that it intends to reject the common position, it shall immediately inform the Council. The Council may convene a meeting of the Conciliation Committee referred to in paragraph 4 to explain further its position. The European Parliament shall thereafter either confirm, by an absolute majority of its component Members, its rejection of the common position, in which event the proposed act shall be deemed not to have been adopted, or propose amendments in accordance with subparagraph (d) of this paragraph;

(d) proposes amendments to the common position by an absolute majority of its component Members, the amended text shall be forwarded to the Council and to the Commission which shall deliver an opinion on those amendments.

3. If, within three months of the matter being referred to it, the Council, acting by a qualified majority, approves all the amendments of the European Parliament, it shall amend its common position accordingly and adopt the act in question; however, the Council shall act unanimously on the amendments on which the Commission has delivered a negative opinion. If the Council does not approve the act in question, the President of the Council, in agreement with the President of the European Parliament, shall forthwith convene a meeting of the Conciliation Committee.

[3] This procedure is required to be used, *inter alia*, in connection with Article 49 of the EC Treaty (measures for the free movement of workers), Article 54(2) (programme in connection with freedom of establishment), Article 57(2) (mutual recognition of diplomas in connection with the right of establishment), Article 66 (mutual recognition of diplomas in connection with the freedom to provide services), Article 100a(1) (approximation of provisions in connection with the internal market) and Article 130s(3) (action programmes in connection with the environment).

4. The Conciliation Committee, which shall be composed of the members of the Council or their representatives and an equal number of representatives of the European Parliament, shall have the task of reaching agreement on a joint text, by a qualified majority of the members of the Council or their representatives and by a majority of the representatives of the European Parliament. The Commission shall take part in the Conciliation Committee's proceedings and shall take all the necessary initiatives with a view to reconciling the positions of the European Parliament and the Council.

5. If, within six weeks of its being convened, the Conciliation Committee approves a joint text, the European Parliament, acting by an absolute majority of the votes cast, and the Council, acting by a qualified majority, shall have a period of six weeks from that approval in which to adopt the act in question in accordance with the joint text. If one of the two institutions fails to approve the proposed act, it shall be deemed not to have been adopted.

6. Where the Conciliation Committee does not approve a joint text, the proposed act shall be deemed not to have been adopted unless the Council, acting by a qualified majority within six weeks of expiry of the period granted to the Conciliation Committee, confirms the common position to which it agreed before the conciliation procedure was initiated, possibly with amendments proposed by the European Parliament. In this case, the act in question shall be finally adopted unless the European Parliament, within six weeks of the date of confirmation by the Council, rejects the text by an absolute majority of its component Members, in which case the proposed act shall be deemed not to have been adopted.

7. The periods of three months and six weeks referred to in this Article may be extended by a maximum of one month and two weeks respectively by common accord of the European Parliament and the Council. The period of three months referred to in paragraph 2 shall be automatically extended by two months where paragraph 2(c) applies.

8. The scope of the procedure under this Article may be widened, in accordance with the procedure provided for in Article N(2) of the Treaty on European Union, on the basis of a report to be submitted to the Council by the Commission by 1996 at the latest.

Article 189c provides:

Where reference is made in this Treaty to this Article for the adoption of an act, the following procedure[4] shall apply:

(a) The Council, acting by a qualified majority on a proposal from the Commission and after obtaining the opinion of the European Parliament, shall adopt a common position.

(b) The Council's common position shall be communicated to the European Parliament. The Council and the Commission shall inform the European Parliament fully of the reasons which led the Council to adopt its common position and also of the Commission's position.

[4] This procedure is required to be used, *inter alia*, in connection with Article 6 (rules to prohibit discrimination on grounds of nationality), Article 75(1) (transport policy) Article 118a (social policy) and Articles 130k-130l (framework programmes in connection with the environment).

If, within three months of such communication, the European Parliament approves this common position or has not taken a decision within that period, the Council shall definitively adopt the act in question in accordance with the common position.

(c) The European Parliament may, within the period of three months referred to in point (b), by an absolute majority of its component Members, propose amendments to the Council's common position. The European Parliament may also, by the same majority, reject the Council's common position. The result of the proceedings shall be transmitted to the Council and the Commission.

If the European Parliament has rejected the Council's common position, unanimity shall be required for the Council to act on a second reading.

(d) The Commission shall, within a period of one month, re-examine the proposal on the basis of which the Council adopted its common position, by taking into account the amendments proposed by the European Parliament.

The Commission shall forward to the Council, at the same time as its re-examined proposal, the amendments of the European Parliament which it has not accepted, and shall express its opinion on them. The Council may adopt these amendments unanimously.

(e) The Council, acting by a qualified majority, shall adopt the proposal as re-examined by the Commission.

Unanimity shall be required for the Council to amend the proposal as re-examined by the Commission.

(f) In the cases referred to in points (c), (d) and (e), the Council shall be required to act within a period of three months. If no decision is taken within this period, the Commission proposal shall be deemed not to have been adopted.

(g) The periods referred to in points (b) and (f) may be extended by a maximum of one month by common accord between the Council and the European Parliament.

Article 203 makes provision for the budget of the Community. In particular, after the procedure for making modifications and amendments to the draft budget, it is open to the European Parliament to reject the draft budget and to ask for a new budget to be submitted (Article 203(8)).

Article 206 provides for parliamentary involvement in the process of discharging the European Commission in respect of the implementation of the budget. In particular, the European Parliament may ask to hear the European Commission give evidence on the execution of expenditure, and the European Commission is required to submit information to the European Parliament if so requested. Further, the European Commission is required to take all appropriate steps to act on the observations of the European Parliament in this connection.

D. *Elections and the European Parliament*

17. Article 138(3) of the EEC Treaty provided, in 1976, that the European Parliament was to draw up proposals for elections. The Council was required to "lay down the appropriate provisions, which it [was to] recommend to Member States for adoption in accordance

with their respective constitutional requirements". Identical provision was made in the European Coal and Steel Community Treaty and the European Atomic Energy Community Treaty.

18. In accordance with Article 138(3), Council Decision 76/787 ("the Council Decision"), signed by the President of the Council of the European Communities and the then member States' foreign ministers, laid down such provisions. The specific provisions were set out in an Act Concerning the Election of the Representatives of the European Parliament by Direct Universal Suffrage of 20 September 1976 ("the 1976 Act"), signed by the respective foreign ministers, which was attached to the Council Decision. Article 15 of the 1976 Act provides that "Annexes I to III shall form an integral part of this Act". Annex II to the 1976 Act states that "The United Kingdom will apply the provisions of this Act only in respect of the United Kingdom".

E. *The application of the Convention to Gibraltar*

19. By a declaration dated 23 October 1953, the United Kingdom, pursuant to former Article 63 of the Convention, extended the Convention to Gibraltar. Protocol No 1 applies to Gibraltar by virtue of a declaration made under Article 4 of Protocol No 1 on 25 February 1988.

PROCEEDINGS BEFORE THE COMMISSION

20. Ms Matthews applied to the Commission on 18 April 1994. She alleged a violation of Article 3 of Protocol No 1, taken alone or in conjunction with Article 14 of the Convention.

21. The Commission declared the application (No 24833/94) admissible on 16 April 1996. In its report of 29 October 1997 (former Article 31 of the Convention), it expressed the opinion that there had been no violation of Article 3 of Protocol No 1 (eleven votes to six) and that there had been no violation of Article 14 of the Convention (twelve votes to five). The full text of the Commission's opinion and of the five separate opinions contained in the report is reproduced as an annex[5] to this judgment.

FINAL SUBMISSIONS TO THE COURT

22. The Government asked the Court to find that there had been no violation of the Convention.

23. The applicant, for her part, asked the Court to find a breach of her rights under Article 3 of Protocol No 1, taken alone or in conjunction with Article 14 of the Convention. She also claimed an award of costs.

[5 The Commission's opinion is not reproduced here.]

THE LAW

I. *Alleged Violation of Article 3 of Protocol No 1*

24. The applicant alleged a breach of Article 3 of Protocol No 1, which provides:

The High Contracting Parties undertake to hold free elections at reasonable intervals by secret ballot, under conditions which will ensure the free expression of the opinion of the people in the choice of the legislature.

25. The Government maintained that, for three main reasons, Article 3 of Protocol No 1 was not applicable to the facts of the present case or, in the alternative, that there had been no violation of that provision.

A. *Whether the United Kingdom can be held responsible under the Convention for the lack of elections to the European Parliament in Gibraltar*

26. According to the Government, the applicant's real objection was to Council Decision 76/787 and to the 1976 Act concerning elections to the European Parliament (see paragraph 18 above). That Act, which had the status of a treaty, was adopted in the Community framework and could not be revoked or varied unilaterally by the United Kingdom. The Government underlined that the European Commission of Human Rights had refused on a number of occasions to subject measures falling within the Community legal order to scrutiny under the Convention. Whilst they accepted that there might be circumstances in which a Contracting Party might infringe its obligations under the Convention by entering into treaty obligations which were incompatible with the Convention, they considered that in the present case, which concerned texts adopted in the framework of the European Community, the position was not the same. Thus, acts adopted by the Community or consequent to its requirements could not be imputed to the member States, together or individually, particularly when those acts concerned elections to a constitutional organ of the Community itself. At the hearing, the Government suggested that to engage the responsibility of any State under the Convention, that State must have a power of effective control over the act complained of. In the case of the provisions relating to the elections to the European Parliament, the United Kingdom Government had no such control.

27. The applicant disagreed. For her, the Council Decision and 1976 Act constituted an international treaty, rather than an act of an institution whose decisions were not subject to Convention review. She thus considered that the Government remained responsible under the Convention for the effects of the Council Decision and 1976 Act. In the

alternative—that is, if the Council Decision and 1976 Act were to be interpreted as involving a transfer of powers to the Community organs—the applicant argued, by reference to Commission case-law, that in the absence of any equivalent protection of her rights under Article 3 of Protocol No 1, the Government in any event retained responsibility under the Convention.

28. The majority of the Commission took no stand on the point, although it was referred to in concurring and dissenting opinions.

29. Article 1 of the Convention requires the High Contracting Parties to "secure to everyone within their jurisdiction the rights and freedoms defined in . . . [the] Convention". Article 1 makes no distinction as to the type of rule or measure concerned, and does not exclude any part of the member States' "jurisdiction" from scrutiny under the Convention (see the *United Communist Party of Turkey and Others* v. *Turkey* judgment of 30 January 1998, *Reports of Judgments and Decisions* 1998-I, pp. 17-18, para. 29).

30. The Court notes that the parties do not dispute that Article 3 of Protocol No 1 applies in Gibraltar. It recalls that the Convention was extended to the territory of Gibraltar by the United Kingdom's declaration of 23 October 1953 (see paragraph 19 above), and Protocol No 1 has been applicable in Gibraltar since 25 February 1988. There is therefore clearly territorial "jurisdiction" within the meaning of Article 1 of the Convention.

31. The Court must nevertheless consider whether, notwithstanding the nature of the elections to the European Parliament as an organ of the EC, the United Kingdom can be held responsible under Article 1 of the Convention for the absence of elections to the European Parliament in Gibraltar, that is, whether the United Kingdom is required to "secure" elections to the European Parliament notwithstanding the Community character of those elections.

32. The Court observes that acts of the EC as such cannot be challenged before the Court because the EC is not a Contracting Party. The Convention does not exclude the transfer of competences to international organisations provided that Convention rights continue to be "secured". Member States' responsibility therefore continues even after such a transfer.

33. In the present case, the alleged violation of the Convention flows from an annex to the 1976 Act, entered into by the United Kingdom, together with the extension to the European Parliament's competences brought about by the Maastricht Treaty. The Council Decision and the 1976 Act (see paragraph 18 above), and the Maastricht Treaty, with its changes to the EEC Treaty, all constituted international instruments which were freely entered into by the United Kingdom. Indeed, the 1976 Act cannot be challenged before the European Court of Justice for the very reason that it is not a "normal" act of the Community, but is

a treaty within the Community legal order. The Maastricht Treaty, too, is not an act of the Community, but a treaty by which a revision of the EEC Treaty was brought about. The United Kingdom, together with all the other parties to the Maastricht Treaty, is responsible *ratione materiae* under Article 1 of the Convention and, in particular, under Article 3 of Protocol No 1, for the consequences of that Treaty.

34. In determining to what extent the United Kingdom is responsible for "securing" the rights in Article 3 of Protocol No 1 in respect of elections to the European Parliament in Gibraltar, the Court recalls that the Convention is intended to guarantee rights that are not theoretical or illusory, but practical and effective (see, for example, the above-mentioned *United Communist Party of Turkey and Others* judgment, pp. 18-19, para. 33). It is uncontested that legislation emanating from the legislative process of the European Community affects the population of Gibraltar in the same way as legislation which enters the domestic legal order exclusively via the House of Assembly. To this extent, there is no difference between European and domestic legislation, and no reason why the United Kingdom should not be required to "secure" the rights in Article 3 of Protocol No 1 in respect of European legislation, in the same way as those rights are required to be "secured" in respect of purely domestic legislation. In particular, the suggestion that the United Kingdom may not have effective control over the state of affairs complained of cannot affect the position, as the United Kingdom's responsibility derives from its having entered into treaty commitments subsequent to the applicability of Article 3 of Protocol No 1 to Gibraltar, namely the Maastricht Treaty taken together with its obligations under the Council Decision and the 1976 Act. Further, the Court notes that on acceding to the EC Treaty, the United Kingdom chose, by virtue of Article 227(4) of the Treaty, to have substantial areas of EC legislation applied to Gibraltar (see paragraphs 11 to 14 above).

35. It follows that the United Kingdom is responsible under Article 1 of the Convention for securing the rights guaranteed by Article 3 of Protocol No 1 in Gibraltar regardless of whether the elections were purely domestic or European.

B. *Whether Article 3 of Protocol No 1 is applicable to an organ such as the European Parliament*

36. The Government claimed that the undertaking in Article 3 of Protocol No 1 was necessarily limited to matters falling within the power of the parties to the Convention, that is, sovereign States. They submitted that the "legislature" in Gibraltar was the House of Assembly, and that it was to that body that Article 3 of Protocol No 1 applied in the context of Gibraltar. For the Government, there was no basis upon which the Convention could place obligations on Contracting Parties in relation to elections for the parliament of a distinct, supranational organisation, and

they contended that this was particularly so when the member States of the European Community had limited their own sovereignty in respect of it and when both the European Parliament itself and its basic electoral procedures were provided for under its own legal system, rather than the legal systems of its member States.

37. The applicant referred to previous decisions of the European Commission of Human Rights in which complaints concerning the European Parliament were dealt with on the merits, so that the Commission in effect assumed that Article 3 of Protocol No 1 applied to elections to the European Parliament (see, for example, *Lindsay* v. *the United Kingdom*, application No 8364/78, decision of 8 March 1979, Decisions and Reports (DR) 15, p. 247, and *Tête* v. *France*, application No 11123/84, decision of 9 December 1987, DR 54, p. 52). She agreed with the dissenting members of the Commission who did not accept that because the European Parliament did not exist when Protocol No 1 was drafted, it necessarily fell outside the ambit of Article 3 of that Protocol.

38. The majority of the Commission based its reasoning on this jurisdictional point. It considered that "to hold Article 3 of Protocol No 1 to be applicable to supranational representative organs would be to extend the scope of Article 3 beyond what was intended by the drafters of the Convention and beyond the object and purpose of the provision. . . . [T]he role of Article 3 is to ensure that elections take place at regular intervals to the national or local legislative assembly, that is, in the case of Gibraltar, to the House of Assembly" (see paragraph 63 of the Commission's report).

39. That the Convention is a living instrument which must be interpreted in the light of present-day conditions is firmly rooted in the Court's case-law (see, *inter alia*, the *Loizidou* v. *Turkey* judgment of 23 March 1995 (*preliminary objections*), Series A No 310, pp. 26-7, para. 71, with further reference). The mere fact that a body was not envisaged by the drafters of the Convention cannot prevent that body from falling within the scope of the Convention. To the extent that Contracting States organise common constitutional or parliamentary structures by international treaties, the Court must take these mutually agreed structural changes into account in interpreting the Convention and its Protocols.

The question remains whether an organ such as the European Parliament nevertheless falls outside the ambit of Article 3 of Protocol No 1.

40. The Court recalls that the word "legislature" in Article 3 of Protocol No 1 does not necessarily mean the national parliament: the word has to be interpreted in the light of the constitutional structure of the State in question. In the case of *Mathieu-Mohin and Clerfayt* v. *Belgium*, the 1980 constitutional reform had vested in the Flemish Council sufficient

competence and powers to make it, alongside the French Community Council and the Walloon Regional Council, a constituent part of the Belgian "legislature", in addition to the House of Representatives and the Senate (see the *Mathieu-Mohin and Clerfayt* v. *Belgium* judgment of 2 March 1987, Series A No 113, p. 23, para. 53; see also the Commission's decisions on the application of Article 3 of Protocol No 1 to regional parliaments in Austria (application No 7008/75, decision of 12 July 1976, DR 6, p. 120) and in Germany (application No 27311/95, decision of 11 September 1995, DR 82-A, p. 158)).

41. According to the case-law of the European Court of Justice, it is an inherent aspect of EC law that such law sits alongside, and indeed has precedence over, domestic law (see, for example, *Costa* v. *ENEL*, 6/64 [1964] ECR 585, and *Amministrazione delle Finanze dello Stato* v. *Simmenthal SpA*, 106/77 [1978] ECR 629). In this regard, Gibraltar is in the same position as other parts of the European Union.

42. The Court reiterates that Article 3 of Protocol No 1 enshrines a characteristic of an effective political democracy (see the above-mentioned *Mathieu-Mohin and Clerfayt* judgment, p. 22, para. 47, and the above-mentioned *United Communist Party of Turkey and Others* judgment, pp. 21-2, para. 45). In the present case, there has been no submission that there exist alternative means of providing for electoral representation of the population of Gibraltar in the European Parliament, and the Court finds no indication of any.

43. The Court thus considers that to accept the Government's contention that the sphere of activities of the European Parliament falls outside the scope of Article 3 of Protocol No 1 would risk undermining one of the fundamental tools by which "effective political democracy" can be maintained.

44. It follows that no reason has been made out which could justify excluding the European Parliament from the ambit of the elections referred to in Article 3 of Protocol No 1 on the ground that it is a supranational, rather than a purely domestic, representative organ.

C. *Whether the European Parliament, at the relevant time, had the characteristics of a "legislature" in Gibraltar*

45. The Government contended that the European Parliament continued to lack both of the most fundamental attributes of a legislature: the power to initiate legislation and the power to adopt it. They were of the opinion that the only change to the powers and functions of the European Parliament since the Commission last considered the issue in the above-mentioned *Tête* decision (see paragraph 37 above)—the procedure under Article 189b of the EC Treaty—offered less than even a power of co-decision with the Council, and in any event applied only to a tiny proportion of the Community's legislative output.

46. The applicant took as her starting-point in this respect that the European Commission of Human Rights had found that the entry into force of the Single European Act in 1986 did not furnish the European Parliament with the necessary powers and functions for it to be considered as a "legislature" (see the above-mentioned *Tête* decision). She contended that the Maastricht Treaty increased those powers to such an extent that the European Parliament was now transformed from a mere advisory and supervisory organ to a body which assumed, or assumed at least in part, the powers and functions of legislative bodies within the meaning of Article 3 of Protocol No 1. The High Contracting Parties had undertaken to hold free elections at reasonable intervals by secret ballot, under conditions which would ensure the free expression of the opinion of the people in the choice of the legislature. She described the powers of the European Parliament not solely in terms of the new matters added by the Maastricht Treaty, but also by reference to its pre-existing powers, in particular those which were added by the Single European Act in 1986.

47. The Commission did not examine this point, as it found Article 3 not to be applicable to supranational representative organs.

48. In determining whether the European Parliament falls to be considered as the "legislature", or part of it, in Gibraltar for the purposes of Article 3 of Protocol No 1, the Court must bear in mind the *sui generis* nature of the European Community, which does not follow in every respect the pattern common in many States of a more or less strict division of powers between the executive and the legislature. Rather, the legislative process in the EC involves the participation of the European Parliament, the Council and the European Commission.

49. The Court must ensure that "effective political democracy" is properly served in the territories to which the Convention applies, and in this context, it must have regard not solely to the strictly legislative powers which a body has, but also to that body's role in the overall legislative process.

50. Since the Maastricht Treaty, the European Parliament's powers are no longer expressed to be "advisory and supervisory". The removal of these words must be taken as an indication that the European Parliament has moved away from being a purely consultative body, and has moved towards being a body with a decisive role to play in the legislative process of the European Community. The amendment to Article 137 of the EC Treaty cannot, however, be taken as any more than an indication as to the intentions of the drafters of the Maastricht Treaty. Only on examination of the European Parliament's actual powers in the context of the European Community legislative process as a whole can the Court determine whether the European Parliament acts as the "legislature", or part of it, in Gibraltar.

51. The European Parliament's role in the Community legislative process depends on the issues concerned (see paragraphs 15-16 above).

Where a regulation or directive is adopted by means of the consultation procedure (for example under Articles 99 or 100 of the EC Treaty) the European Parliament may, depending on the specific provision, have to be consulted. In such cases, the European Parliament's role is limited. Where the EC Treaty requires the procedure set out in Article 189c to be used, the European Parliament's position on a matter can be overruled by a unanimous Council. Where the EC Treaty requires the Article 189b procedure to be followed, however, it is not open to the Council to pass measures against the will of the European Parliament. Finally, where the so-called "assent procedure" is used (as referred to in the first paragraph of Article 138b of the EC Treaty), in relation to matters such as the accession of new member States and the conclusion of certain types of international agreements, the consent of the European Parliament is needed before a measure can be passed.

In addition to this involvement in the passage of legislation, the European Parliament also has functions in relation to the appointment and removal of the European Commission. Thus, it has a power of censure over the European Commission, which can ultimately lead to the European Commission having to resign as a body (Article 144); its consent is necessary for the appointment of the European Commission (Article 158); its consent is necessary before the budget can be adopted (Article 203); and it gives a discharge to the European Commission in the implementation of the budget, and here has supervisory powers over the European Commission (Article 206).

Further, whilst the European Parliament has no formal right to initiate legislation, it has the right to request the European Commission to submit proposals on matters on which it considers that a Community act is required (Article 138b).

52. As to the context in which the European Parliament operates, the Court is of the view that the European Parliament represents the principal form of democratic, political accountability in the Community system. The Court considers that whatever its limitations, the European Parliament, which derives democratic legitimation from the direct elections by universal suffrage, must be seen as that part of the European Community structure which best reflects concerns as to "effective political democracy".

53. Even when due allowance is made for the fact that Gibraltar is excluded from certain areas of Community activity (see paragraph 12 above), there remain significant areas where Community activity has a direct impact in Gibraltar. Further, as the applicant points out, measures taken under Article 189b of the EC Treaty and which affect Gibraltar relate to important matters such as road safety, unfair contract terms

and air pollution by emissions from motor vehicles and to all measures in relation to the completion of the internal market.

54. The Court thus finds that the European Parliament is sufficiently involved in the specific legislative processes leading to the passage of legislation under Articles 189b and 189c of the EC Treaty, and is sufficiently involved in the general democratic supervision of the activities of the European Community, to constitute part of the "legislature" of Gibraltar for the purposes of Article 3 of Protocol No 1.

D. *The application of Article 56 of the Convention to the case*

55. Article 56(1) and (3) of the Convention provide as follows:

> 1. Any State may at the time of its ratification or at any time thereafter declare by notification addressed to the Secretary General of the Council of Europe that the . . . Convention shall, subject to paragraph 4 of this Article, extend to all or any of the territories for whose international relations it is responsible.
>
> . . .
>
> 3. The provisions of [the] Convention shall be applied in such territories with due regard, however, to local requirements.

56. The Government noted, without relying formally on the point, that two members of the Commission had emphasised the constitutional position of Gibraltar as a dependent territory in the context of Article 56 (formerly Article 63) of the Convention.

57. The applicant was of the view that the "local requirements" referred to in Article 56(3) of the Convention could not be interpreted so as to restrict the application of Article 3 of Protocol No 1 in the case.

58. The Commission, which found Article 3 not to be applicable on other grounds, did not consider this point. Two members of the Commission, in separate concurring opinions, both found that Article 56 of the Convention had a role to play in the case.

59. The Court recalls that in the *Tyrer* v. *the United Kingdom* judgment (25 April 1978, Series A No 26, pp. 18-19, para. 38) it found that before the former Article 63(3) could apply, there would have to be "positive and conclusive proof of a requirement". Local requirements, if they refer to the specific legal status of a territory, must be of a compelling nature if they are to justify the application of Article 56 of the Convention. In the present case, the Government do not contend that the status of Gibraltar is such as to give rise to "local requirements" which could limit the application of the Convention, and the Court finds no indication that there are any such requirements.

E. *Whether the absence of elections to the European Parliament in Gibraltar in 1994 was compatible with Article 3 of Protocol No 1*

60. The Government submitted that, even if Article 3 of Protocol No 1 could be said to apply to the European Parliament, the absence

of elections in Gibraltar in 1994 did not give rise to a violation of that provision but instead fell within the State's margin of appreciation. They pointed out that in the 1994 elections the United Kingdom had used a single-member constituency, "first-past-the-post" system. It would have distorted the electoral process to constitute Gibraltar as a separate constituency, since its population of approximately 30,000 was less than 5% of the average population per European Parliament seat in the United Kingdom. The alternative of redrawing constituency boundaries so as to include Gibraltar within a new or existing constituency was no more feasible, as Gibraltar did not form part of the United Kingdom and had no strong historical or other link with any particular United Kingdom constituency.

61. The applicant submitted that she had been completely deprived of the right to vote in the 1994 elections. She stated that the protection of fundamental rights could not depend on whether or not there were attractive alternatives to the current system.

62. The Commission, since it did not find Article 3 of Protocol No 1 to be applicable, did not examine whether or not the absence of elections in Gibraltar was compatible with that provision.

63. The Court recalls that the rights set out in Article 3 of Protocol No 1 are not absolute, but may be subject to limitations. The Contracting States enjoy a wide margin of appreciation in imposing conditions on the right to vote, but it is for the Court to determine in the last resort whether the requirements of Protocol No 1 have been complied with. It has to satisfy itself that the conditions do not curtail the right to vote to such an extent as to impair its very essence and deprive it of effectiveness; that they are imposed in pursuit of a legitimate aim; and that the means employed are not disproportionate. In particular, such conditions must not thwart "the free expression of the people in the choice of the legislature" (see the above-mentioned *Mathieu-Mohin and Clerfayt* judgment, p. 23, para. 52).

64. The Court makes it clear at the outset that the choice of electoral system by which the free expression of the opinion of the people in the choice of the legislature is ensured—whether it be based on proportional representation, the "first-past-the-post" system or some other arrangement—is a matter in which the State enjoys a wide margin of appreciation. However, in the present case the applicant, as a resident of Gibraltar, was completely denied any opportunity to express her opinion in the choice of the members of the European Parliament. The position is not analogous to that of persons who are unable to take part in elections because they live outside the jurisdiction, as such individuals have weakened the link between themselves and the jurisdiction. In the present case, as the Court has found (see paragraph 34 above), the legislation which emanates from the European Community forms part of the legislation in Gibraltar, and the applicant is directly affected by it.

65. In the circumstances of the present case, the very essence of the applicant's right to vote, as guaranteed by Article 3 of Protocol No 1, was denied.

It follows that there has been a violation of that provision.

II. *Alleged Violation of Article 14 of the Convention Taken in Conjunction with Article 3 of Protocol No 1*

66. The applicant in addition alleged that, as a resident of Gibraltar, she had been the victim of discrimination contrary to Article 14 of the Convention, which provides:

> The enjoyment of the rights and freedoms set forth in [the] Convention shall be secured without discrimination on any ground such as sex, race, colour, language, religion, political or other opinion, national or social origin, association with a national minority, property, birth or other status.

67. The Government did not address separately this complaint.

68. In view of its above conclusion that there has been a violation of Article 3 of Protocol No 1 taken alone, the Court does not consider it necessary to consider the complaint under Article 14 of the Convention.

III. *Application of Article 41 of the Convention*

69. Under Article 41 of the Convention,

> If the Court finds that there has been a violation of the Convention or the Protocols thereto, and if the internal law of the High Contracting Party concerned allows only partial reparation to be made, the Court shall, if necessary, afford just satisfaction to the injured party.

A. *Costs and expenses*

70. The applicant did not claim any damages under Article 41, but she did claim costs and expenses before the Court totalling 760,000 French francs (FRF) and 10,955 pounds sterling (GBP), made up as to FRF 760,000 of her representative's fees and expenses (750 hours at FRF 1,000 per hour and FRF 10,000 disbursements), and as to GBP 10,955 of fees and expenses incurred in instructing solicitors in Gibraltar. She also claimed FRF 6,976 and GBP 1,151.50 in respect of travel expenses.

The Government considered that the total number of hours claimed by the applicant's main representative should be reduced by about half, and that the Gibraltar advisers' claims should not have amounted to more than one-third of the sums actually claimed. They also challenged some of the travel expenses.

71. In the light of the criteria established in its case-law, the Court holds on an equitable basis that the applicant should be awarded the sum

of GBP 45,000 from which should be deducted FRF 18,510 already paid by way of legal aid for fees and travel and subsistence expenses before the Court.

B. *Default interest*

72. According to the information available to the Court, the statutory rate of interest applicable in the United Kingdom at the date of adoption of the present judgment is 7.5% per annum.

FOR THESE REASONS, THE COURT

1. *Holds* by fifteen votes to two that there has been a breach of Article 3 of Protocol No 1;
2. *Holds* unanimously that it is not necessary to consider the complaint under Article 14 of the Convention taken together with Article 3 of Protocol No 1;
3. *Holds* unanimously
   (a) that the respondent State is to pay the applicant, within three months, for costs and expenses, 45,000 (forty-five thousand) pounds sterling together with any value-added tax that may be chargeable, less 18,510 (eighteen thousand five hundred and ten) French francs to be converted into pounds sterling at the rate applicable on the date of delivery of the present judgment;
   (b) that simple interest at an annual rate of 7.5% shall be payable from the expiry of the above-mentioned three months until settlement;
4. *Dismisses* unanimously the remainder of the claim for just satisfaction.

Done in English and in French, and delivered at a public hearing in the Human Rights Building, Strasbourg, on 18 February 1999.

In accordance with Article 45(2) of the Convention and Rule 74(2) of the Rules of Court, the joint dissenting opinion of Sir John Freeland and Mr Jungwiert is annexed to this judgment.

JOINT DISSENTING OPINION OF JUDGES SIR JOHN FREELAND AND JUNGWIERT

1. We voted against the finding of a breach of Article 3 of Protocol No 1, essentially for the following reasons.

2. In the first place, and as a general point, the view has throughout weighed heavily with us that a particular restraint should be required of the Court when it is invited, as it is here, to pronounce on acts of the European Community or consequent to its requirements, especially when those acts relate to a matter so intimately concerned with the operation of the Community as elections to one of its constitutional organs.

3. Secondly, as to the interpretation to be given to Article 3 of Protocol No 1, we have considered that the view taken in the Commission, by the substantial majority of eleven votes to six, that "the role of Article 3 is to ensure that elections take place at regular intervals to the national or local legislative assembly" has much to commend it. It is, as reference to the *travaux préparatoires* confirms, a view squarely within the intention of the drafters (who, it should be recalled, were working at a time when about half the countries of Europe—including some in Western Europe—were deprived of free elections). Further, by confining the ambit of the provision to bodies within the domestic area and excluding any supranational representative organ, it avoids the uncertainty and invidiousness involved in analysis by an outside body of the characteristics of such an organ, which as experience has shown are likely to be neither straightforward nor static.

4. If, however, it is justifiable, on the familiar basis that "the Convention is a living instrument which must be interpreted in the light of present-day conditions", to include within the scope of Article 3 of Protocol No 1 a body which was plainly not within the contemplation of the drafters, if only because no such body existed at the time, it becomes necessary to consider whether the body concerned is properly to be regarded as "*the* legislature" (emphasis supplied) within the meaning of the provision. That question may require, in turn, two others. First, is the body a legislature at all? And, secondly, if it is, is it the legislature for the State or territory in question—in this case, Gibraltar?

5. As to the first of these questions, it is in our view intrinsic to the notion of a "legislature" that the body concerned should have the power to initiate legislation and to adopt it (subject, in the case of some national Constitutions, to the requirement of the assent of the head of State). If this power is lacking, the fact that the body may have other powers often exercisable by national legislatures (for example, powers in relation to censure of the executive or to the budget) is not enough to remedy the deficiency. The existence of such other powers may enhance the body's entitlement to be styled as a parliament and its role in promoting an "effective political democracy". But the facts that it is so styled and has such a role are not to be regarded as requiring it to be treated as a "legislature" unless it has in itself the necessary legislative power.

6. With the vestigial and for present purposes insignificant exception of its power under Article 95(3) of the European Coal and Steel Community Treaty, the European Parliament has no power to initiate and adopt legislation. Even in the case of the so-called co-decision procedure (Article 189b) introduced by the Maastricht Treaty—a procedure to which much significance was attached on behalf of the applicant—, while the European Parliament has potential influence on the content of legislation and a power to block legislation to which it objects, it has

neither the sole right to adopt legislation nor the power to force the Council to adopt legislation which the Council does not want. Nor does the procedure provide the Parliament with any opportunity to initiate legislation itself.

7. Thus, even if, as paragraph 50 of the judgment says, the Maastricht Treaty's removal of the words "advisory and supervisory" to describe the powers of the European Parliament "must be taken as an indication that the European Parliament has moved away from being a purely consultative body, and has moved towards being a body with a decisive role to play in the legislative process of the European Community", as matters stand (and stood at the time of the 1994 elections) that Parliament has not in our view reached a stage where it can of itself properly be regarded as constituting a legislature. To borrow the words of Professor Dashwood in his inaugural address at the University of Cambridge in November 1995, "the Community has no legislature, but a legislative process in which the different political institutions have different parts to play". In fact, of the institutions of the Community it is the Council of Ministers which performs the functions most closely related to those of a legislature at national level.

8. If it had become necessary to consider whether, on the hypothesis that it was in the true sense a legislature, the European Parliament qualified to be treated as "the legislature" for Gibraltar within the meaning of Article 3 of Protocol No 1, so that Gibraltar elections were required to be held to it as well as to the local House of Assembly, we would have been influenced in the contrary direction by the exclusion of Gibraltar from substantial parts of the EC Treaty and the limited extent of the areas of Community competence in which the Parliament has, in any event, a significant role (as it does not in the areas of foreign and security policy, justice and home affairs, the implementation of the common commercial policy or the negotiation of trade agreements with other States or international organisations; or in the field of economic and monetary union). We would have been similarly influenced by the small number of measures adopted under the Article 189b procedure and applicable to Gibraltar. But, given the negative view which we have reached on the qualifications of the European Parliament to be regarded as a legislature, there is no need for us to proceed to a conclusion on the further question.

9. We would add only that, to put it no higher, we see a certain incongruity in the branding of the United Kingdom as a violator of obligations under Article 3 of Protocol No 1 when the exclusion from the franchise effected multilaterally by the 1976 Decision and Act—in particular, Annex II—was at that time wholly consistent with those obligations (because on no view could the Assembly, as it was then known, be regarded as a legislature); when at no subsequent time has it been

possible for the United Kingdom unilaterally to secure the modification of the position so as to include Gibraltar within the franchise; and when such a modification would require the agreement of all the member States (including a member State in dispute with the United Kingdom about sovereignty over Gibraltar).

[Report: ECHR Reports of Judgments and Decisions 1999—I, p. 253]

Direct effect—Directives—Interpretation of national law—Duty of national courts to interpret national law consistently with provisions of directive — Scope of obligation — Applicability to national law introduced to implement directive — Council Directive 80/777 on harmonization of legislation on natural mineral water—The law of Austria

Natural Mineral Water Case

(Case No GZ V 136/94)

Austria, Constitutional Court. 12 *December* 1995

SUMMARY: *The facts*:—Section 6 of the Mineral Water Act 1994 appeared to preserve a requirement contained in earlier legislation that natural mineral water should be bottled only in glass bottles. Article 6 of EC Council Directive 80/777 of 1980 on the harmonization of legislation relating to natural mineral water contained no such restriction. In proceedings before the Austrian Constitutional Court, the question arose as to how these two provisions were to be reconciled.

Held:—The Mineral Water Act 1994 was to be interpreted and applied so as to give effect to the provision of the Directive permitting all types of containers to be used in the bottling of natural mineral water.

In accordance with Article 5 of the EC Treaty and the jurisprudence of the European Court of Justice, national courts, including the Constitutional Court, were required to interpret and apply national law in accordance with the requirements of Community law, so far as the national courts were able to do so. This principle applied in particular in proceedings where the ruling on the facts was not only the subject of national legislation but was also regulated by the provisions of an EC directive. In this case, where the 1994 Act had been enacted to incorporate the provisions of the Mineral Water Directive into national law, it was to be interpreted in the same sense as the Directive, in order to harmonize the two provisions in so far as the intent of the Mineral Water Act was open to doubt.

The following is the text of the judgment of the Court:

Section 6 of the Mineral Water Act 1994 (*BGBl* 1994/552) states that the "Glass Bottle Law" of the Mineral Water Act 1935 (*BGBl* 1935/526) also applies to the sale within Austria of natural mineral water. An Austrian producer of mineral water challenged the Act in question in an individual action in the Constitutional Court (in accordance with Section 139(1) of the Law on the Constitutional Court (*BVG*)), as his legal rights were being directly and currently infringed, and there was no means of challenging the Act. He argued, *inter alia*, that Section 6 of the 1994 Act contravenes Directive 80/777 of the Council of the

European Communities of 15 July 1980 on the harmonization of legislation on the production of, and trade in, natural mineral water (*ABl* 1980, No L 229, p. 1). Article 6 of the Directive, which concerns the bottling of mineral water, contains no kind of restriction that natural mineral water may only be sold in glass bottles.

(1) By virtue of the principle arising from Article 5 of the EC Treaty, that domestic law should be interpreted to conform with directives (Rodríguez Iglesias/Riechenberg, "*Zur richtlinienkonformen Auslegung des nationalen Rechts*", *Festschrift Everling*, 1994, p. 1213), the national courts, including the Constitutional Court, are bound to interpret a national law in conformity with the meaning and intention of an enacted directive. It can be inferred from the judgments of the Court of Justice (*von Colson and Kamann* v. *Land Nordrhein-Westfalen*, Case 14/83, [1984] ECR 1981;[1] *Marleasing SA* v. *La Comercial Internacional de Alimentación SA*, Case C-106/89, [1990] ECR I-4135;[2] and *Faccini Dori* v. *Recreb Srl*, Case C-91/92, [1994] ECR I-3325)[3] that Article 5 of the EC Treaty obliges all national courts to interpret and apply the national law in accordance with the requirements of Community law, to the full extent of the judiciary's capability. This principle applies particularly in proceedings where the ruling on the facts is not only the subject of national regulation, but is also regulated by the directive (see von Bogandy, in Grabitz and Hilf, *Kommentar zur Europäischen Union*, Art. 5, footnote 55).

(2) The outlined principle of interpreting national law so as to conform [as far as possible] to EC directives leads, in the current case, to the interpretation of the 1994 Act, which was enacted to incorporate the Mineral Water Directive, in the same sense as the Directive. This will harmonize the Act with the Directive, so far as the content of that Act's intentions remains doubtful. The extension of the "Glass Bottle Law" from the 1935 Act (which is also valid until 31 December 1996) to natural mineral water, as intended by Section 6 of the 1994 Act, is not compatible with the prescribed legal position defined by European Community law and, in particular, the ruling contained in Appendix II Z 2 c-d of the Directive. The Mineral Water Act 1994 is to be interpreted and applied in the sense of the Directive that all containers used in the bottling of natural mineral water are permitted, so far as these containers do not alter the microbial and chemical properties of the natural mineral water [. . .].

[Report: *Europarecht in Fällen*, p. 158 (in German)]

[1 Volume 1, Note, p. 187.]
[2 Volume 1, p. 167.]
[3 See p. 19.]

Direct effect — Directives — Conditions for direct effect — Failure of Member State to implement provisions of directive by specified time—Whether directive may be relied upon by individuals before national courts—The law of Austria

TYROLEAN PROVINCIAL ALLOCATION OFFICE CASE

(Case No GZ B 2477/95)

Austria, Constitutional Court. 12 *June* 1996

SUMMARY: *The facts*:—A Tyrolean Provincial Law on the allocation of Government contracts provided that the chairman of the body responsible for verifying compliance in the allocation of public construction contracts should be "versed in the allocation process" and that one of the members should be a judge. EC Council Directive 89/665 provided that the chairman of such a body should have the qualifications of a judge. The question arose in proceedings before the Constitutional Court as to the effect of the Directive in Austrian law.

Held:—The Directive defined the Tyrolean Law as meaning that the chairman of the body at issue must be qualified as a judge.

Natural law and the jurisprudence of the European Court of Justice required the provisions of the Directive at issue to be given direct effect. The rule contained in the Directive was definite and clearly formulated and gave individuals the right to review of decisions by an impartial body established in a particular way. The Regional Legislature was required to incorporate that provision into national law and, since the time limit for transposition had passed and it was directly effective, it already applied.

The following is the text of the judgment of the Court:

(1) Section 6(1) of the Tyrol Allocation Act (*TVergG*) states that the Provincial Allocation Office (*Landesvergabeamt*) (which is empowered to make decisions) of the Office of the Tyrol Government shall consist of:

(a) a person versed in the allocation process as chairperson;
(b) a civil servant of the Tyrol Provincial Government, versed in the law, as reporter;
(c) a member of the judiciary; and
(d) an advisory member from each of:
 —the Tyrol Chamber of Commerce (*Wirtschaftskammer Tirol*);
 —the Architects and Engineers Legal Advisory Chamber for Tyrol and Vorarlberg (*Architekten- und Ingenieur-konsultenkammer für Tirol und Vorarlberg*);
 —the Tyrol Workers and Employees Chamber (*Kammer für Arbeiter und Angestellte für Tirol*); and

—the Tyrol Municipal Organization (*Tiroler Gemeindeverband*);
—all the above persons to be versed in the allocation process.

(2) The Directive relating to the verification of allocation decisions is EC Council Directive 89/665 of 21 December 1989 on the Coordination of Legal and Administrative Rules for Verification Procedures for the allocation of delivery and building contracts. Article 2(8) states that the chairman of an authority which is not a court must at least have the legal and vocational qualifications of a judge.

Natural law and judicial precedent (*Van Duyn* v. *Home Office*, Case 41/74, [1974] ECR 1337)[1] require this rule to have direct effect. The rule is definite, and its contents are sufficiently clearly formulated (*Pubblico Ministero* v. *Ratti*, Case 148/78 [1979] ECR 1629; *Becker* v. *Finanzamt Münster-Innenstadt*, Case 8/81 [1982] 93 ILR 113),[2] giving the individual the right to supervision by an impartial body established in a particular way. The Tyrol legislator is obliged to incorporate this rule into national law, since the EWR Agreement came into force on 1 January 1994. Although he has not done this, as it is directly applicable, it already applies. (See also *Fratelli Constanzo* v. *Milano*, Case 103/88 [1989] ECR 4311.)

(3) The Directive has therefore defined Section 6(1) *TVergG* as meaning that the chairperson of the State Allocation Office must be versed in the method of allocation and have the legal and vocational qualifications of a judge, referring to the qualifications of a judge in national law.

[Report: *Europarecht in Fällen*, p. 158 (in German)]

[[1] Volume 1, Note, p. 135.] [[2] Volume 1, p. 103.]

National constitutions—Constitutional challenge to national legislation — Austrian Federal Constitutional Law, Section 140(1)—Burgenland Regional Tourism Law 1992—Levy to promote tourism based on VAT yield—Whether compatible with Sixth EC VAT Directive 77/388

Supremacy—Community law and subsequent national law—Consequences for contrary national law—Duty of national courts not to apply conflicting national provisions—Principle that uniformity and full effectiveness of Community law must be ensured — Whether national constitutional court entitled to wait to examine possible incompatibility of domestic provision with Community law until after review of provision for compatibility with the Constitution

Institutions—Court of Justice—Powers—Jurisdiction under Article 177 of EC Treaty—Scope of duty of national courts to make reference to Court of Justice — Whether national constitutional court under duty to make a reference

Institutions — Court of Justice — Effect of decisions in Member States — Role in ensuring uniform application of EC law—The law of Austria

Austrian Tourism Promotion Tax Case

(Case No G 2/97)

Austria, Constitutional Court. 24 *June* 1998

SUMMARY: *The facts*:—Proceedings were instituted before the Austrian Constitutional Court challenging the constitutionality of a provision of the Burgenland Regional Tourism Law 1992, which laid down that a tax to promote tourism in Burgenland was to be calculated by reference to the net yield "within the meaning of the Federal VAT Law". If the tax in question was a form of VAT, it was accepted that it was precluded by Article 33 of the Sixth EC VAT Directive 77/388. The Burgenland Government argued, however, that the tax in question was not in the nature of a turnover tax and therefore did not fall within the scope of the prohibition contained in Article 33 of the Directive.

Held:—The phrase "within the meaning of the Federal VAT Law" was to be annulled on constitutional grounds, irrespective of any possible conflict with EC law.

(1) The principle of the supremacy of Community law, developed by the Court of Justice of the European Community, was intended to ensure the uniform application of Community law in all Member States. Every national court

called upon to rule, in a case involving a question of Community law, was required to observe the priority of Community law in all cases within its jurisdiction and, if necessary, to set aside any conflicting provision of national law. According to the jurisprudence of the Court of Justice, the national court could itself rule on the compatibility with Community law of a provision of national law only if the question was so obvious as to "leave no scope for any reasonable doubt". In any other case, the national court would be required to make a reference to the Court of Justice for a preliminary ruling under Article 177 of the EC Treaty.

(2) The Constitutional Court was also required to observe the prior-ranking application of EC law, although only within the framework of the jurisdiction entrusted to it. It was therefore required itself to decide the question whether an Austrian legal provision should be set aside, because of the prior-ranking application of directly effective rules of Community law, only if the question was relevant for its decision on the merits, an issue which was to be decided in accordance with domestic law. The Constitutional Court therefore had jurisdiction to examine the compatibility of domestic legislation with Community law.

(3) However, the Constitutional Court was always empowered, under Article 140 of the Constitution, to examine first, of its own motion, the compatibility of domestic legislation with the Constitution, wherever this was open to reasonable doubt. This jurisdiction of the Constitutional Court to review legislation was not restricted by Austrian accession to the European Union. In such a review, no final decision was taken as to whether or not to give precedence to EC law or domestic law. If a provision of domestic law which might be in conflict with EC law was set aside because it violated a constitutional rule, the interests of the European Union were in any case served. But even if the domestic provision was not set aside in the review proceedings before the Constitutional Court, the issue of the supremacy of a possibly conflicting rule of Community law could and should then be clarified by the Court exercising its public law jurisdiction with final authority, if necessary after making a reference for a preliminary ruling to clarify the position under Article 177 of the EC Treaty.

The following is the text of the judgment of the Court:

I.1. A complaint under Section 144 of the Federal Constitutional Law (*BVG*) is pending before the Constitutional Court (*VfGH*) (No B2798/96) contesting a notice issued by the Burgenland Government pursuant to the Burgenland Tourism Law 1992 (*Burgenland Tourismusgesetz*), *LBGl* 1992/36, in the version of *LGBl* 1994/7 and 1994/33 [. . .]

2. Following that complaint, the Constitutional Court decided on 5 December 1996 to examine *ex officio* the constitutionality of the words "within the meaning of the Turnover Tax Law (*Umsatzsteuergesetz*)" in Section 27(2) of the Tourism Law 1992.

The Constitutional Court assumed for the purpose of its preliminary review that, in view of the reference by the Burgenland legislature to net yearly turnover "within the meaning of the Turnover Tax Law", Section 27(2) of the Tourism Law 1992 could not be interpreted as being in accordance with the Constitution and that it was not possible to restrict the obligation to pay a levy so as to construe it as applying to turnover that had been achieved in Burgenland. Inclusion, in the basis of assessment for the levy, of turnover achieved in other Federal States would not be justifiable, as that turnover would bear no proper relationship to advantages derived from tourism in Burgenland [. . .] The Constitutional Court therefore adopted the preliminary view that the same reservations would exist in regard to the words "within the meaning of the Turnover Tax Law" in Section 27(2) of the Tourism Law 1992 as those which, in the judgments in Cases 5811/1968, 5995/1969, 11,640/1988 and 12,224/1989, had led to the annulment of the corresponding provisions.

. . .

The Constitutional Court reserved, for clarification in proceedings for the review of the constitutionality of legislation, the question whether the application of the provisions concerning the tourism promotion levy under the Tourism Law 1992 is precluded by the prior-ranking application of EC law (see Article 33 of the Sixth Council Directive of 17 May 1977 on the harmonization of the laws of the Member States relating to turnover taxes—Common system of value added tax: uniform basis of assessment (OJ 1977 L 145, p. 1) in the version of Council Directive 91/680/EEC of 16 December 1991 supplementing the common system of value added tax and amending Directive 77/388/EEC with a view to the abolition of fiscal frontiers (OJ 1991 L 376, p. 1), hereinafter "the Directive"; *cf.* also judgment of the Court of Justice in Case C-200/90 *Dansk Denkavit* [1992] ECR I-2217).

[The Burgenland Government contended that the words in question could be construed as being in accordance with the Constitution. The tourism levy did not infringe Article 33 of the Directive because it was not in the nature of a turnover tax, not being a general tax nor levied on each stage of production and distribution. The levy was applicable only to specified undertakings and depended upon the extent to which the undertakings benefited from tourism. It was based on net yearly turnover in Burgenland. The levy did not therefore fall within the scope of Article 33 of the Directive. It did not therefore infringe that Article.]

5. In view of the general importance of the matter, the Governments of the other Federal States were invited to submit their views on whether application of the provisions concerning the tourism promotion levy pursuant to the Tourism Law 1992 was precluded by the prior-ranking application of EC law. The [Federal State Governments] submitted that the tourism promotion levy was not in the nature of a turnover tax and it could therefore be assumed that the provisions concerning that levy in the Tourism Law 1992 were not precluded by Article 33 of the Directive.

II. The Constitutional Court holds as follows:

A. *Admissibility*

1. Under the first sentence of Section 140(1) of the Federal Constitutional Law, the Constitutional Court is to decide *ex officio* on whether a Federal or State law is unconstitutional, in so far as the Court would have to apply such a law in a pending case. Where the Constitutional Court initiates a review of legislation *ex officio*, a ruling must be given, for the purpose of that provision of the Constitution, on legislative provisions that have been applied reasonably (*in denkmöglicher Weise*) by the defendant authority when it issued the contested notice, even if the authority may have been incorrect to do so.

. . .

2. The defendant company claims that the Tourism Law 1992 is inapplicable on grounds of Community law, because the tourism promotion levy conflicts with Article 33 of the Directive, which is directly applicable.

3. Article 33 is worded as follows:

(1) Without prejudice to other Community provisions, in particular those laid down in the Community provisions in force relating to the general arrangements for the holding, movement and monitoring of products subject to excise duty, this Directive shall not prevent a Member State from maintaining or introducing taxes on insurance contracts, taxes on betting and gambling, excise duties, stamp duties and, more generally, any taxes, duties or charges which cannot be characterised as turnover taxes, provided however that those taxes, duties or charges do not, in trade between Member States, give rise to formalities connected with the crossing of frontiers.

(2) . . .

According to the jurisprudence of the European Court of Justice, Article 33 of the Directive is directly effective. It thus establishes rights for individuals which must be protected by national courts, and is intended to prevent the introduction of taxes, duties and charges which compromise the functioning of the common system of VAT by levying an amount on the movement of goods and services in a way comparable to VAT (Case C-200/90 *Dansk Denkavit*, cited above, paras. 11 and 14) . . .

In its case law (*cf.* . . . Case C-347/90 *Bozzi* [1992] ECR 2947, para. 12 . . .) the Court of Justice has stated that the following features are essential:

— VAT applies generally to transactions relating to goods or services;
— it is proportional to the price of those goods or services;
— it is charged at each stage of the production and distribution process;
— and finally it is imposed on the added value of goods and services since the tax payable on a transaction is calculated after deduction of the tax paid on the previous transaction.

4.1. Section 27 of the Tourism Law 1992 in the version of *LGBl* 1994/7 provides as follows:

(1) In all municipalities of area classification I to III, but in municipalities of area classification IV only where there is a local tourism association, a levy . . . ("tourism promotion levy") will be collected by the Burgenland Tourism Association in accordance with the following provisions:

. . .

(2) . . . The basis of assessment shall be the net annual turnover within the meaning of the Turnover Tax Law . . .

4.2. . . .

In view of the special features of those rules, the defendant authority did not commit an error tantamount to an unlawful act when it assumed that Article 33 of the Directive did not preclude their application. That could have been the case only if the conflict between a provision of Community law and the provision of Austrian law was obviously within the meaning of the *acte clair* doctrine (see *VfGH* of 26 June 1997, B 877/96) . . . When issuing the notice contested before the Constitutional Court the authority did not therefore apply Section 27(2) of the Tourism Law unreasonably (*denkunmöglich*).

This is also clear from the fact that by orders of 12 August 1997 and 27 October 1997 the Administrative Court (*Verwaltungsgerichtshof*) referred to the Court of Justice for a preliminary ruling the question whether Article 33(1) of the Directive precludes a Member State from levying a tourism levy, described in more detail in the order for reference; those applications concern contributions [*inter alia*] under the Tyrol Tourism Law . . .

The Administrative Court is therefore uncertain whether application of the above provisions of Federal State law is precluded by EC law. It should be pointed out in that connection that the provisions of the Burgenland Law at issue here display far fewer features of turnover tax than, for example, the Tyrol rules.

In the present proceedings, therefore, the Constitutional Court would have to apply Section 27 of the Tourism Law 1992 within the meaning of the case-law on Article 140(1), first sentence, of the Federal Constitutional Law.

4.3. That conclusion is not precluded by the fact that provisions of the Member States which conflict with Community law are not to be "applied". The majority of academic writers take the view that this principle applies in full to the Constitutional Court as it does to any other State authority, and especially in regard to its jurisdiction to initiate proceedings to review the constitutionality of legislation . . .

However, the latter view can be based ultimately only on a nominal parallel between the notion of the "prior-ranking application (*Anwendungsvorrang*) of EC law" and the expression "would have to apply" (*anzuwenden hätte*) in Section 140(1) and Section 139(1) of the Federal Constitutional Law. It does not take into account the wholly different objectives served by the prior-ranking application of EC law and by the Constitutional Court's review of the constitutionality of legislation, nor the fact that, through Austria's accession to the EU, the Austrian system of legal protection, in particular genuine Austrian constitutional jurisdiction to review legislation, must be regarded as modified only in so far as is necessary for the purposes of Community law.

The principle of the prior-ranking application of Community law developed by the Court of Justice is intended to ensure the uniform application of Community law in all Member States. Every national court which has to rule on a case or on the legality of acts of the administration must observe this priority of Community law in cases within its jurisdiction and, if necessary, set aside the [conflicting] provision of national law (judgment of the Court of Justice in Case 106/77 *Simmenthal II* [1978] ECR 629).[1] A court within the meaning of the third paragraph of Article 177 of the EC Treaty can rule on the compatibility with Community law of a provision of national law only if the question of interpretation of Community law is so obvious as to "leave no scope for any reasonable doubt" (judgment of the Court of Justice in Case 283/91 *CILFIT* [1982] ECR 3415); in any other case, the national court would have to refer the question of interpretation to the Court of Justice in accordance with Article 177.

The Constitutional Court too must observe the prior-ranking application of EC law (see for example its decisions of 12 April 1997, G 400/96, G 44/97; 4 October 1997, G 322, 323/97; 5 December 1997, G 23-26/97), although only within the framework of the duties which it has to fulfil. It must therefore itself decide the question whether an Austrian legal provision should be set aside, because of the prior-ranking application of directly effective Community law, only if the question is relevant for its decision, an issue which is to be decided in accordance with domestic law (see also the decision, cited above, in Case 106/77 *Simmenthal II* [1978] ECR 629, para. 21,[2] and the decision of the Constitutional Court of 26 June 1997, B 877/96). In so far as the Constitutional Court does not have to take a decision on the lawfulness of an administrative authority's conduct (which, having regard to the fact that the review function is shared between the public-law courts, is the case for example in the area relevant here of the fundamental rights to property and the equality of all citizens before the law), the question whether the defendant authority should have applied ordinary domestic legislation or Community law cannot be material to the decision in the proceedings before it.

Nevertheless, the Constitutional Court must always review legislation in that area too, if application by the authority of the legislation of "doubtful" constitutionality was at least "reasonable" (*denkmöglich*).

[[1] Volume 1, p. 73.] [[2] Volume 1, p. 73 at p. 101.]

Only such a broader understanding of its obligation to rule on the constitutionality of legislation is in keeping with the function of legislative review by the Constitutional Court.

The jurisdiction of the Constitutional Court to review legislation, as a central element of the system of the Austrian Federal Constitution, was not restricted by Austria's accession to the EU. Nor does the requirement for the effectiveness of Community law call for a restrictive interpretation in that regard: in proceedings where the Constitutional Court reviews legislation, no final decision is made as to whether Community law or national law is to be applied in determining the case which has given rise to the review proceedings. If a legal provision is set aside in those proceedings or its unlawfulness established, and if that provision is unobjectionable from the point of view of Community law, there is just as little problem from that point of view as where there is an infringement of Community law. If a national legal provision which, although not clearly contrary is possibly contrary to Community law, is set aside by the Constitutional Court on the ground that it infringes a national rule, that cannot lead to a result contrary to the interests of the Community. Moreover, if that national legal provision is not set aside in the review proceedings before the Constitutional Court, the possible prior-ranking application of Community law is to be clarified by the Court exercising its public law jurisdiction with final authority, if necessary after obtaining a preliminary ruling under the third paragraph of Article 177 of the EC Treaty.

"Application" for the purposes of Article 140(1) of the Austrian Constitution and application within the meaning of the prior-ranking application of Community law must therefore each be understood differently in their specific contexts and in a manner which encompasses all aspects of legal protection. They are derived from two different legal systems and must not be treated mechanically in the same way, but distinguished, as set out above, so as to observe the prior-ranking application of EC law and to harmonize both systems.

Nor is it contrary to the purpose of the prior-ranking application of EC law if the Constitutional Court reviews the legality or compatibility with the Constitution of general legal provisions, which it would have to apply in the proceedings before it and, if appropriate, sets them aside or declares them unlawful, because in such review proceedings no decision is taken as to whether the domestic legislation is precluded by the prior-ranking application of EC law.

. . .

B. *Substance*

The lower court's misgivings that, in view of the Burgenland legislature's reference to net yearly turnover within the meaning of the Turnover Tax Law, the provision could not be interpreted as being compatible with the Constitution, and so the duty to make contributions could not be restricted to a duty to make contributions in respect of turnover achieved in Burgenland, are justified for the reasons given in the order for reference.

The Burgenland Government submits that the words in question are capable of interpretation in accordance with the Constitution because, having regard to the declaration to be given under Section 27(6) of the Tourism Law 1992, it is wholly tenable to argue that the wording in question is to be understood as meaning exclusively net yearly turnover, within the meaning of the Turnover Tax Law, that has arisen in Burgenland.

In decision 6205/1970 the Constitutional Court held that Section 21 of the Burgenland Tourism Law, *LGBl* 1967/5, could still be interpreted as being compatible with the Constitution because that law did not link the notion of "yearly turnover" to "turnover" within the meaning of the Turnover Tax Law. As the Tourism Law had not been amended in that regard in 1986, the Constitutional Court also confirmed that case-law in its decision 11,025/1986.

However, in the currently applicable Tourism Law 1992, the Burgenland legislature expressly refers to "net annual turnover within the meaning of the Turnover Tax Law". As no provision is made in that law for excluding, from the basis of assessment, turnover that has been achieved outside Burgenland, but it is instead laid down that a particular net turnover, namely turnover in accordance with the Turnover Tax Law, is to be used as a basis for calculating the levy, the interpretation proposed by the Burgenland Government would be inconsistent with the clear wording of that law.

That finding is not altered by the fact that under Section 27(6) of the Tourism Law 1992 each undertaking must declare its "relevant turnover". That can only refer to net yearly turnover within the meaning of the Turnover Tax Law.

In summary therefore, the wording used in Section 27(2) of the Tourism Law 1992 does not lead to a result that is justifiable on the merits, because there is no proper relationship between the turnover achieved outside Burgenland, included in the basis of assessment, and the benefit derived from tourism in Burgenland.

[Report: *JBl*, 1999, p. 172 (in German)]

NOTE.—The above judgment appears to be in conflict with the position of the European Court of Justice, in so far as the Constitutional Court considers that it is entitled to wait to examine the possible incompatibility of domestic provisions with EC law until the conclusion of proceedings in which those provisions are reviewed for compatibility with the Constitution (see Note to the judgment by Potacs, *JBl* 1999, p. 176 at p. 178 (in German).

The status of EC law is not regulated by a specific constitutional provision in Austria. Membership of the European Union was possible in principle on the basis of Article 9(2) of the Federal Constitution which provides:

> By a Law or by a State treaty, which must be ratified in accordance with Article 50(1) of the Constitution, specific sovereign rights of the Federation may be transferred to intergovernmental institutions and their organs, and the activity of organs of foreign States in Austria as well as the activity of Austrian organs abroad may be regulated within the framework of international law.

Nevertheless, Austrian ratification of the Treaty of Accession of 24 June 1994 was regarded as involving the modification of a number of basic constitutional principles. It was therefore necessary to follow the procedure laid down for a "total revision" of the Constitution, involving acceptance by a two-thirds majority of the National Council and approval in a referendum of the Austrian people (Article 44 of the Constitution). The necessary amendment to the Constitution was duly approved, 67 per cent of the votes cast in the referendum being in favour of accession. In particular, a new Chapter on the European Union was inserted into the Constitution (Articles 23a to 23e), providing the framework for the exercise of Federal executive and legislative powers in relation to the European Union, determining the manner in which those powers were to be exercised and fixing the division of responsibilities between the Federal and State authorities in that regard. Article 23f expressly provided for Austrian participation in the common foreign and security policy of the European Union (for further discussion see Fisher and Lengauer, The Adaptation of the Austrian Legal System following EU membership, CML Rev 2000, p. 763).

Direct effect—Treaty provisions—EC Treaty, Article 93(3)—Whether conferring rights which may be relied upon by individuals before national courts — State aid — Failure of Member State to observe correct procedure — Whether national constitutional court bound to regard national aid measure as ineffective until correct procedure followed

Institutions—Court of Justice—Powers—Jurisdiction under Article 177 of EC Treaty — Scope of duty of national courts to make reference to Court of Justice — Whether national constitutional court under duty to make a reference—"Court or tribunal of a Member State against whose decision there is no judicial remedy under national law" — Whether constitutional court such a court or tribunal within the meaning of Article 177—The law of Austria

ADRIA-WIEN PIPELINE GMBH AND ANOTHER

(Cases Nos B 2251/97 and 2594/97)

Austria, Constitutional Court. 10 *March* 1999

SUMMARY: *The facts*:—In proceedings before the Austrian Constitutional Court (*VerfGH*), the appellant companies challenged decisions taken against them by the Austrian tax authorities which restricted their right to reimbursement of energy duties under an Austrian statute. The appellants argued that the decisions were in breach of their constitutional right to inviolability of property. In the course of the proceedings, the question arose as to whether the provisions of the statute at issue constituted State aid within the meaning of Article 92 of the EC Treaty so that the duties should have been subject to the procedure laid down in Article 93(3) of the Treaty. The Constitutional Court therefore had to determine whether it was required to make a reference to the Court of Justice of the European Community under Article 177 of the EC Treaty, in order to determine the scope of the applicability of the provisions of the EC Treaty on State aid to national legislative measures of the type at issue.

Held:—The Constitutional Court was required to make a reference for a preliminary ruling to the Court of Justice.

(1) The third paragraph of Article 93(3) of the EC Treaty, concerning the procedure for the adoption of State aid, had direct effect in national law so that its infringement by national authorities affected the validity of the measures implementing the aid in question. The national courts were therefore required to draw the appropriate inferences in favour of individuals, who could rely on such an infringement both as regards the validity of the measures at issue and as regards the recovery of financial support granted in breach of the EC provision or possible interim measures.

(2) The Austrian Constitutional Court was a court within the meaning of the third paragraph of Article 177 of the EC Treaty against whose decisions there was no judicial remedy under national law. A reference to the Court of Justice was therefore obligatory for the Constitutional Court.

(3) According to the case-law of the Court of Justice, a national court of final instance would be released from the obligation to make a reference if it found that the correct application of Community law was so obvious as to leave no scope for any reasonable doubt. It appeared to the Constitutional Court provisionally that application of the Energy Duties Reimbursement Law was precluded by the blocking effect of the third sentence of Article 93(3) of the EC Treaty. However, the questions which required clarification had not been unequivocally answered in the case-law of the Court of Justice and their answers were not so obvious as to leave no scope for any doubt.

The following is the text of the judgment of the Court:

OPERATIVE PART OF THE JUDGMENT

1. The following questions are referred to the Court of Justice of the European Community for a preliminary ruling.

Question 1:

> Are legislative measures of a Member State which provide for partial reimbursement of energy duties on natural gas and electrical energy, but grant that reimbursement only to undertakings whose activity is shown to consist primarily in the production of tangible assets, to be regarded as State aid within the meaning of Article 92 of the EC Treaty?

Question 2:

> If the answer to Question 1 is affirmative: Is such a legislative measure to be regarded as State aid under Article 92 of the EC Treaty even if it is granted to all undertakings, regardless of whether their activity is shown to consist primarily in the production of tangible assets?

2. The proceedings will be continued after the decision of the Court of Justice of the European Community.

I. *Facts of the Main Proceedings*

Two appeals brought under Section 144(1) of the *Bundesverfassungsgesetz* (Federal Constitutional Law, "*BVG*") are pending before the *Verfassungsgerichtshof* (*VerfG*) based on the following facts:

1. *Adria-Wien Pipeline GmbH*

1.1. The object of the appellant company's undertaking is *inter alia* the construction and operation of pipelines for transporting crude oil.

On 18 June 1996 the appellant company made an application to the *Finanzamt Klagenfurt* (Klagenfurt Tax Office) on the basis of the *Energieabgabenvergutungsgesetz* (Energy Duties Reimbursement Law) ("*EavG*") for reimbursement of energy duties on electrical energy for the year 1996. By a decision notified on 1 July 1997 the *Finanzamt Klagenfurt* rejected the application on the ground that a claim for reimbursement under paragraph 2(1) *EavG* exists only for undertakings whose activity is shown to consist primarily in the production of tangible assets. An appeal against that decision was dismissed by the *Finanzlandesdirektion Kärnten* (Tax Office of the *Land* of Carinthia).

1.2. In the appeal under Section 144(1) *BVG* the appellant company submits that there has been a breach of the constitutional right to the inviolability of property and an infringement of rights by application of an unconstitutional law.

1.3. The appeal complains in particular that energy duty is reimbursed only to undertakings whose activity is shown to consist primarily in the production of tangible assets, and not to undertakings which provide services.

2. *Wietersdorfer & Peggauer Zementwerke GmbH*

2.1. The appellant company, whose activity is centred on the manufacture of cement and lime, contests the decision of the *Finanzlandesdirektion Kärnten* dismissing its appeal against the determination of the amount of the energy duty reimbursement for 1996. By application of 12 March 1997 the appellant company sought reimbursement for the calendar year 1996 of energy duties (relating to both natural gas and electrical energy) in the amount of ATS 8,675,202.- under paragraphs 1 and 2 *EavG*. The *Finanzamt* did not grant reimbursement in full and fixed the amount at ATS 8,023,821.-. Calculation of the net production value for the purpose of ascertaining the amount of the energy duty reimbursement took place on the basis of the entire annual turnover for 1996.

2.2. The appeal under Section 144(1) *BVG* claims that there has been a breach of the constitutional rights to equality and inviolability of property, since the net production value should have been ascertained only for the period from which energy duties were levied, namely from 1 June 1996. Consequently, the amount of energy duty reimbursement is ATS 651,381.- more than was fixed.

II. *The Legal Position*

1. The *Elektrizitätsabgabegesetz* (Electricity Duty Law) provides for the taxation of the supply of electrical energy . . .

2.1. The *EavG* provides for partial reimbursement of energy duty on natural gas and electrical energy. Paragraph 1(1) of the *Bundesgesetz über die Vergutung von Energieabgaben* (Federal Law on Reimbursement of Energy

Duties) (Article 62, *Strukturanpassungsgesetz* 1996, *BGBl* No 201) (*EavG*) provides:

(1) Energy duties on natural gas and electrical energy are to be reimbursed, on application, for a calendar year (trading year), in so far as they (in total) exceed 0.35% of the difference between

1. turnover within the meaning of paragraph 1(1)(1) and (2) of the *Umsatzsteuergesetz* (Turnover Tax Law) 1994 [supplies] and

2. turnover within the meaning of paragraph 1(1)(1) and (2) of the *Umsatzsteuergesetz* 1994 which is supplied to the undertaking [input supplies] (the net production value).

2.2. The energy duty reimbursement is not granted to all undertakings, but only to those whose activity is shown to consist primarily in the production of tangible assets . . .

Paragraph 2(1) of that Law, in the version in force at the time of adoption of the contested decision, reads:

(1) Only undertakings whose activity is shown to consist primarily in the production of tangible assets are entitled to reimbursement.

III. *Grounds*

1. *Admissibility*

The *VerfGH* would have to apply paragraph 2(1) of the *EavG* in the two proceedings. In cases B 2251/97 and B 2594/97 the question arises for the *VerfGH* whether the provisions of the *EavG* constitute State aid within the meaning of Article 92 of the EC Treaty. Since, as described in more detail below, there was no notification of those legislative provisions, it is necessary for the *VerfGH* decision to determine initially whether application of the *EavG* is precluded by the blocking effect of the third sentence of Article 93(3) of the EC Treaty for aid which has not been notified.

Article 93(3) of the EC Treaty lays down an obligation on the Member States to inform the Commission, in sufficient time to enable it to submit its comments, of any plans to grant or alter aid. If it considers that any such plan is not compatible with the common market having regard to Article 92 of the EC Treaty, it is to initiate without delay the procedure provided for in Article 93(2). The Member State concerned may not put the proposed measure into effect until the Commission has taken a final decision.

The *VerfGH* assumes provisionally that failure to comply with that procedure has such an effect on the national process of adoption of an aid provision that a law enacted without that procedure is of no effect.

The question set out at point 2 could be material for the *VerfGH*'s decision in so far as it might find itself in a position, on the one hand, to remove the restriction upon reimbursement to undertakings whose activity is shown to consist primarily in the production of tangible assets, which would effectively be equivalent to extending the reimbursement of energy duty to all undertakings, or else, on the other hand, to assess the contested decisions by an interpretation consistent with the requirements of the principle of equality and with Community law.

The *VerfGH* therefore provisionally assumes that such an extension of the reimbursement of energy duties to all undertakings would be permissible only if that extension were not precluded by the blocking effect of the third sentence of Article 93(3) of the EC Treaty for aid which has not been notified.

2. *Substance*

2.1. The *EavG* entered into force at the same time as the *Erdgasabgabegesetz* (Natural Gas Duty Law) and the *Elektrizitätsabgabegesetz* (Electricity Duty Law) and is applicable to events after 31 May 1996.

If the reimbursement of energy duties constituted aid within the meaning of Article 92 of the EC Treaty, it could clearly not be regarded as existing aid under Article 93(1) of the EC Treaty . . . The third sentence of Article 93(3) of the EC Treaty would therefore apply.

2.2. The *VerfGH* asked the *Bundeskanzleramt-Verfassungsdienst* (Constitutional Department of the Federal Chancellor's Office) whether the *EavG* had been notified for the purposes of Article 93(3) of the EC Treaty. The *Bundeskanzleramt-Verfassungsdienst* replied as follows on 7 January 1999:

> In our opinion the reimbursement of energy duties is not State aid within the meaning of Article 92 of the EC Treaty. Nevertheless, in the course of preparation of the measure in question, the *Bundesministerium für Finanzen* (Federal Ministry of Financial Affairs) asked the European Commission informally whether notification would be appropriate. The European Commission said that it would not be, *inter alia* on the ground that Denmark had not notified its energy duty reimbursement either.

2.3. The third sentence of Article 93(3) of the EC Treaty has direct effect. The direct applicability of the prohibition of implementation in that Article affects any aid measure which is put into effect without having been notified, or which, in the event of notification, is put into effect during the preliminary investigation period or, if the Commission initiates a formal procedure, before the final decision is adopted.

Infringement of the third sentence of Article 93(3) of the EC Treaty by the national authorities affects the validity of legal action implementing aid measures.

The national courts must, in accordance with their national law, draw all inferences therefrom in favour of individuals who may rely on such an infringement, both as regards the validity of the legal acts for implementation of the aid measures and as regards the recovery of financial support granted in breach of that provision or possible interim measures (see Case C-354/90 *FNCE* v. *French State* [1991] ECR I-5505, paragraphs 11 and 12).

2.4. The *VerfGH* has cause to interpret and apply the concept of aid, so as to be able to determine whether the legislative measure on reimbursement of energy duty ought to have been subject to the procedure provided for in Article 93(3) of the EC Treaty. In case of doubt, the national courts must, under the second and third paragraphs of Article 177 of the EC Treaty, refer a question of the interpretation of Article 92 of the EC Treaty to the Court of Justice of the European Community for a preliminary ruling (see Case 78/76 *Steinike und Weinlig* [1977] ECR 595, paragraph 14; Case C-189/91 *Kirsammer-Hack* v. *Sidal* [1993] ECR I-6185, paragraph 14; Case C-39/94 *SFEI* v. *La Poste* [1996] ECR I-3547, paragraphs 49 and 51).

IV. *The Reference*

1. The *VerfGH* is a court, within the meaning of the third paragraph of Article 177 of the EC Treaty, against whose decision there is no judicial remedy under national law. A reference to the Court of Justice of the European Community is therefore obligatory for the *VerfGH*.

2. According to the case-law of the Court of Justice, a national court of final instance is released from the obligation to make a reference *inter alia* if it finds that the correct application of Community law is so obvious as to leave no scope for any reasonable doubt. The existence of such a possibility must be assessed in the light of the specific characteristics of Community law, the particular difficulties to which its interpretation gives rise and the risk of divergencies in judicial decisions within the Community (see Case 283/31 *CILFIT* v. *Ministry of Health* [1982] ECR 3415, at p. 3431 *et seq.*).

3. *Question 1*

3.1. The correct application of the said provision in the present case may not be regarded as so obvious that no scope is left for any reasonable doubt, for the following reasons:

3.2. The Commission Notice on the application of the State aid rules to measures relating to direct business taxation (OJ 1998 C 384, p. 3, 10 December 1998) provides indications as to the interpretation of Article 92(1) of the EC Treaty. The criteria for regarding a measure as aid within the meaning of Article 92 of the EC Treaty are described in Point B:

9. Firstly, the measure must confer on recipients an advantage which relieves them of charges that are normally borne from their budgets. The advantage

may be provided through a reduction in the firm's tax burden in various ways, including:

—a reduction in the tax base (such as special deductions, special or accelerated depreciation arrangements or the entering of reserves on the balance sheet);

—a total or partial reduction in the amount of tax (such as exemption or a tax credit);

—deferment, cancellation or even special rescheduling of tax debt.

10. Secondly, the advantage must be granted by the State or through State resources. A loss of tax revenue is equivalent to consumption of State resources in the form of fiscal expenditure. This criterion also applies to aid granted by regional or local bodies in the Member States. Furthermore, State support may be provided just as much through tax provisions of a legislative, regulatory or administrative nature as through the practices of the tax authorities.

11. Thirdly, the measure must affect competition and trade between Member States. This criterion presupposes that the beneficiary of the measure exercises an economic activity, regardless of the beneficiary's legal status or means of financing. Under settled case-law, for the purposes of this provision, the criterion of trade being affected is met if the recipient firm carries on an economic activity involving trade between Member States. The mere fact that the aid strengthens the firm's position compared with that of other firms which are competitors in intra-Community trade is enough to allow the conclusion to be drawn that intra-Community trade is affected. Neither the fact that aid is relatively small in amount, nor the fact that the recipient is moderate in size or its share of the Community market very small, nor indeed the fact that the recipient does not export or exports virtually all its production outside the Community do anything to alter this conclusion.

12. Lastly, the measure must be specific or selective in that it favours "certain undertakings or the production of certain goods". The selective advantage involved here may derive from an exception to the tax provisions of a legislative, regulatory or administrative nature or from a discretionary practice on the part of the tax authorities. However, the selective nature of a measure may be justified by "the nature or general scheme of the system". If so, the measure is not considered to be aid within the meaning of Article 92(1) of the EC Treaty. These various aspects are examined below.

3.3. There does not appear to the *VerfGH* to be any doubt that the measure in question confers on the beneficiaries an advantage, as described in Point B of the Notice, which relieves them of charges normally borne from their budgets, especially as the present case involves reimbursement of a tax which has been paid.

3.4. A further criterion for aid is the granting of the advantage by the State or through State resources. Having regard to the case-law of the Court of Justice on this point (see Joined Cases C-52/97 to C-54/97 *Viscido and Others* v. *Ente Poste Italiane* [1998] ECR I-2629, paragraph 13) this criterion too appears to be fulfilled since the reimbursement of energy duty takes place from budgetary resources.

3.5. Classification of a reimbursement of energy duty as aid appears to the *VerfGH* to be doubtful, however, in that the Commission assumes in its Notice of 10 December 1998 (point 13) that Member States are not restricted in choosing the economic policy which they consider appropriate, and in particular in spreading the tax burden as they see fit across the different factors of production. Measures which pursue general economic policy objectives through a reduction of the tax burden related to certain production costs therefore do not constitute State aid. It is thus questionable in particular whether the energy duty reimbursement which applies to undertakings whose activity is shown to consist primarily in the production of tangible assets, and excludes service firms (even with higher electricity consumption), can be such a measure. It appears to make no difference to the classification of aid, according to the case-law of the Court of Justice (see Case 173/7 *Italy* v. *Commission* [1974] ECR 709), that the measure may contribute to bringing the charges in the relevant sector into line with the charges of its competitors in other Member States (see point 15 of the Notice of 10 December 1998).

3.6. Whether a reimbursement of energy duties affects competition and trade between Member States also appears questionable.

From the point of view of the first proceedings (involving an undertaking which constructs and operates crude oil pipelines) it remains doubtful whether energy duty reimbursement measures are liable to affect trade between Member States. Against the possibility of trade between Member States being affected is the circumstance that services of an installation with a fixed location, in contrast to manufactured goods, cannot be locally substituted. However, the Court of Justice (Case 102/87 *France* v. *Commission* [1988] ECR 4067) does not regard the lack of export activity as a criterion which excludes aid.

From the point of view of the second proceedings, that assessment must be differentiated, as the production of cement and lime can be locally substituted, and a reimbursement of energy duties thus appears more probably liable to affect trade between Member States.

3.7. Finally, it is also doubtful whether an energy duty reimbursement of the present kind is specific or selective: a tax measure which primarily promotes one or more sectors of activity admittedly constitutes aid (see point B 18 of the Notice of 10 December 1998). However, whether or not the differentiation of the energy duty reimbursement between service activities on the one hand, which have no right to reimbursement, and production activities on the other hand satisfies the requirements of selectivity is still unclear, partly because of the case-law of the Court of Justice which is casuistic in this respect.

4. *Question 2*

If it is decisive for classification as aid that a reimbursement of energy duty is restricted to undertakings whose activity is shown to consist primarily in the production of tangible assets, the question arises for the *VerfGH* whether the blocking effect of the third sentence of Article 93(3) of the

EC Treaty would also arise if the *EavG* provided for reimbursement of energy duties for all undertakings.

In other words: could an energy duty reimbursement law which provides for unrestricted reimbursement of duty (that is, for service undertakings too) have been brought into effect without the procedure provided for in Article 93(3) of the EC Treaty?

V. *Conclusion*

The *VerfGH* therefore provisionally assumes that application of the *EavG* is precluded by the blocking effect of the third sentence of Article 93(3) of the EC Treaty, and that the questions referred have not been unequivocally clarified by the case-law of the Court of Justice of the European Community and the answers are not so obvious that no scope is left for doubt. Those questions are therefore referred to the Court of Justice of the European Community for a preliminary ruling under the first paragraph, letter (a), and the third paragraph of Article 177 of the EC Treaty.

[Reports: 26 *EuGRZ* 365 (1999) (in German); 20 Human Rights Law Journal, 1999, p. 281 (English translation)]

National constitutions—Constitutional review concerning Community Treaty — Belgian Constitution — Whether conclusion of Community treaties is subject to constitutional review—Whether there is any rule of international law giving States the right to conclude treaties contrary to their constitutions

National constitutions — Fundamental rights — Belgian Constitution — Protocol of 1962 concerning establishment of European Schools—Possible conflict with Constitution—Whether Belgian Court of Arbitration competent to examine compatibility of Community Treaty with fundamental constitutional rights—The law of Belgium

EUROPEAN SCHOOL *v.* HERMANS-JACOBS
AND HEUVELMANS-VAN IERSEL

(Case No 12/94)

Belgium, Court of Arbitration. 3 *February* 1994

(Melchior, *President*; Blanckaert, Boel, Martens, de Wasseige and de Baets, *Judges*)

SUMMARY: *The facts*:—Proceedings were brought before the Belgian courts by the European School of Mol, which claimed tuition fees from the parents of two children at the school for the year 1989/90. The parents argued that, pursuant to Article 17(3) of the Belgian Constitution[1] and Article 2 of Additional Protocol No 1 to the European Convention on Human Rights, access to education was required to be free. The proceedings were stayed and a reference was made to the Court of Arbitration to determine whether the Laws of Assent approving the Statute of the European School adopted in 1957 by international agreement, which empowered the Governing Council to levy fees, and the Protocol of 1962 concerning the Establishment of European Schools, as well as the Agreement of 1962 between the Belgian State and the Governing Council of the Schools, were compatible with Article 17(3) of the Constitution. Although the European Schools were empowered to charge fees, they were also required to grant an exception to the children of officials of European Community institutions or national officials seconded to an EC institution or representation.

Held:—The laws in question did not violate Article 17(3) of the Constitution.

(1) No rule of international law, which was the creation of States, not even Article 27 of the Vienna Convention on the Law of Treaties, 1969, gave the

[1] For the text of Article 17(3) see p. 158.

power to States to conclude treaties which were contrary to their constitutions. The Court of Arbitration was therefore competent to rule on the compatibility of the Protocol of 1962 with the Constitution.

(2) The European Schools were established by international agreements and were administered by a supranational body acting as the organizing authority. These Schools were financed principally by contributions made by the Contracting Parties in accordance with a division of charges agreed by the Governing Council pursuant to Article 26(1) of the Statute of 1957.

(3) The fact that the Belgian State was bound, pursuant to an Agreement concluded with the Governing Council in 1962, to make available, maintain and equip school buildings, did not mean that the School in question was an institution subsidized by the public authorities to which the guarantee of free access to education enshrined in Article 17(3) of the Constitution applied. Accordingly the charging of fees for the category of children in question did not violate Article 17(3).

The following is the text of the judgment of the Court:

I.—*Object of the Preliminary Question*

By two judgments of 20 April 1993, the justice of the peace for the Canton of Mol asked the following preliminary question:

Article 26 of the Protocol of 12 April 1957 containing the Statute of the European School (approved by the Law of 28 February 1959 (*MB*, 25 June 1959)) provides that tuition fees shall be payable by the parents by a decision of the Governing Council. Does this provision violate Article 17(3) *in fine* of the Belgian Constitution which provides that access to education shall be free up until the completion of compulsory education?

and/or

Is Article 17(3) *in fine* of the Belgian Constitution violated by the Law of 8 November 1975 (*MB*, 7 February 1976) which approves:

1. (a) The Protocol signed in Luxembourg on 13 April 1962 concerning the Establishment of European Schools on the basis of the Statute of the European School signed in Luxembourg on 12 April 1957;

(b) The Protocol concerning the provisional application of the above-mentioned Protocol, signed in Luxembourg on 13 April 1962; and

2. The Agreement between the Government of the Kingdom of Belgium and the Governing Council of the European School, signed in Brussels on 12 October 1962, on the basis of which the European School of Mol-Geel has asked the parents of Belgian children for the payment of a supplement for secondary education?

II.—*The Facts and Procedure*

Proceedings have been instituted by the European School of Mol against Mr and Mrs Hermans-Jacobs and Mr and Mrs Heuvelmans-Van Iersel claiming payment of tuition fees for their children for the school year 1989-90.

Before the judge who has made this reference, the parents alleged in their defence that, pursuant to Article 17(3) of the Constitution and Article 2 of Additional Protocol No 1 to the European Convention for the Protection of Human Rights and Fundamental Freedoms, access to education must be free. The justice of the peace therefore decided to refer to the Court of Arbitration the questions set out above.

With regard to the object of the preliminary question

B.1.—The preliminary question concerns the compatibility with Article 17(3) *in fine* of the Constitution of:

—The Law of 28 February 1959 (in particular, Article 26(4)) approving the Protocol of 12 April 1957 containing the Statute of the European School, pursuant to which the Governing Council of the European Schools may demand tuition fees;

—The Law of 8 November 1975 approving the basic provisions pursuant to which the European School of Mol may charge the parents of Belgian children a supplement for secondary education.

According to the wording of the decision of the justice of the peace making this reference, it concerns exclusively Article 17(3), first paragraph, second phrase, of the Constitution.

With regard to the competence of the Court

B.2.—Article 107 *ter* (2) of the Constitution provides that the Court of Arbitration shall give rulings on the violation by a law, decree or regulation covered by Article 26 *bis*, of Articles 6, 6 *bis* and 17 of the Constitution.

Article 107 *ter* (2) also provides that proceedings may be instituted before the Court by every authority designated by the law, by any person able to justify an interest and, by way of a preliminary question, by any court.

This provision makes no distinction with regard to the extent of constitutional review according to whether the Court is seized by an authority, a person able to justify an interest or a court.

B.3.—Article 107 *ter* (2) of the Constitution provides that the composition, competence and functioning of the Court of Arbitration shall be determined by law. This provision was given effect by the Special Law of 6 January 1989 on the Court of Arbitration. In Title 1 of the Law, concerning the jurisdiction of the Court, Chapter I deals with actions for annulment (Articles 1 to 25) and Chapter II with preliminary questions (Articles 26 to 30). These provisions do not create any further distinctions in the jurisdiction attributed to the Court to review the conformity of legislative norms with Articles 6, 6 *bis* and 17 of the Constitution, according to whether the Court is seized by way of an action for annulment or a preliminary question.

Article 3(2) of the Special Law of 6 January 1989 expressly recognizes the jurisdiction of the Court to rule on actions for annulment brought against a law, decree or regulation covered by Article 26 *bis* of the Constitution by which assent is given to a treaty.

According to Article 26 of the Special Law of 6 January 1989, the Court of Arbitration shall rule, by way of preliminary reference, on questions concerning the violation of a law, decree or regulation covered by Article 26 *bis* of the Constitution, of a constitutional rule concerning competence or Articles 6, 6 *bis* and 17 of the Constitution.

This provision does not in any way exclude laws, decrees or orders by which assent is given to a treaty.

B.4.—Furthermore the Constitution, which prohibits the legislature from adopting domestic legislative norms which are contrary to the norms referred to in Article 107 *ter* of the Constitution, cannot be interpreted so as to authorize the legislature to adopt such norms indirectly by means of the assent given to an international treaty.

Indeed no rule of international law, which is the creation of States, not even Article 27 of the Vienna Convention of 1969 on the Law of Treaties, gives the power to States to conclude treaties which are contrary to their Constitutions.

B.5.—The Court is therefore competent to rule on the question referred to it.

With regard to the preliminary question

B.6.—The Laws of Assent of 28 February 1959 and 8 November 1975 state that the international acts in question "shall have full and complete effect".

The review which the Court must carry out involves an examination of the content of the provisions of the international acts in question which are relevant to the present proceedings. The Court must review the position taking account of the fact that the case at issue involves not a unilateral act of sovereignty but a treaty provision which also has legal effects outside the domestic legal order.

On the merits

B.7.1.—Article 17(3) of the Constitution provides:

> Everyone shall have the right to education respecting fundamental rights and freedoms. Access to education shall be free up until the end of the period of compulsory education.

All students subject to compulsory education have the right, at the expense of the community, to moral and religious education.

B.7.2.—In the explanatory note accompanying the Government draft revision of Article 17 of the Constitution, the proposal to insert a new paragraph 3(1), second phrase, is explained as follows:

Compulsory education includes the right to instruction which shall also be free to the extent that it is compulsory . . .

The Constitution of 1988 now includes a constitutional guarantee of free instruction for which the Court of Arbitration must ensure respect. That guarantee was previously enshrined in the legislation concerning the "education pact", according to which access to instruction must be free for all children of compulsory school age attending schools organized or subsidized by the public authorities.

B.7.3.—Belgium has three European schools. Two of them are in Brussels at Uccle (opened in September 1958) and at Woluwe-Saint Lambert (opened in September 1975). The third is in Mol (opened in September 1960). Pursuant to Article 26(4) of the Statute, the Governing Council of the European Schools imposed tuition fees. These were fixed for the European Schools established in Belgium, for the school year 1989/90, at BF 7,464; 12,940; and 22,031 for kindergarten, primary and secondary education respectively. From the school year 1992/3 the tuition fees have been fixed respectively at BF 25,342; 35,457; and 47,923. Tuition fees at a more or less equivalent level are also demanded by the other European Schools established in Luxembourg, Varése (Italy), Karlsruhe and Munich (Germany), Bergen (Netherlands) and Culham (United Kingdom).

The above-mentioned amounts are reduced to half rate for a second child and quarter rate for a third and subsequent children.

Exemption from tuition fees is granted, however, for the children of certain persons such as staff and officials of the Communities, the European Schools or organizations and institutions with which an agreement has been concluded, as well as national officials of the twelve Member States of the Community "on secondment" in a country where there is a European School (*cf. Recueil des Décisions du Conseil supérieur des Ecoles européennes*, September 1992, p. 139, paragraph c).

In accordance with the possibility created by Article 1(2) of the Protocol of 13 April 1962, other children may in principle also be admitted to the European Schools, including the School in Mol, provided certain conditions are fulfilled, including knowledge of languages, a maximum number of children in each class, and payment of tuition fees.

This Court has only been asked to consider the position of children in this latter category. It will therefore limit its reply to an examination of the position of such pupils.

B.7.4.—The European Schools are organized by or pursuant to international agreements and are administered by a supranational body acting as the organizing authority.

These schools are principally financed through contributions made by the Contracting Parties on the basis of a division of charges decided upon by the Governing Council in accordance with Article 26(1) of the Statute of the European School. Pursuant to an Agreement concluded on 12 October 1962 with the Governing Council of the European School, the Belgian State undertook, in conformity with Article 28 of the Statute, to provide, maintain, insure and equip the school buildings. But this fact does not permit the conclusion to be drawn that the School in question is an establishment subsidized by the public authorities to which the guarantee enshrined in Article 17(3) of the Constitution should be applicable.

By reason of their particular status, European Schools cannot therefore be regarded as providing education to which access must be free in accordance with Article 17(3), paragraph 1, of the Constitution. Article 17(3) does not in any way prevent the Governing Council of the European Schools from fixing tuition fees. Nor does it prevent the European School of Mol from requiring the parents of Belgian children to pay an additional contribution.

For these reasons the Court rules that the following provisions do not violate Article 17(3), first paragraph, of the Constitution:

—The Law of 28 February 1959 approving the Statute of the European School created at the seat of the European Coal and Steel Community and the Protocol of Signature signed in Luxembourg on 12 April 1957, as well as the Appendix containing the regulations for the European Baccalaureate signed in Luxembourg on 15 July 1957, in so far as tuition fees may be charged to the parents of pupils by a decision of the Governing Council taken pursuant to Article 26 of the Statute;

—The Law of 8 November 1975 approving the following international acts:

1. (a) The Protocol signed in Luxembourg on 13 April 1962 concerning the Establishment of European Schools on the basis of the Statute of the European School signed in Luxembourg on 12 April 1957;

(b) The Protocol concerning the provisional application of the Protocol concerning the Establishment of European Schools signed in Luxembourg on 13 April 1962;

2. The Agreement between the Government of the Kingdom of Belgium and the Governing Council of the European Schools signed

in Brussels on 12 October 1962, to the extent that the European School of Mol-Geel is given the right to claim from the parents of Belgian pupils the payment of an additional contribution for secondary education.

[Report: *Journal des Tribunaux* 1994, p. 532 (in French)]

Supremacy—Conflict between Community law and national constitutional law — Belgian Constitution, Article 34 — Whether constitutional provisions taking precedence over Community law

National constitutions—Constitutional challenge to national legislation — Belgian Constitution, Article 34 — Legislation implementing EC Treaty as interpreted by Court of Justice of the European Community—Conflict with Article 10 of Constitution — Whether special constitutional amendment required

Institutions — Court of Justice — Effect of decisions in Member States—Role in ensuring uniform application of EC Treaty

Legal order in general — Special character — Nature of obligations undertaken by Member States under EC Treaty—Requirement of uniform application of Community law in Member States—Whether transfer of sovereignty inherent in membership of European Community is reversible—The law of Belgium

ORFINGER *v.* BELGIAN STATE (MINISTER FOR CIVIL SERVICE)

(Case No 62.922)

Belgium, Conseil d'Etat (Sixth Chamber). 5 *November* 1996

(Willot-Thomas, *President*; Leroy and Wettinck, *Judges*)

SUMMARY: *The facts*:—A Belgian Royal Decree of 26 September 1994 required employment in the public service to be opened up to nationals of Member States of the European Union, whilst reserving for Belgian nationals those posts involving direct or indirect participation in the exercise of powers conferred by public law or duties designed to safeguard the general interests of the State. This Decree basically confirmed the position under Article 48(4) of the EC Treaty, as interpreted in the case-law of the Court of Justice of the European Community. Mr Orfinger applied to the *Conseil d'Etat* for the annulment of the Decree in question on the ground that it was incompatible with Article 10(2) of the Belgian Constitution, which prohibited non-Belgian nationals from obtaining employment in civil and military posts in the public administration, except where this was expressly permitted by specific legislation covering particular cases.

Held:—The application was rejected.

(1) When Belgium first acceded to the EC Treaty, there was no apparent conflict between Article 48 of the Treaty and the Constitution. The conflict had only become apparent since 1980 when, in a series of judgments, the Court of Justice had enunciated the interpretation of Article 48(4) which the Royal Decree at issue was intended to confirm. Consequently the point at issue was the compatibility with the Constitution of an interpretation of a Treaty provision given, a considerable time after the conclusion of the EC Treaty, by the Court of Justice as the authority entrusted by that Treaty with responsibility for giving its provisions a uniform interpretation which was binding on the Member States.

(2) Article 34 of the Constitution permitted the exercise of certain powers to be transferred by a treaty or law to international organizations. This provision, although adopted subsequently to the conclusion of the EC Treaty, provided a constitutional basis for the institutional mechanisms established by the Treaty. Nevertheless, Article 34 determined neither which competences could be transferred nor their limits.

(3) Where there was a conflict between a rule of domestic law and a rule of international law with direct effect in the domestic legal order, the rule established by the treaty had to take precedence. According to the settled case-law of the Court of Justice of the European Community, recourse to provisions of the domestic legal order in order to restrict the scope of the provisions of Community law would have the effect of impairing the unity and efficacy of that law and consequently could not be accepted even if the provisions of domestic law were those of the Constitution.

(4) The authority of the interpretation given to the EC Treaty by the Court of Justice was based on Article 34 of the Constitution even where it restricted the effect of Articles 8 and 10 of the Constitution. The application of the Treaty, in the interpretation given by the Court of Justice, was the consequence of the accession of Belgium to the Community. That application could always be brought to an end, at the initiative of the Belgian authorities, by the renunciation of that membership or renegotiation of its conditions. In the absence of such an initiative, the principle of the rule of law required Community rules to be applied in full. Whilst it was desirable that the Constitution should be adapted to the requirements of Community law, the application of Community law was not dependent upon such an amendment and was obligatory even in its absence.

The following is the text of the judgment of the *Conseil d'Etat*:

Henri Orfinger lodged an application on 26 November 1994 in which he asked for the annulment of a Royal Decree of 26 September 1994 fixing the general principles of the Service Regulations concerning administrative and financial matters for State Officials of National and Regional Governments . . .

[The *Conseil d'Etat* first considered and rejected a ground based on the alleged violation of the principle of the non-retroactivity of laws. The *Conseil d'Etat* held that this principle, enshrined in Article 2 of the Civil Code, was in general applicable to royal decrees. However, where the administrative authorities were, as here, re-enacting a measure which had been annulled by the *Conseil d'Etat*, they could make the new measure retroactive if it was essential for the proper functioning or continuity of the public service, provided the legal basis for the annulment was respected. These conditions appeared to have been satisfied in this case. The *Conseil d'Etat* continued:]

In his third ground, the applicant contends that Article 1(3)(1) of the Decree being challenged violates Article 10(2) of the Constitution. He contends that the Decree is unconstitutional for two reasons. First he argues that it is only the legislature which can alter the nationality condition established for access to public employment. Secondly he considers that the Constitution reserves public employment to Belgian persons save in the case of specific exceptions established by law. With regard to this second point, he argues that the effect of the provision being challenged is to transform this constitutional rule into an exception.

In his further submissions, he argues that the rule that international law takes precedence over the Constitution has no constitutional basis and that the rules of international treaty law are only binding in Belgium by reason of their incorporation into domestic law in accordance with the rules established by the Constitution so that it would be illogical to place those laws above the Constitution. In support of this argument he relies upon the judgment of the Court of Arbitration of 3 February 1994 in Case No 12/94.[1] The applicant points out that there is no rule of international law giving States the power to conclude treaties in conflict with their Constitution. Furthermore, the legislative section of the *Conseil d'Etat*, in its Opinion on the Draft Law of Assent to the Maastricht Treaty, indicated that it would be necessary to modify the Constitution before ratifying the Treaty. Finally, the jurisprudence of the Court of Justice of the European Community does not prohibit the enumeration of those posts open to nationals of other Member States, which would be in conformity with the Constitution, subject to the interpretation to be given to the words "in special cases". Finally, he adds that the provision being challenged, by reason of its abstract and imprecise wording, constitutes an implicit delegation which is unlawful and pernicious from the standpoint of legal security.

In his final written submissions, the applicant states that it would be unacceptable to give precedence to the Treaty over the Constitution because the binding force of the Treaty stems from its adoption in conformity with the rules governing form and substance laid down in the Constitution. He refers to the procedural requirements which constitute a comprehensive framework of democratic guarantees, pointing out that a simple majority vote without any right of amendment cannot modify the Constitution or replace the procedure laid down for its revision. In support of these statements he cites a published article, arguing that if

[[1] See p. 155.]

the European Court were to substitute itself for the legislature and the national or European authorities, it would effectively have the power of last resort which would appear to be contrary to the rule of law. The applicant further contends that the application of the rules on the free movement of workers to certain public posts cannot have been foreseen at the time of the adoption of the Treaty of Rome in 1957. Citing a commentary to the judgment of the Court of Justice of the European Community of 17 December 1980,[2] he states that there is no provision of the Treaty which empowers the organs of the European Union to dictate the status of public officials of the Member States. He stresses that such a course would be incompatible with the principle of subsidiarity enshrined in the Maastricht Treaty. According to the applicant, public officials form part of a hierarchy and all participate in the exercise of public authority. He indicates that the principle of equality prohibits distinctions being made between different officials in this regard. Even accepting recognition of the primacy of the Treaty over the Constitution, he considers that the King would nevertheless not be empowered to establish a derogation from the nationality requirement since such a power is reserved by the Constitution to the legislature.

[The *Conseil d'Etat* then set out the provisions of Articles 8, 10 and 34 of the Constitution and continued:]

The problem raised by this ground does not concern a conflict between the Constitution and a directly applicable rule of treaty law. It is not contested that at the moment when Belgium acceded to the Treaty of Rome there was no apparent conflict between Article 48 of that Treaty and the Constitution. The position challenged in this ground only became apparent from 1980, when the Court of Justice of the European Community gave an interpretation to Article 48 of the Treaty requiring posts in the public service to be opened up to nationals of the European Union where "they do not involve direct or indirect participation in the exercise of powers conferred by public law or duties designed to safeguard the general interests of the State or of other public authorities". The question which this ground raises is therefore the compatibility between the Constitution and the interpretation given to a provision of the Treaty, a considerable time after its conclusion, by the authority entrusted by that Treaty with the responsibility for giving its provisions a uniform interpretation which is binding upon the Member States of the Union.

Article 34 of the Constitution permits the exercise of certain powers to be transferred by a treaty or a law to institutions governed by public international law. Even though this provision was adopted subsequently to the conclusion of the Treaty of Rome, which was approved by a Law of 2 December 1957, it provides a constitutional basis for the institutional

[[2] Case 149/79, *Commission* v. *Belgium* [1980] ECR 3881.]

mechanisms established by the Treaty, which were intended in particular to ensure its uniform interpretation in all the Member States of the European Union. Nevertheless this provision determines neither those competences which may be transferred nor their limits.

The principle of the free movement of workers established by Article 48 of the Treaty of Rome is inapplicable, according to paragraph 4 of that Article, to "employment in the public service". According to the settled interpretation of this provision by the Court of Justice since 1980:

> This provision removes from the ambit of Article 48(1) to (3) a series of posts involving direct or indirect participation in the exercise of powers conferred by public law or duties designed to safeguard the general interests of the State or of other public authorities.[3]

Where a conflict exists between a rule of domestic law and a rule of international law with direct effect in the domestic legal order, the rule established by the treaty must take precedence. According to the settled case-law of the Court of Justice of the European Community, "recourse to provisions of the domestic legal order in order to restrict the scope of the provisions of Community law would have the effect of impairing the unity and efficacy of that law and consequently cannot be accepted" even if the provisions of domestic law are those of the Constitution (CJEC, 2 July 1996, Case C-473/93, *Commission* v. *Grand Duchy of Luxembourg*).[4] From the standpoint of Belgian constitutional law, the authority of the interpretation given to the Treaty of Rome by the Court of Justice is based upon Article 34 of the Constitution, even though that interpretation restricts the effects of parts of Articles 8 and 10 of the Constitution.

This conclusion does not conflict with any of the principles invoked by the applicant in support of this ground. The application of the Treaty of Rome in all its provisions, and in the interpretation given to it by the Court of Justice, is the consequence of the accession of Belgium to the European Union. The application of the Treaty could always be brought to an end, at the initiative of the Belgian authorities, by the renunciation of that membership or by the renegotiation of its conditions. So long as such an initiative has not been taken, the principle of the rule of law requires Community rules to be fully applied. Whilst it is desirable, as the Legislative Section of the *Conseil d'Etat* has pointed out, that the text of the Constitution should be adapted to the requirements of European law, the application of European law is not dependent upon such an amendment and is required even in its absence.

The obligation to open up employment in the public service to nationals of the European Union, with the exception of those positions which involve direct or indirect participation in the exercise of powers conferred

[[3] *Ibid.*, paragraph 11.] [[4] See p. 72.]

by public law and duties designed to safeguard the general interests of the State or of other public authorities, is enshrined in Belgian law by virtue of the Treaty of Rome and the interpretation given to it by the Court of Justice of the European Community. The Decree being challenged does not create that obligation. Its scope, on this point, is not that of a rule of law but rather a notification given to the different public authorities to which the Decree being challenged is directly or indirectly applicable. That notification, as a derogation from the normally applicable legal rules, was legitimately considered by the Government as capable of being disseminated in a legal text in order to avoid any misunderstanding as to the existence of the rule in question. The manner in which the rule is formulated, reserving employment in certain posts to Belgian nationals whilst opening up other posts to citizens of the European Union, is entirely in conformity with the principles outlined in the case-law of the Court of Justice. Since this ground does not challenge a provision with independent legal effect, it is inadmissible.

[The application was rejected.]

[Report: *Journal des Tribunaux* 1997, p. 254 (in French)]

Direct effect—Directives—Interpretation of national law—Duty of national courts to interpret national law consistently with provisions of directive — Scope of obligation — Applicability to national law introduced to implement directive

Institutions — Court of Justice — Powers — Jurisdiction — Article 177 of EC Treaty—Scope of duty of national courts to make reference to Court of Justice—Whether constitutional court under duty to make a reference — The law of Belgium

FÉDÉRATION BELGE DES CHAMBRES SYNDICALES DES MÉDECINS *v.* COUNCIL OF MINISTERS, GOVERNMENTS OF FRENCH AND FLEMISH COMMUNITIES

(Case No 6/97)

Belgium, Court of Arbitration. 19 *February* 1997

SUMMARY: *The facts*:—In proceedings instituted before the Belgian Court of Arbitration, a Belgian medical representative body challenged provisions of a Flemish Community Decree concerning the organization of a common programme of study for medical training which allowed the first year of the second cycle of specific training to be done concurrently with the last year of the first cycle, and therefore prior to obtaining the basic doctor's diploma. The Decree specifically stated that the common programme of study must satisfy the conditions of EC Council Directive 93/16, which was attached to it. But the Court of Arbitration was faced with uncertainty as to the precise nature of the requirements of the Directive with which the provisions of the Decree at issue were supposed to comply.

Held:—Prior to a decision on the merits of the case, a reference should be made to the Court of Justice for a preliminary ruling.

(1) The scope of the provisions of the Decree being challenged had to be interpreted on the basis that they were in conformity with the international obligations of Belgium, in this case contained in EC Council Directive 93/16.

(2) Since it was possible to interpret the provisions of the Directive in several ways it was necessary, prior to examining the grounds of the application, to make a reference to the Court of Justice under Article 177 of the EC Treaty for a ruling on three preliminary questions set out in the operative part of the judgment.

The text of the judgment of the Court commences on the opposite page.

I.—*Object of the Application*

By a request to the Court lodged with the registrar on 29 January 1996, the *Fédération belge des chambres syndicales des médecins*, whose registered office is in Brussels . . . has brought an action for the annulment of Section 4(2) of the Decree of the Flemish Community of 5 April 1995, which amended the Decree of 12 June 1991 on universities in the Flemish Community, concerning the organization of special training in general medicine and other provisions on universities, published in the *Moniteur belge* of 29 July 1995.

. . .

IV.—*In law*

. . .

With regard to the grounds of the application

B.1.—An examination of the grounds requires that the scope of the Decree of 5 April 1995 which is being challenged should first be determined, and in particular the provisions of Section 4(2) which are in dispute.

. . .

B.4.2.—Article 3 of EC Council Directive 93/16 of 5 April 1993, intended to facilitate the free movement of doctors and the mutual recognition of their diplomas, certificates and other evidence of formal qualifications, provides:

> The diplomas, certificates and other evidence of formal qualifications referred to in Article 2 are as follows:
>
> (a) *in Belgium*:
>
> Diploma of doctor of medicine, surgery and obstetrics required by law awarded by the university faculties of medicine, the Central Examining Board or the State University Education Examining Board; . . .

B.4.3.—In Belgian law, according to Section 2(1) of Royal Decree No 78 of 10 November 1967 concerning the exercise of the right to practice, "no one may practice as a doctor unless he has the diploma of doctor of medicine, surgery and obstetrics required by law, obtained in accordance with the legislation on academic grades and the programme of university examinations or, if he has been legally exempted from this condition, unless he fulfils the conditions laid down in Section 7(1) or (2)".

So far as the Flemish Community is concerned, the words "diploma of doctor of medicine, surgery and obstetrics . . . obtained in accordance with the legislation on academic grades and the programme of university examinations" must be read, since the entry into force of the Decree of 12 June 1991, as "diploma of medicine obtained in accordance with the Decree of 12 June 1991" (Court of Arbitration, Judgment No 78/92, paragraph B.5.5.).

B.4.4.—Section 14 of the Decree of 12 June 1991 provides that training in medicine shall consist of a cycle of three years of study followed by a training cycle of four years of study.

B.4.5.—Section 4(2) of the Decree of 5 April 1995, which is being challenged in these proceedings, amends Section 14 of the Decree of 12 June 1991 concerning universities in the Flemish Community, adding a fourth paragraph as follows:

> The total period of studies for training in general medicine shall amount to three years of studies, comprising the fourth year of study of the second training cycle for doctors and two years of study for training in general medicine.

B.4.6.—It was made clear in the explanatory report accompanying the Decree being challenged that only after obtaining a diploma of doctor, that is to say after the fourth year of the second period of medical studies, may the holders of such diplomas practise as salaried doctors (Draft Decree, Flemish Council, *DOC*, 1994–5, No 691/1, p. 3) . . . The first year of specific training in general medicine is therefore given to students when they are completing the last year of their training as a doctor.

B.4.7.—Section 3 of the Decree being challenged adds two additional paragraphs to Section 11 of the Decree of 12 June 1991 as follows:

> The common programme of study for the first cycle of training as a doctor and the first three years of studies for the second cycle of that training must satisfy the conditions laid down in EC Council Directive 93/16 of 5 April 1993, Chapter IV, attached to this Decree. The university authorities shall issue, to those students who have been successful in the annual examination at the end of the third year of studies for the second cycle, a certificate stating that they have successfully completed the cycle of training referred to in Article 23 of the above-mentioned Directive.
>
> This certificate states that its holder has completed six years of studies. It does not authorize that person to practise medicine in Belgium but authorizes them to begin the specific training in general medicine prior to obtaining their diploma as a doctor.

B.4.8.—On the basis of these provisions, it appears that the diploma of medicine is obtained after seven years of studies and that the specific training in general medicine is given over a period of three years of which the first year coincides with the seventh year of studies in medicine.

This organization is in conformity with domestic legislation because, during the first year of specific training in general medicine, the student who holds the certificate mentioned in paragraph B.4.7. above does not practise medicine since he could only do so after obtaining the diploma of a doctor at the end of seven years of studies.

B.5.1.—The scope of the provision being challenged must nevertheless be interpreted on the presumption that it is in conformity with the international obligations of Belgium.

B.5.2.—Article 30 of EC Directive 93/16 provides:

> Each Member State which dispenses the complete training referred to in Article 23 within its territory shall institute specific training in general medical practice meeting requirements at least as stringent as those laid down in Articles 31 and 32, in such a manner that the first diplomas, certificates or other evidence of formal qualifications awarded on completion of the course are issued not later than 1 January 1990.

According to Article 23, to which Article 30 refers:

> 1. The Member States shall require persons wishing to take up and pursue a medical profession to hold a diploma, certificate or other evidence of formal qualifications in medicine referred to in Article 3 which guarantees that during his complete training period the person concerned has acquired:
>
> (a) Adequate knowledge of the sciences on which medicine is based and a good understanding of the scientific methods including the principles of measuring biological functions, the evaluation of scientifically established facts and the analysis of data;
>
> (b) sufficient understanding of the structure, functions and behaviour of healthy and sick persons, as well as relations between the state of health and physical and social surroundings of the human being;
>
> (c) adequate knowledge of clinical disciplines and practices, providing him with a coherent picture of mental and physical diseases, of medicine from the points of view of prophylaxis, diagnosis and therapy and of human reproduction;
>
> (d) suitable clinical experience in hospitals under appropriate supervision.
>
> 2. A complete period of medical training of this kind shall comprise at least a six-year course or 5,500 hours of theoretical and practical instruction given in a university or under the supervision of a university.

B.6.—It is true that the Preamble to the Directive specifies that "it is immaterial whether this training in general medical practice is received as part of, or separately from, basic medical training as laid down nationally". This Court considers, however, that this recital would appear to be incompatible with the provisions of Articles 23 and 30 of the Directive.

B.7.—Furthermore, amongst the conditions which the specific training in general medical practice must satisfy, Article 31(1) mentions:

> (a) Entry shall be conditional upon the successful completion of at least six years' study within the framework of the training course referred to in Article 23; . . .
>
> (d) It shall entail the personal participation of the trainee in the professional activities and responsibilities of the persons with whom he works.

B.8.—Reading of these Articles of EC Directive 93/16 gives rise to the question of whether it is sufficient, in order to obtain entry to the specific training in general medical practice, for a candidate to obtain the certificate referred to in Article 23 of the Directive, guaranteeing that he has successfully completed six years of medical studies, or whether he must first have obtained the diploma in medicine defined in Article 3 of the Directive.

B.9.—Furthermore, if Article 31(1)(d) of the Directive must be interpreted not as simply imposing a trainee obligation but as requiring that, during and from the beginning of the entire period of his training, the candidate assumes the professional responsibilities of a doctor, either in full-time training or in part-time training equivalent to two years of full-time training, as permitted by Article 34 of the Directive, Article 31 would then also imply that the candidate could only begin his specific training if he was the holder of a diploma of doctor. If that is the case, in order to comply with the Directive, the provision in question would have to be interpreted as permitting those persons following a course of specific training to lodge the documentation concerning their practice of medicine from the beginning of their seventh year of studies. That would raise a problem of compatibility with the terms of Royal Decree No 78 which requires, in Section 2(1), that a person working as a medical practitioner must be the holder of a diploma of doctor.

B.10.—It is therefore necessary, prior to examining the grounds of the application, to make a reference to the Court of Justice of the European Community, in application of Article 177 of the EC Treaty, for a ruling on the three preliminary questions set out in the operative part of this judgment below.

For these reasons the Court, prior to giving a ruling on the merits of the case, refers to the Court of Justice of the European Community the following three preliminary questions:

1.—Must Article 31(1)(a) of EC Council Directive 93/16 of 5 April 1993 to facilitate the free movement of doctors and the mutual recognition of their diplomas, certificates and other evidence of formal qualifications, when read in conjunction with Articles 3 and 23 and the other provisions of Chapter IV of that Directive, be interpreted as requiring that specific training in general medical practice cannot commence until the person concerned has obtained, after at least six months of study, the basic diploma referred to in Article 3?

2.—Must Article 31(1)(d) of the same Directive be interpreted in the sense that "the personal participation of the trainee in the professional activities and responsibilities of the person with whom he works" implies that the candidate exercises the activities of a doctor which are reserved to the holders of the diplomas required by Articles 2 and 3 of the Directive?

3.—In the affirmative, must Article 31(1)(d) be interpreted as requiring that the candidate must exercise the activities of a doctor from the beginning of his specific training in general medical practice, whether he is engaged in the full-time training provided for in Article 31 of the Directive or the part-time training provided for in Article 34?

[Report: *Journal des Tribunaux* 1997, p. 430 (in French)]

NOTE:—This judgment appears to represent the first occasion when a court with an exclusively constitutional role has made a reference to the Court of Justice (Lenaerts, *Constitutional Law of the European Union* (Sweet & Maxwell, 1999), p. 516, footnote 49).

In its judgment of 16 July 1998 the Fifth Chamber of the Court of Justice ruled that Article 31 of the Directive did not make access to specific training in general medical practice subject to the condition of first obtaining a basic doctor's diploma ([1998] ECR I-4837).

National constitutions — Constitutional review concerning Community Treaty—Danish Constitution, Article 20—Treaty on European Union, 1992 (Maastricht Treaty)—Amendments to EC Treaty — Compatibility with Constitution — Whether providing satisfactory constitutional basis for accession of Denmark to Treaty on European Union and amendments to EC Treaty — Powers exercised by EC institutions — Recourse of Council to Article 235 of EC Treaty—Recourse of European Court of Justice to judicial legislation—Whether violating constitutional requirement for transfer of powers to international organizations to be "specified by statute"—Scope of permissible transfer of sovereignty to Community institutions — Whether limited by Danish Constitution — Whether transfer of sovereignty by treaty subject to constitutional review by Danish courts — Whether any constitutional assumption that Denmark must remain an independent State—Whether transfer of sovereignty may violate constitutional requirement of democratic system of government—Whether further European integration should be conditional upon additional democratic control

Powers—Extension by treaty—Treaty on European Union, 1992 — Legal basis for extension of powers of European Community — Principle of conferred powers contained in EC Treaty — Definition — Whether Community institutions competent to determine their own powers — Article 235 of Treaty—Scope of application

Institutions—Court of Justice—Powers—Jurisdiction under Articles 173 and 177 of EC Treaty—Role as final authority for interpretation of scope of powers vested in EC institutions—Compatibility with Danish Constitution, Article 20

National constitutions — Fundamental rights — Danish Constitution—Treaty on European Union, 1992 and amended EC Treaty—Possible conflict with fundamental rights under Constitution—Role of European Court of Justice in ensuring respect for fundamental rights — Whether Danish courts retaining ultimate right to secure compatibility of Community legislation with fundamental constitutional rights

Supremacy — Constitutions and Community law — Danish Constitution — Whether fundamental constitutional rights could take precedence over Community law — The law of Denmark

CARLSEN AND OTHERS *v.* RASMUSSEN

(Case No 272/1994)

Denmark, Supreme Court (Admissibility). 12 *August* 1996

(Pontoppidan, Hornslet, Andreasen, Sørensen, Melchior, Blok, Walsøe, Lorenzen and Jensen, *Judges*)

(Case No B-2131/96)

Eastern Provincial Court (Merits). 27 *June* 1997

(Case No I-361/1997)

Supreme Court (Merits). 6 *April* 1998

(Hornslet, Hermann, Andreasen, Pedersen, Sørensen, Melchior, Blok, Nørgaard, Lorenzen, Dahl and Kristensen, *Judges*)

SUMMARY: *The facts*:—In proceedings brought by Mr Carlsen and nine other private citizens against the Danish Prime Minister, a declaration was sought that the procedure followed for the implementation in Denmark of amendments to the Treaty establishing the European Community ("EC Treaty"), as set out in the Treaty on European Union ("EU Treaty"), was unconstitutional.

Proceedings on Admissibility:—The Eastern Provincial Court, in a judgment of 30 June 1994, held that the application to determine the constitutional validity of the implementing law was inadmissible because the law in question did not sufficiently affect the applicants in a concrete and immediate manner. The applicants appealed.

Held (by the Supreme Court, judgment of 12 August 1996):—The appeal was allowed and the case was remitted to the Eastern Provincial Court for a decision on the merits.

The applicants did have the necessary legal interest to have their claims examined because of the vital and general importance of Danish accession to the amended EC Treaty for the population as a whole. Consequently, and contrary to earlier Danish case-law,[1] the right to a determination of the constitutional

[1] See Volume 1, Note at p. 275.

legality of the implementing legislation was not subject to the condition that the applicants were affected by it in a concrete and immediate manner.

Proceedings on the Merits:—Article 20(1) of the Danish Constitution[2] authorized the transfer of powers to international organizations provided the procedure laid down in Article 20(2)[3] was followed, requiring an enhanced five-sixths parliamentary majority or approval in a referendum. But the applicants argued that Article 20(1) only gave authority for transfers of sovereignty "to such an extent as shall be provided by statute" and that this condition had not been complied with. They referred in particular to the powers vested in the Council under Article 235 of the EC Treaty[4] and to the "judicial legislation" engaged in by the European Court of Justice. They also argued that the derogation of sovereignty was on such a scale and of such a nature as to be inconsistent with the Constitution's premise of a democratic form of government. This latter claim did not, however, relate to the third stage of Economic and Monetary Union since Denmark had decided not to participate in it, with the agreement of the other Member States.[5] Accordingly, the applicants argued that the accession of Denmark to the amended EC Treaty could only take place following a constitutional amendment pursuant to Article 88 of the Constitution.

Held (by the Eastern Provincial Court, judgment of 27 June 1997):—The accession to the amended EC Treaty did not exceed the limits authorized by Article 20 of the Constitution and accordingly the claims were dismissed.

(1) It was a fundamental principle of constitutional law that legislative, executive and judicial powers were to be exercised by Danish authorities. Any transfer of these powers to an international organization with supranational authority generally required an amendment of the Constitution unless the transfer of such powers was expressly authorized by the Constitution. Article 20 of the Constitution was introduced in 1953 to enable Denmark to join international organizations with supranational authority without a constitutional amendment being necessary. Article 20 was intended to cover the delegation of powers to supranational authorities to enact directly effective measures forming part of Danish law.

(2) The effect of Article 20 of the Constitution was that only clearly defined powers could be transferred, meaning that powers in specified fields could be transferred together with an indication of the content of those powers. The EC Treaty was based on the principle of legality, which excluded its institutions from determining their own powers. Furthermore, the Treaty contained rules on the exercise of transferred powers. The fact that provisions of the Treaty could give rise to doubt, concerning the extent of the powers transferred, did not imply any departure from the principle of legality which was binding on the Court of Justice in its interpretation of EC law, including the safeguarding of fundamental rights.

(3) Neither from Article 20 of the Constitution, nor from its legislative history, could any requirement be inferred that powers could only be transferred to international organizations to a quantitatively limited extent. Furthermore it

[2] For the text of Article 20(1) see p. 186.

[3] For the text of Article 20(2) see p. 187.

[4] For the text of Article 235 see p. 189.

[5] See Volume 1, Note at p. 275.

did not appear that, when Denmark acceded to the EC Treaty, powers were transferred to the European Community to an extent beyond what must have been foreseen at the time of the adoption of Article 20.

Further Proceedings on the Merits:—The applicants appealed to the Supreme Court, which made several orders for additional information to be provided and for evidence to be given by Government Ministers. The applicants maintained the same basic grounds as those submitted before the Provincial Court.

Held (by the Supreme Court, judgment of 6 April 1998):—The appeal was dismissed and the judgment of the Eastern Provincial Court was affirmed.

(1) Article 20 was included in the Constitution in 1953 so as to enable Denmark, without amending the Constitution in accordance with Article 88, to participate in international organizations, implying that the exercise of legislative, administrative or judicial authority could be entrusted to such organizations with direct effect in Denmark. Since it was impossible to predict with any degree of certainty what forms such international cooperation might assume in the future, no detailed specification was given as to what powers Article 20 covered. Accordingly, it was intended that it should be possible to transfer sovereignty within wide limits. However, it was emphasized in Article 20 that such delegation of powers could only occur "to such extent as shall be provided by statute". Furthermore, the stringent requirements for the adoption of laws under Article 20 provided a far-reaching safeguard.

(2) Article 20 did not permit an international organization to be entrusted with the promulgation of measures which were contrary to provisions in the Constitution, including its rights and freedoms. The term "to such extent as shall be provided by statute" required a positive delimitation of the powers delegated from the standpoint of both the fields of responsibility and the nature of the powers. Such delimitation had to enable an assessment to be made of the extent of the delegation of sovereignty. The fields of responsibility could be described in broad categories and there was no requirement to state the extent of delegation so precisely as to leave no room for discretion or interpretation. The powers delegated could be indicated by means of a reference to a treaty. Article 20(1) did, however, preclude the possibility that the international organization could be left to determine its own powers. On the other hand, it did not mean that Denmark was only authorized to transfer powers to such an organization to a limited or minor extent. The EC Treaty was based on a principle of conferred powers which implied a restriction on the powers of its institutions which complied with the requirement of Article 20 of the Constitution that only specified powers should be delegated.

(3) As the European Court of Justice had itself made clear in Opinion 2/94, Article 235 of the EC Treaty was an integral part of an institutional system based on the principle of conferred powers and could not serve as a basis for widening the scope of Community powers beyond the general framework created by the provisions of the Treaty as a whole and, in particular, by those provisions which defined the activities and tasks of the Community. The Court of Justice had stressed that Article 235 could not be used to circumvent the procedure for amending the Treaty. This interpretation of Article 235 was to be accepted even though, prior to the amendment of the EC Treaty, that provision may have been

applied on the basis of a broader interpretation. At the same time the amendment of the EC Treaty had expanded the areas of activity of the Community and a number of the areas where Article 235 had previously been referred to by the Court of Justice as the basis of competence were now expressly mentioned in the Treaty. Accordingly, the application of Article 235 in accordance with the interpretation outlined above did not constitute a violation of the requirement for specified powers contained in Article 20 of the Constitution.

(4) Pursuant to Article 164 of the Treaty, the European Court of Justice ensured that, in the interpretation and application of the Treaty, the law was observed. Article 173 of the Treaty empowered the Court of Justice to review the legality of acts of the Community institutions. Article 177 of the Treaty gave the Court of Justice jurisdiction to give preliminary rulings concerning the interpretation of the Treaty and the validity and interpretation of acts of the institutions. Any question on the validity of measures adopted pursuant to Article 235 could therefore be brought before the Court of Justice, which would then ensure that the scope of the operation of the Community was observed. The fact that jurisdiction to give rulings on questions concerning the scope of the powers vested in the institutions of the Community was transferred to the European Court of Justice, and that in giving its rulings the Court could take account of factors other than the wording of the provisions at issue, could not of itself be regarded as incompatible with Article 20 of the Constitution.

(5) The applicants argued that the jurisdiction of the European Court of Justice under the EC Treaty, when account was taken of the principle of the supremacy of EC law, implied that Danish courts were prevented from enforcing limits to the transfer of sovereignty contrary to the requirements of Article 20(1) of the Constitution. It was certainly true that, in adopting the Act of Accession to the EC Treaty, it had been recognized that the power to test the validity and legality of EC measures was vested exclusively in the European Court of Justice under the provisions of the Treaty. However, the requirement for specification contained in Article 20(1) of the Constitution, when taken in the light of the power of Danish courts to review the constitutionality of acts, meant that national courts could not be deprived of their right to examine whether a particular EC measure exceeded the limits for the transfer of sovereignty brought about by the Act of Accession. Consequently the Danish courts would be bound to rule that an EC measure was inapplicable in Denmark if the extraordinary situation should arise that it could be established that the measure, even if it had been upheld by the European Court of Justice, was based on an application of the Treaty which lay beyond the transfer of sovereignty brought about by the Act of Accession. A similar interpretation would apply with regard to rules of Community law and legal principles developed in the practice of the European Court of Justice. Accordingly, neither the additional powers delegated to the Council pursuant to Article 235 of the EC Treaty, nor the law-making activities of the Court of Justice, could be regarded as incompatible with the requirement for specified powers contained in Article 20(1) of the Constitution.

(6) According to Article 20 of the Constitution, powers could only be delegated to international bodies established by mutual agreement with other States for the promotion of international rules of cooperation. It was to be assumed that powers could not be transferred to such an extent that Denmark could

no longer be considered an independent State. Whilst the determination of the limits of such a transfer had to rely almost exclusively on considerations of a political nature, it was clear that sovereignty had not been transferred to the Community by the Act of Accession to such an extent as to violate the above-mentioned assumption.

(7) So far as the constitutional assumption of a democratic system of government was concerned, any delegation of part of the legislative powers of the Danish Parliament to an international organization inevitably involved a certain encroachment on the Danish democratic system of government. This fact had clearly been taken into consideration in the drafting of the rigorous requirements for the adoption of laws under Article 20(2) of the Constitution. So far as the EC Treaty was concerned, legislative powers had been transferred primarily to the Council, in which the Government could exercise its influence and was answerable to Parliament. It was reasonable to assume that Parliament had the task of considering whether participation by the Government in further EC integration should be conditional upon any additional democratic control.

The text of the judgment of the Eastern Provincial Court of 27 June 1997 commences on p. 181. The text of the judgment of the Supreme Court of 6 April 1998 commences on p. 185. The following is the text of the judgment of the Supreme Court of 12 August 1996:

Course of the Proceedings

The judgment under appeal was rendered by the Eastern Provincial Court of Denmark.

Nine [Supreme Court] judges have participated in these proceedings: Pontoppidan, Hornslet, Marie-Louise Andreasen, Melchior, Poul Sørensen, Blok, Walsøe, Lorenzen and Jensen.

The Appellants [Hanne Norup Carlsen and nine others] claim that the case should be remitted to the Eastern Provincial Court to be heard on its merits.

The interveners [the Association "Constitution Committee 93" and others] have made statements in support of the claim of the Appellants.

The Respondent claims that the appeal should be dismissed . . .

For the purpose of the proceedings before the Supreme Court statements have been made by Nicolas Fischer, Yvonne Petersen and Arne Würgler and further information has been provided.

In support of his submissions to the Provincial Court, the Respondent stated that, in a case brought before the Danish courts, it is possible for a citizen who is specifically and currently affected by a legislative act emanating from the institutions of the European Union to have examined, not only the question of whether the legislative act is in conflict with the Danish Constitution or reflects an exercise of powers not vested in the institutions concerned, but also the general question of whether the Act of Accession of 28 April 1993 was adopted in accordance with the Constitution.

The Appellants additionally claim that dismissal of the case [as inadmissible] would be contrary to their right to have the case tried by the courts pursuant to Article 6(1) of the European Convention on Human Rights. The Respondent disputes whether this provision is applicable to an action such as the present one.

Grounds of the Judgment

In support of their claims the Appellants contend that the transfer of sovereign powers which took place with Denmark's accession to the Treaty on European Union (*cf.* Section 4(xii) of the Law on Denmark's Accession to the European Communities as amended by Law No 281 of 28 April 1993) could not be enacted pursuant to Article 20 of the Constitution, but only following a constitutional amendment pursuant to Article 88 of the Constitution. In the Appellants' opinion the transfer of sovereignty was not "to such an extent as shall be provided by statute" as required by Article 20(1) of the Constitution.

Regarding the question whether the Appellants should be entitled to have this question examined by the courts, importance must be attached to the fact that accession to the Treaty on European Union implies a transfer of legislative powers in a number of general and important aspects of life, so that it is of vital importance to the Danish population in general. Thus, this case differs from the usual cases in which it is examined whether a law is consistent with the Constitution. Because of the general and vital importance of the Act of Accession, the Appellants have a considerable interest in having their claims examined. The Supreme Court finds that, in these circumstances, there is not a sufficient basis (contrary to the decision in the earlier Supreme Court judgment in *Ugeskrift for Retsvaesen*, 1973, p. 694)[6] for making the right to adjudication by the courts dependent upon the Appellants being able to establish that, pursuant to the Treaty on European Union, legislative acts have been issued which concretely and presently affect their situation. Moreover, the Court finds it important that a requirement to this effect would not be suited to ensuring greater clarification of the question as to the limits to the application of Article 20 of the Constitution, raised by the Appellants.

The Supreme Court therefore finds that the Appellants have the necessary legal interest in having their claims examined. There is not a sufficient basis for establishing that the claims are inadmissible because of their wording or for other reasons.

[6 See Volume 1, Note at p. 275.]

The Appellants' claim, that the case be remitted to the Provincial Court for a hearing on its merits, is therefore allowed.

The Supreme Court therefore rules that the judgment of the Provincial Court [of 30 June 1994] shall be quashed and the case remitted to the Provincial Court for a hearing on its merits . . .

[Report: Unofficial translation prepared by the Danish Ministry of Foreign Affairs]

[The following is the text of the judgment of the Eastern Provincial Court of 27 June 1997:]

Course of the Proceedings

The Danish Supreme Court, by a judgment of 12 August 1996, has remitted the case to the Eastern Provincial Court to be heard on its merits. The plaintiffs, Hanne Norup Carlsen, Ingeborg Fangel, Nicolas Fischer, Jørgen Erik Hansen, Marianne Henriksen, Ole Donbæk Jensen, Yvonne Petersen, Iver Reedtz-Thott, Lars Ringholm and Arne Würgler, have submitted the following final claims:

The Defendant, Prime Minister Poul Nyrup Rasmussen, shall be ordered to acknowledge:

(1) that the transfer of [certain] powers of the Danish authorities, consequent upon Sections 2 and 4 of Danish Law No 447 of 11 October 1972 on Denmark's Accession to the European Communities, together with the overall effect of this Law following the entry into force of Law No 281 of 28 April 1993, is in contravention of the Danish Constitutional Act of 5 June 1953;
(2) that the Defendant is not entitled to ratify the Treaty on European Union of 7 February 1992 on behalf of Denmark; and
(3) that the obligations which result from the Treaty on European Union and from the legislative acts enacted on the basis of the Treaty are not binding on the Plaintiffs.

The Defendant has moved for dismissal of the Plaintiffs' claims.

Grounds of the Judgment

Following the Supreme Court judgment of 12 August 1996, a decision is required in the case before this Court only on whether, as a result of Denmark's accession to the European Communities and European Union, powers have been transferred to the European Community to a wider extent than provided for by Article 20 of the Danish Constitution. In the present case no review can be made of whether individual EC legal acts are in compliance with the Constitution. However, this does not exclude EC legal acts and other decisions from forming part of the basis for the adjudication as to whether, upon the accession of Denmark to the two treaties, powers have been transferred in contravention of Article 20 of the Constitution.

It is a fundamental principle of constitutional law that legislative, executive and judicial powers are to be exercised by Danish authorities. Any transfer of these powers to an international organization with supranational authority generally requires an amendment of the Constitution, unless such transfer of powers is expressly authorized by the Constitution.

Article 20 of the Constitution was introduced by the Constitutional Act of the Kingdom of Denmark of 5 June 1953, to enable Denmark to join international organizations with supranational authority without an amendment of the Constitution being necessary.

In its comments to [the draft of] Article 20, the Constitutional Commission referred to developments in international cooperation, including the supranational Authority for Coal and Steel (the "Schumann Plan"), and stated:

> The "powers of the Realm" [which may be transferred to international organizations] shall mean the legislative as well as the executive and judicial powers. It will hardly be possible to give a narrower definition as it cannot with certainty be predicted what forms international cooperation will assume in the future. However, this Article establishes that sovereignty may only be transferred to such an extent as shall be provided by statute and only to organizations established by mutual agreement with other States for the promotion of international rules of law and cooperation. The more rigorous requirements regarding the adoption of bills of this kind present a comprehensive guarantee.

Paragraph 5 of the Report of the Constitutional Commission, on the transfer of constitutional powers to international organizations (point 52), mentions, *inter alia*, restrictions upon national sovereignty as a way of describing those cases where the international body concerned acts with direct and legally binding effect on the citizens of individual States.

Consequently, Article 20 of the Constitution covers only the delegation of powers by which supranational authorities are given authority to issue legal acts or make decisions which, as part of Danish law, have direct and legally binding effect on Danish citizens, or to exercise other powers which are vested by the Constitution with the authorities of the Realm, for example the authority to conclude treaties with other States. To the extent that an international body makes decisions which are aimed at the Danish State only as an obligation at the level of international law, there is no transfer of powers requiring compliance with Article 20 of the Constitution.

The report of the European Affairs Committee of the Parliament *(Folketing)* of 25 August 1972 concerning the Accession Bill of 1972 states:

The powers assigned to the EC institutions are laid down in the Treaties referred to in Section 4 of the Bill, which have been included as Schedules 1 and 2 to the Bill. Thereby, the requirement of the Constitution that only clearly defined powers may be delegated has been complied with. Pursuant to Article 235 of the EEC Treaty, the Council may in certain cases, acting unanimously, take the appropriate measures "if action by the Community should prove necessary to attain, in the course of the operation of the common market, one of the objectives of the Community".

The Committee has asked questions to the Ministers for Foreign Affairs and Finance on the interpretation of the limitations applying to the use of this provision. On the basis of the reply of the Minister for Foreign Affairs and Finance, reproduced in Appendix 2, the majority finds that the requirements of the Constitution have also been complied with as regards this provision.

In connection with the negotiations which led to the adoption of the Act of 1993 on the incorporation of the Treaty on European Union, a memorandum prepared by the Danish Ministry of Justice on, *inter alia*, the question of the delegation of powers pursuant to Article 20 of the Constitution, was submitted to the European Affairs Committee.

Under Section 2 of the Act of Accession, EC institutions may exercise powers which are vested under the Constitution in the authorities of the Realm, to the extent laid down in the Treaties and instruments mentioned in Section 4 of the Act.

In the case before this Court, the matter under consideration is the delegation of powers consequent upon accession to the [amended] EC Treaty and the Treaty on European Union, Titles I, II and VII (the so-called first pillar).

The activities of the European Community are based on a principle of legality since, pursuant to Articles 3b and 4 of the EC Treaty and Article E of the Treaty on European Union, its institutions, including the Council, the Commission and the Court of Justice, shall act within the limits of the powers conferred upon them by the Treaties. Under Article 189 of the EC Treaty, a regulation is directly applicable in all Member States whereas a directive is addressed to the Member States. However, in its practice the European Court of Justice has established that, subject to certain conditions being fulfilled, the provisions of directives may create directly enforceable rights for individual citizens. A decision is binding upon those to whom it is addressed.

Articles 2 and 3 of the EC Treaty contain a general description of the objectives and activities of the Community (*cf.* also Article B of the Treaty on European Union). More detailed rules on the so-called policies of the Community can be found in Part Three of the EC Treaty which contains, in a number of chapters, detailed provisions on the activities of the Community and the tasks and powers of the institutions in various fields.

Under Article 235, if the Treaty has not provided the necessary powers, the Council may, acting unanimously, take the appropriate measures if this should prove necessary to attain, in the course of the operation of the common market, one of the objectives of the Community.

Under Article 173, the European Court of Justice may review, *inter alia*, the observance of the Treaty by the Council and the Commission, including whether the conditions for recourse to Article 235 have been met.

In connection with the decision as to whether Denmark's accession to the [revised] European Community and the European Union ("first pillar") is constitutional, it should be noted firstly that EC Directives are only covered by Article 20 of the Constitution to the extent that they contain provisions which directly create rights for individual citizens. The jurisdiction of the European Court of Justice under Article 177 to give preliminary rulings, including the interpretation of EC law applicable in Denmark, cannot be considered to be covered by Article 20 of the Constitution since, in this case, no power is exercised which was exercised by the Danish authorities prior to accession.

The principle contained in Article 20 of the Constitution, that only clearly defined powers may be transferred, according to its wording and on the basis of statements contained in the legislative material regarding the purpose of the provision, must be understood to mean that only powers in specified fields may be transferred together with an indication of the content of those powers. As mentioned above, the original Treaty establishing the European Economic Community, as well as the Treaty on European Union, are based on a principle of legality which excludes the institutions from determining their own powers. Furthermore, the Treaties contain rules on the exercise of transferred powers. The fact that provisions in the Treaty may give rise to doubt, concerning the interpretation of the extent of the powers transferred, does not imply a departure from the principle of legality which, as mentioned above, is binding on the Court of Justice in its interpretation of EC law, including its observance of fundamental rights.

In connection with both accession to the EEC in 1972 and accession to the European Union in 1993, the Government gave the *Folketing* detailed information concerning their relationship to Article 20 of the Constitution and the extent of the obligations which would arise from accession to the Treaties, including developments in the European Community. In adopting the Act of Accession, the basis of the decision of the *Folketing* majority must be assumed to have been that accession to the Treaties would not go further than authorized by Article 20 of the Constitution.

On the basis of the above considerations, it must be concluded that the two Acts of Accession transferred only clearly defined powers in accordance with Article 20 of the Constitution.

Neither from Article 20 of the Constitution, nor from its legislative history, can any requirement be inferred that powers can only be transferred to international organizations to a quantitatively limited extent. Furthermore, it does not appear that, when Denmark acceded to the Treaties, powers were transferred to the European Community to an extent which goes beyond what must be assumed to have been foreseen at the time of the adoption of Article 20 of the Constitution.

Taking into account the structure of the EC institutions, including the composition of the Council, and in view of the influence exercised, according to information given by the Danish Parliament's European Affairs Committee on all important matters relating to Denmark's relations to the EC, it is not found that such a limitation of Danish democracy has taken place that the Acts of Accession can be set aside as being invalid on constitutional grounds.

Accordingly, the plaintiffs' claims are dismissed . . .

The Court therefore rules in favour of Prime Minister Poul Nyrup Rasmussen.

Neither party shall pay legal costs to any of the other parties or to the Treasury.

[Report: Unofficial translation prepared by the Danish Ministry of Foreign Affairs]

[The following is the text of the judgment of the Supreme Court of 6 April 1998:]

Course of the Proceedings

In the lower instance, judgment was delivered by the Third Chamber of the Eastern Division of the Danish High Court on 27 June 1997.

Eleven Supreme Court Judges have participated in the proceedings: Hornslet, Hermann, Marie-Louise Andreasen, Wendler Pedersen, Poul Sørensen, Melchior, Blok, Jørgen Nørgaard, Lorenzen, Borge Dahl and Lene Pagter Kristensen.

The Appellants, Hanne Norup Carlsen and [nine] others, claim that the Respondent, Prime Minister Poul Nyrup Rasmussen, should be ordered to recognize that the transfer of the powers of the Danish authorities, which is a consequence of Sections 2 and 4 of Danish Law No 447 of 11 October 1972 on the Accession of Denmark to the European Communities together with the overall effect of this Law following the entry into force of Law No 281 of 28 April 1993, is in contravention of the Danish Constitutional Act of 5 June 1953. The Appellants have withdrawn claims 2 and 3 made before the Provincial Court.[7]

[[7] See p. 181.]

The Prime Minister asks for the dismissal of the Appellants' claim.

The interveners Professor Ole Krarup, Doctor of Laws, and the Association "Constitution Committee 93" acting on behalf of Allan Aabech and others, have made statements in support of the Appellants' claim.

For the purpose of the proceedings before the Supreme Court, additional information has been provided, consequent upon an Order of the Court of 3 November 1997, which required the Respondent to produce a substantial number of documents. Furthermore, in accordance with the Court's Order of 13 January 1998, evidence has been given by the Minister for Foreign Affairs, Mr Niels Helveg Petersen, former Minister Mr Ivar Norgaad and former Ambassador and Secretary-General Mr Niels Ersboll.

. . .

Grounds of the Judgment

9.1. What the Supreme Court is required to consider in this case is whether the implementation in Denmark of the Treaty establishing the European Community ("EC Treaty") as amended by the Treaty on European Union ("EU Treaty") was lawfully enacted pursuant to Article 20 of the Danish Constitution or whether such implementation required an amendment to the Constitution pursuant to Article 88 of the Constitution.

Primarily, the Appellants have pleaded that Article 20(1) of the Danish Constitution grants authority for the transfer of sovereignty only "to such extent as shall be provided by statute", and that this condition has not been complied with. In this connection they have referred, in particular, to the powers vested in the Council under Article 235 of the EC Treaty, and to the law-making activities of the European Court of Justice. Secondly, the Appellants have pleaded that the delegation of sovereignty is on such a scale and of such a nature that it is inconsistent with the Constitution's premise of a democratic form of government.

The Appellants' representations concern only the EC Treaty and therefore involve neither the second pillar of the EU Treaty on the common foreign and security policy, nor the third pillar concerning cooperation in the fields of justice and home affairs. The representations concerning the EC Treaty have no bearing on the third stage of Economic and Monetary Union, since Denmark is not participating therein, *cf.* Sections 4 and 12(a) of the Act of Accession.

9.2. Article 20 of the Danish Constitution provides as follows:

(1) Powers vested in the authorities of the Realm under this Constitutional Act may, to such extent as shall be provided by statute, be delegated to international

bodies established by mutual agreement with other States for the promotion of international rules of law and cooperation.

(2) For the enactment of a Law dealing with the above matter, a majority of five-sixths of the members of the *Folketing* (Parliament) shall be required. If this majority is not obtained, but the majority required for the passing of an ordinary Law is obtained, and if the Government maintains its support for the measure, it shall be submitted to the electorate for approval or rejection in accordance with the rules for a referendum laid down in Article 42 of the Constitution.

Article 20 was included in the 1953 Constitutional Act to enable Denmark, without amending the Constitution in accordance with Article 88, to participate in international cooperation, implying that the exercise of legislative, administrative or judicial authority could be entrusted to an international organization with direct effect in this Kingdom. Since it was impossible to predict with any degree of certainty what forms such international cooperation might assume in the future, no detailed specification was given as to what powers this provision covers. Accordingly, the aim was to enable transfer of sovereignty to be made within wide limits. However, it was emphasized in the provision itself that the delegation of powers can occur only "to such extent as shall be provided by statute". Furthermore, it was considered important that the more stringent requirements for the adoption of laws under the provision [by comparison with the requirements for ordinary laws] offer a far-reaching safeguard.

The application of the special procedure laid down by Article 20 of the Constitution is required to the extent that an international organization is entrusted with the exercise of legislative, administrative or judicial authority with direct effect in Denmark, or the exercise of other powers which, according to the Constitution, are vested in the authorities of the Realm, including the power to enter into treaties with other States.

Article 20 does not permit an international organization to be entrusted with the promulgation of legal acts or the making of decisions which are contrary to provisions in the Constitution, including its rights and freedoms. Indeed, the authorities of the Realm themselves have no power to enact such measures.

The term "to such extent as shall be provided by statute" must be interpreted to the effect that a positive delimitation must be made of the powers delegated, *partly* as regards the fields of responsibility and *partly* as regards the nature of the powers. The delimitation must enable an assessment to be made of the extent of the delegation of sovereignty. The fields of responsibility may be described in broad categories, and there is no requirement for the extent of the delegation of sovereignty to be stated so precisely that there is no room left for discretion or interpretation. The powers delegated may be indicated by means of a reference to a treaty.

The requirement for specification in Article 20(1) precludes the possibility that it can be left to the international organization itself to specify its powers. [On the other hand] the term "to such extent as shall be provided by statute" cannot be interpreted to the effect that powers which are vested in the authorities of the Realm can be entrusted to an international organization only to a limited or minor extent.

9.3. The Act of Accession delegates powers to the European Community to the extent laid down in the EC Treaty. The compatibility of the Act of Accession with Article 20 of the Constitution therefore presupposes that the Treaty meets the requirement that powers have been delegated only "to such extent as shall be provided by statute".

The EC Treaty is based on a principle of conferred powers (*cf.* Article 3b(1) and Article 4(1) of the Treaty). The institutions of the Community may act only within those limits upon the activities of the Community as appear from the provisions of the Treaty, and within those limits the institutions may only exercise such powers as have been conferred upon them by or pursuant to the Treaty.

The principle of conferred powers thus implies a restriction on the powers of the institutions which is in keeping with the demand for specification contained in Article 20 of the Constitution. The Supreme Court finds that the specific rules of competence contained in the EC Treaty meet this requirement.

9.4. However, as stated above, the Appellants specifically claim that the general grant of competence in Article 235 of the EC Treaty enables the incorporation of new areas of responsibility under the powers of the European Community to an extent which implies that the demand for specification in Article 20 of the Danish Constitution has not been observed. They have stated that this appears from the way in which Article 235 has been applied prior to the implementation of the EU Treaty. In this connection they have referred to the material produced in accordance with the order made by the Supreme Court of 3 November 1997. Furthermore, they have stated that the amendments to the EC Treaty which were made by the EU Treaty imply an expansion of the scope of Article 235.

In this connection it should be noted that, as already mentioned, the case concerns the question whether the adoption of the Act on Denmark's Accession to the EC Treaty, with the content given to that Treaty by the EU Treaty, was constitutional. The issue is therefore not whether any transgression of the limits to the powers conferred may have taken place prior to the amendment of the Treaty, as a result of certain legislative acts adopted pursuant to Article 235.

By the amendment of the EC Treaty the areas of activity stated in Article 3 have been expanded and new articles have been added in Part Three of the Treaty on "Community Policies". A number of the areas where Article 235 was previously referred to as the basis of competence for legislative measures are now expressly mentioned in the Treaty. Furthermore, the "second and third pillars" of the EU Treaty also comprise rules on international cooperation in a number of other fields. The field of application of Article 235 must be evaluated against this background.

The wording of Article 235 of the EC Treaty is as follows:

> If action by the Community should prove necessary to attain, in the course of the operation of the common market, one of the objectives of the Community and this Treaty has not provided the necessary powers, the Council shall, acting unanimously on a proposal from the Commission and after consulting the European Parliament, take the appropriate measures.

It appears from the wording of Article 235 that the fact that action by the Community is considered necessary in order to attain one of the objectives of the Community does not in itself constitute a sufficient ground for applying the provision. It is a further condition that the intended action is "in the course of the operation of the common market". This provision, when compared with Article 2 under which the tasks of the Community shall be promoted "by establishing a common market and an economic and monetary union and by implementing the common policies or activities referred to in Articles 3 and 3a", is to be understood as requiring that the intended action shall lie within the scope of the operation of the common market as it appears from the other provisions of the Treaty, including, in particular, Part Three on the policies of the Community and the lists contained in Articles 3 and 3a of the individual activities or areas of operation. This interpretation is in accordance with the Government's Memorandum of 21 January 1997 to the Parliament's European Committee and is confirmed by Opinion 2/94 of 28 March 1996 of the European Court of Justice (plenary session) ([1996] ECR I-1759)[8] which states:

> 29. Article 235 is designed to fill the gap where no specific provisions of the Treaty confer on the Community institutions express or implied powers to act, if such powers appear none the less to be necessary to enable the Community to carry out its functions with a view to attaining one of the objectives laid down by the Treaty.
>
> 30. That provision, being an integral part of an institutional system based on the principle of conferred powers, cannot serve as a basis for widening the scope of Community powers beyond the general framework created by the provisions of the Treaty as a whole and, in particular, by those that define the activities and tasks of the Community. On any view, Article 235 cannot be used as a basis for the adoption of provisions whose effect would, in substance, be to amend the Treaty without following the procedure which it provides for that purpose.

This interpretation of Article 235 must be taken as the basis even though, prior to the amendment of the Treaty, this provision may have been applied on the basis of a wider interpretation.

[[8] See p. 45.]

A legislative act which goes no further than to confer powers to enact legislative measures or decide upon other measures, in accordance with the interpretation of Article 235 given above, does not constitute a violation of the requirement for specification contained in Article 20 of the Constitution.

Any measure adopted pursuant to Article 235 must be by unanimous vote. Therefore the Government may prevent the provision from being applied to the adoption of a measure which is beyond the stated scope of Denmark's delegation of powers to the European Community. The Government cannot participate in the adoption of laws which fall outside this scope and therefore presuppose an additional transfer of sovereignty. On the basis of the objective which Article 235 is intended to pursue, it is unavoidable that the precise delimitation of the scope of the application of that provision may give rise to doubts. Consequently it must be considered that the Act of Accession grants the Government a not insignificant margin of discretion.

9.5. Pursuant to Article 164 of the Treaty, the European Court of Justice shall ensure that in the interpretation and application of the Treaty the law is observed and, under Article 173 of the Treaty, the Court of Justice shall review the legality of acts of the institutions of the Community. Under Article 177 the Court of Justice shall have jurisdiction to give preliminary rulings concerning the interpretation of the Treaty and the validity and interpretation of acts of the institutions of the Community.

Any question on the validity of a legal act or other measure adopted pursuant to Article 235 may therefore be brought before the European Court of Justice, which shall then ensure that the scope of the operation of the Community is observed.

The fact that the detailed determination of the powers vested in the institutions of the Community may give rise to doubt, and that jurisdiction to give rulings concerning the interpretation of such questions is transferred to the European Court of Justice, cannot of itself be regarded as incompatible with the requirement for specification contained in Article 20 of the Constitution.

The fact that the European Court of Justice, in its interpretation of the Treaty, also attaches importance to factors of interpretation other than the wording of the provisions, including the objectives of the Treaty, is not in violation of the assumptions on which the Act of Accession was based, nor is it of itself incompatible with the requirement for specification in Article 20(1) of the Constitution. The same applies to the law-making activities of the European Court of Justice within the scope of the Treaty.

9.6. The Appellants have argued that the jurisdiction of the European Court of Justice under the Treaty, when account is taken of the principle of the supremacy of EC law, implies that Danish courts of law are prevented from enforcing limits for the transfer of sovereignty which has taken place under the Act of Accession and that this must be taken into consideration in determining whether the requirement for specification in Article 20(1) of the Constitution has been observed.

By adopting the Act of Accession it has been recognized that the power to test the validity and legality of EC legal acts is vested in the European Court of Justice. This implies that Danish courts of law cannot hold that an EC act is inapplicable in Denmark without the question of its compatibility with the Treaty having been examined by the European Court of Justice, and that when Danish courts base their decisions on such questions on judgments delivered by the Court of Justice, they act properly within the limits of the transfer of sovereignty.

However, the Supreme Court finds that it follows from the requirement for specification contained in Article 20(1) of the Constitution, taken against the Danish courts' power to review the constitutionality of acts, that the national courts cannot be deprived of their right to examine the question of whether a particular EC legal act exceeds the limits for the transfer of sovereignty brought about by the Act of Accession. Consequently Danish courts must rule that an EC act is inapplicable in Denmark if the extraordinary situation should arise that it can be established with the requisite certainty that an EC act which has been upheld by the European Court of Justice is based on an application of the Treaty which lies beyond the transfer of sovereignty brought about by the Act of Accession. A similar interpretation would apply with regard to rules of Community law and legal principles developed in the practice of the European Court of Justice.

9.7. On the basis of the above considerations, the Supreme Court finds that neither the additional powers delegated to the Council pursuant to Article 235 of the EC Treaty, nor the law-making activities of the Court of Justice, can be regarded as incompatible with the requirement for specification contained in Article 20(1) of the Constitution.

9.8. Under Article 20 of the Constitution any delegation of powers can be made only to "international bodies" established by "mutual agreement" with "other States" for the promotion of "international rules of law and cooperation". It must be regarded as assumed in the Constitution that powers could not be transferred to such an extent that Denmark could no longer be considered an independent State. The determination of the limits of such transfer must rely almost exclusively on considerations of a political nature. The Supreme Court finds beyond any doubt that, by the Act of Accession, sovereignty has not been transferred to the Community to such an extent as to violate the above-mentioned assumption in the Constitution.

9.9. With regard to the question whether the transfer of sovereignty brought about by the Act of Accession is of such a nature as to be in violation of the constitutional assumption of a democratic system of government, it must be noted that any delegation of part of the Parliament's legislative powers to an international organization will inevitably involve a certain encroachment on the Danish democratic system of government. This fact has been taken into consideration in the drafting of the rigorous requirements for the adoption of laws under Article 20(2). In so far as the EC Treaty is concerned, legislative powers have been transferred primarily to the Council, in which the Danish Government can exercise its influence and is answerable to the Parliament. It is reasonable to assume that the Parliament has the task of considering whether participation by the Government in [further] EC integration should be conditional upon any additional democratic control. The Supreme Court does not find any basis in this respect for holding the Act of Accession unconstitutional.

9.10. In view of the above considerations and the fact that the Appellants have made no further submissions which might lead to a different outcome, the Supreme Court hereby affirms the judgment of the Eastern Provincial Court and dismisses the appeal.

Accordingly, the Court rules:

The judgment of the Eastern Provincial Court is affirmed;

Neither of the parties shall pay the costs of the proceedings before the Supreme Court to any other party or to the Treasury.

[Report: Unofficial English translation prepared by the Danish Foreign Office; 1998 *UfR* p. 800 (in Danish)]

Supremacy—Conflict between Community law and national law — Consequences for contrary national law — Duty of national courts not to apply conflicting national provisions— The law of Finland

VAT DEDUCTION RIGHTS CASE

Finland, Supreme Administrative Court (Taxation Chamber).

31 *December* 1996

The text of this judgment of the Supreme Administrative Court is not reproduced here because it is largely concerned with substantive issues of VAT law. It was, however, the first case where a Finnish court set aside provisions of national legislation adopted at the level of an Act of Parliament and gave precedence to provisions of Community law. The Supreme Administrative Court considered that the concept of an economic activity within the meaning of Article 4(1) of the Sixth VAT Directive (77.388/EEC, OJ 1977 L 145/1), as interpreted by the Court of Justice of the European Community in the *Rompelman*[1] and *INZO*[2] judgments, led to wider deduction rights than the corresponding definition in the Finnish VAT Act. The Court observed that "It follows again from the principles expressed in the case-law of the Court of Justice that Article 4 of the Directive must be applied for the benefit of the private party if the national legislation does not lead to the tax treatment required by the Directive." Consequently, the Finnish authorities had to give precedence to the provisions of the Directive over the provision of the Finnish Act. (Report: *KHO* 1996 B 577 (in Finnish); English summary extracted with the permission of the author from Jaaskinen, The Application of Community Law in Finland, 1995-1998, CML Rev 1999, p. 409 at p. 416.)

NOTE.—It is remarkable that the Supreme Administrative Court did not raise any questions of principle which might have affected the unreserved precedence given to Community law in the above judgment. The primacy and direct effect of Community law have, in practice, been clearly recognized by the Supreme Administrative Court, both explicitly and implicitly, in a series of decisions. In a judgment of the Court of 20 March 1996 in *Chiquita Finland*, the direct applicability of Community regulations was expressly confirmed on the basis of Article 189 of the EC Treaty. A banana importer had challenged the legality of a Commission Regulation concerning import quotas but the Court held that it had no competence to declare the Regulation invalid and could proceed on the basis of its presumed validity in the absence of serious reasons for suspecting its invalidity (Jaaskinen, *op. cit.*, p. 420). In a subsequent judgment of 8 July 1997 in *Udenmann Liitto*, the Supreme Administrative Court gave direct effect to EC Council Directives on Conservation and quashed a decision of the Ministry of the Environment ratifying a regional plan concerning territory covered by the Directives (Jaaskinen, *op. cit.*, p. 421).

[1] Case 268/83, [1985] ECR 655.

[2] Case C-110/94, [1996] ECR I-857.

The constitutional procedure resorted to in Finland for accession to the constitutive treaties of the European Community and the European Union, as well as the Act of Accession in 1994, involved the adoption of so-called "Exception Acts" by a special two-thirds parliamentary majority, creating limited derogations from the Constitution without the need to provide specifically for the transfer of powers to EU organs. Such Exception Acts transform treaties into domestic law and automatically take precedence in Finland over all other domestic legislative provisions including the Constitution itself. The same procedure was followed for the ratification of the Amsterdam Treaty in June 1998 (Jaaskinen, *op. cit.*, pp. 408-13). The procedure is now contained in Article 73 of the new Constitution of Finland of 11 June 1999.

Supremacy — Conflict between Community law and subsequent national law — Consequences for contrary national law—Duty of national courts not to apply conflicting national provisions—Finding of European Court of Justice that national provisions violating Article 30 of EC Treaty—Whether national provisions automatically inapplicable—Rules restricting advertising of imported alcoholic products

Enforcement in national courts—Remedies—Claim against Member State — Breach of Community law for which Member State responsible — Restriction of advertising on alcoholic products incompatible with Community law — Whether individuals entitled to claim compensation from national authorities for loss suffered

Institutions — Court of Justice — Effect of decisions in Member States—Declaration that Member State in default of obligations under EC Treaty—Illegality of measures taken pursuant to defaulting national legislation — The law of France

UNITED DISTILLERS FRANCE *v.* AGENT JUDICIAIRE DU TRÉSOR PUBLIC

France, Court of Cassation (Commercial Chamber). 21 *February* 1995

(Bézard, *President*; Huglo, *Rapporteur*; Raynaud, *Advocate-General*)

SUMMARY: *The facts*:—United Distillers and several other whisky manufacturers brought a claim for damages against the French State for losses suffered as a result of a French ministerial circular instructing the authorities to bring criminal proceedings against those advertising alcoholic drinks, including imported ones. The companies argued that the French legislation relied upon by the Minister infringed the prohibition on measures with equivalent effect to quantitative restrictions enshrined in Article 30 of the EC Treaty, as the Court of Justice had expressly held in two judgments in 1980. The *Tribunal de grande instance* and the Court of Appeal of Paris both rejected the claim. The companies appealed to the Court of Cassation.

Held:—The appeal was allowed and the case was remitted to the Court of Appeal of Douai.

(1) According to the settled case-law of the Court of Justice, once a national provision had been found to be incompatible with Community law, the national authorities were absolutely precluded from applying it. The adoption of the ministerial circular at issue therefore constituted wilful misconduct.

(2) So far as State liability was concerned, the Court of Appeal had been wrong to deny any possibility of the companies having suffered loss, without first

examining whether the fact that the companies had refrained from advertising for fear of criminal prosecution did not amount to a harmful distortion of competition.

The following is the text of the judgment of the Court:

According to the judgment under appeal, United Distillers France, Johnny Walker and Sons Limited and Tanqueray Gordon and Company Limited ("the companies") brought a claim for damages against the French State for losses suffered as a result of a circular of 10 October 1980 issued by the Ministry of Justice, which required the *Ministère public* to institute criminal proceedings against any advertising of imported [alcoholic] products which violated Articles L.17 and L.18 of the Code on Alcohol Sales, in the version currently in force. The companies relied on the judgments of the Court of Justice of the European Community of 27 February 1980 (*Commission* v. *France*) and 10 July 1980 (*Commission* v. *France*) which held those provisions to be contrary to Article 30 of the Treaty establishing the European Community.

. . .

On the fifth part of the single ground of appeal

The Court has considered Article L.781-1 of the Code on the Organization of the Judiciary in conjunction with Article 171 of the Treaty establishing the European Community.

[In rejecting the claim for damages] the Court of Appeal held that wilful misconduct (*faute lourde*) was not committed by the Minister in issuing a circular interpreting, however erroneously, the meaning and scope of a judgment of the Court of Justice of the European Community.

By ruling in this manner, the Court of Appeal erred in law and violated the above-mentioned provisions. [The Court of Appeal failed to take into account] the judgment of the Court of Justice of 27 February 1980, also referred to in the judgment of 10 July 1980, which held that the French Republic had failed to comply with its obligations under the Treaty by enacting the rules concerning the advertising of alcoholic drinks contained in Articles L.17 and L.18 of the Code on the Sale of Alcoholic Drinks. The Court of Justice stated that it "deems it unnecessary for the purposes of resolving this dispute to give a ruling on the question whether or not the alcoholic beverages concerned are wholly or partially similar products within the meaning of the first paragraph of Article 95, when it is impossible reasonably to deny that, without exception, they are in at least partial competition with the domestic products to which the application refers . . .". According to the settled jurisprudence of the Court of Justice of the European Community (in particular the judgment of 13 July 1972 in *Commission* v. *Italy*, Case 48/71), the effect of Community law implies, for the competent national authorities, that there is an absolute prohibition on the application of a national provision which has been recognized as incompatible with the Treaty. The circular at issue, by instructing the *Ministère public* to bring criminal proceedings against any advertising of imported alcoholic products violating Articles L.17 and L.18 of the Code on the Sale of Alcoholic Drinks, on the ground that it is the task of the criminal court to determine whether the imported product must be regarded as similar to or in competition with a national product, misinterpreted the scope of the judgments of the Court of Justice of 27 February and 10 July 1980 and its adoption therefore constituted wilful misconduct (*faute lourde*).

On the sixth part of the single ground of appeal

The Court has considered Article L.781-1 of the Code on the Organization of the Judiciary.

In reaching its conclusion, the Court of Appeal held that, in the absence of actual criminal prosecutions against the companies concerned, those companies could not claim to have suffered loss or prejudice as a result of the circular at issue.

[This Court considers, however,] that in reaching this conclusion, without first examining whether the renunciation by the companies of the right to advertise their drinks, by reason of the threat of criminal prosecution contained in the circular at issue, did not amount to a distortion of competition causing loss, the Court of Appeal failed to give a proper legal basis to its decision.

For these reasons, without it being necessary to rule on the other grounds of appeal . . . the Court:

Quashes and annuls, in all its provisions, the judgment rendered between the parties on 11 January 1993 by the Court of Appeal of Paris;

Returns the case and the parties to the state in which they were prior to that judgment;

Remits the case to the Court of Appeal of Douai.

[Report: *Bull. Civ.* 1996 IV, p. 50 (in French)]

Direct effect — Directives — Conditions for direct effect — Failure of Member State to implement provisions of directive by specified time—Whether directive may be relied upon by State against individuals or only by individuals against the State and its organs—Council Directive 89/105—Fixing of prices for medicines—Transparency—The law of France

SA LILLY FRANCE

France, Conseil d'Etat. 26 *June* 1995

(Faure, *Rapporteur*; Maugüé, *Commissaire du Gouvernement*)

SUMMARY: *The facts*:—In France the price of medicines was regulated and requests from drug manufacturers to increase prices had to be notified to certain Ministers for a decision. Such a request was implicitly granted if the Ministers did not oppose it within three months of notification. SA Lilly sought an increase in the price of Prozac, which the Ministers did not oppose within three months of notification. However, the competent Minister informed Lilly that he had decided to apply Article 3(1) of EC Council Directive 89/105 concerning the transparency of decisions relating to the fixing of prices for medicines. This provision allowed national authorities to extend the time limits for objection to price rises by a further sixty days if the number of applications was exceptionally high. Lilly applied to the *Conseil d'Etat* for the annulment of this decision for *ultra vires*.

The *Commissaire du Gouvernement* argued in her submissions that, since the provisions of the Directive had not been transposed into French law, they could not be invoked by the State against individuals. Whilst it was now accepted, according to the jurisprudence of the Court of Justice of the European Community, that provisions of non-implemented directives could be invoked by individuals against the State, once the period for the implementation had expired, this possibility was based on a doctrine of "estoppel" intended to prevent a State from taking advantage of its own failure to comply with Community law. Directives did not therefore enjoy a form of direct effect comparable to the position in relation to international treaty provisions which were "self-executing". Accordingly, as the case-law of the Court of Justice clearly indicated, non-implemented or incorrectly implemented directives were only binding in relation to the Member States to whom they were addressed and could never be invoked against individuals by the State. It was unacceptable for Member States to dispense with the requirement to enact measures of application in good time and instead directly to apply a directive.

Held:—The decision of the Minister was annulled.

The State authorities could not invoke the provisions of an EC Directive which they had not implemented into domestic law. Consequently, the Minister had acted unlawfully in invoking the provisions of the Directive in question to extend the time limit for examination of the application for the price increase requested in this case.

The text of the judgment of the *Conseil d'Etat* commences at p. 203. The following is the text of the relevant part of the opinion of *Commissaire du Gouvernement* Madame Maugüé:

The three applications lodged by Société Lilly France enable the *Conseil d'Etat* to clarify, in the context of a dispute concerning the raising of prices for medicines, the effect to be given to European Community Directives in domestic law. The question at issue is whether the authorities are entitled to rely on the provisions of a directive which they have not transposed into domestic law. This question does not normally arise because it is usually individuals rather than the authorities who invoke the provisions of non-transposed directives.

[1.-2. The *Conseil d'Etat* set out the nature and history of the provisions governing the system of pricing for medicines and the context in which the present dispute had arisen.]

3. This dispute therefore raises the preliminary question of whether the authorities are entitled to invoke directly the provisions of a directive which has not been transposed into domestic law or has been incorrectly transposed.

[3.1. The *Commissaire du Gouvernement* then analysed the origins of the jurisprudence of the Court of Justice of the European Community concerning the direct effect of directives and continued:]

Subsequently, however, the Court of Justice has significantly narrowed the effect of its jurisprudence and adopted a much more restrictive conception of the effect of directives. The first limitation was introduced by the Court of Justice in its judgment of 5 April 1979 in the *Ratti* case[1] in which it was held that an individual can only invoke the provisions of the directive against a Member State once the period for the implementation has expired and no implementing measures have been introduced or there has been incorrect implementation . . . A second, even more important, limitation was introduced by the *Marshall* judgment of 26 February 1986[2] where it was held that a directive could only be invoked against the defaulting State and never against a third party because the essence of directives was that they were addressed exclusively to States . . . The Court of Justice thereby denied any "horizontal" direct effect to directives, which could only be applied in relations between the State and another natural or legal person, to the exclusion of relations between individuals since directives were only endowed with "vertical" direct effect (the terminology used by the Advocates-General of the Court, for instance Advocate-General Slynn in the *Marshall* judgment). The default of the State could arise either where it failed to implement the directive in national law by the end of the period

[1 [1979] ECR 1629.] [2 Volume 1, p. 136.]

prescribed or where it failed to implement the directive properly (paragraph 46 of the *Marshall* judgment) . . .

The theory of vertical direct effect, which has subsequently been confirmed by the Court of Justice in a number of judgments (more recently in the *Faccini Dori* judgment of 14 July 1994),[3] significantly restricts the scope of the direct effect of directives, despite the criticism by some legal writers . . . and certain members of the Court of Justice itself (Advocates-General Van Gerven (2 August 1993, *Marshall* II ([1993] ECR I-4367, paragraph 12 of his opinion),[4] Jacobs (3 March 1994, *Van Eetveld*, [1994] ECR I-763, paragraphs 15 *et seq.* of his opinion) and in particular Lenz (14 July 1994, *Faccini Dori*, paragraphs 43 *et seq.* of his opinion)).[5] According to the Court of Justice, the direct effect of directives is merely and exclusively the penalty for default by the Member State concerned. As stressed by Galmot and Bonichot, in their excellent commentary on the jurisprudence of the Court (*La CJCE et la transposition des directives en droit interne, RFDA* 1988.1), the Court at the beginning of the 1980s even abandoned the formula of "direct effect" and instead subsequently referred to the fact that individuals "could invoke" the provisions of directives against defaulting States.

As Judge Pescatore has pointed out from 1980 onwards, the jurisprudence of the Court of Justice on this question is an expression of the principle generally referred to by the English legal term "estoppel", in its broad meaning (Martin, *L'estoppel en droit international public*), whereas Latin jurists refer to it by the maxim *venire contra factum proprium* or even *nemo auditur* (Pescatore, *L'effet des directives communautaires, Dalloz* 1980, chronique, 171). This principle is particularly clearly expressed in the *Marshall* judgment, both in the opinion of the Advocate-General, who underlines that a State cannot invoke its own failure to confer rights on individuals, and in the judgment itself, which points out that "it is necessary to prevent the State from taking advantage of its own failure to comply with Community law" (paragraph 49).[6]

3.2. The French administrative courts have also accepted that directives may be invoked by individuals, but on the basis of a different reasoning. [The *Commissaire du Gouvernement* then analysed a series of decisions of the *Conseil d'Etat*, including *Cohn-Bendit* of 22 December 1978,[7] *Compagnie Alitalia* of 3 February 1989[8] and *SA Rothmans International France* of 28 February 1992.[9] The *Commissaire du Gouvernement* continued:]

In sum, as foreseen by Boulouis in his illuminating commentary on the *Cohn-Bendit* decision of 1979 (*L'applicabilité directe des directives, à propos d'un arrêt Cohn-Bendit du Conseil d'Etat* in *Revue du Marché Commun*, 1979,

[3 See p. 19.] [4 Volume 1, p. 165.] [5 See p. 19 at p. 31.]
[6 Volume 1, p. 136 at p. 162.] [7 Volume 1, p. 317.]
[8 Volume 1, p. 334, note.] [9 Volume 1, p. 357.]

p. 104), the differences between the jurisprudence of the Court of Justice and that of the *Conseil d'Etat* are very limited so far as their practical effects are concerned (on this point see also Bonichot, *Convergences et divergences entre Conseil d'Etat et Cour de Justice des Communautés européennes*, *RFDA* 1989, p. 579 and Abraham, *Droit international, droit communautaire et droit français*, Paris, 1989). The differences amount in the end to a single case, which only rarely occurs, where there are no domestic provisions covering the objectives fixed by the directive. In such a case, the administrative courts cannot draw any legal consequences from the directive in proceedings for *ultra vires*. In every other case, however, the directive can be relied upon in substitution for national law before the administrative courts and an applicant can always rely on its provisions under domestic law provided the correct procedures are properly invoked. Individuals therefore enjoy before the French administrative courts a guarantee which is equivalent to the rights granted to them by Community law.

Nevertheless, it was on a different basis to that adopted by the Court of Justice that the *Conseil d'Etat* has accepted that an individual can invoke a Community directive before the administrative courts. Whilst directives are capable of producing effects in domestic law, the *Conseil d'Etat* considers that this is not because they directly create rights for individuals, in the same way as provisions of international treaties are recognized as having a direct effect. On the contrary, the *Conseil d'Etat* considers that Article 189 of the Treaty of Rome imposes upon the national authorities an obligation to adapt domestic legislation to directives and failure to comply with this obligation is sanctioned by giving direct effect to the directives as against the laws in question . . . In other words, since the national authorities are bound to adapt national legislation to comply with directives addressed to them, they cannot adopt conflicting regulatory provisions or allow such provisions to remain in force if that would be contrary to the terms of a directive, without violating the obligation to achieve the purpose of the directive (*obligation de résultat*) laid down in Article 189 of the Treaty of Rome.

. . . The reasoning of the *Conseil d'Etat* is, it is true, now very close to that of the Court of Justice since the latter's jurisprudence on the direct effect of directives has evolved in the more restrictive direction referred to above. For both the Court and the *Conseil d'Etat*, the direct effect of directives is a sanction for the defiance by the State, as the addressee of the directive, and directives do not enjoy a direct effect comparable to that of international provisions which are "self-executing". But the Court of Justice and the *Conseil d'Etat* do not draw the same effects from that defiance. Whereas the Court of Justice directly applies directives at the instance of individuals, the *Conseil d'Etat* penalizes the authorities for the non-execution of their obligation to implement the directive . . .

3.3. The question before the *Conseil d'Etat* today is presented in rather different terms. In fact, the directive in this case has not been invoked by the company against the decision being challenged, but by the authorities in support of that decision. The decision at issue is unlawful from the standpoint of the relevant national legislation, which does not provide for the possibility of the extension of the time limit, and the decision being challenged can only be regarded as lawful if the provisions of Article 3(1) of the Directive are taken into account. Instead of adapting the national legislation, in this case the Decree of 4 August 1987, to the requirements of the directive, the authorities have directly applied the Community provisions, which are expressly referred to in the decision to extend the time limit of 12 February 1993 . . . But were the authorities entitled thereby to give direct effect to the provisions of a directive which they had not implemented in domestic law? The reply must be in the negative, having regard to the very clear position adopted by the Court of Justice of the European Community. According to the consistent case-law of the Court of Justice, direct effect can only be applied for the benefit of individuals against the State, and not to their detriment. For a long time, this rule was only enunciated by the Court implicitly in its judgment. In the cases which initially came before the Court, individuals invoked directives against the defaulting State and the Court accepted that, so long as the provisions of the directive in question created obligations for the States which were sufficiently clear and precise, an individual could rely on them before the national courts (*cf.* Court of Justice, 19 January 1982, [1982] ECR 53)[10] . . . The precise scope of these judgments was controversial . . .

The principle that the direct effect of a directive which has not been implemented or has been incorrectly implemented cannot be relied upon against an individual was formulated for the first time in the *Marshall* judgment referred to above.[11] The Court considered that "a directive may not of itself impose obligations on an individual and that a provision of a directive may not be relied upon as such against such a person". Consequently the Court refused to recognize the horizontal effect of directives. This rule was restated and developed in subsequent judgments of the Court in *Pretore di Salo*, 11 June 1987 ([1987] ECR 2545), and *Kolpinghuis Nijmegen*, 8 October 1987 ([1987] ECR 3982) . . . These cases concerned both the possibility of horizontal effect and the possibility that directives could have descending vertical effect and thereby benefit States against individuals. The clear response of the Court is that directives are only binding in relation to the Member States to whom they are addressed. Whether the question and issue concern the relations between an individual and the State or relations between two individuals, the response is the same. A non-implemented directive can never be invoked against individuals. This case-law is the logical consequence of the reasoning which led the Court of Justice to give direct effect

[10 Volume 1, p. 103.] [11 Volume 1, p. 136.]

to directives which had not been implemented or had been incorrectly implemented. Thus, as noted above, the objective of the Court of Justice is to allow individuals to obtain a sanction against States which have failed correctly to implement directives in good time or to prohibit those States from benefiting from their own failure to take the appropriate action. Direct effect is a sanction against the inertia of the State which prevents Community law from becoming a dead letter . . .

It is therefore excluded, according to the case-law of the Court of Justice, that an obligation should be imposed upon individuals on the basis of a directive which has not been implemented or has been incorrectly implemented. Directives can therefore only be enforced, with ascending vertical direct effect, by individuals against the State. Consequently, the Member States cannot dispense with the requirement to enact measures of application in good time and instead directly apply a directive (Court of Justice, *Commission* v. *Kingdom of Belgium* ([1980] ECR 1473)) . . .

[The *Commissaire du Gouvernement* then examined the case-law of the *Conseil d'Etat* and considered that its own conception of the nature of directives prevented the authorities from placing direct reliance on the provisions of a directive which had not been implemented under national law. She therefore proposed that the *Conseil d'Etat* should decide that a State could not rely on the provisions of an unimplemented directive, that such a solution was entirely in conformity with the clear case-law of the Court of Justice and that there was no need to make a reference for a preliminary ruling to that Court. Consequently the competent Minister was not entitled to rely on the provisions of the directive at issue and his decision to do so was unlawful and should therefore be quashed. Finally, she considered that the State should be ordered to pay 20,000 francs to SA Lilly France.]

[The following is the text of the decision of the *Conseil d'Etat*:]

1. In application No 149,226, SA Lilly France asks the *Conseil d'Etat* to annul the decision of 22 April 1993 by which the competent Minister for Health rejected its request of 26 November 1992 for the manufacturer's price (excluding tax) for the pharmaceutical product Prozac 20 to be increased by 10%.

2. In application No 155,083, SA Lilly France asks the *Conseil d'Etat* to annul the decision of 8 November 1993 by which the Minister for Social Affairs, Health and Urbanization rejected its request of 9 July 1993 for a revaluation of the price of Prozac. In addition, Lilly asks for the State to be ordered to pay the sum of 50,000 francs on the basis of the provisions of Section 75-I of the Law of 10 July 1991.

3. A request was presented by the same company to the Administrative Court of Paris and transmitted to the *Conseil d'Etat* where it was

registered under No 162,001, by order of the President. It sought the same relief as application No 155,083.

The *Conseil d'Etat* has considered the Code of Social Security, EC Council Directive 89/105/EEC of 21 December 1988, Law No 91-647 of 10 July 1991, the Code on the Administrative Courts and Administrative Courts of Appeal, Decree No 45-1708 of 31 July 1945, Decree No 53-934 of 30 September 1953 and Law No 87-1127 of 31 December 1987.

[The two applications were joined for a single decision.]

On application No 149,226

Article L.162-38 of the Code of Social Security provides:

> Without prejudice to the provisions of this Code concerning agreements concluded between health insurance agencies and the health professions, the Ministers for the Economy, Health and Social Security may fix by ministerial order the price and profit margin for products and the charges for services whose provision is the responsibility of the social security authorities. The prices and charges fixed shall take account of the progressive development of charges, the level of revenues and the volume of activity of the practitioners or companies concerned . . .

Section 2(2) of the Order of 4 August 1987 (as amended on 12 November 1988 and 2 January 1990) concerning prices and profit margins for refundable medicines and charges on the basis of the provisions of Article L.162-38 of the Code of Social Security provides: "Changes to maximum prices for existing products shall be lodged with the Minister for the Economy, Finance and Health. They shall apply at the end of three months, in the absence of any objection being notified by either of those Ministers." Pursuant to these provisions, the opportunity was given to either of those Ministers, who had received an application on 26 November 1992 from SA Lilly France for a revaluation of the price of Prozac, if they wished to make use of their right to object, to notify that company accordingly prior to the expiry of the period of three months from 26 November 1992.

EC Council Directive 89/105 of 21 December 1988 concerning the transparency of decisions concerning the fixing of the price of medicines for human use and their inclusion within the framework of national systems of health insurance provides:

> Article 3(1), first paragraph: The Member States shall ensure that a decision concerning a request to raise the price of a medicine, duly presented in accordance with the conditions laid down in the Member State concerned by the holder of the right to market that medicine, shall be adopted and notified to the applicant within a time limit of ninety days from its receipt.
>
> Article 3(1), second paragraph: If the number of applications is exceptionally high, the time limit may be extended once only for sixty days. The applicant

shall receive notification of such an extension before the expiry of the initial time limit.

In invoking the terms of the second paragraph of Article 3(1) of the Directive, the deputy Minister of Health, in a letter of 12 February 1993, informed SA Lilly France that the time limit for rendering a decision on the request had been extended by sixty days.

However, the State authorities cannot invoke the provisions of an EC Directive which they have not implemented in domestic law. Consequently the competent Minister of Health did not act lawfully when, in invoking the above-mentioned provisions of the second paragraph of Article 3(1) of the Directive of 21 December 1988, which had not been implemented in domestic law, he extended the time limit for examination of the application lodged by SA Lilly France.

It follows that, following the expiry of the time limit of three months given by the above-mentioned provisions of the order of 4 August 1987 (as amended), which started to run from 26 November 1997, and in the absence of any decision objecting to the proposed price increase within that time limit, the guarded silence of the Ministers for the Economy and Health on the application by the company constituted a decision not to oppose the price increase requested by the company for Prozac. Although, in the exercise of their regulatory powers granted to them by Article L.162-38 of the Code of Social Security, which allowed them at any time to fix, by special order, the price of refundable medicines, the Ministers for the Economy and Health could subsequently abrogate their decision not to oppose such an increase, the deputy Minister of Health was not competent to decide, acting alone, upon that abrogation. Consequently the decision taken on 22 April 1993 was *ultra vires* and must be annulled.

On applications Nos 155,083 and 162,001

Following a new application by SA Lilly France dated 9 July 1993 for a revaluation of the price of Prozac, asking for the price to be fixed at a higher level than that requested in the previous application, the Minister for Social Affairs, Health and Urbanization, in a letter of 8 November 1993, informed the company that its application had been sent to the Directorate of Social Security responsible for rendering a decision in the matter.

After the expiry of the time limit of three months granted by the above-mentioned provisions of 4 August 1987, which began to run on 9 July 1993, and in the absence of any decision to object notified within that time limit, the guarded silence of the Ministers for the Economy and Health on the application of the company constituted a decision not to oppose the price increase lodged by the company for Prozac. In these circumstances, the letter of 8 November 1993 must be regarded as constituting a decision putting an end to the legal position which had arisen from the absence of any objection. Although, in the exercise of their regulatory powers under Article L.162-38 of the Code of Social Security, which allowed them at any moment to fix, by special order, the price of refundable medicines, the Ministers concerned could subsequently abrogate their decision not to oppose the price rise requested, the Minister for Social Affairs, Health and Urbanization was not competent to decide, acting alone, upon such an abrogation. The decision which he took on 8 November 1993 was therefore *ultra vires* and must be annulled.

On the request contained in applications Nos 155,083 and 162,001 for the provisions of Section 75-I of the Law of 10 July 1991 to be applied

In the circumstances of this case it is appropriate to apply the provisions of Section 75-I of the Law of 10 July 1991 and to order the State to pay to SA Lilly France the sum of 20,000 francs to cover the amount spent by that company and not included in its costs . . .

[The decisions being challenged were annulled and the State was ordered to pay to SA Lilly France the sum of 20,000 francs pursuant to Section 75-I of the Law of 10 July 1991.]

[Report: *Receuil Lebon* 1995, p. 257 (in French)]

Direct effect — Directives — Conditions for direct effect — Failure of Member State to implement provisions of directive by specified time — Extension of time limit for implementation—Whether having retroactive effect—Whether directive may be relied upon by individuals before national courts in relation to period prior to extension of time limit—Council Directive 77/388—Harmonization of "VAT"

Enforcement in national courts—Remedies—Claim against Member State — Breach of Community law for which Member State responsible — Failure of authorities in Member State to comply with provisions of Community directive — Enforcement by administrative authorities of national legislation incompatible with Community directive—Whether individuals entitled to compensation for loss suffered—The law of France

MINISTER FOR THE BUDGET *v.* SA JACQUES DANGEVILLE

SA CABINET REVERT ET BADELON

France, Conseil d'Etat. 30 *October* 1996

(Fabre, *Rapporteur*; Goulard, *Commissaire du Gouvernement*)

SUMMARY: *The facts:*[1]—SA Jacques Dangeville was an insurance brokerage firm which paid VAT on its receipts for the first half of 1978, pursuant to Article 256 of the French General Code of Taxation. The Sixth EEC Council Directive on the harmonization of National VAT Legislation of 17 May 1977 provided that such receipts should not be subject to VAT, but at the relevant time France had not yet implemented the Directive. The Court of Justice, in a judgment of 22 February 1984 in *Kloppenburg*, held that the Directive should have been implemented in the Member State by 1 January 1978 and that, although subsequently a Ninth Directive had extended the deadline to 1 January 1979, that extension did not have retroactive effect for the period prior to 30 June 1978.

On the basis that the payment of VAT for the first half of 1978 was in breach of the Sixth Directive, Dangeville instituted administrative proceedings for recovery of the amount paid. But the *Conseil d'Etat*, in a decision of 19 March 1986, held that whatever details they might contain with regard to the intentions of Member States, directives could not be invoked by the nationals of those States in support of claims in tax litigation. Dangeville's subsequent demand for compensation from the Minister for the Budget was rejected and this decision was upheld by the Administrative Court of Versailles in a judgment

[1] The facts are taken from the submissions of *Commissaire du Gouvernement* Goulard printed in RTDE 1997, pp. 171 ff., section I (in French).

of 23 May 1989. However, on appeal by Dangeville, the Administrative Court of Appeal of Paris, in a judgment of 1 July 1992, held that since the provision at issue of the General Code of Taxation was incompatible with the Sixth Directive, the French State could be held liable to pay compensation for the loss arising from the unlawful collection of VAT for the period in question. The Minister for the Budget then applied to the *Conseil d'Etat* for the annulment of this decision.

Commissaire du Gouvernement Goulard, in his submissions relating to the *Dangeville Case*, emphasized that the administrative authorities were precluded from applying provisions contained in domestic legislation which were incompatible with a Community directive, once the date for its implementation had passed. If those authorities nevertheless applied the existing legislative provisions, they committed a wrongful act (*faute*) and the illegality of the individual administrative decision could engage the liability of the State in damages. On this point of principle the *Commissaire du Gouvernement* considered that the reasoning of the Administrative Court of Appeal was correct.

Nevertheless, according to the *Commissaire du Gouvernment*, the decision of the Court could not be upheld because it violated the principle of *res judicata* and the rules concerning the jurisdiction of administrative courts. The applicant had already had his claim for a tax refund rejected by the fiscal courts and the present claim for compensation essentially sought the same remedy in a different court. The principle of national procedural autonomy, recognized in the jurisprudence of the Court of Justice, clearly required the preservation of national jurisdictional rules and a reference to the Court of Justice on this point was not required. The *Commissaire du Gouvernement* therefore concluded that the application should be held to be inadmissible.

In a second, almost identical, case, the *Conseil d'Etat* was called upon to take a decision on the principle of exemption from VAT, for the same period in 1978, of another insurance brokerage firm, *Revert et Badelon*. In a decision in 1982, the Administrative Court of Paris had rejected their claim to exemption from VAT. The *Commissaire du Gouvernement* argued that, in this case, the *Conseil d'Etat* should exclude the application of the provisions of the General Code on Taxation in question, to the extent that they were incompatible with the objectives of the Sixth Directive, and hold that consequently there was no liability to VAT for the first half of 1978. In respect of the second half of that year, however, the *Commissaire du Gouvernement* argued that the extension of the time limit for implementation contained in the Ninth Directive applied, so that the existing domestic legislation continued to be applicable for that period.

First Decision (Minister for the Budget v. *Dangeville)*

Held:—The appeal was allowed and the judgment of the Administrative Court of Appeal of Paris was annulled.

The present claim for compensation, for the loss which the imposition of VAT for the relevant period had caused the applicant, had in reality the same objective as the claim for reimbursement of the tax which had been rejected by the *Conseil d'Etat* in 1986. It was therefore inadmissible.

Second Decision (Cabinet Revert et Badelon)

Held:—The appeal was allowed in part and the judgment of the Administrative Court of Appeal of Paris was amended accordingly.

The provisions of the General Code of Taxation at issue were incompatible with the provisions of the Sixth VAT Directive and could not be applied for the first half of 1978, so that the applicants were entitled to claim exemption for that period, since the Directive should originally have been implemented by 1 January 1978. For the second half of 1978, however, the applicants were not entitled to claim exemption, since the prescribed time limit for implementation had by then been extended by the Ninth Directive to 1 January 1979, and the existing domestic legislation was therefore applicable.

The text of the second decision of the *Conseil d'Etat* commences on p. 210. The following is the text of the first decision of the *Conseil d'Etat*:

This is an application by the Minister for the Budget . . . in which he asks the *Conseil d'Etat* to annul the decision of the Administrative Court of Appeal of Paris of 1 July 1992 in so far as, by that decision, the Court ordered the State to pay to SA Jacques Dangeville . . . compensation of 129,845.86 francs with interest . . .

The *Conseil d'Etat* has considered the documents in the file, the Treaty establishing the European Economic Community, the Sixth EEC Council Directive of 17 May 1977 and the Ninth Council Directive of 26 June 1978, the General Code of Taxation [and various other legislative and administrative enactments].

The *Conseil d'Etat* has heard, in public session, the report of Mr Fabre, *Conseiller d'Etat*, the submissions of Mr Garreau, advocate for SA Jacques Dangeville and the submissions of Mr Goulard, *Commissaire du Gouvernement*.

It appears from the documents in the file submitted by the Administrative Court of Appeal of Paris that, by a decision of 19 March 1986, the *Conseil d'Etat* rejected an application by SA Jacques Dangeville for the refund of value-added tax which that company had paid for the period 1 January to 30 December 1978. The application was based, in particular, on the ground that the company's subjection to the tax in question had been based on the application of legislative provisions which were incompatible with the objectives of the Sixth EEC Council Directive of 17 May 1977 [on the harmonization of the laws of the Member States relating to turnover taxes].

The application by SA Jacques Dangeville on which the Administrative Court rendered the judgment under appeal sought compensation of an amount equal to the value-added tax which had been levied, as compensation for the loss which the imposition of that tax had caused to the company. It was argued that this loss resulted from the delay by the French State in implementing the objectives of the Directive into domestic law. This claim therefore, in reality, had the same objective as the claim for reimbursement of the tax, which had been rejected by the above-mentioned decision of the *Conseil d'Etat* on 19 March 1986. Consequently, in deciding that the fact that the company "had first sought to recover the tax in question in proceedings before the fiscal courts" did not render its claim for compensation inadmissible, since it was based on a loss different from that suffered as a result of the payment of the tax, the Administrative Court of Appeal of Paris committed an error in law, as the Minister for the Budget had argued. The Minister for the Budget was therefore entitled to ask for the judgment under appeal to be annulled in so far as the Administrative Court partly upheld the submissions contained in the application of SA Jacques Dangeville.

In these circumstances, it is appropriate for the *Conseil d'Etat* to render a decision in these proceedings, with regard to the submissions contained in the claim brought by SA Jacques Dangeville before the Administrative Court of Appeal which that Court did not reject.

It results from the above-mentioned considerations that SA Jacques Dangeville is not entitled to complain that, in the judgment being challenged of 23 May 1989, the Administrative Court of Paris wrongly rejected its claim for compensation . . .

The *Conseil d'Etat* decides:

Article 1—Articles 1 and 2 of the operative part of the judgment of the Administrative Court of Appeal of 1 July 1992 are annulled.

Article 2— . . .

Article 3—This decision shall be notified to the Minister for the Economy and Finance and to SA Jacques Dangeville.

[Report: RTDE 1997, p. 171 at p. 184 (in French)]

[The following is the text of the second decision of the *Conseil d'Etat*:]

This is an application by SA Cabinet Revert et Badelon . . . in which it asks the *Conseil d'Etat* to:

1. Annul the judgment of 10 June 1982 by which the Administrative Tribunal of Paris rejected their claim to be exempted from value-added tax to which they had been assessed for the periods 1 to 28 February 1978 and 1 April to 31 December 1978;
2. Hold that the tax in question is not chargeable . . .

The *Conseil d'Etat* has considered the documents in the file, the General Code of Taxation [and various legislative and administrative enactments].

The *Conseil d'Etat* has heard, in public session, the report of Mr Fabre, *Conseiller d'Etat* and the submissions of Mr Goulard, *Commissaire du Gouvernement*.

Pursuant to Article 1 of the Sixth EEC Council of 17 May 1977, the Member States were required to adopt, by 1 January 1978 at the latest, the necessary measures in order to modify their value-added tax systems in accordance with the requirements of the Directive. The Ninth Council Directive of 26 June 1978, notified to France on 30 June of that year, authorized certain Member States including France only to implement the Directive by 1 January 1979. Nevertheless, according to the interpretation given by the Court of Justice of the European Community, the Ninth Directive did not have retroactive effect. Consequently, that Directive could not cover the period prior to 30 June 1978 during which time the French authorities had failed to implement provisions in conformity with the requirements of the Sixth Directive within the prescribed period.

Furthermore, Articles 256 and 261 of the General Code on Taxation . . . , in so far as they maintain the subjection to value-added tax of business done by insurance brokers where they are not remunerated by commission or brokerage fixed by legislative or administrative provision, are incompatible with the requirements of the provisions of Article 13B(a) of the Sixth Directive, which exempt from that tax all insurance and re-insurance business done by brokers and insurance intermediaries. Consequently, and to that extent, the provisions of Articles 256 and 261 must not be applied for the period 1 January to 30 June 1978. It follows that SA Cabinet Revert et Badelon, which is in the business of insurance brokerage, is entitled to claim that the value-added tax levied on its business for the periods 1 to 28 February 1978 and 1 April to 30 June 1978 is without legal foundation.

On the other hand, for the period from 1 July to 31 December 1978, the company is not entitled to invoke the incompatibility of Articles 256 and 261 of the General Code of Taxation with the requirements of the provisions of Article 13B(a) of the Sixth Directive, since the prescribed time limit given to France for adapting its legislation to the Directive had by then been extended to 1 January 1979 by the Ninth Directive. Consequently, the applicant company was correctly assessed for value-added tax for the period from 1 July to 31 December 1978 on the basis of the provisions of Articles 256 and 261 of the General Code of Taxation, which were applicable for that period.

It results from the above-mentioned considerations that SA Cabinet Revert et Badelon is only entitled to claim that, in the judgment being challenged, the Administrative Tribunal of Paris wrongly rejected its claim for the periods from 1 to 28 February 1978 and 1 April to 30 June 1978.

The *Conseil d'Etat* decides:

Article 1—SA Cabinet Revert et Badelon is exempted from the value-added tax to which it was assessed for the periods 1 to 28 February 1978 and 1 April to 30 June 1978;

Article 2—The judgment of the Administrative Tribunal of Paris of 10 June 1982 is amended in so far as it is in conflict with the present decision;

Article 3—Other submissions contained in the application of SA Cabinet Revert et Badelon are rejected;

Article 4—This decision shall be notified to SA Cabinet Revert et Badelon and to the Minister for the Economy and Finance.

[Report: RTDE 1997, p. 171 at p. 185 (in French)]

[The following is the text of the relevant part of the opinion of the *Commissaire du Gouvernement*, Mr Goulard:]

I.—[The *Commissaire du Gouvernement* outlined the facts and the course of the procedure and continued:]

II.—*On State liability*
Subject to a question of admissibility, which will be discussed later, it would appear that the application which the Administrative Court of Appeal of Paris has made of the principle of the liability of the State for failure to comply with obligations arising from Community law is correct in law, both from the standpoint of the obligation to comply with the case-law of the Court of Justice of the European Community and from the logic of the case-law of the *Conseil d'Etat*.

The principle according to which the Member States are required to pay compensation for damage caused to individuals by violations of Community law for which they are responsible has been developed only recently in the case-law of the Court of Justice. Furthermore, the principle has not been confirmed without both nuances and reservations. The prudence of the members of the Court can certainly be explained by their desire not to seriously disrupt the legal orders of the Member States, of which very few accept so broadly the principle of State responsibility.

The *Francovich* judgment (19 November 1991, Case 6/90 and 9/90, [1991] ECR I-5357)[2] represents the point of departure of this developing case-law of the Court of Justice. The effects of this first judgment cannot, however, be correctly understood without taking account of the more recent judgment in *Brasserie du Pêcheur* and *Factortame* (5 March 1996, Case 46/93 and 48/93, [1996] ECR I-1029)[3] by which the Court has specified the scope of the principle of State liability.

This case-law constitutes a coherent whole of minimal requirements of which the essential point can be summarized in two propositions. First, the Member States are required to pay compensation for damage caused to individuals by violations of Community law for which they are responsible, on the double condition that the rule of Community law with which they have failed to comply is intended to confer rights on individuals and that there is a causal link between the failure to comply with the rule of Community law and the damage suffered by the individual who is seeking compensation. Secondly, if the failure complained of is attributable to the national legislature in a domain in which it has

[2 Volume 1, p. 188.] [3 See p. 474.]

a wide discretion, the liability of the Member State is only engaged if the breach is sufficiently serious. The Court then adds that the conditions laid down for the exercise of the right to damages must not be less favourable than those relating to similar domestic claims and "must not be such as in practice to make it impossible or excessively difficult to obtain reparation".[4]

With the possible exception of the notion of a sufficiently serious breach, this case-law should not raise any serious objection on the part of the *Conseil d'Etat*. On the contrary, there is a striking analogy between the principles developed by the Court of Justice and the longer established principles in the case-law of the *Conseil d'Etat*. More than twenty years ago, in confirming the principle already enshrined in many earlier decisions, the *Conseil d'Etat* held that any illegality constituted fault (26 January 1973, *Ville de Paris* v. *Sieur Driancourt, Recueil Lebon*, p. 77). In the words of President Gentot in his submissions in that case:

> citizens have a veritable right to legality and can claim compensation for loss suffered as a result of a violation of that right.

Where the question arose, the *Conseil d'Etat* has not hesitated to extend this rule to the particular form of legality incumbent upon the national authorities in order to respect treaties and international agreements. Consequently, it is the task of the administrative courts, pursuant to Article 55 of the Constitution, to review the compatibility of laws with treaties (*Conseil d'Etat*, 20 October 1989, *Nicolo, Recueil Lebon*, p. 190),[5] with EC regulations (*Conseil d'Etat*, 24 September 1990, *Boisdet, Recueil Lebon*, p. 250)[6] as well as with EC directives (*Conseil d'Etat*, 28 February 1992, *SA Rothmans International France and SA Philip Morris France, Recueil Lebon*, p. 80).[7] Furthermore, treaties and acts derived from them form part of the norms of positive law for which the *Conseil d'Etat* must ensure respect by giving them supremacy over all rules of domestic law. It is therefore clear that the very notion of legality has been enlarged so as to include enactments of both international and Community law. Any failure to comply with those norms therefore constitutes fault.

In fact, this finding is already contained in the case-law of the *Conseil d'Etat*. The reasoning which forms the basis of the decision of the *Conseil d'Etat* of 28 February 1992 in *Arizona Tobacco Products* and *SA Philip Morris*[8] is from this standpoint both simple and convincing. A law whose provisions are incompatible with the requirements of a directive can no longer be applied once the date by which the directive should have been implemented into national law has passed. Consequently, a decree enacted after that date on the basis of those national legislative provisions has no legal basis. Individual decisions taken on the basis of that decree are therefore themselves illegal and that illegality is such as to engage

[4 See p. 474 at p. 581.]
[5 Volume 1, p. 335.]
[6 Volume 1, Note, p. 357.]
[7 Volume 1, p. 357.]
[8 *Ibid.*]

the liability of the State. Put more succinctly, the *Arizona Tobacco Products* decision signifies that the authorities cannot apply the provisions of a law which is incompatible with a directive. If they nevertheless apply those provisions, they commit fault of such a nature as to engage their liability.

It is clear that in the *Arizona Tobacco Products* decision, the failure to implement the directive was attributable to the legislature, according to the most recent case-law of the Court of Justice. The *Arizona Tobacco Products* decision therefore already constituted an application of the *Brasserie du Pêcheur/Factortame* case-law of the Court of Justice, four full years prior to those judgments of the Court of Justice and without the imposition of the restriction that the liability of the State is only engaged if the breach of Community law is sufficiently serious.

In order to confirm the principle of State responsibility enshrined in the judgment of the Administrative Court of Appeal of Paris which is the subject of this appeal, the *Conseil d'Etat* need only reproduce this reasoning, with the single difference that this case does not involve delegated legislation inserted between the law and the individual decision.

[The *Commissaire du Gouvernement* then examined a distinction proposed by the Minister for the Budget between fault committed by the administrative authorities in regulatory action taken on the basis of a law incompatible with a Community directive, which could engage State responsibility, and loss caused by an individual decision taken directly on the basis of a law incompatible with a directive, which could not provide a basis for State liability. He rejected this distinction as unacceptable and continued:]

The case before the *Conseil d'Etat* today appears to offer the opportunity for a ruling, in accordance with the principles set out above, that any administrative decision applying legislative provisions incompatible with a Community directive constitutes fault of such a nature as to engage the responsibility of the State. That would not amount to full liability for fault on the part of the legislature since the existence of an individual decision to impose taxation would still enable the administrative authorities to be regarded as being at fault. Nevertheless, the reasoning adopted by the Administrative Court of Appeal, containing a simple objective finding of a misinterpretation of the obligations arising from Community law, in order to establish the principle of State liability, without any identification of the level of Government responsible for the failure, skilfully avoided the question, which was in reality rather improbable, whether the loss was the result of the direct application of a law without the intervention of a regulatory measure or an individual application.

III.—*On the admissibility of the application*

Nevertheless, what we would regard as the irreproachable reasoning of the Administrative Court of Appeal with regard to State liability is insufficient to enable the judgment under appeal to be confirmed. It appears that the Administrative Court of Appeal, without doubt influenced by an excessive desire to be fair, went beyond what was reasonable with regard to their application of the principles of domestic law. In order to achieve the result mentioned above, the Court in fact took some liberty with two principles whose fundamental nature cannot be ignored. They violated both the principle of *res judicata* and the rules concerning the jurisdiction of administrative courts (*distinction des contentieux*). [The *Commissaire du Gouvernement* then analysed in detail the jurisprudence of the *Conseil d'Etat* in order to demonstrate why the application should be regarded as inadmissible. In particular he pointed out that it would be contrary to the law to allow a taxpayer to obtain reimbursement of tax paid which he was challenging other than through the financial courts. The principle of the procedural autonomy of the Member States, which was recognized as a rule of fundamental importance in the jurisprudence of the European Court of Justice, clearly required the preservation of the jurisdictional rules of the administrative courts as a principle at the heart of the domestic jurisdictional system. This point was clearly established and there was no need to make a reference for a preliminary ruling to the Court of Justice on this question. The *Commissaire du Gouvernement* continued:]

IV.—The holding in the judgment under appeal that new proceedings could be brought must therefore be overruled since the Administrative Court of Appeal erred in law. Nevertheless, before reaching such an abrupt conclusion . . . it is appropriate to lend further support to the view that a claim for fiscal restitution is just as effective, from the standpoint of the effectiveness of Community law, as a claim for compensation.

In order to do this, the ideal would be to be in possession of a case file whose facts were as close as possible to those of the Société Dangeville case. Such a file actually exists and is before the *Conseil d'Etat* today as Case No 45.126 . . . It requires a decision on an identical question to that decided by the *Conseil d'Etat* on 19 March 1986 on the application of Société Dangeville. The period concerned is the same, and the applicable provisions are identical. The applicant company, which operates as Revert et Badelon, runs an insurance brokerage business which is practically identical to that of Société Dangeville.

This case should, in fact, have been decided years ago. But Application No 45.126 was one of those rare files, amongst tens of thousands, which despite the vigilance of officials was buried away for years prior to reappearing . . . The opportunity is now presented for the *Conseil d'Etat* to demonstrate once again its desire not to deprive individuals of the rights granted to them by the treaties establishing the European Communities and the legislative text based thereon.

This application, which is clearly admissible, once again raises the difficult question of the relationship between national law and EC directives. As is well known, the *Conseil d'Etat* held in its plenary decision of 22 December 1978 in *Minister of the Interior* v. *Cohn-Bendit*[9] that directives could not be directly relied upon by individuals against an individual administrative act. The decision in *Cohn-Bendit*, which had the merit of being based upon a literal and precise interpretation of Article 189 of the Treaty of Rome, has long been contested by legal writers who argued correctly that it was hardly compatible with the jurisprudence of the European Court of Justice, and in particular with the judgment of 5 April 1979 in *Ministère Public* v. *Ratti* (Case 148/78, [1979] ECR 1629),[10] which adopted and further developed the jurisprudence of the Court in its earlier judgment in *Franz Grad* (Case 9/70, [1970] ECR 825).[11]

However, the recent jurisprudence of the *Conseil d'Etat* has made it clear that the apparent drawbacks of the *Cohn-Bendit* decision are notably reduced by various indirect methods by which the *Conseil d'Etat* has allowed the provisions of a directive to be relied upon. In proceedings for *ultra vires*, the *Conseil d'Etat* has annulled regulatory acts contrary to the objectives of directives (7 December 1984, *Federation Française Société de protection de la nature, Recueil Lebon*, p. 409) and also annulled a refusal to quash a regulation contrary to the objectives of a directive (Plenary session, 3 February 1989, *Compagnie Alitalia, Recueil Lebon*, p. 44).[12] The Conseil d'Etat has also accepted a defence plea excluding the application of regulations incompatible with the objectives of the directive (8 July 1991, *Palazzi, Recueil Lebon*, p. 276) and even excluding the application of a law incompatible with those objectives (Plenary session, 28 February 1992, *SA Rothmans International France and SA Philip Morris France, Recueil Lebon*, p. 80).[13] The same method, and in particular the latter, have also been held to be applicable in claims for compensation (Plenary session, 28 February 1992, *Société Arizona Tobacco Products and SA Philip Morris France, Recueil Lebon*, p. 78)[14] . . . The application of Société Revert et Badelon gives the *Conseil d'Etat* not only the opportunity to confirm all these judicial decisions but also to take a further step in applying the same reasoning in a case whose significance we will now explain.

In *Société Arizona Tobacco Products*, the *Conseil d'Etat* excluded the application of Article 6 of the Law of 24 May 1976 amending the monopoly on manufactured tobacco products to the extent that it allowed the Government to fix the selling prices of imported tobacco under conditions which were incompatible with the Directive of 19 December 1972. The application of these legislative provisions having been excluded, the Decree of 31 December 1976 enacted for their application was declared unlawful and the individual decisions taken on the basis of that Decree,

[9 Volume 1, p. 317.]
[10 Volume 1, Note, p. 134.]
[11 *Ibid.*]
[12 Volume 1, Note, p. 334.]
[13 Volume 1, p. 357.]
[14 *Ibid.*]

which were themselves unlawful, were regarded as constituting fault of such a nature as to engage the liability of the State.

. . .

On several such occasions, the *Conseil d'Etat* therefore demonstrated that it is prepared to exclude the application of legislative or regulatory provisions to the extent that they provide for the unfavourable treatment of taxpayers and are incompatible with the objectives of the Sixth Directive. The application of Société Revert et Badelon is somewhat different to the extent that the company requests the application of a rule which is favourable to its interests, in the form of an exemption which is contained in the objectives of the Directive but does not figure in the list of exemptions provided for in the General Code on Taxes. Nevertheless, the situation is very similar to other cases referred to above. Article 261 of the General Code on Taxes, which was in force at the relevant time, exempted in sub-section (4)(a) "transactions carried out by insurance brokers where they were remunerated by the payment of commission or brokerage fixed by legislative or regulatory provisions". This provision could be held to be incompatible with the objectives of the Sixth Directive for various reasons.

[The *Commissaire du Gouvernement* then outlined how the solution which he proposed was consistent with various decisions of the *Conseil d'Etat*. He continued:]

I therefore propose that the *Conseil d'Etat* should exclude the application of Articles 256 and 261(4)(a) of the General Code on Taxes, as requested by Société Revert et Badelon, to the extent that their provisions are incompatible with the objectives of the Sixth Directive. This defence of incompatibility should then lead the *Conseil d'Etat* to hold that there is no liability for the value-added tax to which the company was assessed for the period from 1 January to 30 June 1978. With regard to the period from 1 July 1978 to 31 December of the same year, the *Conseil d'Etat* should hold that, since the implementation period for the Sixth Directive was extended by the Ninth Directive, the general objective of exempting transactions carried out by insurance brokers could no longer be relied upon at that date to ask a fiscal court to exclude the application of national law and, to that extent, the *Conseil d'Etat* should reject the submissions of the company.

In reaching such a decision, by applying its already well-established jurisprudence and acting in accordance with the requirements of the jurisprudence of the Court of Justice, the *Conseil d'Etat* will allow Société Revert et Badelon to rely without reservation, before the fiscal court, upon the rights which it derives from Community law. In a field governed by national law but in a case where the provisions of an EEC Directive have not been implemented, the *Conseil d'Etat* will accordingly nevertheless have given precedence to those provisions. Thereby, the *Conseil d'Etat* will conform precisely with the requirements of Community law as laid down in particular in the judgment of the Court of Justice of the European Community in its *Becker* judgment (19 January 1982, Case 8/81, [1982] ECR 53),[15] which dealt specifically with an exemption from turnover tax.

Consequently, the *Conseil d'Etat* should annul the judgment of the Administrative Court of Appeal of Paris which upheld the claim for compensation of Société Dangeville. That company merely had the misfortune to have its claim for fiscal restitution decided too early. I am conscious of the fact that this position may appear unjust but I feel that to uphold the judgment awarding damages would involve a derogation from the principles upon which the jurisdiction of the *Conseil d'Etat* is based, with serious consequences for the stability of legal positions created by the courts. A particular individual case, albeit arising from transitional difficulties, cannot justify such a derogation.

[The *Commissaire du Gouvernement* then explained that his proposal meant that the judgment of the Administrative Court of Appeal should be quashed on grounds of inadmissibility rather than on the ground proposed by the Minister for the Budget, of *res judicata*. He gave two reasons for this conclusion and continued:]

The plea of inadmissibility put forward by the Minister does not give rise to these objections. It therefore justifies the annulment of the judgment under appeal and the rejection, by application of Article 11 of the Law of 31 December 1987, of the application of SA Jacques Dangeville. Having thus accepted the submissions of the Minister, the only course open to the *Conseil d'Etat* will be to reject the submissions in which SA Dangeville asks in defence that the State should be ordered to pay to it the sum of 20,000 francs in unrecoverable costs.

For these reasons the *Commissaire du Gouvernement* concludes as follows:

1. Application No 141.043—the judgment of the Administrative Court of Appeal of Paris should be annulled, the application presented before that Court by SA Jacques Dangeville should be rejected and the submissions made by that company on the basis of Article 75-I of the Law of 10 July 1991 should also be rejected;
2. Application No 45.126—SA Revert et Badelon should be exempted from the value-added tax to which they were assessed for the period from 1 January to 30 June 1978 and the judgment of 10 June 1992 of the Administrative Tribunal of Paris should be amended but only to the extent to which it is in conflict with such an exemption.

[Report: RTDE 1997, p. 171 (in French)]

[15 Volume 1, p. 103.]

National constitutions — Constitutional review concerning Community Treaty — French Constitution, Article 54 — Treaty of Amsterdam, 1997 — Compatibility with French Constitution — Whether affecting essential conditions for exercise of national sovereignty — Whether special constitutional amendments required prior to ratification— Scope of permissible transfer of sovereignty to Community institutions

Powers—Extension by treaty—Treaty of Amsterdam, 1997— Nature of obligations entered into by Member States — Introduction of measures concerning asylum, immigration and the crossing of internal borders of Member States— Provisions for taking such measures by qualified majority voting and the "co-decision" procedure, after a transitional period of five years—Whether requiring transfer of sovereign powers from Member States—The law of France

Re Treaty of Amsterdam, 1997, Amending the Treaty on European Union and the Treaties Establishing the European Communities

(Decision No 97-394 DC)

France, Constitutional Council. 31 *December* 1997

Summary: *The facts*:—The President and the Prime Minister of the French Republic, acting jointly pursuant to Article 54 of the French Constitution,[1] referred to the Constitutional Council the question of whether the authorization to ratify the Amsterdam Treaty amending the Treaty on European Union and the Treaties establishing the EC, signed on 2 October 1997, had to be preceded by a revision of the Constitution because it included clauses which were contrary thereto.

Held:—The authorization to ratify the Treaty, by the enactment of a law, could not take place until after revision of the Constitution.

(1) Respect for national sovereignty did not prevent France, on the basis of the Preamble to the Constitution of 1946 which proclaimed that the French Republic "shall conform to the rules of public international law", from concluding international agreements, subject to reciprocity, with a view to participating in the creation or development of a permanent international organization endowed with its own legal personality and granted powers of decision by means of the transfer of competences agreed to by the Member States. Nevertheless,

[1] For the text of Article 54 see Volume 1, p. 403.

where such international agreements contained a clause contrary to the Constitution or infringed the essential conditions for the exercise of national sovereignty, the authorization to ratify those agreements required a constitutional revision.

(2) It followed from Article 88(2) of the Constitution, inserted by the Constitutional Law of 25 June 1992,[2] that those provisions of the Treaty of Amsterdam which effectively operated, for the benefit of the European Community, to transfer competences which called into question the essential conditions for the exercise of national sovereignty, necessitated a further revision of the Constitution. This was the case either because the transfers of competence were in a domain other than the establishment of the European Economic and Monetary Union or the crossing of common external borders, or because the provisions laid down procedures other than those provided for by the Treaty on European Union signed on 7 February 1992, for the exercise of competences whose transfer was authorized by Article 88(2).

(3) Article 2 of the Treaty of Amsterdam inserted into the Treaty establishing the European Community a new Title IIIa, "Visas, asylum, immigration and other policies related to the free movement of persons". Title IIIa contained Article 73j, paragraphs (1) and (3), as well as Article 73k, which provided for the transfer of powers to the Community in the areas of asylum, immigration and the crossing of internal borders, all of which involved the exercise of national sovereignty and did not fall within the scope of the powers provided for by Article 88(2) of the Constitution.

(4) According to the penultimate paragraph of Article 73k, measures adopted by the Council relating to immigration policy and the right to reside in the Member States "shall not prevent any Member State from maintaining or introducing in the areas concerned national provisions which are compatible with this Treaty and with international agreements". Since these areas did not fall within the exclusive competence of the Community, respect for the principle of subsidiarity enshrined in Article 3b of the EC Treaty required that the Community should only intervene if the objectives of the proposed action could not be sufficiently achieved by the Member States themselves. Nevertheless, the application of this principle did not, of itself, prevent the transfers of powers at issue from having such a broad ambit as to affect the essential conditions for the exercise of national sovereignty.

(5) The essential conditions for the exercise of national sovereignty would not be affected during the transitional period of five years from the entry into force of the treaty, when decisions of the Council would be taken unanimously and the Member States would retain the power of initiative. However, at the end of this transitional period, by virtue of Article 73o(2) the Council would be able to adopt decisions exclusively on the basis of Commission proposals and the Member States would lose their power of initiative. Even more important, all measures decided upon in all or part of the areas outlined above would be adopted by decision of the Council acting by qualified majority vote and in accordance with the so-called "co-decision" procedure laid down in Article 189b of the EC Treaty. This change from unanimity to qualified majority voting and to the procedure of "co-decision" would not require any national act of

[2] For the text of Article 88 see Volume 1, p. 399.

ratification or approval and would therefore not be subject to constitutional review on the basis of the provisions of Article 54 or Article 61(2) of the French Constitution. In these circumstances, the application of the second paragraph of Article 73o could affect the essential conditions for the exercise of national sovereignty.

(6) Equally, with regard to measures contained in Title IIIa concerning the crossing of external borders of the Member States, the automatic change to qualified majority voting and the "co-decision" procedure at the end of a period of five years from the entry into force of the Treaty of Amsterdam, for determining procedures and conditions for the issuing of visas as provided for by the fourth paragraph of Article 73o, constituted in the context of the Treaty on European Union a new procedure for the transfer of powers in areas touching upon national sovereignty, which was not covered by Article 88(2) of the Constitution. The change from the rule of unanimity to qualified majority voting and the "co-decision" procedure in such matters could therefore affect the essential conditions for the exercise of national sovereignty. The same considerations applied to the application of the procedures laid down by the second paragraph of Article 73o to the provisions of subsection (a) of the second paragraph of Article 73j, concerning procedures for carrying out checks at external borders which, for the reasons mentioned above, also infringed the essential conditions for the exercise of national sovereignty.

The following is the text of the decision of the Constitutional Council:

On 4 December 1997 the President of the Republic and the Prime Minister, acting pursuant to Article 54 of the Constitution, referred to the Constitutional Council the question of whether, taking account of the obligations entered into by France and the provisions for their entry into force, the authorization to ratify the Amsterdam Treaty amending the Treaty on European Union, the Treaties establishing the European Communities and certain related acts, signed on 2 October 1997, must be preceded by a revision of the Constitution.

The Constitutional Council has considered the Constitution of 4 October 1958, in particular Title XIV, "The European Communities and the European Union", the Preamble to the Constitution of 27 October 1946, the Ordinance of 7 November 1958 which constitutes the organic law of the Constitutional Council and the [municipal laws authorizing ratification of treaties and decisions entered into by the Member States of the European Communities and the European Union concerning their structure, powers and enlargement, concluded or enacted between 1952 and 1997].

The Constitutional Council has also considered the effect of Decree No 53-192 of 14 March 1953 concerning the ratification and publication of international agreements entered into by France, as amended by Article 3 of Decree No 86-707 of 11 April 1986.

The submissions of the *Rapporteur* have been heard.

On the applicable norms of reference

1. In the Preamble to the Constitution of 1958 the French people solemnly proclaim their attachment to the rights of man and the principle of national sovereignty, as defined in the Declaration of 1789 and confirmed and supplemented by the Preamble to the Constitution of 1946.

2. Article 3 of the Declaration on the Rights of Man and the Citizen proclaims that "the basis of all sovereignty resides essentially in the Nation". Article 3 of the Constitution of 1958 provides that "national sovereignty belongs to the people who shall exercise it through their representatives and by means of a referendum".

3. The Preamble to the Constitution of 1946 proclaims, in paragraph 14, that the French Republic shall "conform to the rules of public international law". Paragraph 15 provides that "subject to reciprocity France consents to those limitations of sovereignty necessary for the organization and defence of peace".

4. Article 53 of the Constitution of 1958 recognizes, in the same manner as Article 27 of the Constitution of 1946, the existence of "treaties or agreements concerning international organization". The President of the Republic can only ratify or approve such treaties or agreements by the enactment of a law.

5. Pursuant to Article 88(1) of the Constitution, inserted by the Constitutional Law of 28 June 1992, "The Republic shall participate in the European Communities and the European Union, which have been established by States having freely chosen, pursuant to the constitutive treaties of those entities, to exercise certain of their powers in common."

6. It results from these constitutional provisions that respect for national sovereignty does not prevent France, on the basis of the provisions of the Preamble to the Constitution of 1946 cited above, from concluding international agreements subject to reciprocity, with a view to participating in the creation or development of a permanent international organization endowed with its own legal personality and vested with powers of decision, by means of the transfer of competences agreed to by the Member States.

7. Nevertheless, where international agreements entered into for this purpose contain a clause which conflicts with the Constitution or infringe the essential conditions for the exercise of national sovereignty, the authorization for their ratification requires a constitutional revision. It is in the light of these principles that the Constitutional Council must examine the treaty signed in Amsterdam on 2 October 1997.

On the provisions of the Treaty relating to visas, asylum and the free movement of persons

8. According to Article 88(2), inserted into the Constitution by the Constitutional Law of 25 June 1992:

Subject to reciprocity, and in accordance with the procedures laid down in the Treaty on European Union signed on 7 February 1992, France agrees to the transfer of the powers necessary for the establishment of the European Economic and Monetary Union as well as for the fixing of rules concerning the crossing of the external borders of the Member States of the European Community.

It follows from Article 88(2) that those provisions of the Treaty of Amsterdam which effectively operate, for the benefit of the Community, to transfer competences which call into question the essential conditions for the exercise of national sovereignty necessitate a further revision of the Constitution. This is the case either because the transfers of competence are in a domain other than the establishment of the Economic and Monetary Union or the crossing of common external borders, or because the provisions lay down procedures other than those provided for by the Treaty on European Union, signed on 7 February 1992, for the exercise of competences whose transfer was authorized by Article 88(2) above.

9. Article 2 of the Treaty of Amsterdam inserts into the Treaty establishing the European Community a new Title IIIa entitled, "Visas, asylum, immigration and other policies related to the free movement of persons".

10. With reference to the free movement of persons the new Title contains Article 73j which authorizes the Council, acting in accordance with the procedure referred to in Article 73o of the same Title, to adopt, within five years after the Treaty of Amsterdam's entry into force, a certain number of measures which are specifically enumerated and which relate to the crossing of the internal and external borders of the Member States, as well as the movement of nationals of third countries within the territory of the Member States.

11. The measures relating to the crossing of internal borders comprise "measures with a view to ensuring, in compliance with Article 7a, the absence of any control on persons, be they citizens of the Union or nationals of third countries, when crossing internal borders".

12. The measures relating to the crossing of external borders of the Member States shall establish "standards and procedures to be followed by Member States in carrying out checks on persons at such borders" and "the rules relating to visas for intended stays of no more than three months, including the list of third countries whose nationals must be in possession of a visa . . ." as well as "the procedures and conditions for issuing visas by Member States", the definition of "a uniform format for visas", and the rules on "a uniform visa".

13. Finally, the measures concerning the movement of nationals of third countries shall set out the conditions under which such nationals shall have the freedom to travel within the territory of the Member States during a period of no more than three months.

14. With regard to asylum and immigration policy, the new Title IIIa contains Article 73k, which provides that the Council, acting in

accordance with the procedure laid down in Article 73o, shall, within five years after the entry into force of the Treaty of Amsterdam, adopt a certain number of measures relating to asylum, refugees and immigration.

15. The measures on asylum concern the "criteria and mechanisms for determining which Member State is responsible for considering an application for asylum submitted in one of the Member States by a national of a third country", the "minimum standards on the reception of asylum seekers in Member States" and "minimum standards with respect to the qualification of nationals of third countries as refugees" as well as "minimum standards on procedures for granting or withdrawing refugee status in Member States".

16. The measures on refugees and displaced persons concern "minimum standards for giving temporary protection" to such persons and measures for "promoting a balance of effort between Member States in receiving and bearing the consequences of receiving" such persons.

17. The measures relating to immigration policy concern "conditions of entry and residence", standards on procedures for the issue by Member States of long-term visas and residence permits, including those for the purpose of family reunion, and measures concerning "illegal immigration and illegal residence including repatriation of illegal residents".

18. Also provided for are "measures defining the rights and conditions under which nationals of third countries who are legally resident in a Member State may reside in other Member States".

19. It is clear from the penultimate paragraph of Article 73k that measures adopted by the Council relating to immigration policy and the right to reside in the Member States "shall not prevent any Member State from maintaining or introducing in the areas concerned national provisions which are compatible with this Treaty and with international agreements".

20. Article 73o lays down the procedure for the adoption by the Council of decisions under Title IIIa. Paragraph 1 provides that "During a transitional period of five years following the entry into force of the Treaty of Amsterdam the Council shall act unanimously on a proposal from the Commission or on the initiative of a Member State and after consulting the European Parliament." Paragraph 2 adds that "After this period of five years the Council shall act on proposals from the Commission" whilst being always required to "examine any request made by a Member State that it submit a proposal to the Council" and that "the Council, acting unanimously after consulting the European Parliament, shall take a decision with a view to rendering the procedure referred to in Article 189b applicable to all or parts of the areas covered by this Title and to adapt the provisions relating to the powers of the Court of Justice".

21. It is specified in paragraph 3 that, by derogation from the rules established in the first two paragraphs, rules relating to the list of third countries whose nationals are required to be in possession of a visa for short stays and rules on a uniform visa shall, from the entry into force of the Treaty of Amsterdam, "be adopted by the Council acting by a qualified majority on a proposal from the Commission after consulting the European Parliament". It is further provided in the fourth paragraph that, by derogation from paragraph 2, measures concerning the procedures and the conditions for the issue of such visas, as well as rules on a uniform format for visas, shall, after a period of five years following the entry into force of the Treaty, be "adopted by the Council, acting in accordance with the procedure referred to in Article 189b".

On the measures concerning asylum, immigration and the crossing of the internal borders of Member States

22. The first and third paragraphs of Article 73j and Article 73k provide, in addition to what has been discussed above, for the transfer of powers to the Community in the areas of asylum, immigration and the crossing of internal borders, all of which involve the exercise of national sovereignty and do not fall within the scope of the powers provided for by Article 88(2) of the Constitution.

23. It is true that since these areas do not fall within the exclusive competence of the Community, respect for the principle of subsidiarity, enshrined in Article 3b of the EC Treaty, whose conditions of application are set out in a Protocol annexed to the Treaty of Amsterdam, requires that the Community shall only intervene if, and to the extent that, the objectives of the proposed action cannot be sufficiently achieved by the Member States. Nevertheless, the application of this principle does not, of itself, prevent those transfers of powers authorized by the Treaty and submitted to the Constitutional Council for examination from having such a broad ambit and taking effect in such a manner as to affect the essential conditions for the exercise of national sovereignty.

24. The essential conditions for the exercise of national sovereignty will not be affected during the transitional period of five years from the entry into force of the Treaty when, in accordance with the first paragraph of Article 73o, decisions of the Council shall be taken unanimously and the Member States retain the power of initiative.

25. On the other hand, at the end of this transitional period, by virtue of the second paragraph of Article 73o, the Council shall adopt decisions exclusively on the basis of Commission proposals and the Member States will thereby lose their power of initiative. Above all, by a simple decision of the Council, all measures decided upon in all or part of the areas outlined above shall be adopted by a qualified majority vote in accordance with the so-called "co-decision" procedure laid down in Article 189b of the EC Treaty. This change from unanimity to qualified majority voting and

to the procedure of "co-decision" will not require, when the time comes, any national act of ratification or approval and will therefore not be subject to constitutional review on the basis of the provisions of Article 54 or Article 61(2) of the Constitution.

26. In these circumstances, and notwithstanding the provisions of the penultimate paragraph of Article 73k, the application of the second paragraph of Article 73o could affect the essential conditions for the exercise of national sovereignty.

27. Consequently, the provisions of the second paragraph of Article 73o, inserted into the EC Treaty by Article 2 of the Treaty of Amsterdam, must be declared contrary to the Constitution to the extent that they apply to measures provided for by the first and third paragaphs of Article 73j and by Article 73k of the EC Treaty.

On the measures concerning the crossing of the external borders of the Member States

28. In its decision of 2 September 1992, the Constitutional Council declared the provisions of Article 100c of the EC Treaty concerning the list of third countries whose nationals must be in possession of a visa and the introduction of a uniform format for visas to be in conformity with the Constitution and in particular with Article 88(2). The authority of *res judicata* of that decision requires that the Constitutional Council should not call into question the provisions of the third paragraph of Article 73o since they simply reproduce the rules contained in Article 100c.

29. On the other hand, the automatic change to qualified majority voting and the "co-decision" procedure at the end of a period of five years from the entry into force of the Treaty of Amsterdam, for determining the procedures and conditions for issuing short stay visas by Member States and the rules on a uniform visa, as provided for by the fourth paragraph of Article 73o, constitutes, in the context of the Treaty on European Union, a new procedure for the transfer of powers in areas touching upon national sovereignty. The change from the rule of unanimity to qualified majority voting and the "co-decision" procedure, in such matters, could therefore affect the essential conditions for the exercise of national sovereignty.

30. It follows from the above considerations that the fourth paragraph of Article 73o, inserted into the EC Treaty by Article 2 of the Treaty of Amsterdam, must be declared contrary to the Constitution.

31. Finally, the change to qualified majority voting and the "co-decision" procedure, simply by Council decision in accordance with the procedure provided for in the second paragraph of Article 73o, with regard to the provisions of subsection (a) of the second paragraph of Article 73j, which establish the "standards and procedures to be followed by Member States in carrying out checks on persons at external

borders", for the reasons mentioned above, infringe the essential conditions for the exercise of national sovereignty. It is therefore necessary to declare the provisions of the second paragraph of Article 73o to be contrary to the Constitution to the extent that they apply to the measures provided for by subsection (a) of the second paragraph of Article 73j.

On the international agreement submitted for examination by the Constitutional Council, taken as a whole

32. None of the other provisions of the international agreement, referred to the Constitutional Council for examination under Article 54 of the Constitution, is contrary to the Constitution.

33. For the above-mentioned reasons, the authorization to ratify the Treaty of Amsterdam by the enactment of a law requires a constitutional revision.

The Constitutional Council decides:

Article 1—The authorization to ratify the Treaty of Amsterdam by the enactment of a law cannot take place until after the revision of the Constitution.

[Reports: *Journal Officiel de la République Française*, 1998, No 2; *Revue du Droit Public*, 1998, p. 345 (in French)]

NOTE.—Following the decision of the Constitutional Council, Constitutional Law No 99-49 was adopted by the French Parliament on 25 January 1999, amending Articles 88(2) and 88(4) of the Constitution.

Article 88(2), as amended, provides:

> Subject to reciprocity, and in accordance with the terms of the Treaty on European Union signed on 7 February 1992, France agrees to the transfer of powers necessary for the establishment of European economic and monetary union.
>
> Subject to the same reservation, and in accordance with the terms of the Treaty establishing the European Community as amended by the Treaty signed on 2 October 1997, the transfer of powers necessary for the determination of rules concerning freedom of movement for persons and related areas may be agreed.

National constitutions—Constitutional review concerning Community Treaty — French Constitution, Article 88(3) — Treaty on European Union, Article 8B — Electoral rights of citizens of European Union in national elections in Member States — EC Council Directive 94/80 concerning the exercise of electoral rights — Organic law giving effect to provisions of Directive—Compatibility with French Constitution — Whether Article 88(3) of Constitution empowering Constitutional Council to ensure compatibility of Organic Law with EC Treaty provisions and secondary Community legislation—The law of France

Re ORGANIC LAW CONCERNING APPLICATION OF ARTICLE 88(3) OF FRENCH CONSTITUTION

France, Constitutional Council. 20 *May* 1998

The text of this judgment of the Constitutional Council is not reproduced here because it is largely concerned with the constitutionality of provisions of electoral law. In April 1998, acting pursuant to Article 61(1) of the French Constitution, the Prime Minister made a reference to the Constitutional Council for a ruling on the constitutionality of the Organic Law determining the conditions for the application of Article 88(3) of the Constitution,[1] concerning the exercise by non-French citizens of the European Union resident in France of the right to vote and stand as a candidate in municipal elections. The Organic Law incorporated the provisions of EC Council Directive 94/80 of 19 December 1994 into domestic law.

The Constitutional Council pointed out that the Directive in question had been enacted by the EC Council pursuant to the provisions of Article 8b of the EC Treaty, inserted into that Treaty by Article G of the Treaty on European Union, 1992. By providing, in Article 88(3) of the Constitution, that the right of citizens of the Union to vote and stand in municipal elections was granted "in accordance with the procedures laid down in the Treaty on European Union", the Constitution had expressly subordinated the constitutionality of the Organic Law enacted for its application to its conformity with norms of Community law. Consequently, the Constitutional Council considered that it was required to ensure that the Organic Law, provided for by Article 88(3) of the Constitution, respected the provisions of both Article 8b of the EC Treaty and the above-mentioned Directive. The Constitutional Council systematically examined the provisions of the Organic Law and concluded that none of them were in conflict either with any constitutional norm or with any of the applicable reference norms of Community law. Accordingly, the Constitutional Council ruled that the Organic Law was in conformity with the Constitution (Report: *AJDA* 1998, p. 531 (in French)).

[1] For the text of Article 88 see Volume 1, p. 399.

Supremacy — Constitutions and Community law — French Constitution, Article 55 — National legislation enacted to give effect to provisions of Council Directive 92/73 on homeopathic medicines—Provision in domestic legislation extending scope of registration procedure for medicines beyond objectives of Directive — Refusal of State to implement domestic provision — Whether justified by requirement to recognize hierarchy of legal norms in Article 55 of Constitution—The law of France

ASSOCIATION OF PATIENTS FOR ALTERNATIVE MEDICINE AND OTHERS

France, Conseil d'Etat. 24 *February* 1999

(Eoche-Duval, *Rapporteur*; Bonichot, *Commissaire du Gouvernement*)

SUMMARY: *The facts*:—An action was brought by the Association of Patients for Alternative Medicine and other bodies seeking the annulment for *ultra vires* of a French Decree giving effect to new provisions in the French Code of Public Health on the regulation of the marketing of homeopathic medicines. The Decree was intended in part to give effect to Council Directive 92/73 on additional provisions relating to homeopathic medicines. The applicants objected, in particular, to the failure of the French authorities to implement Article L.601-4 of the Code of Public Health.

Held:—The application was rejected.

Article L.601-4 of the Code of Public Health was incompatible with the Directive in so far as it extended the scope of the simplified registration procedure for homeopathic medicines beyond the objectives laid down by the Directive. The Government was justified in not implementing this provision since, by giving precedence to the Community measure, it had complied with the requirement to respect the hierarchy of norms in the domestic legal order enshrined in Article 55 of the Constitution.

The following is the text of the relevant part of the judgment of the *Conseil d'Etat*:

This is an application . . . brought by the Association of Patients for Alternative ("anthroposophique") Medicine (and other bodies) in which they ask the *Conseil d'Etat* to annul for *ultra vires* Decree No 98/52 of 28 January 1998 concerning requirements for the marketing of homeopathic medicines . . .

On the ground based on the failure to implement Article L.601-4 of the Public Health Code

Article L.601-3, inserted into the Code of Public Health by Article 12-II of the Law of 18 January 1994 concerning public health and social protection, provides that homeopathic medicines which satisfy a list of specified conditions, and in particular the requirement that they are administered orally or externally, are subject to a simplified registration procedure with the Medicines Agency rather than the authorization regime governing pharmaceutical preparations laid down in Article L.601 of the Code.

Article L.601-4, which was also inserted in the Code of Public Health by Article 12-II of the Law of 18 January 1994, provides that "homeopathic medicines which are not administered in the manner provided for in Article L.601-3, and in particular those administered by injection, may be the subject of registration in accordance with special rules". According to paragraph 12 inserted in Article L.605 of the Code of Public Health by Article 12-III of the aforementioned Law, the *Conseil d'Etat* may issue decrees specifying the conditions for the application of Articles L.601 to L.604 and in particular "the conditions for the presentation of requests for registration of homeopathic medicines as laid down in Articles L.601-3 to L.601-4".

However, paragraph 1 of Article 7 of EEC Directive 92/73 of 22 September 1992 laying down additional provisions on homeopathic medicinal products provides that the procedure for special simplified registration, which the Member States are entitled to establish, is reserved for medicinal products satisfying "all the conditions set out" in that paragraph, including the requirement "that they are administered orally or externally". According to Article 9 of the same Directive, homeopathic medicines other than those specified in Article 7 "shall be authorized and categorized" in accordance with the rules laid down in EEC Directive 65/65 of 26 January 1965 concerning special pharmaceutical preparations.

It follows from these considerations that the above-mentioned provisions of Article L.601-4 of the Code of Public Health, in so far as they extend the scope of the simplified registration procedure beyond the objectives defined by the Directive, are incompatible with that Directive. Consequently, in not enacting the appropriate regulatory measures to bring into force Article L.601-4 of the Code of Public Health, the Government acted, as it was required to do, in conformity with the requirements inherent in the hierarchy of norms in the domestic legal order, based on Article 55 of the Constitution. In these circumstances, the applicant bodies cannot lawfully claim that the decree being challenged is illegal since it fails to render applicable the provisions of Article L.601-4 of the Code of Public Health.

. . .

[The *Conseil d'Etat* rejected various other procedural grounds put forward by the applicants and continued:]

The *Conseil d'Etat* decides:

Article 1: The application of the Association of Patients for Alternative Medicine (and other bodies) is rejected.

[Report: *AJDA* 1999, p. 823 (in French)]

NOTE:—In a decision rendered a few months earlier by a combined session (*Assemblée*) of the *Conseil d'Etat* it was held that, whilst Article 55 of the Constitution laid down that properly ratified treaties were to be accorded superior authority to laws, the supremacy thereby conferred on international agreements over domestic law did not cover provisions of a constitutional nature (*Sarran et Levacher*, 30 October 1998, *Clunet* 1999, p. 745 (in French)). Some commentators have suggested that this decision, which was not concerned with EC law, indicates that the *Conseil d'Etat* might be prepared to give precedence to a national constitutional provision in the event of conflict with secondary EC legislation, which would be contrary to the case-law of the European Court of Justice (see Richards, *Sarran et Levacher*: Ranking Norms in the French Republic, EL Rev 2000, p. 192).

National constitutions — Constitutional challenge to legislation — German Constitution, Article 70 — Legislation of Community institutions enacted pursuant to EC Treaty— Draft EC directive concerning television broadcasting — Dispute between Federal Government and States (*Länder*) concerning competence over broadcasting matters — Whether Federal Government violating rights of *Länder* by agreeing to adoption of EC Council directive restricting competence of *Länder* in broadcasting matters

Powers — Extension by treaty — Legal basis for powers of European Community — Principle of conferred powers contained in EC Treaty—Definition—Articles 100 and 235 of Treaty — Scope of application — The law of the Federal Republic of Germany

Television Broadcasting Directive Case

(Case No 2 BvG 1/89)

Federal Republic of Germany, Federal Constitutional Court (BVerfG)

(Limbach, Böckenförde, Klein, Grasshof, Kruis, Kirchhof, Winter and Sommer, *Judges*)

22 *March* 1995

Summary: *The facts*:—In a dispute concerning the negotiation and adoption of EC Council Directive 89/552 on Television Broadcasting, Bavaria and other German States (*Länder*) applied to the Federal Constitutional Court for a ruling that their legislative rights had been violated by the Federal Government, in particular by its acceptance of quota rules contained in the draft Directive which interfered with the content of television programmes. The *Länder* also sought a declaration that the Directive was inapplicable and without legal effect in Germany. The *Länder* argued that the European Community had no competence in cultural matters (prior to the entry into force of the Maastricht Treaty) so that the Federal Government should not have agreed to the terms of the Directive. In fact, the Federal Government initially strongly defended the position of the *Länder*. Ultimately, however, the Government agreed to the quota provisions contained in the Directive on the basis that they constituted a political objective rather than legally binding rules, although this view was not shared by the EC Commission.

Held:—The Federal Government had violated the rights of the *Länder*.

(1) The claim for a declaration that the Directive was inapplicable and without legal effect in Germany was inadmissible since the German Government had not taken or even envisaged any action to implement it. Where the European

Community claimed a legislative power, it was for the Federal Government to defend the interests of the Federal Republic against the Community and its institutions. Where, under German law, a matter on which the Community claimed the right to legislate was reserved to the legislative competence of the *Länder*, the Federal Government acted in relation to the Community as the representative of the *Länder* and the defender of their rights under the Constitution. If a dispute arose as to the Community's right to legislate in a specific field, the principle of federality required the Federal Government to take account of the legal stance of the *Länder*. According to German constitutional procedure, this legal stance was to be established within the *Bundesrat*, which should give its opinion on all measures of Community legislation. That opinion was then to be taken into account in negotiations by the Federal Government, on the basis of a relationship of cooperation and mutual consideration with the *Länder* making up the Federation (pp. 240-4).

(2) The Federal Government was under a duty to respect the principle that the powers exercised by the Community had to be specifically conferred. Where, as here, an attempt was made to encroach upon a specific area of competence retained by the Member States, and in Germany by the *Länder*, the principle of federality required the Federal Government to oppose such a development. The initial negotiating position adopted by the Federal Government respected this principle by insisting that broadcasting was *a priori* a matter falling within the competence of the *Länder* and outside Community competence, or at least that Community competence could only be based on Articles 100 or 235 of the EC Treaty, which required unanimity in the Council for the adoption of measures, thereby enabling the Federal Government fully to defend the position of the *Länder* by using its veto. At the same time, the Federal Government had been entitled to recognize Community legislative competence in relation to certain specific matters relating to broadcasting, such as advertising and sponsorship, which did not undermine the cultural aspects of broadcasting policy. Accordingly, at the initial negotiating stage, the Federal Government had not violated the rights of the *Länder* (pp. 245-50).

(3) However, the manner in which the Federal Government had exercised the European Community membership rights of the Federal Republic in the Council of Ministers, in relation to the quota rules contained in the Directive, constituted a violation by the Government of the rights of the *Länder*. Once the Federal Government realized that, despite its intensive negotiations, its position would not prevail in the Council and majority voting would be used to override it, the Government should have informed the *Bundesrat* and sought agreement on its subsequent conduct. Its failure to do so constituted a violation of the legislative rights of the *Länder* (pp. 251-2).

The following is the text of the relevant part of the judgment of the Court:

[205] OPERATIVE PART OF THE JUDGMENT

1. The manner in which, following its Resolution of 8 March 1989, the Federal Government exercised the Community membership rights of the Federal Republic in relation to the adoption of the quota rules contained

in Chapter III of Council Directive 89/552/EEC (on the coordination of certain provisions laid down by law, regulation or administrative action in Member States concerning the pursuit of television broadcasting activities) constituted a violation by the Federation of the rights of the Bavarian Free State and its co-applicant *Länder* under Article 70(1) of the Basic Law ["*GG*"] read in conjunction with Article 24(1) *GG*, and of the principle of pro-federal conduct [*bundesfreundliches Verhalten*]

2. In all other respects the applications are rejected.

GROUNDS:

A.

The central issue in the dispute between Federation and *Länder* arising out of the negotiation and adoption of the EEC Council Directive on television broadcasting concerns the obligations incumbent upon the Federal Government in a case where the EEC claims the right to legislate in respect of a matter which, under German law, falls within the legislative competence of the *Länder*, and Federation and *Länder* are unable to agree on the existence or extent of Community competence.

I.

[1.-4.] . . . **[206-210]** [The Court outlined the legislative history of the draft Directive, including an account of the opposition thereto by the German *Länder* and the *Bundesrat* (Federal Council) and of the Federal Government's efforts to represent those views at Community level. The Court continued:]

. . . 5.(a) On 8 March 1989 . . . the Federal Minister of the Interior transmitted to the *Bundesrat* a Federal Government Resolution of the same date . . . The text of that Resolution was as follows:

[211] I. The Federal Government notes the following:

— In consequence of the entry into force on 1 July 1987 of the Single European Act, the Federal Republic of Germany, as a Member of the European Community, committed itself to the achievement, by not later than the end of 1992, of a free internal market in respect of . . . the provision of services.
— In the Federal Republic broadcasting is a public undertaking. It is an institution which contributes to the formation of public opinion and helps to guarantee its diversity. It has an important cultural function; but it also involves an economic activity.
— Pursuant to the unanimous case-law of the European Court of Justice (see Judgments of: 30 April 1974, Case 195/73, *Sacchi* [1974 ECR 409]; 18 March 1980, Case 52/70, *Debauve* [1980 ECR 833]; 18 March 1980, Case 60/79, *Coditel* [*ibid.* 881]; 26 April 1988, Case 352/85, *Kabelregeling* [1988 ECR 2085]) the Federal Government is obliged to recognise that broadcasting

constitutes a service for purposes of the rules on freedom to provide services contained in Articles 59 ff. of the EEC Treaty.

— The European Commission regards the existence of differing regimes governing the distribution and production of television programmes (quotas), advertising and the protection of young people as barriers within the meaning of Articles 59 and 60 of the EEC Treaty which could hinder cross-frontier broadcasting. The Federal Government shares the position of the Commission with regard to *advertising* and *the protection of young people*. Differences in the rules of individual Member States in this regard could result in breaches of the law in receiving States if cross-frontier broadcasting were left unregulated. In this connection particular note should be taken of the rapid growth in the number of private broadcasting stations, and of the fierce competition among them for advertising.

— The Federal Government does not share the Commission's position with regard to the mandatory *quota rules* contained in Chapter II of the draft Directive. To impose quotas is to dictate the composition of programmes, which amounts to controlling the content of broadcasting. This is a matter going beyond the scope of Article 60 of the EEC Treaty. Regulation of the actual content of broadcasts is a matter going primarily to the cultural and socio-political aspects of broadcasting, in relation to which the European Community has no mandate to legislate.

— Any text which prescribes mandatory quotas for Member States or for **[212]** broadcasting companies is unacceptable to the Federal Government on grounds of lack of legislative competence.

— Moreover, the Federal Government considers that the setting of a quota is not an appropriate means of achieving the aim, which it shares, of promoting the creation and distribution of European audiovisual productions.

— If the quota rules were to be formulated as a purely political objective and a satifactory overall solution was achieved, then the Federal Government would be prepared to assent to the terms of the Directive.

II. With regard to the relationship between the proposed European Community Directive and the draft Council of Europe Convention on cross-frontier television, the Federal Government moreover considers, in agreement with the *Länder*, that the latter agreement should be accorded political priority, so that other [non-Community] European States may be included in a European regime.

However, in view of the unanimous case-law [of the European Court], a Council of Europe Convention cannot fully replace the Directive, since the Council of Europe lacks an institution equivalent to the Court of Justice of the European Community.

In order to satisfy the requirements of the European internal market in this regard, the European Community must itself accede to the Council of Europe Convention as a contracting party. This will require a provision in the Convention permitting the European Community to bind itself as a signatory party.

(b) By a judgment of 11 April 1989 this *Senat* refused . . . an application by the Bavarian Government for an interim order temporarily staying the Government from implementing the cabinet Resolution of 8 March 1989 (see 80 *BVerfGE* 74 ff.).

6. [(a) . . .] **[213]** . . .

(b) On 13 April 1989 the Council [of the European Communities] agreed a common position by qualified majority (first reading of the Directive). As a result of pressure from the Federal Government, sound broadcasting was removed from the Directive, while for purposes of the quota rules German companies were permitted to count all productions from the GDR as European works. The fifty-third recital, "This Directive is only a first step . . ." was deleted. The rules governing programme and production quotas were largely brought into line with those contained in Article 10(1) of the European Convention (see Articles 4 and 5 of the Directive). The Government failed in its attempt to have a general declaration included in the minutes to the effect that the quota provisions were not legally enforceable, whether under the Directive or under the Convention. Because of its objections to the quota provisions and to the definition of "European works" (as it then stood), the Federal Government voted against the common position.

(c) . . .

(d) Prior to the second reading on 3 October 1989, the Federal Government sought to have a provision included in the Directive itself making it clear that the quota rules were not binding. However, it found that this would not be acceptable to the majority. The best that it was able to obtain was formal declarations from Council and Commission for inclusion in the minutes, the terms of which were as follows:

[214]—Declaration No 15:

Declaration by the Council and the Commission concerning Articles 4 and 5:

The Council and the Commission agree that the aims pursued in those provisions are to be regarded by Member States as political objectives.

—Declaration No 7:

Declaration by the Council and the Commission concerning Article 4:

The Council and the Commission are of the opinion that the provisions contained in Article 4 are directed towards the aims recognised by the Rhodes and Madrid European Councils, and in particular to the need to extend "efforts to strengthen Europe's capacity in the audiovisual field". They confirm that these provisions leave it to individual Member States to establish, within the framework of their respective constitutional structures, the forms and means for the achievement of these aims. The Council and the Commission agree that these provisions, which are based on the current state of the audiovisual market in Europe, may be adapted to take account of market developments.

—Declaration No 16:

Declaration by the Commission concerning Articles 4 and 5:

The Commission confirms that it will interpret Articles 4 and 5 in light of the joint declaration by the Council and the Commission to the effect that the aims pursued in Articles 4 and 5 are to be regarded by Member States as political objectives, and that the proportion specified in Article 4 relates to every broadcasting undertaking to which this Directive applies.

On this basis the Federal Republic recorded its assent to the Directive, which was adopted by a substantial majority, with only Belgium and Denmark voting against it.

7. In the final version of the Directive (see OJEC, No L 298/23) the rules on quotas for European works were contained in Chapter III (Promotion of distribution and production of television programmes). They included the following:

[215] *Article 4*

1. Member States shall ensure, where practicable and by appropriate means, that broadcasters reserve for European works, within the meaning of Article 6, a majority proportion of their transmission time, excluding the time appointed to news, sports events, games, advertising and teletext services . . .

2. . . .

3. From 3 October 1991, the Member States shall provide the Commission every two years with a report on the application of this Article and Article 5.

That report shall in particular include a statistical statement on the achievement of the proportion referred to in this Article and Article 5 for each of the television programmes falling within the jurisdiction of the Member State concerned, the reasons, in each case, for the failure to attain that proportion and the measures adopted or envisaged in order to achieve it.

The Commission shall inform the other Member States and the European Parliament of the reports, which shall be accompanied, where appropriate, by an opinion. The Commission shall ensure the application of this Article and Article 5 in accordance with the provisions of the Treaty. The Commission may take account in its opinion, in particular, of progress achieved in relation to previous years, the share of first broadcast works in the programming, the particular circumstances of new television broadcasters and the specific situation of countries with a low audiovisual production capacity or restricted language area.

4. . . .

Article 5

Member States shall ensure, where practicable and by appropriate means, that broadcasters reserve at least 10% of their transmission time, excluding the time appointed to news, sports events, games, advertising and teletext services, or alternatively, at the discretion of the Member State, at least 10% of their programming budget, for European works created by producers who are independent of broadcasters . . .

[216] For the rest, Article 6 of the Directive contains a definition of "European works", while Article 7 lays down a minimum "waiting period" for television showings of films produced for the cinema. Further provisions cover television advertising and sponsorship (Chapter IV), the protection of minors (Chapter V) and finally the right of reply (Chapter VI).

8. In the meantime the rules contained in the European Convention and in the Directive have been incorporated in the Agreement between the *Länder* of 31 August 1991 on Broadcasting within the United Germany [*Staatsvertrag der Länder über den Rundfunk im vereinten Deutschland*], which entered into force on 1 January 1992 (see, *inter alia*, *BayGVBl* 1991, 451).

II.

[216-225] [The Court summarized the arguments contained in the Bavarian Government's application and those of the Federal Government in reply.]
[226] . . .

III.

. . .

B.-I.

Points 1 and 2 of the Bavarian Government's application are admissible. The remainder are inadmissible.

1. In a dispute between Federation and *Länder* of a constitutional nature (Article 93(1)(3) of the Basic Law), a *Land* is entitled to apply to the Federal Constitutional Court under Sections 69 and 64(1) of the Law on the Federal Constitutional Court ["*BVerfGG*"] where it claims that, as a result of an act or omission of the Federation, the rights and duties conferred upon it by the Constitution have been violated or directly threatened. In order for the application to be admissible, the *Land* need only show that there is a possibility of its rights being violated or threatened as a result of a material constitutional law relationship involving both *Land* and Federation (see 81 *BVerfGE* 310, at 329).

[227] 2. Where the application relates to the adoption of an EEC instrument which, in consequence of its legal primacy, restricts the exercise of the *Länder*'s internal powers, that instrument cannot in itself be regarded as an act within the meaning of ss. 64 and 69 *BVerfGG* attributable to the Federation. The power of enactment in relation to EEC instruments lies not with the Federation but with the Community. Nonetheless, the Federal Republic's membership of the Community gives the Federation rights of participation and collaboration within the Community and its institutions, and this is just as much the case where a Community instrument affects the powers of the *Länder*. The exercise by the Federal Government of these rights of collaboration can constitute an act capable of challenge by the *Länder*.

3. In regard to broadcasting, the applicant relies on the competence accorded to it under Article 30 *GG*, read in conjunction with Article 70(1), in relation to which the Federation is bound to act in accordance with the principles of pro-federal conduct (*nach den Grundsätzen bundesfreundlichen Verhaltens*). The procedural rules contained in Article 2 of the Law ratifying the Single European Act ("*EEAG*"), which provide for the involvement of the *Bundesrat* in proposed Community legislation and require the Federal Government, in accordance with detailed criteria laid down in its third paragraph, to take account of the *Bundesrat*'s opinion in [Community] negotiations, do not—although the position has never been definitively settled by a decision of this Court—preclude the applicant from claiming against the Federation on account of a violation of its individual rights.

4.(a) It follows that Point 1 of the Bavarian Government's application is admissible. In its Resolution of 8 March 1989 the Federal Government stated that it would agree to the terms of the Television Directive in the event of a "satisfactory overall solution", provided that it was clearly established that the quota provisions constituted a purely political objective. This Resolution provided the Federal Government's representative in the Council of Ministers with authority to vote. Thus, being both attributable to the Federation and having legal consequences for the *Länder*, it constituted a relevant act [for purposes of s. 64(1) *BVerfGG*] (see 3 *BVerfGE* 12 at 17). The Resolution may also have constituted a breach of the Federation's obligation to the *Länder*, pursuant to its constitutional duty of pro-federal conduct, **[228]** to respect the latter's legislative powers.

(b) Point 2 is also admissible. It is stated to be directed against the Federal Government's favourable vote within the [European] Council of Ministers, but what is essentially at issue is the manner in which the Federation exercised its membership rights within the EEC. That constituted a separate legal act [for purposes of s. 64(1) *BVerfGG*], since it involved separate decisional elements, in particular in relation to the manner in which the cabinet Resolution was applied. Here too there may have been a violation of *Länder* rights.

5. Point 3(a) of claim No 3(a) and subsidiary Point 3(b) are inadmissible. For the purposes of ss. 64 and 69 *BVerfGG*, a dispute between Federation and *Länder* can arise only where it is conclusively shown that, as a result of a specific measure or a failure to act in a particular case, there exists a direct threat to a *Land*'s rights or duties.

(a) In its Point 3(a) the Bavarian Government seeks a declaration that the Federation is not entitled to apply the Television Directive, notwithstanding that no federal provision requiring the *Länder* to transpose the Directive into their own law has been adopted or even envisaged. The application accordingly fails to satisfy the requirements laid down by ss. 64 and 69 *BVerfGG* for the admissibility of disputes between Federation and *Länder*.

(b) The subsidiary claim, whereby it is sought to require the Federation, acting through the Federal Government, to recognize that the Directive does not constitute applicable law, is likewise inadmissible. There is no evidence of any action by the Government in this regard which might have violated or directly threatened the rights of the *Land*.

(c) The applicant also relies in support of Points 3(a) and (b) on Article 93(1)(4) *GG*, but that provision is of no assistance either in terms of the claim's admissibility. Under the provisions governing "other disputes involving public law" (Article 93(1)(4)), the admissibility of proceedings is also subject to the condition that there must have been an actual act or omission capable of resulting in a violation of a right or a **[229]** direct threat thereto. However, quite apart from this, admissibility is in any event precluded by the fact that the relationship between the parties to the dispute is one governed by constitutional law. It follows that this is a case which falls within Article 93(1)(3) *GG* and hence outside the scope of the procedural regime of Article 93(1)(4).

[II. and III.]

[The Court ruled that the other applicant *Länder* were entitled to have their applications joined with that of Bavaria. It further rejected as redundant the Federal Government's application for a separate declaration that no violation of the applicants' rights had taken place. The Court continued:]

[230] C.

The manner in which, following its Resolution of 8 March 1989, the Federal Government exercised the Community membership rights of the Federal Republic in relation to the adoption of the quota rules contained in Chapter III of the Council Directive of 3 October 1989 (on the coordination of certain provisions laid down by law, regulation or administrative action in Member States concerning the pursuit of television broadcasting activities (OJ No L 298/23 of 17 October 1989)) constituted a violation by the Federation of the rights of the Bavarian Free State and its co-applicant *Länder* under Article 70(1) *GG* read in conjunction with Article 24(1) *GG*, and of the principle of pro-federal conduct (*bundesfreundliches Verhalten*). In all other respects the applications—in so far as they are admissible—are unfounded.

I.

Where the European Community claims a legislative power, it is for the Federation to defend the interests of the Federal Republic against the Community and its institutions. Where, under German law, a matter on which the Community claims the right to legislate is reserved by the Basic Law to the legislative competence of the *Länder*, then the Federation acts in relation to the Community as the representative (*Sachwalter*) of the *Länder* and the defender of their rights under the Constitution. Where the existence and extent of the Community's right to legislate in a specific field is called into question, the principle of federality (*Bundesstaatsprinzip*) requires that the Federation take account of the legal stance of the *Länder*. In respect of the period prior to the entry into force of Article 23 *GG* as amended by the 38th Amendment to the Basic Law of 21 December 1992 (*BGBl* I, 2086), the position of the Federation in this regard was governed by Article 70(1) *GG* read in conjunction with Article 24(1), and also by the constitutional principle of pro-federal conduct (*bundesfreundliches Verhalten*).

1. The latter principle (see 81 *BVerfGE* 310 at 337 ff.) requires that, in the exercise of their powers, both Federation and *Länder* take necessary and reasonable account of their common interest in the Federal State and of the interests of the *Länder*. It follows that, in the preparatory stages of Community legislation affecting **[231]** the legislative powers of the *Länder*, Federation and *Länder* must work closely together.

However, the Constitution can only provide the bases for the forms and procedures governing this collaboration. Where the European Community seeks to legislate in a particular field, the Federal Government has a duty to defend any contrary rights of the Federal Republic and to represent itself effectively, both in relation to the Community and—within the limits of its institutional powers of collaboration—within the Community institutions. By contrast, the *Länder* have no means of their own for defending the powers accorded to them by the Constitution against the Community institutions. In the event of a dispute concerning the power of the Community to adopt secondary legislation, or the extent of that power, they have to rely on the Federal Government, as their representative, to defend effectively the legislative powers accorded to them by the Constitution and retained by them pursuant to the EEC Treaty [hereafter "ECT"].

2. In order to ensure that the rights of the *Länder* in relation to Community matters were effectively represented by the Federal Government, Federation and *Länder* developed ad hoc methods of cooperation, which have subsequently been formalized in order to make them legally binding and ensure mutual consistency in their application. Thus the *Länder* are expected to represent their position to the Federal Government on a unanimous basis, while the latter is required to deal only with a single representative of the *Länder*'s interests. This has led by stages to a procedure whereby the legal stance of the *Länder* is established within the *Bundesrat* and represented through the latter.

(a) In areas where the *Länder* have power to legislate, Article 32(3) *GG* also gives them a right to conclude treaties. It has always been a matter of dispute whether this right is exclusive to the *Länder* or whether the Federation enjoys a concurrent treaty-making power (see Grewe, *Handbuch des Staatsrechts*, vol. III, 1988, para. 77, **[232]** marginal numbers 84 ff.). Irrespective of this question, the Federation and the *Länder* have come to an arrangement—the so-called "Lindau Agreement" (reproduced in Maunz/Dürig, *Grundgesetz*, Art. 32, marginal number 45)—whereby, before signature of an [international] agreement in any field where the *Länder* have exclusive legislative competence, "the agreement of the *Länder* has to be obtained", pending which the agreement will not be binding in international law. The *Länder* are to be "involved as early as possible in the preparation of the agreement, and in any event in good time before the drafting of the final text". For purposes of this provision a *Länder* Standing Treaty Committee (*Ständige Vertragskommission der Länder*) was set up, and has been in operation since 1958.

(b) With regard to proposed Community legislation, it had already been provided in Article 2 of the Law ratifying the Rome Treaties of 25 March 1957 (*BGBl* II, 753) that the Federal Government must keep the *Bundesrat* informed of developments within the Council of the European Community. After many years of negotiation this procedure involving the *Bundesrat* was supplemented by the so-called "*Länder* participation procedure" (*Länderbeteiligungsverfahren*). In an Exchange of Letters between the Federal Chancellor and the President of the Conference of [*Länder*] Chief Ministers (*Ministerpräsidentenkonferenz*) (reproduced as Document 5 in the Annex to Hürbek/Thaysen [ed.], *Die Deutschen Länder und die Europäischen Gemeinschaften*, 1986, p. 237), it was agreed that, in the case of EC proposals in areas falling wholly or in part within the exclusive legislative competence of the *Länder*, or affecting the latter's essential interests, Federation and *Länder* were under a duty (founded on their relationship of mutual trust) of loyal and close collaboration. The Federation would expect the *Länder* to seek to establish a common position and to make every effort to ensure that their position was consistent with the Federation's aims and needs under its foreign and European integration policies. The Federation would endeavour to reach agreement with the *Länder* on a joint position and would make all possible efforts in the course of [Community] negotiations to represent that position and secure its acceptance. The Federation undertook to depart from the *Länder*'s position only on compelling grounds of foreign and European integration policy, and to inform the *Länder* of the reasons for any decision to that effect. **[233]** Where the proposed measure concerned a field where the *Länder* had exclusive competence the Federation was required, if so requested and in so far as it was possible for it to do so, to bring two representatives of the *Länder* to the negotiations within the relevant consultative bodies at Commission or Council level.

This procedure was founded on the assumption that the *Länder* would be able to agree on a common position. It required an exceptional degree of coordination and did not make direct use of the institutional and organizational possibilities offered by the *Bundesrat*. The *Länder* accordingly sought to bring the procedure under the latter's aegis (see *Bundesrat* debate at the 564th Session of 16 May 1986, Stenographic Record, pp. 299 ff.). This resulted in the *Länder*'s rights of collaboration being incorporated in a *Bundesrat* procedure, while the Federal Government's duties were embodied in Article 2 *EEAG* as follows:

(1) Without prejudice to Article 2 of the Law on the Treaties of 25 March 1957 establishing the European Economic Community and of 27 July 1957 establishing the European Atomic Energy Community (*BGBl* II, 753), the Federal Government shall at the earliest possible moment provide the *Bundesrat* with full particulars of all proposals within the framework of the European Community which could be of interest to the *Länder*.

(2) Before agreeing to any measure of European Community legislation which relates wholly or in its individual provisions to matters in respect of which the *Länder* have exclusive legislative competence, or which affects their essential interests, the Federal Government shall give the *Bundesrat* the opportunity, in good time, to give its opinion.

(3) The Federal Government shall take account of this opinion in negotiations. Where an opinion relates to matters in respect of which the *Länder* have exclusive legislative competence, the Federal Government may depart from the terms thereof only on irrefutable grounds of foreign or integration policy. In all other matters, in formulating its position it shall take account of the requirements of the *Länder* as presented to it by the *Bundesrat*.

(4) Where the Federal Government departs from the terms of the *Bundesrat*'s opinion in a matter in respect of which the *Länder* have exclusive legislative competence, and in all other matters whenever the *Bundesrat* so requests, it shall provide the *Bundesrat* with a statement of the reasons for its actions.

(5) In cases where the Federal Government is required to seek the *Bundesrat*'s opinion then, without prejudice to the existing rules it shall, on request **[234]** and in so far as it is possible for it to do so, bring representatives of the *Länder* to the negotiations within the relevant consultative bodies at Commission or Council level.

(6) Detailed rules with regard to the provision of information and participation shall be agreed between the Federation and the *Länder*.

Detailed rules concerning the "Provision of information to the *Bundesrat* and the *Länder* and their rights of participation" were laid down in an Agreement of 17 December 1987 between the Federal Government and the governments of the *Länder* (*GMBl* 1989, 697 at 698). In this Agreement the parties begin by declaring their support "for the European Union on the basis of the Treaties establishing the European Communities and the law deriving therefrom and for their resultant duty to provide information and act towards one another in a manner reflecting their relationship of mutual trust". Accordingly, they agree to collaborate in a close and loyal manner in relation to legislative proposals put forward within the framework of the European Community.

3. The procedure provided for in Article 2 *EEAG* gives a specific form to the duty of mutual communication incumbent upon Federation and *Länder* within the cooperative federal State (see 1 *BVerfGE* 299 at 315). Even though this procedure is founded merely on statute and hence cannot alter the respective positions of Federation and *Länder* under the Constitution, nonetheless it contributes substantially to defining and interpreting the relationship between Federation and *Länder* deriving from the principle of federal loyalty (*Bundestreue*). Thus Federation and *Länder* are bound by a statutory procedure whereby any proposed European Community legislation which could be of interest to the *Länder* has to be referred to the *Bundesrat*, which then becomes responsible for defending the constitutional rights of the *Länder* vis-à-vis the Federal Government. The question can be left open whether this procedure excludes the defence of additional rights of individual *Länder*, in particular where the latter dissent from the legal position taken by the majority within the *Bundesrat*. The fact remains that every *Land* is entitled, in any case involving the defence of its basic rights under the Constitution, to ensure that the Federal Government complies with the procedure prescribed by Article 2 *EEAG* and **[235]** conducts itself in accordance with the principle of federal loyalty (*Bundestreue*). In so far as Article 2 *EEAG* contains any additional rights, these are exercisable only by the *Bundesrat*.

4. In any case involving the existence or scope of the European Community's right to legislate in a field where the Constitution confers exclusive legislative competence on the *Länder*, the Federal Government, by virtue of its position as the organ of the State representing the Federal Republic within the competent institutions of the European Community and of its responsibility as representative of the rights of the *Länder*, has in particular the following procedural obligations in pursuance of its duties of cooperation and mutual consideration under the principle of federality (*Pflichte zu bundesstaatlicher Zusammenarbeit und Rücksichtnahme*):

(a) As soon as the competent German agencies receive sufficiently precise and reliable information on proposed Community legislation, the Federal Government must undertake a detailed examination in order to ascertain whether, in light of the interests of the State as a whole, the Federal Republic should support the proposed legislation, can accept it or should oppose it. This examination must cover the question of legislative competence, both under German law and in terms of the existence and scope of the relevant Community power. The Government must clarify its stance on this question in light of any changes in the proposed legislation as it progresses through its various stages.

(b) Once it has established its position, the Government must provide a statement of it, including its view of the relevant powers of the *Länder*. The statement must be properly reasoned, so that the *Länder* can then debate it within the *Bundesrat* and, if need be, raise doubts and objections which may cause the Government to reconsider its position. In this regard the *Länder* must, however, take account of the Federal Republic's duty to comply with Community law as interpreted with binding effect by the European Court (see 75 *BVerfGE* 223 at 242 ff.).[1]

(c) The Government must discuss its position with the *Bundesrat*. **[236]** Article 2(2) *EEAG* provides for a procedure within the *Bundesrat* whereby each individual *Land* has the opportunity to state and justify its position, after which the *Länder*'s common position is established by majority vote.

(d) Where, as a result of their discussions, the Government and the *Bundesrat* find themselves in agreement that the Community has no power to legislate, then the Government is bound to represent this view consistently and effectively in negotiations prior to the adoption of the [proposed Community] legislation.

(aa) Where Federation and *Länder* agree that the Community lacks the power, whether totally or in part, to adopt legislation in the field proposed, then the Government is not entitled to deviate from that view. This remains the case even where the Government believes that, notwithstanding the absence of a basis in Community law for the encroachment upon the legislative competence of the *Länder*, it may nonetheless be able, in the course of Community negotiations on the proposed text, to mitigate the effects of such encroachment. Its task is rather to avoid such encroachment completely. Even where it may be possible to negotiate a compromise on the content of the Community measure which in practice would meet the objections of the *Länder* to the substance of the proposed regime, this still does not justify any deviation by the Government from the agreed view that the Community is not competent to legislate in the field in question. Similarly, the Government cannot fulfil its duty as representative of the interests of the *Länder* by agreeing to legislation in one of the forms set out in Article 189 ECT in the expectation that its binding effect will be mitigated by accompanying declarations in the minutes, unilateral reservations or the like. Such procedures, at least so far as external appearances are concerned, involve a recognition in principle of the Community's power to legislate, to the detriment of the legislative powers of the *Länder* under the Constitution, thereby setting a damaging precedent which may be difficult to remedy subsequently.

Where, exceptionally, in the course of the Community negotiations the Federal Government considers that there are compelling reasons of foreign or integration policy for revising the common **[237]** position of Federation and *Länder* to the detriment of the latter, it must allow time for the agreement of the *Bundesrat* to be sought.

(bb) On the other hand, Article 2 *EEAG* does not mean that, where Federation and *Länder* are in agreement as to the lack of Community legislative power, the Federal Government must abstain altogether from participating in Community negotiations or restrict itself to disputing the

[[1] *Kloppenburg*, Volume 1, p. 496.]

Community's right to legislate. Rather, it must avail itself of all the means at its disposal in order to persuade the Community institutions to act in accordance with their powers, and to this end it must make its legal position clear beyond doubt. As a last resort, in cases where Community law allows a majority decision, but such a decision would conflict with the principle of federality (*Bundesstaatlichkeit*) enshrined in the Constitution (Article 79(3) *GG*), the Federal Government must invoke the obligation of reciprocal consideration (*wechselseitige Rücksichtnahme*)[2] deriving from the principle of Community loyalty (*Gemeinschaftstreue*) (see 89 *BVerfGE* 155 at 184).[3] If, however—notwithstanding the Federal Republic's contrary vote—legislation is adopted which in its view falls outside the Community's legislative competence while restricting that of the *Länder*, then the Government is under a continuing duty to use all the means at its disposal at Community level to procure the repeal or amendment of the instrument in question. It must do nothing that might affect, whether in law or in fact, the chances of its view prevailing in an application to the European Court of Justice.

(e) Where the existence or scope of a Community competence is disputed, then the Federal Government must, when deciding what position it should adopt within and in relation to the Community, give serious consideration to the *Bundesrat*'s contrary view. If, however, the Government and the *Bundesrat* are unable to reach agreement, then—notwithstanding the second sentence of Article 2(3) *EEAG*—the Government is entitled to take a view of the legal position different from that held by the *Bundesrat* where it is able to base that view on an **[238]** interpretation of the Treaty [of Rome] established by the case-law of the European Court of Justice. Before finally coming to a decision, the Government must take all possible steps to explain the reasons for its view to the *Bundesrat* and to discuss them with it.

II.

The Federal Government's conduct satisfied these tests as regards its Resolution of 8 March 1989, but failed them in terms of the manner in which it exercised its Community membership rights within the Council of Ministers.

1. The power to adopt statutory guidelines for purposes of safeguarding broadcasting freedom is a matter falling within the legislative competence of the *Länder*. Broadcasting is, however, also a cultural manifestation. In so far as cultural matters are subject to government legislation at all, Articles 70 ff. *GG* confer competence in this regard

[2 In the sense of the duty on the part of the Community institutions to take account of the problems specific to individual Member States, particularly those with a federal structure.]

[3 *Maastricht Treaty 1992 Constitutionality Case*, Volume 1, p. 526 at p. 553.]

upon the *Länder*, subject to any specific constitutional provisions imposing restrictions or exceptions in favour of the federal power (see 12 *BVerfGE* 205 at 229). The question whether such restrictions or exceptions apply in respect of specific individual matters covered by the Television Directive can be left open, since in any case the Directive's main concern is to establish an overall framework for the regulation of broadcasting, and in this regard it encroaches upon the exclusive legislative competence of the *Länder*.

2. The Federal Government's Resolution of 8 March 1989 did not violate the rights of the *Länder*.

(a) The applicants argue that, in adopting a broad approach to the power to issue directives under Articles 66 and 57 ECT, the Federal Government is conceding to the Community a legislative power that is potentially unlimited. They contend that, ultimately, the Community seeks to extend the principle of "freedom to provide services" to every cross-frontier service involving a monetary consideration, thereby also making "culture" (Article 128 ECT) subject to its unrestricted powers under Articles 59 ff. In practice this argument is unfounded.

The Federal Government is under a duty to ensure that the powers specifically conferred upon the Community (see 89 *BVerfGE* **[239]** 155 at 187 f., 191 ff.)[4] are not applied in such a manner that their scope becomes less foreseeable and their restrictive function is lost. In this regard the Government can in general rely on the fact that the EC Treaty is characterized by the principle of limited specific empowerment (*begrenzte Einzelermächtigung*). That principle operates to prevent the Treaty rules from simply being extended to any form of activity having some economic content; rather, there must be a specific grant of tasks, competences and powers within a particular field, and the Government is entitled to assume that this principle will basically be respected. At the same time loyalty to the principle of federality requires that the federal institutions oppose any long-term development which, through the gradual extension of Community competence, and in particular of the so-called "horizontal competences" (*Querschnittskompetenzen*), might result in an encroachment upon those specific areas of competence retained by the Member States, and hence also upon the rights of the *Länder*.

The Federal Government's conduct adhered to these principles. In the negotiations on the Television Directive it emphasized the principle of limited specific empowerment and in particular denied Community competence in relation to Chapter II (now III) programme quotas (see *inter alia* extract from the Minutes of 30/31 October 1986 of the Ad hoc Group [Council Document 10785/86]; Note of 17 December 1987 from the German Delegation to the Secretariat-General). It characterized the Community's efforts to regulate advertising and sponsorship as

[[4] *Ibid.*, pp. 555-6, 558 ff.]

a distortion of competition to the detriment of German media undertakings (see Report from the Federal Interior Minister of 26 February 1988 regarding the federal position), sought to have the Directive limited to television broadcasting, with sound broadcasting being excluded from its scope, and to delete the description of the Directive as a "first step" towards an overall European media policy.

(aa) During the negotiations on the Television Directive the Federal Government basically had no reason to place specific emphasis on the fact that the ECT objective of a free market in services did not in itself give the EEC an infinitely extendable competence in this regard. **[240]** It is generally recognized that the law-making institutions of the EEC cannot act except where expressly so empowered by the founding Treaties. Unlike the legislative organs of States they have no general power, founded on an overall governmental and institutional authority (*Verbands und Organkompetenz*), to legislate in any field whatever and to determine for themselves what form such legislation should take. The Government was entitled to assume that, in fulfilling the tasks "conferred upon it", the EEC will act "in accordance with the Treaty" (see Articles 3, 4, 145, 155 and 189 ECT). This principle of limited specific empowerment means that the Community institutions may act only where the Treaty gives the Community power to legislate and that they must employ the prescribed legislative forms, save in so far as the Treaty allows them freedom of choice in this regard (see Oppermann, *Europarecht*, 1991, para. 6, marginal number 433; Streinz, *Europarecht*, 2nd edition 1995, marginal numbers 436 f.; also now Articles E EUT and 3b(1) ECT and 89 *BVerfGE* 151 at 191 ff.[5]).

(bb) The Federal Government's Resolution was founded on a concern to ensure that in relation to the application of Articles 57 and 66 ECT there should likewise be no deviation from the principle of specific empowerment. At the outset of negotiations within the EC Council the Government, acting with the agreement of the *Länder*, entered a reservation on grounds that broadcasting was a matter falling within the competence of the federal *Länder* and outside that of the Community. It subsequently reserved its position on the question whether the cited legal basis (Articles 57(2) and 66 ECT) was appropriate to cover the entire Directive. In particular it queried whether it was a proper basis for Chapter II (now III). As an alternative it suggested that a more suitable basis might be Articles 100 and 235 ECT, which required a unanimous vote and where the Government would have been able to assert the rights of the *Länder* to their full extent. Further, in the course of subsequent discussions within the Council, the Government expressed fundamental doubts regarding the power of the Community to harmonize the cultural policies of Member States on broadcasting.

[[5] *Ibid*., pp. 558 ff.]

Thus it is clear from the negotiating positions adopted by the Federal Government that **[241]** it constantly, and with increasing insistence as the negotiations continued, emphasized the limits on the legislative powers deriving from Articles 57(2) and 66 ECT and sought to have their content more closely defined. There was never any question of the Government adopting or recognizing, whether as a negotiating stance or a basis for decision, an interpretation of the power to regulate the provision of services which would ultimately have allowed the EEC unlimited competence in relation to all cross-frontier services involving a monetary consideration.

(b) It was perfectly possible for the Federal Government, without violating the applicants' rights, to take the view that the Community was competent to legislate on the right of reply, the regulation of advertising and sponsorship and the protection of young people. To this extent it was entitled to deviate from the position of the *Bundesrat*. In support of its view that in law the broadcasting of television programmes constituted the provision of a service, in respect of which the Community enjoyed legislative competence under Articles 59 ff. ECT, the Government could rely on an established interpretation of the Treaty handed down by the European Court. On this basis it was open to it to come to the conclusion that the Treaty obligation to establish a free internal market in services allowed the Community to adopt provisions liberating cross-frontier television broadcasting and reception in all Member States and that to this end some approximation of law was required, at least in regard to the rules governing advertising and sponsorship, the protection of young people and the right of reply to television broadcasts. In reaching this conclusion, it was perfectly proper for the Government to take the view that, while the proposed legislation was of substantial financial concern to television broadcasting companies, it did not encroach upon the core area of the *Länder*'s right of regulation in regard to the organizational, political and cultural aspects of broadcasting.

(c) Nor did the Government violate the rights of the *Länder* in this regard in its Resolution of 8 March 1989 when it rejected the *Bundesrat*'s claim that **[242]** there was no requirement in law for Community legislation, since priority should be given to adoption of the proposed rules under the [draft] Council of Europe Convention, and these would then be sufficient. Initially, the Government did indeed endorse the doubts expressed by the *Länder* as to the legal necessity for a directive and made its reservations clear at Community level. However, it subsequently accepted that there was a requirement in law for binding Community legislation over and above the rules contained in the impending Council of Europe Convention, but only in relation to advertising, sponsorship, the protection of young people and the right of reply. In terms of *Länder* rights there was nothing constitutionally objectionable in this. Once the Federal Government, in reliance on an interpretation of the

Treaty handed down by the European Court of Justice, had accepted the Community's right in principle to legislate in this field, then there could be no question of it having further deviated from the position of the *Bundesrat* in also now accepting that there was a legal requirement for such legislation. Rather, in light of the undisputed need (acknowledged even by the applicants) for international legislation in this field, it is clear that the Government's stance derived from the view that a Council of Europe Convention—even if this were to be accorded political priority in order to bring other [non-Community] European States within its ambit—was no true substitute for a [Community] directive, since the Council of Europe lacked an institution equivalent to the European Court of Justice capable of overseeing its application.

(d) As regards the quota provisions, in its Resolution of 8 March 1989 the Government continued to adhere to the view that these were not covered by Articles 59 and 60 ECT and that the material content of broadcasts was primarily a cultural and socio-political matter. This was an area in which the European Community had no power to legislate. Accordingly, a regime which imposed mandatory quotas upon Member States and broadcasting companies was unacceptable to the Government. The Government further stated that it did not consider the setting of quotas to be an appropriate means of achieving the aim, which it shared, of promoting the creation and **[243]** distribution of European audiovisual productions.

The Government further made it clear that, if a satisfactory overall solution could be found, it could accept the Directive, provided that the quota provisions were formulated purely in terms of a political objective. However, this still did not amount to a deviation from the agreed common stance on competence sufficient to violate, or even directly threaten, the rights of the *Länder*. Thus the Government took the view that, while the latest draft of the quota rules was formulated in terms that in practice mitigated their binding effect, this still did not constitute a satisfactory solution, and it was not certain whether such a solution would be achieved. It was also still not clear whether the Government would succeed in its demand for the quota regime to be formulated in terms of a purely political objective, or within what legal framework this would be done. It was even possible that solutions would be found that did not involve EEC legislation at all and left the legislative powers of the *Länder* undisturbed. The agreed common stance of Federation and *Länder* on the question of competence continued to govern the position. In the event that the Community negotiations produced a result that, from its point of view, the Government considered satisfactory, it might have felt that this was an indication that it should abandon the common stance. However, all it was entitled to do at this stage was to put the new result of the negotiations to the *Bundesrat* with a view to seeking a new agreement.

3. Nevertheless the fact remains that, in relation to the quota provisions, the Federal Government did indeed violate the rights of the *Länder* through the manner in which it exercised the membership rights of the Federal Republic within the Council.

(a) The Government failed to represent consistently and effectively the common position agreed by it with the *Länder*, to the effect that the Community lacked the power to legislate under Articles 57(2) and 66 ECT (see I.4(d) above).[6] It did indeed succeed, in the **[244]** negotiations following the cabinet Resolution, in having the quota regime watered down to some extent. Thus, as a result of the pressure which it brought to bear, at the Council meeting of 13 April 1989 it was agreed that the entire field of sound broadcasting should be removed from the scope of the Directive, and that German broadcasting companies would be allowed to count all productions from the GDR in their quotas as European works. Also, the rules governing programme quotas, and hence likewise those for production quotas, were largely brought into line with Article 10(1) of the European Convention. However, the Government's representatives abandoned their attempts to have the quota provisions removed altogether. Although, prior to the second reading of the Directive on 3 October 1989, it was still not clear from the text whether the quota rules were no longer binding, the German representatives were content to accept formal declarations in the minutes by the Council and the Commission, to the effect that the aims pursued in those provisions "were to be regarded by Member States as political objectives".

The Government takes the view that the quota rules are not binding. But all those involved are aware that this view is of questionable validity. The rules form part of a directive, which under Article 189(3) ECT is binding as to the objectives to be achieved, and the text of the Directive contains no limitation on that binding effect. In these circumstances it remains at the very least doubtful whether the declarations in the minutes (which unlike the Directive have not been published) would alone be sufficient to deprive the Directive of binding force. These doubts were confirmed by the evidence given at the oral hearing by Director-General Dewost, head of the Legal Service of the Commission of the European Communities. Mr Dewost stated that, under the established case-law of the European Court, declarations in the minutes were considered to be of only limited legal force and certainly could not be opposed to the express terms of the Directive. He further stated that in the Commission's view the Directive was clearly binding on Member States in its entirety, and that Articles 4 and 5 simply allowed Member States a large measure of **[245]** discretion in terms of the measures to be adopted in order to achieve the prescribed objectives.

[[6] See p. 245.]

(b) Once the Federal Government realized that, despite its intensive negotiations over the quota issue, it could not count on majority support in the Council for its position, although it did appear that it would be possible to have restrictive declarations by both Council and Commission recorded in the minutes, it should then, before taking any decision on its subsequent action, have informed the *Bundesrat* of the outcome of the negotiations. Its failure to do so and to seek agreement on its subsequent conduct (see I.4(d) above)[7] constituted a breach of the rights of the *Länder*.

[Report: 92 *BVerfGE* I p. 203 (in German). Translated by T. F. K. Johnston MA, LL B]

[[7] *Ibid*.]

National constitutions — Constitutional review concerning Community Treaty — Treaty of Accession of new Member States, 1994 — Provisions concerning allocation of seats in European Parliament — Compatibility with Basic Law of Federal Republic of Germany — Whether violating constitutional principle of equal voting rights—Whether democratic legitimacy of European Union currently provided primarily by national parliaments or European Parliament

Institutions — European Parliament — Representatives — "Weighted" distribution of seats between different Member States—Whether any requirement for distribution of seats in different Member States to reflect fully their respective population sizes

Legal order in general — Special character — Contrast with regimes established by other international treaties — Effect of Community legal order on sovereignty of Member States—Whether Member States retaining status as fully independent States recognized with formal equality under public international law—The law of the Federal Republic of Germany

EUROPEAN PARLIAMENT UNEQUAL REPRESENTATION CASE

(Case No 2 BvR 635/95)

Federal Republic of Germany, Federal Constitutional Court (BVerfG) (Third Chamber)

(Limbach, *President*; Klein and Grasshof, *Judges*)

31 *May* 1995

SUMMARY: *The facts*:—The complainant lodged a constitutional complaint against the manner in which the seats in the European Parliament were allocated to the Member States. By the Act of Accession of new Member States of 24 June 1994, the number of seats in the European Parliament was increased to 567 with the allocation to Germany being fixed at 99 seats. The Act of Accession was approved by the German Parliament, but the complainant challenged this approval on the basis that it infringed the constitutional principle of equal voting rights since Germany, following its reunification, represented 22 per cent of the population of the whole European Union whereas it had only been allocated 16 per cent of the seats in the European Parliament.

Held:—The constitutional complaint was inadmissible.

(1) The composition of the European Parliament did not violate the principle of equal voting rights but merely reflected the composition of the European Union as a union of sovereign Member States. Consequently the composition of the European Parliament could not be judged by the same criteria as those laid down in the Federal Basic Law for German parliamentary elections.

(2) Equal voting rights in Germany were derived from the principle of the political equality of citizens. But the European Union had no "citizenry" in this sense. Article 137 of the European Community Treaty referred to MEPs as representatives of the "peoples of the States brought together in the Union". At the current stage of the development of the European Union, the exercise of the Union's sovereign powers derived legitimacy from the peoples of the democratic Member States primarily via their national parliaments. Equality of voting rights, which ensured this legitimacy, was thus guaranteed by the right to vote in national elections.

(3) The "weighted" distribution of seats in the European Parliament recognized that the European Union was more than the sum of its individual Member States by taking some account of population size. Nevertheless, the basis of the European Union remained its Member States, which continued to exist as independent States and for which the principle of the formal equality of individual States under public international law continued to apply, irrespective of the size of their populations.

The following is the text of the judgment of the Court:

OPERATIVE PART OF THE JUDGMENT

The Court declines to rule on the constitutional complaint.

GROUNDS

The basis of the constitutional complaint is that the principle of equal voting rights is infringed by the manner in which the seats in the European Parliament are allocated to the Member States.

I.

Article 137 of the Treaty of 25 March 1957 establishing the European Community ("ECT"), as amended by the Treaty on European Union of 7 February 1992 ("EUT"), provides that the European Parliament is to consist of "representatives of the peoples of the States brought together in the Community". Article 138(1) provides for the Members of Parliament ("MEPs") to be elected by universal suffrage. Article 138(2) established the number of those Members to be elected by each Member State as follows:

Belgium	24	Ireland	15
Denmark	16	Italy	81
Germany	81	Luxembourg	6
Greece	24	Netherlands	15
Spain	60	Portugal	24
France	81	United Kingdom	81

By a European Council Decision of 1 February 1993 the number of seats in the Parliament was increased to 567. Ninety-nine seats were allocated to Germany. The German Parliament (*Bundestag*) approved this Decision on 13 August 1993 (*BGBl* II, 1242). It came into force for Germany on 1 May 1994 (*BGBl* II, 619). Article 11 of the Act of 24 June 1994, concerning the Conditions of Accession of the Kingdom of Norway, the Republic of Austria, the Republic of Finland and the Kingdom of Sweden, and the Adjustments to the Treaties on which the European Union is founded, amended the number of MEPs to be elected by each Member State as follows:

Belgium	25	Luxembourg	6
Denmark	16	Netherlands	31
Germany	99	Norway	15
Greece	25	Austria	21
Spain	64	Portugal	25
France	87	Finland	16
Ireland	15	Sweden	22
Italy	87	United Kingdom	87

By Article 1 of the Law of 2 September 1994 (*BGBl* II, 2022), published on 16 September 1994, the *Bundestag* approved the Act of Accession of 24 June 1994, including the Declarations written into the Final Act of the same date.

II.

The constitutional complaint, received on 8 March 1995, contests that approval. The complainant argues that Article 11 of the Act of Accession infringes the principle of equal voting rights and thus also Article 3(1) of the Basic Law (*Grundgesetz*), since the complainant's vote would be of less weight in elections to the European Parliament than the votes of citizens of other Member States. He contends that, with the European Parliament now exercising a stronger influence over policy in Europe, it is particularly important that its elections should respect the principle of equal voting rights. This principle requires that each vote should have not only the same numerical value as every other, but also the same chance of influencing the outcome. Thus Germany, with a population of 22% of the entire European Union, should have 137 of the 626 seats in the European Parliament, whereas the disputed provisions allow for only 99 seats for Germany, just 16% of the total.

III.

The conditions for a ruling on the constitutional complaint under Section 93a(2) *BVerfGG* are not satisfied. The complaint does not raise any fundamental principles of constitutional law. Nor are any basic rights involved which would require this Court to examine the complaint. It is clear from the Court's case-law (see in particular 89 *BVerfGE* 155 (*EuGRZ* 1993, 429))[1] that this complaint has no prospect of success.

It is not necessary to decide whether or to what extent the organs of the German State, in approving acts of the European Union, are bound by general principles of equality or by the specific principle of formally equal voting rights. The current composition of the European Parliament does not offend against the principle of equal voting rights: it merely reflects the composition of the European Union itself, as a union of sovereign Member States (see EUT, Article F(1)). For this reason the composition of the European Parliament cannot be judged by the same criteria as those laid down by the Basic Law for parliamentary elections in the Federal Republic of Germany.

1. The principle of equal voting rights (Basic Law, Articles 28(2)(2) and 38(1)(2)) requires that all citizens shall exercise their voting rights in parliamentary and local elections in a manner which is formally equal, and that any vote cast under a system of proportional representation must not only be of the same value as any other but also have the same chance of influencing the outcome (see established case-law, most recently 85 *BVerfGE* 148 at 157 (*EuGRZ* 1992, 79 at 81)). From a historical perspective, equal voting rights are derived from the principle of the political equality of all citizens (41 *BVerfGE* 1 at 12 (*EuGRZ* 1976, 94 at 95)). In this sense, however, the European Union has no "citizenry" (*Staatsvolk*) (see 89 *BVerfGE* 155 at 188 (*EuGRZ* 1993, 429 at 439)).[2] Thus, Article 137 of the ECT refers to MEPs as representatives of the "peoples of the States brought together in the Community". At the current stage of integration of the European Union, the European Parliament serves merely to provide additional political underpinning for the policies of the Union. Exercise of the Union's sovereign powers derives legitimacy from the peoples of the democratic Member States, first and foremost via their national parliaments (89 *BVerfGE* 155 at 184-5 (*EuGRZ* 1993,

[1 Volume 1, p. 526.] [2 *Ibid*., p. 557.]

429 at 437 ff.)).[3] Equality of voting rights, which assures this legitimacy, is thus guaranteed by the right to vote in national elections.

2. The distribution of seats in the European Union according to a so-called "weighted key" is a compromise similar to that underlying the differential weighting of Council Members' votes in qualified majority voting under Article 148(2) of the ECT. The basis of the European Union is the Member States, which continue to exist as States and for which, in public international law, the principle of formal inter-State equality continues to apply, independently of the size of their populations. At the same time, as a union of States, the European Union amounts to more than the sum of the individual members (89 *BVerfGE* 155 at 181 (*EuGRZ* 1993, 429 at 436));[4] and this fact is recognized by taking population sizes into account.

There can be no appeal against this Decision.

[Report: *EuGRZ* 1995, p. 566 (in German); translated by T. F. K. Johnston, MA, LL B]

[3 *Ibid.*, p. 551.]

[4 *Ibid.*, p. 550.]

National constitutions — Constitutional review concerning Community Treaty — Treaty on European Union, 1992 (Maastricht Treaty) — Provisions governing European Monetary Union ("EMU") — Implementation of third stage of Monetary Union and creation of common currency — Constitutional legitimacy under Basic Law of the Federal Republic of Germany — Whether involving additional transfer of sovereign powers to European Community not provided for by Articles 23(1) and 88(2) of the Basic Law — Responsibility for ensuring that economic convergence criteria laid down in Maastricht Treaty are satisfied — Decisions of German Government and Parliament in relation to EMU — Whether subject to constitutional review — Whether subject to adequate democratic control

National constitutions — Fundamental rights — Basic Law of the Federal Republic of Germany — Treaty on European Union, 1992 — Provisions on transition to EMU and common currency — Possible conflict with fundamental rights under Basic Law — Right to participate in democratic process (Article 38(1)) and property rights (Article 14(1)) under Basic Law — Whether violated by procedure for transition to third stage of EMU

Powers—Extension by treaty—Treaty on European Union, 1992—Nature of obligations entered into by Member States—Provisions for implementation of third stage of EMU — Whether requiring further transfer of sovereign powers from Member States—The law of the Federal Republic of Germany

EUROPEAN MONETARY UNION CONSTITUTIONALITY CASE

(Cases Nos 2 BvR 1877/97 and 50/98)

Federal Republic of Germany, Federal Constitutional Court (BVerfG)

(Limbach, *President*; Grasshof, Kruis, Kirchhof, Winter, Sommer, Jentsch and Hassemer, *Judges*)

31 *March* 1998

SUMMARY: *The facts*:—Four German university professors lodged constitutional complaints against the participation of Germany in the third stage of European Monetary Union from 1 January 1999. They argued that, in giving its approval to those States which should enter the EMU, Germany had failed to ensure that the strict economic convergence criteria laid down in the Treaty on European Union, 1992 ("EUT") were applied. Accordingly they claimed that German participation in the EMU violated their democratic rights under Article 38(1) of the Basic Law of the Federal Republic (*Grundgesetz*) and their property rights under Article 14(1) of the Basic Law.

Held:—The constitutional complaints were rejected as manifestly unfounded.

(1) As the Federal Constitutional Court had already held,[1] German participation in the EMU was adequately provided for in the EUT and permitted in principle by Articles 23 and 88(2) of the Basic Law. In order to permit completion of this undertaking, the EUT laid down the criteria to be met and procedures to be followed for entry into the third stage of Monetary Union and, in particular, for the decision as to which States should participate in that Union. The EUT thereby left scope for economic and political assessment and forecasting. The Federal Government and Parliament, from the constitutional standpoint, assumed responsibility for making that assessment and for ensuring the protection of financial property. The owner of financial property did not, however, acquire the right to an examination of that decision in constitutional complaint proceedings (p. 262).

(2) Under the EUT, the sovereign authority necessary for the establishment of the EMU had been transferred to the European Community. Furthermore, the conditions for participation in the third stage of Monetary Union laid down in the EUT had obtained binding force as a result of the ratifying legislation enacted by the German Parliament. In addition to authorizing German participation in the EMU, the Basic Law secured a supervisory role for the German Parliament in relation to the exercise of German membership rights in European Community organs. Accordingly, the implementation of the provisions governing entry into the EMU did not require any additional transfer of sovereignty and could not violate the right to participate in the democratic process enshrined in Article 38(1) of the Basic Law (pp. 262-4).

(3) Property rights under Article 14(1) of the Basic Law were not infringed by the EMU. The German Parliament, in ratifying the EUT, had done no more than determine the precise content of those property rights in relation to money. Like any other holder of German Marks, under the EMU arrangements the complainants would obtain the right to convert German Marks to an equivalent amount of Euros, with the guarantor of that money henceforth being the States participating in the EMU rather than the German State. Article 14(1) did not guarantee the value of money as a fundamental right. Equally, Article 14(1) did not require the German political organs to secure the stability of the EMU in a different way or to postpone its start. In relation to the economic and political assessments to be made in evaluating whether or not the convergence criteria were met, the German Government and Parliament enjoyed a margin of discretion and their decisions were not subject to scrutiny from the standpoint of the basic rights of individuals (pp. 264-8).

The text of the relevant part of the judgment of the Court commences on the following page.

[1] See *Maastricht Treaty 1992 Constitutionality Case*, Volume 1, p. 526.

[350] Professor Rupp (Complaint No 2 BvR 1877/97) . . . and Professors Hankel, Nölling, Schachtschneider and Starbatty (Complaint No 2 BvR 50/98) . . . have entered constitutional complaints . . . against the failure of the Federal Government to ensure that the necessary strict economic convergence criteria were fulfilled by Germany, and the other Member States of the European Community, prior to their being allowed to proceed to the achievement of the third stage of Economic and Monetary Union . . . The complainants have also applied for a temporary injunction to be issued.

[351] OPERATIVE PART OF THE JUDGMENT

The complaints of unconstitutionality are dismissed.

GROUNDS

A.

The complaints of unconstitutionality are directed against the participation of Germany in European Monetary Union from 1 January 1999.

I.

On 7 February 1992, in Maastricht, the Member States of the European Communities signed the Treaty on European Union [hereinafter the "EUT"]. This Treaty also amended the Treaty establishing the European Community [hereinafter the "ECT"] which, in Title VI, Chapter 2, Articles 105 *et seq.*, provides for a common monetary policy for the Member States. The EUT entered into force on 1 November 1993.

The common monetary policy is intended to establish a European Monetary Union in stages and ultimately a common monetary policy under the direction of the European System of Central Banks (ESCB). The first two stages of the transition to monetary union have already been achieved. Currently, implementation of the third stage, the introduction of a single currency, is under preparation.

[The Constitutional Court detailed the decision-making procedure required by the ECT for the introduction of a single currency, as set out especially in Article 109j. In particular, Article 109j(1) required the achievement of a high degree of sustainable economic convergence by the Member States by reference to the fulfilment of four criteria:

—a high degree of price stability without excessive inflation;
—sustainable government finances without an excessive deficit;

— successful participation in the Exchange Rate Mechanism of the European Monetary System for at least two years;
— durable convergence reflected in long-term interest rate levels.

Details of these four criteria were set out in a Protocol on the Convergence Criteria referred to in Article 109j(1), and annexed to the ECT.

The Court then summarized the steps which had already been taken, including the publication on 25 March 1998 of the Convergence Report of the European Monetary Institute and the Recommendation made by the European Commission on the basis of that Report, that eleven Member States fulfilled the conditions for the introduction of a single currency. Subsequently the German Central Bank, at the request of the Federal Chancellor, had issued its opinion that entry into the Monetary Union from 1999 was feasible from the point of view of economic stability. The Federal Government had then decided, on 27 March 1998, to recommend that the Report of the European Monetary Institute and the Recommendation of the European Commission should be followed. The consent of the two houses of the German Parliament had then been requested.

When approving the EUT on 2 December 1992, the lower house of the Federal Parliament (*Bundestag*) and the upper house (*Bundesrat*) had passed almost identical Resolutions on Economic and Monetary Union calling for the stability criteria agreed at Maastricht to be strictly observed and stressing that their consenting votes were required for transition to the third stage of Economic and Monetary Union and must be respected.

The vote in the *Bundestag* on the participation of Germany in Monetary Union was scheduled for 23 April 1998. The *Bundesrat* was to decide on 24 April. The recommendations of the European Council of Ministers were to be made on 1 May and the position of the European Parliament was to be determined at a special session in Brussels on 2 May. Finally, on 3 May 1998, the participating States were to be confirmed by the European Council, meeting in its composition of Heads of State and Government. The Constitutional Court continued:]

[362] II.

The complaints of unconstitutionality concern the participation of Germany in Monetary Union from as early as 1 January 1999. The first complainant alleges a violation of his rights guaranteed by Article 38(1) of the Basic Law. The second complainants allege a violation of their basic rights under Articles 2(1) and 14(1) as well as their rights guaranteed by Article 38(1) of the Basic Law.

[The Constitutional Court set out the arguments put forward by the complainants as well as the view of the Federal Government that the complaints were clearly inadmissible. The Court continued:]

[368] B.

It need not be decided whether the imminent prospect of acts of State justifies considering the complaints of unconstitutionality as admissible. They are in any case manifestly unfounded so that they can be dealt with under Section 24 of the Law on the Federal Constitutional Court (*BVerfGG*) (*cf. BVerfGE* 53, 100 at 106; 79, 223 at 231; 96, 1 at 5). The applications for the issue of an interim injunction can also be dealt with at the same time.

Germany's participation in the Monetary Union is provided for in the EUT and permitted in principle by Articles 23 and 88(2) of the Basic Law (*cf. BVerfGE* 89, 155 at 199).[2] In order to permit completion of this legal undertaking, the EUT sets out the criteria to be met and procedures to be followed for entry into the third stage of Monetary Union and, in particular, for the decision on which States are to participate in Monetary Union. It thereby leaves scope for economic and political assessment and forecasting. The Federal Government and Parliament assume responsibility for this in order to ensure the protection of financial property. The owner of financial property does not, however, acquire the right to an examination of this decision in constitutional complaint proceedings. Parliament alone is responsible for that decision.

I.

Article 38(1) of the Basic Law is not infringed.

1. Article 38(1) and (2) of the Basic Law grants to those entitled to vote the subjective right to take part in the election of deputies to the German *Bundestag*. This guarantee also extends to the fundamental democratic content of this right in that, through elections in accordance with arrangements set out in more detailed legislative provisions, those entitled to vote are guaranteed participation in the legitimation of State authority at federal level and influence over the exercise of that authority. Article 38 of the Basic Law precludes, within the scope of application of Article 23 of the Basic Law, the legitimation of State authority and the influence over its exercise by means of elections from being undermined by the transfer of tasks and powers of the *Bundestag* to such an extent that the principle of democracy is violated, in so far as **[369]** Article 79(3) in conjunction with Article 20(1) and (2) of the Basic Law declares this principle inviolable (*BVerfGE* 89, 155 at 171 *et seq.*).[3]

[2 *Ibid.*, p. 565.]

[3 *Ibid.*, pp. 543-4.]

Democracy presumes an ongoing free dialogue between opposing social forces, interests and ideas, through which political goals are also clarified and developed, and from which public opinion gives shape to the political will. It also presumes that the decision-making process of the organs exercising sovereign authority and the political objectives which are followed as a result are generally clear and understandable (*BVerfGE* 89, 155 at 185).[4] Such overriding constitutional assumptions are not, however, guaranteed as equivalent to basic rights under Article 38(1) of the Basic Law.

2.a) The establishment of European Monetary Union is the object of the EUT. Germany concluded this Treaty with the other Member States, placed the Treaty on a constitutionally valid foundation by enacting Article 23(1) of the Basic Law and, in the ratifying legislation, declared it applicable in Germany pursuant to Article 23(1), second and third sentences, of the Basic Law. The protection of German membership rights in European organs is secured on a parliamentary basis through the participation rights of the *Bundestag* (Article 23(2) and (3) of the Basic Law). In this way entry into the third stage of monetary union is legitimated on an adequate democratic basis (*cf. BVerfGE* 89, 155 at 190 and 199 *et seq.*).[5]

b) This is also true for the decision on the specific form of monetary union on the basis of the EUT, by which monetary union is established without political union either resulting simultaneously or following immediately afterwards. If it emerges that in reality monetary union cannot be achieved without political union, this would require a new political decision, which would have consequences for monetary union and for the form of the Treaty. A Treaty amendment would be required for such a decision and this could only be effected with the consent of the national State organs in exercise of their political responsibility (*BVerfGE* 89, 155 at 207).[6]

c) According to these guidelines the Member States and the European Union now need to decide whether to introduce monetary union **[370]** in a still to be ascertained number of participating States. The standard for and manner of entry into the third stage of monetary union are regulated in the Treaty and have acquired legally binding force in Germany by virtue of the ratifying legislation for which the *Bundestag* and *Bundesrat* were responsible. The *Bundestag* has no further competence or powers in relation to the protection of the sovereign authority which has already been transferred under the EUT. In this respect a violation of Article 38(1) of the Basic Law does not come into question.

d) In so far as the first complainant alleges that the political objectives followed by the Federal Government were not generally clear or understandable, this concerns the fundamental prerequisites for democracy.

[4 *Ibid.*, p. 553.] [5 *Ibid.*, p. 558.] [6 *Ibid.*, p. 570.]

These cannot, however, be enforced as the equivalent of constitutionally guaranteed basic rights under Article 38(1) of the Basic Law. Accordingly, the stage by stage introduction of monetary union envisaged in the ECT as well as the explanations of the Federal Government, the *Bundestag*, the *Bundesrat* and the *Länder* (States) as to its objectives, given at the time of parliamentary consultation over the EUT and the related constitutional amendments, do not require consideration.

II.

The legislation ratifying the EUT amends the definition of the substance and limits of financial property in German Marks, within the meaning of Article 14(1), second sentence, of the Basic Law. If, in application of the EUT, the assessment and forecasting of the responsible State organs leads to the conclusion that the envisaged monetary union will result in a community of stability, then an owner of financial property is not entitled to require the Federal Constitutional Court to scrutinize those assessments and evaluations by means of a complaint of unconstitutionality.

1. Article 14(1) of the Basic Law affords the right to own, use, administer and dispose of tangible and financial property.

a) The guarantee of the right to property, contained in Article 14(1), first sentence, of the Basic Law, ensures the privately controlled economic foundation of individual freedom. The guarantee of the right to property, **[371]** within the overall context of basic rights, "entitles the holder of a basic right to protection of his freedom of action in the field of the law of property thereby enabling him to pursue the responsible development of his life" (*BVerfGE* 50, 290 at 339; 53, 257 at 290). In contemporary society the great majority of citizens are assured the economic basis of their existence and freedoms "less through tangible assets than through earned income and the associated collectively borne public services, which have historically been closely associated with the concept of property" (*BVerfGE* 40, 65 at 84; 53, 257 at 290).

Accordingly, the guarantee of the right to property not only protects physical objects but also monetary claims. The holders enjoy the exclusive right to their private use, based on individual achievement, and to provide a material basis for their personal freedom (*BVerfGE* 40, 65 at 82 *et seq*. . . .). A substantive guarantee of the freedom of property is directly contained in the possibility of exchanging goods and money. The equivalence of tangible and financial property is also one of the functional bases of Article 14 of the Basic Law. Money is the coinage of freedom since it can be freely exchanged for things.

b) Certainly the value of money is linked to and dependent on the community in a particular manner. Its value is established in the context of State sovereignty over monetary and financial policy, as well as through the conduct of the holders of basic rights themselves, in particular in relation to prices, wages, interest rates, economic assessment and evaluation. The external value of money is established by relating the national currency to other currencies and their State, economic and social foundations. Under these conditions the State cannot guarantee the value of money as a fundamental right. In the same way that Article 14(1) of the Basic Law can guarantee only the right of the property owner to dispose of his assets and not the availability of demand for those assets, the basic right of the property owner even in a monetary sense can only be secured through the institutional structure and its individual regulation.

[372] 2. If the German Mark is replaced by another currency, and the sovereign guarantee of its redeemability is thereby exchanged, this alters the legal framework which secures the freedom of development which is given substance through money in the sphere of property law. In future the currency's redeemability is no longer guaranteed by the State-constituted legal community of the Federal Republic of Germany, but rather by another legal community and the economic strength which underpins it. Whether and to what extent this sovereign regulated exchange of currencies affects the rights protected under Article 14(1) of the Basic Law does not require a conclusive evaluation here. In any case, an adequate constitutional basis is provided by Article 88, second sentence, of the Basic Law, by the ratification of the EUT by the *Bundestag* and *Bundesrat* pursuant to Article 23(1), second and third sentences, of the Basic Law, and by those chambers' legal enactments implementing the Treaty pursuant to Article 23(2) of the Basic Law.

a) The EUT regulates a continually developing European Union, which is upheld by the constitutions of the Member States and their earnest willingness to achieve it (*cf. BVerfGE* 89, 155 at 200).[7] The Basic Law recognizes and justifies in Article 23(1), first sentence, the participation of Germany in this development of the European Union. After the Act amending the Basic Law of 21 December 1992 (*BGBl* I, 2086) gave a formal constitutional basis to European integration in Article 23 of the Basic Law, the next move towards integration confronting the legislature, in amending the Constitution, was the decision on European Monetary Union (*BTDrucks* 12/3338, p. 5). Article 88, second sentence, of the Basic Law expresses the will of those amending the Constitution to transfer the tasks and authority of the German *Bundesbank* to a European Central Bank on condition that the European Central Bank is independent and is bound by the primary objective of price stability. The further development of the European Union, which is thus constitutionally legitimated, is established by a decision on the entry of selected States into monetary union.

[7 *Ibid.*, p. 565.]

[373] b) In giving its consent to monetary union, the German legislature has, according to Article 14(1), second sentence, of the Basic Law, determined the content and limits of financial property in such a way that Germany can be included in monetary union under closely regulated legal conditions (Article 109j ECT). On this basis the German Mark can be converted into the Euro after the introduction of a single currency and become absorbed into this independent currency. Thereby every holder of financial property in German Marks is placed in a legal position which envisages its inclusion in the European Monetary Union. This provision has the legal consequence that the guarantor of this money ceases to be the German State and the prevailing strength of the economy in Germany. Henceforth this national guarantor is to be replaced by the States participating in monetary union and their national economies (cf. *BVerfGE* 89, 155 at 174).[8]

c) The ECT and the Basic Law regulate the standards and procedure for entry into the third stage of monetary union in clear legal terms and thereby stress the competence and responsibility of the Federal Government and Parliament.

aa) For the decision which must be taken on the start of monetary union with selected participating States, Article 109j in conjunction with Article 104c ECT essentially requires a critical assessment of the long-term stability of monetary union on the basis of the legal and economic convergence of the participating States. The Treaty has determined the criteria for this convergence in clear constituent detail as a legally binding basis for decision-making (Article 109j(1) in conjunction with Article 104c as well as the Protocol on the Convergence Criteria under Article 109j ECT and the Protocol on the Excessive Deficit Procedure). Admittedly this legal standard does open up scope for assessment, evaluation and prognosis (*BVerfGE* 89, 155 at 203).[9] The examination and assessment of the data provided by the European Monetary Institute and the Commission require empirical determination, assessment and evaluation, which can only rely approximately on empirical knowledge. The critical assessment of these developments requires analysis and projections based on practical common sense, which only permit a finding of probability and cannot be certain. **[374]** The overall assessment of a high degree of long-term convergence and the related forecast of an ongoing community of stability require decisions by the responsible organs involving the overlapping of assessments of facts, evaluations of experience and deliberate models. In so far as the Treaty also specifies a particular *rapprochement* of the reference values in the criteria concerning the budget deficit and the stock of government debt according to Article 104c, paragraph 2, ECT, the decision is based on a prognosis which can only be an assessment of probability and must therefore be made

[8 Volume 1, p. 526 at p. 545.] [9 *Ibid.*, p. 567.]

on an ongoing basis in accompanying examinations and decisions. In this sphere of legally defined factors involving economic judgment and political evaluation the Basic Law assigns the responsibility for decision-making to the Government and Parliament (Article 23(2) *GG*).

bb) The requirement of a long-term overall prognosis on the basis of assessments and evaluations of economic, social and political factors, and of forecasts of future performance of the economy and society, as well as financial economic discipline of the participating States, has caused the *Bundestag* and *Bundesrat* to reserve the right to make their own assessment regarding passage to the third stage of monetary union (*BVerfGE* 89, 155 at 202).[10]

Primary responsibility for the transfer of monetary sovereignty to the European Community and for continuing development through amendment of its treaty basis lies with the legislature (Article 23(1) of the Basic Law), whereas responsibility for the enforcement of the Treaty lies with the Federal Government (*BVerfGE* 92, 203 at 230 *et seq.*). If the Federal Government exercises Germany's membership rights within the European institutions, the *Bundestag* is thereby involved in the formation of the will of the Federation in this integration process, according to the requirements of Article 23(2) and (3) of the Basic Law and the Implementing Law on Cooperation between the Federal Government and the *Bundestag* in European Union affairs of 12 March 1993 (*BGBl* I, 311). The participation of the *Bundesrat* in this process is governed by Article 23(2), (4) and (5) of the Basic Law. These **[375]** interlinked competences are to be exercised in a manner consistent with institutional loyalty (*BVerfGE* 89, 155 at 199 *et seq.*)[11]

cc) The decision of the [European] Council, meeting in its composition of Heads of State and Government according to Article 109j(4) of the ECT, concerning those Member States participating in monetary union, is a legislative act in the sense of Article 23(3) of the Basic Law which applies the Treaty in legally binding form and concerns the Federal Republic of Germany as a Member State. The Federal Government must therefore take into account the opinion of the *Bundestag* under Article 23(3), second sentence, and of the *Bundesrat* under Article 23(5), first sentence, of the Basic Law. The understanding of December 1992 between the *Bundestag* and the *Bundesrat* on the one hand, and the Federal Government on the other, was reached within the framework of the amendment of Article 23, in force since 22 December 1992, on cooperation with the *Bundestag* and *Bundesrat* in a manner consistent with institutional loyalty.

d) In so far as Article 109j(1), second sentence, in conjunction with Article 107 and Article 108 ECT, requires the "legal convergence" (*cf. Bundesbank*, Information Bulletin on European Economic and Monetary

[10 *Ibid.*, p. 568.] [11 *Ibid.*, p. 558.]

Union, No 10, February 1998, p. 3) of the European Central Bank and national central banks, and in particular their legally secured independence as a condition of monetary union, this provision also contains a primary mandate for the Federal Government and Parliament to act as examiner and guarantor to follow and account for the continuing development of monetary union politically. Article 88, second sentence, of the Basic Law requires that the European Central Bank shall be independent and have as its primary aim the safeguarding of price stability. The ECT expands this requirement of independence and extends it beyond the European Central Bank to the central banks of the Member States (Article 107 ECT). It also clarifies the primary objective of price stability in specific substantial institutional requirements (Article 105 *et seq.*, ECT). However, this legal convergence is to be realized under both Community law and the law of other Member States, quite apart from what is required of the German *Bundesbank*. This convergence will be primarily achieved by political agreement with the other Member States.

[376] e) The Federal Government, together with the *Bundestag* and *Bundesrat*, through their mandate to assist the formation of monetary union as a community of stability and thereby fulfil the requirements of Article 88, second sentence, of the Basic Law, contribute to the legally objective safeguarding of financial property and thereby to the guarantee contained in Article 14(1) of the Basic Law. The complainants misjudge the reach of the fundamental legal title guaranteed in Article 14(1) of the Basic Law when, in reliance on Article 14, they seek to oblige the politically responsible organs to secure the stability of European Monetary Union in a different manner and to postpone the start of this Union. The Federal Government and Parliament are required, under Article 109j(1), third sentence, ECT, to examine and evaluate economic data, to observe and assess developments in their wider context under Article 109j(1), fourth sentence, ECT, to make a detailed forecast for States ready to participate and an overall forecast of the stability of the planned monetary union, and finally to work towards legal convergence within the Community and in the legal regime of the Member States. The decisions which need to be made in this regard cannot be taken at the individualized level of a basic right. It is the political organs responsible for the overall assessment of general developments which are answerable and are able to scrutinize and correct their decisions as developments unfold.

III.

Equally, the remaining basic rights and guarantees equivalent to basic rights do not entitle the complainants to the postponement of monetary union which their application seeks.

1. In so far as the complainants accrue salary and pension rights as civil servants *vis-à-vis* the public authorities, Article 33(5) of the Basic Law protects the legal status of the value of money (*BVerfGE* 52, 303 at 344 *et seq.*). Article 33(5) of the Basic Law requires that due regard be given to the traditional principles of the professional civil service and thereby permits a continuing development under which public service law conforms in its detailed form to changed circumstances **[377]** (*cf. BVerfGE* 43, 154 at 168). In the transparency of these developments the legal status of the value of money owned by a civil servant is subject to the same reservation as a common European currency under Article 14 of the Basic Law.

2. In so far as the complainants rely on Article 2(1) of the Basic Law they are also unsuccessful. Regardless of the question of how the guarantees inherent in Article 2(1) of the Basic Law are to be defined in detail and how violation of this basic right is to be distinguished from its merely being affected by an illegal encumbrance assessed in a legally objective manner, general freedom of action together with all other basic rights offer no protection against the enforcement of the ECT by a decision on the introduction of a European Monetary Union in particular Member States. Such a decision is based on politically accountable determination, assessments, evaluations and prognoses and, within the framework of the Basic Law, is the responsibility of the Federal Government, the *Bundestag* and the *Bundesrat*. Long-term economic developments and the consequences which follow therefrom for the stability of a currency cannot be assessed from the point of view of an individual and isolated intervention, but must be constantly moulded and continually scrutinized. This is not a matter for the courts but for the Government and Parliament.

[Reports: 97 *BVerfGE*, p. 350; *EuGRZ* 1998, p. 164 (in German)]

National constitutions — Constitutional challenge to legislation of Community institutions enacted pursuant to EC Treaty — Basic Law of Federal Republic of Germany, Article 23 — Whether Community secondary legislation subject to constitutional review

Human rights—Scope of protection within the Community—Case-law of the Court of Justice of the European Community — Whether adequately ensuring protection of fundamental rights

National constitutions—Fundamental rights—Basic Law of Federal Republic of Germany—EC Treaty and secondary legislation — Possible conflict with fundamental rights under Basic Law — Whether Community legislation subject to constitutional review by national courts to establish compatibility with fundamental constitutional rights — Whether protection of fundamental rights now adequately safeguarded by the Court of Justice so as to satisfy requirements of Basic Law—The law of the Federal Republic of Germany

BANANA MARKET ORGANIZATION CONSTITUTIONALITY CASE

(Case No 2 BvL 1/97)

Federal Republic of Germany, Federal Constitutional Court (BVerfG) (Second Chamber)

(Limbach, *President*; Sommer, Jentsch, Hassemer, Bross, Osterloh and Di Fabio, *Judges*)

7 *June* 2000

SUMMARY: *The facts*:—In 1993, pursuant to EC Council Regulation 404/93, a common organization of the market for bananas entered into force, replacing the disparate national regimes which had hitherto applied in the Member States of the Community. The preferential regime which had been granted to imports into the Federal Republic of Germany under a "Banana Protocol" to the EC Treaty was thereby discontinued. Instead, a regime was established which gave a measure of preferential treatment to so-called "ACP Bananas" (originating from certain African, Caribbean and Pacific States associated with the European Community under the Lomé Conventions) and "Community Bananas" (originating in the Member States) over "third-country bananas" (originating mainly in the Central American countries which had previously been the main suppliers of the German market).

Both the Federal Republic of Germany and a group of companies which traditionally imported third-country bananas into Germany ("the Atlanta Group") challenged the legality of the new tariff quotas applicable to traders in third country bananas under the Regulation, on the basis that they violated fundamental rights and general principles of law recognized by European Community law. Germany applied to the Court of Justice of the European Community for the annulment of the relevant provisions of the Council Regulation. In October 1994, in *Germany* v. *Council* ([1994] ECR I-4973), the European Court of Justice dismissed the application, upholding the legality of the Regulation and rejecting arguments that it violated the principles of non-discrimination and proportionality as well as the right to property, acquired rights and freedom to pursue a trade. At the same time, the Atlanta Group brought proceedings before the Administrative Court (*VwG*) of Frankfurt against the Federal authorities, challenging the import quotas allocated to them. The Administrative Court made a reference to the Court of Justice for a preliminary ruling on the validity of the provisions of the Regulation at issue. In November 1995, in *Atlanta Fruchthandelsgesellschaft* v. *Bundesamt für Ernährung* ([1995] ECR I-3799), the Court of Justice upheld the validity of the Regulation, simply confirming its earlier judgment.

Notwithstanding this ruling, the Administrative Court of Frankfurt then made a reference to the Federal Constitutional Court in October 1996, arguing that the judgments of the Court of Justice appeared to result in a failure to protect fundamental rights guaranteed by the Federal Constitution (*GG*) and raising the issue of the scope of the application of Community secondary legislation in Germany under Article 23(1) *GG*, in the event of a possible conflict with fundamental rights protected by the Constitution. The Administrative Court argued that its reference was admissible since, in its *Maastricht Treaty Constitutionality Case*[1] judgment, the Federal Constitutional Court had in effect reversed its position in *Solange II*[2] and was once again prepared to exercise its power of constitutional review in order to secure compliance with the standard of fundamental rights unconditionally required by the Constitution. The Administrative Court argued that the provisions of the Regulation violated the applicant companies' rights under Article 3(1) (right to equality), Article 12(1) (freedom to practise an occupation) and Article 14 (right to property) *GG*. Accordingly, in the view of the Administrative Court, the quota system at the heart of the new Common Market organization for bananas had brought about a structural deficit in the protection of fundamental rights in Germany.

Held:—The reference to the Federal Constitutional Court was inadmissible.

(1) In its *Maastricht Treaty* judgment in 1993, the Federal Constitutional Court had emphasized that it ensured, through its jurisdiction exercised in cooperation with the Court of Justice, that effective protection of fundamental rights was secured generally for residents in Germany as against the sovereign powers of the European Community. This was substantially similar to the protection of fundamental rights required unconditionally by the Constitution and safeguarded the essential content of those rights. In practice, however, the Federal Constitutional Court would exercise this jurisdiction only if and when the Court

[1] Volume 1, p. 526. [2] Volume 1, p. 461.

of Justice should depart from the standard of fundamental rights laid down by the Constitutional Court in its *Solange II* judgment in 1986 (pp. 281-3).

(2) Consequently, constitutional complaints and references from courts, alleging the infringement of fundamental rights enshrined in the Federal Constitution by secondary Community law, were inadmissible *ab initio* if their grounds failed to show that the development of European law, and in particular the jurisprudence of the Court of Justice since the *Solange II* judgment of the Federal Constitutional Court, had fallen below the required standard of fundamental rights protection (p. 283).

(3) Accordingly, the grounds for a reference by a national court or a constitutional complaint must specify how the minimum protection of fundamental rights unconditionally required by the Constitution was in general not ensured. This required a comparison of the protection of fundamental rights at the national and the Community level, in the manner carried out by the Federal Constitutional Court in *Solange II*. The Federal Constitutional Court had not altered its position on this point and the *Maastricht Treaty* judgment was fully consistent with the judgment in *Solange II*. The amended Article 23(1) *GG* confirmed this case-law. It was not necessary that the specific fundamental rights protected under the Constitution should be covered to exactly the same extent by Community law and jurisprudence (pp. 283-4).

The following is the text of the relevant part of the judgment of the Court:

[148] OPERATIVE PART OF THE JUDGMENT

The reference is inadmissible.

GROUNDS

A.

This reference concerns the question whether the application of the European Community's common organization of the market for bananas in the Federal Republic of Germany is in accordance with the German Constitution.

I.

1. Until 1993 the market for bananas within the European Community was subject to different rules in the various Member States. Some markets, for example France, were closed markets with guaranteed prices. Others, for example Germany, were open markets without quota restrictions. Under the "Banana Protocol" to the EC Treaty the Federal Republic of Germany was able to import duty free a particular quantity

of bananas . . . (see Case C-283/93 R, *Germany* v. *Council* [1993] ECR I-3668).

On 1 July 1993, pursuant to the second sentence of Article 33 of Council Regulation (EEC) No 404/93 of 13 February 1993 (OJ 1993 L 47, p. 1), the common organization of the market for bananas entered into force and the duty-free quota allowed under the Banana Protocol was discontinued (Article 21(2) of Regulation No 404/93).

The Regulation distinguishes bananas according to their area of origin: "Community bananas" are those produced within the European Community. "ACP bananas" are those which originate in certain States in Africa, the Caribbean and the Pacific, which as "ACP States" have for some time been associated with the European Community through special, multilateral agreements (Lomé Convention Agreements; . . .) **[149]** (see Article 179(3) EC Treaty in the version of the Treaty of Amsterdam; . . .). "Traditional" ACP bananas refers to a tariff quota of up to a total weight of 857,700 tonnes (see the Annex to Regulation No 404/93), which corresponds to the traditional quantity imported from the ACP States. Imports exceeding that quantity are referred to as "non-traditional" ACP bananas. Lastly, "third-country" bananas have their origin neither in the Community nor in the ACP States.

Community and ACP bananas cannot compete in price and quality with third-country bananas. Primarily third-country bananas were consumed on the German market . . . The common organization of the banana market was intended to support the production of bananas in the Community and to make it possible for bananas from traditional ACP States to be imported duty free, but without undermining imports of third-country bananas and non-traditional ACP bananas (see the second recital *et seq.* to Regulation No 404/93).

2. Aid rules are to be drawn up for that purpose for Community bananas (Article 10 *et seq.* of Regulation No 404/93). Like all bananas produced outside the Community, traditional ACP bananas require an import licence (Article 17 of Regulation No 404/93), but are imported duty free (Article 17).

Non-traditional ACP bananas and third-country bananas may be imported, within a particular tariff quota, at low or duty-free rates. Imports in excess of that quota are subject to a high rate of duty. Under Article 18 of Regulation No 404/93 the yearly quota was originally 2 million tonnes. Within that quota non-traditional ACP bananas could be imported duty free, third-country bananas at a rate of 100 ecu per tonne. For imports in excess of that quota, ACP bananas were subject to a duty rate of 750 ecu per tonne, third-country bananas to a rate of 850 ecu per tonne.

The customs quota for non-traditional ACP bananas and third-country bananas is divided according to operators and economic **[150]** activity. Pursuant to Article 19 of Regulation No 404/93, the tariff quota is divided amongst operators as follows:

—66.5% for the category of operators who marketed third-country bananas and/or non-traditional ACP bananas;
—30% for the category of operators who marketed Community bananas and/or traditional ACP bananas;
—3.5% for the category of operators established in the Community who commenced marketing bananas other than Community bananas and/or traditional ACP bananas from 1992.

Article 2 of Commission Regulation (EEC) No 1442/93 of 10 June 1993 laying down detailed rules for the application of the arrangements for importing bananas into the Community (OJ L 142 of 12 June 1993, p. 6) refers to those three categories as Categories A, B and C respectively. [The Court explained that market participants in Categories A and B were also divided according to economic activity and their import licences determined in accordance with Articles 5 and 6 of Regulation No 1442/93. The Court continued:]

[151] 3. The common organization of the banana market was subsequently supplemented and amended on several occasions.

For example, with effect from 1 January 1995, Regulation No 3290/94 reformulated some articles of Regulation No 404/93. Article 18 of Regulation No 404/93 (new version) reduced the rate of duty on the import of third-country bananas within the quota to 75 ecu per tonne and increased the yearly customs quota from 2 million tonnes to 2.1 million tonnes for 1994 and to 2.2 million tonnes thereafter (see Council Regulation (EEC) No 3290/94 of 22 December 1994 . . . OJ 1990 L 349, p. 105, annex XV, point 4; on the entry into force of the amendment, see Article 6(2)(d) of Regulation No 3290/94). Further increases in the customs quota on the basis of forecast needs remained possible. The quotas in 1997 in fact amounted to 2.553 million tonnes . . . With regard to quantities in excess of the tariff quota, the original fixed rates of 750 ecu per tonne for non-traditional ACP bananas and 850 ecu per tonne for third-country bananas were replaced, in the new version of Regulation No 404/93, by a complex rule (Article 18(2) in conjunction with Article 15 of Regulation No 404/93 in the version of Regulation No 3290/94), which nevertheless still provided that, with regard to imports in excess of the quota, the rate of duty for non-traditional ACP bananas was to be fixed at 100 ecu per tonne below the rate of duty for third-country bananas . . .

[152] In connection with the initiation of arbitration proceedings within the framework of the GATT (so-called second Banana Panel), the European Community concluded a framework agreement on bananas with four Latin American States (Colombia, Costa Rica, Venezuela, Nicaragua). The framework agreement was transposed into Community law with effect from 5 March 1995 by Commission Regulation (EC) No 478/95 of 1 March 1995 on additional rules for the application of Regulation No 404/93 as regards the tariff quota arrangements for imports of bananas into the Community and amending Regulation No 1442/93 (OJ 1995 L 49, p. 13) . . . [Article 1(1) of Regulation No 478/95 divided the customs quota for third-country bananas and non-traditional ACP bananas amongst individual export countries.] . . .

Article 3(2) of Regulation No 478/95 also provided, pursuant to the framework agreement, that products of operators in Categories A and C originating in Colombia, Costa Rica or Nicaragua could be imported only upon presentation of an export licence issued by those countries.

The costs associated with the issue of the export licence resulted in the price paid by those operators for bananas being 33% higher than the price paid by operators in Group B. In two judgments of 10 March 1998 the Court of Justice declared **[153]** that requirement for special export licences for imports from the above-mentioned countries to be invalid to the extent to which it required Category A and C operators, but not Category B operators, to obtain export licences, on the ground that it infringed the general prohibition of discrimination laid down in the second subparagraph of Article 40(3) of the EC Treaty, which is merely the specific enunciation of the general principle of equality (Case C-122/95 *Germany* v. *Council* [1998] ECR I-973 = ZIP 1998, 524, and Joined Cases C-364/95 and C-365/95 *T Port GmbH & Co. KG* v. *Hauptzollamt Hamburg-Jonas* [1998] ECR I-1023). Those two judgments did not call into question the validity of the common organization of the Banana market in any other respect.

II.

1. The plaintiffs in both of the original proceedings are nineteen undertakings in the "Atlanta Group". As importers of bananas, they are active at all stages of the transport, ripening and marketing of bananas. Thirty per cent of their turnover relates to the marketing of bananas. Between 1989 and 1991 the Atlanta Group imported on average 410,000 tonnes of third-country bananas.

After the entry into force of the common organization of the market, the plaintiffs were included in Category A and awarded an interim quota for the third quarter of 1993. Objections to the consequent limit on the amount which they could import were rejected on the basis of Community law. In their action to contest the rejections of their objections the plaintiffs initially claimed, in the first set of proceedings, that Regulation No 404/93 infringed Community law. The *Verwaltungsgericht* (Administrative Court) referred the question to the Court of Justice of the European Community. At the same time it awarded the plaintiffs, by way of interim protection, additional import licences for third-country bananas at a duty rate of 100 ecu per tonne for November and December 1993 which, should they be unsuccessful in the main proceedings, were to be set against the reference amounts to which the plaintiffs were entitled under Community law. The second set of proceedings relates to the import licences awarded to the plaintiffs for 1995.

2. In its judgment of 9 November 1995 in Case C-466/93 **[154]** *Atlanta* v. *Bundesamt für Ernährung und Forstwirtschaft*, the Court of Justice held, largely referring to its judgment of 5 October 1994 in Case C-280/93 *Germany* v. *Council* [1994] ECR I-4973, that there were no grounds for questioning the validity of Regulation No 404/93. In both sets of proceedings the plaintiffs are now seeking a declaration that the notices issued to them are unlawful in so far as they restrict the import by them of bananas from third countries into the European Community. They allege that application of the import rules under Regulation No 404/93 and Regulation No 478/95 is unconstitutional because it infringes Article 2(1), Article 14(1), Article 12(1) and Article 3(1) *GG* (*Grundgesetz*) (Basic Law).

III.

By order of 24 October 1996 the *Verwaltungsgericht* (Administrative Court) of Frankfurt am Main stayed proceedings and referred to the Federal Constitutional Court primarily the question whether the application in Germany of Articles 17 to 19 and Article 21(2) of Regulation No 404/93 and of Regulation No 478/95 was compatible with Article 23(1), first sentence, Article 14(1), Article 12(1) and Article 3(1) *GG*. If the Constitutional Court were to hold that reference inadmissible or to answer the question in the affirmative, that would raise the question whether the German laws acceding to the EC Treaties are incompatible with the Constitution to the extent that they transferred to the Community legislature the power to put into force the above Community rules in Germany.

In essence, the Administrative Court gave the following reasons for making the reference:

1. The reference is admissible under Article 100(1) *GG*.

a) Article 100(1) *GG* permits formal laws of the Federal State or *Länder* that postdate the entry into force of the Constitution to be referred to the Federal Constitutional Court for review. In principle, therefore, it is not possible to refer rules of secondary Community law to the Federal Constitutional Court under Article 100(1) *GG*. The court with jurisdiction in that respect is the Court of Justice of the European Community. However, the Administrative Court considers that if the Court of Justice holds that there is no infringement of Community law, **[155]** then the case-law of the Court of Justice may fail to ensure the protection of fundamental rights to be afforded under the Constitution, not give effect to the Federal Republic of Germany's international obligations under the GATT and fail to counter action by the Community legislature that is outside the scope of the EC Treaty or infringes its provisions. The question then arises as to the limits of the prior application of Community law. For the Federal Republic of Germany, those limits are laid down in Article 23(1) *GG*.

b) There is a difference in two respects between the decisions of the Constitutional Court in *BVerfGE* 73, 339 (*Solange II*)[3] and in *BVerfGE* 89, 155; *ZIP* 1993, 1636 (*Maastricht*).[4] First, since the *Maastricht* decision the Constitutional Court now extends its power of review and annulment also to sovereign acts of the Community that take effect in Germany, and thereby ensures the protection of fundamental rights for Germans where sovereign powers are exercised by national or Community institutions. Second, the Constitutional Court, unlike after the *Solange II* decision, is now once again expressly exercising its power of review, albeit in cooperation with the Court of Justice. Consequently, constitutional complaints and references by courts under Article 100(1) *GG* are admissible in any event if it is shown that acts of the Community infringe fundamental rights of a citizen in Germany which are protected by the Constitution and that the protection of fundamental rights allowed by the case-law of the Court of Justice in respect of that infringement does not correspond to the level unconditionally required by the Constitution. The question whether such a level of fundamental rights is ensured can be clarified only at national level. No specific procedure for ruling on that question is provided for in German law. Since the Constitutional Court has sole competence to declare German laws invalid on the ground that they infringe the Constitution, the existing gap in the law should be filled by the analogous application of Article 100(1) *GG*.

However, the Federal Constitutional Court **[156]** does not ensure protection of fundamental rights against secondary Community law merely where the protection of fundamental rights allowed by the Court of Justice and that allowed by the Constitutional Court are not coextensive or where the Court of Justice gives no protection to a fundamental right in the particular case. The content of the fundamental right must have been infringed generally by the Community, that is to say there must be a structural deficit in the protection of fundamental rights.

The reference is made on the basis that the case-law of the Court of Justice does not ensure protection of the fundamental rights of the plaintiffs individually and does not do so generally in the area of the law relating to the common organization of the markets.

2. As a result of the import rules in Section 4 of Regulation No 404/93 and Regulation No 478/95 in conjunction with the import rules in Regulation No 1442/93, the plaintiffs' fundamental rights under Article 14(1), Article 12(1) and Article 3(1) *GG* have been infringed. It was and is still not possible for them to achieve through the Community courts the protection of their fundamental rights which corresponds to the standard of fundamental rights unconditionally required by the Constitution.

a) Under the import regulations resulting from the common organization of the banana markets the plaintiffs are now able to import only less than 50% of the quantity of third-country bananas which they had previously imported into Germany. That state of affairs entered into force with permanent effect and without transitional rules on 1 July 1993. It is not possible to find a substitute

[[3] Volume 1, p. 461.] [[4] Volume 1, p. 526.]

through the import of Community or ACP bananas, because the producers of those bananas are already bound under long-term contracts with traditional marketers and importers of Community and ACP bananas. The regulation itself has not made any provision for the possibility of such substitutes, for example by the allocation of tariff quotas.

The reduction in quantities without transitional arrangements means that the plaintiffs' existing installations, some of which are required only for the marketing of bananas—such as loading terminals, refrigerated warehouses and ripening plants—can no longer be used at all or **[157]** only uneconomically. As a result, individual businesses or branches have to be closed and employees laid off.

b) The import rules and their consequences constitute a de facto interference with property.

Until the banana market rules had entered into force, the Federal Republic's Banana Protocol had guaranteed for operators in Germany the duty-free import of bananas up to a particular amount. Pursuant to Article 239 of the EC Treaty (now Article 311), the Protocol is part of the EC Treaty. The plaintiffs set up their businesses and acquired the necessary operating plant in reliance on that protocol. The import regulations in Section IV of Regulation No 404/93 mean that it was no longer possible to operate those businesses or to do so economically.

The rules in Regulation No 404/93 do not represent a permissible definition of the content and limits of property for the purposes of Article 14(1), second sentence, *GG*. It is indeed necessary to take into account the fact that Article 40 of the EC Treaty (now Article 34) provides for the creation of a common organization of the agricultural markets in order to attain the objectives of the Community's common agricultural policy for the purposes of Article 39 of the EC Treaty (now Article 33). Under the second sentence, point (c), of Article 40(1) of the EC Treaty (now Article 34(1), second sentence, point (c)), a European market organization is also one of the permissible forms of organization. Against that background, the plaintiffs had to reckon with the possibility that the Community legislature would create a common organization of the market for bananas. It is also recognized at national level that in the case of such a new organization of an area of law the legislature enjoys a particularly wide discretion. It may restrict or redefine legal positions if there are public interest reasons for doing so which deserve precedence over justified reliance in the continuation of a long-standing right. However, pursuant to the principle of proportionality, a careful transitional regime must then be adopted (reference to *BVerfGE* 58, 300, 351), the extent of which depends on a balance between the loss suffered as a result of that reliance and the public interest **[158]** (reference to *BVerfGE* 70, 101, 114). The Community legislature has infringed the principle of proportionality because it has not adopted any transitional regime for the benefit of third-country operators.

c) The import regulations and their consequences also infringed the right to exercise a trade or profession in accordance with Article 12(1) *GG*. Although the right to choose a trade or profession was not affected, the import regulations nevertheless restricted the freedom to exercise a trade or profession, in a manner contrary to the Constitution.

d) Article 3(1) *GG* is also infringed.

Section IV of Regulation No 404/93 treats operators from third countries differently from operators in the Community and the ACP. The Community and ACP group are allocated 30% of the tariff quota for third-country bananas, even though that category has hitherto not had any trading relationships with third-country producers. At the same time, the existing marketing monopoly of that group with respect to Community and ACP bananas is still, de facto, unaffected, because third-country operators, owing to the existing contractual relationships between the ACP and Community operators, on one hand, and the corresponding producers, on the other, are unable to enter into contractual relations with Community and ACP producers to any material extent. As a result, the plaintiffs in the main proceedings, being third-country operators, had available to them only around 50% of the quantity of bananas which they had previously imported. On the other hand, Community and ACP operators have, in addition to Community and ACP bananas, an extra 30% of the import quota of third-country bananas at their disposal.

3. The protection which the plaintiffs have received and could have received from the Court of Justice in respect of the above infringements of their fundamental rights does not correspond to the standard of fundamental rights unconditionally required by the Constitution.

The protection of fundamental rights is one of the general principles of Community law. The right to property, the freedom to exercise a trade or profession **[159]** and the general principle of equality are all fundamental rights in the Community and recognized in the case-law of the Court of Justice. However, in the law relating to the common organization of markets there is a structural deficit between the protection of fundamental rights to be guaranteed under the Constitution as interpreted by the Federal Constitutional Court, on the one hand, and the protection of fundamental rights under Community law, as interpreted by the Court of Justice, on the other.

4. The applicability of Regulation No 404/93 and Regulation No 478/95 is also material to the decision. If they are applicable, the plaintiffs' action for a declaration that the notices were unlawful would have to be dismissed, because no error in applying the law is discernible. On the other hand, if those regulations are not applicable, the action would have to be upheld, because there would be no restrictions on imports of third-country bananas into the Federal Republic of Germany and the notices would be unlawful. No other possibility of deciding in favour of the plaintiffs exists.

IV.

1. By letter of 26 March 1997 it was pointed out to the Administrative Court that, following the reference for a preliminary ruling, the Court of Justice had delivered its judgment of 26 November 1996 (Case C-68/95 *T Port GmbH & Co. KG* v. *Bundesanstalt für Landwirtschaft und Ernährung* [1996] ECR I-6065), in which it had held that Article 30 of Regulation No 404/93 requires the Commission to lay down all necessary transitional measures. Those transitional measures ought to solve the problems which had arisen after introduction of the common organization of the market, but whose origin lay in the state of national markets before the

regulation had been adopted. It was suggested that the decision might be significant in view of the lack of transitional arrangements to which the Administrative Court had referred.

2. In his reply, the President of the relevant chamber of the Administrative Court stated, referring to the **[160]** content of that court's order for reference, that Article 30 of Regulation No 404/93 was of no assistance in remedying the infringements of fundamental rights. It was not a case of hardship in an individual case which the legislature had not intended, but of hardship which the legislature had in fact intended. Only by restricting imports of third-country bananas was it possible to ensure that producers of Community and ACP bananas received the necessary protection.

Unlike in the case decided by the Court of Justice, the plaintiffs in the main proceedings were not seeking the application of a reference period other than that provided for in the regulation, but sought a general increase in the reference quantities in order to remove hardship generally associated with the introduction and allocation of the tariff quota. Ultimately therefore, it was a hardship which affected all importers of third-country bananas in the Federal Republic of Germany in the same way. Article 30 of Regulation No 404/93 therefore still did not provide any assistance in preventing infringements of fundamental rights. Moreover, after the introduction of the common organization of the market the Federal Republic of Germany had unsuccessfully sought the adoption of hardship rules by the Commission on account of the difficulties experienced by German banana importers. For that reason too, there was no prospect of success in referring the plaintiffs to hardship rules adopted under Article 30 of Regulation No 404/93 and a corresponding action before the Court of Justice.

V.

. . .

B.

The reference is inadmissible.

[161] I.

References to the Constitutional Court under Article 100(1) *GG* for review of the constitutionality of rules of secondary European Community law are admissible only if the referring court's statement of reasons shows that the present development of the law on protection of fundamental rights under European Community law, in particular the case-law of the European Court of Justice, does not ensure generally the protection of fundamental rights unconditionally required.

The Administrative Court has indeed set out its conviction, in a manner which satisfies the requirements of Section 80(2), first sentence, *BVerfGG*, that it considers the application of the relevant rules of law to be unconstitutional, and the reasons for that view (see *BVerfGE* 37, 328, 333; *BVerfGE* 66, 265, 269; *BVerfGE* 84, 160, 165; *BVerfGE* 86, 52, 57). The reference for a ruling also clearly expresses the court's view that the decision to be made by it turns on the answer to the question referred to the Federal Constitutional Court (*BVerfGE* 97, 49, 60; *BVerfGE* 98, 169, 199). It is, however, not possible to concur with its view that the provisions of Articles 17 to 19 and Article 21(2) of Regulation (EEC) No 404/93 and other rules of secondary Community law may be referred to the Federal Constitutional Court under Article 100(1) *GG* for review of their constitutionality.

II.

1. In its decision of 29 May 1974 (2 BvL 52/71, *BVerfGE* 37, 271—*Solange I*)[5] the Chamber concluded in regard to the facts that the process of integration in the Community was not yet at a stage where Community law contained a catalogue of fundamental rights, agreed upon by a Parliament and actually in force, which was adequate in comparison with the catalogue of fundamental rights contained in the Constitution. It accordingly held that it was admissible and necessary for a court in the Federal Republic of Germany to refer a case to the Federal Constitutional Court in proceedings for constitutional review, after obtaining a ruling of the Court of Justice under Article 177 of the EC Treaty (now Article 234 EC), **[162]** if the German court regarded the provision of Community law which was relevant to its decision as inapplicable in the interpretation given by the Court of Justice because and in so far as it conflicted with one of the fundamental rights in the Constitution (*BVerfGE* 37, 271, 285).[6]

2.a) In its decision of 22 October 1986 (2 BvR 197/83, *BVerfGE* 73, 339—*Solange II*)[7] the Chamber held that in the meantime a measure of protection of fundamental rights had been established within the sovereign jurisdiction of the European Communities which, in its conception, substance and manner of implementation was essentially comparable to the standard of fundamental rights in the Constitution. There were no compelling reasons to conclude that the standard of fundamental rights then achieved under Community law was not adequately consolidated and was only of a transitory nature (*BVerfGE* 73, 339, 378).[8]

[[5] Volume 1, p. 419.]
[[6] *Ibid.*, p. 448.]
[[7] Volume 1, p. 461.]
[[8] *Ibid.*, p. 487.]

Referring to individual decisions of the Court of Justice, the Chamber made findings as to the standard of fundamental rights at European level which the case-law of the Court of Justice of the European Community had formulated in content, consolidated and adequately guaranteed (*BVerfGE* 73, 339, 378-81).[9] In so doing it commented on the case-law of the Court of Justice on fundamental rights and freedoms relating to economic activities, such as the right to property and freedom to pursue economic activities (*BVerfGE* 73, 339, 380), freedom of association, the general principle of equal treatment and the prohibition of arbitrariness, religious freedom, protection of the family, principles of the prohibition of excessive action and of proportionality as general legal principles in reaching a balance between the common-interest objectives of the Community legal system and the safeguarding of the essential content of the fundamental rights in the German Constitution (*BVerfGE* 73, 380).

The Senate summarized the position as follows: so long as the European Communities and especially the case-law of the Court of Justice of the European Community generally ensure an effective protection of fundamental rights as against the sovereign powers of the Communities, which is to be regarded as substantially similar to the protection of fundamental rights required unconditionally by the German Constitution **[163]** and, in particular, generally safeguards the essential content of the fundamental rights, the Federal Constitutional Court will no longer exercise its jurisdiction to decide on the applicability of secondary Community law cited as the legal basis for acts of German courts and authorities within the Federal Republic of Germany and will no longer review that legislation by the standard of the fundamental rights contained in the Constitution. References (of secondary Community legislation) to the Federal Constitutional Court under Article 100(1) *GG* are therefore inadmissible (*BVerfGE* 73, 387).[10]

b) The Chamber maintained that view in the *Maastricht* decision (*BVerfGE* 89, 155). The Chamber emphasized there that the Federal Constitutional Court ensures, through its jurisdiction exercised in cooperation with the European Court of Justice, that effective protection of fundamental rights is secured generally for residents in Germany also as against the sovereign powers of the Communities and that this is to be regarded as substantially similar to the protection of fundamental rights required unconditionally by the German Constitution and in particular safeguards the essential content of the fundamental rights. In that way, the Federal Constitutional Court secures that essential content also as against the sovereign powers of the Community (*BVerfGE* 89, 155, 174,[11] with reference to *BVerfGE* 37, 271, 280 and *BVerfGE* 73, 339, 376, 386). Subject to the reservation set out by the Chamber in *BVerfGE* 73, 339—*Solange II*, the Court of Justice also has jurisdiction to protect the fundamental rights of citizens of the Federal Republic of Germany

[9 *Ibid.*, pp. 487-90.] [10 *Ibid.*, p. 494.]
[11 Volume 1, p. 526 at pp. 545-6.]

against measures of national (German) public authorities adopted on the basis of secondary Community law. The Federal Constitutional Court will resume its jurisdiction only if and when the Court of Justice of the European Community should depart from the standard of fundamental rights which the Chamber laid down in *BVerfGE* 73, 339, 378 to 381.

c) Article 23(1), first sentence, *GG* (introduced by the Law of 21 December 1992, *BGBl*, 2086) confirmed that case-law. Accordingly, with a view to establishing a united Europe, the Federal Republic of Germany is to contribute to the development of a **[164]** European Union that is committed to democratic, social and federal principles, to the rule of law, and to the principle of subsidiarity, and that guarantees a level of protection of basic rights essentially comparable to that afforded by the Constitution. It is not necessary that the individual areas of fundamental rights in the Constitution be covered to exactly the same extent by European Community law and by the case-law of the Court of Justice thereon. In accordance with the conditions set out in *BVerfGE* 73, 339, 340, 387,[12] the requirements of the Constitution are satisfied if the case-law of the Court of Justice generally ensures an effective protection of fundamental rights as against the sovereign powers of the Communities which is to be regarded as substantially similar to the protection of fundamental rights required unconditionally by the Constitution and, in particular, generally safeguards the essential content of the fundamental rights.

d) Consequently, the Chamber's decision in *BVerfGE* 89, 155,[13] also held that constitutional complaints and references from courts are inadmissible *ab initio* if the statement of reasons for them does not show that the development of European law, including the case-law of the Court of Justice of the European Community after delivery of the *Solange II* decision (*BVerfGE* 73, 339, 378-81),[14] has fallen below the necessary standard of fundamental rights. The statement of reasons for a reference by a national court or for a constitutional complaint which asserts an infringement by Community law of fundamental rights in the Constitution must therefore show in detail that the minimum protection of fundamental rights unconditionally required in the particular case is not generally ensured. This requires a comparison of the protection of fundamental rights at national level with that at Community level in the manner carried out by the Federal Constitutional Court in *BVerfGE* 73, 339, 378-81.[15]

III.

This requirement is not satisfied here.

1. The statement of reasons for the reference fails from the very start to satisfy the specific requirements for admissibility, because it is based

[12 Volume 1, p. 494.]
[13 Volume 1, p. 546.]
[14 Volume 1, pp. 487-90.]
[15 *Ibid*.]

on a misunderstanding of the *Maastricht* decision. The Administrative Court **[165]** considers that, after the *Maastricht* decision and contrary to the *Solange II* decision, the Federal Constitutional Court is now expressly exercising its power of review, even if in cooperation with the Court of Justice.

That view cannot be inferred from the *Maastricht* decision. In the passage on which the Administrative Court relies, the Chamber expressly quotes its *Solange II* decision with the statements concerning the restricted exercise of its jurisdiction. It is not borne out that the Chamber, either there or in any other passage in the *Maastricht* decision, had ceased to maintain the view set out in *BVerfGE* 73, 339[16] concerning the division of competence between the Court of Justice of the European Community in relation to the Federal Constitutional Court and vice versa, and this is also clear from the preceding considerations (*BVerfGE* 89, 155, 174).[17] After all, the Chamber raises these questions in the section concerning the admissibility of remedies under constitutional law and not in the section concerning the merits of the case (*BVerfGE* 89, 155, 174). In that respect too, the assumption that there is a conflict between the decisions in *Solange II* and *Maastricht* has no sound basis.

2. In the present case, in addition to these requirements, there was particular reason to give detailed arguments concerning a negative development in the standard of fundamental rights in the case-law of the European Court of Justice. In its judgment on the reference for a preliminary ruling of 26 November 1996 (Case C–68/95 *T Port GmbH & Co. KG* v. *Bundesanstalt* [1996] ECR I-6065) the Court of Justice had required the Commission to adopt under Article 30 of Regulation No 404/93 all necessary transitional measures it considered necessary. Such transitional measures ought to be able to solve the problems that have arisen after introduction of the common organization of the market, but whose origin lies in the state of the national markets before adoption of the regulation. The Federal Constitutional Court itself raised with the Administrative Court this decision and its possible consequences for the admissibility of the reference by the Administrative Court.

[166] By that stage at the latest, the Administrative Court should have recognized the inadequacy of the statement of reasons for its reference and have remedied this (*BVerfGE* 51, 161, 163; *BVerfGE* 85, 191, 203). An answer simply from the President of the Chamber was in itself insufficient procedurally, because, just as one member of a collegiate court may not draw up the order for reference on his own (see *BVerfGE* 1, 80, 81; *BVerfGE* 21, 148, 149), it is not right that only he should monitor and deal with the admissibility of the reference until the time when the Federal Constitutional Court makes its decision. His arguments are also wrong in substance. They conflict with the statement of reasons for the

[16 Volume 1, p. 461.]

[17 Volume 1, p. 526 at pp. 545-6.]

reference, which also criticizes in particular the absence of transitional measures and infers from this that Regulation No 404/93 is contrary to the Constitution. Indeed, it would not have been possible, against the background of that decision of the Court of Justice, for the Administrative Court to infer a general lowering of the standard of fundamental rights in the case-law of the Court of Justice.

Moreover, the Administrative Court should have realized that the decision of the Court of Justice preceded the order of the First Chamber of the Second Chamber of the Federal Constitutional Court of 25 January 1995 (2 BvR 2689/94 and 2 BvR 52/95, 1995, 126). The view of the Court of Justice as to the need for temporary hardship rules arising out of the right to property was similar to that of the Federal Constitutional Court. Both decisions thus illustrate the interlocking nature of the protection of fundamental rights at European level afforded by national courts and the Community judicature.

C.

This decision has been adopted unanimously.

[Report: 102 *BVerfGE*, p. 147 (in German)]

Supremacy — Conflict between Community law and subsequent national law—National administrative measure restricting right of free movement between Member States—Whether compatible with Community law—Scope of public policy exception to free movement rules

Institutions—Court of Justice—Powers—Jurisdiction under Article 177 of EC Treaty — Role of Court in ensuring observance of fundamental rights by national authorities—Scope of jurisdiction in relation to protection of human rights

Human rights — Scope of protection within the European Community — Case-law of the Court of Justice — Whether protection of human rights within the Community limited to situations falling within the field of application of Community law—The law of Greece

DIAMANTOPOULOS *v.* IKA

(Case No 247/1997)

Greece, Council of State (Fourth Chamber). 28 *January* 1997

(Fattouros, *Vice-President*; Pararas, *Rapporteur*)

(Case No 4674/1998)

Council of State (Plenary Session). 27 *November* 1998

(Botopoulos, *President*; Pararas, *Rapporteur*)

SUMMARY: The *facts*:—Mr Diamantopoulos, a Greek citizen, was the managing director of Transatlantic plc, a Greek company which owed a large sum in unpaid pension contributions to the Greek National Insurance Institution. Pursuant to a Greek law of 1990, an administrative measure was issued against him by the police, at the request of the Greek tax authorities, forbidding him to leave the country whilst the debt remained unpaid. Mr Diamantopoulos challenged the measure before the Fourth Chamber of the Council of State on the ground that Article 5 of the Greek Constitution prohibited such a measure as a breach of the right of Greek citizens to leave the country.[1]

Held (by the Fourth Chamber of the Council of State, by four votes to three):— The measure at issue violated both the Greek Constitution and Community law

[1] For the text of the relevant part of Article 5 see p. 289.

and accordingly should be annulled. However, because of the importance of the matter, the case should be referred to the Plenary Session of the Council of State.

(1) According to Article 5(4) of the Greek Constitution, it was only possible exceptionally to forbid Greek citizens to leave the country by individual administrative measure, where the measure was aimed at preventing a crime and was based on a judgment of a criminal court, where the measure was imposed by act of the public prosecutor on persons subject to criminal charges, or where the measure had been adopted in order to protect public health or sick persons. Those reasons, since they involved a substantial limitation of personal freedom otherwise guaranteed by the Constitution, were to be narrowly interpreted and did not apply to the case at issue. Consequently the measure in question was not constitutionally justifiable, even though it might serve the public interest (p. 292).

(2) The restrictions on the freedom to leave the country imposed by the Greek legislation at issue violated the rights to freedom of movement and freedom of establishment enshrined in Articles 48 and 52 of the EC Treaty as well as various EC Council Directives, and the general right of European Union citizens to move and reside freely within the territory of the Member States enshrined in Article 8A(1) of the Treaty on European Union. The restriction at issue did not fall within the terms of the public policy exceptions to the Community rules on freedom of movement. The restriction at issue was therefore contrary to the Community legal order, which was superior to the Constitution (p. 290).

(3) The restriction also violated Article 5(1) of the European Convention on Human Rights and Article 1 of the First Additional Protocol, which only permitted measures against the debtor's goods in such circumstances and not against his person. Those provisions had become primary Community law as a result of the direct reference made to them in Article F(2) of the Treaty on European Union (pp. 290-1).

Dissenting Opinion:—Three judges considered that the measure at issue fell within the public policy exception to the Community rules on freedom of movement and that the measure was not contrary to the provisions of the European Convention and Protocol in question since those provisions did not cover the type of restriction involved in this case (pp. 292-3).

Held (by the Plenary Session of the Council of State, by twenty-one votes to seven):—The restriction at issue was lawful both from the standpoint of the Constitution and from the standpoint of Community law. The case was referred back to the Fourth Chamber for a decision on the merits.

(1) (by twenty-one votes to seven) The measure at issue did not violate Article 5(4) of the Constitution since it was of a temporary and urgent nature, was justified in the public interest and was a general rather than an individual administrative measure (pp. 293-4).

Dissenting Opinion:—Seven judges considered that the measure at issue violated Article 5(4) of the Constitution, for identical reasons to those given by the majority in the decision of the Fourth Chamber (paragraph (1) of the summary, above) (pp. 294-5).

(2) (by twenty-six votes to two) The right of citizens of the European Union to move freely within the territory of the Member States (Article 8A(1)) was

a fundamental principle of Community law of which the provisions on free movement of workers (Article 48) and freedom of establishment (Article 52) were specific expressions. However, according to the case-law of the Court of Justice, the provisions on free movement were not applicable to situations which did not fall within the field of application of Community law. There was no connection between the case at issue and Community law since it involved a Greek citizen challenging a Greek measure preventing him leaving Greece where he resided. Whilst the applicant had argued that the restriction at issue prevented him visiting England for medical treatment for his heart condition, and travelling to France and Germany on business, the purely hypothetical prospect of exercising the right of free movement did not, according to the case-law of the Court of Justice, establish a sufficient connection with Community law (pp. 295-6).

Dissenting Opinion:—Two judges considered that the measure at issue violated the provisions of the Community law in question, for identical reasons to those given by the majority in the decision of the Fourth Chamber (paragraph (2) of the summary, above) (pp. 296-7).

(3) (by twenty-six votes to two) Article 5(1) of the European Convention and Article 1 of the First Additional Protocol were not intended to impair the right of a State to enforce such laws as it deemed necessary to secure the payment of taxes or other contributions or penalties (p. 298).

Dissenting Opinion:—Two judges considered that the restriction at issue violated the provisions of the European Convention in question, for identical reasons to those given by the majority in the decision of the Fourth Chamber (paragraph (3) of the summary, above) (pp. 298-9).

The text of the relevant part of the judgment of the Plenary Session of the Council of State commences on p. 293. The following is the text of the relevant part of the judgment of the Fourth Chamber of the Council of State:

The Facts

The Director of the Third Payments Office for Collecting Revenue of the National Insurance Institution asked the Police Directorate of the Ministry of Public Order to forbid the managing director and chairman of the board of directors of "Transatlantic plc" to leave the country because of debts to the National Insurance Institution amounting to 6,042,950 drachmas . . .

According to Law No 395/1976 . . . "It shall be permitted to forbid Greek nationals to leave the country, if they are in debt to the State and the debt exceeds the amount of one hundred thousand drachmas . . ." Article 27 of Law No 1882/1990 provides:

(1) It shall be permitted to forbid the following natural persons to leave the country if they are in debt to the State, to limited companies, to unions

or co-operatives, or to foreign legal persons, if they are of Greek nationality: managing directors, directors, or administrators of limited companies, or any person appointed directly or indirectly either by law or by private mandate, to the administration or management of such companies . . .

(2) The measure of forbidding the natural persons mentioned in the previous paragraph to leave the country may be taken for debts of the companies and other legal persons to the State of over one million drachmas, which have either been certified by the tax office or the customs authorities . . .

(3) For the application of the above-mentioned measure, which shall be incorporated into the procedure for collecting public revenue and serves the public interest, it shall not be necessary previously to notify the persons to whom it relates.

(4) The procedure for taking such measures, the conditions for their removal and any other necessary details for the implementation of this Article shall be regulated by Decisions of the Minister of Finance, published in the Official Journal of the Greek Government. The level of the debts for which this measure may be taken may be amended either generally or for certain categories of debtors by similar Decisions.

In accordance with paragraph (4) above . . . Decision 1106544/7010/0016/9.8.1993 of the Deputy Minister of Finance was issued, amending the amount of one million drachmas to ten million drachmas. According to Article 21(7) of Law No 1902/1990, the provisions of Law No 395/1976 and Article 27 of Law No 1882/1990 are applicable *mutatis mutandis* to the National Insurance Institution's claims arising from contributions . . .

Article 5 of the Constitution provides in part as follows:

(3) Personal liberty is inviolable. No one shall be prosecuted, arrested, imprisoned or otherwise confined except when and as the law provides.

(4) Individual administrative measures restricting freedom of movement or residence in the country, and the freedom to enter and leave the country, of any Greek national shall be prohibited. Such measures may be imposed in exceptional cases of emergency, but only in order to prevent the commission of criminal acts, following a ruling by a criminal court and as specified by law. In extremely urgent cases, such a ruling may be issued after the administrative measure has been imposed and within three days thereof at the latest.

According to the Interpretative Clause of Article 5 of the Constitution it is specified that "Paragraph 4 does not preclude any prohibition on leaving the country for persons being prosecuted on criminal charges by act of the public prosecutor, or the imposition of measures necessary for the protection of public health of sick persons, as specified by law."

From the Grounds of the Judgment

5. The Treaty establishing the European Community, to which Greece acceded by the Treaty of 28 May 1979, ratified by Law No 945/1979, provides in Article 48 for the free movement of workers within the Community "subject to limitations justified on grounds of public policy, public security or public health", and in Article 52 for the right of establishment of nationals of a Member State in the territory of another Member State. Also, Council Directive 68/360/EEC (OJ 1968, L 257/13) on the abolition of restrictions on movement and residence within the Community for workers of Member States and their families stipulates that "Member States shall grant the nationals referred to in Article 1 (nationals of the Member States of the Community as defined in Council Regulation 68/1612/EEC, (OJ 1968 L 257/2)) the right to leave their territory in order to take up activities as employed persons and to pursue such activities in the territory of another Member State" (Article 2) and that "Member States shall not derogate from the provisions of this Directive save on grounds of public policy, public security or public health" (Article 10). Furthermore, Council Directive 73/148/EEC (OJ 1973, L 172/14) on the abolition of restrictions on movement and residence within the Community for nationals of Member States with regard to establishment and the provision of services, stipulates that "The Member States shall, acting as provided in this Directive, abolish restrictions on the movement and residence of: (a) nationals of a Member State who are established or who wish to establish themselves in another Member State in order to pursue activities as self-employed persons, or who wish to provide services in that State; (b) nationals of Member States wishing to go to another Member State as recipients of services . . ." (Article 1). "Member States shall grant the persons referred to in Article 1 the right to leave their territory. Such right shall be exercised simply on production of a valid identity card or passport . . ." (Article 2). "Member States shall not derogate from the provisions of this Directive save on grounds of public policy, public security or public health" (Article 8) (see also the relevant Presidential Decrees by which Greek legislation was adjusted to comply with the above provisions, Nos 525/1983, 499/1987, 30/1990 and 278/1992).

In addition, the Treaty establishing the European Community, as amended by the Treaty on the European Union signed in Maastricht on 7 February 1992 and ratified by Law No 2077/1992, stipulates in Article 8A(1) that "Every citizen of the Union shall have the right to move and reside freely within the territory of the Member States, subject to the limitations and conditions laid down in this Treaty and the measures adopted to give it effect." The Treaty on the European Union provides in Article F(2) that "The Union shall respect fundamental rights, as guaranteed by the European Convention for the Protection of Human Rights and Fundamental Freedoms signed in Rome on 4 November 1950 and as they result from the constitutional traditions common to the Member States, as general principles of Community Law." Finally, the European Convention of 4 November 1950, ratified by Legislative Decree No 653/1974, stipulates in Article 5(1) that "Everyone has the right to liberty and security of person." Furthermore, the First Additional Protocol of Paris of 20 March 1952, ratified by the same Legislative Decree, stipulates in Article 1 that "Every natural or legal person is entitled to the peaceful enjoyment of his possessions. No one shall be deprived of his possessions except in the public interest and subject to the conditions provided for by law and by the general principles of international law. The preceding provisions shall not, however, in any way impair the right of a State to enforce such laws as it deems necessary to control the use of property in accordance with the general interest or to secure the payment of taxes or other contributions or penalties."

6. According to the [majority] opinion that has prevailed in this Court, the restrictions on the freedom to leave the country imposed by the Greek legislation at issue are an obstacle to the free movement and establishment of Greek nationals within the European Community, as guaranteed by the above provisions of the Treaty establishing the European Community and the Treaty on European Union. It must therefore be accepted that, after the entry into force of these Treaties, those restrictions are contrary to the Community legal order, which is superior to the Constitution, and cannot be tolerated. In addition, those restrictions are contrary to the above-mentioned provisions of Article 5(1) of the European Convention on Human Rights (which establish the natural freedom of movement of persons, see European Court of Human Rights, *Engel Case*, 1976, Series A22, para. 28) and the above-mentioned Article 1 of the First Additional Protocol (both of these texts have become primary Community law because of the direct reference to them contained in the Maastricht Treaty). Neither of these Articles tolerates the imposition of such restrictions against persons since, in order to secure the payment of tax and contributions, they allow legislative measures only in relation to the use of the debtor's goods. Furthermore, the case of a debt to the National Insurance Institute cannot be considered as one of the exceptional cases mentioned by Community law (public policy, public security, etc.) which would allow the Member States to take measures forbidding someone to leave the country, as here. Consequently, the above-mentioned provisions of Laws Nos 1902/1990, 1882/1990 and 395/1976, in so far as they forbid debtors of the State or the National Insurance Institute to leave the country, are invalid after the enactment of the Treaty establishing the European Community and the Treaty of Maastricht. Consequently, they cannot provide a legal basis for the decision in question which accordingly should be annulled, even though

this reason is not mentioned in the application for annulment, because the national judge must examine of his own motion the compatibility of national law with Community law (European Court of Justice, Cases C-87/90, 88/90, 89/90, [1991] ECR I-3757 *et seq.*).

7. Furthermore, according to the same [majority] opinion, the above-mentioned provisions of Article 5(4) of the Constitution and the Interpretative Clause, which focus especially on the issue of Greek citizens entering and leaving the country, according to their wording generally forbid the Administration to take individual measures implementing existing legislation limiting Greek citizens' freedom to move or establish themselves in any part of Greece, or preventing them from entering or leaving the country. Only exceptionally is it possible to forbid Greek citizens to leave the country, by adopting an individual administrative measure, if that measure aims to prevent a crime and is based on a judgment of a criminal court or, as stated in the Interpretative Clause, if the measure is imposed either by an act of the public prosecutor on persons being prosecuted on criminal charges or by an individual administrative measure adopted under legislation which prohibits leaving the country for the specific reasons of the protection of public health or the health of sick persons. Only for such reasons, which must be interpreted narrowly since they result in a substantial limitation of personal freedom, is it possible according to the Constitution to forbid someone to leave the country. Such a prohibition cannot be imposed for other reasons, even if they serve the public interest or aim to fulfil other constitutional obligations like the payment of taxes (Article 4(5) of the Constitution). In view of all these considerations the circumstances in which it is permitted to forbid someone to leave the country, under the legislative provisions referred to in paragraph 4 above, do not fall within any of the constitutional justifications for limiting the right to leave the country and accordingly violate Article 5(4) and the Interpretative Clause of the Constitution. Therefore the measure under review should also be annulled on this ground.

[8. According to the **Dissenting Opinion** of President of the Chamber Chr. Fattouros and two associate judges, St. Charalambous and Sp. Xrisikopoylos, with regard to the Community legal order, the Treaty establishing the European Community (Article 48) and the above-mentioned Council Directives allow the imposition of the restriction at issue for reasons of public policy, which includes the prompt payment of public revenue and national insurance contributions. Furthermore, the above-mentioned Treaty on European Union (Maastricht Treaty), which reaffirms the already established regimes of freedom of movement and establishment for nationals of the Member States within the Community, also maintains in force the limitations and conditions applicable to the exercise of this right. Consequently, the measure allowing restrictions on the freedom of someone to leave the country is still in force, even after the ratification of this Treaty by Law No 2077/1992. Furthermore, as previously held, the enactment of measures forbidding debtors of the State to leave the country is not contrary to Article 5 of the European Convention on Human Rights since that Article concerns cases of restrictions of freedom by means of arrest or imprisonment (Council of State Decisions Nos 2565/1990 and 1545/1995). In addition, Article 1 of the Additional Protocol does not concern cases such as the present, involving forbidding debtors of the State or the National Insurance Institute to leave the country (see Council of State Decision No 1545/1995).]

9. Because of the importance of the matters arising in this case . . . the Chamber considers that it must be referred to the Plenary Session of the Council of State . . .

[Report: Archives of the Council of State, Fourth Chamber Decision No 247/1997 (in Greek)]

The following is the text of the relevant part of the judgment of the Plenary Session of the Council of State:

[The Council of State repeated the statement of facts contained in the judgment of the Fourth Chamber of the Council of State and continued:]

7. According to the above-mentioned constitutional provisions, personal freedom is a fundamental constitutional principle. However, it is permitted to impose restrictions on that freedom through legislation in a general and objective manner. Especially with regard to freedom of movement or establishment throughout the country, as well as in relation to the freedom of every Greek to enter and leave the country, the legislature is not allowed to enact such restrictions in the form of "individual administrative measures". According to the preparatory discussions during the enactment of Article 5 of the Constitution, the constitutional legislature wanted to prevent the granting through legislation to administrative bodies of any discretionary authority to adopt individual administrative measures which would restrict such freedom (see the successive wordings of Article 5 contained in the original and the second Government Drafts and the Drafts of the Sub-Committees and the Plenary Session of the Committee of the Fifth Revising Parliament) . . . Consequently, legislation which introduces restrictions to free movement and establishment throughout the country, as well as to freedom to enter and leave the country, does not contravene the Constitution provided it merely allows the administrative bodies to verify if the conditions, set by law in a general, specific, clear and objective manner, are satisfied in order to issue an individual administrative measure restricting the above-mentioned freedom and only so long as those restrictions are in accordance with the provisions of paragraphs (1) and (2) of Article 5 of the Constitution . . .

8. In the light of the above considerations the measures at issue, taken in relation to Greek debtors of the State or the National Insurance Institution (for debts concerning social security contributions) or Greek nationals involved in the administration or management of companies owing similar debts, and forbidding them to leave the country, are of a temporary and urgent nature and are aimed at resolving a major national problem, namely the collection of public revenue and social insurance contributions. Consequently these measures do not contravene Article 5 of the Constitution and especially paragraphs (3) and (4) . . . since such individual measures forbidding someone to leave the country are not "individual administrative measures" within the meaning of the provisions of Article 5(4) of the Constitution and the Interpretative Clause of this Article, as explained above . . . More specifically, this may clearly be concluded from a statement of the Minister of Justice that it was "self-evident" that forbidding debtors of the State to leave the country, as provided for by the legislation in force . . . , is a general and not an individual administrative measure and consequently the possibility of restricting their ability to travel is not covered by the Interpretative Clause of Article 5(4) of the Constitution (see pp. 780-1 of the Minutes of the Plenary Session of the Fifth Revising Parliament). Furthermore, such a restriction of personal freedom is justified by the need to achieve obvious objectives of particularly important public and social interest, namely the collection on time of public revenue and contributions to the Social Insurance Institution . . .

[Members of the Council of State Pararas, Christoforos, Karalis, Papaevaggeloy, Rozos, Rantos and Rammos were of the following **Dissenting Opinion:**

The above-mentioned provisions of Article 5(4) and the Interpretative Clause of the Constitution, which regulate measures restricting the freedom of Greek citizens to enter and leave the country, in general forbid the adoption of individual administrative measures under existing legislation, which would restrict the freedom of Greek citizens to move in or establish themselves in any area of Greece or would prevent them from leaving or entering the country. Only in exceptional circumstances is it possible to forbid Greek citizens to leave the country by the adoption of an individual administrative measure where that measure aims to prevent a crime and is based on a judgment of a criminal court or . . . is imposed either by act of the public prosecutor for persons being prosecuted on criminal charges, or by an individual administrative measure issued by virtue of legislation which forbids someone to leave the country on the specific ground of protecting public health or the health of sick persons. Only for these reasons, which must be interpreted narrowly since they restrict personal freedom, is it possible according to the Constitution to forbid someone to leave the country. Such a measure cannot be imposed for any other reason, even where the public interest is involved or the aim is to ensure the fulfilment of other constitutional obligations such as the payment of taxes (Article 4(5) of the Constitution). Consequently the prohibition on leaving the country, contained in the above-mentioned provisions, does not fall within the constitutionally justifiable reasons for depriving someone of the right to leave the country and contravenes Article 5(4) and the Interpretative Clause of the Constitution. Accordingly, the measure under review should be annulled.]

9. The right of the citizens of the European Union to move and reside freely within the territory of the Member States, which is enshrined in Article 8A of the Treaty establishing the European Community, is a fundamental principle of Community law, specific expressions of which are the provisions of Articles 48, 52 and 59. According to Article 8A(1) the right of free movement and residence is established subject to the limitations and conditions laid down in the Treaty and the measures adopted to give it effect, namely the exceptions included in Articles 48(3), 56(1) and 66, and under the conditions laid down by the relevant Regulations and Directives. According to the case-law of the European Court of Justice, it is only permitted to invoke these provisions where a situation regulated by national legislation falls within the scope of Community law, in particular in the sphere of the free movement of persons. Consequently, the provisions of primary and secondary Community law concerning free movement are not applicable in situations which do not have any connection with any of the situations contemplated by Community law (Case 35, 36/82, *Morson and Jhanjan*, [1982] ECR 3736, paragraph 15; Case 180/83, *Moser*, [1984] ECR 2539, paragraph 15; Case C-299/95 *Kremzow*, [1997] ECR I-2645, paragraph 15).[2] In this case the situation of the applicant does not have any connection with any of the situations regulated by the provisions of the Treaty, namely those relevant to free movement of persons, since the case concerns a Greek citizen challenging a measure of a Greek authority according to which he is not allowed to leave Greece, where he resides, because of debts owed to a Social Insurance Organization under national legislation which has not been enacted in order to ensure the implementation of Community law provisions. The applicant has not included anything in his application to establish a relationship between this case and Community law. Only in a memo of 3 May 1997, submitted after the hearing of the case before the Fourth Chamber, does he submit, vaguely and without proof, that forbidding him to leave the country does not allow him a) to go to England for health reasons, given that he has had a heart operation and b) to pay visits for professional reasons, as managing director of Transatlantic SA, to various Member States of the European Union (England, France, Germany). Whilst it is true that every prohibition on leaving the country may, by its very nature, prevent the person concerned from exercising

[[2] See p. 70.]

the right of free movement, from the case-law of the European Court of Justice it is clear that a purely hypothetical prospect of such an exercise does not establish a sufficient connection with Community law to justify the application of Community provisions (see the above-mentioned judgments in the cases of *Moser* and *Kremzow*). Consequently, in this case, the national legislative provision contained in Article 27 of Law No 1882/1990, according to which the applicant was forbidden to leave Greece, concerns a situation which does not fall within Community law.

[Members of the Council of State Oikonomoy and Pararas were of the following **Dissenting Opinion**:

The Treaty establishing the European Community, to which Greece acceded by the Treaty of Accession of 28 May 1979 ratified by Law No 945/1979, provides in Article 48 for the free movement of workers within the Community "subject to limitations justified on grounds of public policy, public security or public health" as well as, in Article 52, for the right of establishment of nationals of a Member State on the territory of another Member State. Council Directive 68/360/EEC (OJ 1968, L 257/13) on the abolition of restrictions on movement and residence within the Community for workers of Member States and their families provides that "Member States shall grant the nationals referred to in Article 1 (meaning nationals of the Member States of the European Community according to Council Regulation 68/1612/EEC) (OJ 1968 L 257/2) the right to leave their territory in order to take up activities as employed persons and to pursue such activities in the territory of another Member State" (Article 2). In addition, "Member States shall not derogate from the provisions of this Directive save on grounds of public policy, public security or public health" (Article 10). Council Directive 73/148/EEC (OJ 1973, L 172/14) on the abolition of restrictions on movement and residence within the Community for nationals of Member States provides, with regard to establishment and the provision of services, that:

> The Member States shall, acting as provided in this Directive, abolish restrictions on the movement and residence of:
>
> (a) nationals of a Member State who are established or who wish to establish themselves in another Member State in order to pursue activities as self-employed persons, or who wish to provide services in that State;
>
> (b) nationals of Member States wishing to go to another Member State as recipients of services . . . [Article 1]
>
> Member States shall grant the persons referred to in Article 1 the right to leave their territory. Such right shall be exercised simply on production of a valid identity card or passport . . . [Article 2]
>
> Member States shall not derogate from the provisions of this Directive save on grounds of public policy, public security or public health. [Article 8] [See also the relevant Presidential decrees by which Greek legislation was adjusted to conform with the above provisions . . .]

The Treaty establishing the European Community, as amended by the Treaty on the European Union signed in Maastricht on 7 February 1992 and ratified by Law No 2077/1992, provides in Article 8A(1) that "Every citizen of the Union shall have the right to move and reside freely within the territory of the Member States, subject to the limitations and conditions laid down in this Treaty and by the measures adopted to give it effect." The Treaty on the European Union provides in Article F(2) that "The Union shall respect fundamental rights, as guaranteed by the European Convention for the Protection of Human Rights and Fundamental Freedoms signed in Rome on 4 November 1950 and as they result from the constitutional traditions common to the Member States, as general principles of Community Law." In the light of these provisions, the imposition of restrictions on the right freely to leave the country by Greek legislation limits the free movement and establishment of Greek citizens within the boundaries of the European Union established by the Treaty of Maastricht and, after the entry into force of that Treaty on 1 November 1993, contravenes the Community legal order, which is superior to the Constitution so that such a contravention is intolerable. Because of the universality and superior value of the individual Community right of the Union's citizens (inherent in the dignity and capacity of the Union's citizens) to move freely within the territory of the Union (unless, as mentioned above, there are contrary reasons of public policy, etc.), this right is at the same time a primary institutional and ideological commitment of the Member States. Therefore the above-mentioned primary Community law is applicable regardless of whether or not this particular case falls within the field regulated by substantive Community law.

Furthermore, in the opinion of Member of the Council of State Pararas, the case under review (debt to the Social Insurance Institution) cannot be considered as included in the exceptions mentioned by Community legislation (public policy, public security, etc.), for which the Member States may enact measures forbidding someone to leave the country, as in this case. Consequently, the above-mentioned provisions of Laws Nos 1902/1990, 1882/1990 and 395/1976, in relation to their provisions forbidding debtors of the Social Insurance Institution to leave the country, are invalid after the entry into force of the Treaty of Maastricht and cannot be considered as providing a proper legal basis for the measure under review, which should be annulled for that reason, even though it has not been advanced by the applicant, because the national judge is required to rule *ex officio* on the compatibility of national legislation with Community legislation. (Joined Cases C-87/90, C-88/90, C-89/90, *Verholen and Others*, [1991] ECR I-3757.)

In the opinion of Member of the Council of State Oikonomoy, however, the need to collect the social security contributions on time, which is a necessary condition for the realization of the aims of the Social

Insurance Institution to cover the whole population, which is a fundamental social interest whose satisfaction is the aim of the measure forbidding Greek debtors of the Institution from leaving the country, is a reason of public policy within the meaning of the Community provisions which justifies the restriction of the right of free movement of the citizens of the European Union. Therefore, in his opinion, the above-mentioned national provisions enabling someone to be forbidden to leave the country are not contrary to Community law.]

10. The European Convention for the Protection of Human Rights and Fundamental Freedoms of 4 November 1950, ratified by Legislative Decree No 653/1974, provides in Article 5(1) that "Everyone has the right to liberty and security of person. No one shall be deprived of his liberty save in the following cases and in accordance with a procedure prescribed by law . . ." The First Additional Protocol, signed in Paris on 20 March 1952 and ratified by the same Legislative Decree, provides in Article 1 that "Every natural or legal person is entitled to the peaceful enjoyment of his possessions. No one shall be deprived of his possessions except in the public interest and subject to the conditions provided for by law and by the general principles of international law." The preceding provisions shall not, however, in any way impair the right of a State to enforce such laws as it deems necessary to control the use of property in accordance with the general interest or to secure the payment of taxes or other contributions or penalties.

11. The measure of forbidding someone to leave the country, as prescribed by the above-mentioned national provisions, does not fall within the field of application of Article 5 of the European Convention, since that Article refers to cases of deprivation of a person's liberty by arrest or imprisonment and does not concern other restrictions of the right of every person to leave any country, including his own (see European Court of Human Rights, *Engel Case*, 1976, Series A Vol. 22, paragraph 58). Equally the provisions of Article 1 of the Additional Protocol are not applicable in this case. The right of free movement and establishment and the more specific right of a person to leave a country, even his own, are established by Article 2 of the Fourth Protocol to the Convention (with the restriction provided for in paragraph 3 of that Article), which has not been ratified by the Hellenic Republic.

[In the **Dissenting Opinion** of Members of the Council of State Pararas and Christoforos, the above-mentioned restrictions are contrary to Article 5(1) of the European Convention on Human Rights (which establishes the natural freedom of movement of a person, see European Court of Human Rights, *Engel Case*, 1976, Series A Vol. 22, paragraph 58) and also contrary to Article 1 of the relevant Additional Protocol (both provisions have become primary Community law as a result of the direct reference to them by the Treaty of Maastricht), given that both these Articles do not tolerate such restrictions against persons and only permit the enactment of measures relating to the use of the debtor's goods for the payment of taxes or contributions.]

12. Since the legal issues discussed have now been resolved, the case is referred back to the Fourth Chamber for judgment on the merits.

[Report: Archives of the Council of State, Plenary Decision No 4674/1998 (in Greek)]

NOTE.—The judgment of the Plenary Session of the Council of State has been the subject of a critical comment by Maganaris, The Greek Council of State—Europhobic or Simply Over-protective?, 25 EL Rev 2000, p. 200.

Supremacy — Constitutions and Community law — Greek Constitution, Article 28—Whether constitutional prohibition could take precedence over right given by Community law — Decision of national administrative body refusing recognition of foreign law degree — Ban on operation of foreign universities in Greece under Greek Constitution, Article 16 — Whether compatible with fundamental right of free movement under Community law — Scope of applicability of Community law to education and vocational training

Institutions—Court of Justice—Powers—Jurisdiction under Article 177 of EC Treaty — Scope of duty of national courts to make reference to Court of Justice—Court against whose decision there is no judicial remedy under national law—The law of Greece

KATSAROU *v.* DI.KATSA

(Case No 3458/1998)

Greece, Council of State (Plenary Session). 25 *September* 1998

(Botopoulos, *President*)

SUMMARY: *The facts*:—Mrs Katsarou, a Greek citizen, applied to DI.KATSA (the Greek recognizing body) for recognition of her law degree obtained from the University of Lille in France. The first two years of her course had been completed at the premises of a private law school in Greece which was affiliated with the University of Lille and she had then moved to Lille and completed the last two years of her studies in France. The recognizing body rejected the application for recognition of the degree on the ground that the first two years had been completed in Greece at a private school without university status. She was merely allowed to enter the third year of any Greek law school in order to complete a Greek law degree.

Mrs Katsarou challenged the decision before the Sixth Chamber of the Council of State, on the ground that it violated Articles 48 and 52 of the EC Treaty and Directive 89/48 on the mutual recognition of legal qualifications. The Sixth Chamber considered that there was a conflict between Article 16(5) of the Greek Constitution[1] (which prohibited the provision of higher education in Greece by foreign universities) and the relevant provisions of EC law. However, the Chamber took the view that the supremacy of EC law only covered ordinary national law and did not extend to constitutional provisions. Article 28 of the Greek Constitution[2] provided for the superiority of ratified international treaties

[1] For the text of Article 16(5) see p. 303.
[2] For the text of Article 28 see Volume 1, p. 577, note 1.

over domestic law. But for treaty provisions to be superior even over a constitutional provision would require a constitutional amendment. Nevertheless, the Sixth Chamber recommended that a reference should be made to the Court of Justice of the European Community to obtain a preliminary ruling under Article 177 of the EC Treaty. However, because of the importance of the matter, the Sixth Chamber referred the case to the Plenary Session of the Council of State.

Held (by a majority of seventeen votes to twelve):—The application for recognition of the degree was rejected. There was no reason to make a reference to the Court of Justice for a preliminary ruling.

(1) Article 16(5) of the Constitution prohibited a period of study completed in Greece at the premises of an establishment affiliated to a foreign university from being recognized as equivalent to a period of study at a national university.

(2) Article 126 of the EC Treaty provided that the Community fully respected "the responsibility of the Member States for the content of teaching and the organization of education systems and their cultural and linguistic diversity". Article 126 also provided that the Council was merely empowered to adopt incentive measures, excluding the harmonization of national laws and regulations. A literal interpretation of these provisions indicated that the Member States were exclusively responsible for the organization of their higher education systems, which therefore fell outside the sphere of Community regulations.

(3) It was therefore acceptable for national regulatory control of this area to restrict the application of the free movement rules contained in the EC Treaty. This flowed from the preservation of cultural and linguistic diversity in the Member States. Consequently, not only the content and organization of the educational systems of the Member States, but also the closely related matter of the recognition of the equivalence of foreign degrees, were the responsibility of the national legislature and were governed in Greece by Article 16 of the Constitution.

Dissenting Opinion:—Twelve judges considered that the question at issue was governed by Community law and that a reference should be made to the Court of Justice under Article 177.

(1) Whilst education and education policy fell outside the competence of Community organs, access to and participation in education, and especially vocational training, were not outside the scope of Community law. Access to vocational training was capable of promoting the free movement of persons throughout the Community, by allowing them to obtain qualifications in the Member State where they intended to practise their profession. Consequently, the conditions of access to vocational training fell within the sphere of regulation of Community law.

(2) The term "vocational training" applied to any training which provided the necessary qualifications or skills for a specific profession, including university education. According to the case-law of the Court of Justice, the free movement rules contained in the EC Treaty constituted fundamental freedoms whose effectiveness would be hampered if Member States were allowed to exclude their own nationals from benefiting from provisions of Community law to obtain vocational training in another Member State.

(3) Accordingly, the Council of State was obliged, pursuant to Article 177 of the EC Treaty, to make a reference for a preliminary ruling to the Court of Justice, in order to determine whether the issue of the equivalence of the degree in question with the corresponding national law degree was governed by Community law and, if so, whether the refusal of the Greek recognizing body to grant recognition of the French degree in question was compatible with Community law.

The following is the text of the judgment of the Council of State:

Facts

Mrs Katsarou is a Greek citizen who submitted an application to DI.KATSA (the recognizing body) seeking recognition of the equivalence of her law degree as well as the postgraduate degree which she had obtained from the University of Lille in France. The application for recognition of the equivalence of those degrees with the relevant Greek law degree was unsuccessful. The recognizing body argued that since the first two years of her basic law degree were completed in Greece at the premises of what was effectively a private school with no university status, it could not recognize the qualifications obtained as equivalent to a Greek law degree. Mrs Katsarou was only allowed to enter directly the third year of any Greek law school, in order to achieve a national law degree. Mrs Katsarou went before the Sixth Chamber of the Council of State and sought to have this decision of the recognizing body annulled, arguing that it was in breach of Community law provisions, namely Articles 48 (now 39) (free movement of workers) and 52 (now 43) (freedom of establishment) of the EC Treaty and Directive 89/48 (mutual recognition of qualifications in relation to the legal profession). The application of Mrs Katsarou came before the Chamber on 8 July 1997 (Council of State, Decision 2809/1997 of 8 July 1997). The judges initially analysed Articles 16 (prohibition of provision of higher education by non-Greek State universities) and 28 (superior status of ratified international treaties) of the Greek Constitution and Articles 48 (now 39), 52 (now 43) and 126 (now 149) of the EC Treaty (cooperation between Member States for the development of quality education) and Directive 89/48. The outcome of this analysis was that the domestic constitutional provisions and the European provisions concerning the specific matter at issue were in conflict. The judges argued that the applicable law in this instance was the domestic one because, in their opinion, the principle of supremacy of Community law could not stretch as far as covering the provisions of the Greek Constitution. However, the interaction of national and European law in relation to the circumstances surrounding the issue under examination forced the Chamber to recommend that the opinion of the Court of Justice should be sought under Article 177 (now 234) of the EC Treaty. Finally the judges of the Sixth Chamber, considering the importance of the circumstances of this case, concluded that the matter should be decided by a plenary session of the Council of State and referred the case accordingly. The case came before the Plenary Session of the Council of State on 6 March 1998.

From the Grounds of the Judgment

. . .

2. The application under examination has been referred to the Plenary Session of the Council of State as a result of Decision No 2809/1997 of the Sixth Chamber of the Council . . .

4. Article 16(5) of the [Greek] Constitution provides that: "Higher education shall exclusively be provided by state institutions which are self-regulating. These institutions are subject to the supervision of the State, are entitled to financial aid and should operate in accordance with the laws relating to their organization . . .". Paragraph (8) of the same Article provides that: "Private parties are prohibited from establishing universities."

5. Following both a literal and a teleological interpretation of the above-mentioned provisions of Article 16 of the Constitution, it is to be inferred that DI.KATSA, which is the body that controls the procedure of recognition of the equivalence of foreign university degrees to the relevant national ones, cannot recognize the period of study completed in Greece at the premises of an establishment affiliated to a foreign university and operating as a private school as a period of study completed in a foreign university equivalent to a national one. Consequently, the decision of DI.KATSA to decline recognition of the equivalence of the degree under examination to the national one is lawful. Indeed, a decision favouring recognition of the equivalence of a degree obtained from a foreign university under the above-mentioned circumstances would result in the recognition of degrees that have been completed in Greece at the premises of a private school affiliated to a foreign university, which would constitute a breach of the constitutional prohibition on the establishment in Greece by private parties of institutions providing higher education . . .

16. Article 126 (now 149) of the EC Treaty provides that the Community fully respects "the responsibility of the Member States for the content of teaching and the organization of education systems and their cultural and linguistic diversity" and the Council shall merely adopt incentive measures, excluding any harmonization of the laws and regulations of the Member States. In addition, the Treaty expressly distinguishes education and the organization of education systems [Article 126 (now 149)] from vocational training [Article 127 (now 150)]. A literal

interpretation of the provisions of Article 126 (now 149) indicates that the Member States are exclusively responsible for the organization of their educational systems, higher education included. It is therefore understood that since the content of teaching and the organization of the educational system falls outside the sphere of Community regulation, and remains within the regulatory control of the Member States, this could result in the restriction of the application of the freedom of movement of persons, capital and services, established by the relevant provisions of the Treaty. This results from the fact that the preservation of the cultural and linguistic diversity of the Member States referred to in Article 126(1) (now 149(1)) is considered by the Treaty as being of paramount importance. The importance of the preservation of cultural and linguistic diversity can also be inferred from the provisions of Article 128 (now 151) . . . which mentions the "flowering of the cultures of the Member States while respecting their national and regional diversity" as being a cultural aim. The participation of education is clearly necessary for the preservation of the national identity and the linguistic and general cultural heritage of each State. In this respect the contribution of higher education is extremely significant to the extent that, within its context, the necessary conditions for the development of the above-mentioned matters (national identity, linguistic and general cultural heritage) are formed and mature, as a result of the simultaneous presence in the same place of teachers and students.

Consequently it is clear that the issue of the content and organization of the educational system of each Member State, specifically with regard to higher education, as well as the closely related matter of the recognition of the equivalence of foreign degrees to the relevant national ones, is the responsibility of the national legislator and is regulated in Greece, as already mentioned, by Article 16 of the Constitution and other secondary legislation emanating from it. The latter includes the legislation already mentioned regulating the operation of DI.KATSA. Consequently the above-mentioned considerations, which can be inferred without any reasonable doubt from the provisions of the Treaty and especially Article 126 (now 149), should inform the relevant provisions of secondary Community law [Directive 89/48/EEC]. In any case, there is no indication that the provisions of Directive 89/48 EEC, which mentions in its preamble Articles 49 (now 40), 57(1) (now 47(1)) (issuing of directives for the mutual recognition of higher education diplomas) and 66 (now 55) of the Treaty, refer to matters relating to Article 126 (now 149) of the Treaty and specifically to the organization of higher education. In view of the above considerations, it is clear that no reason exists to refer a question for a preliminary ruling to the European Court of Justice under Article 177 (now 234) of the Treaty.

17. In the light of the above considerations [the majority of the Plenary Session of] the Council of State concludes that the application under examination must be rejected in its entirety . . .

For these reasons the Council of State rejects the application under examination.

Members of the Council of State L. Economou, A. Tsambasis, F. Arnaoutoglou, G. Papamentzelopoulos, N. Sakellariou, A. Gotsis, A. Randos, D. Briolas, E. Sarp, C. Rammos, N. Markoulakis and K. Kousoulis were of the following **Dissenting Opinion**:

The European Court of Justice has accepted the following principles, in the light of the provisions of Articles 48 (now 39), 52 (now 43), 126 (now 149) of the Treaty and Directive 89/48/EEC:

1. The free movement of persons and freedom of establishment, guaranteed by Articles 48 (now 39) and 52 (now 43) of the EC Treaty, are integral to the European Community framework, and would not be able to operate fully if Member States were allowed to prevent their use, by those of their nationals who have taken advantage of the freedoms available to them by virtue of the provisions of Community law, to obtain vocational training in another Member State. Consequently these provisions are violated by any national measure relating to the terms of use of a university degree completed in another Member State, even in situations where such a measure is applied in a non-discriminatory manner in respect of the nationality of the individual, wherever it could prevent or reduce the scope of the exercise of the above-mentioned fundamental freedoms.
2. . . .
3. Whilst it is true that education and education policy fall outside the jurisdiction of the Community organs, the issue of access to and participation in education, especially when it comes to vocational training, is not outside the scope of Community law.
4. Access to vocational training is capable of promoting the freedom of movement of persons throughout the Community and of allowing them to obtain qualifications in the Member State where they intend to practise their vocation, providing them with the opportunity to complete their education and develop their special talents in the Member State where the appropriate vocational training is available. Consequently, the conditions of access to vocational training fall within the sphere of regulation of Community law.
5. The term vocational training applies to any kind of vocational training that leads to a qualification or provides a particular skill for the practice of a profession.

6. University education does, generally speaking, qualify as vocational training.
7. . . .
8. A year of study that forms part of a course, that is an educational unit, and leads to a qualification or provides a particular skill for the practice of a profession, can be classified as vocational training in the context of the EC Treaty.
9. . . .
10. The demand by certain Member States that individuals possess a qualification in order to practise specific professions poses an obstacle to the effective application of the fundamental freedoms guaranteed by the Treaty, an obstacle that must be removed by virtue of the issuing of directives that will lead to the mutual recognition of diplomas, certificates or other qualifications. The fact that such directives have not as yet been issued does not mean that a Member State is allowed to decline recognition of the beneficial effects of these freedoms in relation to individuals who are subject to Community law, when those freedoms could easily be secured in that Member State because of the existence of legislative instruments specifically regulating the recognition of the equivalence of foreign qualifications to national ones.
11. . . .
12. Additionally, the European Court of Justice has decided that free movement of persons and freedom of establishment, which are secured by Articles 48 (now 39) and 52 (now 43) of the EC Treaty, constitute fundamental freedoms within the Community legal system, whose full potential could not be achieved if the Member States were able to prevent their nationals from benefiting from the effect of the provisions of Community law where they have availed themselves of the opportunities provided by the relevant provisions of Community law to obtain vocational training in another Member State. The European Court of Justice has also decided that the position of a Community citizen who is in possession of a university degree obtained in another Member State which facilitates access to the practice of a profession, or at least an economic activity, is governed by Community law, even when it comes to the relationship between that Community citizen and the Member State of which he is a citizen (see the decisions of the Court of Justice in *Kraus Steen* v. *Deutsche Bundespost* and *Saunders*).

On the basis of the above-mentioned case-law of the European Court of Justice, it should be concluded that the degree under examination, which was obtained under the conditions referred to above, is governed by Community law so far as the issue of the recognition of its equivalence with the equivalent national degree is concerned. This Court is therefore obliged, pursuant to Article 177 (now 234) of the EC Treaty, to refer a question for a preliminary ruling to the European Court of Justice, in order for the latter to decide whether the recognition of equivalence of the degree under examination indeed falls within the sphere of influence of the relevant provisions of Community law and, if the response to this question is in the affirmative, whether the refusal by DI.KATSA to recognize the degree, obtained on the basis that part of the studies towards its achievement was completed in Greece at the premises of a private school affiliated to a foreign university, taking into account that pursuant to Article 16 of the Greek Constitution university education cannot be offered in Greece by private schools, can be reconciled with Community law.

According to the opinion of the Member of Council Sakellariou, irrespective of the possible consequences that a breach of Community law could have for Member States (see Articles 169 (now 226) and 171 (now 228) of the EC Treaty), since the responsibility for the uniform application of Community law rests with the European Court of Justice, it is not possible to argue validly that, in situations like the one under examination which by virtue of the previous involvement of the European Court of Justice are deemed to be regulated by Community law, avoiding referring a question to the European Court by utilizing dubious methods of interpretation does not fall foul of Community law.

Finally, according to Member of the Council Randos, a referral to the European Court of Justice under Article 177 (now 234) EC is in this instance necessary simply because of the fact that the presence of a significant number of dissenting voices in the Council indicates that the issue of Community law under examination is not sufficiently clear and free from doubt, so that the conditions for the national courts not to make a referral, laid down in the decision of the Court of Justice in the *CILFIT Case*, are not fulfilled.

[Report: Archives of the Council of State, Plenary Decision No 3458/1998 (in Greek)]

NOTE.—The judgment of the Plenary Session of the Council of State has been the subject of a critical comment by Maganaris, The Principle of Supremacy of Community Law in Greece—From Direct Challenge to Non-application, 24 EL Rev 1999, p. 426.

Supremacy — Constitutions and Community law — Irish Constitution, Article 29(4)(5) — Executive order implementing Community directive — Whether taking precedence over existing national law implicitly amended thereby—Whether executive order in substance a measure of Community law in the form of domestic law — Implementation of Council Directive 81/602 prohibiting use of certain hormonal substances on farm animals

National constitutions — Constitutional challenge to legislation—Irish Constitution, Articles 15(2) and 29(4)(5)—European Communities Act 1972, Section 3(2)—Appropriate method for implementation of provisions of Council Directive — Whether ministerial regulation sufficient or parliamentary legislation required—Scope of delegated powers of Member States in relation to implementation of Community law—The law of Ireland

MEAGHER *v.* MINISTER FOR AGRICULTURE AND ATTORNEY GENERAL

Ireland, Supreme Court. 18 *November* 1993

(Finlay, *Chief Justice*; O'Flaherty, Egan, Blayney and Denham, *Justices*)

SUMMARY: *The facts*:—The applicant was a farmer whose farm was searched in March 1991 by Irish Department of Agriculture officials, acting under a search warrant. Various veterinary products were seized for investigation to ascertain whether they contained certain hormonal substances prohibited for use on cattle by two Irish regulations of 1988 and 1990 which had implemented various European Community directives. Subsequently, the applicant was prosecuted for violation of the Regulations and he brought judicial review proceedings seeking a declaration that Section 3(2) of the European Communities Act 1972 violated Article 15 of the Irish Constitution, in so far as it permitted ministerial regulations to amend existing law, and that consequently the regulations at issue were *ultra vires* and void. The High Court held that Section 3(2) was unconstitutional and the Minister appealed to the Supreme Court.

Held:—The appeal was allowed.

(1) Section 2 of the European Communities Act 1972 secured the application in Ireland of the law of the European Communities as a basic obligation necessitated by membership of the European Community. Having regard to the large number of Community measures requiring implementation into Irish law, the obligations of membership required that in some cases, and possibly the majority, implementation should be achieved by ministerial regulation rather than legislation. Accordingly, the power to make regulations contained in Section 3(2) of the 1972 Act was necessitated by the obligations of membership and, by

virtue of Article 29(4)(5) of the Constitution, could not be impugned. Whether it was appropriate for a specific Community measure to be implemented by ministerial regulation could be determined by recourse to proceedings for *ultra vires*. The issue to be determined was whether or not the power constitutionally conferred upon the Minister had been exercised in the correct manner in each particular case (pp. 313-14).

(2) Recourse to ministerial regulation to determine the procedures for search and prosecution in relation to the substances at issue was appropriate and justifiable in this case. Section 3(2) of the 1972 Act conferred upon the Minister an express power to include in regulations such incidental and consequential provisions as appeared necessary for the purposes of the regulations, including repealing or amending the existing regulation (pp. 317-18).

(3) The Irish Regulations of 1988 were derived from a Council directive which was binding on the State, from the moment of its adoption, as to the result to be achieved. This required Member States to create effective sanctions for the enforcement of measures contained in the directive. If this necessitated a measure which impliedly amended existing legislation, that measure would take precedence over conflicting domestic law. The Irish Regulation at issue derived its force from the Directive and took precedence over other domestic legislation because it was in substance a measure of Community law (p. 320).

(4) Article 189 of the EC Treaty required that the form and method chosen for implementation of a directive by the State should be appropriate. If the methods chosen were not appropriate, or the measures went beyond what was required, they would be open to constitutional challenge (pp. 320-1).

The following is the text of the judgment of the Court:

[347] FINLAY CJ

This is an appeal by the respondents in an application by way of judicial review against an order made in the High Court by Johnson J on the 1st April, 1993, whereby he declared that such portion of sub-s. 2 of s. 3 of the European Communities Act, 1972, as entitles a Minister by regulation to repeal or amend or apply with or without modification other law exclusive of that of the said Act is unconstitutional.

The application for judicial review in which this declaratory order was made had sought a declaration that the European Communities (Control of Oestrogenic, Androgenic, Gestagenic and Thyrostatic Substances) Regulations, 1988, and the European Communities (Control of Veterinary Medicinal Products and their Residues) Regulations, 1990, are *ultra vires* and void.

The application also sought an order of certiorari quashing a search warrant purportedly granted by a judge of the District Court pursuant to those regulations, and in addition, sought an order of prohibition of the first respondent from proceeding to prosecute the applicant in respect of summonses alleging offences against the regulations.

The learned trial judge, having reached a conclusion that the particular sub-section of the European Communities Act, 1972 ("the Act of 1972") was invalid having regard to the provisions of the Constitution, did not make any declaration with regard to the questions of *ultra vires*, nor did he make an order quashing the warrant or prohibiting the prosecution.

The respondents in appealing against the order of the learned trial judge declaring the subsection of the Act of 1972 invalid having regard to the Constitution, maintained in the alternative that if the Court were to conclude that the statutory instruments concerned were *ultra vires* or constituted an unconstitutional exercise of the power to legislate by regulation then the statutory instruments, alone, should be condemned but the subsection of the statute should not.

The applicant for judicial review who is the respondent on this appeal, has not served any notice to vary, but was permitted in the interests of justice by the Court to make the case that even if his challenge to the constitutional validity of the subsection of the Act of 1972 were to fail he should be entitled to maintain a challenge, which he submitted was correct, against the validity of the regulations made pursuant to that subsection and that, accordingly, the warrant of search provided under them and the summons for an offence against them would both be invalid.

[348] This decision, which is the decision of the Court, pronounced pursuant to Article 34, s. 4, sub-s. 5 of the Constitution, deals only with the challenge to the constitutional validity of the impugned subsection of the Act of 1972.

The Impugned Legislation

The relevant provisions of the European Communities Act, 1972, are:

Section 2

From the 1st day of January, 1973, the treaties governing the European Communities and the existing and future acts adopted by the institutions of those Communities shall be binding on the State and shall be part of the domestic law thereof under the conditions laid down in those Treaties.

Section 3

(1) A Minister of State may make regulations for enabling section 2 of this Act to have full effect.

(2) Regulations under this section may contain such incidental, supplementary and consequential provisions as appear to the Minister making the regulations to be necessary for the purposes of the regulations (including provisions repealing, amending or applying, with or without modification, other law exclusive of this Act).

The Constitutional Provisions Involved

The constitutional provisions involved are the provisions contained in Article 29, s. 4, sub-ss. 3, 4 and 5 of the Constitution, which are in the form consequent upon the Eleventh Amendment of the Constitution enacted by the Eleventh Amendment of the Constitution Act, 1992, which came into force on the 16th July, 1992, and also Article 15, section 2.

Article 29, sub-s. 4

3. The State may become a member of the European Coal and Steel Community (established by Treaty signed at Paris on the 18th day of April, 1951) the European Economic Community **[349]** (established by Treaties signed at Rome on the 25th day of March, 1957) and the European Atomic Energy Community (established by Treaty signed at Rome on the 25th March, 1957). The State may ratify the Single European Act (signed on behalf of the Member States of the Communities at Luxembourg on the 17th day of February, 1986, and at the Hague on the 28th day of February, 1986).

4. The State may ratify the Treaty on European Union signed at Maastricht on the 7th day of February, 1992, and may become a member of that Union.

5. No provision of this Constitution invalidates laws enacted, acts done or measures adopted by the State which are necessitated by the obligations of membership of the European Union or of the Communities, or prevents laws enacted, acts done or measures adopted by the European Union or by the Communities, or by institutions thereof, or by bodies competent under the Treaties establishing the Communities, from having the force of law in the State.

Article 15, s. 2, sub-s. 1

The sole and exclusive power of making laws for the State is hereby vested in the Oireachtas; no other legislative authority has power to make laws for the State.

The Challenge to the Validity of the Statute

The broad nature of the challenge made to the constitutional validity of s. 3, sub-s. 2 of the Act of 1972 may thus be summarised.

1. If Article 29, s. 4, sub-s. 5 of the Constitution does not apply to this subsection, then it would be invalid having regard to the provisions of Article 15, s. 2 of the Constitution because a power provided by statute to a Minister to make laws by regulation or statutory instrument which included provisions either repealing, amending or modifying other law, including statute law enacted by the Oireachtas, would constitute an invasion of the sole and exclusive power of making laws vested in the Oireachtas. In support of this contention reliance was placed on the decision of this Court in *Harvey* v. *The Minister* **[350]** *for Social Welfare* [1990] 2 IR 232; *Cooke* v. *Walsh* [1984] IR 710; and

Cityview Press v. *An Chomhairle Oiliúna* [1980] IR 381. In respect of the last two decisions reliance was placed in particular upon the fact that the Act of 1972 did not in any of its other provisions lay down principles or policy which could be said to restrict the discretion vested in the Minister in the making of regulations pursuant to s. 3, sub-s. 2 to application and administration of given guidelines.

2. It is submitted that Article 29, s. 4, sub-s. 5 of the Constitution cannot protect the impugned subsection from the invalidity arising by reason of its inconsistency with Article 15, s. 2 because, whereas in general terms the obligations of memberships of the Union and Communities imposes upon the State a duty to apply the laws enacted and to implement acts done or measures adopted by those bodies which then become acts on the part of the State, necessitated by those obligations of membership, the obligations of membership never entail mandatory direction to the State to carry out its duty of applying or implementing laws, acts or measures by any particular legal procedure applicable within the national law of the State. It is, therefore, submitted that the choice purporting to be vested in the Minister by sub-s. 2 of s. 3, for the purpose of enabling s. 2 of the Act to have full effect, to make regulations which include the repealing or amending or modifying of a statute of the Oireachtas, cannot be an act done or a measure adopted by the State which is necessitated by the obligations of membership. All that is necessitated, it is urged, is the implementation: the method of it is a choice to be made by the State within its own national law framework, and must be consistent with the Constitution.

The Submissions of the Respondents

The respondents made to the claim for a declaration of constitutional invalidity of s. 3, sub-s. 2 a number of submissions in the alternative. Some of those were directed to and interwoven with the issues which arose in this case with regard to the validity of the statutory instruments actually made.

[351] The primary and fundamental response to the claim of invalidity may, however, be summarised as follows. It cannot be disputed that upon joining the Communities and subsequently joining the Union, the State took upon itself an obligation to apply and implement fully and efficiently and with expedition laws enacted, acts done or measures adopted by the Communities or, subsequently, by the Union. That obligation fell into a broad necessity for two separate actions. One was in the case where laws enacted or acts done by the Communities or Union were done according to Community law, in such a fashion as to have direct application within the State. In those instances significant minor administrative regulations may be necessary to facilitate the entry of such legal provisions into the legal structure of the State, carrying with them, of course, a primacy over any conflicting or inconsistent national legal principles or provisions. In such instances, it is said, as one example at least, the repeal, amendment or modification of any existing law by a simple ministerial regulation would be a strict necessity arising from the obligations of the State as a member of the Community and Union. In other instances, it is urged, where directives may require to be implemented by the State the terms of such directives may be sufficiently specific and clear to require simple administrative application, something which would be again, appropriately done by regulation.

In these circumstances it is urged that the entire of the Act of 1972, which has subsequently been amended, is necessitated by the obligations of the State to the Community, and now to the Union. No provision of the Constitution, therefore, it is submitted, including in particular, Article 15, s. 2, can be brought to bear on the provisions of that Act so as to invalidate any part of it.

The Decision

The Court has considered these submissions and has come to the following conclusions.

The power to make regulations contained in section 3, sub-s. 1 of the Act of 1972 is exclusively confined to the making of regulations for one purpose, and one purpose only, that of enabling s. 2 of the Act to have full effect. Section 2 of the Act which provides for the application of the Community law and acts as binding on the State and as part of the domestic law subject to conditions laid down in the Treaty which, of **[352]** course, include its primacy, is the major or fundamental obligation necessitated by membership of the Community. The power of regulation-making, therefore, contained in s. 3 is *prima facie* a power which is part of the necessary machinery which became a duty of the State upon its joining the Community and therefore necessitated by that membership.

The Court is satisfied that, having regard to the number of Community laws, acts done and measures adopted which either have to be facilitated in their direct application to the law of the State or have to be implemented by appropriate action into the law of the State, the obligation of membership would necessitate facilitating of these activities, in some instances, at least, and possibly in a great majority of instances, by the making of ministerial regulation rather than legislation of the Oireachtas.

The Court is accordingly satisfied that the power to make regulations in the form in which it is contained in s. 3, sub-s. 2 of the Act of 1972 is necessitated by the obligations of membership by the State of the Communities and now of the Union and is therefore by virtue of Article 29, s. 4, sub-ss. 3, 4 and 5 immune from constitutional challenge.

In so far as it may be possible to point to hypothetical instances of certain types of laws, measures or acts of the Community or Union which in their implementation or application within the national law might not, as to the method of implementation or application, be necessarily carried out by ministerial regulation, but rather should have been carried out by enactment of law by the Oireachtas, the Court is satisfied, without deciding that such instances do occur, that the principles laid down by this Court in the decision of *East Donegal Co-operative Livestock Marts Ltd* v. *Attorney General* [1970] IR 317, must be applied to the construction of the impugned subsection in the manner in which it was applied by the decision of this Court in *Harvey* v. *The Minister for Social Welfare* [1990] 2 IR 232 to the construction of the section of the statute impugned in that case, namely, s. 75 of the Social Welfare Act, 1952. That principle is that it must be implied that the making of regulations by the Minister, as is permitted by the section, is intended by the Oireachtas to be conducted in accordance with the principles of constitutional justice, and therefore that it is to be implied that the Minister shall not in exercising the power of making regulations pursuant to the section, contravene any provisions of the Constitution.

If therefore in such an instance challenge were to be made to the validity of a ministerial regulation having regard to the absence of **[353]** necessity for it to be carried out by regulation instead of legislation and having regard to the nature of the content of such regulation it would have to be a challenge made on the basis that the regulation was invalid as *ultra vires* being an unconstitutional exercise by the Minister of the power constitutionally conferred upon him by the section.

Having reached the conclusion that the challenge to the constitutional validity of this subsection has not been established, and the Court not being satisfied that the subsection is invalid having regard to the Constitution, it is not appropriate for the Court to deal with any of the alternative submissions in defence of the constitutional validity of the subsection which were put forward on behalf of the respondents, since those are involved in the other aspect of this appeal, namely, the challenge to the validity of the statutory instruments which have been made by the Minister in pursuance of s. 3 of the Act of 1972.

Such statutory instruments are not laws within the meaning of Article 34, s. 4, sub-s. 5 of the Constitution and, therefore, may be the subject matter of separate judgments.

FINLAY CJ

I agree with the judgments about to be delivered by Blayney and Denham JJ.

O'FLAHERTY J

I agree.

EGAN J

I agree.

BLAYNEY J

On the 24th August, 1992, the applicant was served with twenty District Court summonses relating to offences under the European Communities (Control of Veterinary Medicinal Products and their Residues) Regulations 1988 and 1990. The offences were alleged to have been committed on the 27th March, 1991, being the date on which a number of officers of the Department of Agriculture, acting on the **[354]** authority of a search warrant granted by the District Court pursuant to art. 16 of the Regulations of 1988, had carried out a search of the applicant's farm at Baptist Grange, Lisronagh, Clonmel in the County of Tipperary.

The applicant immediately applied for and was granted leave to seek by way of judicial review the following reliefs:

1. A declaration that the Regulations of 1988 and 1990 are *ultra vires* and void.
2. A declaration that the provisions of s. 3, sub-s. 1 and s. 3, sub-s. 2 of the European Communities Act, 1972, are contrary to the Constitution of Ireland and are void.
3. An order of certiorari quashing the search warrant granted by the District Court pursuant to art. 16 of the Regulations of 1988.
4. An order of prohibition restraining the Minister for Agriculture from proceeding with the twenty summonses issued against the applicant.

The motion seeking these reliefs was heard by Johnson J and by order dated the 1st April, 1993, it was declared "that such portion of s. 3, sub-s. 2 of the European Communities Act, 1972, which entitles a Minister by regulation to repeal or amend or applying [*sic*], with or without modification, other law exclusive of that of the said Act is unconstitutional." The Minister appealed against that order and during the hearing the Court accepted that it would deal not only with the constitutional issue but also with the other reliefs which had been sought in the High Court but in respect of which no order had been made.

The constitutional issue having been dealt with in the decision of the Court which has just been pronounced by the Chief Justice, what remains to be considered is the other reliefs which are claimed and these were narrowed down in the course of the argument to a single issue: whether the Regulations of 1988 and 1990 are *ultra vires* the Minister for

Agriculture and Food under s. 3 of the European Communities Act, 1972, in so far as they authorise the District Court to grant a search warrant and permit a summons to be brought in the District Court within two years of the commission of the offence notwithstanding s. 10, sub-s. 4 of the Petty Sessions (Ireland) Act, 1851. Mr Hogan, on behalf of the applicant, stated that he did not take objection to any of the other provisions of the regulations. His sole claim, accordingly, is that art. 16 of the Regulations of 1988, which is the article authorising the issue of search warrants by the District Court, and art. 32, para. 8 of the Regulations **[355]** of 1988 and art. 11, para. 4 of the Regulations of 1990, both of which provide the two year time limit for issuing summonses, are *ultra vires*.

The Law

The relevant law to be considered is the same as had to be considered on the constitutional issue but it would probably be helpful if I were to set it out again.

1. *Article 189 of the Treaty of Rome*

A directive shall be binding, as to the result to be achieved, upon each Member State to which it is addressed, but shall leave to the national authorities the choice of form and methods.

2. *Article 29, s. 4, sub-s. 5 of the Constitution*

No provision of this Constitution invalidates laws enacted, acts done or measures adopted by the State necessitated by the obligations of membership of the European Union or of the Communities, or prevents laws enacted, acts done or measures adopted by the European Union or by the Communities, or by institutions thereof, or by bodies competent under the Treaties establishing the Communities, from having the force of law in the State.

3. *European Communities Act, 1972*
Section 2:

From the 1st day of January 1973 the Treaties governing the European Communities and the existing and future acts adopted by the institutions of those Communities shall be binding on the State and shall be part of the domestic law thereof under the conditions laid down in those Treaties.

Section 3:

(1) A Minister of State may make regulations for enabling section 2 of this Act to have full effect.

(2) Regulations under this section may contain such incidental, supplementary and consequential provisions as appear to the Minister making the regulations to be necessary for the purposes of the regulations (including provisions repealing, amending or applying with or without modification, other law, exclusive of this Act).

[356] The submissions made in the course of the hearing were directed both to the constitutionality of the impugned provision in sub-s. 2 of s. 3 of the Act of 1972 and to the issue with which this judgment is concerned and it would be rather difficult to segregate them. Rather than attempt to do so I propose to proceed directly to the question that has to be addressed and I will refer to the different submissions as occasion arises.

In considering whether the two statutory instruments are *ultra vires*, the first thing that has to be done is to see exactly what power the Minister is given by s. 3 of the Act of 1972. The power is a very wide one. It is to enable s. 2 of the Act to have full effect and since that section provides that "the Treaties governing the European Communities and the existing and future acts adopted by the institutions of those Communities shall be binding on the State and shall be part of the domestic law thereof under the conditions laid down in those Treaties" the relevant power of the Minister in the context of the present case is to ensure that the EC directives referred to in the two statutory instruments are part of our domestic law under the conditions laid down in the Treaties. Furthermore, under sub-s. 2 of s. 3, the Minister has express power to include in the regulations such incidental, supplementary and consequential provisions as appear to him to be necessary for the purposes of the regulations "including provisions repealing, amending or applying, with or without modification, other law, exclusive of [the 1972] Act."

These being the powers of the Minister, had he power to include in the regulations the provision authorising the District Court to grant a search warrant, and the provision allowing a period of two years for instituting prosecutions for offences? The answer in my opinion clearly is that he had such power provided that it was necessary for the purpose of giving effect to the directives. Accordingly the directives have to be looked at to see if these provisions are necessary for their implementation and when this is done it becomes quite clear that they are.

I start with the power given to the District Court to issue a search warrant. This is clearly required by some of the provisions of Council Directive 85/358/EEC of the 16th July, 1985, which is one of the directives implemented by the Regulations of 1988. Two of the recitals in the preamble to the directive are as follows:

> Whereas provisions should be made for the official taking of samples at the slaughterhouse; whereas, furthermore, where there **[357]** is a justified suspicion of infringement, provision should be made for the possibility of taking such samples at the farm of origin; . . .
>
> Whereas, where the presence of prohibited substances or of the residues of such substances is confirmed, an investigation should be made at the farm of origin in order to exclude the meat in question from human and animal consumption and to place the prohibited substances under official control.

The relevant articles of the directive provide as follows:

Article 1

The Member States shall ensure that official on-the-spot random controls are made on the substances referred to in Directive 81/602/EEC at the manufacturing, handling, storage, transport, distribution and sales stages for the presence of prohibited substances and veterinary pharmaceutical preparations containing prohibited substances which may be intended to be administered to animals for fattening purposes . . .

Article 3

Member States shall ensure that:

1. where there is justified suspicion of an infringement, the competent departments make or arrange to have made:

— random controls on animals on their farms of origin, particularly in order to detect traces of implants;

— an official control for the presence of the substances the use of which is prohibited on farms where animals are reared, kept or fattened;

— such controls may include the official taking of samples;

2. random samples are taken from animals from fattening farms.

Article 5 then provides for the samples referred to in art. 3 to be analysed in a laboratory approved by the competent authorities.

Finally, art. 6 provides as follows:

1. Where the analysis referred to in Article 5 confirms the presence of prohibited substances or of residues either exceeding the maximum natural physiological levels for the authorised substances or proving that authorised substances have been used abusively, the competent authority shall be informed immediately of:

[358] (a) all the particulars needed to identify the animal and its farm of origin. These particulars shall be determined in accordance with the procedure laid down in Article 10;

(b) the result of the analysis.

2. The competent authorities shall then ensure that:

(a) an investigation is made at the farm of origin to determine the reason for the presence of hormone residues;

(b) an investigation of the source or sources of the substance concerned is made, as necessary, at the manufacturing, handling, storage, transport, distribution or sales stage.

It is clear that these provisions could not be implemented without creating a power to enable a compulsory search to be made of farms where animals are kept. It follows that the Minister had power to include in the Regulations of 1988, art. 16 which gives the District Court power to issue search warrants.

As regards the two year period for instituting proceedings for an offence under the regulations, it is relevant to note firstly that no objection was taken to the fact that the regulations create a number of offences. It is accordingly accepted by counsel for the applicant that this was required for the implementation of the relevant directives. And it must follow logically that the implementation required in addition that the offences could be effectively prosecuted. So the regulations had to be in a form to enable this to be done and if it was necessary for this purpose to allow a period of two years the Minister clearly had power to allow such a period.

The only evidence on this point, which is uncontested, is that of Ms Maura Waters, an assistant principal of the Department of Agriculture and Food. In an affidavit sworn on the 19th February, 1993, she deals in detail with the unavoidable delays in the investigation of offences under the regulations by reason of the necessity for analyses to be carried out in the State laboratory and says that experience "had shown that in carrying out the type of investigation necessary having regard to the inquiries which would be required and the possible need to avail of very sophisticated analytical procedures which had waiting lists for the service the six-month statutory period for instituting proceedings would not be met in many cases."

She then goes on to deal with other possible causes of delay in the final paragraph of her affidavit:

> **[359]** 4. In particular the directives require investigations to be carried out in more than one Member State if it is suspected that the offence may have connections outside the State where initially detected and organising the necessary co-operation from another State may be time-consuming. For these reasons an opinion was formed that in order to fully implement the directives to the extent of exercising sanctions against offenders and to determining the source of the problem (where possible) that it was necessary to extend the period during which proceedings may be instituted. Accordingly recourse was made to the enabling power in s. 3, sub-s. 2 of the European Communities Act, 1972, to provide that the time limit in s. 10, sub-s. 4 of the Petty Sessions (Ireland) Act, 1851, would not apply and to substitute a two year period in its place.

It is quite clear from Ms Waters' affidavit that if the power of prosecution given in the Regulation was to be effective, the six-month period was too short and so it was necessary to extend it. It follows that the Minister had power to provide for a longer period and so had power to extend the six months to two years.

It was submitted by Mr Hogan that there was nothing in the directive which expressly required a two-year time limit and for that reason it was not justified. I reject that submission. The directive clearly required, as Mr Hogan accepted, that offences had to be created and obviously, as I said earlier, it had to be possible for these offences to be effectively prosecuted. Accordingly, the implementation of the directive required that the Regulations should provide for an adequate time for the preparation of the prosecutions. It was not necessary that the directive should itself fix a time. It was a matter for the State to decide on the length of time required to enable the prosecution to be brought and that is what the Minister has done in providing for a period of two years.

Mr Hogan also submitted that s. 10 of the Act of 1851 could not be amended except by statute. The decision of the Court already delivered has upheld the constitutional validity of the part of s. 3, sub-s. 2 of the Act of 1972 which gives the Minister express power to include in a regulation a provision amending other law. In so far therefore as this submission may be construed as meaning that the portion of the Regulation amending s. 10 of the Act of 1851 is invalid, it seems to me that it should be rejected for the following reasons.

[360] It is well established that Community law takes precedence over our domestic law. Where they are in conflict, it is the Community law that prevails. See *Marleasing SA* v. *La Commercial Internacional de Alimentacion SA* (Case C-106/89) [1990] ECR 1-4135, and *Francovich* v. *Italy* (Case C-6/90) [1991] ECR 1-5357. The relevant directives here were binding on the State, from the moment they were adopted, "as to the result to be achieved". One result to be achieved clearly was the creation of effective sanctions for the enforcement of the measures contained in the directives. So the State was bound to introduce effective sanctions, and if this necessitated adopting a measure which impliedly amended an existing statute, that measure would prevail over the statute because it was in substance a measure of Community law. It is only in form that it is part of the domestic law. It derives its force from the directive which is binding on the State as to the results to be achieved. Such in my opinion is the character of art. 32, para. 8 of the Regulations of 1988 providing for the two-year period for instituting prosecutions.

Finally, I would not accept Mr Hogan's submission that merely because Article 189 of the Treaty of Rome leaves to the State the choice of the form and methods of implementing a directive, what is done by way of implementation is not necessitated by the State's obligations of membership and so may be subjected to constitutional challenge. The Article obliges the State to implement the directive and equally obliges the State, in exercise of the discretion given to it, to choose an appropriate method of implementation. If the State were free not to implement the directive, then clearly, if it were to do so, it would be a voluntary act not necessitated by the obligations of membership and would not be protected by Article 19, s. 4, sub-s. 5 of the Constitution. But the State is not free. It is obliged to implement the directive and so is obliged to choose a method of implementation and, provided the method it chooses is appropriate for the purpose of satisfying the obligation of the State and the measures it incorporates do not go beyond what is required to implement the directive, it is correctly categorised as being necessitated by the directive. In any instance where the method was not appropriate, or its measures went beyond what was required, it would not be necessitated and would be open to constitutional challenge. This is not such a case.

For all these reasons I would refuse all the relief sought by the applicant by way of judicial review.

[361] DENHAM J

The Court in the decision which has just been pronounced by the Chief Justice having rejected the constitutional challenge to the validity of s. 3, sub-s. 2 of the European Communities Act, 1972, this judgment deals with the remaining issue as to the validity of the regulations made by the Minister pursuant to that section.

The issue for determination is whether the European Communities (Control of Veterinary Medicinal Products and their Residues) Regulations, 1988 and 1990 are *ultra vires* the powers of the Minister for Agriculture and Food under s. 3 of the European Communities Act, 1972, in so far as they authorise the procedure for the granting of a search warrant, and in so far as they extend the time within which a summons can be sought thereby amending s. 10, sub-s. 4 of the Petty Sessions (Ireland) Act, 1851.

The facts and issues have been fully set out by the Chief Justice and Blayney J. The directives relevant to this case are Council Directive 81/602/EEC of the 31st July, 1981, Council Directive 81/851/EEC of the 28th September, 1981 (in so far as it relates to substances with oestrogenic, androgenic, gestagenic or thyrostatic action), Council Directive 85/358/EEC of the 16th July, 1985, Council Directive 86/469/EEC of the 16th September, 1986, Council Directive 88/146/EEC of the 7th March, 1988, and Council Directive 88/299/EEC of the 17th May, 1988. Section 3 of the European Communities Act, 1972, and the said directives are the basis upon which the Minister made the regulations in issue in this case.

Law

The sources of the law in issue are national, constitutional and statutory, and European, however all are part of the domestic law. The relevant sections have been set out previously but for analysis I re-state them.

(1) *Bunreacht na hÉireann, Article 15, s. 2, sub-s. 1*:

The sole and exclusive power of making laws for the State is hereby vested in the Oireachtas: no other legislative authority has power to make laws for the State.

[362] (2) *Bunreacht na hÉireann, Article 29, s. 4*

3. The State may become a member of the European Coal and Steel Community (established by Treaty signed at Paris on the 18th day of April, 1951), the European Economic Community (established by Treaty signed at Rome on the 25th day of March, 1957) and the European Atomic Energy Community (established by Treaty signed at Rome on the 25th day of March, 1957). The State may ratify the Single European Act (signed on behalf of the Member States of the Communities at Luxembourg on the 17th day of February, 1986, and at the Hague on the 28th day of February, 1986).

4. The State may ratify the Treaty on European Union signed at Maastricht on the 7th day of February, 1992, and may become a member of that Union.

5. No provision of this Constitution invalidates laws enacted, acts done or measures adopted by the State which are necessitated by the obligations of membership of the European Union or of the Communities, or prevents laws enacted, acts done or measures adopted by the European Union or by the Communities, or by institutions thereof, or by bodies competent under the Treaties establishing the Communities, from having the force of law in the State.

(3) *The European Communities Act, 1972*

2.—From the 1st day of January, 1973, the treaties governing the European Communities and the existing and future acts adopted by the institutions of those Communities shall be binding on the State and shall be part of the domestic law thereof under the conditions laid down in those treaties.

3.—(1) A Minister of State may make regulations for enabling section 2 of this Act to have full effect.

(2) Regulations under this section may contain such incidental, supplementary and consequential provisions as appear to the Minister making the regulations to be necessary for the purposes of the regulations (including provisions repealing, amending or applying, with or without modification, other law, exclusive of this Act).

[363] (4) *The Treaty of Rome, Article 5*:

Member States shall take all appropriate measures, whether general or particular, to ensure fulfilment of the obligations arising out of this Treaty or resulting from action taken by the institutions of the Community. They shall facilitate the achievement of the Community's tasks.

They shall abstain from any measure which could jeopardise the attainment of the objectives of this Treaty.

(5) *The Treaty of Rome, Article 189*:

In order to carry out their task the Council and the Commission shall, in accordance with the provisions of this Treaty, make regulations, issue directives, take decisions, make recommendations or deliver opinions.

A regulation shall have general application. It shall be binding in its entirety and directly applicable in all Member States.

A directive shall be binding, as to the result to be achieved, upon each Member State to which it is addressed, but shall leave to the national authorities the choice of form and methods . . .

This case is not about a balance of power between Community authorities and national authorities. It was accepted by the parties that Community law has primacy.

The issue to be determined is the balance within the national forum of s. 2 and s. 3 of the Act of 1972, Article 15, s. 2 and Article 29, s. 4, sub-s. 5 of Bunreacht na hÉireann and Articles 5 and 189 of the Treaty of Rome. Thus the kernel is the word "necessitated" in Article 29, s. 4, sub-s. 5 and the "choice" afforded in Article 189.

Facts

On the facts of the case there was no contest. There was no replying affidavit to either of the affidavits filed by the State.

The State set out facts which established that under the directive an extension of time within which to apply for a summons was necessary, as was a power to search.

I am satisfied that on the facts of the case, as set out by the State and not controverted by the applicant, it was necessary in view of the substance of the directive to both extend time within which a summons could be issued and to authorise search warrants.

[364] Thus, while, in general, facts may be judicially reviewable they were not in contest in this case.

"Necessitated"

It is clear that on the facts of this case it was necessary (a) to amend the Petty Sessions (Ireland) Act, 1851, as to the time limits within which to apply for a summons and (b) to create a right of search.

There is no doubt that these two factors must be brought into Irish domestic law under its obligations under Community law.

However, the fact that they were "necessitated" under the directive to be incorporated into national law is not the end of the matter.

"Choice"

Article 189 leaves to the national authorities the choice of form and methods. In choosing the form and method the Minister has to act in accordance with the law and the Constitution. Thus the Minister must balance the relevant Articles of the Constitution, which in this case are Article 15, s. 2 and Article 29, s. 4, sub-section 5. His choice, under

Article 189, must be in acordance with national law, the Constitution and Community law. His decision is judicially reviewable.

The fact that the substance of the directive is binding as to the result to be achieved, and that a Minister must initiate an enabling national process, does not determine the issue of choice of method. Whereas the State is required to implement the substance of the directive into law, the State is not required by Community law to choose any particular form or method.

Form or Method

In determining the form or method the State, Minister, must have due regard to the Constitution, both Article 15, s. 2 and Article 29, s. 4, sub-section 3.

Under Bunreacht na hÉireann as enacted in 1937 the sole and exclusive power of making law for the State was vested in the Oireachtas. This is a fundamental aspect of democratic government, based on the separation of powers.

That basic tenet has been qualified by membership of the European Community which has established other law making authorities. *Inter* **[365]** *alia* it has established law making in the form of directives, which are binding on the State, as to the result to be achieved, leaving to the national authorities the choice of form and methods.

Were the Constitution still in its 1937 form the State, Minister, would have no choice—he would have to initiate a process of legislation through the Oireachtas. However, the Constitution has been amended, and Community law has been introduced to the domestic law, and the situation is not now governed by Article 15, s. 2 alone. Article 15, s. 2 cannot be read in isolation.

The term "necessitated" in Article 29, s. 4, sub-s. 5 together with Article 189 of the Treaty make it clear that in balancing the two the mere fact that the substance in laws enacted, acts done or measures adopted, is necessary to be incorporated into domestic Irish law, is not the end of the matter.

The term "necessitated" is relevant to the choice of method, however membership has not itself obligated a special form and method of implementation. Article 15, s. 2 and the choice of form and methods of Article 189 must then be read together with Article 29, s. 4, sub-section 5.

Article 29, s. 4, sub-s. 5 refers to "laws enacted, acts done or measures adopted." Clearly this refers to legislation through the Oireachtas and other methods of implementation, including the two sets of regulations herein.

The Minister made the regulations under s. 3 of the Act of 1972. The directive is "binding" on the State as to the result to be achieved. The principles and policies are set out in the directive. Under s. 3, sub-s. 2 the Minister's regulations may contain such incidental, supplementary and consequential provisions as appear to the Minister to be necessary for the purposes of the regulations, including amending an Act (exclusive of the Act of 1972). Clearly incidental, supplementary and consequential provisions are not foundation principles and policies.

If the directive left to the national authority matters of principle or policy to be determined then the "choice" of the Minister would require legislation by the Oireachtas. But where there is no case made that principles or policies have to be determined by the national authority, where the situation is that the principles and policies were determined in the directive, then legislation by a delegated form, by regulation, is a valid choice. The fact that an Act of the Oireachtas has been affected by the policy in a directive, is a "result to be achieved" wherein there is now no choice between the policy and the national act. The policy of **[366]** the directive must succeed. Thus where there is in fact no choice on a policy or a principle it is a matter appropriate for delegated legislation. If the directive or the Minister envisaged any choice of principle or policy then it would require legislation by the Oireachtas.

The appropriate test is as set out by O'Higgins CJ in *Cityview Press* v. *An Chomhairle Oiliúna* [1980] IR 381 at p. 399, where he stated:

> In the view of this Court, the test is whether that which is challenged as an unauthorised delegation of parliamentary power is more than a mere giving effect to principles and policies which are contained in the statute itself. If it be, then it is not authorised; for such would constitute a purported exercise of legislative power by an authority which is not permitted to do so under the Constitution. On the other hand, if it be within the permitted limits—if the law is laid down in the statute and details only are filled in or completed by the designated Minister or subordinate body—there is no unauthorised delegation of legislative power.

Applying the test to this situation the test is whether the ministerial regulations under s. 3 of the Act of 1972 are more than the mere giving effect to principles and policies of the said Act and the directives which are part of domestic law as to the result to be achieved.

If the regulations contained material exceeding the policies and principles of the directives then they are not authorised by the directives and would not be valid under s. 3 unless the material was incidental, supplementary or consequential. In those circumstances if they were not incidental, supplementary or consequential the regulations would be an exercise of legislative power by an authority not so permitted under the Constitution. If it be within the permitted limits, if the policy is laid down in the directive and details only are filled in or completed by the regulations, there is no unauthorised delegation of legislative power.

Democracy

The separation of powers is a fundamental principle of Bunreacht na hÉireann. The power to legislate for the State is solely within the Oireachtas—save where that authority has been assigned under the Constitution to Community authorities and organs of the State to act in accordance with Community law as integrated into national law.

[367] There was no question in this case that the principles and policies of the directives were not within the Treaties.

In the directives herein the policies and principles have been determined. Thus there is no role of determining policies or principles for the Oireachtas. While the directive must be implemented there is no policy or principle which can be altered by the Oireachtas, it is already binding as to the result to be achieved.

That being the case the role of the Oireachtas in such a situation would be sterile. To require the Oireachtas to legislate would be artificial. It would be able solely to have a debate as to what has already been decided, which debate would act as a source of information. Such a sterile debate would take up Dáil and Seanad time and act only as a window on Community directives for the members of the Oireachtas and the Nation. That is not a role envisaged for the Oireachtas in the Constitution.

Consequently, solely because the Minister is making a regulation which repeals a statute, does not of itself invalidate the regulation which as a vehicle, as a choice, can be *intra vires* the Constitution under Article 29, section 4. To say that the regulations breach Article 15, s. 2, sub-s. 1 simply because it repeals or amends a statute is to hold the false premise that the Minister is determining principles or policy.

The regulations in this case being within the policies and principles of the directives the substance of the regulation is within the directives. There are no policies and principles enunciated in the regulations that are not within the directives. There are no policies and principles in the regulations additional to the directive.

Consequently, to state that such an action—effectively an administrative implementation of policies and principles of a directive—is superior legislation as envisaged in Article 15, s. 2, sub-s. 1—is a misnomer. Superior legislation involves a decision on policies and principles by the legislature and an implementation thereof in the form of a statute. Here what is at issue in essence is subordinate legislation as delegated under Community law.

No constitutional right, other than the process under Article 15, s. 2 of Bunreacht na hÉireann, was submitted as part of the argument, or as being in issue. Nor was any issue raised as to the validity of the directives and their principles and policies under the Treaties.

I am satisfied that the regulations in issue in this case were not *ultra vires* the power of the Minister for Agriculture and Food under s. 3 of the European Communities Act, 1972, in so far as they authorised the **[368]** procedure for the granting of the search warrant, and in so far as they extended time thereby amending s. 10, sub-s. 4 of the Petty Sessions (Ireland) Act, 1851, being as they were implementations of policies and principles in the relevant directives.

I am in agreement with the judgment of Blayney J and consequently I would allow the appeal.

[Report: [1994] 1 Irish Reports 347]

Legal order in general — Incorporation into national legal order — Irish Constitution, Article 29(4)(3) — European Communities Act 1972, Section 2—Whether EC Treaty now forming part of Irish law as statute law or Community law

Direct effect — Directives — Conditions for direct effect — Improper implementation of directive in national law — Whether directive may be relied upon by individuals before national courts—Council Directive 79/7 on equal treatment in social security matters

Enforcement in national courts—Remedies—Claim against Member State — Breach of Community law for which Member State responsible—Failure of Member State to implement provisions of Community directive properly — Whether individuals entitled to damages for loss suffered—Whether national rules on statutory limitation applicable—The law of Ireland

TATE AND ROBINSON *v.* MINISTER FOR SOCIAL WELFARE AND ATTORNEY GENERAL

Ireland, High Court. 3 *February* 1995

(Carroll, *Justice*)

SUMMARY: *The facts*:—The plaintiffs were married women who sought declarations that they were entitled to receive the same social security benefits, under the same rules, as married men and that Ireland had failed properly to implement Council Directive 79/7 on equal treatment in social security matters. They also sought damages from the Irish State. The Directive should have been implemented by the end of 1984 but was, in fact, only partially implemented by Irish regulations which came into force in 1986 and 1992. The plaintiffs argued that the 1992 regulations had failed to remove the discrimination which they had suffered by comparison with men living in similar circumstances.

Held:—The plaintiffs were entitled to rely on the direct effect of the Directive, and either to sue directly for their entitlements under the Directive or to claim damages for the State's failure to implement it.

(1) The rights of the plaintiffs were derived not from the Constitution or the legal order of Ireland but from the Directive itself, construed in the light of the Treaty, which had effect in Irish law by virtue of Article 29(4)(3) of the Constitution and Section 2 of the European Communities Act 1972. The function of this constitutional amendment was to allow the entire body of Community law to have effect in Ireland notwithstanding any provision in the Constitution. Section 2 of the Act then served as a conduit through which

Community law became part of domestic law. But Community law did not thereby become constitutional law. It rather retained its status as Community law, forming part of domestic law (pp. 338-40).

(2) The tort committed by the State, in continuing the discrimination by failing to implement the Directive fully, was a wrong arising from Community law which had domestic effect. The breach of the duty to implement the Directive approximated to a breach of constitutional duty and gave rise to State liability to make good the loss caused to individuals, in accordance with the principles laid down in the *Francovich* judgment of the European Court of Justice. Every type of action which would be available under national law to ensure the observance of that law was available to ensure observance of the Directive, once it took on the mantle of direct effect. An action for damages based on the State's failure to implement the Directive was a claim in tort rather than for breach of statutory duty and, as such, it was subject to the domestic rules on statutory limitation (pp. 340-4).

(3) Where a directive was not properly implemented, despite the deadline for its implementation having passed, and it satisfied the conditions for direct effect, there was also a cause of action based on direct effect which entitled a person to sue directly for the entitlement which had been withheld, relying on the Directive to preclude the application of any national provision inconsistent with it (p. 343).

The following is the text of the judgment of the Court:

[425] CARROLL J

This claim arises out of Council Directive 79/7/EEC of the 19th December, 1978, dealing with the principle of equal treatment for men and women in matters of social security.

Article 4, sub-art. 1 of the Directive provides that:

> The principle of equal treatment means that there shall be no discrimination whatsoever on grounds of sex, either directly or indirectly by reference in particular to marital or family status, in particular as concerns:
> (i) the scope of the schemes and the conditions of access thereto,
> (ii) the obligation to contribute and the calculation of contributions,
> (iii) the calculation of benefits including increases due in respect of a spouse and for dependants and the conditions governing the duration and retention of entitlement to benefits.

Article 8 of the Directive required the Member States to implement the Directive within six years of notification. The relevant date for Ireland was the 23rd December, 1984.

Ireland did not implement any part of the Directive by that date. Certain changes were made by the Social Welfare (No 2) Act, 1985, the provisions of which came into force on varying dates at the end of 1986. For the period between the 23rd December, 1984, and the varying dates in 1986 the following differences existed in the treatment of married women and married men for matters coming within the Directive:

(1) There was a difference in the personal rate of social welfare benefits;
(2) Men were entitled to receive employment benefits for 390 days whereas married women were only entitled to receive the same for 312 days;
[426] (3) Married women had to show they had an adult dependant in order to qualify for unemployment assistance, whereas no such qualifying condition was imposed on married men;
(4) A married man was automatically entitled to an increase in his rate of benefit for an adult dependant if his wife lived with him or was wholly or mainly maintained by him. A married woman was only entitled to an increase if her husband was incapable of self-support and was wholly or mainly maintained by her;
(5) A married man was entitled to an automatic increase in his rate of benefit in respect of a qualified child who normally resided with him. A married woman had to show an incapacity on the part of the child's father to self-support before she could claim an increase in respect of a child residing with her.

Following the coming into effect of the Social Welfare (No 2) Act, 1985, these five differences were removed prospectively. But the Minister for Social Welfare introduced the Social Welfare (Preservation of Rights) (No 2) Regulations, 1986, which granted an increase in the rate of benefit up to a maximum of £20.00 for those who had been in receipt of an adult dependant allowance but who ceased to be entitled to the same after the coming into effect of the Act of 1985. The regulations were expressed to be transitional in nature and the provisions of same were renewed from time to time by subsequent orders made by the Minister for Social Welfare with a decreasing amount of benefit payable. They finally expired in July, 1992. The benefits paid under these regulations were effectively only paid to married men as they were the only people who ceased to be entitled to adult dependancy allowances by virtue of the Act of 1985. They only applied to persons who were in receipt of benefit on particular weeks in November, 1986, and for so long as they were continuously in receipt of benefit.

On 24th March, 1987, the Court of Justice of the European Communities in an Article 177 reference in *Cotter and McDermott* v. *Minister for Social Welfare (No 1)* (Case C-286/85) [1987] ECR 1453 held (1) that Article 4, sub-art. 1 of Directive 79/7/EEC had direct effect from the 23rd December, 1984, and (2) that in the absence of measures implementing art. 4, sub-art. 1 women were entitled to have the same rules applied as are applied to married men.

Prior to that judgment Mrs Cotter and Mrs McDermott had instituted further proceedings seeking, *inter alia*, declarations that they were entitled to the same increases in their social welfare benefits as married men in their circumstances received before the entry into force of the Social **[427]** Welfare (No 2) Act, 1985, and that they were entitled to the transitional compensatory payments which some men received after that date. The Supreme Court referred questions on these issues to the European Court of Justice.

On the 13th March, 1991, the Court of Justice held that after expiry of the period allowed for implementation of the Directive, (1) where married men have automatically received increases and social security benefits in respect of a spouse and children deemed to be dependants without having to prove actual dependancy, married women without actual dependants are entitled to the same increases even if in some circumstances that will result in double payment of the increases, and (2) that where there is a transitional provision providing for compensatory payments to married men who have lost their entitlement to an increase in their social security benefits in respect of a spouse deemed to be dependant because actual dependancy cannot be shown to exist, married women in the same family circumstances are entitled to the same payments even if that infringes the prohibition on unjust enrichment laid down by national law.

Subsequent to this judgment the State settled the claims of Mrs Cotter and Mrs McDermott by the payment of sums of money and costs without admission of liability.

On the 22nd July, 1988, Mrs Teresa Emmott instituted judicial review proceedings against the State making essentially the same claims as Mrs Cotter and Mrs McDermott. The State took a preliminary point that her application for judicial review was out of time because of the provisions of O. 84, r. 21 of the Rules of the Superior Courts, 1986. This provides:

> (1) An application for leave to apply for judicial review shall be made promptly and in any event within three months from the date when grounds for the application first arose, or six months where the relief sought is certiorari, unless the Court considers there is a good reason for extending the period within which the application shall be made.

A question on the matter was referred by the High Court to the European Court of Justice pursuant to Article 177. On the 25th July, 1991, the Court of Justice held that the State was precluded from relying on national procedural rules relating to time limits for bringing proceedings so long as Directive 79/7 had not been properly transposed into its domestic legal system.

This case too was settled without admission of liability.

[428] On the 18th June, 1992, the Minister for Social Welfare made the European Communities (Social Welfare) Regulations, 1992 (the "Regulations of 1992"), which granted some additional payments in respect of the differences in the rates of benefits paid to married men and married women between 1984 and 1986 but did not provide for all the differences.

For those who made claims under the Regulations of 1992, they received:

1. The difference in the personal rate at which the social welfare benefits were paid to them between December, 1984, and November, 1986, and the personal rate paid to married men in similar circumstances during the same period;
2. Unemployment benefit for additional periods between 312 and 390 days at the rate paid to married men in the period 1984 to 1986, and
3. In some cases (where the husband was earning more than £50 per week) one half of the child dependancy allowance a married man in similar family and social welfare circumstances would have received between December, 1984, and November, 1986. This was now part of what was called "household supplement".

The payments made in 1993 (and in some cases 1994) were paid at the rates current between 1984 and 1986 and there was no provision for compensation by reason of the delay.

The Regulations of 1992 did not make any provision for:

(1) Any payments to married women in respect of the transitional payments made to married men pursuant to the Social Welfare (Preservation of Rights) Regulations, 1986;
(2) There was no payment of the adult dependancy allowance which was paid to married men between 1984 and 1986 because under the Regulations of 1992 payment to the husband of this amount (as part of the household supplement) was deemed to be payment to the wife;
(3) There was no payment of an additional half of the child dependancy allowance to women who received half under the Regulations of 1992 to equate with what married men had received. There was no payment of any child dependancy allowance to women with a dependant spouse or with a spouse on social welfare;
(4) For those entitled to unemployment assistance they were not paid at the relevant personal rate increased by an adult dependancy **[429]** allowance and the full child dependancy allowance less the appropriate means test in accordance with the means test used by the Department of Social Welfare pre-November, 1986, as married men in similar circumstances would have been paid. The 1992 Regulations deleted the special provision that applied to married women but placed a limit on the total amount payable to a couple and applied a post-November, 1986, means test.

The plaintiffs all of whom are married women accordingly now claim declarations:

That they are entitled to receive the same benefits and to have the same rules applied to them that were paid and applied to married men in the same situation from the 23rd December, 1984, under the Social Welfare Acts and Regulations, 1981-1992.

That the State has failed to fully or properly implement Directive 79/7/EEC.

That the Regulations of 1992, in particular arts. 4 and 5, are *ultra vires* the powers of the Minister for Social Welfare and therefore null and void.

Alternatively that the Regulations of 1992 are repugnant to Article 15, s. 2 of the Constitution of Ireland, 1937, and are thereby null and void.

Alternatively that the Regulations of 1992 are repugnant to Article 40, s. 3 of the Constitution and are thereby null and void.

They claim damages for the failure by the State to fully or properly implement Directive 79/7/EEC, for breach of the duty of care and/or constitutional duty and/or statutory duty.

They claim interest under the Courts Act, 1981.

A claim for an account was dropped.

The action by Esther Robinson and others originally comprised 79 plaintiffs. Of these 9 discontinued the action, *viz.* Penelope Reilly, Jennifer Woods, Gemma Elders, Diana Delaney, Ann Smith, Mary Murray, Helen Kelleher, Margaret Fox and Imelda Hendrick. One of the plaintiffs, Elizabeth Hayden, died and is now represented by her husband and personal representative, James Hayden. In the action by Rosaleen McClean and Teresa Tate, the action by Rosaleen McClean was discontinued.

The following facts were admitted:

The plaintiffs are persons who:

1. Were all married women on dates between the 23rd December, 1984, and the 21st November, 1986, and subsequent thereto.

[430] 2. All had husbands living with them on dates between the 23rd December, 1984, and the 21st November, 1986, and subsequent thereto.

3. Some of them had eligible children living with them between the 23rd December, 1984 and the 21st November, 1986, and subsequent thereto.

Teresa Tate and 60 of the plaintiffs in the other action all fall into one or more of the following categories:

1. They were in receipt of social welfare benefits (unemployment, disability and invalidity) on dates between the 23rd December, 1984, and the 21st November, 1986.
2. They had husbands in employment on dates between the 23rd December, 1984, and the 21st November, 1986.
3. They had husbands in receipt of social welfare benefits on dates between the 23rd December, 1984, and the 21st November, 1986.
4. They were in receipt of social welfare benefits in November, 1986, on benefit weeks beginning the 17th, 19th, 20th or 21st November, 1986, and continued to be in receipt of social welfare benefits until various dates up to and including the 31st July, 1992.

The remaining ten plaintiffs, Mary Brennan, Noreen Clarke, Anne Dunne, Catherine Hughes, Marie O'Brien, Martina O'Brien, Pauline O'Connell, Margaret O'Rourke, Alice Stamp and Margaret Taaffe were unemployed but not in receipt of social welfare benefits on dates between the 23rd December, 1984, and the 21st November, 1986.

The plaintiffs did not seek to prove the extent of each individual's actual entitlement to social welfare benefit. That was left over to be dealt with as a matter of detail on an individual basis by the Department of Social Welfare. They sought recognition of their right to claim and to be paid if they were entitled.

Evidence was given by nine of the plaintiffs, as a sample of the different types of plaintiffs. Apart from Marian Redmond, these had heard about the equality arrears between 1991 and 1992.

A question arose about letters written to the Department and replies thereto. According to the Department's records, six plaintiffs wrote to the Department of Social Welfare at different times between 1989 and 1992. These were Rose Teague, Kathleen Corcoran, Christina Murphy, Ann Berminghan, Teresa Dunne and Marie Shannon. Some letters were proved in evidence which were replies from the Department of Social Welfare concerning the implementation of the equal treatment provisions. In the **[431]** letter to Marian Redmond (who was not on the Department's list) dated the 2nd October, 1989, the Department said:

> However, while your interest has been duly noted no further action can be taken in relation to previous claims at this point in time until relevant issues which are before the Courts have been adjudicated on.

Marian Redmond wrote again on the 27th July, 1991, and got no reply.

Another example was the reply to Mrs Theresa O'Donnell (also not on the Department's list) dated the 23rd March, 1992, in which the Department said:

> While your interest has been noted, no further action is possible as the matter is still before the Courts.

Mr Owen O'Broin, principal officer in the planning unit of the Department of Social Welfare, was involved with the matter since August, 1986. He gave evidence that the Department had commenced calculating the cost of implementing the Directive in 1985 in the context of the *Cotter and McDermott* v. *The Minister for Social Welfare (Nos 1 & 2)* (Cases 286/85 and C-377/89) [1987] ECR 1453 and [1991] 1 ECR 1155. Claims were made on an ongoing basis from 1987 on. The Department did not process any claims. He agreed that the only message given to women who inquired was that the Department could not do anything, as the matter was before the courts. In 1992 it was decided that provision would be made for equality for the period of delay. Prior to the decision to introduce the Regulations of 1992, decisions were made on an ongoing basis to defend proceedings or to settle without admission of liability. Since the case of *Cotter and McDermott*, 2,700 claims were settled.

Mr O'Broin supplied the figures on which a statistical analysis was made by Mr Bohan, assistant principal officer in the Department of Social Welfare responsible for the statistics section in the planning unit. Mr O'Broin said that the number of women actually paid under the Regulations of 1992 was taken to be the number of potential beneficiaries. They identified those women who qualified for Social Welfare between December, 1984 and 1986. The figure which formed the basis of the estimate was 69,152. This did not include the 2,700 women who settled. He arranged for a survey of a sample of the women concerned, computed the sample and gave it to Mr Bohan. The sample was done in two phases; initially with 200 and later with a further sample of another 200. The number of women who had initiated proceedings (apart from those who settled) was approximately 8,500.

[432] Mr Bohan's evidence as to the potential cost of paying arrears as claimed by the plaintiffs was objected to by Ms Finlay. Mr Fennelly for the State submitted that the European Court of Justice would have regard to the financial exposure of the Irish State. I allowed the evidence on the basis that, while it was not relevant before me, it might be relevant before the European Court of Justice. But I must emphasise that for the State to try and avoid its responsibilities on the basis of cost would not be acceptable in the courts in this State.

On the assumption that the number of potential beneficiaries would be based on the number of married women who received payments under the Regulations of 1992, Mr Bohan estimated that the net cost of payment for the period of delay of adult and child dependant allowances and also transitional payments would amount to £354,000,000 on one estimate or £265,000,000 on another estimate. The breakdown (rounded to the nearest million) was calculated as follows:

For the period of delayed payments of adult and child dependency benefits	£142,000,000
Less benefits already paid	£17,000,000
Balance	£125,000,000
Plus,	
Transitional payments	£96,000,000
Plus, either	
Interest under the Courts Act, 1981	£133,000,000
Total	£354,000,000
or,	
Alternatively, estimated additional cost on a CPI basis	£44,000,000
Total	£265,000,000

These figures represent a worst case scenario. There was no estimate of the likely percentage of those entitled who would actually apply.

The first issue to be decided is whether the plaintiffs suffered discrimination by reason of the fact:

(a) That married men in similar circumstances received payments which they did not get, and
(b) That the plaintiffs failed to get any additional payment in 1992 to compensate for late payment.

The State did not contest the plaintiffs' claim about the continuation of discrimination after the 23rd December, 1984, but submitted that the **[433]** State fully implemented the Directive prospectively from December, 1986. The main arguments of the State were directed to the plea that the plaintiffs' claims arising prior to six years before the issue of proceedings were statute-barred or that the plaintiffs were guilty of *laches* or that they did not suffer any damage.

It is established that Directive 79/7/EEC could be relied on from the 23rd December, 1984, in the absence of implementation and that women were entitled to have the same rules applied as applied to married men in the same situation. (See *Cotter and McDermott* v. *The Minister for Social Welfare (No 1)* (Case 286/85) [1987] ECR 1453.

It is also established that where married men after the 23rd December, 1984, automatically received benefits in respect of a spouse and children without having to prove actual dependency, married women are entitled to have the same rules applied even if this results in double payments. Also that where transitional provisions provided for compensatory payments to married men who had lost entitlement to a dependant wife's allowance, married women in the same family circumstances were entitled to the same payment even if it infringed the prohibition on unjust enrichment laid down by national law. (See *Cotter and McDermott* v. *The Minister for Social Welfare (No 2)* (Case C-377/89) [1991] 1 ECR 1155.

The claim that the State had fully implemented the Directive prospectively from December, 1986, cannot be sustained. The payments under the Regulations of 1992 cannot be ignored. It was not until July, 1992, when these payments were eliminated that the State implemented the Directive prospectively. The Directive was binding as to the result to be achieved but left the choice of form to the national authorities. Until such time as the Directive was implemented, the same rules as applied to men had to be applied to women since in the absence of compliance with the Directive those rules remained the only valid point of reference. The State has only itself to blame. It not only failed to eliminate discrimination retrospectively in 1986 but it invented a new form of payment for men only which it continued to pay until July, 1992.

Based on those principles the plaintiffs continued to suffer the following discrimination:

1. The residual discrimination in respect of the period 23rd December, 1984, to the end of 1986. This comprises, as already stated, failure to pay the entire adult dependency allowance, half, or in some cases all, the child dependency allowance and unemployment assistance in accordance with the pre-November, 1986, means test.

[434] 2. Failure to pay the transitional compensatory payments to married women in the same circumstances as married men who received it from December, 1984, to July, 1992.

3. Since the payments made under the Regulations of 1992 were paid at the rates current between 1984 and 1986 the question of provision for compensation by reason of delay arises (for example, the CPI shows that the value of £1 mid-November, 1984, equalled £1.32 in mid-November, 1993).

A relevant case to consider is the case of *Marshall* v. *The Southwest Hampshire Area Health Authority (No 2)* (Case C-271/91) [1993] ECR I-4367.

In that case one of the questions asked was whether compensation for damage sustained should include an award of interest on the principal amount from the date of the unlawful discrimination to the date when compensation is paid. The answer given by the European Court of Justice with regard to interest, was:

> that full compensation for the loss and damage sustained cannot leave out of account factors such as the effluxion of time which may in fact reduce its value. The award of interest in accordance with the applicable national rules must therefore be regarded as an essential component of compensation for the purposes of restoring real equality of treatment.

Therefore, on the basis that European law imputes an obligation to include an element of compensation where money due is reduced in real terms, the failure to include any compensation for late payment must also be viewed as continuing discrimination.

The next two issues are interrelated, namely, what is the nature of the right conferred on the plaintiffs by the Directive after the date for implementation is passed, and, as a corollary to that, what is the nature of the wrong committed by the State in failing to implement the Directive in time.

Ms Finlay submitted that the State is liable to compensate the plaintiffs for loss and damage suffered by reason of the State's failure to implement the Directive 79/7/EEC. (See *Francovich* v. *The Italian Republic* (Cases C-6190 and C-9/90) [1991] 1 ECR 5357.) The conditions for State liability where a Member State has failed to take all the measures necessary to achieve the result prescribed by a Directive, as laid down in that judgment, are fulfilled here:

1. The Directive 79/7/EEC entails a grant of rights to individuals,
[435] 2. It is possible to identify the content of those rights on the basis of the provisions of the Directive, and
3. There is a causal link between the breach of the State's obligation and the loss and damage suffered by the plaintiffs (see paragraph 40).

That judgment also provided that the nature of the plaintiffs' entitlement to damages should be determined in accordance with national rules, which must not be less favourable than those relating to similar domestic claims and must not be framed so as to make it virtually impossible or excessively difficult to obtain compensation.

Ms Finlay submitted there are as yet no national rules relating to damages for a breach by the State of its obligations under community law, and that the State in continuing to fail to implement the Directive fully is in breach of Article 40, s. 3 of the Constitution. This provides:

1. The State guarantees in its laws to respect and as far as practicable by its laws to defend and vindicate the personal rights of the citizen.
2. The State shall, in particular, by its laws protect as best it may from unjust attack and in the case of injustice done, vindicate the life, person, good name and property rights of every citizen.
3. (Not relevant).

She said the right acquired by an individual at the end of the period allowed for implementation was either a personal right or a property right within the meaning of Article 40, section 3.

It was also pleaded that the Minister owed a duty of care regarding the transposing of the Directive into Irish law by the 23rd December, 1984.

On the other hand Mr Fennelly submitted that the rights of the plaintiffs derive from the Directive and not from the Constitution. The concept of the duty of care taken from the common law of negligence has no bearing on the legal issues in the case. The meaning and effect of the Directive and the relevant Treaty provisions are to be construed and interpreted by the European Court of Justice. The rights as interpreted by that court derive not from the Constitution or the legal order of a Member State but from the Directive construed in the light of the Treaty. The Directive has effect in Irish law by virtue of Article 29, s. 4, sub-s. 3 of the Constitution and s. 2 of the European Communities Act, 1972. The function of the Constitutional amendment was to allow the entire body of European Community law to have effect in

Ireland in spite of any **[436]** provision in the Constitution. It did not confer any new constitutional right; rather its tendency is to qualify those rights.

I prefer Mr Fennelly's view. We are concerned here with a whole new legal order.

The nature of the existence of State liability under Community law is set out in *Francovich* v. *The Italian Republic* (Case C-6/90 and C-9/90) [1991] 1 ECR 5357 at paragraphs 31 to 37:

The existence of State liability as a matter of principle

31. It should be borne in mind at the outset that the EEC Treaty has created its own legal system, which is integrated into the legal systems of the Member States and which their courts are bound to apply. The subjects of that legal system are not only the Member States but also their nationals. Just as it imposes burdens on individuals, Community law is also intended to give rise to rights which become part of their legal patrimony. Those rights arise not only where they are expressly granted by the Treaty but also by virtue of obligations which the Treaty imposes in a clearly defined manner both on individuals and on the Member States and the Community institutions (see the judgments in Case 26/62 *Van Gend en Loos* [1963] ECR 1 and Case 6/64 *Costa* v. *ENEL* [1964] ECR 685).

32. Furthermore, it has been consistently held that the national courts whose task it is to apply the provisions of Community law in areas within their jurisdiction must ensure that those rules take full effect and must protect the rights which they confer on individuals (see in particular the judgments in Case 106/77 *Amministrazione delle Finanze dello Stato* v. *Simmenthal* [1978] ECR 629, paragraph 16, and case C-213/89 *Factortame* [1990] ECR I-2433, paragraph 19).

33. The full effectiveness of Community rules would be impaired and the protection of the rights which they grant would be weakened if individuals were unable to obtain redress when their rights are infringed by a breach of Community law for which a Member State can be held responsible.

34. The possibility of obtaining redress from the Member State is particularly indispensable where, as in this case, the full effectiveness of Community rules is subject to prior action on the part of the State and where, consequently, in the absence of such action, **[437]** individuals cannot enforce before the national courts the rights conferred upon them by Community law.

35. It follows that the principle whereby a State must be liable for loss and damage caused to individuals as a result of breaches of Community law for which the State can be held responsible is inherent in the system of the Treaty.

36. A further basis for the obligation of Member States to make good such loss and damage is to be found in Article 5 of the Treaty, under which the Member States are required to take all appropriate measures, whether general or particular, to ensure fulfilment of their obligations under Community law. Among these is the obligation to nullify the unlawful consequences of a breach of Community law (see, in relation to the analogous provision of Article 86 of the ECSC Treaty, the judgment in Case 6/60 *Humblet* v. *Belgium* [1960] ECR 559).

37. It follows from all the foregoing that it is a principle of Community law that the Member States are obliged to make good loss and damage caused to individuals by breaches of Community law for which they can be held responsible.

The European Communities Act, 1972, s. 2 provides:

From the 1st of January, 1973 the Treaties governing the European Communities and the existing and future acts adopted by the institutions of those communities shall be binding on the State and shall be part of the domestic law thereof under the conditions laid down in those Treaties.

This section is the conduit pipe through which Community law became part of domestic law. The Constitution was amended to enable accession to the Community, the European Communities Act, 1972, was passed and the Treaty of Accession was agreed, and thereby the whole body of Community law, past, present and future, was incorporated into domestic law. But Community law did not thereby become constitutional law or statute law. It is still Community law governed by Community law but with domestic effect. And it is in that form that it is part of domestic law.

In *Meagher* v. *The Minister for Agriculture* [1994] 1 IR 329, Blayney J touches on the matter when he says at p. 360:

The relevant directives here were binding on the State from the moment they were adopted "as to the result to be achieved" . . . So the State was bound to introduce effective sanctions, and if this necessitated adopting a measure which implied amending an existing statute **[438]** that measure would prevail over the statute because it was in substance a measure of Community law. It is only in form that it is part of domestic law. It derives its force from the directive which is binding on the State as to the results to be achieved.

Therefore, the rights of the plaintiffs in this case come from the Directive which had direct effect as from the 23rd December, 1984, because the State failed in its obligation to implement the Directive under Article 5 of the Treaty of Rome.

In my opinion, the concept of the duty of care under the law of negligence is not applicable. The plaintiffs' claim does not arise as a breach of constitutional right (as in *Conway* v. *The Irish National Teachers Organisation* [1992] 2 IR 305). The plaintiffs' right to sue the State derives from the Directive itself once the date for implementation had passed and this right must be interpreted in accordance with Community law as enunciated by the European Court of Justice.

Therefore, as from the 23rd December, 1984, the plaintiffs were entitled to rely on the provisions of the Directive to preclude the application of any national provision inconsistent with art. 4, sub-art. 1 of the Directive (see *Cotter and McDermott* v. *The Minister for Social Welfare (No 2)* Case

C-377/89 [1991] 1 ECR 1155, a right which was conferred by European law).

That being so, what was the nature of the wrong committed by the State in failing to implement the Directive within the time limited? Here again the wrong belongs to the new order.

In my opinion, the wrong committed by the State in continuing the discrimination by failing to fully implement the Directive is a wrong arising from Community law which has domestic effect. It is not a breach of constitutional rights; it is not a breach of statutory duty and it is not a breach of the duty of care. It is a breach of duty to implement the Directive and it approximates to a breach of constitutional duty. Every type of action which would be available in the national domestic law to ensure the observance of national law is available to ensure observance of the Directive once it took on the mantle of direct effect.

The next issue is whether the State can claim that the plaintiffs' claim is statute-barred. This has two aspects,

(a) does the Statute of Limitations, 1957, apply to this type of claim? and
(b) is the State precluded from relying on the statute by virtue of *Emmott* v. *The Minister for Social Welfare* Case C-208/90 [1991] 1 ECR 4269 or by estoppel?

[439] The State claims that it is entitled to rely on the Statute of Limitations, 1957, to bar the right of the plaintiffs to recover any sum of money due in respect of the delay in implementation of the Directive from 1984 to 1986 and also to bar any sum claimed in respect of the transitional compensatory payments paid to men which fell due more than six years before the issue of proceedings. In Mrs Tate's case, the relevant date is the 16th July, 1987, and for the other plaintiffs, the 17th September, 1987.

Mr Fennelly submitted that if this is a claim for money due under statute then s. 11, sub-s. 1(e) applies. That provides:

> The following actions shall not be brought after the expiration of six years from the date on which the cause of action accrued . . .
> (e) Actions to recover any sum recoverable by virtue of any enactment, other than . . . [does not apply].

If this is a claim for damages, s. 11, sub-s. 2(a) applies. This provides:

> Subject to paragraphs (b) and (c) of this subsection, an action founded on tort shall not be brought after the expiration of six years from the date on which the cause of action accrued.

Subparagraphs (b) and (c) do not apply.

Mr Fennelly submitted that this is an action founded in tort. A tort is a civil wrong and it is undefined in the Act. A breach of duty is mentioned in sub-s. 2(b) of s. 11, but only in the context of personal injuries. He claimed that the wrong first occurred on the 24th January, 1984. This was a breach of statutory duty imposed by the European Communities Act, 1972. Although there is no specific provision in the Statute of Limitations for a breach of statutory duty, it is accepted that it is a tort (Ms Finlay agreed with this).

Mr Fennelly referred to the judgment of Lord Diplock in *Garden Cottage Foods Ltd* v. *The Milk Marketing Board* [1984] AC 130 in reference to Article 86 of the EC Treaty (concerning the prohibition of abuse of a dominant position) which had direct effect. Lord Diplock said (at p. 175) that a breach of duty imposed by Article 86 could be categorised in English law as a breach of statutory duty that is imposed not only for the purpose of promoting the general economic prosperity of the common market but also for the benefit of private individuals to whom loss or damage is caused by breach of that duty.

Mr Fennelly also referred to *Rewe Zentralfinanze* v. *Landwirtschaftskammer für das Saarland* (Case 33/76) [1976] ECR 1989 which concerned the refusal to repay the equivalent of customs duties wrongfully charged. It was held that in the then state of Community law, there **[440]** was nothing to prevent a citizen who contests before a national court a decision of a national authority on the ground that it is incompatible with Community law, from being confronted with the defence that limitation periods laid down by national law have expired, it being understood that the procedural conditions governing the action may not be less favourable than those relating to similar actions of a domestic nature. (In this case, it was the period for challenging an administrative decision which had expired.)

The court said (at paragraph 5) that in the absence of measures of harmonisation, the right conferred by the Community law must be exercised before the national courts in accordance with conditions laid down by national rules. The position would be different only if the conditions and time limits made it impossible in practice to exercise the rights which the national courts are obliged to protect. This is not the case where reasonable periods of limitation of actions are fixed. The laying down of such time limits with regard to actions of a fiscal nature is an application of the fundamental principle of legal certainty protecting both the tax payer and the administration concerned.

Another case cited by Mr Fennelly is *Rewe-Handelsgesellschaft Nord* v. *Hauptzollamt Kiel* [1981] ECR 1805. It was stated (at para. 44) that "although the Treaty made it possible in a number of instances for private persons to bring direct action where appropriate before the Court of Justice, it was not intended to create new remedies in the national courts to ensure observation of community law other than those already laid down by national law. On the other hand, the system of legal protection established by the Treaty, as set out in Article 177 in particular, implies that it must be possible for every type of action provided for by national law to be available for the purpose of ensuring observance of community provisions having direct effect, on the same conditions concerning the admissibility and procedure as would apply were it a question of ensuring observance of national law."

Ms Finlay on the other hand, submitted that there was no part of s. 11 which would bar the plaintiffs from applying to enforce their rights relying on the direct effect of the Directive once the time for implementation had passed. She claimed two distinct causes of action:

1. Direct effect, and
2. The State's failure to implement the Directive.

She said this is not a breach of statutory duty. The Directive should have been implemented by December, 1984, but since it was not, it had never been given analogous statutory force. It is a new cause of action **[441]** emanating from Community law and does not emanate from within the domestic legal system. She said the cause of action is a right to assert a right against the State and the relief sought is a separate question from the cause of action.

Ms Finlay argued that the other cause of action (i.e. failure to implement the Directive) is not a tort since tort does not include a breach of duty imposed by European law which is not yet part of domestic law.

While Mr Fennelly says breach of constitutional duty is also a tort, Ms Finlay replies that the Supreme Court makes a distinction between torts and breach of constitutional rights. (See *Conway* v. *Irish National Teachers Organisation* [1992] 2 IR 305 at 316 and *Hanrahan* v. *Merck Sharp and Dohme (Ireland) Ltd* [1988] ILRM 629 at page 636).

It seems to me that Ms Finlay is correct in saying there are two distinct causes of action but I do not agree that the relief sought is a separate question. I think the relief sought indicates which cause of action is being pursued.

I agree there is a cause of action based on direct effect which entitles a person who is discriminated against to sue directly for the entitlement which is withheld relying on the Directive to preclude the application of any national provision inconsistent with the Directive.

If this were the cause of action being pursued, what the plaintiffs would have to claim would be the actual benefits awarded by the Social Welfare Acts and Regulations to men in a similar situation on the basis that the same rules should be applied to them. Here it should be noted that among the "rules" which would apply to men would be s. 11, sub-s. 1(e) of the Statute of Limitations, 1957. This bars actions to recover sums recoverable by virtue of any enactment where the cause of action arose more than six years previously. On the basis that what is sauce for the gander, is sauce for the goose, this "rule" would also have to apply to women making this type of claim.

However, the plaintiffs have based their claim squarely in damages and the claim for an account was dropped. Therefore the plaintiffs have opted for the cause of action based on the State's failure to implement the Directive.

So, is this a breach of statutory duty as claimed by Mr Fennelly or some other kind of tort which might or might not be included in the Statute of Limitations?

I do not accept that the breach of obligation by the State to implement the Directive is a breach of statutory duty. It is, as I already said earlier, a wrong arising from Community law which has domestic effect and **[442]** approximates to a breach of constitutional duty. While the Supreme Court did speak separately of torts and breach of constitutional rights in *Conway* v. *Irish National Teachers Organisation* [1992] 2 IR 305, it was not in the context of the Statute of Limitations. I would be surprised if there was no limitation period affecting a breach of a constitutional right. Just as the word "tort" in the Statute of Limitations is sufficiently wide to embrace breach of statutory duty even though not specifically mentioned, so also, in my opinion, the word "tort" is sufficiently wide to cover breaches of obligations of the State under Community law. There is nothing strange in describing the State's failure to fulfil its obligations under the Treaty as a tort.

Therefore I am satisfied that s. 11, sub-s. 2 of the Statute of Limitations does apply to a breach of obligation to observe Community law. This also means that the plea of *laches* is no longer relevant.

The next point by Ms Finlay is that if the Statute of Limitations does apply to this action there is a new cause of action by virtue of the Regulations of 1992. The State belatedly adopted measures in 1992 to implement the Directive. In doing so they were obliged to respect the rights of individuals granted under the Directive. The regulations are defective because they fail to fully implement the Directive. She cited the case of *De Weerd* v. *Bestuur van de Bedrijfsvereniging voor de Gezondheid* (Case C-343/92) [1994] 1 ECR 571:

> A Member State may not impose in national legislation intended to implement Article 4 under the Directive adopted after the expiry of the time limit set by the Directive, conditions which deprive married women of the rights which they derive as from the expiry of that period, from the direct effect of that provision of Community law.

She claims a fresh breach of duty occurred insofar as the Regulations of 1992 failed to respect the plaintiffs' rights. It is true that the regulations deprive married women of rights under the Directive, therefore I accept the argument that a fresh cause of action arose. The regulations, while purporting to provide for equality of treatment for the delay in implementation, deprived women of the right to the full child allowance making provision only for half (and in some case for none) and they deprived women of the entire adult dependant's allowance. They also changed the means test for social assistance.

Can it be said that failure to provide in the Regulations of 1992 for payment of the transitional payments gave rise to a fresh cause of action? That I doubt. The failure to include any provision for the payment to women of the equivalent of the transitional payment is an omission not a **[443]** positive act. Since there is no new positive act, I do not think there can be a fresh cause of action.

Since this means that transitional payments falling due more than six years before action brought are barred, that gives rise to the next question. Does the judgment in *Emmott* v. *The Minister for Social Welfare* (Case C-208/90) [1991] 1 ECR 4269 preclude the State from pleading the Statute of Limitations or has the law in that regard been changed by the two subsequent cases, *Steenhorst-Neerings* (Case C-33/91) [1993] 1 ECR 5475 and *Johnson* v. *The Chief Adjudication Officer (No 2)* (Unreported, European Court of Justice, 6th December, 1994).

Mr Fennelly conceded that on a literal reading of the *Emmott* case, the State could not succeed but he said the law has been changed by the two later cases.

The facts of the *Emmott* case are as follows. Mrs Emmott wrote on the 24th March, 1987, to get the same amount of benefits as those paid to a married man in an identical situation. On the 16th June, 1987, the Minister replied that since the Directive was still the subject of litigation before the High Court no decision could be taken. On the 22nd June, 1988, she got leave to issue proceedings by way of judicial review of that decision and was met with a plea that she had failed to observe the time limit for instituting proceedings under O. 84, r. 21(1) of the Rules of the Superior Courts, 1986.

The question asked of the European Court of Justice was a general one, whether the ruling of the Court in *Cotter and McDermott* v. *The Minister for Social Welfare (No 1)* [1987] ECR 1453 was to be understood as meaning that in a claim relying on art. 4, sub-art. 1 "it is contrary to the general principles of community law for the relevant authorities of a Member State to rely on national procedural rules, in particular, rules relating to time limits, in bringing claims in defence of that claim such as to restrict or refuse such compensation".

The Court of Justice said that the laying down of reasonable time limits which if unobserved bar proceedings, in principle satisfies the condition, provided the conditions are no less favourable than those relating to similar actions of a domestic nature and not framed so as to render it virtually impossible to exercise rights conferred by Community law. Although Article 189, sub-art. 3 of the EEC Treaty leaves Member States free to choose the means of implementing a Directive, they must adopt within the framework of their national legal system all the measures necessary to ensure that the Directive is fully effective.

[444] Member States are required to ensure the full application of Directives in a sufficiently clear and precise manner so that where Directives are intended to create rights for individuals, they can ascertain the full extent of those rights. So long as a Directive has not been properly transposed into national law individuals are unable to ascertain the full extent of those rights.

The Court said, at paragraphs 22 and 23:

> (22) Only the proper transposition of the Directive will bring that state of uncertainty to an end and it is only on transposition that the legal certainty which must exist if individuals are to be required to assert their rights is created.
>
> (23) It follows that until such time as a Directive has been properly transposed, a defaulting Member State may not rely on an individual's delay in initiating proceedings against it in order to protect rights conferred on him by provisions of the Directive and that a period laid down by national law within which proceedings must be initiated cannot begin to run before that time.

Those words are very clear.

So do the cases of *Steenhorst-Neerings* (Case C-33/91) [1993] 1 ECR 5475 and *Johnson* (Unreported, European Court of Justice, 6th December, 1994) alter the law?

In *Steenhorst-Neerings* the European Court of Justice was asked whether Community law precludes the application of a national rule of law according to which benefits for incapacity for work are paid not earlier than one year before the date of claim where an individual seeks to rely on rights conferred directly by art. 4, sub-art. 1 of the Directive 79/7 with effect from the 23rd December, 1984, and where on the date of claim the Member State had not yet properly transposed that provision into national law. Mrs Steenhorst-Neering had applied for welfare benefits under the AAW (the general law on incapacity for work). That law provided that benefits were payable not earlier than one year before the date on which claimed or on which they were automatically granted.

The Court distinguished *Emmott* v. *The Minister for Social Welfare* (Case C-208/90) [1991] 1 ECR 4269 by saying that Mrs Emmott relied on the judgment in *Cotter and McDermott* and the national authorities had declined to adjudicate on her claim because proceedings were pending before a national court and then claimed her proceedings were out of time even though the Directive had still not been correctly transposed into national law. The Court noted that unlike the rule of domestic law fixing time limits for bringing actions, the rule referred for a preliminary ruling **[445]** in the *Steenhorst-Neerings* case, did not affect the right of individuals to rely on Directive 79/7 in proceedings before the national courts against a defaulting Member State. It merely limited the retroactive effect of claims made for the purpose of obtaining the relevant benefits.

The Court also said, at para. 22, that the *Emmott* judgment indicates that the requirement of a time limit which ensures administrative decisions cannot be challenged indefinitely, cannot prevail over the need to protect rights conferred on individuals by direct effect as long as the Member State has not properly transposed the Directive into national law. On the other hand it said the aim of the rule restricting the retroactive effect of claims for benefits for incapacity for work is quite different from that of a rule imposing mandatory time limits for bringing proceedings. Accordingly, the court answered the question by saying that Community law did not preclude the application of a national rule of law whereby benefits for incapacity for work are payable not earlier than one year before the date of claim where the individual relies on art. 4, sub-art. 1 of Directive 79/7 and where the Member State has not yet properly transposed that provision into national law.

In *Johnson* v. *The Chief Adjudication Officer (No 2)* (Unreported, European Court of Justice, 6th December, 1994) Mrs Johnson had been entitled to an invalidity benefit (NCIB) which ceased to be payable when she began cohabiting with a male friend. A different test was applied to her than would have been applied to a man. In 1984 invalidity benefit was abolished and a new Severe Disablement Allowance (SDA) was introduced.

Persons entitled to the old NCIB automatically qualified without being required to prove that they satisfied the new conditions.

Mrs Johnson applied on the 17th August, 1987, for the SDA and was turned down. She made a claim before the European Court of Justice and it held that it had been possible since the 23rd December, 1984, to rely on art. 4 of Directive 79/7 in order to have set aside national regulations which made entitlement to a benefit subject to the previous submission of a claim in respect of a different benefit which had since been abolished and which had entailed a condition discriminating against female workers.

Following that case she was granted the SDA but only with effect from twelve months prior to her claim. This curtailment was based on a rule that said no person should be entitled in respect of any period more than twelve months before the date on which the claim is made.

[446] She appealed and since there were the two decisions apparently conflicting, *Emmott* and *Steenhorst-Neering*, the matter was referred to the European Court of Justice.

The Court observed that in the *Johnson* case the wording of the contested rule showed it was of general application and it merely limited the period prior to the bringing of a claim in respect of which arrears of benefit are payable and did not make it virtually impossible to bring an action relying on Community law.

The Court said it was clear that the solution adopted in *Emmott* v. *The Minister for Social Welfare* (Case C-208/90) [1991] 1 ECR 4269 was justified by the special circumstances of that case in which a time bar had the result of depriving the applicant of any opportunity whatever to rely on her right to equal treatment.

It held the rule adversely affecting Mrs Johnson was similar to that at issue in *Steenhorst-Neerings* (Case C-33/91) [1993] 1 ECR 1. Neither rule constituted a bar to proceedings. They merely limited the period prior to the bringing of the claim in respect of which arrears of benefit were payable.

In this case, while s. 11 of the Statute of Limitations does provide that no tort action shall be brought after the expiration of six years from the date on which the cause of action accrued, and so it is a "rule imposing mandatory time limits for bringing proceedings", the reality is that where there is a continuing breach it too, in effect, limits the period in respect of which arrears of benefit can be claimed. The effect is that a claim can be made for six years' arrears. This is very different to the original *Emmott* case where Mrs Emmott decided to proceed by way of judicial review and the time bar pleaded was one which applied to judicial review. If she had issued a plenary summons in 1988 she would not have been barred from claiming her entitlement from the 24th December, 1984.

So it appears to me that the reference in the *Johnson* case to the particular circumstances of the *Emmott* case makes me believe that it does not have the wide general application which it appears to have on first reading. Also bearing in mind *Rewe Zentralfinanz* v. *Landwirtschaftskammer für das Saarland* (Case 33/76) [1976] ECR 1989 it seems to me that the European Court of Justice would now find nothing wrong in having a limitation period of six years even though the Directive has not yet fully been implemented.

It follows that I believe *Emmott* v. *The Minister for Social Welfare* (Case C-208/90) [1991] 1 ECR 4269 does not prevent the State from **[447]** pleading the Statute of Limitations in respect of the transitional payments which fell due more than six years before action brought.

In respect of a small number of plaintiffs who made claims prior to the passing of the Regulations of 1992, it is pleaded that the State is estopped from relying on the Statute of Limitations to defeat their claims.

Mr Fennelly accepted that if these plaintiffs were misled by unambiguous promises that the State could not rely on the Statute of Limitations and therefore if they did not issue proceedings within time, estoppel would apply: but he said there was no such evidence. He cited *Doran* v. *Thompson & Sons Ltd* [1978] IR 223. In that case Henchy J, at p. 225, gave the underlying reason for estoppel and said "it would be dishonest or unconscionable for the defendant having misled the plaintiff into a feeling of security on the issue of liability and, thereby, into a justifiable belief that the statute would not be used to defeat his claim, to escape liability by pleading the statute."

Nothing like that has happened here. The most the State did was to write saying no further action was possible because the matter was before the court. There were no words or conduct which could have misled any of these plaintiffs to infer liability would be admitted. Accordingly, this plea fails.

The next issue is what are the appropriate damages? Mr Fennelly said that damages are not appropriate at all. He said the amounts being claimed are greater than the plaintiffs would have been entitled to if the Directive had been implemented in time. He said the plaintiffs are claiming the benefit of unjust enrichment and this goes beyond compensatory damages. He said the sums being claimed are not sums the plaintiffs were caused to lose, rather they are sums they gained. But this argument does not stand up to examination. What the plaintiffs are entitled to is to have the same rules applied to them as applied to married men in the same circumstances. That is their legal entitlement. As long as the State did not transpose the Directive, the rules applying to men are the only reference. This means they are entitled to be paid the same sums that would have been paid to married men in the same situation,

(a) between December, 1984, and the end of 1986, and,
(b) the transitional payments paid to married men from six years before action brought to July, 1992.

The State cannot complain if there is any element of double payment or unjust enrichment since this was dealt with by the European Court of Justice in *Cotter and McDermott* v. *The Minister for Social Welfare (No 2)* (Case C-377/89) [1991] 1 ECR 1155.

[448] The plaintiffs are also entitled, following the judgment already mentioned in *Marshall* v. *South West Hampshire Area Health Authority (No 2)* (Case C-271/91) [1993] 3 CMLR 293, to compensation for the delay in payment. I consider the best way to bring the payments due for earlier years up to date is to apply to them the consumer price index which has been admitted in evidence. This means that payment received will equate in real terms with the payments received in former years by their male counterparts. The amounts due, increased by the CPI, are in fact nothing more than compensatory damages. There is no element of punitive or exemplary damages included. Even though the State has wriggled for ten years in its efforts to avoid paying the same to women as to men, in view of the very large sums involved, I do not intend to add any element of punitive or exemplary damages.

The question of referring the matter to the European Court of Justice for an opinion does not arise. Mr Fennelly asked that I would submit a case in relation to the interpretation of the *Emmott, Steenhorst Neering* and *Johnson* cases. Ms Finlay asked me not to. In the event, Mr Fennelly's view of those cases prevailed, so I do not see any necessity for a reference by me.

The last issue is whether the Regulations of 1992 are void on the basis that they are *ultra vires* the Minister for Social Welfare. His powers under s. 3 of the European Communities Act, 1972, are limited to making regulations enabling s. 2 of the Act to have effect, i.e. in furtherance of Community law: not in derogation of it. Mr Fennelly submitted there was nothing wrong with deeming payments to the husband to be payments to the wife and he said equality was given retrospectively in 1992 for the period of 1984 to 1986, neither of which submissions I would accept. He submitted that the court cannot eliminate certain provisions if what is left does not represent the legislative intent, i.e. the court cannot legislate by deletion.

However, I do not think it is necessary to declare the Regulations of 1992 *ultra vires* and void. Money has been paid out under them even though this did not fully compensate for breach of the Directive. I agree that the court should not legislate by deletion. The regulations are so convoluted that to delete any section or subsection could well have a domino effect on the whole edifice. What I do intend to do is to declare that the State is not entitled to rely on any portion of the Regulations of 1992 which has the effect of not recognising the plaintiffs' rights under the direct effect of the Directive.

The relief which I will grant is:

[449] (1) A declaration that the defendants have failed to fully or properly implement Directive 79/7/EEC.

(2) A declaration that the plaintiffs were entitled as from the 23rd December, 1984, to receive the same benefits and to have the rules under the Social Welfare Acts and Regulations, 1981 to 1992 that were paid and applied to married men in the same situation paid and applied to them.

(3) A declaration that the defendants are not entitled to rely on any portion of the European Communities (Social Welfare) Regulations, 1992, which has the effect of not recognising the plaintiffs' rights under the direct effect of the Directive.

(4) Damages equivalent to the benefits or assistance which married men in the same circumstances received and which they did not receive, for the period commencing the 23rd December, 1984, and ending on the relevant date at the end of 1986 increased by the appropriate amount under the CPI to date of payment.

(5) Damages equivalent to the transitional payments which married men in the same circumstances received and which the plaintiffs did not receive, from the 16th July, 1987, for Teresa Tate and from the 17th September, 1987, for all other plaintiffs increased by the appropriate amount under the CPI to date of payment.

The plaintiffs will now have to apply to the Department of Social Welfare to have their applications for entitlement considered in the light of the declarations made.

Liberty to apply.

Costs.

[Reports: [1995] 1 Irish Reports 425]

Supremacy—Community law and subsequent national law—Whether Community law automatically prevailing over conflicting national law even if national law subsequently enacted

Direct effect — Directives — Interpretation of national law — Duty of national courts to interpret national law consistently with provisions of directive — Scope of obligation — Applicability to national law introduced to implement directive — Council Directive 76/207 on equal treatment in employment—The law of Ireland

NATHAN *v.* BAILEY GIBSON LTD, IRISH PRINT UNION AND ANOTHER

Ireland, Supreme Court. 29 *February* 1996

(Hamilton, *Chief Justice*; Blayney and Barrington, *Justices*)

SUMMARY: *The facts*:—The plaintiff applied for a post as a machine operator with the first defendant, which had a "closed shop" agreement with the second defendant requiring vacancies to be filled as far as possible from union members. The plaintiff was not a union member and was not offered the post, which went to a male member of the union, whose membership was overwhelmingly male. The plaintiff lodged a complaint arguing that she had been the victim of indirect discrimination. Although such discrimination was not expressly mentioned in the Employment Equality Act 1977, the plaintiff argued that the Act had been introduced to implement EC Council Directive 76/207 in Ireland and the definition of discrimination should be determined by reference to the Directive and the case-law of the European Court of Justice interpreting its provisions. The Labour Court and the High Court rejected the complaint and the plaintiff appealed to the Supreme Court.

Held:—The appeal was allowed and the case was referred back to the Labour Court.

(1) It was well established that Community law took precedence over domestic law and that, where they were in conflict, Community law prevailed (p. 361).

(2) It was also well established that national courts, in interpreting a provision of national law intended to implement the provisions of a directive, should do so in the light of the wording and purpose of the directive in order to achieve the result envisaged by it. In accordance with the case-law of the European Court of Justice, this approach was required by the duty of Member States to take all appropriate measures to ensure the fulfilment of their Community obligations, enshrined in Article 5 of the EC Treaty (pp. 361-2).

(3) Having regard to the terms of the Directive, the provisions of the Act at issue were to be interpreted as prohibiting cases of both direct and indirect discrimination (pp. 363-4).

The following is the text of the judgment of the Court:

[164] HAMILTON CJ

This is an appeal brought by the above named Breda Nathan (hereinafter referred to as the appellant) against the judgment of Murphy J delivered on the 8th October, 1992 and the order made in pursuance thereof on the 15th October, 1992.

The matter came before the High Court by way of appeal by the appellant on a point of law arising from a determination by the Labour Court made on the 8th April, 1991, in a dispute which had been referred to it by the first respondent in accordance with the provisions of s. 19 of the Employment Equality Act, 1977.

The facts relevant to the determination of the issues before the Court are not disputed and are contained in the affidavit of the appellant, the report of the equality officer, the determination of the Labour Court and are summarised in the judgment of the learned trial judge as follows:

> The business of the first respondent includes, among other things, the manufacture of cartons. One of the machines used by the first respondent for that purpose is described as "the carton folder/gluer machine". That machine was operated by a man who was a member of the second respondent for many years up to his retirement from his employment with the first respondent in January, 1988. For ten years prior to his retirement the operative had been assisted in his work on the machine by the [appellant]. When the post became vacant the [appellant] applied for it.
>
> It appears that the printing industry generally and the first respondent's business in particular, is fully unionised. The craft workers were organised into specific unions, including the second respondent, while non-craft employees were in general organised on a gender basis with male non-craft employees organised by the ITGWU and **[165]** female non-craft employees organised by the Irish Women Workers Branch of the FWUI. The second respondent is not and was not based on gender discrimination. The objective of the union is to keep its existing membership employment be they male or female.
>
> The first respondent entered into a "closed shop" agreement with the second respondent the result of which was that vacancies as machine operators of the category in question must be offered first, to suitable candidates holding the second respondent's membership cards, secondly to unemployed members of the second respondent subject to certain training requirements and then, but only then, to non-union members. If and when a non-union member selected in accordance with that procedure is employed, the union grant membership to him or her without any distinction whatsoever on the basis of sex.
>
> The first respondent was most anxious that the [appellant] should be appointed to the available post and made strenuous representations to the second respondent to that end. The second respondent was unwilling to waive the term of the closed shop agreement or to sacrifice the rights of their existing membership. In the circumstances the first respondent interviewed certain qualified

members of the second respondent none of whom was willing to accept the post. Subsequently, the first respondent interviewed certain unemployed members of the second respondent, one of whom was selected for training and subsequently appointed to the vacant post on the 1st September, 1988.

In those circumstances, the [appellant] contacted the Employment Equality Agency who, on the 28th February, 1989, referred a complaint of discrimination in regard to the recruitment process to the Labour Court. In turn the Labour Court referred the case to the equality officer for investigation and recommendation.

As appears from para. 58 of the equality officer's conclusions and recommendations dated the 6th February, 1990, the equality officer had held that:

(1) Bailey Gibson Ltd, the first respondent herein, did not discriminate directly against the [appellant] in terms of s. 2(a) of the Act and in contravention of s. 3 of the Act in appointing a male to the position of carton folders/gluer operator on the 1st September, 1988.
(2) The Irish Print Union, the second respondent herein, did not directly discriminate against the [appellant] in terms of s. 2(a) of **[166]** the Act and in contravention of s. 5 of the Act in not granting her membership.
(3) Bailey Gibson Ltd, the first respondent herein, indirectly discriminated against the [appellant] in terms of s. 2(c) of the Act and in contravention of s. 3 of the Act by making it a requirement that access to the vacant position of carton folder/gluer operator in 1988 be confined to persons who held membership of the second respondent.

The first respondent appealed to the Labour Court against the equality officer's findings and recommendation and the appellant also appealed against the recommendations but the Court is not concerned with the adequacy or otherwise of the equality officer's recommendations in these proceedings with regard to remedy.

As appears from the determination by the Labour Court, the Labour Court found that there was no direct discrimination against the worker in the terms of s. 2(c) or in contravention of s. 3 of the Act of 1977.

The Labour Court based its determination on the following grounds:

1. In the Irish printing industry, craft workers were organised in specific unions, including the second respondent, while non-craft employees were in general organised on a gender basis, with male non-craft employees organised by the ITGWU and female non-craft employees organised by the Irish Women Workers Branch of the FWUI. Membership of the second respondent was not based on gender. The second respondent grants membership to non-craft workers

in particular circumstances, and when it does so, membership is granted irrespective of the sex of the employee. However, its first objective is to keep its existing members in employment, be they male or female.

2. In pursuance of that objective, the second respondent had an agreement with the first respondent that certain procedures be observed in relation to recruitment. The equality officer was satisfied that the policy of recruitment resulted in the same difficulties for applicants, whether the candidate for employment was male or female, the first respondent could only recruit independently with a guarantee of a membership card for the proposed employee if the agreed procedures had first been implemented to the satisfaction of the second respondent.
3. The fact of the matter is that there are many more male members of the second respondent than there are female members. This is because, historically, the craft area of the printing industry attracted **[167]** more men, and it is only in recent years that women have entered this employment area. Therefore, if the first respondent could only recruit someone with a union card, inevitably the pool of people who could comply with the requirement to have a union card was going to contain more men than women.
4. The equality officer has pointed out in her recommendation that currently in excess of 80% of the second respondent's membership is male. (In this context the Court notes the second respondent, at the hearing of the appeal, indicated that 82% of its membership is male and 18% is female.) The equality officer was satisfied that it was therefore reasonable to conclude that the reason females were substantially more affected by the requirement to have a card than males was related to an attribute of their sex. The Court does not agree with the logic of this argument. We take the view that the worker first had to show that there was a causal link between the requirement to have a union card and her sex. Only then would it become relevant whether the proportion of men able to comply with the requirement was substantially higher. But what was this "attribute" of her sex? In *North Western Health Board* v. *Martyn* [1987] IR 565, an age requirement was the relevant attribute. But this Court finds that there are no conditions for membership of the second respondent or for apprenticeship in the industry which are more onerous on women than on men. It is a fact that more men than women have the second respondent's union cards, but this is simply because historically males occupied the craft positions in the Irish printing industry. The requirement for certain employees to hold a union card was agreed between the second respondent and the first respondent. But that requirement which was craft based and which was imposed on the

worker by the first respondent bore no relationship to the sex of the worker. It was imposed in circumstances in which, had the agreed procedures not resulted in the recruitment of a member of the second respondent (male or female), it was a matter of indifference to the second respondent whether a male or a female was recruited for the job, the person would automatically have been given membership of the second respondent and the training necessary to carry out the work concerned (in other words, craft status would have been conferred without the need for a formal apprenticeship being entered into).

[168] 5. We find, in effect, that the disproportionate impact of the requirement on women is not causally linked with sex, but is historic. It was not because she was a woman that the worker could not become a member of the second respondent; it was because she was a non-craft worker in a non-craft union, and because there were existing members of the second respondent available for employment. In *Revenue Commissioners* v. *Kelly* (EE 9/1987 Labour Court, Unreported, 2nd December, 1987), the requirement imposed on applicants for a job was that they hold a full driving licence. In that case the equality officer was unable to establish any attribute of their sex which would result in a lower proportion of females than males being able to comply with the requirement. In this case, the requirement was to hold a union card. But unless the union was discriminating between men and women in those to whom they gave cards, and only gave them to men, or imposed conditions which made it more difficult for women to obtain them, the worker could not claim that the requirement to have a card discriminated against her. Historical circumstances which have resulted in more men than women in a craft industry do not lead to the conclusion that the small number of women in the industry now is an attribute of their sex.

6. In the light of its findings at paras. 4 and 5 above that the requirement imposed on the workers was not causally related to the sex of the worker, the other matters raised by the appeals and by the second respondent's submissions are irrelevant.

The important findings contained in the aforesaid determination by the Labour Court were that:

(a) the requirement that certain employees held a union card was agreed between the second respondent and the first respondent;
(b) that requirement which was craft based and which was imposed on the worker by the company bore no relationship to the sex of the worker;
(c) the worker had to show that there was a causal link between the requirement to have the union card and her sex;

(d) if the worker failed to establish that, the question whether the proportion of males able to comply with requirement was substantially higher than females did not arise for consideration;

[169] (e) the disproportionate impact of the requirement on women was not causally linked with sex but was historic;

(f) historical circumstances which have resulted in more men than women in a craft industry do not lead to the conclusion that the small number of women in the industry now is an attribute of their sex.

The appellant appealed to the High Court on a point of law arising from such determinations of the Labour Court.

In the special endorsement of claim on the special summons issued on behalf of the appellant, it is alleged on her behalf that:

7. In reaching its determination in respect of the said appeals the Labour Court was wrong in law in so much as it—

(a) held that to constitute discrimination against the [appellant] pursuant to s. 2(c) and s. 3 of the Employment Equality Act, 1977, the requirement imposed on the [appellant] in respect of access to the particular position sought by her must be causally connected to the sex of the [appellant];

(b) held that the [appellant] was obliged to show that there was a causal link between the requirement imposed on the [appellant] in respect of access to the position which she sought and the sex of the [appellant];

(c) failed to hold that the requirement imposed on the [appellant] in respect of access to the position sought by her constituted discrimination contrary to the provisions of s. 2(c) and s. 3 of the Employment Equality Act, 1977 in circumstances where the disproportionate impact of such requirement on members of the female sex arose from historical reasons;

(d) took into account the reason why the particular requirement imposed on the [appellant] in respect of access to the position which she sought had a disproportionate impact on women.

The appellant claimed:

(a) an order declaring that the imposition by the first respondent of the requirement that she hold a membership card of the second respondent in respect of access to the position sought by her constituted unlawful discrimination contrary to the provisions of s. 2(c) and s. 3 of the Employment Equality Act, 1977;

(b) an order remitting this matter to the Labour Court in regard to the question of remedy;

[170] (c) in the alternative, an order remitting this matter to the Labour Court to be determined in accordance with the findings of law made by this Honourable Court.

The issue in the High Court centred on the interpretation of s. 2(c) and s. 3 of the Act of 1977 and the learned trial judge held that the interpretation thereof by the Labour Court was correct and that the Labour Court was correct in the decision which it gave.

In the course of his judgment, the learned trial judge stated:

> Whilst it seems to me that para. (c) of s. 2 of the Act of 1977 is not happily expressed, it would not be possible to interpret that paragraph by treating the words "because of his sex or marital status" as mere surplusage. Those words must be given some meaning notwithstanding the provisions of the European directive and in my view they clearly connote a causal link as the Labour Court held in their decision reversing the determination of the equality officer.

and

> I accept that to constitute discrimination, the requirement need not be imposed because of sex or marital status, but, as I say, the inclusion of those words in the Irish section, unlike the comparable United Kingdom legislation, it seems to me to lead inescapably to the conclusion that there must be a causal connection between the sex or marital status of a person and the treatment afforded to him.
>
> If women were excluded from the second respondent or if they were treated less favourably in their quest for membership thereof, then the appropriate causal link would be established and the figures extracted by the equality officer would be of decisive importance. However, it seems to me that the Act of 1977 requires this basic connection between sex and treatment and does not deem discrimination to have occurred merely because historical factors (other than sex or marital status) have limited the eligible candidates to a pool which contains a larger number of the members of one sex than the other.

The appellant has appealed to this Court against the findings of the learned trial judge on the grounds that:

(1) the learned trial judge was wrong in law in the manner in which he construed the provisions of the Employment Equality Act, 1977 and in particular ss. 2 and 3 thereof.

(2) The learned trial judge was wrong in law in holding that the appellant was obliged to show that there was a causal link between the requirement imposed on her in respect of access to the position which she sought and her sex.

[171] (3) The learned trial judge was wrong in law in failing to hold that the requirement imposed on the appellant in respect of access to the position sought by her constituted discrimination contrary to the provisions of s. 2(c) and s. 3 of the Employment Equality Act, 1977 in circumstances where the disproportionate impact of such requirement on members of the female sex arose from historical reasons.

(4) The learned trial judge was wrong in law in failing to properly and adequately construe the provisions of the Employment Equality Act, 1977, in the light of the relevant provisions of Community law.

(5) That in construing the provisions of the Employment Equality Act, 1977, the learned trial judge failed to do everything possible in view of the wording and objectives of Directive No 76/207/EEC to achieve the result laid down by the said Directive and thereby comply with the requirements of Article 189(3) of the Treaty of Rome.

Before dealing with the facts of the case, it is desirable to set forth the relevant provisions of the Employment Equality Act, 1977 (the "Act of 1977").

Section 2 of the Act of 1977 provides that:

For the purposes of this Act, discrimination shall be taken to occur in any of the following cases—

(a) where by reason of his sex a person is treated less favourably than a person of the other sex;

(b) where because of his marital status a person is treated less favourably than another person of the same sex;

(c) where because of his sex or marital status a person is obliged to comply with a requirement, relating to employment or membership of a body referred to in section 5, which is not an essential requirement for such employment or membership and in respect of which the proportion of persons of the other sex or (as the case may be) of a different marital status, but of the same sex able to comply, is substantially higher.

(a) and (b) of this section have no application to the proceedings herein.

Section 3(1) of the Act provides that:

A person who is an employer or who obtains under a contract with another person, the services of employees of that other person, shall not discriminate against an employee or a prospective employee **[172]** or an employee of that other person in relation to access to employment, conditions of employment (other than remuneration or any condition relating to an occupational pension scheme), training or experience for or in relation to employment, promotion or re-grading in employment or classification of posts in employment.

Section 3(2) of the Act provides that:

An employer shall not, in relation to his employees or to employment by him, have rules or instructions which would discriminate against an employee or class of employee, and shall not otherwise apply or operate a practice which results or would be likely to result in an act which is a contravention of any provision of this Act when taken in conjunction with section 2(c).

Though not expressly stated in the Act, it is accepted by all parties to these proceedings that the purposes of the Act were to secure compliance with Council Directive of the 9th February, 1976, on the implementation of the principle of equal treatment for men and women as regards access to employment, vocational training and promotion and working conditions.

Article 2.1 of the said directive provides that:

For the purposes of the following provisions, the principle of equal treatment shall mean that there shall be no discrimination whatsoever on grounds of sex either directly or indirectly by reference in particular to marital or family status.

Article 3.1 of the said directive provides that:

Application of the principle of equal treatment means that there shall be no discrimination whatsoever on grounds of sex in the conditions, including selection criteria, for access to all jobs or posts, whatsoever the sector or branch of activity, and to all levels of the occupational hierarchy.

Article 5 of the said directive provides that:

1. Application of the principle of equal treatment with regard to working conditions, including the conditions governing dismissal, means that men and women shall be guaranteed the same conditions without discrimination on grounds of sex.

Article 6 provides that:

Member States shall introduce into their national legal systems such measures as are necessary to enable all persons who consider themselves wronged by failure to apply to them the principle of equal treatment within the meaning of Articles 3, 4 and 5 to pursue their **[173]** claims by judicial process after possible recourse to other competent authorities.

The case made on behalf of the appellant in this Court can be summarised as follows:

(1) The requirement that the appellant, before being appointed to the position which she sought, be a member of the second respondent and the holder of a union card amounted to indirect discrimination against the appellant by reason of the disproportion between male and female members of the said union, the membership of which was 82% male and 18% female, unless the first respondent can show that this requirement is based on objectively justified factors unrelated to any discrimination on the grounds of sex or marital status.
(2) The provisions of Council Directive 76/207/EEC prohibit discrimination on grounds of sex either directly or indirectly.
(3) The purpose of the said directive was to put into effect in the member states the principle of equal treatment for men and women as regards access to employment, including promotion, and to vocational training and as regards working conditions.
(4) In applying the national law and in the interpretation thereof national courts are required to interpret such law in the light of the wording and the purpose of the directive which was to put into effect in the member states the principle of equal treatment for men and

women as regards access to employment, including promotion, and to vocational training and to achieve the result envisaged by the directive.

(5) The provisions of the said directive prohibited any discrimination whatsoever on the grounds of sex whether direct or indirect.

(6) The learned trial judge failed to have regard to or apply the provisions of the directive in interpreting the provisions of s. 2(c) of the Act and in holding that there must be a causal connection between the sex or marital status of a person and the requirement referred to in the said sub-section, thereby precluding the Labour Court from inquiring into the question whether the requirement that the appellant be a member of the second respondent before obtaining the post which she sought was necessary and could amount to indirect discrimination against her on the grounds of her sex.

As stated by Blayney J in *Meagher* v. *Minister for Agriculture and Food* [1994] 1 ILRM 1, it is well established that Community law takes **[174]** precedence over our domestic law and that where they are in conflict it is the Community law which prevails.

It is also well established that national or domestic courts in interpreting a provision of national law designed to implement the provisions of a directive, should interpret their national law in the light of the wording and the purpose of the directive in order to achieve the result envisaged by the directive.

The European Court of Justice stated, in the case of *Von Colson and Kamann* v. *Land Nordrhein-Westfalen* [1984] ECR 1891, at para. 26:

> However the Member States' obligation arising from a directive to achieve the result envisaged by the directive and their duty under Article 5 of the Treaty to take all appropriate measures, whether general or particular, to ensure the fulfilment of that obligation, is binding on all the authorities of Member States including, for matters within their jurisdiction, the courts. It follows, that in applying the national law and in particular the provisions of a national law specifically introduced in order to implement Directive No 76/207 national courts are required to interpret their national law in the light of the wording and the purpose of the directive in order to achieve the results referred to in the third paragraph of Article 189.

The European Court came to a similar conclusion in the more recent case of *Marleasing SA* v. *La Commercial International de Alimentación SA* [1990] ECR 4135, where the Court stated at para. 8 of its judgment:

> In order to reply to that question, it should be observed that, as the Court pointed out in its judgment in Case 14/83 *Von Colson and Kamann* v. *Land Nordrhein Westfalen* [1984] ECR 1891, paragraph 26, the Member States' obligation arising from a directive to achieve the result envisaged by the directive and their duty under Article 5 of the Treaty to take all appropriate measures, whether

general or particular, to ensure the fulfilment of that obligation, is binding on all the authorities of Member States including, for matters within their jurisdiction, the courts. It follows that, in applying national law, whether the provisions in question were adopted before or after the directive, the national court called upon to interpret it is required to do so, as far as possible, in the light of the wording and the purpose of the directive in order to achieve the result pursued by the latter and thereby comply with the third paragraph of Article 189 of the Treaty.

The learned trial judge had been referred to this latter case and was concerned about its implications.

[175] He stated in the course of his judgment that:

Reference was also made to the judgment of the European Court given on the 13th November, 1990, in *Marleasing SA* and *La Commercial Internacional de Alimentación SA*. That was a far-reaching decision in so far as it determined that national courts are bound to interpret their national laws in the light of the wording and purpose of the relevant EEC directive even where the national law in question was adopted before the directive was given. That was, as I say, a far-reaching application of the general rule on interpretation which itself is not open to challenge.

The learned trial judge also seemed to consider that the provisions of s. 2(c) of the Act of 1977 might be in conflict with the provisions of the said directive because he further stated that:

Whilst it seems to me that para. (c) of s. 2 of the Act of 1977 is not happily expressed, it would not be possible to interpret that paragraph by treating the words "because of his sex or marital status" as mere surplusage. These words must be given some meaning notwithstanding the provisions of the European directive and in my view they clearly connote a causal link as the Labour Court held in their decision reversing the determination of the equality officer.

He also referred to "the problems in construing this important legislation" and at the conclusions of his judgment stated:

Having regard to the existing ambiguities and the importance of the principles involved, I would like to think that the facts which in this case have been carefully analysed in the decisions of the equality officer and the Labour Court might be reviewed by the Supreme Court and an authoritative decision obtained as to correct principles to be followed.

This Court is in the same position and under the same obligations as any other national court to interpret the provisions of s. 2(c) and s. 3 of the Act, as far as possible, in the light of the wording and the purpose of the directive in order to achieve the result pursued by the directive *viz.* establishing that there shall be no discrimination on grounds of sex either directly or indirectly by reference in particular to marital or family status.

The question of direct discrimination does not arise in this case and it is not sought, nor could it be sought, by the appellant that this Court should hold that the first respondent directly discriminated against her.

What is sought by her is an interpretation of the provisions of s. 2(c) and s. 3 of the Act of 1977 which would oblige the Labour Court to consider the question, as to whether the requirement that the appellant be **[176]** a member of the second respondent before being appointed to the post which she sought constituted indirect discrimination against her contrary to the provisions of the directive.

While this Court is not called upon to decide the question whether or not, on the facts of this case, the requirement imposed by the first respondent amounted to indirect discrimination against the appellant, it is desirable to refer briefly to the submissions made by counsel for the appellant in regard thereto.

These submissions were:

(1) that the appellant was indirectly discriminated against by reason of the requirement that she be a member of the second respondent before being appointed to the post;
(2) that this requirement was indirectly discriminatory because it adversely affects a far higher proportion of women than of men;
(3) that, as appears from the findings of the equality officer, 21 male employees of the first respondent could satisfy such requirement by reason of their membership of the second respondent and no female employee could satisfy such requirement;
(4) if the available pool for such employment were extended to the membership of the second respondent the number of male members eligible for such employment was 2,337 and the number of females eligible was 283;
(5) that a requirement which adversely affects a much larger number of women than of men is prohibited by the directive unless the requirement is justified by objectively justified factors unrelated to any discrimination on the grounds of sex;
(6) that the onus lies on the employer, where a requirement adversely affects a much larger number of women than of men, to show that the requirement is based on objectively justified factors unrelated to sex.

Counsel on both sides have drawn the attention of the Court to a number of decisions of the European Court of Justice with regard to what constitutes indirect discrimination and the onus of proof in regard thereto.

I do not however consider it necessary to deal with these cases because this Court is not concerned to ascertain whether, on the facts of this case, the requirement of the first respondent amounted to indirect discrimination against females, including the appellant.

As appears from the determination of the Labour Court, the reference to the Labour Court of the dispute by the appellant was a reference under ss. 2 and 3 of the Act of 1977.

[177] Section 3(1) of the Act provides that an employer shall not discriminate against an employee or a prospective employee.

Having regard to the provisions of the directive, and in interpreting that section in the light of the wording and purpose thereof, I am satisfied that the discrimination referred to therein refers to both direct and indirect discrimination.

Section 3(2) of the Act provides that:

> An employer shall not, in relation to his employees or to employment by him, have rules or instructions which would discriminate against an employee or class of employee, and shall not otherwise apply or operate a practice which results or would be likely to result in an act which is a contravention of any provision of this Act when taken in conjunction with section 2(c).

The primary and clear obligation placed on an employer by this sub-section is not to have rules or instructions which would discriminate either directly or indirectly against an employee.

The effect of the second provision of that sub-section *viz.* "that he shall not otherwise apply or operate a practice which results or would be likely to result in an act which is a contravention of any provision of this Act when taken in conjunction with s. 2(c)" does not in any way limit the general obligation imposed by s. 3(1) and (2) of the Act of 1977 but is merely a specific and separate obligation imposed by the Act.

The obligations imposed on an employer by virtue of s. 3 of the Act of 1977 are not in any way limited by the provisions of s. 2 of the Act.

This section provides that for the purposes of the Act, discrimination shall be taken to occur in the cases set forth at (a), (b) and (c) of the section.

The cases referred to therein are clearly cases of direct discrimination and cannot be regarded as an exhaustive description of direct discrimination and do not cover cases of indirect discrimination.

Cases of indirect discrimination are clearly prohibited by the directive and s. 3(1) and (2) of the Act of 1977 cannot be interpreted as containing no prohibition against indirect discrimination but must be interpreted as prohibiting cases of both direct and indirect discrimination.

A requirement, relating to employment or membership of a body which is not an essential requirement for such employment or membership and in respect of which the proportion of persons of the other sex or (as the case may be) of a different marital status but of the same sex able to comply is substantially higher may amount to indirect discrimination **[178]** even when a person is obliged to comply therewith for reasons other than a person's sex or marital status.

Section 2(c) only applies where the obligation is imposed on a person because of his sex or marital status.

When the obligation was imposed for reasons other than a person's sex or marital status, the issue falls to be considered in the light of the provisions of the directive and s. 3 of the Act of 1977.

Consequently, I am satisfied that the Labour Court and the learned trial judge erred in law in holding that there must be a causal connection between the requirement and the sex or marital status of the employee.

In such a case the worker is not required, in the first instance, to prove a causal connection between the practice complained of and the sex of the complainant. It is sufficient for him or her to show that the practice complained of bears significantly more heavily on members of the complainant's sex than on members of the other sex. At that stage the complainant has established a *prima facie* case of discrimination and the onus of proof shifts to the employer to show that the practice complained of is based on objectively verifiable factors which have no relation to the complainant's sex.

I would allow the appeal and refer the matter back to the Labour Court for consideration by them in the light of the provisions, not of s. 2(c) of the Act but of s. 3 of the Act of 1977.

BLAYNEY J

I agree.

BARRINGTON J

I also agree.

[Report: [1998] 2 Irish Reports 164]

[*Reporter's note*: The Labour Court issued its determination on the 14th August, 1997, and held, *inter alia*, that no discrimination had taken place within the terms of section 3. It allowed the respondent's appeal and dismissed the appellant's cross-appeal against the recommendations of the equality officer. This decision is under appeal.]

National constitutions — Constitutional challenge to legislation — Italian Constitution, Article 11 — Regional law on vineyards — Incompatibility with EC Regulation — Whether regional legislation subject to constitutional challenge on grounds of violation of EC law

Enforcement in national courts—Remedies—Claim against Region of Member State—Draft regional legislation in breach of EC law—Whether Member State would be in breach of its obligations under EC Treaty if regional law enacted — Whether Member State entitled to obtain Constitutional Court declaration that regional law is unconstitutional by reason of breach of EC law—The law of Italy

PRESIDENT OF COUNCIL OF MINISTERS *v.* UMBRIAN REGION

(Case No 384/94)

Italy, Constitutional Court. 10 *November* 1994

(Casavola, *President*)

SUMMARY: *The facts*:—The President of the Council of Ministers applied to the Constitutional Court for a ruling on the constitutionality of a draft Umbrian Regional Law on vineyards. The Italian Government considered that the draft Law infringed EC Regulations on the replanting of vineyards and, if it became law, would place the Italian State in breach of its obligations under EC law. On this account the Government argued that the Law violated Article 11 of the Constitution. The Umbrian Region argued that the application was inadmissible since the alleged conflict between EC law and national law did not raise any constitutional issue and merely required the competent court to refuse to apply the incompatible national provision.

Held:—The application was admissible and succeeded on the merits.

(1) In relation to the European Community, it was the State which was responsible for violations of Community law, even where they arose from the exercise of legislative powers by the regions. According to the jurisprudence of the European Court of Justice, the maintenance in force within the national legal order of a measure incompatible with EC legislation derived from the EC Treaty constituted a violation by the State of that Treaty. Furthermore, as the Constitutional Court had previously held, the legislative power of the regions could not be exercised in such a manner as to conflict with the rules and limits laid down by EC law.

(2) The President of the Council had therefore been correct to refer the matter to the Constitutional Court, in order to preclude *ab initio* any risk of non-compliance with Community obligations by the State, even before the law at issue entered into force. The question of alleged incompatibility between

directly applicable Community legislation and an *existing* provision of national law was a separate issue which was a matter for the ordinary courts to deal with in proceedings on the merits.

(3) The provisions of the national legislation at issue clearly violated the EC Regulations in question, were a material breach of the obligations incumbent upon Italy as a member of the European Community, and accordingly were objectionable as infringements of Articles 11 and 117 of the Constitution.

The following is the text of the relevant part of the judgment of the Court:

In Law—1. The President of the Council of Ministers, represented by the Advocate-General, has applied for a ruling on the constitutionality, in relation to Articles 11 and 117 of the Constitution and Articles 6 and 7 of EEC Regulation No 822/87, as supplemented by Regulation No 1325/90, of a [draft] Umbrian Regional Law, approved for the second time as amended . . . on 31 March 1994, which lays down special rules . . . for the replanting of vineyards in the Umbrian production areas for wines of controlled . . . designation of origin. The President considers that the draft law may contravene the Community rules on the replanting and extension of vineyards, placing the Italian State in breach of its Community obligations and hence of Articles 11 and 117 of the Constitution.

The Umbrian Region contends that the application is inadmissible. It argues that . . . any conflict between a Community regulation directly applicable in Italy and an allegedly incompatible provision of domestic law is not to be treated as raising an issue of constitutionality. It is simply for the competent judicial and administrative authorities to refuse to apply the incompatible provision. In support of this contention the Region cites this Court's Decision No 170 of 1984 (*Foro Italiano* 1984 I, 2062),[1] and also Decisions Nos 168 of 1991 (*idem* 1992 I, 660), 389 of 1989[2] (*idem* 1991 I, 1076), 113 of 1985[3] (*idem* 1985 I, 1600), Order No 391 of 1992 (*idem*, *Repertorio* 1993, *Regione*, No 287) and, finally, Decision No 115 of 1983 (*ibid.*, *Cooperativa*, No 34).

2. We will deal first with the question of admissibility. Notwithstanding the Region's persuasive argument on this point, we are unable to accept it.

Without wishing to become involved in a discussion of Decision 170/84 (which modified the previous case-law, whereby provisions of national law which contravened prior Community legislation were ruled unconstitutional on grounds of violation of Article 11), we nonetheless feel bound to add some remarks concerning the implications of the obligation to ensure that domestic law complies with Community law,

[1 *Spa Granital* v. *Amministrazione delle Finanze dello Stato*, Volume 1, p. 642.]
[2 *Provincia di Bolzano* v. *Presidente Consiglio Ministri*, Volume 1, Note, p. 652.]
[3 *Spa BECA* v. *Amministrazione delle Finanze dello Stato*, Note, *ibid.*]

pursuant to Article 11 of the Constitution as interpreted by this Court, and the manner in which the legislative power of the regions is to be exercised in fields where Community law applies.

It should be borne in mind that, in relation to the European Community, it is the State that is responsible for violations of Community law, even where these arise out of the exercise of the legislative power of the regions. Thus the maintenance within the domestic legal order of a measure incompatible with legislation deriving from the EEC Treaty, as well as creating an ambiguous situation in practice, is regarded by the jurisprudence of the European Court of Justice as a breach of the State's obligations under the Treaty itself. Further, as regards regional powers, this [Constitutional] Court has specifically made it clear that these may be exercised only in so far as this does not result in a conflict with the rules and limits laid down by Community law and by the relevant [national] implementing measures (see, most recently, Decision No 224 of 1994, "*In Law*", points 5 and 8, *idem* 1994 I, 2025).

We are not concerned here, as the Region contends in its defence, to establish a legislative hierarchy (in this case between Community legislation and regional laws), but to examine whether completion of the regional legislative procedure would result in the introduction into the Italian legal order of legislation which, on an objective view, is incompatible with pre-existing Community regulations. In these circumstances prior decisions of this Court on admissibility are irrelevant: in the present case, the regional law under challenge had not yet entered into force, and the President of the Council was correct in referring the matter to the Court during the final phase of the legislative procedure, in order to preclude *ab initio* any risk of non-compliance with Community obligations. By contrast, the decisions cited by the Region all concern cases where the provision of domestic law ruled inapplicable on grounds of incompatibility with Community law was already in force.

Thus the question of alleged incompatibility between directly applicable Community legislation and an existing provision of domestic law is a separate issue, and a matter for the [ordinary] courts dealing with the case on the merits. The situation is totally different where it is sought to review the lawfulness of the legislative deliberations of regional councils [while these are still in progress]. Here, pending the result of the challenge by the Government before the Constitutional Court, the legislative process is blocked and the measure in question cannot be formally adopted and given effect through publication. We cannot accept the argument that compliance with Community obligations—and hence with Article 11 [of the Constitution]—could still be ensured if this Court were to declare the issue inadmissible but motivate its decision in terms which made it clear that provisions of domestic law incompatible with those of Community law may not in any event be applied by the competent public agencies (that is, not only the courts but also administrative bodies: on this latter point, see this Court's Decision No 389 of 1989[4] cited above and the Judgment of the European Court of Justice of 22 June 1989,[5] *idem* 1991 IV, 129). Such a decision would both be illogical and generate uncertainty as to the manner in which it was to be applied in practice. These are directly instituted constitutional proceedings [*giudizio di legittimità costituzionale instaurato in via principale*]. Thus we are not dealing here with a situation where the court, in ruling on a specific case, declares a law to be inapplicable. In such circumstances this Court's decision (on the obligation to apply the Community provisions) would be addressed to the regional administration. However, in the meantime the measure under challenge would have been enacted (notwithstanding that it had been ruled inapplicable), and thus incorporated into domestic law, in clear violation of the principles of legal certainty and clarity, and of the obligations incumbent upon the Italian State, in particular its obligation to ensure that domestic law accords with Community law.

It follows that the Government is entitled to seek the review of a regional law that has not yet entered into force where that law is suspected of violating Community legislation. It is hardly necessary to add that the converse does not apply. The region cannot challenge a State law that is already in force, and any conflict between the latter and Community law is a matter for the courts dealing with the merits (see Decision No 115 of 1993 *supra*).

3. [The Court then dealt with and dismissed the Region's procedural objection to admissibility. The Court continued:]

4. On the merits, the application succeeds.

The provision under challenge, even in its second [revised] version, constitutes a clear breach of the rules introduced by the cited Community Regulations for the purpose of curbing over-production in the wine sector . . . [After a brief discussion of the relevant technical provisions, the Court continued:] This regime . . . represents a material breach of the obligations incumbent upon the Italian State by virtue of its membership of the European Union and an unlawful exercise of regional legislative power, and is accordingly objectionable on grounds of violation of Articles 11 and 117 of the Constitution.

For these reasons, the Constitutional Court hereby declares unconstitutional the [draft] Umbrian Regional Law, approved for the second time as amended . . . on 31 March 1994, laying down special rules . . . for the replanting of vineyards in the Umbrian production areas for wines of controlled . . . designation of origin.

[Report: *Il Foro Italiano* 1994 I, p. 3289 (in Italian). Translated by T. F. K. Johnston, MA, LL B]

[4 *Provincia di Bolzano* v. *Presidente Consiglio Ministri*, Note, *ibid*.]

[5 Case No 103/88, *Fratelli Costanze SpA* v. *Comune di Milano*, 1989 ECR 1839.]

NOTE.—The same approach was followed by the Constitutional Court in a subsequent judgment raising similar issues of the compatibility of regional legislative proposals with EC law. The Constitutional Court held that proceedings instituted directly before it by the local representative of the Italian Government were admissible where they claimed a possible violation of Article 11 of the Constitution on account of an alleged breach by Italy of its Community obligations. However, on the merits, the Constitutional Court held that obligations in relation to the notification procedure for State aid, laid down under Article 93 of the EC Treaty, were not breached by the manner in which the legislative proposals had been notified to the European Commission (*State Commissioner for Sicily* v. *Region of Sicily*, Case 94/95, 30 March 1995, *Il Foro Italiano* 1995, p. 1081 (in Italian)).

On the other hand, in a later case involving a dispute between two regions and the Italian State regarding their respective powers in relation to vocational training schemes financed by the European Social Fund, the Constitutional Court refused to exercise jurisdiction to review the constitutionality of circulars issued by the State Ministry of Employment concerning the schemes. The Court confirmed that Community law could legitimately depart from constitutional provisions on the distribution of powers between the State and the Regions where this was necessary to meet the needs of the European Community. The circulars at issue merely transposed Community instruments and therefore enjoyed full "Community protection" by virtue of their origin. As such they were not amenable to constitutional review unless they could be shown to be incompatible with fundamental constitutional principles (*Umbrian and Marches Regions* v. *Italian State*, Case 93/97, 26 March 1997, *Giur. Cost*. 1997, p. 923 (in Italian)).

Enforcement in national courts—Remedies—Claim against Member State — Breach of Community law for which Member State responsible — Duty of national courts to provide effective remedies for the enforcement of rights of individuals under Community law — Whether requiring national courts to allow claim for compensation to be brought by individuals against State — Principle of State responsibility for harm caused to individuals by such breach — Conditions for liability — Whether governed by national law

Supremacy—Conflict between Community law and national law — Consequences for contrary national law — Duty of national courts not to apply national provision in conflict with general principle of Community law—Right of individuals to compensation for loss suffered as a result of breach of Community law by a Member State—Scope of right—The law of Italy

President of Council of Ministers *v.* Mariotti and Others

(Case No 10617/95)

Italy, Court of Cassation (Labour Section). 11 *October* 1995

(De Rosa, *President*)

Summary: *The facts*:—In 1980 the European Community enacted EEC Council Directive 80/987 which was intended to guarantee a minimum level of protection for employees in the event of the insolvency of their employers. Italy did not implement the Directive before the prescribed deadline (23 October 1983). The Court of Justice subsequently ruled that Italy was in default of its obligations under the EC Treaty (Case 22/87, *Commission* v. *Italy*, [1989] ECR 143). The Directive required the Member States to take the measures necessary to guarantee the payment of outstanding wage claims of employees in the event of insolvency. Italian workers subsequently instituted proceedings before the Italian courts claiming payment of their arrears of wages, or alternatively compensation, from the Italian State.

On a reference from the Italian courts for a preliminary ruling under Article 177 of the EC Treaty, the Court of Justice held that individuals could not rely on the provisions of the Directive at issue against Italy because those provisions did not have direct effect in the national legal order since they did not identify the institution liable to provide the guarantee in question. Nevertheless the Court of Justice held that Member States could be liable, subject to certain conditions, to pay compensation to individuals for breaches of Community law giving rise to an infringement of rights created for them by Community law. The Court of Justice held that it was for the internal legal order of each Member State to lay down the procedure enabling the right to compensation to be claimed (Cases C-6/90 and 9/90, *Francovich and Bonifaci* v. *Italian Republic*, [1991] ECR I-5357).[1]

Following the *Francovich* judgment, Italy enacted Decree No 80/1992 to implement the Directive. Article 2(7) provided for the payment of compensation to individuals who had suffered loss as a result of the failure of Italy to transpose the Directive within the time limit. This Decree failed, however, to make clear whether it was the State itself or the National Insurance Board (*INPS*) which should be responsible for the payment of compensation. Subsequently various groups of workers instituted proceedings before the Italian courts against both the Italian State and *INPS*. The Examining Magistrate (*Pretore*) and the Tribunal of Florence both held that the right of action lay against the State and not against *INPS*. Italy appealed in cassation.

Held:—The appeal was allowed. *INPS*, as administrator of the Guarantee Fund, was responsible for the payment of any indemnity provided for in the Decree at issue.

(1) It followed from the ruling of the Court of Justice in *Francovich* that the Member States could be liable to pay compensation for loss suffered by individuals as a result of the non-implementation of a Community directive, provided certain conditions were fulfilled. However, whilst the right to compensation was derived from Community law, the substantive and procedural conditions governing the payment of compensation were to be determined by the rules of national law. Consequently the specific form of the protection to be accorded by the Italian courts to individual rights derived from Community law was to be determined by national law.

(2) Italian law did not recognize individuals as acquiring subjective rights, on the basis of Community law, either to the enactment of legislative acts or to compensation from the State under Article 2043 of the Civil Code for unlawful conduct by the State in the exercise of its legislative powers.

(3) Consequently the current regime of Italian law was in conflict with general principles of Community law inasmuch as it failed to provide individuals with an adequate remedy for losses suffered as a result of the State's failure to implement a Community directive. In such circumstances the national regime could be disregarded by the national courts since, in case of a conflict between a rule of Italian law and a directly effective rule of Community law, the Italian courts could refuse to apply the national rule, although the Italian law in question did not thereby become void.

(4) In this case, however, it was possible to resolve the conflict between Italian law and the general principles of Community law by interpreting Article 2 of the Italian Decree at issue so as to make *INPS* responsible for the payment of an indemnity as an administrative authority, without any obligation to pay compensation being imposed upon the State itself.

The text of the relevant parts of the judgment of the Court commences on the opposite page.

[1] Volume 1, p. 188 at pp. 238-44.

[511] *Course of the Proceedings*—Giuliano Mariotti [and others] applied to the Pistoia District Judge [*Pretore*], sitting as a labour court, for an order against the Italian Republic for compensation in an amount corresponding to that outstanding in respect of unpaid remuneration **[512]** following their employer's insolvency. By way of subsidiary claim, the applicants sought an order against the State, and against the *INPS* (National Insurance Board) as administrator of the Guarantee Fund, for an amount representing their final three months' salary. The applicants founded their claim on Decree-Law No 80 of 27 January 1992, which provides for the payment of an indemnity equivalent to the loss suffered as a result of the failure to implement by the prescribed date Council Directive No 80/987/EEC on the protection of employees in the event of the employer's insolvency.

The *Pretore*, in two judgments to like effect, accepted the applications in relation to the Italian State, while ruling that there was no right of action against the *INPS*.

. . . The Italian Republic's [joined] appeals were rejected by the Florence Tribunal [*Tribunale*], which interpreted the Decree-Law as **[513]** meaning that compensation for losses suffered in respect of insolvency proceedings commenced prior to its entry into force was excluded from the scope of payments to be made out of the Guarantee Fund administered by the *INPS*. The Tribunal stated that its decision was based both on the Decree-Law's express terms and on the consideration that, whereas the Fund had been set up to make good an insolvent employer's obligation to pay his employees the remuneration due to them, responsibility for compensating workers who had suffered loss as a result of the late implementation of the Directive, and consequent exclusion *ratione temporis* from the benefit of the Fund, could attach only to the State.

The Tribunal accordingly rejected the subsidiary appeals by the employees against the *INPS*.

The Italian Republic has appealed in cassation against the [Tribunal's] decision **[514]** . . .

Grounds of decision—In its sole ground of appeal, based on the violation and wrongful application of the seventh paragraph of Article 2 of Decree-Law No 80 of 27 January 1992, the Italian Republic contends that payment of the indemnity provided for therein is properly the responsibility of the *INPS*, as administrator of the Fund.

The Court considers that the appeal is well founded. Under the powers delegated to it by Article 48 of Law No 428 of 29 December 1990 (Community legislation for 1990), the Government adopted Decree-Law No 80 of 27 January 1992, implementing Council Directive No 80/987/EEC on the protection of employees in the event of the employer's insolvency. The Decree-Law's provisions for the protection of staff of **[515]** . . . [insolvent undertakings] differ according to whether the insolvency proceedings commenced before or after its entry into force.

Thus Articles 1 and 2 of the Decree-Law provide for two different situations. Sums owed to employees in respect of their employment are to be paid out of the [*INPS*] Guarantee Fund, but this applies only to insolvency proceedings commenced after the Decree-Law's entry into force (Article 2, sixth para.). For proceedings commenced prior to that date, employees are to receive an indemnity [*indennità*], in an amount substantially equivalent to that expressly charged to the Fund . . . , "on account of the loss suffered in consequence of the failure to implement Directive EEC/80/987" (Article 2, seventh para.).

It is this latter provision . . . that has given rise to the dispute as to who should be liable for payment of the amount in question.

The decision under appeal is founded partly on the language **[516]** [of the paragraph in question] and on the express exclusion of retroactive effect in relation to the new regime, but above all on the systemic difference between proceedings against the Guarantee Fund for payment of a debt and a claim for damages under Article 2043 [of the Civil Code][2] on account of failure to implement the Directive. [The Tribunal took the view that] in the latter case, in the absence of an express provision imposing liability on some other agency, such a claim should properly be addressed to the author of the unlawful act.

[The Court, having examined in detail **[516-517]** the terms of the paragraph, and the effect of the references therein to other paragraphs of the same Article, held that, notwithstanding the differing nature of the two types of claim, on a true construction, both were payable out of the Fund. In relation to the Tribunal's argument that the nature of the obligation was such that it could attach only to the Italian State, the Court continued:]

The systemic argument relied on by the Tribunal must also be rejected. The indemnity payable to those who have suffered loss as a result of the failure to implement the Community Directive is not to be characterized in law as compensation for a breach of civil liability.

In its Judgment of 19 November 1991 in joined Cases Nos C-6/90 and C-9/90[3] *Foro Italiano* 1992 IV, 145) the European Court of Justice interpreted the provisions of Council Directive No 80/987/EEC of 20 October 1990 (on the approximation of the laws of Member States relating to the protection of employees in the event of the insolvency of their employer), defining the rights of employees as meaning that, where no implementing measures had been adopted within the prescribed period, the persons concerned could not enforce the rights in question against

[[2] Article 2043, "Compensation for unlawful acts", which governs civil liability in general under Italian law, provides: "Any fraudulent, malicious or negligent act that causes an unjustified injury to another obliges the person who has committed the act to pay damages."]

[[3] *Francovich and Bonifaci* v. *Italian Republic*, Volume 1, p. 188.]

the State before national courts. The Court stated that, while the provisions of the Directive were unconditional and sufficiently precise with regard to the identity of the persons entitled to the guarantee and to the latter's content (it being understood that the option whereby Member States may limit the amount of the guarantee to sums not going beyond the social objective of the Directive could not be relied on [so as to defeat the rights of beneficiaries] by a State which had failed to exercise that option because of its failure to implement the Directive), they did not, however, identify the person liable to provide that guarantee; the State could not be considered liable on the sole ground that it had failed to adopt the necessary implementing provisions within the prescribed period.

However, the Court further held that any breaches by a Member State of its duty under Articles 5 and 189 of the EC Treaty to take all appropriate measures, whether general or particular, to ensure fulfilment of its obligations under Community law would make that State liable to pay compensation for harm caused to individuals on whom implementation of the Directive would have conferred rights, where the content of those rights was clearly identifiable on the basis of the provisions of the Directive and there existed a causal link between the breach of the State's obligations and the harm suffered. In this regard the Court further stated that, while the right to compensation was founded directly on Community law, the rules and conditions, both substantive and procedural, governing the payment of compensation were to be determined in accordance with national law. In regard to the particular case before it, the Court concluded that a Member State was required to pay compensation for the harm suffered by individuals as a result of the failure to implement Directive 80/987.

It therefore follows that the specific form of the protection to be accorded by the Italian courts to individual rights deriving from Community law must be determined under the rules of Italian law.

Community law, by its very nature, does not distinguish between "actual" or "simple" interests [*interessi di fatto o semplici*], "legitimate interests" [*interessi legittimi*] and "subjective rights" [*diritti soggettivi*]. It simply lays down the rules and principles to be observed by Member States and their agencies; that is to say, it provides for the achievement of a specific "result", but the nature of the individual rights deriving therefrom is determinable solely by reference to the criteria laid down by Italian law (see plenary Cassation Decision No 8383 of 27 July 1993, *idem*, *Repertorio* 1993, *Giurisdizione civile*, No 110).

In establishing basic rules for the organization and operation of the State, the Constitution regulates the legislative function, sharing it between government and parliament as the expression of a political power which may be exercised without restriction as to the ends to be achieved, and hence free of any form of judicial control (see Article 31 of Royal Decree No 1054 of 26 June 1924, consolidating the laws on the Council of State). The exercise [by the State] of its political power **[518]** takes precedence over any subjective rights of individuals (see plenary Cassation Decision No 124 of 8 January 1993, *idem* 1993 I, 2866). It follows that Community law, as interpreted by the Court of Justice, cannot have the effect of giving individuals subjective rights under Italian law in relation to the exercise of legislative power, or of characterizing as unlawful conduct (within the meaning of Article 2043 of the Civil Code), attributable to the State personally, a matter pertaining to the latter's exercise of its legislative powers.

Thus, under Italian law, a claim by an individual for compensation in respect of losses suffered as a result of [the State's] failure to implement a Community directive (assuming that the conditions laid down by the Court of Justice are satisfied) cannot be regarded as anything other than a claim to be indemnified on account of a financial loss resulting from the exercise of a power not susceptible of review by the courts.

In other words, the current regime under Italian law conflicts with general rules of Community law as established by an interpretative decision of the European Court of Justice in exercise of its institutional powers under Articles 169 and 167 of [the Treaty of Rome] . . . , inasmuch as it fails to provide individuals with an adequate remedy in respect of losses suffered by them in consequence of [the State's] failure to implement a [Community] directive.

To this extent and subject to these limits, the domestic regime may be disregarded by the national courts (see Constitutional Court Decisions Nos 170 of 8 June 1984,[4] *idem* 1984 I, 2062; 113 of 23 April 1985,[5] *idem* 1985 I, 1600; 389 of 11 July 1989, *idem* 1991 I, 1076). Thus, where a rule of Italian law conflicts with a directly applicable provision of Community law, the question of constitutionality does not arise, for the effect of that conflict is not that the Italian law thereby becomes void, but that the Italian courts may refuse to apply it (Constitutional Court Decision No 168 of 18 April 1991,[6] *idem*, 1992 I, 660).

The case with which we are dealing here presents certain similarities with that settled by the intervention of the Constitutional Court through its Decision No 307 of 22 June 1990 (*idem*, 1990 I, 2694). There, the Court declared Law No 51/65 on compulsory vaccination against poliomyelitis to be unconstitutional, on the ground that it made no provision for the State to compensate victims of damage resulting from vaccination in circumstances not covered by Article 2043. This Decision led to the enactment of Law No 210 of 25 February 1992, on compensation for persons having suffered irreversible damage to their health as a result

[[4] *Spa Granital* v. *Amministrazione delle Finanze dello Stato*, Volume 1, p. 642.]
[[5] *Spa BECA* v. *Amministrazione delle Finanze*, Volume 1, Note, p. 652.]
[[6] *Provincia di Bolzano* v. *Presidente Consiglio Ministri*, Note, *ibid.*]

of compulsory vaccinations, transfusions or the administration of blood products.

The conflict between Italian law and the general rules of Community law, as interpreted by the Court of Justice, was in effect resolved precisely by the provision in the seventh paragraph of Article 2 of Decree-Law No 80/92 which made the Fund responsible for payment of an indemnity consisting of a sum of money determinable by reference to the amount of the guarantee payable under the terms of the Directive.

In reaching our decision as to who should bear responsibility for payment of the sums provided for in the said seventh paragraph, we consider that to place that obligation not upon the State itself but upon one of the public-law agencies forming part of the indirect administrative machinery of the State does not conflict with the law's requirements of coherence and rationality, inasmuch as it has not been sought to burden an agency different from the author of the unlawful act with civil liability under Article 2043 of the Civil Code.

[The Court concluded by holding that its interpretation of the Decree-Law as imposing liability on the *INPS* rather than the State was also in accordance with Italian constitutional law. In support of this view it cited Constitutional Court Decision No 285 of 16 June 1993 (*idem* 1993 I, 2393), as well as two of its own decisions on the issue of jurisdiction in the matter.]

[Report: *Il Foro Italiano* 1996, p. 503 (in Italian). Translated by T. F. K. Johnston, MA, LL B]

NOTE.—The above judgment of the Court of Cassation, inasmuch as it appears to limit the right of individuals to claim compensation against the State for breaches of Community law, has been the subject of critical comment (Malferrari, State Liability for Violations of EC Law in Italy, *ZaöRV* 1999, p. 809 at pp. 814-21 (in English); also Adinolfi, The Judicial Application of Community Law in Italy, CML Rev 1998, p. 1313 at p. 1337, footnote 99).

By a judgment of 22 July 1999, the Court of Cassation has considerably expanded the scope of State liability under Article 2043 of the Civil Code, holding that the public authorities may be subject to claims not only where the subjective rights (*diritti soggettivi*) of individuals have been violated but also where their legitimate interests (*interessi legittimi*) have been infringed. Accordingly, Article 2043 is now applicable to the infringement by the State of all significant individual interests under the legal order. The judgment of the Court of Cassation does not refer to the decision of the Court of Justice in *Francovich*, nor indeed does it contain any reference to Community law. Nevertheless it has been argued that the reference by the Court of Cassation to the legal order covers both the national and the Community legal order so that Article 2043 should now provide a basis for claims in State liability for breaches of Community law (for a detailed analysis of the effect of the judgment of the Court of Cassation on State liability for breaches of Community law see Malferrari, State Liability, *ibid*. pp. 832-6).

Direct effect—Directives—Interpretation of national law—Duty of national courts to interpret national law consistently with provisions of directive — Scope of obligation — Applicability to national law introduced to implement directive — Whether national constitutional court bound to resolve incompatibility between directive and provisions of national law

Institutions—Court of Justice—Powers—Jurisdiction under Article 177 of EC Treaty—Scope of duty of national courts to make reference to Court of Justice—Whether constitutional court under duty to make such a reference—"Court or tribunal of a Member State against whose decision there is no judicial remedy under national law" — Whether constitutional court such a court or tribunal within the meaning of Article 177—The law of Italy

MESSAGGERO SERVIZI SRL *v.* OFFICE OF REGISTRAR OF PADUA

(Case No 536/95)

Italy, Constitutional Court. 29 *December* 1995

(Ferri, *President*; Granata, *Rapporteur*)

SUMMARY: *The facts*:—In the course of proceedings challenging the imposition of certain taxes on company property transactions, a reference was made to the Italian Constitutional Court concerning the compatibility of certain provisions of Italian tax law with EEC Council Directive 69/335 concerning indirect taxes on the raising of capital. It was argued that, even if the provisions of the Directive at issue did not have direct effect, the conflicting national provisions should be set aside since an Italian Revenue Law of 1971 had provided that the revenue system should be brought into line with the Directive, but without fixing a deadline for the Directive to come into force.

Held:—The Constitutional Court declined either to examine the case itself or to refer it for a preliminary ruling to the European Court of Justice, and remitted the case to the trial court for a decision.

(1) It was not the task of the Constitutional Court to interpret Community norms, unless it was possible to do so on the basis of clear evidence, nor to resolve irreconcilable differences in interpretation, such as those in this case, in relation to those norms. In such circumstances it was necessary to refer the matter to the European Court of Justice for an interpretation which would be binding on all the Member States.

(2) Contrary to the suggestion made in one of its previous decisions,[1] the Constitutional Court considered that a question of Community law could not

[1] See Volume 1, Note, p. 667.

be referred by it to the Court of Justice for a preliminary ruling. The function of the Constitutional Court was to act as the guarantor of the Constitution and it was not a "court or tribunal of a Member State" within the meaning of Article 177 of the EC Treaty. It was a matter for the court seized of a conflict between national law and a Community norm to refer the question directly to the Court of Justice for a ruling.

The following is the text of the relevant part of the judgment of the Court:

In the course of an action brought by Messaggero Servizi Srl and Others, challenging the action of the Office of the Registry in imposing mortgage and land registry taxes, as well as capital duty, attributable to an increase in the company's capital by means of the acquisition, *inter alia*, of real estate, the Revenue Commission of Padua raised the incidental issue of the constitutional legitimacy of [certain provisions of Italian tax law] from the standpoint of Article 76 of the Constitution, to the extent that those provisions failed to provide for exemption from duty in such circumstances as required by EEC Council Directive 69/335 of 17 July 1969 concerning indirect taxes on the raising of capital.

In the opinion of the appellant Revenue Commission, the provision of the EEC Directive at issue should not be interpreted as having direct effect in national law. Nevertheless, according to the Commission, although the Directive does not have direct effect, its legal substance applies in another form because the law providing for the reorganization of the revenue system (Law No 825 of 9 October 1971) provides in Article 7 that the regime governing mortgage and land registry taxes should be brought into conformity with EEC Directive 335 of 1969. Accordingly, the Revenue Commission considers that, since the legislature has not set a date for the Directive to come into force, the offending national provisions must be rendered ineffective due to an unlawful delegation of powers.

The President of the Council of Ministers has intervened, represented by the Advocate General of the State, and requests that the incidental issue raised should be declared inadmissible or unfounded . . .

The issue of constitutionality raised, since it is founded on the interpretation of the above-mentioned Directive, requires that the substance of the norms contained in the Community legislation must be completely and unambiguously identified in accordance with the rules expressly laid down in that legislation, so that their substance is presented in a clear and reliable manner, capable of correcting the revealed defects contained in the offending provisions of national law.

It is not the task of this Court to provide an interpretation of Community norms, unless it is possible to do so on the basis of "clear evidence" (Decision No 168 of 1991),[2] or to resolve irreconcilable differences in

[[2] *Ibid.*]

interpretation (such as those in this case) in relation to those norms. It is necessary in such circumstances to refer the matter to the European Court of Justice for an interpretation which is binding on all the Member States.

Contrary to the suggestion made in its prior decision (No 168 of 1991), a question of Community law cannot be referred by the Constitutional Court to the Court of Justice for a preliminary ruling. The Constitutional Court "essentially exercises a function of constitutional control, ultimately guaranteeing the observance of the Constitution of the Republic by the constitutional organs of the State and the Regions" (Decision No 13 of 1960).

It is not possible to recognize the Constitutional Court as a "national jurisdiction" within the meaning of Article 177 of the EC Treaty because "the differences in the role performed by the Court, which cannot truly be regarded as either an ordinary or a special judicial organ, are profound and without precedent in the Italian judicial system, a fact which is well understood and historically established . . ." (Decision No 13 of 1960).

Instead it is for the judge seized of the case, once he has identified an issue of constitutional legitimacy based on [a conflict between] a norm of Community law [and provisions of national law], in the absence of a specific precedent decision on the point by the European Court of Justice, to make a reference to the Court of Justice in order to ensure an interpretation of the scope of the Community norm at issue which is certain, reliable and of practical (as opposed to hypothetical or uncertain) significance and is not manifestly unfounded on the basis of doubtful constitutional legitimacy regarding a domestic provision which [from the standpoint of a constitutional yardstick] falls within the scope of the Community provision.

Accordingly, the case should be remitted to the judge who referred it . . .

For these reasons, the Constitutional Court orders that this case shall be remitted to the judge who referred it.

[Report: *RDI* 1996, p. 502 (in Italian)]

Direct effect — Directives — Conditions for direct effect — Failure of Member State to implement provisions of directive by specified time—Whether directive may be relied upon by individuals against other individuals or only against the State and its organs—Scope of legal effects of non-implemented directive which cannot be invoked by individuals — Council Directive 85/577—Consumer protection—Right of cancellation

Direct effect—Directives—Interpretation of national law—Duty of national courts to interpret national law consistently with provisions of directive—General principles of equity—Whether requiring national courts to apply provisions of non-implemented directive on consumer protection—The law of Italy

RECREB SRL *v.* SALUSTRI

(Case No 2369/96)

Italy, Court of Cassation (First Civil Section). 20 *March* 1996

(Cantillo, *President*)

SUMMARY: *The facts*:—The defendant signed a contract in his home for the purchase of foreign language instructional materials. He subsequently sought to cancel the contract and the supplier, Recreb srl, brought proceedings claiming the amount due under the contract. The *Giudice Conciliatore* (Judge-Assessor) of Rome held that, even though EC Council Directive 85/577 concerning the protection of the consumer in respect of contracts negotiated away from business premises had not yet been implemented in Italy, its provisions giving a right to consumers to cancel the contract in such circumstances governed the case as a matter of equity, the contract was oppressive, and accordingly no binding legal obligation had arisen. Recreb appealed to the Court of Cassation.

Held:—The appeal was dismissed.

(1) At the time of the signature of the contract at issue, Directive 85/577 had not yet been implemented in Italy. The European Court of Justice had held, in its judgment of 14 July 1994,[1] that in those circumstances the Directive could not be relied upon by the consumer against the private company before the national courts since the direct effect of directives was not recognized in relations between private parties (so-called "horizontal relations"). Accordingly, under Italian law as enshrined in the Italian Civil Code, a person signing a contract without reservation was bound to perform it.

(2) However, a rule corresponding to that contained in the Directive, giving a right of cancellation in the circumstances of the case, was applicable under a

[1] *Faccini Dori* v. *Recreb srl*, p. 19.

general principle of equity which required that consumer contracts such as the one at issue would be deemed to be void if they did not give the purchaser a right of cancellation for a limited period following their conclusion. This equitable principle provided an adequate basis for the decision under appeal despite the fact that the position in strict law was different.

(3) Accordingly, the issue of the direct effect of Community directives in municipal law had to be approached in a broader manner. Respect for international obligations was enshrined in the Constitution. Accordingly, even where directives had not been incorporated into municipal law and could not be directly invoked as rules of law governing relations between private parties, they were not totally deprived of legal effect, at least from the date prescribed for their implementation. As the European Court of Justice had made clear in the abovementioned judgment,[2] in interpreting the provisions of national law in force, the courts of the Member States were under a duty to take account of Community directives wherever possible, even where they had not yet been transposed into municipal law. Once the deadline for their implementation had expired, their provisions were automatically brought within the orbit of the domestic legal order and became one of the sources on which national law could draw, even before their transposition into municipal law. Accordingly, they could no longer be disregarded in determining the guiding principles of institutions governed by law.

The following is the text of the relevant parts of the judgment of the Court:

[1666] *Course of the Proceedings*—On 29 April 1989 the *Giudice Conciliatore* [Judge-Assessor] of Rome, on an application by Recreb srl, issued an order against Carlo Salustri directing him to pay to the applicant sums due under a contract for the purchase of instructional materials in respect of a foreign-language course.

On 5 June 1992, following opposition proceedings by Salustri, the *Conciliatore* revoked the order. Evidence submitted to the court showed that Salustri had been assured at the time when he signed the contract, which had been presented to him at his home by a representative of the vendor company, that his signature was not binding. In consequence the *Conciliatore* held that in equity the matter was governed by the principles established by EEC Directive No 85/577 of 20 December 1985, even though at the time of the events in question that Directive had not yet been formally incorporated into Italian law. He accordingly ruled that, in view of the circumstances in which the contract had been signed (a contract which he found to be of an "oppressive" ["*giugulatorio*"] nature as far as the purchaser was concerned), no binding legal obligation on the latter could be derived from it.

Recreb appealed in cassation against that decision . . .

Grounds of the Decision—1. The appellant company, alleging breaches of Article 13, second paragraph of the Code of Civil Procedure and

[2] *Ibid.*, paragraph 26, p. 42.

Articles 1329, 1331 **[1667]** and 1427 ff. of the Civil Code . . . , challenges the *Conciliatore*'s decision on the ground that it is founded on a Community directive which is not directly applicable in national law and incompatible with the legal principles in force under national law at the time of the decision.

The appellant further contends that the reasoning in the decision under challenge is flawed, in that the *Conciliatore*, while citing in general terms the Community regime governing so-called "doorstep sales" and referring to "equity", failed to indicate the actual *rule* of equity by reference to which he resolved the dispute. Moreover, without giving any reasons, he described as "oppressive" a contract freely subscribed to by Salustri, whose terms were formulated in the clearest of language and contained no provision **[1668]** incompatible with the guiding norms and principles of Italian law.

2. The Court finds that the appeal fails.

Under . . . Article 113 of the Code of Civil Procedure (as amended by Article 3 of Law No 399 of 30 July 1984), the *Conciliatore* must reach his decision in equity in compliance with the principles governing the area of law concerned. His decisions, while not subject to the normal process of appeal, may be challenged in cassation (CCP, Art. 339, final para.). However, in view precisely of the equitable nature of his jurisdiction, such a challenge may be founded only—apart from cases of procedural error—on a violation of the governing principles in question (as well as, *a fortiori*, on any breach of norms or principles of a constitutional nature). Thus no challenge may be made to the *choice* [emphasis added] of the equitable rule on the basis of which the *Conciliatore* reached **[1669]** his decision. Nor can his decision be attacked on grounds of misinterpretation of a rule of law expressly or implicitly held applicable in accordance with the principles of equity. Since a decision in equity is, by its very nature, dependent on the merits of the particular case, and is not susceptible of review for defects *in iudicando* (see, *inter alia*, Court of Cassation, plenary Decisions Nos 6794 of 1991, *Foro italiano* 1991 I, 2717; 8883 of 1994, *idem*, *Repertorio* 1994, *Sentenza civile*, No 32; 9986 of 1994, *ibid.*, *Cassazione civile*, No 29; and 7545 of 1995, *idem*, *Massime*, 870) . . .

[After considering further the nature and scope of the *Conciliatore*'s equitable jurisdiction under Italian domestic law and the limits on its own power of review of his exercise thereof, the Court continued:]

3. In the present case the *Conciliatore* had to decide whether a consumer was bound by his acceptance of an offer for the sale of goods made to him at his home by a representative of the vendor company (a so-called "doorstep" sale). The *Conciliatore* settled the matter by applying a rule corresponding to that laid down in European Community Directive No 85/577 of 20 December 1985. The contract made no provision for a right of cancellation on the consumer's part whereas, under Articles 4, 5 and 6 of the said Directive, consumers in cases of this kind are entitled

to such a right, which cannot be excluded by the terms of the contract. The *Conciliatore* accordingly held that the contract was void: the consumer was not bound by his signature and was not obliged to pay the sum demanded of him by the vendor.

The rule of equity which the *Conciliatore* intended to apply in this case is thus clearly identifiable. As has already been pointed out, no standard formula is required. It is sufficient that, where the reasoning underlying the decision is questioned, it clearly emerges what precisely was the equitable ground on which it was based. In this case the *Conciliatore* clearly stated the equitable ground for his decision, namely the requirement of consumer protection deriving from the aforementioned Community regime governing "doorstep sales", by virtue of which, *inter alia*, contracts are deemed void where they do not include a provision giving the purchaser a period following signature during which he may exercise a right of cancellation. The *Conciliatore*'s further findings with regard to the "oppressive" nature of the contract and the assurances given to the consumer at the time of signature of the contract are of minor relevance, for his decision was based primarily on the rule contained in the Community Directive—applied as a principle of equity—pursuant to which a contract that fails to give the consumer a right of cancellation is invalid.

The appellant's challenge to the decision is founded essentially on the fact that, at the time when it was made, the Community Directive had not yet been incorporated into Italian law, and accordingly could not be invoked in order to settle a dispute arising out of a relationship governed solely by Italian law, which at that time provided to the contrary. **[1670]** It is perfectly true that Community Directive No 85/577 was incorporated into Italian law only by Decree-Law No 50 of 15 January 1992, and hence at a time subsequent to the signature of the contract at issue in this case, to which the new law could not apply, since it had not been endowed with retroactive effect. It is also true, as the European Court of Justice held in its Judgment of 14 July 1994 in Case 91/92[3] (*idem* 1995 IV, 38), that, while the provisions of the Directive were unconditional and sufficiently precise, they were not directly applicable under the national law of Member States because they dealt with relations between private parties (so-called "horizontal relations"), and this remained the case until national implementing provisions were adopted. Hence, as the Judgment also made clear, in the absence of such implementing provisions, an individual consumer could not invoke the Directive in order to claim a right of cancellation in respect of a contract concluded by him with a private trader.

In cases similar to the present one, this Court has applied that principle, ruling that consumers could not benefit from any right of cancellation

[[3] *Ibid.*, p. 19 at p. 41.]

prior to the adoption in Italy of the aforementioned Decree-Law No 50 of 1992 (see [Cassation] Decisions Nos 2275 of 1995, *idem* 1995, *Massime*, 298; and 5289 of 1995, *ibid.*, 638). And there would be no reason to depart from that approach if the decision now before us were one founded exclusively in law, for it is undeniable that, in terms solely of the rules of contract law deriving from the Civil Code, a person who accepts a contractual offer without reservation remains bound by the obligation to perform the duties arising under the contract thus concluded and hence, subject to such exceptions as are specifically provided by law, cannot be released from that obligation save by mutual consent (Article 1372, Civil Code, first paragraph).

However, as we have repeatedly pointed out, the *Conciliatore*'s decision was founded not in law but in equity. Thus the fact that the principle applied by him in order to resolve the particular dispute before him is not consistent with the rules of law laid down in the Code is not of itself sufficient to justify annulment of the decision under challenge. On the contrary, what we have to ask ourselves is whether the equitable principle on which the *Conciliatore* based his decision was compatible not with one or more specific rules of law in force at the relevant time, but with the overall principles governing that particular area of the law. These may not necessarily accord with the regime imposed by individual legal norms. Rather, they are identifiable solely by reference to the guidelines established by the relevant legal institutions at the time in question, that is to say the time when the events with which the decision is concerned took place, since it is a general principle, not subject to exception save where specifically so provided, that new rules cannot be applied to pre-existing relationships.

Posed in these terms, the issue of the direct effect of Community directives in internal law has to be approached from a different standpoint. In effect, it should always be borne in mind that respect for international obligations is enshrined in the Constitution. It follows from this constitutional requirement that, even where directives which the Italian State is required to incorporate into domestic law cannot be invoked directly as rules of law governing relations between private citizens, they are not totally deprived of effect for purposes of domestic law—at least from the date prescribed for their implementation (the deadline for implementation of Directive No 577/85 was 23 December 1987). Evidence of this is provided by the fact that, certainly in terms of so-called "vertical relations" (that is, relations between the citizen and the public administration), it is now generally accepted that, where such directives contain clear and unconditional provisions, these are applicable immediately even where they have not yet been formally incorporated into national law. This approach is confirmed by the terms of the Judgment of the European Court of Justice cited above, where the Court made it clear that, in interpreting provisions of national law still in force, the courts of

Member States are under a duty to take account of Community directives whenever possible, even where these have not yet been transposed into national law.[4]

This is sufficient to enable us to state that, once the period for implementation of a directive has expired, then, even where the latter has not yet been formally incorporated into national law and cannot yet be applied directly **[1671]** to legal relations between private persons, it has nonetheless now been brought within the orbit of the domestic legal order [*inserita nel circuito giuridico nazionale*]. The effect of this is that henceforth the directive itself (independently of its subsequent transposition into national law) becomes one of the sources on which national law may draw, and thus cannot be disregarded for purposes of determining the guiding principles of the institutions governed by that law. And in fact the Directive on consumer protection with which we are here concerned is a good example of this. Thus it is apparent from the *travaux préparatoires* which preceded the relevant implementing law, and from the doctrinal commentaries on that law, that already in 1989 certain trade associations of firms operating in the home-sales sector, anticipating the Directive's incorporation into Italian law, had signed a memorandum of agreement establishing a uniform regime complying with the rules laid down in that Directive governing contracts concluded away from business premises. This is clear evidence that since that date those rules, and the requirement of consumer protection deriving therefrom, have been accepted as effectively compatible with the principles underlying the national legal corpus.

This conclusion finds further support from another quarter. It should not in effect be forgotten that, even before the entry into force of Decree-Law No 50 of 1992, other similar examples of the consumer's right to withdraw from a contract had already been introduced into Italian law: in particular by Article 18 *ter* of Law No 216 of 7 June 1974 (renewed in 1985), governing home sales of securities offered direct to the investing public. In relation to this provision the more perceptive of doctrinal writers had already distinguished the gradual emergence of a general principle of consumer protection, whereby the consumer was entitled to a right of cancellation in all cases of "doorstep sales" involving movable goods or securities wherever he was in a position of substantial contractual inferiority. This approach was subsequently confirmed by the terms of Article 8 of Law No 1 of 2 January 1991, governing financial management contracts.

Thus, in light of the foregoing, it can be persuasively argued in doctrine that it is no longer possible to rely on a uniform law of contract as laid down in the Code, there now being, in place of or in addition to the latter, a multiplicity of models, depending in each case on the status of the

[4 *Ibid.*, paragraph 26, p. 42.]

contracting party (for example: "consumer"), or on the circumstances in which the contract was concluded (for example: through acceptance of a "doorstep" offer), or on the subject-matter of the contract (for example: movable goods or securities), or on various combinations of these elements.

It follows that the principles governing a particular field of contract law—within whose parameters the *Conciliatore* is bound to remain in reaching his decision in equity—cannot be identified solely by reference to the general model laid down in the Code but must also take account of the specific contractual situation in question. Thus, in the case of contracts for the sale of goods between a commercial company and an individual consumer, signed in the latter's home, account must be taken of the principles of consumer protection inherent in the regime governing such contracts—as influenced by EEC Directive No 577/85 and by the specific legislation referred to above—even in respect of cases which arose before the entry into force of Decree-Law No 50 of 1992.

4. Applying this principle, we find that the *Conciliatore*'s decision withstands the appellant's grounds of objection.

The appeal is accordingly dismissed.

[Report: *Il Foro Italiano* 1996, p. 1665 (in Italian). Translated by T. F. K. Johnston, MA, LL B]

National constitutions — Constitutional challenge to legislation — Italian Constitution, Article 11 — Council Directive concerning recognition of professional qualifications — Alleged incompatibility with Constitution — Whether EC legislation subject to constitutional review

National constitutions — Fundamental rights — Italian Constitution, Articles 3 and 4—Possible conflict between provisions of Council Directive and the Constitution—Scope of jurisdiction of Constitutional Court—Limitation to cases of alleged conflict between fundamental constitutional rights or principles and EC treaty norms—Ultimate remedy of withdrawal from European Union

Supremacy — Conflict between Community law and national law—Consequences for contrary national law—Duty of national courts not to apply conflicting national provisions — Whether conflicting national provisions automatically inapplicable — Whether fundamental constitutional rights could take precedence over Community law

Institutions—Court of Justice—Powers—Jurisdiction under Article 177 of EC Treaty—Effect of judgments in national legal order—The law of Italy

TALAMUCCI *v.* MINISTER OF HEALTH

(Case No 1512/98)

Italy, Court of Cassation (Plenary Session). 13 *February* 1998

(La Torre, *President*)

SUMMARY: *The facts*:—Prior to 1978, the dental profession in Italy was unregulated and ordinary doctors could practise dentistry. Under EC Council Directives governing mutual recognition of qualifications enacted in 1978, special account was taken of this situation and transitional arrangements were made for Italy to enable it to establish a new training system for dentists. The new Community system came into force on 28 January 1980 and Article 19 of the Recognition Directive established transitional arrangements for Italy applicable to medical students who had begun their studies prior to 28 January 1980. However, an Italian law of 1988 extended the category of exceptions, beyond those contained in Article 19 of the Directive, to those enrolling on medical courses beginning up to and including 1984/85.

In a judgment of 1 June 1995, in proceedings brought by the European Commission against Italy (Case C-40/93), the Court of Justice of the European Community held that the new Italian Law created a category of dentists which was not provided for by the Directive and Italy was therefore in breach of its obligations under Community law. An Italian student sought to be inscribed on the Register of Dentists on the basis of qualification under the 1988 Law. The Central Commission of Dentists refused his application on the grounds that the Law had been held to be incompatible with the EC Directives in question and the judgment of the Court of Justice was binding on the Italian courts. The applicant appealed to the Court of Cassation, arguing that the decision of the Central Commission violated his fundamental constitutional rights to work and to equality of treatment. In its judgment the Court of Cassation took the opportunity to review the guidelines given by the Constitutional Court on the relationship between the national and Community legal orders and their respective courts.

Held:—The appeal was dismissed.

(1) The Italian and Community legal orders were separate and coordinated on the basis of the division of powers laid down in the Community Treaties. Within those areas in which the organs of the Community were competent, the Community rule took precedence over conflicting national rules. The direct effect of Community law in Italy was founded on Article 11(2) of the Constitution.

(2) A conflict between national provisions and Community rules did not render the latter invalid but rather led to their non-application. In other words, they could not be taken into account by the national courts in the resolution of the case at issue.

(3) Any judgment of the Court of Justice of the European Community, in which it applied or interpreted Community law, had the character under Article 164 of the EC Treaty of a declaratory statement of Community law, in which the Court of Justice authoritatively determined the significance of its judgment and the final effect, scope and content of its possible application. Its judgments thereby constituted a source of Community law with *erga omnes* application throughout the Community.

(4) The powers of constitutional review of the Constitutional Court did not apply to Community provisions, which were not part of the domestic legal order, and was only exercisable in relation to statutes implementing treaties whose application might provoke a violation of the fundamental principles of the Italian constitutional order or of inalienable human rights. In the event of an alleged conflict between a Community norm and fundamental constitutional principles, the national courts were required to examine, in order to determine whether or not a reference to the Constitutional Court was appropriate, whether the alleged conflict with the Constitution was potentially so serious as to justify the radical remedy of Italian withdrawal from the European Union.

The following is the text of the relevant part of the judgment of the Court:

The applicants challenged, before the Court of Cassation, a decision of the Central Commission of the Society of Medical and Dental

Surgeons denying them the right to be inscribed on the Register of Dentists . . .

By a Law No 471 of 31 October 1988, it was provided that graduates in medicine and surgery enrolled on courses in medicine and surgery in the academic years from 1980/81 to 1984/85 should be entitled to be inscribed on the Register of Dental Practitioners provided they exercised that right by 31 December 1991 . . .

The applicants criticized the decision being challenged in so far as it held that Law No 471 of 1988 could not be applied because it was in conflict with EC Council Directives Nos 686 and 687/1978, as the Court of Justice of the European Community had held in a judgment of 1 June 1995 in Case C-40/93.

The applicants argued that Law No 471/1988 had been enacted to avoid a disparity of treatment [between medical students enrolled prior to 1980/81 and those who had enrolled subsequently up until 1984/85].

They therefore argued that the application of Community law would lead to a violation of Article 3 of the Constitution since substantially similar situations would be treated in a dissimilar manner.

The applicants argued that the primacy of Community law over national law did not extend to fundamental principles of the State order such as the principles contained in Articles 3 and 4 of the Constitution . . .

[The applicants also argued that the application of the Community Directives in question would violate their constitutional right to work. The applicants had been admitted to a degree course in surgery and medicine for the academic year 1983/84 and sought to exercise the right to be admitted to the Register of Dental Practitioners under the 1988 Law, which had been held by the Court of Justice of the European Community in the above-mentioned judgment to be contrary to EC Council Directives 686 and 687/1978. The Court of Cassation analysed in detail the effect of various provisions of the Directives and continued:]

VI. The Court of Justice of the European Community, in a judgment of 1 June 1995 in Case C-40/93, held that

> By deferring, by Law No 471 of 31 October 1988, until 1984/1985, with regard to diplomas in medicine and surgery, the final date set in Article 19 of Council Directive 78/686/EEC of 25 July 1978, concerning the mutual recognition of diplomas, certificates and other evidence of the formal qualifications of practitioners of dentistry, the Italian Republic has failed to fulfil its obligations under that Article and under Article 1 of Council Directive 78/687/EEC of 25 July 1978 concerning the coordination of provisions laid down by law, regulation or administrative action, in respect of the activities of dental practitioners.

This ruling must be interpreted and applied in accordance with the standards laid down in the principles set out below, as elaborated in the doctrine and jurisprudence, in particular by the Constitutional Court, as it has enunciated both the relationship between the norms of national and Community law and the relationship between the Court of Justice of the European Community and the national courts.

A) The Italian and Community legal orders are separate and are coordinated on the basis of the division of powers laid down in the Treaties establishing the European Community, now known as the European Union (*cf.* Constitutional Court, 8 June 1984, Case No 170;[1] 11 July 1989, No 389;[2] and 18 April 1991, No 168[3]).

B) Within those areas in which the organs of the Community are competent, the Community rule takes precedence over any rule of national law.

The direct applicability of Community law in Italy is essentially founded upon . . . Article 11(2) of the Constitution which establishes that Italy "consents to those limitations of sovereignty necessary to international organizations for assuring peace and justice between nations" . . . (*cf.* the cases cited above and Constitutional Court, 27 December 1973, Case No 183).[4]

C) A conflict between national provisions and Community rules does not render the former invalid but rather leads to their disapplication or, in more precise terminology, to their non-application . . . (*cf.* Constitutional Court, Case No 168/1991, *loc. cit.*).

With this orientation, the Constitutional Court abandoned its original approach which had required a ruling that the Community rule abrogated the pre-existent national provision incompatible with it. This, in turn, had required a determination [by the Constitutional Court itself] that the offending national provision was unconstitutional by virtue of its violation of Article 11 of the Constitution (*cf.* Constitutional Court Cases Nos 232/1975[5] and 163/1977).

According to its more recent approach, however, the Constitutional Court has taken the position that the Community rule "did not abrogate or invalidate a provision of municipal law which was incompatible with it, but merely prevented that provision from being taken into consideration for the resolution of the case before the national judge" (*cf.* Constitutional Court Case No 170/1984)[6] . . .

D) The interpretation of Community law, with binding effect for all authorities (both judicial and administrative) of the Member States, is within the competence *ultra partes* of the Court of Justice.

According to the terms of Article 164 of the EC Treaty, the Court of Justice shall ensure that in the interpretation and application of the Treaty the law is observed. It is to be deduced from this provision that any judgment of the Court which applies or interprets a Community

[1 Volume 1, p. 642.]
[2 Volume 1, Note, p. 652.]
[3 Volume 1, Note, p. 667.]
[4 Volume 1, p. 629.]
[5 Volume 1, Note, p. 641.]
[6 Volume 1, p. 642 at p. 649.]

norm unquestionably has the character of a declaratory statement of Community law in the sense that the Court, as the competent interpreter of that law, authoritatively specifies the significance of its own judgments and thereby determines with final effect the scope and content of their possible application.

The Constitutional Court has previously held that

> The fundamental requirements of equality and legal certainty demand that Community provisions, which cannot be categorized as being derived from either international law, foreign law or municipal law, should have compulsory efficacy and direct application in all Member States, without the necessity for reception or adaptation, as acts having the force of law in every Member State of the Community, to the extent that they should enter into force everywhere simultaneously and receive equal and uniform application in all the States to which they are addressed. (Judgment of the Constitutional Court No 183 of 1973.)[7]

It follows from these principles that the judgments of the Court of Justice have the force of further sources of Community law, not as *ex novo* Community norms but rather as indications of the significance and limits of their application with *erga omnes* effect throughout the Community.

This effect has been recognized in relation to both preliminary rulings of the Court of Justice under Article 177 of the Treaty (judgment of the Constitutional Court No 113/1985)[8] and rulings in contentious proceedings brought under Article 169 of the Treaty (judgments of the Constitutional Court Nos 389/1989[9] and 168/1991).[10]

It is in the light of these premises that the consequences of the judgment of the Court of Justice of 1 June 1995 referred to above are to be determined for the purpose of resolving the present dispute.

The Court of Justice, as stated by the Republic of Italy, ruled that "by enacting by Law No 471 of 31 October 1988, deferring until the academic year 1984/1985 the final date set in Article 19 of the Council Directive concerning mutual recognition, with regard to diplomas in medicine and surgery, Italy has failed to fulfil the obligations incumbent upon it pursuant to that Article and Article 1 of the Directive concerning the coordination of provisions". Thereby the Court of Justice has determined that the Italian norm laid down in Law 471/1988 referred to above must be assumed to be inapplicable by the Italian administrative and judicial authorities.

The declaration that a Member State has failed to fulfil its Community obligations entails, for both the judicial and administrative authorities of the Member State in question, a prohibition having the full force of law against applying a national rule held to be incompatible with Community

[[7] Volume 1, p. 647.] [[8] Volume 1, Note, p. 652.] [[9] *Ibid.*]
[[10] Volume 1, Note, p. 667.]

law (Court of Justice of the European Community, 19 January 1993, Case C-101/91).

According to the Court of Justice, Italy has unlawfully created a new category of dentists (enrolled on courses in medicine after 28 January 1980) not permitted by the provisions of the Directive in question of 1978 . . .

The applicants' contention appears to be that the inapplicability of Law No 471/1988 and the consequent application of the Community norm referred to above would lead to a disparity of treatment between medical students enrolled prior to the academic year 1980/81 and those who enrolled subsequently up until 1984/1985, with the result that there would be a violation not only of Article 3 of the Constitution but also of Article 4, in so far as there would be a restriction on the right to work . . .

[This Court considers that] the proceedings brought by the applicants cannot succeed.

According to the principles stated above, the constitutional legitimacy of a Community norm cannot be referred to the Constitutional Court under Article 134 of the Constitution, which only gives the Constitutional Court competence to examine national or regional laws but not Community norms . . .

According to the Constitutional Court, the only question which may be referred is that of the legitimacy of statutes implementing treaties, where their application might provoke a violation of the fundamental principles of the Italian constitutional order or of inalienable human rights (*cf.* judgments of the Constitutional Court No 183/1973[11] and, in particular, No 232/1989 of 21 April 1989).[12]

Where the question raised involves an alleged conflict between a Community norm and the fundamental principles of the Italian Constitution, the national courts must examine, for the purpose of deciding whether it is appropriate to make a reference [to the Constitutional Court], because a plea of unconstitutionality is not manifestly unfounded, . . . whether the conflict appears to be so serious that the Treaty itself is in conflict with the Constitution, justifying the radical and disruptive remedy of the withdrawal of Italy from the European Union.

In this case, however, such an examination does not lead to this conclusion.

[The Court of Cassation examined the Directive at issue. The Court held that, in moving from the old regime to the new regime of recognition of dental qualifications, it was legitimate to fix time limits governing the application of each and that, in particular, the provisions of Article 19 of Directive No 686/78 were sufficiently precise to constitute the giving of proper notice, to new students enrolling in degree courses in medicine, that any degree obtained at the end of courses starting after

[11 Volume 1, p. 629.] [12 Volume 1, p. 653.]

28 January 1980 would not give them the automatic right to enrolment on the register of dentists. Accordingly there was no conflict between the provisions of the Directive and the constitutional rights to work and equality of treatment contained in Articles 3 and 4 of the Constitution. The application was dismissed.]

[Report: *Jiust. civ.*, 1998, I, p. 1935 (in Italian)]

Supremacy — Conflict between Community law and subsequent national law — Consequences for contrary national law—Duty of national courts not to apply national provision even if subsequently enacted

Direct effect—Treaty provisions—Articles 48 and 52 of EC Treaty—Whether conferring rights which may be relied upon by individuals before national courts

Legal order in general — Incorporation into national legal order—Nature of obligations undertaken by Member States under EC Treaty — Requirement of uniform application of Community law in Member States—Role of national courts in application of Community law—The law of Luxembourg

SOARES TEIXEIRA *v.* LE FOYER SA

Luxembourg, Court of Appeal (Civil). 2 *July* 1997

(Mousel, *President*; Have and Wivenes, *Judges*; Klopp, *Ministère Public*)

SUMMARY: *The facts*:—Soares Teixeira, a Portuguese national living in Luxembourg, was involved in a car accident in 1990 for which a Luxembourg court held he was solely responsible. Although he had lived in Luxembourg since 1988, he had failed to exchange his Portuguese driving licence for a Luxembourg licence, as required by a Luxembourg Regulation of 1982. In these circumstances the Luxembourg court held that, according to provisions of the Luxembourg Automobile Insurance Regulations, Soares Teixeira was to be regarded as not having been in possession of a valid driving licence at the time of the accident so that he was liable to indemnify his insurance company for any compensation payable by it as a result of the accident. Soares Teixeira appealed against the decision of the court, arguing that the provision in question was inapplicable since it violated the principle of the equality of European citizens before the law.

Held:—The Luxembourg Regulations at issue were inapplicable and the appeal was accordingly allowed.

(1) The national courts were the jurisdictions of ordinary law responsible for the application of Community law. It followed from the principles of the primacy and uniform application of Community law that a court of a Member State, seized of a dispute which raised questions of Community law, was required to ensure respect for the rules of Community law, and in particular the rules concerning the free movement of persons, services and capital.

(2) In accordance with the case-law of the Court of Justice of the European Community on Article 52 of the EC Treaty, the provisions of the Luxembourg

Automobile Insurance Regulations, which treated the failure to exchange a driving licence issued in Portugal within a prescribed time limit as equivalent to not holding a licence, thereby preventing the insured from relying on his automobile insurance, constituted discrimination based on nationality and an unjustifiable restriction on the freedom of movement of workers contrary to Article 48 of the EC Treaty, since the appellant was a worker within the meaning of that provision.

(3) According to the case-law of the Court of Justice, it followed from the principle of the supremacy of Community law that every court, seized with a case over which it was competent to exercise jurisdiction, had the obligation to apply Community law fully and to protect the rights conferred by it upon individuals by immediately setting aside any conflicting provision of national law.

The following is the text of the relevant part of the judgment of the Court:

[The Court summarized the course of the proceedings arising from an automobile accident. In a judgment of the Local District Court of 4 May 1994, Bernardino Soares Teixeira was held liable for the accident and ordered to indemnify his insurance company, Le Foyer, for the amount of damages awarded against him, on the ground that he had not been in possession of a valid driving licence on the date of the accident. Soares Teixeira appealed, both against the finding that he had been responsible for the accident and against the order that he should indemnify his insurance company. Le Foyer also appealed, seeking an increase in the amount of the indemnity payable to it by Soares Teixeira, in order to cover all amounts paid out to cover damage suffered by third parties as a result of the accident. The Court of Appeal dismissed the appeal against the finding that Soares Teixeira was liable for the accident and continued:]

On the appeal of Le Foyer against Bernardino Soares Teixeira

. . .

It appears from the documents submitted in the proceedings at first instance that Bernardino Soares Teixeira has lived continuously in Luxembourg since 15 February 1988.

It has been established that he failed to exchange his driving licence issued in Portugal for a Luxembourg licence prior to the accident on 31 August 1990, although the Regulations of the Grand Duchy of Luxembourg of 18 December 1982, which were applicable on the date of the accident, required such an exchange to take place within one year of the arrival of the person concerned in Luxembourg.

Pursuant to the provisions of Article 74 of the Traffic Code, Bernardino Soares Teixeira was to be regarded as not having been in possession of a valid driving licence on the date of the accident.

According to Section 21(f) of the General Conditions for civil liability insurance for automobile vehicles (1976), approved by the ministerial decrees of 23 July and 16 December 1976, which were applicable on the date of the accident and are identical to Section 11(2) of the General Conditions contained in the Regulations of the Grand Duchy of 20 December 1991, damage is not covered by the insurance policy where it is caused by a driver who does not hold a driving licence as required by the Regulations.

According to Section 21(2) of the General Conditions of 1976, which is identical to Section 11(2), last paragraph, of the General Conditions of 1991, this exclusion cannot be relied upon against the persons injured but the insurance company retains a right of indemnity against the insured.

Bernardino Soares Teixeira invokes the inapplicability of this provision on the ground that it infringes the principle of equality of European citizens before the law. According to the appellants, the holder of a valid Luxembourg driving licence who is resident in Portugal and has failed to exchange his driving licence [for a Portuguese licence] is covered by the law whereas the holder of a valid Portuguese driving licence resident in Luxembourg, who has failed to exchange his licence for a Luxembourg licence, runs the risk of not being covered by the law.

It is clear that the principle of non-discrimination on the grounds of nationality enshrined in Article 6 of the EC Treaty (formerly Article 7 of the EEC Treaty) and given concrete effect in the various provisions of the Treaty concerning the free movement of persons, in particular Article 48 on the freedom of movement of workers, requires that the Member States of the Community shall not treat the nationals of other Member States less favourably than their own nationals.

Furthermore, it is undisputed that Bernardino Soares Teixeira is a migrant worker within the meaning of Article 48 of the EC Treaty.

The principle of non-discrimination enshrined in Article 48 does not require a Member State of the Community to grant to a national of another Member State the same treatment as that accorded in the latter State to nationals of the former State.

The terms of comparison, with regard to the principle of non-discrimination, are not the treatment accorded in the various Member States to the nationals of other Member States, but rather the treatment accorded in each State to the nationals of other Member States in comparison with the treatment accorded to their nationals.

The national courts are the jurisdictions of ordinary law responsible for the application of Community law.

It follows from the principles of the primacy and uniform application of Community law, that a court of a Member State seized of a dispute which raises questions of Community law is required to ensure respect for the rules of Community law, and in particular the rules concerning the free movement of persons, services and capital (*cf.* judgment of the

Court of Justice of the European Community of 27 April 1994, *Almelo*, C-393/92, [1994] ECR 1477).

In these circumstances, the Court of Appeal must examine whether the Luxembourg Regulations, which treat the failure to exchange a driving licence issued in Portugal as equivalent to not holding a valid licence, with all the resultant consequences as far as automobile insurance is concerned, constitute direct or indirect discrimination on grounds of nationality or an unjustifiable restriction on the free movement of workers.

The Court of Justice of the European Community has held that "prior to the implementation of EEC Council Directive 91/439 of 29 July 1991 on driving licences (OJ, No 237, p. 1), Article 52 of the EC Treaty does not preclude a Member State from requiring the holder of a driving licence issued by another Member State to exchange that licence for a licence of the host Member State within one year of taking up normal residence in that State in order to remain entitled to drive a motor vehicle there" (judgment of the Court of Justice of the European Community of 29 February 1996, *Skanavi*, C-193/94, [1996] ECR I-929 at 953).

The Court of Justice also held however, in the same judgment, that in view of the resultant consequences which might arise in the national legal system in question, Article 52 of the Treaty "precludes the driving of a motor vehicle by a person who could have obtained a licence from the host State in exchange for the licence issued by another Member State, but did not make that exchange within the prescribed period, from being treated as driving without a licence and thus rendered punishable by imprisonment or a fine" (*loc. cit.*, p. 955).

That finding in relation to Article 52 of the Treaty, concerning the right of establishment of independent economic operators, is equally applicable to Article 48 concerning the freedom of movement of workers.

The Court of Justice justified this conclusion on the following grounds:

Under the provisions of EEC Council Directive 80/1263 of 4 December 1980 on the introduction of a Community driving licence (OJ 1980 L 375, p. 1), a driving licence issued by a Member State is recognized by the other Member States in which the holder is not normally resident and, for one year, also in the State in which he takes up normal residence.

Although the holder may be required to have his licence exchanged in order to remain entitled to drive motor vehicles within the territory of the host Member State after the expiry of the one-year period, his original licence remains valid in the Member State which issued it and continues to be recognized by the other Member States.

Member States may indeed refuse to exchange licences in certain circumstances expressly set out in the Directive, but that possibility cannot affect the entitlement of licence holders to have their licences exchanged if there are no such exceptional circumstances.

It follows that the issue of a driving licence by a Member State in exchange for a licence issued by another Member State does not constitute the basis of the right to drive a motor vehicle in the territory of the host State, which is directly conferred by Community law, but evidence of the existence of such a right. In those circumstances, the obligation to exchange driving licences which Member States may impose under the Directive is essentially a way of meeting administrative requirements (*loc. cit.*, p. 954).

The Court of Justice ruled, in the *Skanavi* judgment, that "Treating a person who has failed to have a licence exchanged as if he were a person driving without a licence, thereby causing criminal penalties even if only financial in nature . . . would also be disproportionate to the gravity of that infringement in view of the ensuing consequences" (*loc. cit.*, p. 955).

According to the Court of Justice, "a criminal conviction may have consequences for the exercise of a trade or profession by an employed or self-employed person, particularly with regard to access to certain activities or certain offices, which would constitute a further, lasting restriction of freedom of movement" (*loc. cit.*, p. 955).

This Court of Appeal considers that the conclusions drawn by the Court of Justice of the European Community from the EC Treaty, on the hypothesis that failure to exchange the driving licence within the requisite period would result in criminal penalties, are equally valid in these proceedings where the failure to exchange the licence gives rise, pursuant to the general conditions of automobile insurance contracts approved by the public authorities, to a right of action for the insurance company against the insured for an indemnity covering the whole of the loss for which the insurance company has paid compensation.

In fact, the central point of the reasoning of the Court of Justice is the finding that failure to exchange the driving licence cannot be treated as a failure to hold a licence.

The fact that, in the *Skanavi* judgment, the national law which is regarded as incompatible with the EC Treaty provided for criminal penalties is not decisive since consequences of a financial nature, such as those arising from the national regulations in the case at issue, are equally capable of constituting a significant restriction on the freedom of movement of workers.

According to the jurisprudence of the Court of Justice, it follows from the principle of the primacy of Community law that every court, seized with a case over which it is competent to exercise jurisdiction, has the obligation to apply Community law fully and to protect the rights conferred by it upon individuals by setting aside any conflicting provision of national law (judgment of 9 March 1978, *Simmenthal*, 106/77 [1978] ECR 629).[1]

[[1] Volume 1, p. 73.]

In these circumstances, the Court of Appeal holds that Section 21(f), in conjunction with Section 21(2), of the General Conditions of 1976 referred to above, which have been invoked by Le Foyer in support of its appeal against Bernardino Soares Teixeira, are inapplicable.

It is therefore necessary to amend the judgment under appeal on this point and to dismiss the appeal lodged against the insured by Le Foyer.

. . .

For these reasons . . .

[Order accordingly]

[Report: *Pas Lux* 1998, p. 458 (in French)]

Supremacy — Community law and subsequent national law—Whether national courts bound not to apply conflicting national provisions — Whether supremacy applies even where rule of Community law is not directly effective — Right of Council of European Community to confidentiality under its Rules of Procedure—Whether taking precedence over right of access to public documents under national law

Legal order in general — Special character — Nature of obligations undertaken by Member States under EC Treaty—Requirement of uniform application of Community law in Member States — The law of the Netherlands

METTEN *v.* MINISTER OF FINANCE

Netherlands, Council of State (Administrative Law Division). 7 *July* 1995

(Cleton, *President*; Lauwaars and Hoekstra, *Members*)

SUMMARY: *The facts*:—The appellant was a member of the European Parliament who sought to obtain access to the minutes of meetings of the Council of the European Community on Economics and Financial Affairs ("Ecofin Council") from the Netherlands' Minister of Finance, in reliance on the Dutch Act on Open Government. The Minister refused to give access, on the basis of the confidentiality clause in the Rules of Procedure of the Ecofin Council,[1] taking the view that the clause took precedence over the provisions of national law. The appellant challenged this decision before the Council of State.

Held (by the President of the Administrative Law Division and confirmed by the full Division):—The appeal was dismissed and a reference to the Court of Justice for a preliminary ruling was refused.

(1) The confidentiality clause in the Rules of Procedure of the Council of the European Community was a binding obligation which formed part of Community law, even though it was not enacted in one of the legislative forms provided for in Article 189 of the EC Treaty. As such, even though it was not directly effective, this clause took precedence over a conflicting rule of national law.

(2) The overriding requirement that Community law should be given uniform application in all Member States meant that it could not have been intended that the granting or refusal of access to EC Council documents should be dependent on the law of the Member State where access was requested. Under its Rules of Procedure, the Council of the European Community was given the right to waive the confidentiality of its documents, and the appellant should have

[1] The text of Article 18 of the Rules of Procedure appears at p. 403. It was replaced by Article 5 of the revised Rules of Procedure, which was the subject of several judgments of the Court of Justice of the European Community, including Case T-194/94, *John Carvel and Guardian Newspapers Ltd* v. *Council of the European Union*, 19 October 1995, [1995] ECR II-2765.

requested waiver by that body and, if necessary, he could then have made use of the possibilities of appeal provided for under the EC Treaty.

The following is the text of the decision of the Council of State:

In his decision of 2 October 1992 (No WJB 92/1250), the defendant Minister rejected the appellant's request, which was based on the provisions of the Act on Open Government, to provide him with access to the minutes of meetings of the Council of the European Communities (Economic and Financial Affairs: Ecofin Council).

The appellant lodged a notice of objection against this decision with the defendant on 23 October 1992. The defendant declared the objection unfounded in his decision No WJB 92/1365 of 9 December 1992. The appellant has lodged an appeal against this decision by notice of 7 January 1993, which was received at the Council of State on 8 January 1993. The defendant has lodged a notice of reply, which was received on 25 October 1993.

By notice of 8 December 1994, the appellant addressed himself to the President of the Division with the request to apply Article 107 of the Act on the Council of State to the decision of 9 December 1992.[2] In his decision of 6 February 1995, the President of the Division rejected the request to apply Article 107 of the Act on the Council of State. The case was heard at a public hearing of the Division on 1 June 1995, during which the appellant, in person and through his representative, and the defendant through his representatives, civil servants of the relevant Ministry, put forward their views. At the request of the appellant, Professor VerLoren van Themaat and Professor Curtin have also been heard in their capacity as expert witnesses.

In law

. . .

The appellant considers it desirable for the fulfilment of his duty as a Member of the European Parliament to become acquainted with the minutes of a number of meetings of the Ecofin Council which he has specified. The appellant bases himself on the view that the defendant has the obligation under the Act on Open Government (*WOB*) to provide him with access to these documents.

The appellant cannot agree with the view of the defendant that the *WOB* does not apply to the minutes of the meetings of the Ecofin Council because meetings of the Council of the European Community, under Article 18 of the Rules of Procedure of the Council, are subject to secrecy and because the doctrine of primacy of Community law over national

[[2] Article 107 of the Act provides for the possibility of a provisional order by the President of the Division in summary proceedings.]

law also applies to the Rules of Procedure. He is of the opinion that such primacy can be derived from the case-law of the Court of Justice of the European Community and the system of the EC Treaty only with respect to treaty provisions and acts of the Community's institutions, which have direct effect for the Member States and/or other natural or legal subjects. In this connection, the appellant has recourse to the acts enumerated in Article 189 of the EC Treaty, for which Articles 190 to 192 contain the necessary guarantees for proper law and administration. The appellant is of the opinion that primacy of the Rules of Procedure, over national acts of parliament which grant rights to citizens, could only exist if the Rules of Procedure had been established in the form of a regulation in the sense of Article 189 of the EC Treaty.

The appellant has proposed that the Division should seek a preliminary ruling on this issue from the Court of Justice. Finally, the appellant has also submitted that the provisions of the *WOB* itself, contrary to what the defendant has alleged, do not stand in the way of providing him with the information requested.

The President based his decision of 6 February 1995 on the following grounds:

The Council of the European Community was created by the Treaty establishing a single Council and a single Commission of the European Communities, the so-called Merger Treaty [1965]. Pursuant to Article 5 of this Treaty, the Council draws up its Rules of Procedure. At the time of the disputed decision, the Rules of Procedure in the version of 24 July 1979 applied.

Article 18 of these Rules provides as follows:

> Without prejudice to other applicable provisions, the deliberations of the Council shall be covered by the obligation of professional secrecy, except in so far as the Council decides otherwise.
>
> The Council may authorize the production of a copy or an extract from its minutes for use in legal proceedings.

The Court of Justice of the European Community has established in several judgments that the legal order of the European Community is an integral part of the legal systems of the Member States, and that precedence must be accorded to Community law over national provisions. In this connection, the judgments of 5 February 1963, No 26/62 (*Van Gend en Loos*) ECR [1963] 3;[3] 15 July 1964, No 6/64 (*Costa* v. *ENEL*) ECR [1964] 585[4] and 9 March 1978, No 106/177 (*Simmenthal*) ECR [1978] 629[5] may be mentioned.

Not only the treaties establishing the European Community, but also acts of the institutions, are part of Community law. The Rules established by the Council of the European Community, on the basis of Article 5

[[3] Volume 1, p. 27.] [[4] Volume 1, p. 50.] [[5] Volume 1, p. 73.]

of the Merger Treaty, amount to such an act and are therefore part of Community law. The provisions contained in those Rules in any case, in so far as the Member States are bound to them, therefore take precedence over national provisions.

The Council of State, taking into account the documents in the file and the public hearings, finds no reason to depart from the views of the President. This conclusion is based on the following grounds:

The primacy of Community law is one of the essential characteristics of the Community legal order. According to *Costa* v. *ENEL*, the law of the Treaty, which flows from an autonomous source, cannot be set aside by any provision of national law "without being deprived of its character as Community law and without the legal basis of the Community itself being called into question". The Court added that later unilaterally promulgated legislative measures which are incompatible with the "concept of the Community" cannot prevail (1964 ECR 594).[6]

In its judgment of 13 February 1969 (*Walt Wilhelm and Others* v. *Bundeskartellamt*, No 14/68, 1969 ECR 1) the Court of Justice based this view on the following grounds:

> [T]he EEC Treaty has established its own system of law, integrated into the legal systems of the Member States, and which must be applied by their courts. It would be contrary to the nature of such a system to allow Member States to introduce measures capable of prejudicing the practical effectiveness of the Treaty. The binding force of the Treaty and of measures taken in application of it must not differ from one State to another as a result of internal measures, lest the functioning of the Community system should be impeded and the achievement of the aims of the Treaty placed in peril.

In this context, the Court referred to the principle that Community law takes precedence (1969 ECR, 14-15).

In the second *Simmenthal* judgment the Court said that "if national measures which encroach upon the field within which the Community exercises its legislative power or which are otherwise incompatible with the provisions of Community law had any legal effect, that would amount to a corresponding denial of the effectiveness of obligations undertaken unconditionally and irrevocably by Member States pursuant to the Treaty and would thus imperil the very foundations of the Community" (1978 ECR 643, paragraph 18).[7]

The Council of State concludes from this case-law that the principle of primacy of Community law also holds for provisions which are not directly effective.

Specifically with respect to the Rules of Procedure, the Council of State holds that these are binding, at least as regards the obligation

[6 Volume 1, p. 50 at p. 67.]

[7 Volume 1, p. 73 at p. 100.]

of secrecy under Article 18 of those Rules, notwithstanding the fact that they are not given the form of one of the instruments of Article 189, first to fourth paragraphs, of the EC Treaty. In the light of the aim of ensuring the uniform effect of Community law in all Member States, it cannot have been the intention that the granting or refusal of permission to have access to documents of the Council be dependent on the law of the Member State where the request for such access is filed. Otherwise, it would detract from the full effect [*effet utile*] of the provision at issue. This is a principle which forms one of the bases of the primacy of Community law, as is apparent from the judgment in the *Walt Wilhelm and Others* v. *Bundeskartellamt*, quoted above. The Council of State also refers to the judgment of 23 February 1988, in the so-called *Hormones Case* (*United Kingdom* v. *Council*, No 68/86, 1988 ECR 855). Although this case concerned another provision of the Rules of Procedure (Article 6, first paragraph), which provides that the Council can take decisions in urgent matters by means of a written vote when all members of the Council agree to that procedure in the relevant case, the Council of State attaches importance to the express statement that the Council has the obligation to abide by this procedural rule. The Court of Justice added that the Council cannot depart therefrom without formally changing the Rules of Procedure which are an act based on Article 5 of the Merger Treaty (*loc. cit.* 902 paragraph 48). The Advocate General referred in his conclusion in this case expressly to the purpose and intention of the relevant rule (*loc. cit.* 884).

By way of *obiter dictum*, the Council of State points to the competence which Article 18 of the Rules of Procedure vests in the Council to waive the obligation of secrecy. The appellant could have requested the Council for a copy or an abstract of the minutes of the meetings of the Ecofin Council, and could have made use of the possibilities for appeal provided in the EC Treaty in the event of a refusal.

As to the appellant's view that the Rules of Procedure have only internal effect and are therefore not directly effective, the Council of State does not feel obliged to make a decision as it has been established above that provisions of Community law which are not directly effective also take precedence over national law, while the secrecy clause binds the members of the Council and hence the State.

Having regard to the above considerations the judges of the Council of State hold that, on the basis of the Community secrecy clause, the defendant rightfully rejected the request of the appellant for access to the minutes of the meeting of the Ecofin Council, based on the *WOB*. The Council of State does not find that there is any reason to put a preliminary question on this issue to the Court of Justice.

As it is apparent that the decision being challenged does not require annulment on one of the grounds of Article 8, first paragraph, of the Administrative Decisions Appeals Act, the appeal must be dismissed.

Decision

The Division of Administrative Justice of the Council of State, rendering judgment in the name of the Queen, dismisses the appeal.

[Report: *Maastricht Journal of European and Comparative Law* 1996, p. 179 (English translation reproduced with permission)]

NOTE.—Pursuant to the Amsterdam Treaty, Article 255 (formerly Article 191a) has been inserted in the EC Treaty and provides for a new Treaty-based right of access to the documents of EC institutions. It has been argued that the effect of this provision, when read in conjunction with Article 1 of the Treaty on European Union, is that EC law cannot detract from the *status quo* so far as national laws on the right of access are concerned and that consequently the *Metten* case would be decided differently today (Curtin, Citizens' Fundamental Right of Access to EU Information, CML Rev 2000, p. 7 at p. 15).

Direct effect — Directives — Conditions for direct effect — Failure of Member State to implement provisions of directive by specified time—EC Treaty, Article 189—Whether directive may be relied upon by individuals before national courts—Whether provisions sufficiently precise and unconditional—Directive conferring margin of discretion on Member States—Council Directive 79/409—Conservation of wild birds—The law of Portugal

League for Environmental Protection *v.* Council of Ministers

(Case No 31.535)

Portugal, Supreme Administrative Court (First Section). 14 *March* 1995

(Vaz Rebordão, *President*)

Summary: *The facts*:—The League for Environmental Protection appealed against a decision of the Portuguese Council of Ministers concerning the location of a new bridge over the estuary of the River Tagus. They argued that the decision infringed Article 4(4) of EC Council Directive 79/409 on the Conservation of Wild Birds, which required Member States to establish Zones of Special Protection within which activities with a potential to cause harm to resident wild birds would be prohibited. The deadline for Portugal to implement the Directive into domestic law expired in April 1988. Shortly thereafter, the Portuguese Government announced the creation of various zones of special protection, including one in the Tagus Estuary Region, which was considered an important wetland area. But the designation of the zones was not followed by legal regulation.

The appellants argued that Article 4(4) of the Directive was applicable and could be relied upon by individuals, on the basis of the doctrine of vertical direct effect, since the period for its implementation had expired and the rule it contained was clear, precise and unconditional. The appellants argued that the construction of the bridge would result in significant deterioration in the habitat of the protected birds and cause them harm, thereby infringing Article 4(4). The Government replied that the announcement of the creation of zones was a declaration of intent without legal consequences and the provision of the Directive relied upon was insufficiently precise to have direct effect.

Held:—The decision of the Council of Ministers did not infringe the Directive and the appeal was dismissed.

(1) In accordance with the jurisprudence of the Court of Justice, the provisions of Community directives could have direct effect and be relied upon by individuals once the time limit for their implementation into municipal law had expired, provided the provision relied upon was sufficiently clear, precise and unconditional.

(2) Article 4(4) of the Directive at issue imposed a duty on the Member States to take measures to avoid environmental damage and disturbance which might have a "significant effect" on the objectives of the Article. But the Member States retained a broad margin of discretion in determining what factors might be taken into account in contributing to such a "significant effect", which was a vague and indeterminate concept and certainly did not prohibit all activities with a potential to harm wild birds. The provision in question was therefore insufficiently clear and precise to have direct effect.

The following is the text of the judgment of the Court:

The League for Environmental Protection appeals against the decision of the Council of Ministers, taken at a meeting of 13 August 1992, by which it approved Law No 220/92 of 15 October, which provides, in Section 1, under the heading "Location of new bridge over the Tagus":

It is confirmed that the new bridge over the Tagus will be situated between the areas of Samouco, in the district of Alcochete, and Sacavem, in the district of Loures, in accordance with the terms of the Annex, which forms an integral part of this document.

Submissions of the Parties

The Appellant states that 2 April 1979 saw the publication of European Community Directive 79/409/EC, the objective of which was the conservation and protection of wild birds common to the territory of the European Community. It imposed upon Member States the duty to implement a series of measures designed to fulfil that objective, the most prominent of which was the obligation of each Member State to set up protected areas, known as "Zones of Special Protection" ("the Zones"), in which Member States would be under a duty to prohibit any type of activity which might cause harm to the wild birds actually living there.

Following the accession of Portugal and Spain to the European Community, Council Directive 86/122/EC added a new Annex to Directive 79/409/EC, containing the Spanish and Portuguese names for the relevant wild birds. The Directive entered into force in Portugal on 8 April 1986.

From that date onwards Portugal had a period of two years to bring into force the legislative, regulatory and administrative measures necessary in order to comply with the Directive. Despite this, Law No 75/91, intended to give effect to Directive 79/409/EC in Portuguese law, was restricted to imposing limitations on the suppression and commercialization of wild birds, and only made provision for the creation of the Zones at some future date.

Ultimately, in view of the fact that the two-year deadline period for the implementation of the Directive had elapsed, and keen to avoid putting itself in a position of non-compliance, the Portuguese Government, by a Dispatch of 30 April 1988 from the then Secretary of State for the Environment and Natural Resources, drawn up on the basis of information received from the National Service for Parks, Reserves and the Conservation of Nature, set up 18 Zones. This was without prejudice to the subsequent enactment *ab initio* of legislation designed to apply the Directive.

The Portuguese Government then proceeded to classify the Zones but failed to define which legal regime was applicable to them. Nevertheless this does not mean that the Zones are unregulated by law, in view of the fact that their origin is Article 4(4) of Directive 79/409/EC, which can be directly invoked by private individuals in each Member State, given the theory of vertical direct effect and the fact that the rule is clear, unconditional and complete.

One of the Portuguese Zones is situated in the Tagus Estuary Region, which is considered one of the most important wetland areas in Europe from the viewpoint of the conservation of wild aquatic birds, and is used by tens of thousands of birds annually for the purposes of feeding, shelter and nesting.

Of considerable importance as areas for food and shelter are the salt pans, including those which continue to be exploited and those which have been abandoned. The Samouco salt complex is particularly important. But they all provide important nesting sites for numerous species of birds. Furthermore, the type of vegetation which exists in the Tagus Estuary Zone is preferred by a large number of species for the purpose of shelter and refuge during the winter months.

Of the tens of species of wild birds which are to be found in the Tagus Estuary Zone, a significant number are listed in Annex 1 of Directive 79/409/EC, and as such are the object of special protection.

The richness and diversity of bird life in the Tagus Estuary Zone arises from the biological potential of the region which is closely dependent on the surrounding conditions characterized, on the edge of the Tagus, by a low density of human population.

The construction of a new bridge over the River Tagus, whose location is approved by the Law at issue and which will cut across the entire length of the Tagus Estuary Zone, will inevitably result in the significant deterioration of existing habitats and the consequent disturbance of protected birds, all of which would be a clear infringement of Article 4(4) of Directive 79/409/EC.

The results of the construction work would be as follows: The Samouco salt complex, which lies at the point where the bridge will meet the south bank of the river, would be completely destroyed. The upheaval necessary for the laying of the foundation structures would provoke movement of sediments on the river bed, giving rise to resuspension phenomena. The concentration of solids on the surface of the water, many of which are highly toxic, in addition to the foreseeable use of pollutant substances in the construction work, would give rise to unfavourable alterations in water quality, which would in turn provoke the disappearance of an incalculable number of dependent living organisms and bring about alterations in the birds' food chain.

The danger that the existing habitats would be destroyed also emerges, more seriously, from the great changes which would occur in the type of human activity practised in the Zone, such as the restructuring and re-ordering of urban and rural areas resulting in a reduction in air quality arising from the consequent increase in pollution levels.

The Appellant also alleges that the act complained of violates legislation regulating environmental impact assessment which requires the Ministry of Public Works, Transport and Communications to make an evaluation of environmental impact for submission to the Ministry for the Environment. The Ministry for the Environment ought then to nominate an entity with responsibility for drawing up a report, so that a public enquiry can be commenced. This procedure was in no way observed, thereby constituting a breach of Sections 3(1) and (3) of Law No 186/90 of 6 June 1990 and Article 2 of Regulatory Decree No 38/90 of 27 November 1990; Sections 3(2) and (4) of Law No 186/90 and Article 3 of the Regulatory Decree; and Article 4(6) of Regulatory Decree No 38/90 and Section 5 of Law No 186/90.

In reply the Respondent defended its decision and denied the existence of a Zone in the Tagus Estuary, alleging that the Dispatch from the Secretary of State for the Environment and Natural Resources of 30 April 1988 was a preparatory act in the process leading to the future establishment of the Zones. It also denied the direct applicability of the rule contained in Article 4(4) of Directive 79/409/EC on the basis that the direct applicability of directives, prior to their incorporation into domestic law, depends upon whether they are, of themselves, prescriptive, complete, self-executing, precise and unconditional. The rule in question possessed none of these characteristics. The Respondent denied any infringement of that rule on the grounds that the act complained of is not an activity directly linked to the deterioration of the habitats and the disturbance of the birds. The construction of a bridge could never be regarded as such an activity and is, furthermore, a project whose object is to promote the greater public interest, a more valuable goal than that envisaged by the implementation of the prohibitions contained in the Directive.

Finally, the Appellant alleges a failure to abide by the formalities relative to the process of evaluating environmental impact, arguing that the applicable administrative procedure does not apply to a matter *sub judice* such as the approval of the location of the new bridge over the Tagus.

The Appellant maintains its original position and formulates the following conclusions:

In view of the content of the present allegations and the notice of appeal, it is concluded that the decision of the Council of Ministers regarding the location of the new bridge over the Tagus violated the following legal rules:

a) Article 4(4) of Directive 79/409/EC;
b) Sections 3(1) and (3) of Law No 186/90 of 6 June and Article 3 of Regulatory Decree No 38/90 of 27 November;
c) Sections 3(2) and (4) of Law No 186/90 and Article 3 of Regulatory Decree 38/90;
d) Article 4(6) of Regulatory Decree 78/90;
e) Section 5 of Law No 186/90.

The Respondent challenges the appeal and defends its previous actions.

Opinion of the Advocate-General of the Ministry of Public Affairs, attached to the Supreme Court

We would accept the Respondent's denial of the allegations made against it, on the following grounds:

—the inexistence of a Zone of Special Protection in the Tagus Estuary;
—the fact that Directive 79/409/EC is not directly applicable;
—and the observance of the proportionality principle regarding the decision as to the location of the new bridge.

On the other hand it is impossible to argue, in our opinion, that the construction of the bridge can be excluded from that category of projects which ought to be subjected to the Environmental Impact Evaluation process. It is unquestionable that Law No 186/90 of 6 June subjects the construction of motorways, expressways and main roads to prior environmental impact evaluation.

The type of bridge which would be built across the Tagus is naturally going to be incorporated within an expressway or motorway and should therefore be the subject of an environmental impact study either separately or in the wider context of the road system of which it forms a part.

Having said that, we accept that it is not the location decision process which ought to be subjected to the Environmental Impact Evaluation, but the actual construction itself or, at least, the planning phase of the construction project. We therefore agree with the Respondent on the facts before us, having found that there has been no infringement of procedural formalities. Furthermore, the reports, on pages 120-5 and 137-72, do not portray the bridge, of itself, as being a cause of significant damage, in that there is no proof that it would destroy wetland habitats and cause significant damage to the salt pans.

According to the first report, the impact of the bridge on the north bank is considered negligible and in relation to the south bank it is made clear that "the most serious negative effects will certainly be linked to the structural influences of the area and to the human activities in the south bank sector" with the encroachment of urban influence upon those areas of greatest ecological value on the left bank of the estuary. This is a problem to be safeguarded against at the planning stage of the bridge project and is only indirectly caused by the bridge.

We would therefore recommend that this appeal be dismissed.

GROUNDS OF THE JUDGMENT

The Facts

a) The Appellant is an association for the protection of the environment registered on the National Register of Associations for the Protection of the Environment, at the National Institute of the Environment.

b) Council Directive 86/122/EC of 8 April 1986, pursuant to the accession of Spain and Portugal to the EC, added a new annex to Directive 79/409/EC, which contains the names, in Spanish and Portuguese, of the wild birds which the Directive seeks to protect.

c) Directive 86/122/EC came into force in Portugal on 8 April 1986 and Portugal had two years to bring into force the legislative, regulatory and administrative rules necessary to comply with it.

d) The Permanent Representative of Portugal attached to the European Community addressed a communication dated 28 December 1987, to the Foreign Minister, concerning the application of Directive 79/409/EC in Portugal . . .

e) The National Service for Parks, Reserves and Nature Conservation drew up a Memorandum of 1 March 1988 which, in fulfilment of Article 4 of Directive 79/409/EC, proposed *inter alia* the establishment of a Zone of Special Protection for the Tagus Estuary.

f) Regarding that information document the Secretary of State for the Environment and Natural Resources sent the following dispatch dated 30 March 1988: "Seen. I agree. To be considered by His Excellency the Secretary of State for European Integration, for fulfilment of Community obligations."

. . .

h) The above Dispatch was brought to the attention of the Secretary of State for European Integration by a communication dated 31 March 1988.

. . .

l) Law No 14-A/91 of 9 January established the Committee for the Crossing of the Tagus in Lisbon (GATTEL), whose principal mandate was the "performance, coordination and control of activities necessary for the promotion of the construction and use of the second Tagus road crossing in the Lisbon Region".

m) In September 1991 GATTEL drew up a document entitled "Evaluation of the Routes—Conclusions and Recommendations", in which it suggested that the bridge solution ought to be adopted without indicating a clear preference for any of the crossing routes considered: Trafaria/Alges, Chelas/Barreiro or Olivais/Montijo.

n) The location of the new bridge across the Tagus was approved by the Council of Ministers, in the terms of Section 1 of Law No 220/92 of 15 June. It was decided that it should be situated between Samouco, in the district of Alcochete, and Sacavem, in the district of Loures.

In Law

Having outlined the facts it is important to define the scope of the appeal, which, as we have already seen, centres on the decision of the Council of Ministers, taken at a meeting of 13 August 1992, which approved the location of the new bridge over the Tagus, situated between Samouco, in the district of Alcochete, and Sacavem, in the district of Loures.

. . .

Leaving, for the moment, the question of whether the Portuguese State set up Zones of Special Protection in the Tagus Estuary in fulfilment of Directive 79/409/EC, it is first necessary to decide whether the Directive is effective within the domestic order so as to permit the appellant to invoke it as an obligation imposed on the State, failure to conform with which would render a decision illegal. In other words, it must be decided whether the provision contained in the Directive has direct effect.

Article 8(3) of the Constitution of the Republic of Portugal states:

> Rules enacted by the competent organs of international organizations of which Portugal is a member are directly effective in domestic law in so far as the constitutive treaties so provide.

Commenting on this constitutional rule, Gomes Canotilho and Vital Moreira, in *Constituicao de Republica Portuguesa Anotada*, 3rd edition, page 89, write that "this ought to be read in conjunction with Article 7(5) in the text of the third constitutional revision (1992), which introduced the clause detailing the division of powers necessary for the development of the European Union. It attempts to define one of the legal consequences (perhaps the most important) of membership of an organization of that type, namely, direct and immediate submission to the rules laid down by it, in accordance with the terms of the applicable governing treaties."

Caseiro Alves, in *Revista de Direito e Economia*, vol. 9, pp. 216-17, writes that "Article 8(3) grants direct application in the Portuguese legal order to all rules laid down by international organizations whenever direct application is expressly provided for in the applicable governing treaties. These are the only rules which will be directly applicable."

In other words, these are the only rules which will automatically come into force as part of domestic law. This is not to say that other rules, whose direct application is not expressly provided for, cannot in certain circumstances have direct effect even though they are not directly applicable in the strict sense. Nor does it allow the legislator, in bringing constitutional law into line with the rules of "international organizations" (which is, after all, the purpose of Article 8(3)), to deny direct applicability to any rules which have automatic direct effect.

Amongst the rules which can, in certain circumstances, have direct effect within the Member States of the Community, are directives. Fausto Quadros in *Direito das Comunidades Europeias e Direito Publico Internacional*, p. 420 *et seq.*, defines the concepts of "direct applicability" and "direct effect" in Community law. He states that "direct applicability" is expressly defined in Article 189 EC and signifies immediate entry into force independent of any legislative or administrative act. He also confirms that "direct effect" signifies the ability of private individuals to invoke a rule of Community legislation which does not benefit from direct applicability (i.e. directives and decisions) in the national courts in order to overturn the application of a domestic law rule, if the "nature, context and wording" of the Community rule so permits. Rules benefiting from this exception neither will be directly applicable nor will their contents have been implemented by any act of domestic law, whether legislative or administrative. "Direct effect" is not defined in the treaties, being derived from the jurisprudence of the European Court of Justice, with particular reference to directives.

The directive is defined in Articles 189 of the EC Treaty and 161 of the EEA Treaty as being an act which binds all Member States as to the result to be achieved, but leaves national governments the discretion as to the choice of form and methods. Thus, in principle, the "directive" only has legal effect as regards the relations between the Member States and is not, of itself, a normative act. It is executed by national governments by means of normative or individual acts. Furthermore, the directive is normatively characterized as being an incomplete act, requiring the intervention of national governments in order for its objectives to be achieved, and indeterminate, failing to specify the type of implementation which the national governments ought to adopt (see Pedro Malaquias, in *Directivas no Ordenamento Juridito Comunitario Europeus*, vol. 3, pp. 334 *et seq.*).

In this light it is legitimate to assume that national courts will not be able to recognize rights for individuals based on Community directives unless those rights arise from national rules adopted to give effect to the directive in the domestic order of the Member State (see Mota de Campos, in *Direito Comunitario,* vol. 2, 4th edition, p. 290).

That said, Community jurisprudence has come to hold the view that, provided that strict conditions are observed, the Community "directive" can produce immediate effects, susceptible to judicial scrutiny, within the legal sphere of private litigants. The first time the European Court addressed this matter was in its decision of 17 December 1970, Case No 33/70, *Spa SACE* ([1970] ECR 1213). It stated:

> A directive, the objective of which is to impose on a Member State a deadline for the implementation of a Community obligation, is not confined to relations between the Commission and that State, but also entails legal consequences of which both the other Member States concerned in its performance and individuals may avail themselves when, by its very nature, the provision establishing this obligation is directly applicable, as are Articles 9 and 11 of the Treaty.

This jurisprudence has been confirmed on several occasions. The reply to the question of whether a community "directive" can produce direct effects in favour of private litigants is to be found, for example, in the decision of 22 February 1990 in the *Busseni Case* ([1990] ECR I-495), in which the Court summarized the essential jurisprudence relevant to the matter in the following terms:

> According to the jurisprudence of the Court, where the Community authorities have, by means of a directive, placed the Member States under a duty to adopt a certain course of action, the effectiveness of such a measure would be diminished if private persons were prevented from relying upon it in proceedings before a court and national courts were prevented from taking it into consideration as an element of Community law. Consequently, a Member State which has not adopted the implementing measures required by the directive within the prescribed period may not plead, as against individuals, its own failure to fulfil the obligations which the directive entails. Thus, wherever the provisions of a directive appear, as far as their subject-matter is concerned, to be unconditional and sufficiently precise, those provisions may, in the absence of implementing measures within the prescribed period, be relied upon against any national provision which is incompatible with the directive or in so far as the provisions define rights which individuals are able to assert against the State.

Thus the current situation as regards Community "directives" may be summed up as follows: The general rule is that in all cases in which a directive is correctly adopted within domestic law, private litigants can take advantage of its effects without needing to examine whether the provision as adopted into domestic law meets the conditions to which it would otherwise be subordinated. In the case of a directive which has not been correctly implemented by the Member State, private litigants may sometimes also have the right to invoke it before the national courts.

In all cases in which the provisions of a directive are, from the point of view of their contents, unconditional and sufficiently precise, they can be invoked, in the event of measures of application not having been taken within the due period, against any national provision which does not conform with the directive, or if the directive produces rights which an individual wishes to protect as against the national government.

Thus, direct effect is dependent on the existence of a series of conditions, namely:

1) that the period specified for the adoption of the domestic implementation measures has expired;
2) that the Member State has failed to adopt the aforesaid measures or has adopted rules which do not conform with Community requirements;
3) that the wording of the directive, on the basis of its contents, can be considered unconditional and sufficiently precise and clear.

As Mota de Campos writes, *loc. cit.*, p. 288, "a perfectly clear precise and unconditional obligation is, of itself, capable of giving rise to rights beneficial to private litigants since its application in a given, concrete situation may substitute for the failure of a Member State to adopt domestic implementation measures".

Given these principles, it is important to analyse whether Article 4(4) of Directive 79/409/EC can be relied upon by the Appellant as providing the basis of a contentious appeal against the decision of the Council of Ministers as to the location of the new bridge over the Tagus, situated on land classified as a Zone of Special Protection.

Before proceeding any further it should be noted that Law No 75/91 of 14 February, which refers in its preamble to the adoption of Directive 79/409/EC concerning the conservation of wild birds, as adapted to the accession of Portugal by Directive 86/122/EC, purports in Section 1 to establish measures for the protection of birds, nests and eggs and the safeguard of applicable habitats, but ignores the matters referred to in Article 4(4) of the Directive which states:

> Member States shall take adequate measures to avoid the pollution or deterioration of habitats in the Zones of Protection referred to in Sections 1 and 2 and other disturbances which affect the birds, since they may have a significant effect on the objectives of this Article. Member States shall also have regard to the avoidance of pollution or the deterioration of habitats outside the Zones of Protection.

The failure to adopt this provision into domestic law gives rise to a situation in which the Appellant may be able to invoke the Directive itself in order to overturn the decision of the Council of Ministers. However, it is first necessary to have regard to the necessary requirements and, in particular, to verify whether the contents of the provision are unconditional and sufficiently precise.

The purpose of Article 4(4) of the Directive is the avoidance of the pollution or deterioration of the habitats and other disturbances which affect the birds both inside and outside the established Zones of Special Protection, Member States being obliged to take adequate measures to this effect.

That said, such obligations are only imposed on the Member States to the extent that pollution, deterioration of habitats or other disturbances which affect the birds may have a "significant effect" on the objectives laid down in the rule, which states: "The species mentioned in Annex 1 are the object of special conservation measures with regard to their habitat, so as to permit their survival and reproduction in their distribution area."

Consequently, the desired objective does not have a precise and unconditional character, in the sense that the provision does not specify which activities and situations capable of causing pollution, deterioration of habitats and disturbances constitute the "significant effect" alluded to by the rule.

The Member States therefore have a broad margin of discretion as to which factors may satisfy the concept of "significant effect", requiring consideration of the diverse general interests likely to be affected by the creation of a Zone of Special Protection and the implementation of the Directive in other non-Zonal areas which contain habitats of the birds mentioned in Annex 1 of the Directive.

Accordingly, and contrary to the argument of the Appellant, the rule does not result in the condemnation of all activities which may potentially give rise to the disturbance of the wild birds, but only those activities having "significant effect", a vague and indeterminate concept which causes the rule to lack precision in its content, not being sufficiently precise and unconditional to permit this Court to conclude that the decision of the Council of Ministers violates the aforementioned rule of the Directive.

Article 4(4) of the Directive is not, in terms of content, an unconditional and sufficiently precise provision. It is therefore not directly effective, is not breached, and the first group of allegations are consequently inapplicable.

The Appellant further alleges that the decision as to the location of the new bridge over the Tagus infringed [various provisions of domestic law concerning the procedure for obtaining an environmental impact assessment].

[The Court examined the legislative provisions governing the administrative procedure for obtaining an environmental impact assessment and concluded that they applied only to the approval of the construction phase of any project and not to the approval of the location. The Court therefore concluded that the further grounds of appeal were inadmissible and dismissed the appeal.]

[Report: *Acórdãos Doutrinais do Supremo Tribunal Administrativo* 1996, p. 826 (in Portuguese)]

NOTE.—In a subsequent judgment of 22 June 1999, the Supreme Administrative Court recognized the so-called "vertical" direct effect of various provisions of EC Directive 93/37 on procedures for the award of public works contracts because they had not been correctly transposed into national law. The President of the National Assembly had awarded a contract for the completion of an extension to its building to a competitor of the applicant, who sought the annulment of the decision on the basis that the national legislation providing the basis for the decision failed to transpose the requirements of the Directive concerning criteria for the assessment of tenders correctly. Referring expressly to the principle of the supremacy of Community law, the Court held that this implied that the direct effect of incorrectly transposed provisions of a directive should be recognized if they were clear, complete, precise and unconditional. The Court therefore quashed the decision being challenged on the ground that it violated the provisions of the Directive relied upon (*National Assembly Works Contract Case* (Nos 44.140, 44.147), *Acórdãos Doutrinais do Supremo Tribunal Administrativo* 1999, p. 1380 (in Portuguese)).

Direct effect—Treaty provisions—EC–Morocco Cooperation Agreement, 1976, Article 41 — Whether capable of creating rights which may be relied upon by individuals — Criteria for determining which treaty provisions have direct effect — Applicability in proceedings concerning unemployment rights

National constitutions — Fundamental rights — Spanish Constitution, Article 14 — Right to non-discrimination on grounds of nationality — EC–Morocco Cooperation Agreement, Article 41(1) — Relationship between Community treaty norms and fundamental rights under national constitution—The law of Spain

Moroccan Seaman Case

(Case No 130/95)

Spain, Constitutional Court. 11 *September* 1995

SUMMARY: *The facts*:—The appellant, a Moroccan seaman employed by a Spanish company, applied for constitutional protection, alleging that he had been discriminated against on grounds of nationality, in decisions of both the administrative authorities and the lower Spanish courts which had denied him the right to Spanish unemployment benefit. He argued that this violated his right to equality of treatment enshrined in Article 14 of the Spanish Constitution.

Held:—The appeal was allowed and the decisions being challenged were quashed.

Article 41(1) of the EC–Morocco Cooperation Agreement gave Moroccan workers the right to non-discriminatory treatment in the field of social security by comparison with nationals of the Member State where they were employed. In accordance with the case-law of the European Court of Justice, this provision had direct effect within the Community since it contained a clear and precise obligation which was not subject in its implementation or effects to the adoption of any subsequent measure by the Member State. The denial of unemployment benefit in the circumstances of this case therefore violated the right to equality of treatment enshrined in Article 14 of the Constitution.

The following is the text of the relevant part of the judgment of the Court:

1. The appellant, a Moroccan national, worked as a crewman for the Spanish company Fanbar SA. His application for unemployment benefit was rejected by both the Navy Social Fund and the Social Security Tribunals and he invokes those decisions to show that those bodies have

discriminated against him on account of his nationality. He therefore appeals to enforce his right to equality of treatment in accordance with Article 14 of the Constitution.

This raises the question of the applicability of Article 14 to a foreign worker in relation to social security benefits, particularly unemployment benefits, on the basis that the applicant claims that he has been the victim of unequal treatment by comparison with Spanish nationals working in the same company. He bases this proposition on the fact that, like them, he worked regularly, was in possession of the necessary administrative authorization and paid contributions towards social security, including unemployment benefit. Nevertheless, both the Superior Court of Justice of Valencia and a lower court upheld administrative decisions refusing the appellant unemployment benefit on termination of his contract of employment with the company, by reason of the fact that the Treaty on Social Security between Spain and the Kingdom of Morocco (6 November 1979, *Boletin Oficial del Estado* 13 October 1982) does not include unemployment benefit amongst the social security benefits to which Moroccans living in Spain are entitled (Article 2).

2. What arises here is the question of equality of foreign citizens in relation to Spanish nationals, namely whether they ought to receive equal treatment with regard to the provision of unemployment benefits. It is worth remembering that, according to the jurisprudence of this Court, there are rights which are granted equally to Spanish nationals and foreigners and whose regulation ought to be the same for both (those essential to guarantee human dignity). There also exist rights which are unavailable to foreigners in any circumstances whatsoever (those recognized in Article 23 of the Constitution as provided for in Article 13(2)). Then there are other rights which may or may not be available to foreigners, the difference in treatment between Spanish nationals and foreigners being permissible depending upon the provisions laid down in treaties and laws. This requires that the availability of the right to obtain unemployment benefit on an equal footing with Spanish nationals working in the same sector, whose breach the appellant seeks to invoke (by reason of discrimination on account of his Moroccan citizenship), is dependent upon that right being granted to him by law or applicable international treaty. If this is the case, he will have the same entitlement as a Spanish national to social security benefits of the type referred to in Article 41 of the Constitution.

Accordingly, constitutional protection of the right invoked by the appellant is subordinate to whether or not it is recognized by law or treaty. In other words, if there is no such recognition, it would not be possible for the appellant to demand equality of treatment . . .

3. The denial of the right invoked by the appellant is based substantially on the fact that unemployment benefit is not one of the contingencies expressly provided for under the Bilateral Treaty on Social Security

between Spain and Morocco of 6 November 1979, despite the fact that the Treaty provides that Moroccan nationals are subject to Spanish social security law "under the same conditions as Spanish nationals". Equally ILO Agreement 97/1949 on migrant workers is inapplicable since it is also silent on the subject of unemployment benefit, limiting itself in Article 2(2) to a declaration that Member States should use their best endeavours to protect this group (i.e. the excluded category of "seamen").

4. However, in addition to the international treaty law referred to above, it must also be borne in mind that Spain has been a Member State of the European Community since 1 January 1988, in conformity with the provisions of Article 93 of the Constitution. Accordingly, Spain is subject to Community legal norms which possess direct effect in relation to its citizens and take precedence over domestic law as held by the European Court of Justice (Judgments of 5 February 1963 in *Van Gend en Loos*[1] and 15 July 1964 in *Costa* v. *ENEL*)[2] and this has been recognized by the Constitutional Court (Cases Nos 28/91[3] and 64/91[4] amongst others).

Consequently, as the Procurator Fiscal has correctly argued, it must be borne in mind that, by Regulation 2211/1978, the EC Council has approved the Cooperation Agreement between the Community and the Kingdom of Morocco signed in Rabat on 27 April 1976. Article 41(1) of that Agreement formulates a provision which must be regarded as being directly applicable within the Community since it contains "a clear and precise obligation which is not subject, in its implementation or effects, to the adoption of any subsequent measure on the part of the Member States", as held by the Court of Justice in its judgment of 31 January 1991 (*Kziber Case*).[5]

5. It is therefore necessary to examine the provisions of Article 41(1) of the Agreement referred to in which it is stated that workers of Moroccan nationality and any members of their families living with them in a Member State of the EC "shall enjoy, in the field of social security, treatment free from any discrimination based on nationality in relation to nationals of the Member States in which they are employed". This provision has been interpreted by the European Court of Justice in the judgment of 31 January 1991 referred to above. The Court of Justice held there that the principle of no discrimination based on nationality means that a person who satisfies all the conditions laid down by national law for the purposes of entitlement to unemployment benefit "shall not be refused those benefits on the ground of his nationality". This finding of the Court of Justice in Luxembourg gave rise to Circular 11/94, issued by the Directorate General of the Navy Social Fund on 24 March 1994, which recognizes that maritime workers of Moroccan nationality are

[[1] Volume 1, p. 27.] [[2] Volume 1, p. 50.]
[[3] Volume 1, p. 702.] [[4] Volume 1, p. 705.]
[[5] [1991] ECR I-199.]

protected against the contingency of unemployment to the extent that they enjoy the same rights which Spanish legislation gives to workers of Spanish nationality.

6. It must therefore be concluded that a worker of Moroccan nationality, employed by a Spanish company, cannot be denied unemployment benefit to which Spanish workers are entitled, provided that he or she satisfies all the legal requirements governing this type of benefit. By not finding this to be the case both the decisions of the Navy Social Fund and the judgments of lower courts confirming those decisions wrongly denied the appellant his right to equality before the law guaranteed by Article 14 of the Constitution. Accordingly, this Court must allow this appeal, quash the decisions and judgments under appeal, and recognize the right of the appellant to the non-discriminatory application of the rules governing unemployment benefit.

[Report: *REDI* 1996, p. 212 (in Spanish)]

Supremacy — Conflict between Community law and subsequent national law — Consequences for contrary national law—Whether ordinary courts under automatic duty not to apply conflicting national provisions—Whether Community law endowed with constitutional rank and force

National constitutions—Constitutional complaint against national court—Failure to apply EC Regulation—Failure to interpret national legislation in conformity with regulation—Whether providing admissible basis for constitutional complaint — "Infra-constitutional" nature of Community law—Scope of right of parties to translation of documents—EC Council Regulation 1408/71 on social security schemes

Direct effect — Regulations — Interpretation of national law — Duty of national courts to interpret national law consistently with Community law—Scope of obligation—The law of Spain

MARTINEZ PEREZ

(Case No 45/96)

Spain, Constitutional Court. 25 *March* 1996

SUMMARY: *The facts*:[1]—The applicant, a Spanish national resident in Germany but affiliated to the Spanish social security system, applied to the German authorities in 1987 for an invalidity pension. For this purpose he sought to have contributions made whilst he was working in Spain taken into account. The Spanish authorities provided a calculation of his pension entitlement which he challenged before the Spanish courts. In those proceedings he produced documents relating to his incapacity compiled by the German authorities. These documents were apparently not considered by the Spanish court since they had not been submitted together with a translation obtained by the applicant which, according to the court, was required by Article 601 of the Spanish Civil Code. The applicant appealed to the Constitutional Court, arguing that this treatment violated his right to be able to use appropriate evidence in support of his case (Article 14(2) of the Constitution in conjunction with the provisions of EC Council Regulation 1408/71 on the application of social security schemes to persons moving within the Community).

Held:—There had been no breach of the Constitution and the appeal was dismissed.

[1] Further facts have been taken from the section in the judgment outlining the facts, which has not been translated here.

(1) The concept of the direct applicability of regulations, enshrined in Article 189(2) of the EC Treaty, gave national courts responsibility for the selection and interpretation of the norms they contained, subject to the competence of the European Court of Justice. But the Spanish trial court, in rendering its decision in this case, had not disregarded the domestic applicability of the EC Regulation at issue, but had rather applied it in conjunction with the domestic rules of civil procedure so as to reach the conclusion that a court was only required to obtain a translation itself if this was requested by the party concerned. From the standpoint of Article 24(2) this interpretation of the position did not appear unreasonable or arbitrary and was therefore not open to review by the Constitutional Court.

(2) A possible violation of European Community legislation by subsequently enacted national legislation could not convert into a constitutional matter something which was essentially a conflict of "infra-constitutional" norms, which had to be resolved by the ordinary courts.

Dissenting opinion of Judge Gonzalez Campos:—The appeal should be allowed.

(1) National courts were required, in accordance with the case-law of the European Court of Justice, to interpret domestic legislation in conformity with Community legislation, in so far as they were given the discretion to do so under national law. In this case, attention should therefore have been paid to the objectives of the EC Regulation in question in order to arrive at an appropriate interpretation of the national legislation at issue.

(2) To regard a conflict between rules of Community and national law as a conflict between "infra-constitutional" norms was hardly reconcilable with the principle of the supremacy of both primary and secondary rules of Community law, which meant that the rules of Community law must always prevail over domestic law, whatever its rank. This principle required that, in case of a conflict, the rule of domestic law should automatically be held to be inapplicable.

The following is the text of the relevant part of the judgment of the Court:

IN LAW

1. The applicant alleges that documents relating to his incapacity compiled in German by a German administrative organ were adduced in Spain as evidence in the trial which has given rise to this appeal, arguing that such documents were in fact ignored by the court in reaching its judgment, thereby giving rise to a violation of his right to utilize evidence appropriate to his defence in accordance with the provisions of the law (Article 24(2) of the Constitution and, in this case, EC Council Regulation 1408 of 14 June 1971).

Article 84(4) of EC Regulation 1408/71 (social security for migrant workers) provides, in effect, that the courts of a Member State shall not reject petitions or other documents submitted to them solely on the ground that they are written in the official language of another Member State.

. . .

4. In the instant case the Social Security Tribunal understood that it was the responsibility of the party himself to provide translations of the documents, in accordance with both Article 601 of the Civil Code, which makes express reference to the matter, and established case-law on the subject. The Court concluded that it was for the party to attach the translation to his pleadings and that any failure by the Court to consider the evidence [in the absence of such a translation] would arise from the party's passivity and failure to act . . .

The question which gives rise to the allegation of the violation of the right to have evidence considered therefore has its source in the Tribunal's interpretation of the content of two provisions: Article 601 of the Civil Code, which states that documents written in a foreign language must be accompanied by a translation (obtained privately); and Articles 81(b) and 84(4) of EC Regulation 1408/71, from which the applicant deduces not only the obligation not to reject documents written in the language of another Member State, but also the procedure to be followed, namely to send such documents for translation as a matter of course by the Administrative Commission for the Social Security of Migrant Workers . . .

5. It should be made clear from the outset that it is not possible to deprive national courts of their right to interpret both domestic and Community norms. The concept of direct applicability in the Member States (Article 189(2) of the Treaty of Rome) gives them responsibility for the selection and interpretation of those norms (Article 117(3) of the Constitution), albeit without prejudice to the competence of the European Court of Justice in this regard.

In this case the High Court of Justice of Galicia, without disregarding the domestic applicability of the EC Regulation in question, proceeded, in relation to the presentation before the Court of documents in the German language and following the admission of those documents, to apply the provision of Article 601 of the Civil Code, which imposes a duty on the party adducing documents to have them translated . . .

6. The question which goes to the heart of this appeal is whether the precedence of the EC Regulation in the normative hierarchy permits the Social Security Tribunal to reach the decision which it did or whether the latter has failed to apply it to restrict the domestic law rules of procedure . . .

It is the responsibility of the courts to determine the norm applicable to an issue which is in dispute. This is exactly what the Social Security Tribunal has done. Rather than applying the Community Regulation in a vacuum . . . it has applied this norm in conjunction with Article 601, reaching the conclusion that the translation ought not to be performed as a matter of course but only at the request of the party . . . This is an interpretation which this Court is to review since, from the standpoint of Article 24(2) of the Constitution, it does not appear to be unreasonable or arbitrary . . .

Furthermore, this Court refers to its earlier statement in its judgment in Case No 28/1991 (*RTC* 1991, 28) that: "A possible violation of European Community legislation by subsequently enacted national or regional legislation or norms cannot convert into a constitutional matter something which is essentially a conflict of 'infra-constitutional' norms, which must be resolved by the ordinary courts."[2]

It cannot therefore be accepted that there has been a breach of Article 24(2) of the Constitution and accordingly the Court must dismiss this appeal.

[The following is the text of the relevant part of the dissenting opinion of Judge Gonzalez Campos:]

1. In their judgment in this case, the majority applies the case-law contained in the earlier judgment of this Court in Case No 180/1993 and my dissenting view in the present case is similar to that expressed in that earlier case [by three judges] . . . The present case clearly demonstrates the relevance of a requirement derived from the obligations assumed by Spain as a Member State of the European Community (in particular Article 5 of the EC Treaty) to interpret domestic law in conformity with the content of Community norms. This requirement was clearly formulated in the judgment of the European Court of Justice of 10 April 1984 (Case 14/83, *Von Colson and Kamann*)[3] and confirmed in the judgments of the Court of Justice of 13 November 1990 (Case C-106/89, *Marleasing*)[4] and 16 December 1993 (Case C-334/92, *Wagner Miret*). As stated in the first of those judgments, "It is for the national court to interpret and apply domestic legislation . . . in conformity with the requirements of Community law, in so far as it is given discretion to do so under national law." That should have meant in this case, according to my understanding, paying attention to the social objectives which inspired EC Regulation 1408/71 in order to arrive at the appropriate interpretation for the resolution of this case.

2. My dissenting view covers, in particular, the passage cited "by the majority of this Court" from the judgment of the Constitutional Court in Case No 28/91, ground 5,[5] in which the Court took the view that "a possible violation of a rule of Community law by subsequently enacted national legislation cannot convert into a constitutional dispute something which is essentially a conflict of 'infra-constitutional' norms, which

[2 Volume 1, p. 702.]
[3 Volume 1, Note, p. 187.]
[4 Volume 1, p. 167.]
[5 Volume 1, p. 702 at p. 704.]

must be resolved by the ordinary courts". That is a position which is certainly difficult to accept from the standpoint of the rules of both primary and secondary Community law (judgment of the Court of Justice of 14 December 1971 in Case 43/71, *Politi*), which prevail over municipal legislation, whatever its rank (judgment of the Court of Justice of 15 July 1964, Case 6/64, *Costa* v. *ENEL*).[6] [This principle] results in not the nullity of the municipal norm but rather its non-application to the case at issue . . .

[Report: *BOE*, No 102, 27 April 1996, Case No 45/1996 (in Spanish)]

NOTE.—The above judgment has been the subject of critical comment (see *REDI* 1997, p. 201 and *Revista de Derecho Comunitario Europeo* 1997, p. 275 (in Spanish)).

In a subsequent judgment of 30 November 2000, the Constitutional Court ruled on an application by the Spanish Ombudsman for the annulment of certain provisions of the Organic Law on the Protection of Personal Data, 1999. The Ombudsman argued that the discretion left to the authorities by the Organic Law was too broad and thereby violated the fundamental right to privacy enshrined in the Constitution (Article 18(1)) and the right of the individual to the protection of his personal data (Article 18(3)). The Constitutional Court accepted the argument and annulled the relevant provisions of the Organic Law, holding that the Constitution (Article 53(1)) required parliamentary legislation if the fundamental right to personal data protection was to be restricted.

Although the Organic Law in question was apparently intended to implement EC Directive 95/46 on the Protection of Personal Data, the Constitutional Court repeated its previously adopted position (*Electoral Law Constitutionality Case*, 1991, Volume 1, p. 702) that Community secondary legislation did not have the same status as constitutional law and could not therefore constitute a yardstick for constitutional review of legal norms. Nevertheless, such legislation did provide a criterion whereby the meaning and scope of a specific fundamental right could be determined (paragraph 3 of the judgment). Accordingly, in defining the content of the right to personal data protection, the Constitutional Court referred to a number of international instruments, including the EC Directive in question and Article 8 of the Charter of Fundamental Rights of the European Union (paragraph 4 of the judgment) (*Data Protection Law Constitutionality Case*, No 292/00, *Diario La Ley* No 5213/2000).

[6 Volume 1, p. 50.]

Supremacy — Conflict between Community law and subsequent national law — Consequences for contrary national law — Duty of national courts not to apply national provisions—Principle that effectiveness of Community law must be ensured

Human rights—Scope of protection within the Community—Case-law of the Court of Justice of the European Community — Article F(2) of Treaty on European Union, 1992 — Fundamental rights as general principles of Community law—Basis in constitutional traditions common to Member States—European Convention on Human Rights, 1950, Articles 6 and 13 — Status within Community legal order — Right of judicial control as general principle of Community law—The law of Sweden

LASSAGARD AB

(Case No 219/1997)

Sweden, Supreme Administrative Court. 25 *November* 1997

(Werner, von Bahr, Baekkevold, Eliason and Hulgaard, *Judges*)

SUMMARY: *The facts*:—Swedish legislation, enacted to implement EC Regulations concerning the Common Agricultural Policy, provided for the National Board of Agriculture to enact rules for the grant of agricultural area aid to farmers. The rules enacted for 1995 required applications to be lodged with the County Administrative Board before 25 April. No provision was made to cover the treatment of applications lodged after the deadline. The relevant EC Regulation provided for a 1 per cent reduction per working day in the amount of aid entitlement for late applications and stated that if the delay was more than twenty days the application should be considered inadmissible.

An application by Lassagard AB for agricultural area aid for 1995 was rejected by the County Administrative Board because it had been lodged more than twenty days late. This decision was upheld on appeal by the National Board of Agriculture, which also ruled that there was no further right of appeal. An appeal lodged by the company before the County Administrative Court was summarily dismissed on the ground that the application for aid was out of time. On further appeal by the company, the Administrative Court of Appeal held that the administrative courts had no competence to consider appeals from decisions of the Board of Agriculture.

The company then appealed to the Supreme Administrative Court, arguing that the right to agricultural aid was a civil right within the meaning of Article 6 of the European Convention on Human Rights and that the Convention rule requiring judicial review to be available for decisions determining entitlement to such a right was directly applicable as part of Community law. The company contended that, in such circumstances, the case-law of the Court of Justice of the European Community required national courts to set aside any national rule which obstructed the exercise of the right of judicial review derived from Community law.

Held:—The appeal was allowed, the judgment under appeal was quashed and the case was remitted for further proceedings.

(1) The Court of Justice of the European Community had held, specifically in relation to claims for agricultural aid, that there was a requirement of judicial control by national courts over every decision of a national administrative authority. This reflected a general principle of Community law which stemmed from the constitutional traditions common to the Member States and had been enshrined in Articles 6 and 13 of the European Convention on Human Rights. The obligation of Member States of the European Union to respect fundamental rights in such circumstances was now enshrined in Article F(2) of the Maastricht Treaty. To preclude court proceedings in such circumstances would be contrary to the principle of the uniform application of Community law.

(2) Article 33 of the Swedish Agricultural Regulation excluded a right of appeal against decisions of the National Board of Agriculture. Whilst this provision was not contrary to any right expressly granted by a Community regulation, it was incompatible with the above-mentioned general principle of Community law, which took precedence over national law. Accordingly, in accordance with the case-law of the Court of Justice, the provision of national law excluding a right of appeal should not be applied. There was no reason to request a preliminary ruling on the matter.

The following is the text of the judgment of the Court:

Background

Relevant provisions on agricultural subsidies

The Act (1994:1710) concerning Community Regulations on Agricultural Products ("the Agricultural Act") contains the provisions necessary for the implementation in Sweden of the price and market regulation which forms a part of the common agricultural policy of the European Communities. Community Regulations on Agricultural Products include regulations issued by the Community concerning the market regulation of agricultural products (Section 1). In relation to the Community Regulations on Agricultural Products the Government, or the public authority designated by the Government, may prescribe supplementary provisions and provide for their enforcement (Section 2). The Agricultural Act also contains provisions on the obligation to supply information (Section 3), supervision and control (Sections 4-9), interest on payments made after their due date or on the repayment of subsidies (Section 10), charges for supervision etc. (Section 11), penalties (Sections 12-14) and appeals (Section 15).

The Agricultural Act contains no rules as to what kind of subsidies are available or as to the conditions that must be met for agricultural subsidies to be paid. Certain provisions of this type can be found, however, in the Government Regulation (1994:1715) on Community Regulations on Agricultural Products ("the Agricultural Regulation") (*cf.* Section 2 of the Agricultural Law). In the Agricultural Regulation it is stipulated that applications for agricultural area aid to farmers should be decided by the County Administrative Board (Article 9) and that provisions for the supplement and enforcement of the Community regulations on agricultural area aid to farmers shall be prescribed by the National Board of Agriculture (Article 10). Furthermore, it is provided that a decision of the County Administrative Board on aid can be appealed to the National Board of Agriculture and that there is no appeal against the decision of the National Board of Agriculture (Article 33). With regard to other decisions of the National Board of Agriculture the general rule is that they can be appealed to an administrative court and that leave to appeal is required for an appeal to an administrative court of appeal (Article 34 in the amended version in *SFS* 1997:763).[1]

In the provisions enacted by the National Board of Agriculture on agricultural area aid to farmers who grow crops eligible for benefits and on forage area (*SJVFS* 1995:21),[2] it is stated that basic provisions on agricultural area aid to farmers are contained in specified Community Regulations as well as in the Agricultural Act and the Agricultural Regulation (Article 1). According to those provisions, an application for agricultural area aid for 1995 should be made on a prescribed form and submitted to the County Administrative Board by 25 April at the latest (Article 3 in the amended version in *SJVFS* 1995:54).

It does not appear from the provisions enacted by the National Board of Agriculture how an application for agricultural area aid should be treated if it is lodged too late. There are, however, rules on this question in one of the Community Regulations to which the provisions refer, namely Commission Regulation (EEC) No 3887/92 of 23 December 1992 laying down detailed rules for applying the integrated administration and control system for certain Community aid schemes. Article 8(1) of that Regulation states that, except in cases of *force majeure*, late lodgement of an aid application shall lead to a 1% reduction per working day in the amounts affected by the application, to which the farmer would have been entitled if the application had been lodged within the deadline. If the delay amounts to more than 20 days the application shall

[1 *SFS* is the abbreviation of *Svensk Forfattningssamling*, which is the publication where all acts decided upon by the *Riksdag* (the Swedish Parliament) and most Government regulations are published.]

[2 *SJVFS* is the abbreviation of *Statens Jordbruksverks Forfattningssamling*, which is the publication where the National Board of Agriculture publishes its enactments and decisions.]

be considered inadmissible and no aid shall be granted. The Regulation contains no provision on appeals.

The Facts of the Case

In an application received by the County Administrative Board of the County of Halland on 18 May 1995, Lassagard AB (the Company) applied for agricultural area aid for 1995. By a decision of 10 July 1995 the County Administrative Board dismissed the application by reference to Article 8(1) of Commission Regulation (EEC) No 3887/92 (referred to above) and to the fact that the application had been lodged more than 20 days late. The Company appealed. The National Board of Agriculture rejected the appeal on 31 January 1996 and stated that the decision could not be appealed.

The Company appealed against the decision of the National Board of Agriculture to the County Administrative Court in the County of Jonkoping. The Court ruled, in a decision of 7 May 1996, that the right to agricultural area aid was to be regarded as a civil right according to Article 6 of the European Convention for the Protection of Human Rights and Fundamental Freedoms (ECHR). It followed that there was a right to have the case heard by a court and that the prohibition against appeals contained in Article 33 of the Agricultural Regulation could therefore be set aside by application of the rules on judicial review of constitutionality contained in Chapter 11, Article 14, of the Instrument of Government.[3] Even if there were strong reasons indicating that the appeal by the Company in the first instance should be heard by a county administrative court it was, however, not evident according to the Court which county administrative court would be competent to handle the case. It was in any case not evident that it would be the County Administrative Court in the County of Jonkoping. The appeal by the Company was therefore dismissed.

The Company appealed. The Administrative Court of Appeal of Jonkoping ruled, in a decision of 15 August 1996, that the provisions of Chapter 11, Article 14, of the Instrument of Government supported a modification of the applicable rules on competence and that the appeal by the Company should be allowed and the case should be heard by the County Administrative Court of the County of Halland. In a judgment of 16 September 1996, the County Administrative Court examined the appeal by the Company on its merits but found, as the National Board

[[3] Chapter 11, Article 14, of the Swedish Instrument of Government reads as follows: "If a court or any other public body considers that a provision is in conflict with a provision of a fundamental law or with a provision of any other superior statute, or that the procedure prescribed was set aside in any important respect when the provision was introduced, that provision may not be applied. However, if the provision has been approved by the *Riksdag* (Parliament) or by the Government, it may be set aside only if the error is manifest."]

of Agriculture had done, that the application by the Company had been lodged more than 20 days late. The Court therefore dismissed the appeal.

The Company appealed against the judgment of the County Administrative Court, claiming that the application for agricultural area aid had been lodged within the time limit of 20 days. In a decision of 6 December 1996, the Administrative Court of Appeal of Gothenburg held that an administrative court could not be considered as competent to hear the appeal by the Company. The Administrative Court of Appeal therefore quashed the judgment of the County Administrative Court and dismissed the appeal by the Company.

Arguments of the Appellant

The Company appeals against the decision of the Administrative Court of Appeal of Gothenburg and requests that the Supreme Administrative Court establish that a general administrative court should hear the Company's claim despite the exclusion of appeals contained in Article 33 of the Agricultural Regulation and also asks the Supreme Administrative Court to examine the issue of law in question on its merits. Furthermore, the Company requests the Supreme Administrative Court to make a reference for a preliminary ruling under Article 177 of the EC Treaty if it concludes that the Community law in force does not in all aspects elucidate the questions of Community law which arise in the case.

As grounds for its appeal the Company argues as follows: The area aid is a benefit from the European Union and not from the Swedish State. As a result, the question whether the Company's benefit constitutes a civil right cannot only be determined from a national perspective. Furthermore, it appears from the standard commentary to the ECHR that the concept of civil rights should be interpreted broadly (see van Dijk/van Hoof, Theory and Practice of the European Convention on Human Rights, 2nd edn 1990 p. 294 ff.). The rules of the ECHR are now also part of Swedish law (*SFS* 1994:1219). Moreover, the provisions of the Convention on the right to judicial review are directly applicable in Swedish law since they form part of Community law (see Case 222/86, *Heylens* [1987] ECR 4097). From this case it follows that Community law requires that an individual should have the right to judicial review in relation to rights derived from Community law. To obtain area aid under Community Regulations is no doubt a right derived from Community law. It must therefore be concluded that the right to judicial review according to Community law is clear and unconditional. Swedish national rules on the competence of administrative courts must not in any way hinder the exercise of rights derived from Community law. This evidently follows from the principle of the primacy of Community law over national law (see Case 106/77, *Simmenthal*, [1978] ECR 629).[4] The inescapable conclusion is that national courts are obliged to set aside any national rule which can hinder or jeopardize the full impact of the Community rule in national law. In the judgment of the Court of Justice of the European Community in Case C-213/89, *Factortame* ([1990] ECR I-2433)[5] these principles have once again been confirmed. From this latter judgment it follows that a national court is obliged by Article 5 of the EC Treaty to take all measures necessary to give full effect to provisions of Community law. Since Article 6 ECHR gives a right to judicial review, and since the Convention forms part of Community law, a national court must take all the measures necessary to ensure the observance of the provision in question. If this is not done, it constitutes a breach of Community law that is evident and serious from the standpoint of the consistent case-law of the Court of Justice of the European Community.

Grounds of the Judgment

The right to agricultural area aid is regulated, as stated above, partly in the [Swedish] Agricultural Act and Agricultural Regulation and partly in a number of Community Regulations on agricultural products. The latter regulations are binding and directly applicable in all Member States of the European Union (*cf.* Article 2 of the Act 1994:1500 concerning Sweden's accession to the European Union).[6]

The main question in this case is whether the Company, in spite of the exclusion of appeals contained in Article 33 of the Agricultural Regulation, has a right to have its application for agricultural area aid examined by a court and, if so, which court. In this matter it should firstly be noted that the provision contained in Article 15 of the Agricultural Act, that certain decisions can be appealed to an administrative court, does not cover decisions on agricultural area aid. The latter provision is therefore not applicable in this case.

The Supreme Administrative Court must then consider the question whether or not the exclusion, in Article 33 of the Agricultural Regulation, of appeals against decisions of the National Board of Agriculture is compatible with Community law. There is no explicit provision which states in the relevant Community regulations that those who have been denied agricultural area aid or similar subsidies have a right to have their case examined by a court. This does not, however, necessarily mean that there is no such right. The general principles of Community law, as they have been interpreted and developed by the Court of Justice of the European Community, must also be taken into consideration.

[[4] See Volume 1, p. 73.] [[5] See Volume 1, p. 823.]

[[6] This is a reference to the Government's Bill submitted to the *Riksdag* on constitutional amendments with a view to Swedish membership of the European Union and to the Report by the *Riksdag*'s Standing Committee on the Constitution concerning that Bill.]

The action brought by the Company also concerns a claim based on Community law for economic support related to agricultural production. The Court of Justice of the European Community has stated in its case-law (Case C-97/91, *Borelli* [1992] ECR I-6313) that anyone who alleges a claim of this kind has a right to have his case heard by a court. The Court of Justice of the European Community held that the requirement for judicial control of every decision by a national authority reflected a general principle of Community law which stems from the constitutional traditions common to the Member States and had been enshrined in Articles 6 and 13 ECHR (see paragraph 14 of the judgment). This connection between Community law and other sources of law is closely reflected in the amendment of the Rome Treaty which results from the Treaty on European Union signed on 7 February 1992 (the Maastricht Treaty). In Article F(2) of the Common Provisions contained in the Maastricht Treaty it is stated that the Union shall respect fundamental rights, as guaranteed by the European Convention on Human Rights and as they result from the constitutional traditions common to the Member States, as general principles of Community law. Article 6 ECHR provides, *inter alia*, that everyone is entitled in the determination of his or her civil rights and obligations to a fair and public hearing within a reasonable time by an independent tribunal established by law.

What has been stated above speaks strongly in favour of the Company having a right to have its application for agricultural area aid examined by a court. To this should be added that it is only a "court" which, according to Article 177 of the EC Treaty, may or shall request the Court of Justice of the European Community for a preliminary ruling. The exclusion of court proceedings would be contrary to the uniform application of the Community regulations on agricultural products.

Against this background, the Supreme Administrative Court finds that the provision in Article 33 of the Agricultural Regulation excluding appeals against the decisions of the National Board of Agriculture is incompatible with the general principles of Community law as expressed, for example, in the *Borelli Case*. Community law takes precedence in such a case (*cf. Prop* 1993/94: 114 p. 13, *Bet*, 1993/94 *KU*21 p. 17). The provision excluding appeals must therefore not be applied. There is no reason to ask for a preliminary ruling by the Court of Justice of the European Community.

The Supreme Administrative Court accordingly finds that, notwithstanding Article 33 of the Agricultural Regulation, the Company has a right to have its application for agricultural area aid examined by a court.

The question then arises which court shall be deemed competent to hear the appeal against the decision of the National Board of Agriculture in this case. According to Article 34, second paragraph, of the Agricultural Regulation, the general rule is that decisions by the National Board of Agriculture can be appealed to an administrative court and that leave of appeal is required for appeals to an administrative court of appeal. The possibility clearly presents itself to apply the provision also in relation to decisions referred to in Article 33 of the same Regulation. The Supreme Administrative Court finds that this provision shall be applied and that the decisions of the National Board of Agriculture taken under Article 14 of the Act (1971:289) on General Administrative Courts shall therefore be appealed to the County Administrative Court within whose circuit the case was first heard. The County Administrative Court in the County of Halland is therefore the competent court for an application for agricultural area aid first heard by the County Administrative Board in the County of Halland.

The County Administrative Board in the County of Halland has, in its decision of 19 September 1996, already heard the application by the Company for agricultural area aid. The case shall therefore be remitted to the Administrative Court of Appeal in Gothenburg to determine whether leave of appeal should be granted on account of the appeal made by the Company against the judgment of the County Administrative Court.

Ruling

The Supreme Administrative Court quashes the decision of the Administrative Court of Appeal in Gothenburg and remits the case to the Administrative Court of Appeal to determine whether leave of appeal should be granted on account of the appeal lodged by the Company against the judgment of 19 September 1996 delivered by the County Administrative Court of the County of Halland.

[Report: *Regeringsrattens Arsbok* 1997, No 65 (in Swedish)]

NOTE.—Following the conclusion of negotiations for Sweden to join the European Community in April 1994, a consultative referendum was held, resulting in a small majority in favour of membership (52 per cent for and 47 per cent against). Subsequently the Swedish Parliament ratified the Accession Treaty, after the constitutional amendment set out below had been adopted at the end of 1994. Whilst not specifically regulating at constitutional level the status of EC law in Sweden, the first paragraph of Article 5 of Chapter 10 of the Swedish Instrument of Government provides:

> The *Riksdag* may entrust decision-making powers to the European Community so long as the Community makes provision for the protection of rights and freedoms corresponding to the protection provided under this Instrument of Government and the European Convention for the Protection of Human Rights and Fundamental Freedoms. The *Riksdag* may authorize such a transfer of powers by a decision taken with the support of at least three-quarters

> of those voting. The *Riksdag* may also take such a decision in the manner prescribed for the adoption of a fundamental law.

It is no coincidence that the European Community and not the European Union is mentioned as the addressee of the transfer of decision-making powers. Only cooperation under the first pillar was regarded as requiring such delegation. The question of whether the position should be changed has been the subject of deliberation by a Governmental Commission, which has proposed that the reference to the European Community should be replaced by a reference to the European Union. The decision to transfer decision-making powers was taken by the adoption of the Act concerning Sweden's Accession to the Union (1994:1500). Article 3 provides:

> The European Communities may, after Sweden's accession to the European Union, take decisions that are valid here in Sweden to the extent and with the effect that follows from the Treaties and other Instruments listed in Article 4.

The list in Article 4 includes the three basic Treaties and all the amendments made to them up to and including the Amsterdam Treaty.

The effect of the *acquis communautaire* is regulated by Article 2 which provides:

> The Treaties and other Instruments listed in Article 4, as well as all legal acts, agreements and other decisions adopted by the European Communities, prior to Sweden's accession to the European Union, are valid in Sweden with the effect that follows from those Treaties and other Instruments.

(Further discussion of the position in Sweden is contained in Bernitz, Sweden and the European Union: On Sweden's Implementation and Application of European Law, CML Rev 2001, p. 903.)

Supremacy — Conflict between Community law and subsequent national law — Consequences for contrary national law — Whether existing national provisions automatically inapplicable — Whether declaration that conflicting national provisions incompatible with Community law sufficient — Employment discrimination — EC Treaty, Article 119—Equal Pay Directive 75/117—Equal Treatment Directive 76/207

National constitutions—Constitutional review concerning Community Treaty — United Kingdom — Enforcement of treaty obligations—Whether properly the subject of judicial review proceedings — European Communities Act 1972, Section 2—Scope

Enforcement in national courts — Remedies — Scope of remedies in judicial review proceedings before national courts — Whether declaration that Government in breach of obligations under Community law available in judicial review proceedings—The law of England

REGINA *v.* SECRETARY OF STATE FOR EMPLOYMENT, *ex parte* EQUAL OPPORTUNITIES COMMISSION AND ANOTHER

England, House of Lords. 3 *March* 1994

(Lords Keith of Kinkel, Jauncey of Tullichettle, Lowry, Browne-Wilkinson and Slynn of Hadley)

SUMMARY: *The facts*:—The Equal Opportunities Commission ("EOC") was the statutory body responsible for securing equality of treatment by the elimination of discrimination between men and women in the workplace. The EOC considered that the threshold provisions of the Employment Protection (Consolidation) Act 1978 discriminated against women because the rights to unfair dismissal compensation and redundancy pay under that Act were only available to full-time employees working over sixteen hours per week. The vast majority of those working part-time and less than sixteen hours each week were women. The Secretary of State rejected a request for the Act to be amended and the EOC then challenged the legislation in judicial review proceedings, seeking a declaration that it violated Article 119 of the EC Treaty, the Equal Pay Directive 75/117 and the Equal Treatment Directive 76/207. The Divisional Court and the Court of Appeal rejected the application and the EOC appealed to the House of Lords.

Held:—The appeal was allowed.

(1) Recourse to judicial review was available in order to challenge, as incompatible with Community law, certain United Kingdom primary legislation, and in order to seek a declaration to that effect. The *Factortame* litigation before the European Court of Justice and the House of Lords provided authority for such recourse (p. 444).

(2) It was contended that the Divisional Court, in judicial review proceedings, had no jurisdiction to declare that the United Kingdom was in breach of an obligation under Community law. But such a declaration was not required. It was sufficent to grant a declaration that the threshold provisions of the 1978 Act were incompatible with Community law, on the basis of the precedent in *Factortame* (pp. 444-5).

(3) The facts at issue did not involve an attempt by the EOC to enforce the international treaty obligations of the United Kingdom. The application simply sought a ruling reflecting the primacy of Community law enshrined in Section 2 of the European Communities Act 1972 and determining whether the relevant United Kingdom law was compatible with the directives at issue (p. 445).

(4) The Divisional Court, as the court to which applications for judicial review were brought and therefore the only court in which the applicant could pursue the remedy sought, was therefore the appropriate forum to decide the substantive issues at stake. The fact that the European Commission could institute proceedings against the United Kingdom before the European Court of Justice under Article 169 of the EC Treaty was not a bar to proceedings before the Divisional Court (p. 445).

(5) A declaration should therefore be made that the threshold provisions of the 1978 Act were incompatible with Article 119 and the Directive in question. But it was not appropriate in these proceedings to make a declaration that the Secretary of State was in breach of his obligations under Community law so as to provide a basis for a claim for compensation against the United Kingdom. Such a claim should be pursued in separate proceedings under the *Francovich* principle, brought by individuals who believed they had a good claim to compensation against the Attorney General (p. 450).

The following is the text of the judgment of the Court:

[413] This was an appeal by the applicants, the Equal Opportunities Commission and Mrs Patricia Elizabeth Day, by leave of the House of Lords from the decision of the Court of Appeal (Dillon, Kennedy and Hirst LJJ) [1993] 1 WLR 872 given on 6 November 1992 affirming by a majority (Dillon LJ dissenting) in the case of the commission and unanimously in the case of Mrs Day the decision of the Divisional Court of the Queen's Bench Division (Nolan LJ and Judge J) [1992] ICR 341 given on 10 October in respect of the first of two applications for judicial review directed to the respondent, the Secretary of State for Employment.

The Court of Appeal refused the applicants leave to appeal from their decision, but on 25 February 1993 the Appeal Committee of the House of Lords (Lord Templeman, Lord Jauncey of Tullichettle and Lord Woolf)

[1993] 1 WLR 872, 908 allowed a petition by them in respect of the first application for leave to appeal.

The facts are stated in the opinion of Lord Keith of Kinkel.

Their Lordships took time for consideration.

LORD KEITH OF KINKEL. My Lords, article 119 of the EEC Treaty (Cmnd 5179-II) provides:

Each member state shall during the first stage ensure and subsequently maintain the application of the principle that men and women should receive equal pay for equal work. For the purpose of this article, "pay" means the ordinary basic or minimum wage or salary and any other consideration, whether in cash or in kind, which the worker receives, directly or indirectly, in respect of his employment from his employer. Equal pay without discrimination **[414]** based on sex means: (*a*) that pay for the same work at piece rates shall be calculated on the basis of the same unit of measurement; (*b*) that pay for work at time rates shall be the same for the same job.

The Council Directive of 10 February 1975 (75/117/EEC) ("the Equal Pay Directive") spells out the right to equal pay in greater detail. Article 2(1) of the Council Directive of 9 February 1976 (76/207/EEC) ("the Equal Treatment Directive") provides:

For the purposes of the following provisions, the principle of equal treatment shall mean that there shall be no discrimination whatsoever on grounds of sex either directly or indirectly by reference in particular to marital or family status.

Article 5(1) and (2) provide:

1. Application of the principle of equal treatment with regard to working conditions, including the conditions governing dismissal, means that men and women shall be guaranteed the same conditions without discrimination on grounds of sex. 2. To this end, member states shall take the measures necessary to ensure that: (*a*) any laws, regulations and administrative provisions contrary to the principle of equal treatment shall be abolished; . . .

Section 2 of the European Communities Act 1972, so far as material for present purposes, provides:

(1) All such rights, powers, liabilities, obligations and restrictions from time to time created or arising by or under the Treaties [see section 1(2)], and all such remedies and procedures from time to time provided for by or under the Treaties, as in accordance with the Treaties are without further enactment to be given legal effect or used in the United Kingdom shall be recognised and available in law, and be enforced, allowed and followed accordingly; and the expression "enforceable Community right" and similar expressions shall be read as referring to one to which this subsection applies. (2) . . . at any time after its passing Her Majesty may by Order in Council, and any designated minister or department may by regulations, make provision—(*a*) for the purpose of implementing any

Community obligation of the United Kingdom, or enabling any such obligation to be implemented . . . or (*b*) for the purpose of dealing with matters arising out of or related to any such obligation or rights . . . or the operation from time to time, of subsection (1) above; and in the exercise of any statutory power or duty, including any power to give directions or to legislate by means of orders, rules, regulations or other subordinate instrument, the person entrusted with the power or duty may have regard to the objects of the Communities and to any such obligation or rights as aforesaid. In this subsection "designated minister or department" means such minister of the Crown or government department as may from time to time be designated by Order in Council in relation to any matter or for any purpose, but subject to such restrictions or conditions (if any) as may be specified by the Order in Council. . . . (4) The provision that may be made under subsection (2) above includes . . . any such provision (of any such extent) as might be made by Act of Parliament, and any enactment passed or to be passed, other than **[415]** one contained in this Part of this Act, shall be construed and have effect subject to the foregoing provisions of this section; . . .

By the European Communities (Designation) (No 3) Order 1982 (SI 1982 No 1675) the Secretary of State for Employment was designated for purposes of section 2(2) of the Act of 1972 in relation to measures to prevent discrimination between men and women as regards terms and conditions of employment.

The United Kingdom legislation aimed at preventing such discrimination is to be found in the Equal Pay Act 1970 and the Sex Discrimination Act 1975, but nothing in the present case turns on any provision of either of these Acts. What is in issue is those provisions of the Employment Protection (Consolidation) Act 1978 which set out the conditions which govern the right not to be unfairly dismissed, the right to compensation for unfair dismissal and the right to statutory redundancy pay. These conditions require that an employee should have worked a specified number of hours a week during a specified period of continuous employment. In general, the qualifying periods for entitlement to each of the rights in question are (a) two years of continuous employment for employees who work for 16 or more hours per week, and (b) five years of continuous employment for employees who work between eight and 16 hours per week. Employees who work for fewer than eight hours per week do not qualify for any of the rights in question. The provisions of the Act which set out these conditions are to be found in sections 54, 64, 68, 71, 81 and 151, and Schedule 13, which need not be referred to in detail. It is common ground that the great majority of employees who work for more than 16 hours a week are men, and that the great majority of those who work for less than 16 hours a week are women, so that the provisions in question result in an indirect discrimination against women.

On 21 March 1990 the chief executive of the appellant Equal Opportunities Commission ("EOC") wrote to the Secretary of State for Employment referring to the provisions of the Act of 1978 concerning redundancy pay and compensation for unfair dismissal and expressing the view that these constituted indirect discrimination against women employees, contrary to Community law. The Secretary of State was asked to give urgent consideration to that matter and to inform the EOC whether the government would be willing to introduce the necessary legislation to remove the discrimination inherent in the Act of 1978, giving reasons for his decision if the reply was in the negative. The Secretary of State replied by letter dated 23 April 1990, stating, inter alia:

> [We do not accept that] statutory redundancy pay and statutory compensation for unfair dismissal constitute "pay" within the meaning of article 119 . . . or . . . that they fall within the Equal Treatment Directive . . . we believe that our current statutory thresholds are entirely justifiable. These thresholds have existed in one form or another ever since employment protection legislation was first introduced. Their purpose is to ensure that a fair balance is struck between the interests of employers and employees. We have no plans to change the thresholds.

On 6 June 1990 the EOC obtained leave to move for judicial review, the matter in respect of which relief was sought being stated as:

> The decision of the Secretary of State for Employment dated 23 April 1990 declining to accept that the United Kingdom is in **[416]** breach of its obligations under Community law by providing less favourable treatment of part-time workers than of full-time workers in relation to the conditions for receipt of statutory redundancy pay and compensation for unfair dismissal.

The substantive relief sought was expressed in these terms:

> 1. A declaration that the United Kingdom is in breach of its obligations under article 119 of the [EEC Treaty] and [Council] Directive (75/117/EEC) by providing less favourable treatment of part-time workers (most of whom are women) than of full-time workers (most of whom are men) in relation to the conditions for receipt of statutory redundancy pay and compensation for unfair dismissal.
> 2. A declaration that the United Kingdom is in breach of its obligations under [Council] Directive (76/207/EEC) by providing less favourable treatment of part-time workers (most of whom are women) than of full-time workers (most of whom are men) in relation to the conditions for receipt of statutory redundancy pay and compensation for unfair dismissal.

At a later stage the application was amended so as to bring in as second applicant Mrs Day, who had been employed by Hertfordshire County Council as a cleaner for just under five years working 11 hours a week and had been made redundant, and so as to seek certain further declarations and also mandamus to compel the Secretary of State to introduce legislation to abolish the discriminatory provisions of the Act of 1978.

The application was heard by a Divisional Court consisting of Nolan LJ and Judge J [1992] ICR 341 who on 10 October 1991 dismissed it. On appeal by the EOC and Mrs Day to the Court of Appeal [1993] 1 WLR 872 the decision of the Divisional Court was by a majority affirmed (Kennedy and Hirst LJJ, Dillon LJ dissenting). The EOC and Mrs Day now appeal to your Lordships' House.

The principal issue of substance raised by the proceedings is whether the indirect discrimination against women involved in the relevant provisions of the Act of 1978 has been shown to be based upon objectively justified grounds, that being the test propounded by the European Court of Justice in *Bilka-Kaufhaus GmbH* v. *Weber von Hartz* (Case 170/84) [1987] ICR 110 for determining whether or not measures involving indirect discrimination constitute an infringement of article 119 of the EEC Treaty. A number of procedural points were, however, argued in the courts below and before this House.

It is convenient first to consider whether Mrs Day is properly joined in the present proceedings against the Secretary of State. Redundancy pay is "pay" within the meaning of article 119 of the Treaty: *Barber* v. *Guardian Royal Exchange Assurance Group* (Case C 262/88) [1991] 1 QB 344. If the discriminatory measures in the Act of 1978 are not objectively justified, Mrs Day has a good claim for redundancy pay against her employers, the Hertfordshire Area Health Authority, under article 119, which by virtue of section 2(1) of the Act of 1972 prevails over the discriminatory provisions of the Act of 1978. She would also have a good claim under the Equal Pay Directive and the Equal Treatment Directive, which are directly applicable against her employers as being an emanation of the state: *Marshall* v. *Southampton and South West Hampshire Area Health Authority (Teaching)* (Case 152/84) [1986] **[417]** QB 401. Mrs Day's claim against her employers is a private law claim, and indeed she has already started proceedings to enforce it in the appropriate industrial tribunal, these having been adjourned to await the outcome of the present case. The industrial tribunal has jurisdiction to decide questions as to objective justification for discriminatory measures, and has done so on many occasions, in particular in the *Marshall* case. I see no good reason why a purely private law claim should be advanced in the Divisional Court against the Secretary of State, who is not the claimant's employer and is not liable to meet the claim, if sound. The determination of such claims has been entrusted by statute to the industrial tribunal, which is fully competent to deal with them. It is suggested that different industrial tribunals might reach different decisions on the facts in relation to objective justification, but a suitable test case upon the question of principle, supported by the EOC under the power conferred upon it by section 75 of the Act of 1975, would be capable of settling the question definitively. I conclude that the Divisional Court was not the appropriate forum to adjudicate upon what so far as Mrs Day is concerned is her private law claim, and would dismiss her appeal, but without costs.

Turning now to the position of the EOC, the procedural points taken by the Secretary of State are (1) that the EOC has no locus standi to bring the present proceedings, (2) that the EOC's case does not involve any decision or justiciable issue susceptible of judicial review, (3) that the Divisional Court had no jurisdiction to declare that the United Kingdom or the Secretary of State was in breach of any obligations under European Community law, and (4) that the Divisional Court was not the appropriate forum to determine the substantive issues raised by the application.

Dealing first with the question of locus standi, RSC, Ord. 53, r. 3(7) provides that the court shall not grant leave to apply for judicial review "unless it considers that the applicant has a sufficient interest in the matter to which the application relates." Section 31(3) of the Supreme Court Act 1981 contains a provision in the same terms. The matter to which the EOC's application relates is essentially whether the relevant provisions of the Act of 1978 are compatible with European Community law regarding equal pay and equal treatment. Has the EOC a sufficient interest in that matter? Under section 53(1) of the Act of 1975 the duties of the EOC include:

> (*a*) to work towards the elimination of discrimination, (*b*) to promote equality of opportunity between men and women generally . . .

If the admittedly discriminatory provisions of the Act of 1978 as regards redundancy pay and compensation for unfair dismissal are not objectively justified, then steps taken by the EOC towards securing that these provisions are changed may very reasonably be regarded as taken in the course of working towards the elimination of discrimination. The present proceedings are clearly such a step. In a number of cases the EOC has been the initiating party to proceedings designed to secure the elimination of discrimination. The prime example is *Reg.* v. *Birmingham City Council, Ex parte Equal Opportunities Commission* [1989] AC 1155, where the EOC successfully challenged the policy of the council as regards the relative availability of grammar school places for girls and for boys, in proceedings which reached this House and in which it was **[418]** not suggested at any stage that the EOC lacked locus standi. In *Reg.* v. *Secretary of State for Defence, Ex parte Equal Opportunities Commission* (unreported), 20 December 1991, it was common ground that the EOC had locus standi. Another instance is *Reg.* v. *Secretary of State for Social Security, Ex parte Equal Opportunities Commission* (Case C 9/91) [1992] ICR 782, which went to the European Court of Justice. In my opinion it would be a very retrograde step now to hold that the EOC has no locus standi to agitate in judicial review proceedings questions related to sex discrimination which are of public importance and affect a large section of the population. The determination of this issue turns essentially upon a consideration of the statutory duties and public law role of the EOC as regards which no helpful guidance is to be gathered from decided cases. I would hold that the EOC has sufficient interest to bring these proceedings and hence the necessary locus standi.

The next question is whether there exists any decision or justiciable issue susceptible of judicial review. The EOC's application sets out the Secretary of State's letter of 23 April 1990 as being the reviewable decision. In my opinion that letter does not constitute a decision. It does no more than state the Secretary of State's view that the threshold provisions of the Act of 1978 regarding redundancy pay and compensation for unfair dismissal are justifiable and in conformity with European Community law. The real object of the EOC's attack is these provisions themselves. The question is whether judicial review is available for the purpose of securing a declaration that certain United Kingdom primary legislation is incompatible with European Community law. It is argued for the Secretary of State that Ord. 53, r. 1(2), which gives the court power to make declarations in judicial review proceedings, is only applicable where one of the prerogative orders would be available under rule 1(1), and that if there is no decision in respect of which one of these writs might be issued a declaration cannot be made. I consider that to be too narrow an interpretation of the court's powers. It would mean that while a declaration that a statutory instrument is incompatible with European Community law could be made, since such an instrument is capable of being set aside by certiorari, no such declaration could be made as regards primary legislation. However, in the *Factortame* series of cases (*Reg.* v. *Secretary of State for Transport, Ex parte Factortame Ltd* [1990] 2 AC 85; *Reg.* v. *Secretary of State for Transport, Ex parte Factortame Ltd (No 2)* (Case C 213/89) [1991] 1 AC 603; *Reg.* v. *Secretary of State for Transport, Ex parte Factortame Ltd (No 3)* (Case C 221/89) [1992] QB 680) the applicants for judicial review sought a declaration that the provisions of Part II of the Merchant Shipping Act 1988 should not apply to them on the ground that such application would be contrary to Community law, in particular articles 7 and 52 of the EEC Treaty (principle of non-discrimination on the ground of nationality and right of establishment). The applicants were companies incorporated in England which were controlled by Spanish nationals and owned fishing vessels which on account of such control were denied registration in the register of British vessels by virtue of the restrictive conditions contained in Part II of the Act of 1988. The Divisional Court (*Reg.* v. *Secretary of State for Transport, Ex parte Factortame Ltd* [1989] 2 CMLR 353), under article 177 of the Treaty, referred to the European Court of Justice a number of questions, including the question whether these restrictive conditions were compatible with articles 7 and **[419]** 52 of the Treaty. The

European Court [1992] QB 680 answered that question in the negative, and, although the final result is not reported, no doubt the Divisional Court in due course granted a declaration accordingly. The effect was that certain provisions of United Kingdom primary legislation were held to be invalid in their purported application to nationals of member states of the European Economic Community, but without any prerogative order being available to strike down the legislation in question, which of course remained valid as regards nationals of non-member states. At no stage in the course of the litigation, which included two visits to this House, was it suggested that judicial review was not available for the purpose of obtaining an adjudication upon the validity of the legislation in so far as it affected the applicants.

The *Factortame* case is thus a precedent in favour of the EOC's recourse to judicial review for the purpose of challenging as incompatible with European Community law the relevant provisions of the Act of 1978. It also provides an answer to the third procedural point taken by the Secretary of State, which maintains that the Divisional Court had no jurisdiction to declare that the United Kingdom or the Secretary of State is in breach of obligation under Community law. There is no need for any such declaration. A declaration that the threshold provisions of the Act of 1978 are incompatible with Community law would suffice for the purposes sought to be achieved by the EOC and is capable of being granted consistently with the precedent afforded by *Factortame*. This does not involve, as contended for the Secretary of State, any attempt by the EOC to enforce the international treaty obligations of the United Kingdom. The EOC is concerned simply to obtain a ruling which reflects the primacy of European Community law enshrined in section 2 of the Act of 1972 and determines whether the relevant United Kingdom law is compatible with the Equal Pay Directive and the Equal Treatment Directive.

Similar considerations provide the answer to the Secretary of State's fourth procedural point by which it is maintained that the Divisional Court is not the appropriate forum to decide the substantive issues at stake. The issues at stake are similar in character to those which were raised in *Factortame*. The Divisional Court is the only English forum in which the EOC, having the capacity and sufficient interest to do so, is in a position to secure the result which it desires. It is said that the incompatibility issue could be tested in proceedings before the European Court of Justice instituted by the European Commission against the United Kingdom under article 169 of the EEC Treaty. That may be true, but it affords no reason for concluding that the Divisional Court is an inappropriate forum for the application by the EOC designed towards a similar end and, indeed, there are grounds for the view that the Divisional Court is the more appropriate forum, since the European Court of Justice has said that it is for the national court to determine whether an indirectly discriminatory pay practice is founded on objectively justified economic grounds: see *Bilka-Kaufhaus GmbH* v. *Weber von Hartz* (Case 170/84) [1987] ICR 110, 126.

I turn now to the important substantive issue in the appeal, which is whether or not the threshold provisions in the Act of 1978 have been shown to be objectively justified, the onus of doing so being one which rests on the Secretary of State.

[420] In *Bilka-Kaufhaus GmbH* v. *Weber von Hartz*, the European Court of Justice said, at p. 126:

36. It is for the national court, which has sole jurisdiction to make findings of fact, to determine whether and to what extent the grounds put forward by an employer to explain the adoption of a pay practice which applies independently of a worker's sex but in fact affects more women than men may be regarded as objectively justified economic grounds. If the national court finds that the measures chosen by Bilka correspond to a real need on the part of the undertaking, are appropriate with a view to achieving the objectives pursued and are necessary to that end, the fact that the measures affect a far greater number of women than men is not sufficient to show that they constitute an infringement of article 119.

Somewhat broader considerations apply where the discriminatory provisions are to be found in national legislation. In *Rinner-Kühn* v. *FWW Spezial-Gebäudereinigung GmbH & Co. KG* (Case 171/88) [1989] ECR 2743, the question at issue was whether German legislation which permitted restrictions on the right of part-time workers to sick pay contravened article 119 of the EEC Treaty, considering that a great majority of part-time workers were women. The court said, at pp. 2760-1:

12. In such a situation, it must be concluded that a provision such as that in question results in discrimination against female workers in relation to male workers and must, in principle, be regarded as contrary to the aim of article 119 of the Treaty. The position would be different only if the distinction between the two categories of employees were justified by objective factors unrelated to any discrimination on grounds of sex (see the judgment of 13 May 1986 in *Bilka-Kaufhaus GmbH* v. *Weber von Hartz* (Case 170/84) [1986] ECR 1607). 13. In the course of the procedure, the German Government stated, in response to a question put by the court, that workers whose period of work amounted to less than 10 hours a week or 45 hours a month were not as integrated in, or as dependent on, the undertaking employing them as other workers. 14. It should, however, be stated that those considerations, in so far as they are only generalisations about certain categories of workers, do not enable criteria which are both objective and unrelated to any discrimination on grounds of sex to be identified. However, if the member state can show that the means chosen meet a necessary aim of its social policy and that they are suitable and requisite for attaining that aim, the mere fact that the provision affects a much greater number of female workers than male workers cannot be regarded as constituting an infringement of article 119. 15. It is for the national court, which has sole

jurisdiction to assess the facts and interpret the national legislation, to determine whether and to what extent a legislative provision, which, though applying independently of the sex of the worker, actually affects a greater number of women than men, is justified by reasons which are objective and unrelated to any discrimination on grounds of sex. 16. The reply to the question referred by the national court must therefore be that article 119 of the EEC Treaty must be interpreted as precluding national legislation which permits employers to exclude employees whose normal working hours do not exceed 10 hours a week or 45 hours a **[421]** month from the continued payment of wages in the event of illness, if that measure affects a far greater number of women than men, unless the member state shows that the legislation concerned is justified by objective factors unrelated to any discrimination on grounds of sex.

The original reason for the threshold provisions of the Act of 1978 appears to have been the view that part-time workers were less committed than full-time workers to the undertaking which employed them. In his letter of 23 April 1990 the Secretary of State stated that their purpose was to ensure that a fair balance was struck between the interests of employers and employees. These grounds are not now founded on as objective justification for the thresholds. It is now claimed that the thresholds have the effect that more part-time employment is available than would be the case if employers were liable for redundancy pay and compensation for unfair dismissal to employees who worked for less than eight hours a week or between eight and 16 hours a week for under five years. It is contended that if employers were under that liability they would be inclined to employ less part-time workers and more full-time workers, to the disadvantage of the former.

The bringing about of an increase in the availability of part-time work is properly to be regarded as a beneficial social policy aim and it cannot be said that it is not a necessary aim. The question is whether the threshold provisions of the Act of 1978 have been shown, by reference to objective factors, to be suitable and requisite for achieving that aim. As regards suitability for achieving the aim in question, it is to be noted that the purpose of the thresholds is said to be to reduce the costs to employers of employing part-time workers. The same result, however, would follow from a situation where the basic rate of pay for part-time workers was less than the basic rate for full-time workers. No distinction in principle can properly be made between direct and indirect labour costs. While in certain circumstances an employer might be justified in paying full-time workers a higher rate than part-time workers in order to secure the more efficient use of his machinery (see *Jenkins* v. *Kingsgate (Clothing Productions) Ltd* [1981] 1 WLR 1485) that would be a special and limited state of affairs. Legislation which permitted a differential of that kind nationwide would present a very different aspect and considering that the great majority of part-time workers are women would surely constitute a gross breach of the principle of equal pay and could not possibly be regarded as a suitable means of achieving an increase in part-time employment. Similar considerations apply to legislation which reduces the indirect cost of employing part-time labour. Then as to the threshold provisions being requisite to achieve the stated aim, the question is whether on the evidence before the Divisional Court they have been proved actually to result in greater availability of part-time work than would be the case without them. In my opinion that question must be answered in the negative. The evidence for the Secretary of State consisted principally of an affidavit by an official in the Department of Employment which set out the views of the Department but did not contain anything capable of being regarded as factual evidence demonstrating the correctness of these views. One of the exhibits to the affidavit was a report with draft Directives prepared by the Social Affairs Commissioner of the European Commission in 1990 (COM(90) 228 final—SYN 280 and SYN 281, Brussels, 13 August 1990; **[422]** Official Journal 1990 No C 224, pp. 4-8). This covered a wide range of employment benefits and advantages, including redundancy pay and compensation for unfair dismissal, but proposed a qualifying threshold for those benefits of eight hours of work per week. The basis for that was stated to be the elimination of disproportionate administrative costs and regard to employers' economic needs. These are not the grounds of justification relied on by the Secretary of State. The evidence put in by the EOC consisted in large measure in a report of the House of Commons Employment Committee, "Part-Time Work," vol. 1 in 1990 (HC 122-I, 10 January 1990) and a report of the House of Lords Select Committee on the European Communities, "Part-Time and Temporary Employment," in 1990 (HL Paper 7, 4 December 1990). These revealed a diversity of views upon the effect of the threshold provisions on part-time work, employers' organisations being of the opinion that their removal would reduce the amount available with trade union representatives and some employers and academics in the industrial relations field taking the opposite view. It also appeared that no other member state of the European Community, apart from the Republic of Ireland, had legislation providing for similar thresholds. The Republic of Ireland, where statute at one time provided for an 18-hour-per-week threshold, had recently introduced legislation reducing this to eight hours. In the Netherlands the proportion of the workforce in part-time employment was in 1988 29.4 per cent and in Denmark 25.5 per cent, neither country having any thresholds similar to those in the Act of 1978. In France legislation was introduced in 1982 providing for part-time workers to have the same rights as full-time, yet between 1983 and 1988 part-time work in that country increased by 36.6 per cent, compared with an increase of 26.1 per cent over the same period in the United Kingdom. While various explanations were suggested on behalf of the Secretary of State for these statistics, there is no means of ascertaining whether these explanations have any validity.

The fact is, however, that the proportion of part-time employees in the national workforce is much less than the proportion of full-time employees, their weekly remuneration is necessarily much lower, and the number of them made redundant or unfairly dismissed in any year is not likely to be unduly large. The conclusion must be that no objective justification for the thresholds in the Act of 1978 has been established.

A subsidiary issue of substance in the appeal is whether or not compensation for unfair dismissal is "pay" within the meaning of article 119 of the Treaty and the Equal Pay Directive. The definition of "pay" in article 119 has been set out above. In *Arbeiterwohlfahrt der Stadt Berlin eV* v. *Bötel* (Case C-360/90) [1992] IRLR 423, 425, the European Court of Justice said:

> 12. According to the case law of the court . . . the concept of "pay" within the meaning of article 119 of the Treaty comprises any consideration whether in cash or in kind, whether immediate or future, provided that the employee receives it, albeit indirectly, in respect of his employment from his employer, whether under a contract of employment, legislative provisions or made ex gratia by the employer.

In *Barber* v. *Guardian Royal Exchange Assurance Group* (Case C 262/88) [1991] 1 QB 344 the court held that redundancy pay was pay within the meaning of article 119 on the ground (paragraph 18 of the judgment, at p. 400) that receipt of it arose "by reason of the existence of the employment relationship." There is much to be said in favour of the view that compensation for unfair dismissal is of a comparable nature, but the European Court of Justice has not yet pronounced upon this issue, and there may be a question whether the answer to it can properly be held to be acte clair, or whether resolution of it would require a reference to the European Court under article 177 of the Treaty. **[423]**

Such a reference is in any event, however, unnecessary for the disposal of the present appeal. Discrimination as regards the right to compensation for unfair dismissal, if not objectively justified, is clearly in contravention of the Equal Treatment Directive.

In the light of the foregoing I am of the opinion that the appeal by the EOC should be allowed and that declarations should be made in the following terms: (1) that the provisions of the Employment Protection (Consolidation) Act 1978 whereby employees who work for fewer than 16 hours per week are subject to different conditions in respect of qualification for redundancy pay from those which apply to employees who work for 16 hours per week or more are incompatible with article 119 of the EEC Treaty and the Council Directive of 10 February 1975 (75/117/EEC); (2) that the provisions of the Employment Protection (Consolidation) Act 1978 whereby employees who work for fewer than 16 hours per week are subject to different conditions in respect of the right to compensation for unfair dismissal from those which apply to employees who work for 16 hours per week or more are incompatible with the Council Directive of 9 February 1976 (76/207/EEC).

It remains to note that the EOC proposed that the House should grant a declaration to the effect that the Secretary of State is in breach of those provisions of the Equal Treatment Directive which require member states to introduce measures to abolish any laws contrary to the principle of equal treatment. The purpose of such a declaration was said to be to enable part-time workers who were employed otherwise than by the state or an emanation of the state, and who had been deprived of the right to obtain compensation for unfair dismissal by the restrictive thresholds in the Act of 1978, to take proceedings against the United Kingdom for compensation, founding upon the decision of the European Court of Justice in *Francovich* v. *Italian Republic* (Cases C-6/90, C-9/90) [1991] ECR I-5357. In my opinion it would be quite inappropriate to make any such declaration. If there is any individual who believes that he or she has a good claim to compensation under the *Francovich* principle, it is the Attorney-General who would be defendant in any proceedings directed to enforcing it, and the issues raised would not necessarily be identical with any of those which arise in the present appeal.

LORD JAUNCEY OF TULLICHETTLE. My Lords, the Equal Opportunities Commission was established by the provisions of Part VI of the Sex Discrimination Act 1975. Section 53(1) of the Act provides that it should have the following duties:

> (*a*) to work towards the elimination of discrimination, (*b*) to promote equality of opportunity between men and women generally, and (*c*) to keep under review the working of this Act and the Equal Pay Act 1970 and, when they are so required by the Secretary of State or otherwise think it necessary, draw up and submit to the Secretary of State proposals for amending them.

[424] Section 55 requires the commission to keep under review the discriminatory aspects of provisions in health and safety legislation and to report to the Secretary of State on any matter specified by him. Section 56 requires the commission to make an annual report to the Secretary of State on its activities. Section 57(1) provides:

> Without prejudice to their general power to do anything requisite for the performance of their duties under section 53(1), the commission may if they think fit, and shall if required by the Secretary of State, conduct a formal investigation for any purpose connected with the carrying out of those duties.

Section 60(1) provides:

> If in the light of any of their findings in a formal investigation it appears to the commission necessary or expedient, whether during the course of the investigation or after its conclusion . . . (*b*) to make to the Secretary of State any

recommendations, whether for changes in the law or otherwise, the commission shall make those recommendations accordingly.

The commission is also empowered by section 75 to provide assistance to claimants in proceedings under the Act.

In pursuance of its statutory duties the commission has in the past initiated judicial review proceedings without challenge to its capacity so to do. This House upheld its right to obtain a declaration that a provision by a local education authority of selected secondary education was unlawful: *Reg.* v. *Birmingham City Council, Ex parte Equal Opportunities Commission* [1989] AC 1155. In a Divisional Court hearing in December 1991 (*Reg.* v. *Secretary for Defence, Ex parte Equal Opportunities Commission* (unreported), 20 December 1991) on an application for judicial review of a decision made on behalf of the Secretary of State for Defence in relation to pregnant service women it was accepted by the Crown that the commission had legal standing. However, the fact that the commission may properly initiate judicial review proceedings in pursuance of their duties against local authorities or other ministers is not, in my view, conclusive of its ability so to do in relation to the Secretary of State.

The provisions of the Act to which I have referred envisage the commission performing its duties on its own initiative or, in certain cases, as required by the Secretary of State. Section 53(1)(*c*) empowers or requires the commission to submit proposals to the Secretary of State and section 60(1) similarly empowers or requires the commission to make recommendations to the Secretary of State. The Act neither requires the Secretary of State to implement these proposals or recommendations nor confers power on the commission to have them implemented. Thus, vis-à-vis the Secretary of State, the role of the commission is advisory and it is no part of its duties to initiate proceedings against him in matters relating to sex discrimination. The broad words of section 53(1)(*a*) which might be thought habile to cover any steps taken by the commission against anybody towards the specified end must, so far as the Secretary of State is concerned, be read in the context of the particular relationship which has been created between him and the commission. The Act makes the commission answerable to the Secretary of State and not vice versa. If Parliament had intended that the commission should be empowered to challenge decisions of the Secretary of State and impose **[425]** its will upon him it is quite remarkable that Part VI of the Act which sets out in some detail the powers and duties of the commission, both at large and in relation to the Secretary of State, should have remained totally silent upon this particular matter.

While reluctant to disagree with your Lordships I am driven to the conclusion, in agreement with Kennedy LJ in the Court of Appeal, that the commission does not have the capacity to pursue these proceedings. I would therefore dismiss the appeal. I should only add that if I had reached a different conclusion in relation to this preliminary matter I should have been in entire agreement with the reasons given by my noble and learned friends Lord Keith of Kinkel and Lord Browne-Wilkinson for allowing the appeal.

LORD LOWRY. My Lords, I have had the advantage of reading in draft the speech prepared by my noble and learned friend, Lord Keith of Kinkel. I agree with it and for the reasons which he gives I, too, would allow the appeal and make the declarations which he proposes.

Accepting as I do the analysis of my noble and learned friend, I do not find it necessary to consider the question (which I think is arguable) whether the Secretary of State's letter of 23 April 1990 was a "decision" for the purposes of judicial review. I would, however, take the opportunity of expressing my respectful and complete agreement with the observations on procedure which are about to be delivered by my noble and learned friend, Lord Browne-Wilkinson.

I feel bound, however, to add (as can perhaps be inferred from my speech in *Roy* v. *Kensington and Chelsea and Westminster Family Practitioner Committee* [1992] 1 AC 624) that I have never been entirely happy with the wide procedural restriction for which *O'Reilly* v. *Mackman* [1983] 2 AC 237 is an authority, and I hope that that case will one day be the subject of your Lordships' further consideration.

LORD BROWNE-WILKINSON. My Lords, I agree with the speech of my noble and learned friend, Lord Keith of Kinkel but wish to add a few words on the procedural question whether the court can make a declaration on an application for judicial review even though in the circumstances of the case the court could not grant one of the prerogative orders.

The question arises in this way. It being established (for the reasons given by my noble and learned friend, Lord Keith of Kinkel) that the Equal Opportunities Commission has locus standi to bring proceedings for judicial review but has not demonstrated that there is any "decision" by the Secretary of State which can be quashed, has the court got jurisdiction to make a declaration that the domestic law of the United Kingdom is not in conformity with European law?

Before 1977, there were two routes whereby relief could be sought from the courts in the field of what is now known as public law. The first was by application to the Queen's Bench Divisional Court for one of the prerogative orders. The second was by way of a civil action in the High Court for a declaration. This procedure in a civil action for a declaration was under what is now RSC, Ord. 15, r. 16, which provides:

> No action or other proceeding shall be open to objection on the ground that a merely declaratory judgment or order is sought **[426]** thereby, and the court may make binding declarations of right whether or not any consequential relief is or could be claimed.

As early as 1911 it was established that, in a civil action brought by a competent plaintiff, the court could grant declaratory relief against the Crown as to the legality of actions which the Crown proposed to take: *Dyson* v. *Attorney-General* [1911] 1 KB 410. Of course, in such civil proceedings in the High Court there could be no question of the plaintiff being entitled to any of the prerogative orders, which could only be made in proceedings on the Crown side.

Civil proceedings for a declaration as to public rights were a widely adopted method down to 1977. Indeed, many of the most recent developments in public law were made in such civil actions brought to obtain declaratory relief only; see, for example, *Ridge* v. *Baldwin* [1964] AC 40; *Anisminic Ltd* v. *Foreign Compensation Commission* [1969] 2 AC 147; see also *Zamir & Woolf*, *The Declaratory Judgment*, 2nd ed. (1993), pp. 29–31.

The ability to obtain a declaration of public rights in civil proceedings was restricted by the need to show sufficient locus standi. Although the plaintiff did not have to show an actual or threatened infringement of his private rights, he did have to show that any actual or threatened infringement of public rights would cause him special damage: *Gouriet* v. *Union of Post Office Workers* [1978] AC 435. However, questions of locus standi are not what I am now considering.

In 1977 the new Order 53 was introduced, laying down the modern procedure for judicial review. Ord. 53, r. 1(2) expressly provides that an application for a declaration can be made in judicial review proceedings and gives the Divisional Court power to make a declaration if it considers it just and convenient

> having regard to—(*a*) the nature of the matters in respect of which relief may be granted by way of an order of mandamus, prohibition or certiorari, (*b*) the nature of the persons and bodies against whom relief may be granted by way of such an order, and (*c*) all the circumstances of the case . . .

This rule was given statutory confirmation by section 31 of the Supreme Court Act 1981.

In the period between the introduction of the new Order 53 and the decision in *O'Reilly* v. *Mackman* [1983] 2 AC 237 there were therefore two routes whereby a declaration of public rights could be obtained. The first was in judicial review proceedings under Order 53; the second was by civil proceedings for declaratory relief under Ord. 15, r. 16. As to the latter, the position remained as it was before 1977. During this period, civil proceedings for a declaration as to public rights continued to be brought. Thus, in *Royal College of Nursing of the United Kingdom* v. *Department of Health and Social Security* [1981] AC 800 civil proceedings were brought in the Queen's Bench Division for a declaration as to the correctness in law of a circular from the DHSS purporting to explain to the medical profession the effect of the Abortion Act 1967. No one contended that such a declaration could not be made even though, as in the present case, none of the prerogative orders could have been made even if the proceedings had been brought under Order 53. This House restored a declaration as to the legality of the circular which had been made by the trial judge.

[427] Accordingly, right down to the decision of this House in *O'Reilly* v. *Mackman* the two procedures for obtaining declaratory relief, the one by way of civil proceedings in the High Court the other by way of judicial review in the Divisional Court, continued. In *O'Reilly* v. *Mackman* itself this House was considering the propriety of four civil actions brought in the High Court for declarations as to matters of public law. This House held that in such public law cases it is an abuse of process to proceed by way of civil action and that such proceedings must be brought by way of judicial review. In so deciding, Lord Diplock reviewed the law affecting declaratory judgments in both civil proceedings and judicial review proceedings. He said, at p. 283:

> Nevertheless, there may still be cases where it turns out in the course of proceedings to challenge a decision of a statutory authority that a declaration of rights rather than certiorari is the appropriate remedy. *Pyx Granite Co. Ltd* v. *Ministry of Housing and Local Government* [1960] AC 260 provides an example of such a case. So Order 53 since 1977 has provided a procedure by which every type of remedy for infringement of rights of individuals that are entitled to protection in public law can be obtained in one and the same proceeding by way of an application for judicial review, and whichever remedy is found to be the most appropriate in the light of what has emerged upon the hearing of the application can be granted to him.

In my judgment, this passage makes it clear that under Order 53 any declaration as to public rights which could formerly be obtained in civil proceedings in the High Court can now also be obtained in judicial review proceedings. If this were not so, the effect of the purely procedural decision in *O'Reilly* v. *Mackman*, requiring all public law cases to be brought by way of judicial review, would have had the effect of thenceforward preventing a plaintiff who previously had locus standi to bring civil proceedings for a declaration as to public rights (even though there was no decision which could be the subject of a prerogative order) from bringing any proceedings for such a declaration. No statutory provision has ever removed the right to seek such a declaration which right has been established and exercised from 1911. Ord. 53, r. 1(2) does not say that a declaration is only to be made in lieu of a prerogative order. All it requires is that the court should have regard to "the nature of the matters in respect of which" prerogative orders can be made. In the second *Factortame* case, *Reg.* v. *Secretary of State for Transport, Ex parte Factortame Ltd (No 2)* (Case C 213/89) [1991] 1 AC 603, this House, admittedly without argument to the contrary, plainly envisaged that a declaration as to public rights could be made, even though on the facts of that case none of the prerogative orders could have been made.

Finally, the terms of Ord. 15, r. 16 itself indicate the same result. Judicial review proceedings under Order 53 are "proceedings." Therefore the effect of Ord. 15, r. 16 is that the court in judicial review proceedings for a declaration can make a declaratory order "whether or not any consequential relief . . . *could* be claimed."

I have sought to demonstrate that the history of declaratory relief, authority and the terms of Ord. 15, r. 16 all point to the court having power to make a declaratory judgment in judicial review proceedings brought by a plaintiff who has locus standi, whether or not the court **[428]** could also make a prerogative order. The only indications to the contrary are certain dicta in *Reg.* v. *Inland Revenue Commissioners, Ex parte National Federation of Self-Employed and Small Businesses Ltd* [1982] AC 617. The only matter at issue in that case was locus standi to bring proceedings under Order 53. It was suggested in argument that Lord Diplock had indicated, obiter, that a declaration was only available as an alternative to mandamus. I do not so read his speech and, in the light of the passage I have quoted from his speech in *O'Reilly* v. *Mackman* a year later, it would be surprising if he meant so to indicate. Lord Scarman, at p. 648, clearly expressed the view that a declaration could be granted in judicial review proceedings

> only in circumstances in which one or other of the prerogative orders can issue. I so interpret RSC, Ord. 53, r. 1(2) because to do otherwise would be to condemn the rule as ultra vires.

There was no examination of the history of the declaratory judgment in that case and the reason given by Lord Scarman (that otherwise Ord. 53, r. 1(2) would be ultra vires) ceased to have any force when shortly thereafter section 31 of the Act of 1981 was enacted and gave the provision statutory force. Therefore, in my judgment this obiter dictum should not lead your Lordships to reach a conclusion different from that indicated by the other arguments I have mentioned.

For these reasons and the reasons given by my noble and learned friend, Lord Keith of Kinkel, I would allow the appeal and make the declarations that are proposed.

LORD SLYNN OF HADLEY. My Lords, for the reasons given by my noble and learned friend, Lord Keith of Kinkel, I, too, would allow this appeal and make the declarations he proposes.

Appeal of Equal Opportunities Commission allowed with costs.
Declarations accordingly.
Appeal of Mrs Patricia Elizabeth Day dismissed.
No order as to costs.

[Report: [1994] 2 WLR 409]

Direct effect — Directives — Conditions for direct effect — Failure of Member State to implement directive correctly— Whether directive may be relied upon by individuals before national courts — Bodies against which directive may be relied upon—Emanation of the State—Definition— Whether definition laid down by European Court of Justice conclusive—Council Directive 77/187 on Acquired Rights— The law of England

NATIONAL UNION OF TEACHERS AND OTHERS *v.* GOVERNING BODY OF ST MARY'S CHURCH OF ENGLAND (AIDED) JUNIOR SCHOOL AND OTHERS

England, Court of Appeal (Civil Division). 12 *December* 1996

(Beldam, Ward and Schiemann, Lords Justices)

SUMMARY: *The facts*:—Three teachers were made redundant and thereby dismissed when the State-aided school in which they were employed was closed down and replaced by a new school. The authority for the actions of the governors of the old school, its closure and its replacement by the new school, were all provided by orders made by the Secretary of State for Education. The teachers claimed unfair dismissal against the school governors. The Transfer of Undertakings (Protection of Employment) Regulations 1981 provided that dismissal following the transfer of an undertaking was to be treated as unfair, but this provision only applied to commercial undertakings. It subsequently transpired that this limitation constituted an incorrect transposition of Council Directive 77/187 on Acquired Rights and was therefore a breach of Community law. Consequently the teachers instituted proceedings for unfair dismissal in reliance on the Directive itself, invoking the doctrine of vertical direct effect to argue that it conferred rights for individuals upon which they could rely. The industrial tribunal and Employment Appeal Tribunal both held that the governors of a State-aided school were not emanations of the State so that the Directive could not be relied upon directly. The teachers appealed to the House of Lords.

Held:—The appeal was allowed.

(1) In *Foster* v. *British Gas*[1] the European Court of Justice laid down a so-called tripartite test for what constituted an emanation of the State: a body which was made responsible, pursuant to a measure adopted by the State, for providing a public service under the control of the State and had, for that purpose, special powers beyond those normally applicable between individuals. But this test was not to be adopted as if it were a conclusive statutory definition of an emanation of the State. Rather it was to be regarded as merely indicative (pp. 471-3).

(2) Education was clearly a public service and the powers of the Secretary of State and local education authorities amounted to State control. But although

[1] Volume 1, Note, p. 165.

it could not be said that the governors had special powers beyond those which applied between individuals, they were still to be regarded as emanations of the State for the purposes of the doctrine of vertical direct effect (pp. 472-3).

The following is the text of the judgment of the Court:

[631] SCHIEMANN LJ: This appeal from the Employment Appeal Tribunal arises from the dismissal of three teachers. They were employed at a school which was closed along with its neighbour and were dismissed allegedly for reasons of redundancy. On the day after the closure of their school a new school opened its doors. Most of the teachers who had been employed at the two schools which had been closed down were thereafter employed at the new school. Not so the three appellants. They had no job to go to. On the face of it there was **[632]** no answer to the assertion that they had been dismissed by the governors of the old school for reasons of redundancy.

Appellants and respondents are agreed that the determinative question before us is whether the governing body of a voluntary aided school can be regarded as an emanation of the state in the context of the doctrine that an individual can rely on the provisions of a European Community Directive as against the state or an emanation of the state.

The background to the matter is as follows. In general the law provides some protection for employees whose former employer's undertaking is transferred to someone else. That protection springs from the Acquired Rights Directive 77/187.[1] That Directive was transposed into UK legislation by the Transfer of Undertakings (Protection of Employment) Regulations 1981.

In particular those regulations provided by Regulation 8 that:

[1] The preamble to the Directive ([1977] OJ L61/26) recites that:

> Whereas economic trends are bringing in their wake at both national and community level, changes in the structure of undertakings, through transfers of undertakings, business or parts of businesses to other employers as a result of legal transfers or mergers;
>
> Whereas it is necessary to provide for the protection of employees in the event of a change of employer, in particular to ensure that their rights are safeguarded.
>
> Whereas differences still remain in the Member States as regards the extent of the protection of employees in this respect and these differences should be reduced;
>
> Whereas these differences can have a direct effect on the functioning of the Common Market;
>
> Whereas it is therefore necessary to promote the approximation of laws in this field while maintaining the improvement described in Article 117 of the Treaties.

Article 1 provides:

> This Directive shall apply to the transfer of an undertaking, business or part of a business to another employer as a result of a legal transfer or merger.

And Article 4 provides:

> The transfer of an undertaking, business or part of a business shall not in itself constitute grounds for dismissal by the transferor. . . . this provision shall not stand in the way of dismissal that may take place for economic, technical or organisational reasons entailing changes in the workforce.

Where either before or after a relevant transfer, any employee of the transferor . . . is dismissed, that employee shall be treated . . . as unfairly dismissed if the transfer or a reason connected with it is the reason or principal reason for his dismissal.

The regulations only apply to a transfer from one person to another of an "undertaking". In Regulation 2 at the relevant time it was stated that "undertaking":

Includes any trade or business *but does not include any undertaking or part of an undertaking which is not in the nature of a commercial venture* (emphasis supplied).

Since the running of the old school could not be described as a commercial venture the applicants were unable to obtain the benefit of these regulations.

In due course the United Kingdom government became aware **[633]** that it had incorrectly transposed the Directive into national legislation and therefore repealed the underlined words in the definition of "undertaking" by the Trade Union Reform and Employment Rights Act of 1993 as from 30 August 1993. That however did not help these applicants who had been dismissed some months before.

So it was that the applicants came before the Industrial Tribunal seeking to rely on rights which had been given to them by the Directive.

The jurisprudence of the European Court of Justice establishes that directives can in certain circumstances give rights to individuals:

If domestic law falls short of what is required by the directive, the Member State is in breach of its treaty obligation to give effect to it. Thus, if the individual asserts before his domestic court a right or immunity *vis-à-vis* the Member State which is not available under the domestic law but which would have been available if the Member State had brought its domestic law into line with the directive then the individual is entitled to have his case adjudged as if the Member State had performed its obligation: *i.e.* in accordance with the Directive.[2]

However the case law also establishes that those rights cannot be enforced against other individuals. There are of course innumerable bodies in different Member States which fall in a grey area somewhere in between on the one hand being private bodies and on the other being completely identifiable as the state or its agencies. The case law indicates that some of these are regarded as being equivalent for this purpose to the state whereas others are regarded as being equivalent for this purpose to individuals. Those bodies which are regarded as being equivalent for this purpose to the state are sometimes described in a useful term, which I[3] shall adopt, as being an emanation of the state.

[2] *Rolls Royce plc* v. *Doughty* [1992] ICR 538 at 541 per Mustill LJ.
[3] Conscious of the warning of Mustill LJ in the *Rolls Royce* case at p. 553D.

It is undisputed law that the decision on whether a body falls within the concept of an emanation of the state is for the national court. This court will be guided by the emerging case law. If it cannot reach a decision in the light of that case law and the writings of the academics then it will refer a question to the European Court of Justice. Both parties agree that the existing jurisprudence is sufficient to enable this court to reach an answer to the determinative question. Neither has suggested that we should refer any question to the European Court of Justice.

I propose therefore first to examine the case law, second to indicate what are the presently relevant features of the relationship between the governors of a voluntary aided school such as the present and the state, third to describe what happened before the tribunals below, and finally to consider whether such a school, which is admittedly in the grey area which I have mentioned, is to be regarded as **[634]** an emanation of the state for the purposes of the doctrine to which I have adverted and which is known as the doctrine of direct effect.

Before doing so, it is worth noting that since the development of the doctrine of direct vertical effect there has developed another means of giving effect as against the state to the rights given to individuals by directives. This is an action for damages against the state for the failure by national legislation to enact or to give the required effect to a directive. It may be that had the action for damages for non-implementation of directives been established as part of Community jurisprudence in its early years the concept of direct vertical effect would not have developed in the way that it has. That is speculation. This court must apply the concept until such time, if any, as the European Court of Justice modifies it.

Thus an individual whose rights have been infringed has two possible courses of action open to him:

1. He can rely on the doctrine of vertical direct effect and seek to sue the Member State or emanation of the state in which case the latter are inhibited under the jurisprudence developed by the European Court of Justice from relying on the failure of the state correctly to transpose the Directive;
2. He can sue the state for damages for failure correctly to transpose the Directive, relying on the case law of the European Court of Justice which started with Case C-6/90, *Francovich* v. *Italy*[4] and of which the most recent example is Case C-5/94, *R* v. *Ministry of Agriculture, Fisheries and Food, ex parte Hedley Lomas (Ireland) Ltd*.[5]

In the present case the plaintiff chose the former route.

[4] [1991] ECR I-5357; [1993] 2 CMLR 66.
[5] [1996] ECR I-2553; [1996] 2 CMLR 391.

The Case Law

Guidelines by the light of which the national court is to come to its decision as to what is an emanation of the state appear from a series of cases which have emerged from the European Court of Justice relating to national tax authorities,[6] local or regional authorities,[7] public authorities for providing health services,[8] constitutionally independent authorities for maintaining public order such as the Police[9] and a local land consolidation committee responsible for awarding public works contracts.[10] It is clear from those cases that the **[635]** concept of an emanation of the state for the purposes of the doctrine of vertical effect is a very broad one and certainly in my judgment extends to local authorities. Mr Straker, who appears for the respondents, did not formally concede this point, but did not argue to the contrary.

The European Court of Justice has not promulgated a formula which can be applied to all situations. It has preferred to adopt the approach of the Common Law and of the French Conseil d'Etat of moving from case to case to establish principles and refine them as it goes along. Most of the case law has been developed on references to the European Court of Justice under Article 177 EEC. The only ineluctable task of the European Court of Justice on such a reference is to provide a ruling in sufficiently wide terms to enable the national court to reach a decision in the case in which the reference was made. There is a perpetual tension between the desirability of legal certainty which militates towards the laying down of broadly framed rules and the desire to move cautiously and to take stock of the effect of rulings. It is also important to remember that while the decision whether or not a particular body is properly regarded as an emanation of the state is a matter for the national court the proper development of the Community requires that all national courts should proceed upon the same principles when applying Community law.

Each party before us relied upon *Foster* v. *British Gas plc*[11] which was decided by the House of Lords after having obtained an opinion from the European Court of Justice. The issue which faced the court in that case was whether the applicants could rely as against the British Gas Corporation on an unimplemented Council Directive. Although the gas industry had been privatised by the time of the litigation and the rights and liabilities of the British Gas Corporation had been transferred to British Gas plc the courts had to consider the position of a nationalised

[6] Case 8/81, *Becker* v. *Finanzamt Munster-Innenstadt*: [1982] ECR 53; [1982] 1 CMLR 499.

[7] Case 103/88, *Fratelli Costanzo* v. *Comune di Milano*: [1989] ECR 1839; [1990] 3 CMLR 239.

[8] Case 152/84, *Marshall* v. *Southampton and South West Hampshire Area Health Authority (Teaching)*: [1986] ECR 723; [1986] 1 CMLR 688.

[9] Case 222/84, *Johnston* v. *Chief Constable of the Royal Ulster Constabulary*: [1986] ECR 1651; [1986] 3 CMLR 240.

[10] Case 31/87, *Beentjes BV* v. *Netherlands* [1988] ECR 4635; [1990] 1 CMLR 287.

[11] [1991] 2 AC 306.

industry. The House of Lords held that the Corporation was a body against which the Directive could be enforced, thus overruling all the lower courts. The case is important in a number of respects:

1. Van Gerven AG summarised the jurisprudence up to the time of the delivery of his opinion;
2. The European Court of Justice held in paragraph 15 of its decision:

> The Court of Justice has jurisdiction in proceedings for a preliminary ruling to determine the categories of persons against whom the provisions of a Directive may be relied on. It is for the national courts, on the other hand, to decide whether a party to proceedings before them falls within one of the categories so defined.

3. The ruling of the court was expressed thus in paragraph [20] of the judgment:

> A body, whatever its legal form, which has been made responsible, **[636]** pursuant to a measure adopted by the state, for providing a public service under control of the state and has for that purpose special powers beyond those which resulted from the normal rules applicable in relations between individuals is included among the bodies against which the provisions of a Directive capable of having direct effect may be relied upon.

It is clear from the wording of paragraph [20] and in particular the words "is included among" that the formula there used was not intended to be an exclusive formula.

In order to discover what the appropriate principles are which should govern a case such as the present which is not concerned with a nationalised or de-nationalised commercial undertaking but rather with the provision of a service such as public education, it is useful to start with the decision of the European Court of Justice in Case 152/84, *Marshall* v. *Southampton and South West Area Health Authority*. In that case the claimant sought to rely on the Equal Treatment Directive against the area health authority. It was held that she could do so under the doctrine of vertical direct effect. The ECJ stated in paragraph [47] of its decision that in *Becker* it had decided that a Member State which has not adopted the implementing measures required by the directive within the prescribed period may not plead, as against individuals, its own failure to perform the obligations which the directive entails.

The European Court of Justice went on to hold in paragraph [49] that where a person involved in legal proceedings is able to rely on a directive against the state he may do so regardless of the capacity in which the latter is acting, whether employer or public authority. In either case it is necessary to prevent the state from taking advantage of its own failure to comply with Community Law.

From this one can move to the Opinion of Van Gerven AG in *Foster*. At paragraph 21 he said:

> . . . The point of departure must be the reasoning behind *Marshall's* case and *Johnston's* case: A Member State, but also any other public body charged with a particular duty by the Member State from which it derives its authority, should not be allowed to benefit from the failure of a Member State to implement the relevant provisions of the directive in national law. That, however, raises the question how far the expressions "public body" "charged with a particular duty" and "from which it derives its authority" precisely extend. Moreover, it is not entirely possible to give those expressions a precise Community meaning: whether someone forms part of the government, whether a particular duty is a public duty and whether someone derives his authority from the state (whether or not in the sense that he exercises authority delegated by the state) are difficult matters to define, and their meaning differs significantly not just from one Member State to another and within each Member State from one period to another but also in Community Law, in so far as they are used there, according to the matter in issue.
>
> In the cases I have referred to, the court did not attempt to define those concepts in the abstract, and I think it was right not to do so. Nevertheless it appears from those cases that the concept of a public body must be **[637]** understood very broadly and that all bodies which pursuant to the constitutional structure of a Member State can exercise any authority over individuals fall within the concept of "the state". In that respect it is immaterial how that authority (which I shall call public authority) is organised and how the various bodies which exercise that authority are related. In the light of the *Marshall*, *Johnston* and *Costanzo* judgments (and Case 271/82, *Auer* v. *Ministère Public*:[12] and the Opinion of Mancini AG,[13] which preceded them) there can be no doubt that they all fall under the concept of "the state", and there is no need for any criterion of delegation or control by other public authorities. That much is certain.

He went on to propose a test which was not accepted by the court which instead formulated a test of its own, which I have already quoted, and which was adequate to enable the national court to decide the question before it. Lord Templeman delivering a judgment with which all the other members of the Judicial Committee concurred stated this in *Foster* v. *British Gas plc*:[14]

> The principle laid down by the European Court of Justice is that the state must not be allowed to take advantage of its own failure to comply with Community law. The policy of the BGC which involved discrimination against women in breach of the Directive, was no doubt thought to be in the financial and commercial interests of the BGC. The advantages of that policy would accrue indirectly to the State which provided through the BGC a supply of gas for all citizens generally and which was entitled to the surplus revenue of the BGC. If the BGC were allowed to escape the consequences of an admitted breach of the

[12] [1983] ECR 2727, at p. 2745; [1985] 1 CMLR 123, para. [19].
[13] At p. 2751.
[14] Cited above, at p. 15.

Directive the State would be taking advantage of its own failure to comply with Community law. I can see no justification for a narrow or strained construction of the ruling of the European Court of Justice which applies to a body "under the control of the state" . . . I decline to apply the ruling of the European Court of Justice, couched in terms of broad principle and purposive language characteristic of Community law in a manner which is, for better or worse, sometimes applied to enactments in the United Kingdom parliament.

The respondent relied heavily on the decision of this court in *Rolls Royce plc* v. *Doughty*.[15] That was a case in which the applicant sought to sue the company relying on the same Council Directive 76/207. At the relevant time all the shares in the company were held by nominees of the Crown. Mustill LJ, delivering a judgment with which other members of the court agreed, stated at page 550 that there were two questions confronting the court:

1. Is the applicant correct in contending that the sole test or at any rate the sole test material for present purposes, of whether the entity in question falls within the doctrine of *Becker* . . . and *Marshall* . . . is whether it is under the control of the state?
2. If this contention is not correct, to what extent does the answer furnished by the Court of Justice in paragraph [22] of its judgment in **[638]** *Foster* constitute an exhaustive statement of the criteria for determining the status of the entity; and if it is not exhaustive, what test should be applied to the present case?

He held that the answer to the first question was in the negative. For present purposes it is his approach to the second question which is of interest. He said this at page 552:

On behalf of the employer Mr Pannick was disposed to accept, rightly in my view, that this test was not intended to provide the answer to every category of case. The words "is included among" in paragraph [20] make this clear enough. Nevertheless, at least in a case of the same general type as *Foster* the court's formulation must always be the starting point and will usually be the finishing point. If all the factors identified by the court are present it is likely to require something very unusual to produce the result that an entity is not to be identified with the state. Conversely, although the absence of a factor will not necessarily be fatal, it will need the addition of something else not contemplated by the formula, before the principle in *Marshall*'s case . . . has a prospect of being brought into play.

The Position of Voluntary Aided Schools in the State School System

The background to the present case was the closure of two schools—one for 4-7 year olds and one for 7-11 year olds—and their replacement by a new all-through school for children between 4 and 11. The problem before the court springs from the fact that we are not concerned with

[15] Cited above.

county schools established and maintained by a LEA but rather with voluntary aided schools—schools over which the Church has some measure of control. It is conceded by the respondents that had the appellants been employed at a county school both established and maintained by the LEA and had that county school been closed and replaced by another county school they would have been able to rely on the doctrine of vertical direct effect against the LEA at any event until 1988. It is common ground that a LEA is an emanation of the state for the purposes of this doctrine. But the respondents assert that the connection between the governors of the junior school and the state is too loose for the former to be regarded as an emanation of the latter.

The machinery of the state education system in this country is set out in the detailed provisions of the Education Acts 1944-1994 which comprise no fewer than 29 statutes.[16]

The modern system of education in this country is founded upon **[639]** the Education Act ["EA"] 1944 which is still in force albeit much amended and supplemented. The Act is divided into several parts. Part I deals with central administration and in particular the Secretary of State,[17] Part II deals with the statutory system of education in which are included provisions relating to county schools and schools of the

[16] We are directly concerned in the present case with church schools. Originally nearly all the education that was provided was provided by the Church. Gradually the state took an interest and the 1870 Education Act ordained that, for the first time, a school should be placed within the reach of every English child. In order to achieve that, it was desired to make use of all the schools which had been provided by the Church over the centuries. The Church for its part wanted to keep control of its schools but could not afford to provide good new buildings. The compromise that has been worked out is typically English in that rather than dismantling the existing structure and starting afresh, parliament enacted legislation the effect of which in very broad terms is to enable the church schools to opt into the state system on terms.

[17] The duties of the Secretary of State are currently set out in the Education Act 1993. Section 1 provides that:

> The Secretary of State shall promote the education of the people of England and Wales

and section 2 provides that:

> The Secretary of State shall exercise his powers in respect of those bodies in receipt of public funds which:
> (a) carry responsibility for securing that the required provision for primary, secondary or further education is made in schools . . . in or in any area of England and Wales, or
> (b) conduct schools . . . in England and Wales,
> for the purpose of promoting primary, secondary and further education in England and Wales.

So far as teaching is concerned the primary provisions are now contained in the Education Reform Act 1988 ("the ERA"). Section 1 provides:

> (1) It shall be the duty—
> (a) of the Secretary of State as respects every maintained school;
> (b) of every local education authority as respects every school maintained by them; and
> (c) of every governing body or head teacher of a maintained school as respects that school;
> to exercise their functions . . . with a view to securing that the curriculum for the school satisfies the requirements of this section.
> (2) The curriculum for a maintained school satisfies the requirements of this section if it is a balanced and broadly based curriculum which—
> (a) promotes the spiritual, moral, cultural, mental and physical development of pupils at the school and of society; and
> (b) prepares such pupils for the opportunities, responsibilities and experiences of adult life.

type with which we are presently concerned and Part III deals with Independent Schools.

The body with primary responsibility for the provision of education in a given area is the local education authority ("LEA"). The Education Acts place various duties on LEAs relating to the provision of education in their area and LEAs have a wide range of powers to enable them to perform these duties. Under section 8 EA 1944, for example, there is a duty "to secure that there shall be available for their area sufficient schools" for providing primary and secondary education in their area. In the fulfilment of that duty the LEA relies on schools provided by them and schools provided by others. Some of those others are wholly independent of LEA funds; others are dependent to a small degree; others to a very large degree.

Section 9 EA 1944 empowers LEAs "for the purpose of fulfilling their functions under this Act . . . to maintain . . . schools whether established by them or otherwise."

Schools which are maintained by the LEA for this purpose but **[640]** which were not actually established by the LEA are known as voluntary schools (section 9(2) EA 1944).

The concept of "maintaining" a school is defined under the 1944 Act section 114(2). Essentially it means that the LEA defrays the expenses of maintaining the school, save for those expenses that, by virtue of the Act or any agreement thereunder, the governors are required to meet. In the context of the present case it is noteworthy that, by virtue of section 46 of the ERA [Education Reform Act] 1988, the costs of meeting redundancy payments for teachers are carried by the LEA. The system of local government finance is such that those costs are largely if not entirely met by the grant from central government. Until the ERA 1988 one of the distinctions between schools provided by the LEA and voluntary schools which had opted into the state system was that the LEA had much tighter control over the management of county schools than over voluntary schools. Thus the LEA was responsible for managing that part of the expenses of schools which it provided pursuant to section 9 EA 1944 whereas voluntary schools had a board of governors who were responsible for the management. Under the provisions of Chapter 3 ERA 1988 provision was made for very much more devolution of responsibility in the case of county schools.

Voluntary schools choose of their own volition to come within the state system. However, once within the system, they are subject to a very considerable degree of control and influence by the Secretary of State for Education and the LEA.

The following are examples of areas in which central or local government control the activities of voluntary aided schools:

(1) The governors of a school maintained by local education authority cannot change the character or significantly enlarge the premises of the school or transfer it to a new site without the approval of the Secretary of State (EA 1980 section 13).
(2) They are subject to instruments of government and articles of government made by order of the LEA (Education (2) Act 1986 section 1(2)) and the instrument of government regulates the composition of their boards of governors (*ibid*. section 4).
(3) The instrument sets out the principles governing the curriculum which are exactly the same as those contained in section 1(2) of the 1988 Education Act and section 2(1) of the same Act applicable to other schools.
(4) They cannot charge for education with a few exceptions: section 106 ERA 1988.
(5) There are detailed arrangements relating to financing, *e.g.* under sections 15 and 65 EA 1944 and Chapter III ERA 1988.
(6) Section 68 EA 1944 gives power to the Secretary of State when satisfied that:

> The . . . governors of any . . . voluntary school have acted or are proposing to act unreasonably with respect to the exercise of any **[641]** power conferred or the performance of any duty imposed by or under this Act to . . . give such directions as to the exercise of the power or the performance of the duty as appear to him to be expedient.

(7) Section 99 of the same Act provides that if the Secretary of State is satisfied that the:

> governors of any . . . voluntary school have failed to discharge any duty imposed upon them by or for the purposes of this Act [the Secretary of State] may make an order declaring . . . the . . . governors . . . to be in default in respect of that duty and giving such directions for the purpose of enforcing the execution thereof as appear to [the Secretary of State] to be expedient; and any such direction shall be enforceable, on an application made on behalf of [the Secretary of State], by mandamus.

(8) Section 22 of the EA 1944 gives the LEA the right to direct the governing body of any aided school to provide free of charge accommodation on the school premises for purposes connected with education for not more than three days in any one week. The same Section allows the LEA to give directions to the governing body of any aided school as to the number and conditions of service of persons employed at the school for the purposes of the care and maintenance of the school premises.[18]

[18] It is an oddity inherent in the respondents' submissions that whereas they accept that voluntary school caretakers employed by the LEA may rely on the Directive (because the LEA is an emanation of the state), they submit that schoolteachers employed by the governors may not (because the governors are not an emanation of the state).

(9) The governors of a voluntary aided school cannot even close it down without first obtaining the approval of the Secretary of State.

The Case in the Tribunals Below

The EAT [Employment Appeal Tribunal] was hearing an appeal from an industrial tribunal which had decided, on the hearing of a preliminary issue, that the governing body was not an emanation of the state for the purposes of enabling the Applicants to enforce the Directive's provisions directly. The tribunal proceeded on the basis of the following undisputed facts:

(1) At all material times the individual applicants were members of the NUT [National Union of Teachers].
(2) Until 18 April 1993 when they were all dismissed, the applicants were teachers at St Mary's (Aided) Junior School ("the Junior School") for children between the ages of 7 and 11. The respondents claim to have dismissed the applicants by reason of redundancy.
(3) The Junior School was situated in Swanley. In adjoining premises there was a county school, St Mary's Infant School ("the Infants' School") for children between the ages of 4 and **[642]** 7. The Junior School was a Church of England voluntary aided school. Its existence had been promoted by the diocesan board of education of the Diocese of Rochester.
(4) The Kent County Council as local education authority published a notice on 14 November 1991 proposing the closure of the Junior School and of an Infants' School adjoining it. On the same day the diocesan board published a notice proposing the creation of a new voluntary aided school to be known as St Mary's Church of England (Aided) Primary School ("the New School"). It was to be an all-through school for children between ages of 4 and 11.
(5) On 15 July 1992 the Secretary of State for Education gave approval for the closure of the Infants' School and the Junior School and for the establishment of the New School.
(6) On 24 July 1992, the Secretary of State modified the previously arranged implementation date for the closure of the Infants' and Junior Schools and the opening date of the New School to 19 April 1993.
(7) A temporary governing body of the New School was established pursuant to section 12 and Schedule 2 of the Education (2) Act 1986. The temporary governing body first met on 4 September 1992.
(8) Thereafter the individual applicants all applied for posts at the New School. Mr Fidge, who had been Headmaster of the Junior School, applied for the post of Headmaster. The other individual applicants, who had been classroom teachers at the Junior School, applied for

similar posts at the New School. None of their applications were successful. On 18 April 1993 all the individual applicants were dismissed by reason of redundancy.

The decision of the Industrial Tribunal

It seems that the tribunal heard legal argument covering the following issues:

(1) Do the 1981 regulations apply to the exercise of the procedures under sections 12 and 13 of the Education Act 1980?
(2) Does the Directive have direct effect?
(3) If the Directive has direct effect, can it be relied on against the governing body of a voluntary aided school?
(4) Was there a transfer of undertaking in the present case?

Although the tribunal heard arguments on all the points set out above it did not find it necessary to reach a decision on them all. The tribunal dealt with the points in the following way:

(1) The 1981 regulations, in their unamended form, had no **[643]** application to the case because the definition of an undertaking in Regulation 2(1) did not include "any undertaking or part of an undertaking which is not in the nature of a commercial venture".
(2) The applications therefore had to be based on the Directive. The tribunal assumed, without deciding, that the Directive was *capable* of having a direct effect.
(3) The Directive was only capable of enforcement against the state or an organ or emanation of the state. The governing body of a voluntary aided school was not an emanation of the state.
(4) This question did not need to be decided.

The Employment Appeal Tribunal decision

The Employment Appeal Tribunal ("EAT") indicated that the tribunal's desire to avoid hearing all questions of law and fact had led it to take a course which might be regarded as inconvenient. However the EAT proceeded on the same assumptions as the tribunal had made. Before the EAT the parties before us were represented by solicitors and not by the Queen's Counsel whom we have had the advantage of hearing. It was common ground before the Employment Appeal Tribunal, as is recorded in its decision at page 11, that: *The* (emphasis supplied) proper test whether a body is an emanation of state is as laid down by the European Court of Justice and applied by the House of Lords in *Foster* v. *British Gas plc*.[19]

The EAT concluded that the Industrial Tribunal had not erred in its decision that the Directive cannot be enforced by the applicants against

[19] [1991] 1 QBD 405 and [1991] 2 AC 306.

the governing body of a voluntary aided school. Their reasons for this conclusion they set out as follows:

(1) The rationale for the doctrine that provisions of a Directive, which are unconditional and sufficiently precise may have vertical effect is that the state, to whom the Directive is addressed, cannot properly rely, as against an applicant, on its own failure to implement the Directive addressed to it.

(2) *The* (emphasis supplied) test of the European Court of Justice for determining whether the body, against whom it is sought to enforce the Directive is an emanation of the state consists of a tripartite, cumulative set of criteria namely:
   (a) Has the body been made responsible pursuant to a measure adopted by the state for providing a public service?
   (b) Is that service under the control of the state?
   (c) Does the body for that purpose have special powers beyond those which apply between individuals?

(3) The provision of education in voluntary aided schools is a public service. But at a voluntary aided school, that service is provided by the governing body, not by the state or pursuant to its measures or under its control. The governing body is not under the control of the state. It exists by virtue of the constitution in the form of articles of **[644]** government made under the authority of legislation. The governing body does not have a monopoly of education. It is not an agency of the state. The provision of state funds is not determinative of control. The state has no right to require the governors to adopt an employment position (for example, as stated in the Directive) which is not incorporated into the general law by legislation of the Member State. It is for the governing body to adopt an employment position in conformity with the general law applicable as between individuals and non-state bodies. It has no special powers.

(4) The cases in which a body has been held to be an emanation of the state for the purposes of the doctrine of direct effect are far removed from the present case: see for example the decision in *Marshall* . . . in which an area health authority was held to be an emanation of the state; and *Foster* . . . in which the British Gas Corporation was held to be an emanation of the state; *cf. Rolls Royce* v. *Doughty*[20] in which it was held that Rolls Royce plc was not an emanation of the state.

(5) The state is the supreme civil power of a nation. Under its law and through its institutions, it is vested with ultimate effective political control of the organisation and machinery of the government of its affairs, both internal and external. The state and its agencies have special legal powers, exceptional in quality and degree and different from powers exercisable by individuals and non-state bodies. The powers exercised in the organisation and running of (a) voluntary aided school are a far cry from state powers of this kind. Its governors' powers are not exceptional in a relevant sense. They are only special in the sense that those who govern schools have powers which pupils, teachers and parents do not have. The governing body of a voluntary

[20] Cited above.

aided school exists within a state, providing a public service, but it is not an emanation or agency of the organisation of the state. It is under the control of the state only in the same sense that other citizens are. Like the Industrial Tribunal, we have been unable to find any "special powers" in the sense used in the case of *Foster*. So far as the articles of government are concerned they provide that the conduct of the school, its internal organisation and management, should be under the direction of the governing body. The governing body, though financially maintained by the local education authority, is not established or controlled by it. We have been unable to find any "special powers" of the governing body in the relevant education legislation ranging from the 1944 Act to the 1993 Act.

Conclusions

The appellants submit that:

1. Since the present case is not of "the same general type" as *Foster* the tripartite test promulgated therein and adopted in *Rolls Royce* is not directly applicable;
2. If the tripartite test is applicable then it is fulfilled in the present case.

The respondents invite the Court to reject each of those submissions.

[645] I do not regard the present case as of the same general type for present purposes as *Foster*. That case and *Rolls Royce* were both concerned with commercial undertakings in which the Government had a stake. The present case is not concerned with any commercial undertaking but rather with the provision of what would generally in the Community be regarded as the provision of a public service. Mr Straker, who appeared for the respondents, submitted that, since the European Court of Justice in deciding *Foster* had relied on *Marshall*, it followed that the European Court of Justice regarded the case involving the gas industry as being of the same type as a case involving the national health service. He went on to submit that the present case was of the same type as *Marshall*. While I accept the latter submission I do not accept the former. All that the European Court of Justice did in *Foster* in relation to *Marshall* was to draw on it as well as on other cases in the course of formulating a test which would enable the national court to decide the problem posed by *Foster*. Similarly, this court ought to look at the decided case law in order to see whether, on those principles, there is enough material to enable this court to decide the present case.

I do not consider it necessary or appropriate for this court to attempt to add a new formulation to the existing ones. What emerges from the case law is a number of indicia which point to the appropriateness of treating the body in question as an emanation of the state, none of which indicia is conclusive. To quote the Advocate General in *Foster*, ". . . The point of departure must be the reasoning behind *Marshall*'s case[21] and *Johnston*'s case.[22] A Member State, but also any other public body charged with a particular duty by the Member State from which it derives its authority, should not be allowed to benefit from the failure of the Member State to implement the relevant provision of a directive in national law".

In the present case, the Governors of the old junior school derived their authority from the Diocese of Rochester Voluntary Aided Schools (Instrument of Government) No 2 Order made by the Secretary of State for Education in the exercise of powers conferred by sections 17(2) and 11 of the EA 1944. The governors of the new primary school derive their authority from an amendment to that Instrument of Government which was made by the LEA under powers given to the LEA by section 1(2) of the Education No 2 Act 1986. True it is that in each case the governors volunteered for the task and true it is that the diocese might have chosen not to subject the school to the regime set out in that Order. But the diocese did not so choose but chose instead to enter the state system. True it is that, in certain circumstances and subject to certain conditions, the diocese was still free to withdraw the school from the state system, but it did not do so. Whilst the school was **[646]** in the state system the governors were a public body charged by the state with running the school and with exercising their functions with a view to securing that the school provided the national curriculum.

The legislation already referred to gives extensive powers which may be exercised by the LEA or the Secretary of State to control the actions of the governors. Duties are imposed on the Governors both by the general legislation and by the statutory instrument by virtue of which they exercise their powers. The financial position is that the failure to transpose the Directive will, if the present appeal is dismissed, have the effect of allowing the LEA and the state to benefit from the failure to transpose the Directive. The *Rolls Royce* case indicates that the mere fact that some incidental benefit may arise to the state from a failure to implement a Directive does not necessarily bring the doctrine of vertical direct effect into play. In the present case the benefit is direct to the LEA, as is conceded because of the provisions of section 46 of the ERA, and the LEA, as is further conceded, is an emanation of the state for the purposes of the doctrine of direct vertical effect.

The Employment Appeal Tribunal rightly identified in its first finding the rationale behind the doctrine of direct effect. In my judgment it was wrong in adopting the tripartite test in *Foster* as if it were a statutory definition of an emanation of the state. It was understandable that it did so since the parties before it all proceeded on that basis. In my judgment it did not fully appreciate the significance of the undoubted fact that the Community case law indicates that a body may be an emanation

[21] Cited above.

[22] Cited above.

of the state although it is not under the control of central government. Its failure to appreciate the significance of this point is shown by the disquisition on the nature of the state at the beginning of paragraph 5 of its reasoning. In my judgment it is not appropriate to apply the tripartite test in *Foster* as though it were a statutory definition. However I ought briefly to record the parties' submissions on each of the three elements of that test and my reaction to them.

1. Have the governors been made responsible pursuant to a measure adopted by the state for providing a public service?

   Mr Straker submits that they have not because the diocese was free to decide whether or not to apply to make the school a voluntary aided school. He submitted that in England no one person was responsible for the provision of education. That responsibility was shared between parents, schools, LEAs and the Secretary of State.

   Mr Hand, for the appellants, submits that once the diocese asks for and obtains voluntary aided status for one of its schools then the governors have been made responsible.

   As indicated above, I prefer the latter submission. The statutory instrument, made by the LEA under statutory powers, **[647]** can be regarded as a measure adopted by the state. Education can be regarded as a public service.
2. Is that service under the control of the state?

   Mr Straker submits that education is not under our complicated statutory system under the control of the state.

   I am not inclined to accept that submission. As I have sought to show, the Secretary of State has duties and powers in respect of the provision of education and so do LEAs. Those powers amount to sufficient control by the state for present purposes to come within the concept of control.
3. Do the governors have special powers beyond those which apply between individuals?

   Mr Hand submitted that the governors had the power to spend public money and that this was a special power for present purposes. I am not presently persuaded that this was the sort of power which the European Court of Justice had in mind in *Foster*.

However, as I have already indicated, I think it inappropriate to apply the tripartite test as though it were a definition section. In my judgment for the purposes of the doctrine of direct vertical effect the governors of the schools must be regarded as emanations of the state and I therefore consider that this appeal must be allowed.

WARD LJ: I agree.

BELDAM LJ: I also agree.

[Report: [1997] 3 CMLR 631]

Enforcement in national courts—Remedies—Claim against Member State — Breach of Community law for which Member State responsible — Principle of State liability for damage caused to individuals — Whether inherent in treaty system—Whether applicable even where provision of European Community law breached is directly effective and can be relied upon by individuals before national courts—Whether applicable where breach attributable to national legislature — Whether State regarded as single entity in respect of liability for breaches of international commitments irrespective of organ responsible — Article 215 of EC Treaty concerning non-contractual liability of Community institutions — Whether evidence of general principle that public authorities should make good damage caused in performance of their duties

Enforcement in national courts—Remedies—Claim against Member State — Breach of Community law for which Member State responsible—Conditions for State liability—Whether governed by Community law or national law—Whether conditions in principle the same whether Member State or Community institution incurring liability—Requirement that breach of Community law be sufficiently serious — Test of whether Member State or Community institution has manifestly and gravely disregarded the limits of its discretion — Whether any requirement to prove fault—Deliberate adoption of legislation in breach of Community law — Test of whether national legislature clearly able to determine that legislation is contrary to Community law at the time of its adoption — Relevance of position already taken by Court of Justice and Commission

Institutions—Court of Justice—Powers—EC Treaty, Article 164 — Task of Court of Justice — Interpretation of Treaty by reference to fundamental principles of Community legal system and general principles common to legal systems of Member States

Enforcement in national courts—Remedies—Claim against Member State — Breach of Community law for which Member State responsible — Damages — Grounds for awarding damages — Loss suffered by individuals — Scope of right to reparation under Community law — Scope of

applicability of national rules on liability — Requirement that conditions should be no less favourable than those applicable to similar domestic claims — Community rules governing claims brought before national courts against Member States — Requirement that reparation must be commensurate with loss or damage sustained — Requirement that loss of profits must be claimable — Requirement that exemplary or other special damages must be available if such damages could be awarded under domestic law — Requirement that reparation should also cover loss sustained prior to court judgment finding infringement of Community law — The law of the European Community — The law of the Federal Republic of Germany — The law of England

BRASSERIE DU PÊCHEUR SA *v.* FEDERAL REPUBLIC OF GERMANY

REGINA *v.* SECRETARY OF STATE FOR TRANSPORT, *ex parte* FACTORTAME LTD AND OTHERS

(Joined Cases C-46/93 and C-48/93)

Court of Justice of the European Communities. 5 *March* 1996

(Rodríguez Iglesias, *President and Rapporteur*; Kakouris, Edward and Hirsch, *Presidents of Chambers*; Mancini, Schockweiler, Moitinho de Almeida, Gulmann and Murray, *Judges*; Tesauro, *Advocate-General*)

BRASSERIE DU PÊCHEUR SA *v.* FEDERAL REPUBLIC OF GERMANY

(Case No III ZR 127/91)

Federal Republic of Germany, Federal Supreme Court (BGH) (Civil Chamber)

24 *October* 1996

REGINA *v.* SECRETARY OF STATE FOR TRANSPORT, *ex parte* FACTORTAME AND OTHERS

England, House of Lords. 28 *October* 1999

(Lords Slynn of Hadley, Nicholls of Birkenhead, Hoffmann, Hope of Craighead and Clyde)

SUMMARY: *The facts*:—In Case C-46/93 Brasserie du Pêcheur SA, a French company, claimed that it had been forced to discontinue beer exports to Germany in 1981 because the competent German authorities considered that the beer it produced did not comply with purity requirements contained in the Law on Beer Duty 1976 since it contained certain additives. In proceedings brought by the Commission against Germany for failure to fulfil treaty obligations, the prohibition on marketing beers which did not comply with purity requirements was held to be contrary to Article 30 of the EC Treaty (judgment of the Court of Justice of 12 March 1987).[1] Brasserie du Pêcheur then brought an action before the German courts against the Federal Republic for reparation of the loss suffered by it between 1981 and 1987 as a result of the import restriction.

In Case C-48/93 Factortame Ltd, a British company, challenged the compatibility of Part II of the Merchant Shipping Act 1988 with Community law, in particular Article 52 of the EC Treaty, in proceedings brought before the Divisional Court of the High Court of Justice in the United Kingdom. The Merchant Shipping Act provided for the introduction of a new register for British fishing vessels and made their registration subject to certain conditions relating to the nationality, residence and domicile of vessel owners. Vessels ineligible for registration were deprived of their right to fish. The conditions in question were held to be contrary to Community law (judgment of the Court of Justice of 25 July 1991).[2] At the same time, the Court held that it was not contrary to Community law to stipulate, as a condition for registration, that vessels must be managed and their operations directed and controlled from within the United Kingdom. Separate proceedings were also brought by the Commission under Article 169 of the EC Treaty against the United Kingdom, concerning the new system of registration, and the Court of Justice held (judgment of 4 October 1991)[3] that the United Kingdom had failed to fulfil its obligations under Article 52 of the Treaty. In further proceedings before the Divisional Court of the High Court of Justice, Factortame and a large number of Spanish fishermen sought damages from the Secretary of State for Transport for losses incurred due to their inability to obtain registration and operate their fishing vessels between April 1989 and November 1992, when the new United Kingdom legislation had been amended to make it compatible with Community law.

The Federal Supreme Court (*BGH*) (Case C-46/93) and the Divisional Court of the High Court of Justice (Case C-48/93) decided to stay the proceedings in the cases before them and to make references to the Court of Justice for preliminary rulings under Article 177 of the EC Treaty. Both national courts considered that, if their respective national laws were applied in their present state, there would be no remedy, basically because the damage caused was the result of acts and omissions of the national legislature rather than the administration. The relevant German legislation imposed a condition for State liability that the act

[1] Case 178/84, *Commission* v. *Germany* [1987] ECR 1227.

[2] *Regina* v. *Secretary of State for Transport, ex parte Factortame Ltd*, Case 221/89 [1991] ECR I-3905, Volume 1, Note, p. 909. For earlier proceedings before the Court of Justice in the same case, concerning the extent of the duty of national courts to grant interim relief where rights under Community law were at issue, see Volume 1, p. 823.

[3] Case 246/89, *Commission* v. *United Kingdom* [1991] ECR I-4585.

or omission in question should be referable to an individual situation whilst the British legislation required proof of misfeasance in public office.

The Court of Justice decided to join the two sets of proceedings because of the similarity of the issues which they raised. By their questions, the national courts essentially sought a ruling on:

(i) whether the principle of Community law (established in the Court of Justice's judgment of 19 November 1991 in the *Francovich* case)[4] that Member States were obliged to make good loss and damage caused to individuals by breaches of Community law for which they could be held responsible was applicable where the national legislature was responsible for the infringement in question;
(ii) under what conditions a right to reparation of loss or damage caused to individuals by breaches of Community law attributable to a Member State was, in the particular circumstances, guaranteed by Community law; and
(iii) according to what criteria the extent of the reparation payable by the Member State responsible for the breach should be determined.

Judgment of the Court of Justice

The German, Irish and Netherlands Governments contended before the Court of Justice that the Member States were only required to pay damages to individuals for breaches of Community law where the provisions breached were not directly effective. In *Francovich* the Court of Justice had simply sought to fulfil a lacuna in the protection of individual rights where there was no remedy already available, rather than to create a principle of broader scope. The German Government further argued that a general right to reparation for individuals could only be created by legislation and not by judicial decision.

Opinion of the Advocate-General:—Advocate-General Tesauro pointed out that the Court now had to establish whether the principle of State liability in damages for infringements of Community law established in *Francovich* should be confined to cases of failure to implement a directive whose provisions could not be relied on directly by individuals or should be extended to cases, such as those now before the Court, in which the loss or damage suffered arose out of the application of a national law conflicting with Community provisions which could be relied on directly in the national courts. The Advocate-General argued that every individual right had a substantive content and a financial content which could generally be quantified. The substantive reinstatement of a right which had been impaired was the optimum means of protection for an individual. But at times this was not enough to ensure effective judicial protection. The principle of the State's financial liability to make good damage caused by its infringement of provisions of Community law applied as a remedy which was both alternative and additional to substantive protection. Consequently, a claim to establish State financial liability should be available whether or not the provision infringed had direct effect (pp. 519-30).

[4] Case 6/90, *Francovich* v. *Italian Republic*, 19 November 1991, Volume 1, p. 188.

In their respective reference orders, the national courts indicated that their national law did not allow them to award damages because the infringements of Community law at issue were attributable to the legislature which had failed to amend a national law to align it with Community provisions (Case C-46/93, *Brasserie du Pêcheur*) or had passed a national law inconsistent with Community law (Case C-48/93, *Factortame*). The Advocate-General argued that there was no reason why the *Factortame* principle should not apply equally irrespective of whether the acts or omissions of the State causing loss or damage were the responsibility of the legislature or the executive. Under international law, a State whose liability for breach of an international treaty commitment was in issue was viewed as a single entity. It made no difference whether the infringement which gave rise to the damage was attributable to the legislature, the judiciary or the executive. Moreover, the same approach could be seen in the Court's own case-law on Article 169 of the EC Treaty. The Community legal order had a contractual basis founded on the conclusion of traditional international instruments which conferred rights on individuals not only where they were expressly granted but also as a result of the obligations imposed by the Treaty on the Member States. It followed that State liability for legislative acts or omissions in breach of obligations which the States had themselves contractually entered into was perfectly consistent with, and indeed inherent in, the fundamental characteristics of the Community legal order. Whilst it was true that this approach meant that Community law required a remedy to be created in the judicial systems of the Member States which was not at present available, the Advocate-General pointed out that this was not a new problem and there were clear precedents in the rulings of the Court in *Simmenthal*[5] and *Factortame I*.[6] The Member States' autonomy in relation to judicial remedies for the infringement of rights conferred by Community law was subject to derogations wherever these were necessary to ensure the effective protection of individual rights and thereby the proper implementation of Community law (pp. 531-7).

The Advocate-General then turned to the necessary conditions for the Member States to be liable to pay compensation, pointing out that, as made clear in *Francovich*,[7] at least the minimum conditions must be identified and defined in Community law itself, although they might vary in their application from case to case. Three basic conditions were laid down by the Court in *Francovich*,[8] but this did not mean that these conditions were exhaustive so far as the requirements of Community law were concerned. In particular the Court had not specified the limits of State liability, especially the Community criteria for judging whether the conduct of the State was unlawful. In *Francovich* itself, there was no doubt that the omission on the part of the State was unlawful since the result sought by the directive at issue had not been attained and the case was therefore particularly straightforward. But it could never have been intended that every infringement of Community law affecting the financial interests of individuals should automatically entail a right to reparation. In determining the conditions governing the right to compensation for loss caused by State legislative activity in contravention of Community law, it was appropriate to refer to the Court's case-law under Article 215(2) of the EC Treaty concerning the non-contractual liability

[5] Volume 1, p. 73.
[6] Volume 1, p. 823.
[7] Volume 1, p. 188 at pp. 243-4.
[8] *Ibid.*, p. 243.

of Community institutions. The Advocate-General considered that there was no reason to apply different criteria depending on whether the infringement of Community law in question was attributable to a State or a Community institution. Whenever a Member State acted in a field in which it enjoyed broad discretion, its liability for infringements of Community law should be subject to the same restrictive conditions as those applicable to Community institutions in comparable situations. Harmonization of the preconditions for liability was essential (pp. 537-46).

So far as the substantive Community criteria governing State liability were concerned, from the Court's case-law on non-contractual liability it was clear that Community liability could not arise unless a sufficiently serious breach of a superior rule of law for the protection of individuals had occurred. A finding of State liability was therefore essentially dependent, according to the Advocate-General, on two criteria: a manifest and serious breach was required together with fault as the element necessary to characterize the breach of the Community provision as serious. Wherever a Member State enjoyed a broad margin of discretion it would be necessary to establish that it had manifestly and gravely disregarded the limits on its discretion. The Advocate-General further argued, following both the prevalent approach of national legal systems and the Court itself in relation to the non-contractual liability of Community institutions, that the liability of Member States for infringements of Community law should be strict. By this he meant that, whilst it was necessary to assess State conduct on the basis of objective factors, including negligence where appropriate, in order to establish a breach of Community law, there was no requirement to prove the existence of fault as a subjective component of State conduct (pp. 546-54).

It was then recalled by the Advocate-General that in *Francovich* the Court had stressed that Community law laid down those conditions sufficient to give rise to a right to reparation for individuals. Community law thus confined the Member States' autonomy in this context to laying down the other substantive and procedural conditions concerning the reparation of damage. This role of the Member States was limited by the requirement to secure real and effective protection for individuals. Accordingly, the conditions laid down by national law should be no less favourable than those relating to similar domestic claims and should not be so framed as to make it virtually impossible or excessively difficult to obtain reparation. Furthermore, the reparation payable by the Member State should not be merely symbolic but should correspond to the damage suffered. Finally, the obligation on Member States to pay compensation could not be made dependent upon the existence of a judgment of the Court finding the infringement in question and thereby limiting the time, from which the obligation to make reparation started, until after the delivery of such a judgment (pp. 555-64).

Held:—(1) It was a principle of Community law that Member States were obliged to make good loss and damage caused to individuals by breaches of Community law for which they could be held responsible. This principle applied even where the provision of Community law breached was directly effective. The right of individuals to rely on directly effective provisions of Community law before national courts was only a minimum guarantee and was not sufficient in itself to ensure the full and complete implementation of Community law.

The purpose of that right was to ensure that provisions of Community law prevailed over national provisions. It could not, in every case, secure for individuals the benefit of the rights conferred on them by Community law and, in particular, avoid them sustaining damage as a result of a breach of Community law attributable to a Member State (pp. 574-5).

(2) Since the Treaty contained no provision expressly and specifically governing the consequences of breaches of Community law by Member States, it was for the Court, in pursuance of the task conferred on it by Article 164 of the Treaty of ensuring that in the interpretation and application of the Treaty the law was observed, to rule on such a question in accordance with generally accepted methods of interpretation, in particular by reference to the fundamental principles of the Community legal system and, where necessary, general principles common to the legal systems of the Member States. Those general principles were referred to in Article 215 of the Treaty as the basis of the non-contractual liability of the Community for damage caused by its institutions or servants. They included the obligation on public authorities to make good damage caused in the performance of their duties. The protection of the rights which individuals derived from Community law could not vary depending on whether a national authority or a Community authority was responsible for the damage. Accordingly, the principle of State liability for loss and damage caused to individuals as a result of breaches of Community law for which the State could be held responsible was inherent in the system of the Treaty (pp. 575-8).

(3) The principle of State liability held good for any case in which a Member State breached Community law, whatever the organ of the State whose act or omission was responsible for the breach. Furthermore, in view of the fundamental requirement of the Community legal order that Community law be uniformly applied, the obligation to make good damage caused to individuals by breaches of Community law could not depend on domestic rules as to the division of powers between constitutional authorities. In international law, a State whose liability for breach of an international commitment was in issue would be viewed as a single entity, irrespective of whether the breach which gave rise to the damage was attributable to the legislature, the judiciary or the executive. This must apply *a fortiori* in the Community legal order since all State authorities, including the legislature, were bound in performing their tasks to comply with the rules laid down by Community law directly governing the situation of individuals. Consequently, the principle that Member States were obliged to make good damage caused to individuals by breaches of Community law attributable to the State was applicable where the national legislature was responsible for the breach in question (pp. 576-7).

(4) In order to determine the conditions under which State liability gave rise to a right to reparation, account first had to be taken of the principles inherent in the Community legal order which formed the basis for that liability. These were firstly the full effectiveness of Community rules and the effective protection of the rights which they conferred and secondly the obligation to cooperate imposed on Member States by Article 5 of the Treaty. Reference was also to be made to the rules defined in the case-law of the Court of Justice on the non-contractual liability of the Community in so far as, pursuant to Article 215 of the Treaty, they were constructed on the basis of the general principles common to the laws of the Member States. It was inappropriate, in the

absence of particular justification, to have different rules governing the liability of the Community and the liability of Member States in like circumstances (p. 577).

(5)(a) Accordingly, where a Member State acted in a field where it had a wide discretion, comparable to that of the Community institutions in implementing Community policies, the conditions under which it could incur liability must, in principle, be the same as those under which the Community institutions incurred liability in a comparable situation. In such circumstances, Community law conferred a right to reparation where three conditions were met: the rule of law infringed had to be intended to confer rights on individuals; the breach had to be sufficiently serious; and there had to be a direct causal link between the breach of the obligation incumbent upon the Member State and the damage sustained by individuals (pp. 578-9).

(b) The decisive test for finding that a breach of Community law was sufficiently serious was whether the Member State or the Community institution concerned had manifestly and gravely disregarded the limits on its discretion. The factors which the competent court could take into consideration included the clarity and precision of the rule breached, the measure of discretion left by that rule to the national or Community authorities, whether the infringement or the damage caused was intentional or involuntary, whether any error of law was excusable or inexcusable, the fact that the position taken by a Community institution may have contributed towards the omission, and the adoption and retention of national measures or practices contrary to Community law. On any view, a breach of Community law would be sufficiently serious if it had persisted despite a judgment finding the infringement in question to be established, or a preliminary ruling or settled case-law of the Court on the matter from which it was clear that the conduct in question constituted an infringement (pp. 579-80).

(6)(a) The right to reparation thus flowed directly from Community law where the conditions referred to in the preceding paragraph were satisfied. Where such a right existed the State was required, in the absence of relevant Community provisions, to make reparation for the consequences of the loss and damage caused in accordance with the domestic rules on liability, provided that the conditions for reparation laid down by national law should not be less favourable than those relating to similar domestic claims and should not be such as in practice to make it impossible or excessively difficult to obtain reparation. Any condition imposed by national law on State liability requiring either proof of misfeasance in public office or that the act or omission was referable to an individual situation would in practice make it impossible or extremely difficult to obtain reparation where the act or omission was the responsibility of the legislature itself (pp. 581-2).

(b) Certain objective and subjective factors connected with the concept of fault under a national legal system could well be relevant for the purpose of determining whether or not a given breach of Community law was serious (see paragraph (5)(b) above). But the obligation to make reparation for loss or damage caused to individuals could not depend upon a condition based on any concept of fault going beyond that of a sufficiently serious breach of Community law. Imposition of such a supplementary condition would be tantamount to calling into question the right to reparation founded on the Community legal order (p. 583).

(7) Reparation by Member States of loss or damage caused to individuals as a result of breaches of Community law should be commensurate with the loss or damage sustained. National legislation which generally limited the damage for which reparation could be granted to damage done to certain specifically protected individual interests, not including loss of profit by individuals, was incompatible with Community law. Moreover, it should be possible to award specific damages, such as the exemplary damages provided for by English law, pursuant to claims or actions founded on Community law, if such damages could be awarded pursuant to similar claims or actions founded on domestic law (pp. 584-5).

(8) The obligation for Member States to make good loss or damage caused to individuals by breaches of Community law attributable to the State could not be limited to damage sustained after the delivery of a judgment of the Court finding the infringement in question, without calling into question the right to reparation conferred by the Community legal order. Furthermore, a requirement that there must have been a prior finding by the Court of an infringement of Community law would be contrary to the principle of the effectiveness of Community law since it would preclude any right to reparation so long as the presumed infringement had not been the subject of an action brought by the Commission under Article 169 of the Treaty. Such a requirement would also violate the rights of individuals arising from Community provisions having direct effect in the domestic legal systems of the Member States (pp. 585-6).

Judgment of the German Supreme Court (Brasserie du Pêcheur)

Following the ruling of the Court of Justice clarifying the three conditions under which State liability could be incurred, giving rise to a right to reparation against the Member State which had breached Community law, the German Supreme Court was required to decide whether the Federal Republic of Germany was liable to compensate Brasserie du Pêcheur for its loss. The lower German courts had held that there was no liability to pay compensation and Brasserie du Pêcheur had appealed to the Supreme Court, which had made the reference for a preliminary ruling to the Court of Justice.

Held:—The appeal was dismissed.

(1) The key question for consideration was whether it could be established that there had been a sufficiently serious breach of Community law to provide a basis for a right to compensation. The decisive test laid down by the Court of Justice where, as here, the case concerned the enactment of legislation, was whether the Member State had manifestly and gravely disregarded the limits imposed on the exercise of its discretion (pp. 592-3).

(2) In its ruling on the reference from the German Supreme Court, the Court of Justice stated (paragraph 59) that, although it was for the national courts to decide how to characterize the breaches of Community law at issue, it might be taken into account that a distinction should be drawn between the two types of German legislative provisions at issue. As regards the legislation relating to the designation of the product marketed, it would be difficult to regard the breach

of Article 30 as an excusable error since the incompatibility of such rules with that Article was manifest from earlier judgments of the Court of Justice dating from 1979. By contrast, with regard to the legislation prohibiting additives, the criteria available to the national legislature, to determine whether the prohibition was contrary to Community law, were significantly less conclusive prior to the judgment of the Court of Justice of March 1987 (p. 593).

(3) The measures taken against Brasserie du Pêcheur consequent upon the legislative provision which contravened Community law did not relate to the designation of the product marketed. Accordingly, the requirement of a direct causal connection between the legislative prohibition relating to designation and the loss suffered by the claimant was not satisfied (p. 594).

(4) With regard to the legislative prohibition on additives, the Court of Justice had held in its judgment of March 1987 that it could not be justified on grounds of the protection of public health under Article 36 of the EC Treaty. There was nothing, however, in that judgment to indicate that the Federal Government's position was so far removed from the requirements of Community law that there had been a manifest and grave disregard for the limits imposed upon the discretion of the national legislature. Consequently, the breach of the Treaty committed by the Federal Republic was insufficiently serious to provide a basis for State liability (pp. 594-5).

Judgment of the English House of Lords (Factortame)

Following the ruling by the Court of Justice clarifying the conditions under which State liability could be incurred, the Divisional Court held a further hearing. In a judgment of 31 July 1997 the Divisional Court held that the breaches of Community law by the United Kingdom Government were sufficiently serious to give rise in principle to liability for damage caused to the applicants, although there was no entitlement to exemplary damages. The Court of Appeal dismissed an appeal against this decision brought by the United Kingdom Government, which appealed to the House of Lords.

Held:—The appeal was dismissed.

(1) The key question for consideration was what constituted a sufficiently serious breach of Community law and whether the Divisional Court and the Court of Appeal were right to hold that the breaches here were sufficiently serious. The decisive test laid down by the Court of Justice where, as here, the case concerned the enactment of legislation, was whether the Member State had manifestly and gravely disregarded the limits placed upon the exercise of its discretionary powers. It was clear that it was not necessary to establish fault or negligence on the part of the Member State going beyond what was relevant to show a sufficiently serious breach (pp. 605-8).

(2) In the present case, the United Kingdom was entitled to consider how it would exercise the margin of discretion left to it under Community law in the application of the common fisheries policy and also, subject to those limits, how it would exercise its rights under international law to provide for registration as a British fishing vessel. But the three conditions (nationality, domicile and residence), which had been held by the Court of Justice to be in breach of

the EC Treaty, had to be considered separately for the purposes of liability to pay compensation, even if taken in conjunction they reflected what the British Government was trying to do (pp. 608-9).

(3) In determining whether, in imposing a nationality requirement, the United Kingdom had committed a sufficiently serious breach, it had to be noted that the prohibition on discrimination on grounds of nationality was contained in Article 7 of the Treaty, which was a clear and unambiguous provision. The adoption of this provision in the 1988 Act by the British Government was not done inadvertently but after anxious consideration and consultation. Even if it was accepted that it was adopted in good faith, in order to protect British fishing communities, the nationality condition was obviously discriminatory and in breach of the right of establishment enshrined in Article 52 of the Treaty (p. 609).

(4) The Commission had warned the United Kingdom Government that the provisions were *prima facie* contrary to Community law, prior to the Act receiving its royal assent. Ignoring the Commission's firm and consistent view in this regard meant that a court was more likely to find that the breach was sufficiently serious. It was true that the Government's own legal advisers had taken the view that there was a reasonably good prospect of the proposed legislation being upheld by the Court of Justice. However, it nevertheless appeared to be clear in the circumstances that the deliberate adoption of legislation which was obviously discriminatory on the ground of nationality, and inevitably violated Article 52, was a manifest and grave breach of the Treaty and therefore constituted a sufficiently serious breach. The same applied to the domicile and residence requirements (pp. 610-14).

The texts of the judgments and opinions given in the course of the litigation are set out as follows:

JUDGMENT OF THE COURT OF JUSTICE OF THE EUROPEAN COMMUNITY OF 5 MARCH 1996

REPORT FOR THE HEARING

in joined Cases C-46/93 and C-48/93*

* Languages of the cases: English and German.

[1035] I. *Background to the Disputes*

A. *Case C-46/93*

1. *Facts and procedure*

1. Brasserie du Pêcheur SA, the appellant in the main proceedings in Case C-46/93, is a French brewery based at Schiltigheim (Alsace). Until 1981, it exported beer to the Federal Republic of Germany. At the end of 1981 it was forced to discontinue those exports, since the German authorities objected that the beer it produced did not comply with the German Reinheitsgebot (purity requirement) (Biersteuergesetz—Law on Beer Duty—, codification of 14 March 1952, BGBl. I, p. 149, in the version dated 14 December 1976, BGBl. I, p. 3341, p. 3357, hereinafter "the BStG"), in particular Paragraphs 9 and 10 thereof.

2. The Commission, regarding the aforesaid paragraphs of the BStG as contrary to Article 30 of the EEC Treaty, brought an action against the Federal Republic of Germany for failure to comply with its obligations under the Treaty, with regard both to the prohibition against the marketing, under the designation of "Bier" (beer), of beers lawfully manufactured in other Member States according to different rules and to the prohibition against the importation of beers containing additives.

3. In the judgment in Case 178/84 *Commission* v. *Germany* [1987] ECR 1227, the Court held that the prohibition against the marketing of beers imported from other Member States which did not comply with Paragraphs 9 and 10 of the BStG was incompatible with Article 30.

4. Brasserie du Pêcheur consequently brought an action against the Federal Republic of Germany for compensation for the loss suffered by it as a result of that import restriction between 1981 and 1987, in the sum of DM 1,800,000, representing a fraction of the loss actually suffered. That action was dismissed by the lower courts. Brasserie du Pêcheur is pursuing the same claims in its appeal before the Bundesgerichtshof (Federal Court of Justice).

2. *National Law*

5. The first sentence of Paragraph 839(1) of the Bürgerliches Gesetzbuch (German Civil Code, hereinafter "the BGB") provides:

> If an official wilfully or negligently commits a breach of official duty incumbent upon him as against a third party, he shall compensate the third party for any damage arising therefrom.

[1036] Article 34 of the Grundgesetz (Basic Law, hereinafter "the GG") provides:

If a person infringes, in the exercise of a public office entrusted to him, the obligations incumbent upon him as against a third party, liability therefor shall attach in principle to the State or to the body in whose service he is engaged. Where such infringement is wilful or results from gross negligence, a right of recourse is reserved against the person committing the same. A right of appeal to the ordinary courts shall not be excluded for the purposes of proceedings for compensation or an action by way of recourse.

In the Federal Republic of Germany, State liability may be incurred under the combined provisions of the BGB and the GG mentioned above. In the present case, however, the legislature, in enacting the BStG, merely took upon itself tasks which concern the public at large, and which do not relate to any particular person or class of persons who might be regarded as "third parties" within the meaning of those provisions.

6. Furthermore, State liability may also be incurred by reason of unlawful interference, akin to expropriation, on the part of the public authority. This involves a principle developed by the case-law of the Bundesgerichtshof (BGHZ 90, p. 17, p. 29 et seq.). According to that case-law, however, that principle is not such as to enable an order to be made for the payment of compensation for loss resulting from a statute which is contrary to the constitution (BGHZ 100, p. 136, pp. 145 and 146).

7. Consequently, the national court does not consider that German law affords any basis for the payment of compensation for the loss suffered by the claimant.

3. *Questions referred for a preliminary ruling*

8. The Bundesgerichtshof, doubtful as to the interpretation of the principle of State liability for damage caused to individuals by infringements of Community law attributable to the State, as derived from the judgment in Joined Cases C-6/90 and C-9/90 *Francovich and Others* [1991] ECR I-5357 (hereinafter "the *Francovich* judgment"), decided to stay the proceedings and to refer the following questions to the Court for a preliminary ruling:

1. Does the principle of Community law according to which Member States are obliged to pay compensation for damage suffered by an individual as a result of breaches of Community law attributable to those States also apply where such a breach consists of a failure to adapt a national parliamentary statute to the higher-ranking rules of Community law (this case concerning a failure to adapt Paragraphs 9 and 10 of the **[1037]** German Biersteuergesetz to Article 30 of the EEC Treaty)?

2. May the national legal system provide that any entitlement to compensation is to be subject to the same limitations as those applying where a national statute breaches higher-ranking national law, for example where an ordinary Federal law breaches the Grundgesetz of the Federal Republic of Germany?

3. May the national legal system provide that entitlement to compensation is to be conditional on fault (intent or negligence) on the part of the organs of the State responsible for the failure to adapt the legislation?

4. If Question 1 is to be answered in the affirmative and Question 2 in the negative:

(a) May liability to pay compensation under the national legal system be limited to the reparation of damage done to specific individual legal interests, for example property, or does it require full compensation for all financial losses, including lost profits?

(b) Does the obligation to pay compensation also require reparation of the damage already incurred before it was held in the judgment of the European Court of Justice of 12 March 1987 in Case 178/84 *Commission* v. *Germany* [1987] ECR 1227 that Paragraph 10 of the German Biersteuergesetz infringed higher-ranking Community law?

B. *Case C-48/93*

1. *Facts and procedure*

9. On 16 December 1988 a number of individuals and companies incorporated under the laws of the United Kingdom, together with the directors and shareholders of those companies, brought an action before the High Court of Justice, Queen's Bench Division, Divisional Court (hereinafter "the Divisional Court"), in which they challenged the compatibility of Part II of the Merchant Shipping Act 1988 with Articles 7, 52, 58 and 221 of the EEC Treaty. The new system of registration of British fishing vessels imposed certain conditions relating to the nationality, residence and domicile of the owners of the vessels. Fishing boats ineligible for registration in the new register were deprived of the right to fish. The new system entered into force on 1 December 1988, but registration in the new register was not required until, at the latest, the end of a transitional period expiring on 31 March 1989.

[1038] 10. By order of 10 March 1989, the Divisional Court suspended the application of the new registration system and stayed the proceedings pending a preliminary ruling by the Court of Justice on the questions of Community law raised by the claimants. In the judgment in Case C-221/89 *Factortame II* [1991] ECR I-3905, the Court of Justice held that it was contrary to Community law and, in particular, to Article 52 of the EEC Treaty, for a Member State to impose conditions as to the nationality, residence and domicile of the owners of fishing vessels such as those laid down by the new registration system in the United Kingdom.

11. The grant of an interlocutory injunction by the Divisional Court was set aside by the Court of Appeal. Following the claimants' appeal to the House of Lords, that court referred to the Court of Justice, by judgment of 18 May 1989, for a preliminary ruling two questions concerning the extent of the jurisdiction of a national court to grant interim

relief where rights conferred by Community law are in issue. In the judgment in Case C-213/89 *Factortame I* [1990] ECR I-2433, the Court of Justice ruled that "Community law must be interpreted as meaning that a national court which, in a case before it concerning Community law, considers that the sole obstacle which precludes it from granting interim relief is a rule of national law must set aside that rule". On 11 October 1990, the House of Lords affirmed the interlocutory injunction granted by the Divisional Court pending the determination of the substantive case.

12. In the meantime, the Commission brought an action on 4 August 1989 against the United Kingdom under Article 169 of the EEC Treaty in relation to the conditions imposed by the new system of registration in the United Kingdom as to the nationality of the owners of fishing vessels, on the ground that those conditions were contrary to Articles 7, 52 and 221 of the EEC Treaty. By separate document, the Commission also applied, pursuant to Article 186 of the EEC Treaty and Article 83 of the Rules of Procedure of the Court of Justice, for interim measures requiring the United Kingdom to suspend the application of the nationality requirements at issue in relation to nationals of other Member States and in respect of fishing vessels which until 31 March 1989 were pursuing a fishing activity under the British flag. By order of 10 October 1989 in Case 246/89 R *Commission* v. *United Kingdom* [1989] ECR 3125, the President of the Court granted that application. Pursuant to that order, the new registration system was amended by regulation with effect from 2 November 1989. By judgment of 4 October 1991 in Case C-246/89 *Commission* v. *United Kingdom* [1991] ECR I-4585, the Court of Justice held that, by imposing the conditions as to the nationality of the vessel owners, the United Kingdom had failed to fulfil the obligations incumbent upon it under Articles 7, 52 and 221 of the EEC Treaty.

13. Meanwhile, on 2 October 1991, the Divisional Court made an order giving effect to the judgment of the Court of Justice in *Factortame II*, in respect of the registration of the fishing vessels of 79 of the claimants. At the same time, it directed the claimants to give detailed particulars of their claims for damages against the Secretary of State for Transport. By order of 18 November 1992, it gave leave to a number of companies and **[1039]** various other persons to be joined as parties to the proceedings and/or to claim damages. By that order of 18 November 1992, it also gave Rawlings (Trawling) Limited, the 37th claimant in Case C-48/93 (hereinafter "Rawlings"), leave to amend its claim for compensation to include a claim for exemplary damages for unconstitutional behaviour by the public authorities.

14. The compensation sought by the claimants is based on various heads of damage including, in particular, expenses and losses incurred from the entry into force of the new legislation on 1 April 1989 until its repeal on 2 November.

2. *National law*

15. There is no legislation in the United Kingdom by virtue of which the State may incur liability. However, the possibility of such liability has been developed by case-law.

16. First, the State may incur liability for misfeasance in public office. However, in *Bourgoin* v. *Minister of Agriculture, Fisheries and Food* [1986] QB 716, the Court of Appeal held that the State was not required as a matter of English or Community law to compensate the victims of acts which had been found by the Court of Justice to be contrary to Community law, unless the Minister were shown to have acted in the knowledge that the act in question was invalid and with the intention or knowledge that it would injure the claimants. More recently, in *Kirklees Metropolitan Borough Council* v. *Wickes Building Supplies Limited* [1992] 3 WLR 170, 188, C to D, the House of Lords stated *obiter* that:

> . . . since the decision of the European Court of Justice in *Francovich* v. *Republic of Italy* . . . there must now be doubt whether the *Bourgoin* case was correctly decided.

17. An action for damages is unlikely to lie for purely financial loss occasioned by the negligent exercise of administrative, let alone legislative, powers, though that possibility has been left open by the courts: see in particular *Rowling* v. *Takaro Properties Ltd* [1988] AC 473. An action for such compensation is conditional on the existence of a duty of care on the part of the public authorities. The concept and scope of that duty of care are presently being developed in the case-law of the courts of the United Kingdom (*Lonhro* v. *Tebbit* [1992] 4 All ER 280).

[1040] 18. The national court considers that if English law as expressed in the *Bourgoin* decision were to be applied in the present case, the complainants would have no remedy in damages.

3. *Questions referred for a preliminary ruling*

19. The national court, doubtful as to the interpretation of the principle of State liability for damage caused to individuals by infringements of Community law attributable to the State, as derived from the *Francovich* judgment, decided to stay the proceedings and to refer the following questions to the Court for a preliminary ruling:

> 1. In all the circumstances of this case, where:
> (a) a Member State's legislation laid down conditions relating to the nationality, domicile and residence of the owners and managers of fishing vessels, and of the shareholders and directors in vessel-owning and managing companies, and
> (b) such conditions were held by the Court of Justice in Cases C-221/89 and C-246/89 to infringe Articles 5, 7, 52 and 221 of the EEC Treaty,
>
> are those persons who were owners or managers of such vessels, or directors and/or shareholders in vessel-owning and managing companies, entitled as a

matter of Community law to compensation by that Member State for losses which they have suffered as a result of all or any of the above infringements of the EEC Treaty?

2. If Question 1 is answered in the affirmative, what considerations, if any, does Community law require the national court to apply in determining claims for damages and interest relating to:

(a) expenses and/or loss of profit and/or loss of income during the period subsequent to the entry into force of the said conditions, during which the vessels were forced to lay up, to make alternative arrangements for fishing and/or to seek registration elsewhere;
(b) losses consequent on sales at an undervalue of the vessels, or of shares therein, or of shares in vessel-owning companies;
[1041] (c) losses consequent on the need to provide bonds, fines and legal expenses for alleged offences connected with the exclusion of vessels from the national register;
(d) losses consequent on the inability of such persons to own and operate further vessels;
(e) loss of management fees;
(f) expenses incurred in an attempt to mitigate the above losses;
(g) exemplary damages as claimed?

II. *Procedure before the Court of Justice*

20. The orders for reference were received at the Court Registry on 17 February 1993 in Case C-46/93 and on 18 February 1993 in Case C-48/93.

21. Pursuant to Article 20 of the Protocol on the Statute of the Court of Justice of the EEC, written observations were submitted on behalf of:

— Brasserie du Pêcheur SA, by H. Büttner, Rechtsanwalt, Karlsruhe,
— complainants 1 to 36 and 38 to 84 in Case C-48/93, by D. Vaughan QC, G. Barling QC and D. Anderson, Barrister, instructed by S. Swabey, Solicitor,
— complainants 85 to 97 in Case C-48/93, by N. Green, Barrister, instructed by N. Horton, Solicitor,
[1042] — the 37th complainant in Case C-48/93, by N. Forwood QC and P. Duffy, Barrister, instructed by Holman Fenwick & Willan, Solicitors,
— the Government of the Federal Republic of Germany, by E. Röder, Ministerialrat in the Federal Ministry of Economic Affairs, acting as Agent, and J. Sedemund, Rechtsanwalt, Cologne,
— the United Kingdom, by J. E. Collins, Assistant Treasury Solicitor, acting as Agent, and by S. Richards, C. Vajda and R. Thompson, Barristers,
— the Danish Government, by J. Mølde, Legal Adviser in the Ministry of Foreign Affairs, acting as Agent,

— the Spanish Government, by A. J. Navarro González, Director-General for Community Legal and Institutional Affairs, and R. Silva de Lapuerta and G. Calvo Díaz, Abogados del Estado, of the State Legal Service, acting as Agents,
— the French Government, by J.-P. Puissochet, Director of Legal Affairs in the Ministry of Foreign Affairs, and C. de Salins, Deputy Director of the Foreign Affairs Directorate in that Ministry, acting as Agents,
— Ireland, by M. A. Buckley, Chief State Solicitor, acting as Agent,
— the Netherlands Government, by A. Bos, Legal Adviser in the Ministry of Foreign Affairs, acting as Agent,
— the Commission of the European Communities, by C. Timmermans, Assistant Director-General of its Legal Service, J. Pipkorn, Legal Adviser, and C. Docksey, of its Legal Service, acting as Agents.

22. By order of 22 March 1993, the President of the Court decided that the two cases should be joined for the purposes of the written procedure, the oral procedure and the judgment.

[1043] 23. Upon hearing the report of the Judge-Rapporteur and the views of the Advocate General, the Court decided to open the oral procedure without any preparatory inquiry.

III. *Written observations submitted to the Court*

A. *Summary of the arguments and proposed answers*

24. *Brasserie du Pêcheur* considers that no distinction is to be made according to the nature of the State institution to which the infringement is attributable and that, consequently, the activities of the legislature may give rise to compensation. The conditions governing the right to reparation may be those laid down by national law in the case of an infringement of a national provision, subject to the proviso that any rule of national law which imposes conditions which are more restrictive as regards claims based on Community law, or which make it impossible or excessively difficult to obtain reparation, must be disapplied (*Francovich*, paragraphs 42 and 43). It follows that a rule having the effect of wholly excluding the legislature's obligation to pay compensation must be incompatible with Community law. The obligation to pay compensation may be dependent on the existence of fault, but the burden of proving fault cannot be imposed on the victim and, in any event, in Case C-46/93, the mere fact of the application of legislation incompatible with Community law objectively constitutes fault. Compensation for the damage must extend, at the very least, to the fundamental loss caused by the breach of Community law, which, in Case C-46/93, lies essentially, if not exclusively, in loss of profit. The appellant's rights derive from the breach of a provision having direct effect, and thus arose at the time when the breach was committed.

25. *Brasserie du Pêcheur* submits that the answers to the questions referred in Case C-46/93 should be as follows:

1. Community law obliges Member States to make good the damage caused to individuals by breaches of Community law attributable to those States, including breaches caused by a national parliamentary statute which is inconsistent with the rules of Community law.

2. The legislature may decide that the claim for compensation should be subject to the same restrictions as result from a national law when there is a breach of a higher-ranking rule of national law, but only to the extent that such a restriction does not have the effect of making it impossible or extremely difficult to exercise the right to reparation of damage caused by a breach of Community law. It is the task of the national courts to disapply a rule of national law which would have the consequence that the right to reparation could not be asserted or could only be asserted with great difficulty.

[1044] 3. Even if Community law does not preclude the conditions for an obligation to provide compensation being defined by national law and in particular being dependent on proof of fault, that condition must be regarded as fulfilled if the breach of Community law has been found by a judgment of the Court of Justice of the European Communities. Accordingly, the victim of such a breach of Community law cannot be required to provide proof of the exact nature of the fault for that breach.

4.(a) The obligation to protect rights which claimants derive from a breach of Article 30 of the Treaty means that the compensation for the damage resulting from that breach relates to all material elements of the damage, including loss of profit.

(b) The obligation to pay compensation covers the damage suffered from the date when the liability to pay compensation arose, that is, from the time when the Member State breached its obligations under Community law, regardless of when such a breach of Community law was found by the Court of Justice.

26. The *claimants in Case C-48/93 other than Rawlings (hereinafter "Factortame and others")*[1] consider that non-compliance with a substantive provision of Community law (Articles 30 and 52 of the EEC Treaty) is more serious, and more deserving of compensation, than a breach of a procedural obligation (the case of *Francovich* involved Article 189 of the EEC Treaty). In their view, there is no reason why damages should not be awarded for the act of a national legislature. The criteria for compensation established by the case-law relating to the liability of the Community under Article 215 of the Treaty, and in particular the requirement, in relation to legislative measures involving choices of economic policy,

[1] Those applicants include all those companies and individuals, as well as persons claiming to be shareholders or directors of such companies, to whom leave was granted by the Divisional Court to bring proceedings and claim damages, apart from Rawlings. Rawlings, the 37th applicant, to whom leave was granted to include a claim for exemplary damages, was separately represented in the main proceedings and submitted separate observations to the Court.

that a sufficiently flagrant breach be proven, are irrelevant in the present context, since the United Kingdom adopted legislation aimed at an identifiable group of Community nationals and there was no question of any choice of economic policy. More particularly, the liability of a State should not be dependent on its knowledge of the unlawfulness of the act; the breach of a provision of the Treaty must be enough to found such liability. In any event, the Merchant Shipping Act 1988 satisfies the applicable criteria regarding liability on the part of the Community legislature. Factortame and others further state that, as regards their particular situation, the fact that they were granted interim relief is no bar to their being awarded damages, since those two forms of relief are not alternatives. That conclusion **[1045]** is inevitable, particularly since the interim relief was granted over a year after the vessels were excluded from the register. In any event, some applicants were not the beneficiaries of the interim measures. Factortame and others assert that the Court should lay down certain guidelines as to the specific heads of claim for compensation, in the light of the principle laid down in the *Francovich* judgment that the applicable national rules must be no less favourable than those relating to similar claims under national law and must not be such as to render the recovery of damages impossible or excessively difficult (paragraph 43 of the *Francovich* judgment).

27. *Factortame and others* submit that the answers to the questions referred in Case C-48/93 should be as follows:

Question 1: Yes

Question 2: The claims for damages and interest as specified in Question 2, in particular paragraphs (a) to (f), are all recoverable as a matter of Community law.

28. *Rawlings* considers that the ultimate test of a right is whether effective measures exist for its protection and enforcement—*Ubi jus, ibi remedium*—; a right without an effective remedy is in reality no right at all. In its view, the Court is bound to confirm that any infringement by a Member State of a directly applicable provision of Community law gives rise to a right to compensation. The criteria established by the Court's case-law in the context of Articles 178 and 215 of the EEC Treaty are inapplicable in the present case, but, in any event, the conditions of liability laid down by that case-law, together with any other condition which may be deemed appropriate, are nonetheless fulfilled by reason of the manifest and grave nature of the facts on which Rawlings' claim is based. As regards the specific heads of claim, the principles laid down in paragraphs 42 and 43 of the *Francovich* judgment should be complied with. As regards, more particularly, its claim for exemplary damages, Rawlings considers that to deny the possibility of exemplary damages

for breaches of Community law while retaining it for certain breaches of English law would go contrary to the requirement that rights under Community law must not be treated less favourably than similar claims under national law.

29. *Rawlings* submits that the questions referred in Case C-48/93 should be answered as follows:

1. When legislation of a Member State, in breach of Articles 5, 7, 52 and 221 of the **[1046]** EEC Treaty, lays down in relation to the owners and managers of fishing vessels and the shareholders and directors in vessel-owning and managing companies conditions which unlawfully discriminate, directly or indirectly, between citizens of Member States according to their nationality, the Member State concerned is in principle liable to provide effective compensation for losses suffered as a result of the unlawful discrimination.

2. In the absence of any applicable Community legislation, the competent national courts must adjudicate upon claims for such compensation in accordance with the foregoing principle, but otherwise according to substantive and procedural conditions laid down by the national law for similar claims under the internal legal order of the State. Such conditions may not, however, be so framed as to make it virtually impossible, or excessively difficult, to obtain effective compensation for losses which have actually been sustained as a result of the unlawful measures.

3. Where the law of a Member State provides for the possibility of an additional award of damages in respect of oppressive, arbitrary or unconstitutional conduct by public authorities, national courts must ensure similar protection where the conduct in question is contrary to a fundamental principle of Community law. For this purpose,

(i) the rule prohibiting discrimination on grounds of nationality, as expressed *inter alia* in Articles 7, 52 and 221 of the EEC Treaty, constitutes one of the fundamental principles upon which the Community is based and which is designed for the protection of the individual. Disregard of that essential principle should always be regarded as seriously as similar fundamental provisions in a national constitution or its equivalent;

and

(ii) failure by a Member State to take prompt and effective steps to implement an order of the Court of Justice is a serious infringement of the fundamental principle of respect for the rule of law which is one of the essential foundations of the Community.

30. The *Danish Government* considers that the *Francovich* judgment lays down a general principle of Community law requiring Member States to make good the loss and damage caused to individuals by breaches of Community law. The procedural and substantive conditions governing an action for compensation are a matter of national civil law, provided that the compensation must not be rendered illusory. However, it would not be reasonable if Member States could incur more extensive liability than that **[1047]** incurred by the Community institutions, as defined by the Court in its case-law relating to Article 215 of the EEC Treaty.

That case-law establishes the requirement of the existence of fault, in the sense that liability is not incurred unless there is a "sufficiently serious" infringement of a superior rule of law protecting the individual and the institution concerned has "manifestly and gravely" disregarded the limits on the exercise of its powers.

31. The *Danish Government* does not submit any proposed answers to the questions referred to the Court, confining itself to giving its views on the fundamental issues.

32. The *German Government* considers that it was not the intention of the Community legislature to establish any general liability on the part of Member States for infringements of Community law. It points out that during the negotiations concerning the Maastricht Treaty the Member States did not adopt any rules in that regard. The new version of Article 171 of the EC Treaty merely provides for the imposition of penalties on Member States which do not comply with the Court's judgments. The German Government further states that an extension of Community law by judge-made law going beyond the bounds of the legitimate closure of lacunae would be incompatible with the division of competence between the Community institutions and the Member States laid down by the Treaty, and with the principle of the maintenance of institutional balance. The institutions having legislative competence, in particular the Council and the Parliament, cannot be excluded from the establishment of a general right to compensation, which requires democratic legitimation. Furthermore, such a principle requires an alteration of the Treaty entailing financial implications which also necessitate the consent of the national parliaments.

In the German Government's view, the *Francovich* judgment is only concerned with the imposition of penalties in respect of provisions which are not directly applicable, the Court having sought in that judgment to close a lacuna in the system for the safeguarding of rights. Inasmuch as a right of action is accorded for the purposes of asserting rules of Community law, there is no need for the grant of a right to compensation. Consequently, the views expressed by the German Government in relation to the questions referred for a preliminary ruling are put forward only as alternative observations. As regards the conditions governing entitlement to compensation, reference should be made to the criteria laid down in the *Francovich* judgment and to other procedural and substantive conditions deriving both from Community law (case-law relating to Article 215 of the Treaty) and from national law, subject to the restrictions laid down by the Court in paragraph 43 of the *Francovich* judgment. More particularly, the requirement of fault, in the sense that the State must be shown to have acted intentionally or negligently, constitutes a fundamental and intrinsically legitimate condition of the right to compensation. In any event, there cannot exist any obligation to make good loss and damage arising prior to delivery of the judgment of the Court in

Commission v. *Germany*, cited above, according to which a Member State is obliged to remedy an infringement of the Treaty only *ex nunc*.

[1048] 33. The *German Government* submits that the questions referred for a preliminary ruling in Case C-46/93 should be answered as follows:

1. Where a national parliamentary statute such as Paragraphs 9 and 10 of the German Biersteuergesetz is not adapted to a directly effective rule of Community law such as Article 30 of the EEC Treaty, there is no obligation under Community law for a Member State to repair the damage suffered by an individual as a result of that failure.

and, in the alternative:

2. The national legal system may provide that, as regards not only the establishment of liability and its consequences but also the procedure to be followed, the right to compensation under Community law is to be subject to the same limitations as those applying where a national law infringes higher-ranking national law, in so far as those conditions are not so framed as to make it virtually impossible or excessively difficult to obtain compensation.

3. The national legal system may provide that entitlement to compensation under Community law is to be conditional on fault on the part of the Member State, provided that this condition is not framed in such a way as to make it impossible or excessively difficult to obtain compensation.

4.(a) Liability under Community law to provide compensation may be limited in scope by the national legal system, provided that such liability constitutes an effective sanction for ensuring the enforcement of Community law.

(b) The right to compensation under Community law does not generally require damage which had already arisen before the Court of Justice of the European Communities found that Community law had been infringed to be made good.

(or, at all events, if Questions 1 and 4(b) are answered in the affirmative)

The liability of the Federal Republic of Germany for breach of Article 30 of the EEC Treaty by Paragraphs 9 and 10 of the Biersteuergesetz extends only to damage arising after the delivery of this judgment, unless **[1049]** the injured parties previously commenced an action or sought analogous remedies.

34. The *German Government* considers that the answer to the first question referred by the Divisional Court to the Court of Justice should be the same as that given to the first question referred by the Bundesgerichtshof. As regards the Divisional Court's second question, the German Government considers that the amount of the damages to be awarded falls to be determined in accordance with the rules of domestic law, provided that they are not so framed as to make it virtually impossible or excessively difficult to obtain compensation.

35. The *Greek Government*, which has not lodged any written pleading before the Court but which has presented oral submissions, considers that, in order to have any effect, the principle of reparation, which is based directly on Community law (paragraph 41 of the *Francovich*

judgment), must ensure the removal of all consequences, of whatever kind, flowing from the infringement of Community law, and must fully protect the rights of individuals. The Greek Government takes the view that the conditions governing reparation must not differ fundamentally from those laid down in the *Francovich* judgment. The procedural rules of the Member States, which must not make the exercise of Community law impossible or excessively difficult, cannot relate to the conditions giving rise to the reparation obligation, but must be restricted to specific issues, such as the extent of the damage or the sharing of liability. The reparation criteria established by case-law where the Community incurs liability under Article 215 of the EC Treaty, and in particular the requirement as to proof of a manifest and sufficiently serious breach of a superior rule of law, are not relevant to the liability of Member States, inasmuch as it is not easy to establish whether there has been a breach of Community law. The Greek Government further states that, in order for liability to arise, it is enough that there should be an objective breach of a provision of Community law. In its view, compensation should be payable both for financial losses and for loss of profits. Lastly, the Greek Government considers that no temporal limitation should be applied to the right to compensation until a judgment has been delivered by the Court.

36. The *Spanish Government* considers that the principle of the liability in damages of Member States, including their legislatures, has been acknowledged by the Court of Justice. The criteria for compensation have been referred by the Court to the national legal systems. In that regard, the very great normative diversity amongst the Member States is such that there is a need for Community harmonization, since it is not enough simply to apply the principle of national treatment. The scope of such liability has to be examined on a case-by-case basis and, in any event, it is necessary to take account of the nature and scope of the prejudicial act, the damage caused and the existence of a causal link between that act and the damage suffered.

37. The *Spanish Government* requests the Court to reply to the questions referred to it for a preliminary ruling in the terms set out in the observations submitted by it.

[1050] 38. The *French Government* considers that the acts or omissions of the legislature should not be exempted from a general obligation to pay compensation, but that, nevertheless, it is necessary to take into account the difficulties which prompted the Member State in question to disregard Community law. If the criteria for compensation required under national law are such as to render the Community principle of compensation wholly ineffective, those criteria are not compatible with Community law. The Court could develop criteria analogous to those which it has laid down pursuant to Article 178 of the EEC Treaty, but it should confine itself to the concept of a "breach of Community law", without requiring national courts to classify such a breach as one involving "fault". As regards specific heads of compensation, the French Government observes that the Court has allowed claims for loss of profits. Lastly, no obligation to pay compensation can arise unless there has been a serious breach. Consequently, that question falls to be assessed on a case-by-case basis by the national court.

39. The *French Government* submits that the questions referred for a preliminary ruling in Case C-46/93 should be answered as follows:

1. The principle developed by the Court, to the effect that Member States are obliged to repair damage caused to individuals by breaches of Community law which are attributable to them, may also apply where the breach arises from the non-adaptation of a formal parliamentary statute to the provisions of Community law.

2. A national legal system may not make a right to compensation subject to the same restrictions as those applicable where a statute infringes national provisions of a constitutional nature if, by subjecting the right to those requirements, it deprives of all effect the principle of the obligation to make reparation.

3. Where, as in the two cases referred to it, a breach of Community law does not involve the non-implementation of a directive, national courts may make the right to compensation subject to the condition that there must be a serious breach of Community law, that the damage should go beyond the bounds of the risks inherent in the business activities of traders in the sector concerned and, where appropriate, that it should be of a special nature.

4.(a) The obligation to pay compensation may relate to all damage which is proved by the plaintiff to have resulted directly from the breach found to have been committed.

(b) The obligation to make reparation may extend to damage arising prior to a judgment of the Court in which it is held that the national legislation at issue constitutes a breach of an obligation laid down by Community law. However, the concept of a "serious breach" may lead a national court to consider that that criterion is not satisfied until the Court has delivered **[1051]** its judgment establishing the breach or a judgment giving a clear interpretation of the Community provisions said to have been infringed, and to rule that the right to compensation for the damage should run from the date of that judgment.

40. The *French Government* considers that the answers which it proposes that the Court should give to the first three questions referred by the Bundesgerichtshof will enable the first question referred by the Divisional Court to be answered. Its proposed answer to the Bundesgerichtshof's fourth question will enable the Divisional Court's second question to be answered.

41. The *Irish Government* considers, primarily, that the question of the payment of compensation by a Member State for an infringement of a directly effective provision of Community law is a matter for national law, on condition that the Community remedy is treated not less favourably than the comparable remedies under national law, and that the

procedural and substantive conditions should not be such as to render it impossible or excessively difficult to obtain redress. The right to compensation has, basically, a secondary role to play in affording protection, particularly where there is an infringement of Community rules which are not directly effective, as in the case of the provisions of the directive at issue in the *Francovich* judgment. The Irish Government points out that the Member States did not adopt any rule regarding general liability in the course of the negotiations concerning the Maastricht Treaty. The amended wording of Article 171 of the EEC Treaty is limited to providing for the imposition of penalties on Member States which do not comply with judgments of the Court. The Irish Government submits alternative observations in the event that the Court rules that there exists under Community law an obligation to pay compensation for the breach of a directly effective provision. In those circumstances, there should be taken into account, as regards the criteria for the payment of compensation, the Court's case-law relating to Article 215 of the EEC Treaty, as well as national case-law.

42. The *Irish Government* submits that the questions referred for a preliminary ruling in the two cases should be answered as follows:

(a) It is for national law to settle the question of liability for compensation on the part of a Member State for an infringement of a directly applicable rule of Community law for which that State is responsible, on condition that national law treats the Community remedy not less favourably than the comparable national remedy, and that the procedural and substantive conditions imposed by national law are not such as to render it **[1052]** impossible, or excessively difficult, for the wronged claimant to obtain redress.

and, in the alternative:

(b) If and insofar as damages are recoverable in Community law against a Member State for infringements of that law, the conditions laid down by national law, both as to substance and as to form, for the recovery of damages (including the heads of damage, questions of interest, exemplary damages etc.), apply, subject to these conditions being no less favourable than those relating to similar claims under national law and to their not being so framed as to render the recovery of damages excessively difficult or impossible in practice.

43. In the view of the *Netherlands Government*, it is not yet clear whether the principle of compensation, as developed by the Court in the *Francovich* judgment, can be simply transposed to a situation involving the enactment by the national legislature of legislation which is contrary to Community law. The right to compensation has, basically, a secondary role to play in affording protection, particularly where there is an infringement of provisions of Community law which do not have direct effect, as was the case with the provisions of the directive at issue in the

Francovich judgment. Where directly applicable provisions are involved (Articles 30 and 52 of the EEC Treaty), individuals can in principle have recourse to domestic legal remedies enabling them to secure compliance therewith. The Netherlands Government points out that, when the Treaty on European Union was being drawn up, the Member States discussed the question of the effective application of Community law, and that the negotiations resulted in the amendment of Article 171 of the EEC Treaty. If the principle of the payment of compensation falls to be applied in the present case, the conditions set forth by the Court in its case-law regarding Article 215 of the EEC Treaty could usefully be taken as a frame of reference. However, it is open to the national court to base its decision on national law and to apply a stricter system of liability, within the limits laid down in paragraph 43 of the *Francovich* judgment.

44. The *Netherlands Government* restricts itself, in its observations, to the submission of a number of arguments, without proposing any specific answers to the questions referred to the Court.

45. The *United Kingdom* considers that where, in the case of acts of a legislature charged with the responsibility of weighing up competing interests, directly applicable provisions of the Treaty are found to have been infringed, the enactment of such legislative acts gives rise to liability under Community law only if the following conditions are **[1053]** satisfied: (1) the provision of the Treaty which has been infringed is a superior rule of law for the protection of the individual; (2) there has been a sufficiently serious breach of that provision, in that the measures were adopted or maintained in force in manifest and grave disregard of the Member State's obligations under the Treaty; (3) there is a direct causal link between the breach of the State's obligations and the damage suffered by individuals upon whom rights were conferred by the provision of the Treaty in question.

46. The *United Kingdom* submits that the questions referred should be answered as follows:

—in Case C-48/93:

1. Where a Member State enacts legislation involving the exercise of legislative discretion it does not, as a matter of Community law, incur liability in damages in respect of such legislation subsequently held to be incompatible with Community law unless there has been a sufficiently serious breach of a superior rule of law for the protection of the individual whereby the State concerned has gravely and manifestly disregarded its obligations under the Community Treaties. Where:

(i) a Member State's legislature enacted primary legislation relating to the nationality, domicile and residence of the owners and managers of fishing vessels, and of the shareholders and directors in vessel-owning and managing companies which came into effect on 1 December 1988 and

(ii) the Member State complied with the order of the President of the Court in Case 246/89 R *Commission* v. *United Kingdom* [1989] ECR 3125 and the judgment of the Court in Case C-221/89 *The Queen* v. *Secretary of State for Transport* ex parte *Factortame* [1991] ECR I-3905,

the Member State does not, as a matter of Community law, incur liability in damages.

2. Where a Member State is liable, as a matter of Community law, to compensate individuals who suffer loss as the result of legislation which is subsequently held to be incompatible with Community law the conditions as to both substance and form for the recovery of damages are, in the absence of Community rules, a matter for national law **[1054]** subject to those conditions being no less favourable than the conditions relating to similar claims under national law and not being so framed as to render the recovery of damages excessively difficult or virtually impossible in practice.

—in Case C-46/93:

1. Community law requires that a Member State incurs liability in damages for failure to adopt legislation involving the exercise of a legislative discretion where there has been a sufficiently serious breach of a superior rule of law for the protection of the individual whereby the State concerned has gravely and manifestly disregarded its obligations under the Community Treaties.

2. Where a Member State is liable, as a matter of Community law, to compensate individuals who suffer loss as the result of that State's failure to adapt legislation which is subsequently held to be incompatible with Community law the conditions as to both substance and form for the recovery of damages are, in the absence of Community rules, a matter for national law subject to those conditions being no less favourable than the conditions relating to similar claims under national law and not being so framed as to render the recovery of damages excessively difficult or virtually impossible in practice.

3. The answer to this question is the same as the answer to Question 1 above.

4. The answer to this question is the same as the answer to Question 2 above.

47. The *Commission* considers that it is generally contrary to Community law, at all events in the situations with which the main proceedings are concerned, for Member States, in the event of an infringement of Community law, to apply systematically and without limitation, and with a view to redressing the damage caused by the acts of the legislature, general restrictions imposed by national law. As regards the criteria governing entitlement to compensation, the Commission considers that it is necessary to take account of the rules of national law within the limits established in the *Francovich* judgment, and that it may be appropriate to rely on the Court's case-law in relation to Article 215 of the EEC Treaty. The detailed rules for the calculation of loss are derived from national law, but must not fall short of the minimum requirements laid down by the case-law relating to Article 215 of the EEC Treaty. The obligation to pay compensation exists from the time when the authorities should have known, and could have had no excuse for not knowing, that they were taking action in areas covered by Community law and that they were encroaching on rights conferred by that law.

[1055] 48. The *Commission* submits that the questions referred should be answered as follows:

—in Case C-46/93:

1. A Member State must compensate the damage to the individual which arises from the interference by the organs of the State with an individual right granted by Community law, including the case where this interference is the consequence of a failure to adapt formal legislation to Community law.

2. In the present state of Community law, it is the responsibility of the Member States to determine the precise material conditions governing such a right to compensation. The relevant national rules must not be less favourable than those applicable to similar legal rights protected by purely national laws. In addition, those rules must not render this legal protection virtually impossible or excessively difficult in that, in cases of interference with Community law rights, they apply restrictions which are valid in the national framework for legislative conduct.

3. Community law does not prohibit a national rule according to which the right to compensation is subjected to a requirement of fault, provided that the rules governing liability, taken as a whole, do not fall short of the minimum standard applied under the second paragraph of Article 215 of the EEC Treaty in the case of legal acts of the Community having general effect.

4. The effective legal protection required by Community law is excessively curtailed if the obligation to compensate is confined to the reparation of damage to certain individual assets such as property. This also applies to cases where national liability laws generally rule out compensation for loss of profit, even where such loss is adequately substantiated.

5. The effective legal protection required by Community law is also excessively curtailed if compensation is made dependent on the breach of law having been formally established in proceedings pursuant to Article 169 of the EEC Treaty.

—in Case C-48/93:

1. A Member State must compensate the damage to the individual which arises from the interference by the organs of the State with an individual right granted by Community **[1056]** law, including the case where this interference is the consequence of the adoption of a legislative act.

2. In the present state of Community law, it is the responsibility of the Member States to determine the additional conditions governing such a right to compensation. The relevant national rules should however be applied without discrimination and must not render this legal protection virtually impossible or excessively difficult in that, in cases of interference with Community law rights, they apply restrictions which are valid in the national framework for legislative conduct.

3. Community law does not prohibit a national rule according to which the right to compensation is subjected to a requirement of fault, provided that the rules governing liability, taken as a whole, do not fall short of the minimum standard applied under Article 215(2) of the Treaty in the case of legal acts of the Community having general effect.

4. In the present state of Community law, it is the responsibility of the Member States to determine the rules governing claims to damages and interest. The relevant national rules should however be applied without discrimination and should not render this legal protection virtually impossible or excessively difficult. Where national law provides for the award of special or exemplary damages, the rules relating to such damages must be applied without discrimination in the case of interference with Community law rights.

B. *Applicability of the principle of State liability to the measures enacted by the legislature (Question 1 in Case C-46/93 and in Case C-48/93)*

49. *All the parties* accept that the principle of State liability applies to the national legislature (the conditions in which such liability is accepted as being capable of arising are summarized in C and D below).

50. *Brasserie du Pêcheur* considers that any uncertainty has now been removed by the *Francovich* judgment, since the Court draws no distinction according to the function of the State institutions which are responsible for the breach of Community law. In that judgment, the breach was attributed to the Italian Republic, when it resulted from an error on the part of the Italian legislature. This point of view is all the more compelling in that any other solution would have the consequence of creating discrepancies in the protection of rights and would endanger the uniform application of law in the Community.

[1057] 51. *Factortame and others* and *Rawlings* consider that there is often no difference for the individual concerned between whether the unlawfulness is contained in primary legislation, or in secondary legislation adopted pursuant to the powers granted to the executive, or in the simple exercise of those powers. An unlawful act is unlawful however it is adopted and whether or not it has widespread political support.

52. The *French Government* submits in that regard that the fact that a statute is adopted or is not amended, which does not in any way prejudge the nature of the breach of Community law, cannot in itself justify a general exoneration from any obligation to pay compensation.

53. The *Commission* considers that infringements such as those alleged against the Member States in the two cases referred to the Court do not in fact concern the exercise of national legislative sovereignty in the classical sense of the term but failure to observe the principle of the supremacy of Community law. Having regard to the obligation to observe that supremacy, which is incumbent on all the institutions of the Member States, entitlement to compensation should not be made subject to restrictions which have been developed in national law in order to safeguard legislative autonomy and which have no bearing on Community law. The legislature is subject to the objectives of Community law from a practical standpoint, that is to say, not from the point of view of its constitutional position but from that of the executive when adopting general measures to implement Community law.

C. *Conditions governing State liability (Question 2 in Case C-46/93 and Question 1 in Case C-48/93)*

54. The observations of the *German and Irish Governments* in relation to the conditions governing the application of the principle of State liability are submitted only in the alternative, since those governments consider that the principle of Community law established in the *Francovich* judgment is concerned merely with sanctions against provisions which are not directly applicable.

55. *Brasserie du Pêcheur*, the *Danish, German, Spanish, Netherlands and United Kingdom Governments* and the *Commission* observe that the Court did not intend, in the *Francovich* judgment, to establish a universal, complete and fixed system relating to the conditions governing entitlement to compensation. On the contrary, in the absence of Community harmonization, the Court referred to the procedural and substantive conditions laid down by the legal systems of the Member States. However, they go on to state that the Court sought to lay down two limitations. The first requirement imposed by Community law is that the criteria laid down by the national legislatures must not be less favourable than those relating to similar claims under national law. The second requirement imposed by Community law is that those criteria must not be so framed as **[1058]** to make it virtually impossible or excessively difficult to achieve reparation (paragraphs 42 and 43 of the *Francovich* judgment).

56. *All the governments* and the *Commission* consider that the Court's case-law relating to Articles 178 and 215 of the EEC Treaty could be applied, wholly or in part, in determining the liability of Member States. In their view, in the case of legislative acts involving choices of economic policy in fields where a wide discretion exists, Member States, like the Community institutions, should only incur liability where the infringement of Community law amounts to a "serious" breach, that is to say, "manifest and grave". The Danish, German, Netherlands and United Kingdom Governments further state that it would not be reasonable if Member States could incur more extensive liability than that incurred by the Community institutions in comparable situations.

Factortame and others and *Rawlings* consider, on the other hand, that the Court's case-law relating to Articles 178 and 215 of the EEC Treaty is not applicable for the purposes of defining State liability. They consider that, in any event, Part II of the Merchant Shipping Act 1988 easily satisfies the conditions as to Community legislation laid down by the case-law of the Court.

57. The *Danish, Spanish, French, Irish and Netherlands Governments* and the *Commission* consider that a breach of Community law is "manifest" either where the Community-law provisions which have been disregarded are clear in themselves or where the Court has clarified them in a preliminary ruling or in Treaty infringement proceedings, but above all where the Court has previously found the national rule at issue to be incompatible

with Community law. However, the mere existence of a judgment of the Court confirming such incompatibility is not enough in itself to give rise to liability on the part of the State; on the other hand, it is not necessary for the breach to have been the subject of Treaty infringement proceedings.

The *Danish and United Kingdom Governments* and the *Commission* consider that it is very difficult to resolve the question of the attribution of liability to the State where national legislation conflicts with a provision of the EEC Treaty, since fresh questions of interpretation are constantly arising. If questions of interpretation are shrouded in uncertainty and a Member State exercises its discretion in a reasonable way, it would seem unreasonable for it to incur liability if it is later held that Community law precludes the national law or administrative practice in question. Unblameworthy legal mistakes should not lead to liability to make reparation.

58. The *German Government* considers, in Case C-46/93, that the position regarding the compatibility of Paragraphs 9 and 10 of the BStG with Article 30 of the EEC Treaty was **[1059]** by no means clear. On the contrary, when delivering its judgment in Case 178/84, cited above, the Court took the opportunity in that case to redefine in fundamental terms the scope of Articles 30 and 36 of the EEC Treaty as they apply in food law and to lay down procedural rules in relation to the marketability of foodstuffs containing prohibited additives. There was thus no conscious and deliberate infringement by the Federal Republic of Germany of a clear and unequivocal rule of Community law. Since Article 30 of the EEC Treaty was directly applicable, the plaintiff could have asserted its rights before the national courts. Evidently, the reason why it did not do so is because, in the beginning, neither the Commission nor the plaintiff thought that Article 30 had clearly been infringed by the German legislation.

As regards the facts in Case C-46/93, the *Commission* considers that it is necessary to examine separately, on the one hand, the prohibition on describing as "beer" any beer not brewed in accordance with the Reinheitsgebot and, on the other hand, the prohibition on the importation of beer containing additives. As regards the rule concerning the description of the beverage on the sale thereof, it appears that the German authorities should have known, in the light of the settled case-law on the point, that import barriers resulting from such a prohibition cannot be justified under Community law. As regards, on the other hand, the prohibition on the marketing of beers containing additives, it was not made entirely clear until the judgment in Case 178/84 was delivered that such a prohibition was not covered by the exemptions allowed under Article 36 of the EEC Treaty.

59. *Factortame and others* and *Rawlings* consider, in Case C-48/93, that the United Kingdom is liable whatever criteria are applied, for the following reasons: first, the contested provisions of the Merchant

Shipping Act 1988 constitute a manifest breach of Articles 7, 52 and 221 of the EEC Treaty, having regard to the judgments of the Court in Cases C-221/89 and C-246/89; second, the proposed legislation was objected to by the complainants, by the Commission and by another Member State at an early stage, yet such objections were ignored by the United Kingdom, which enacted the legislation and refused to collaborate in any way with the Commission; lastly, the Act was deliberately drafted so as to preclude any exemption and without any amendment in relation to acquired rights, with the intention of reducing the possibility of anticipated legal action and of the grant of interim measures and, finally, with the purpose of causing damage to a specific group of Community nationals, many of whom had been lawfully established in the United Kingdom for many years.

The *Irish and United Kingdom Governments* consider, on the other hand, that the United Kingdom Parliament was faced with two competing interests under Community law: on the one hand, the British fishing communities, who relied on the principle of "relative stability" underlying the common fisheries **[1060]** policy, and, on the other, those who were not part of the British fishing communities, who sought to rely on the principle of non-discrimination on grounds of nationality in access to an economic activity. The Merchant Shipping Act 1988 sought to uphold the first of those principles. The history of the subsequent legal proceedings confirms how uncertain the legal position was. At the time when the 1988 Act was passed, the extent to which the power of a Member State to lay down rules for the registration of vessels fell within the scope of Community law had not yet been determined. A number of experienced English judges were unable to form a precise view as to whether Community law had been infringed. In Case C-221/89, five Member States intervened in favour of the United Kingdom and one Member State intervened in favour of the complainants and the Commission.

The *Commission* observes that it wrote to warn the United Kingdom that the proposed provisions for the registration of vessels were contrary to the prohibition of discrimination on grounds of nationality and that, in any event, it became clear, following the judgment in *Factortame I*, cited above, that discrimination with regard to residence was unacceptable.

60. *Rawlings* considers that, whatever conditions may be held to be appropriate to enable individuals to obtain reparation for damage caused by national legislation contrary to Community law, there can be no doubt that it satisfies those conditions. In its view, it is in a different position from the other applicants, since the only reason given by the United Kingdom authorities for their refusal to authorize its continued ownership and operation of a British fishing vessel was the fact that Mr Ramón Yllera, a shareholder and director of the company, was a Spanish national. The application to Rawlings of the Merchant Shipping Act 1988 involved direct and manifest discrimination on grounds of nationality.

D. *The condition as to "fault" (Question 3 in Case C-46/93)*

61. *Brasserie du Pêcheur* observes that the reference by the Court in the *Francovich* judgment to the autonomy of national rules of procedure may result in national law making the reparation of damage dependent on proof of fault on the part of the administrative authorities. However, it goes on to state that, even where the national rules require the existence of fault on the part of the administrative authorities as a condition of the payment of compensation for the damage, such fault is objectively constituted by the fact of the application of legislation which is incompatible with Community law. That is the position, in particular, where the breach has been established by a judgment of the Court. An exception to the responsibility of the administrative authorities could arise only if they had no discretion in the matter **[1061]** whatever. If that were the case, the legislature would then incur direct responsibility. Lastly, it considers that, in the present case, the infringement of Article 30 of the EEC Treaty arising from the prohibition of the marketing of the imported beer clearly constitutes, in any event, a sufficiently flagrant breach of a rule of Community law such as to impose on Germany an obligation to pay compensation for the damage.

62. The *Danish Government* considers that the principle that the Community cannot incur liability "unless there is a sufficiently serious breach", as laid down by the Court in its case-law relating to Articles 178 and 215 of the EEC Treaty, amounts to a requirement as to the existence of fault (*culparegel*). It further states that the Court has confirmed that the fact that a regulation is held to be invalid does not *per se* suffice to render the Community liable.

63. The *German Government* considers that the requirement of fault, whether intentional or not, committed by State institutions constitutes a fundamentally admissible substantive condition for entitlement to compensation which a Member State may lay down in addition to the conditions laid down by Community law. The only restriction is that the requirement of fault must not make it virtually impossible or excessively difficult to obtain compensation. In its view, German law satisfies that condition.

64. The *Spanish Government* considers that, where acts of the legislature are concerned, fault does not appear to be a factor by which those acts can be defined, since a legislative act cannot be attributed to natural persons who are the agents of the legislature.

65. The *French Government* considers that, taking into account the strong reservations harboured hitherto by Member States about making the legislature liable for wrongful conduct, it is important that the Court, in formulating any criteria, should confine itself to the concept of a "breach of Community law", without requiring national courts to classify such a breach as one involving "fault". However, it further states that the Court could develop from its case-law on non-contractual

liability criteria which national courts could apply as conditions governing entitlement to compensation. In particular, the infringement should be serious, the damage should go beyond the bounds of the risks inherent in business activities in the sector concerned and the damage should constitute special damage, in the sense that it should affect only a limited number of injured parties.

66. The *Netherlands Government* considers that, since the present proceedings are concerned not with the attainment of a Community objective (such as the transposition of a directive) but with an obligation on the part of a Member State to abstain from adopting measures contrary to Community law in the **[1062]** realization of national aims, it would seem appropriate to require that the infringement by the Member State must be actually culpable.

67. In the view of the *Commission*, it would seem appropriate to refer to the Court's case-law on the award of compensation and to regard State liability as corresponding to the minimum standard of liability on the part of Community institutions required under Article 215 of the EEC Treaty. It appears from those decisions of the Court, relating to legislative action involving choices of economic policy where wide discretionary powers or complicated issues are involved, that the criteria governing liability concern, *inter alia*, factors entailing, in many national legal systems, the concept of fault.

68. *Brasserie du Pêcheur, Factortame and others* and the *Commission* further state that to require proof of fault on the part of the national authorities, in the sense of an intention to cause damage to the injured parties, cannot be consistent with Community law. The conditions governing the exercise of a right to compensation should not be such as to make it virtually impossible or excessively difficult to exercise that right (judgment in Case 199/82 *Amministrazione delle Finanze dello Stato* v. *San Giorgio* [1983] ECR 3595). It would be almost impossible to prove an intention to cause damage or knowledge of the unlawfulness of an act without obtaining access to the government's documents showing its innermost secrets, which no doubt would be sought to be protected with great tenacity.

E. *The substantive scope of the obligation to make reparation (Question 4(a) in Case C-46/93 and Question 2 in Case C-48/93)*

69. The *German, Spanish and United Kingdom Governments* and the *Commission* observe that it is apparent from the *Francovich* judgment that the criteria applicable to the determination of the scope of reparation are covered by national law. The Spanish Government further states that the jurisdiction to determine the extent of the harm and therefore of the compensation obtainable lies not with the Court of Justice but with the national courts of the Member States.

70. *Brasserie du Pêcheur, Factortame and others* and *Rawlings* consider, however, that it is apparent from paragraphs 42 and 43 of the *Francovich*

judgment that the criteria governing compensation must be no less favourable than those relating to similar claims under national law and must not be so framed as to render the recovery of damages virtually impossible or excessively difficult. They further state that the national rules must be such as to ensure that rights to compensation are granted full and effective protection.

71. *Brasserie du Pêcheur* considers that the rights of a claimant are not fully safeguarded if compensation is not given for the fundamental element of the loss or damage arising from the breach of Community law, and that **[1063]** that fundamental element must be defined according to the nature of the right which has been infringed.

72. *Factortame and others* further state that a measure of guidance is necessary in order to minimize what could otherwise be unacceptable divergences in the application of the damages remedy in different Member States, because this is not an area in which any Community harmonization may be expected in the foreseeable future. Guidance from the Court could also obviate a further reference for a preliminary ruling, with the delay which that would entail.

73. The *German Government* considers that there is nothing to preclude the restriction of liability to breaches of specific individual legal interests, in the sense of absolute rights akin to property rights. Community law does not require full reparation of all losses, since even a limited right can achieve the objective of the effective enforcement of Community law.

The *Commission*, on the other hand, considers that the reference to national legal systems is qualified by the need for compliance with the minimum requirements laid down by the Court's case-law in relation to Article 215 of the EEC Treaty, and that those requirements would not be met if the obligation to pay compensation were to be limited to making good the damage to certain individual assets protected by law, such as property.

74. *Brasserie du Pêcheur, Rawlings*, the *French Government* and the *Commission* consider that, as is apparent from the case-law of the Court, lost profits (*lucrum cessans*) must be taken into account in determining the criteria governing reparation. Brasserie du Pêcheur further states that it has been deprived of any opportunity of exporting its products and that the damage suffered by it is therefore based essentially, if not exclusively, on the principle of loss of profit. Rawlings adds that interest on lost profits should also be taken into account. The Commission considers that, even though lost profits should be taken into account, the losses suffered as a result of the breach should none the less be proved.

75. The *French Government* considers that the concept of repairable damage is not subject to limitation, and that the possibility of non-material damage should be recognized, provided that it results directly from the breach which is found to have been committed.

76. The *Irish and United Kingdom Governments* observe, in relation to Rawlings' claim for exemplary damages in Case C-48/93, that there is no principle of Community law according to which such compensation must be paid by Member States over and above compensation for loss actually suffered by **[1064]** the plaintiff. That concept appears to exist only in the common law systems of England, Wales and Ireland and is not, therefore, a principle of ordinary law in the legal systems of the Member States.

Rawlings and the *Commission* consider, on the other hand, that to deny the possibility of exemplary damages for breaches of Community law whilst retaining it for certain breaches of English law would go contrary to the requirement that Community law rights must not be treated less favourably than similar claims under national law.

F. *The temporal scope of the obligation to pay compensation (Question 4(b) in Case C-46/93)*

77. *Brasserie du Pêcheur* considers that, in the present case, entitlement to compensation for damage results from the breach of a directly applicable provision of the Treaty and thus accrued at the time when the breach was committed. The judgment establishing the breach of Community law is merely declaratory.

78. The *French Government* and the *Commission* likewise consider that entitlement to compensation for the damage caused by such a breach is not conditional on the prior existence of a judgment of the Court establishing that breach. Instead, it seems necessary to consider at what point in time the authorities should have known, and could have had no excuse for not knowing, that they were acting in breach of Community law.

79. The *Spanish Government* considers in that regard that entitlement to compensation is conditional on, and is triggered by, a judgment establishing the breach or interpreting the provision of Community law at issue. The Spanish Government further states that the principle of legal certainty is such that extreme caution is required in the recognition of the retroactive effect of declarations of unlawfulness.

80. The *German Government*, for its part, considers that, having regard to the Court's case-law on the consequences of a judgment delivered in infringement proceedings, the effect of such a judgment is to oblige the Member State to remedy the infringement only *ex nunc* and is not such as to require it to remedy the consequences of that infringement in the past as well. In the alternative, if Questions 1 and 4(b) in Case C-46/93 are answered in the affirmative, it considers that the application of the ruling in *Francovich* to the present case would have immeasurable financial repercussions and that, for compelling reasons of legal certainty, restrictions must be placed on the possible recovery by parties concerned of compensation for damage caused prior to delivery of the judgment.

It is necessary, therefore, to restrict that possibility to cases in which the injured parties **[1065]** have previously commenced an action or sought analogous remedies.

81. In the view of the *Danish Government* and of the *Commission*, it is also necessary to consider whether the claimant passively accepted the damage for many years without complaining of the alleged infringement and thus did not seek to have a directly applicable provision of the Treaty enforced before the national courts (duty of diligence).

OPINION OF ADVOCATE GENERAL TESAURO

delivered on 28 November 1995*

[1067] 1. State liability for infringements of Community law and the resultant obligation to make reparation to individuals, which is the subject of *inter alia* the well-known judgment in *Francovich*,[1] continues to arouse great interest. That judgment, however, has not cleared up every aspect; many question marks remain, some relating to important issues.

The questions from the Bundesgerichtshof (Federal Court of Justice, Case C-46/93) and the High Court of Justice (Case C-48/93), which raise the issue once again of infringements of the Treaty already found in preceding judgments of this Court, consequently afford an opportunity, if not of resolving all the remaining difficulties associated with this complex subject, at least of providing further clarification, in particular about the existence of State liability in cases other than failure to implement a directive and about the *Community* preconditions for an individual's right to reparation.

As a result, the Court will have to consider a number of important institutional aspects, in particular the relationship between Community law and the national legal systems. Consequently, this is an area in which the correct operation of the Community legal system as a whole has to be assessed.

I *Facts, National Legislation, Questions referred for a Preliminary Ruling*

2. Whilst referring to the Report for the Hearing for a detailed account of the relevant **[1068]** legislation and the facts which have given rise to these proceedings, I shall confine myself to those aspects which are most relevant for present purposes.

(a) *Case C-46/93* (Brasserie du Pêcheur)

3. Brasserie du Pêcheur SA, a French brewery the seat of which is at Schiltigheim (Alsace), claims that it was forced to discontinue exports of

* Original language: Italian.

[1] Judgment in Joined Cases C-6/90 and C-9/90 *Francovich and Bonifaci* [1991] ECR 1-5357.

beer to Germany in late 1981 because the beer produced by it did not comply with the "purity" requirements laid down in Paragraphs 9 and 10 of the Biersteuergesetz[2] (Law on Beer Duty, hereinafter "the BiStG"). More specifically, as emerged at the hearing, the persistent checks carried out by the German authorities at retailers' premises and the resultant claims that the beer in question did not satisfy the requirements laid down caused the brewery's German sole importer to refuse to renew the distribution contract.

Following the judgment of 12 March 1987[3] in which the Court held that the prohibition against the marketing of beers imported from other Member States which did not comply with the BiStG was incompatible with Article 30 of the Treaty, Brasserie du Pêcheur brought an action against the Federal Republic of Germany for compensation for the loss suffered by it as a result of that import restriction between 1981 and 1987, in the sum of DM 1,800,000, which is presumably a fraction of the loss actually incurred. That action was dismissed by the lower courts. Brasserie du Pêcheur is pursuing the same claim in its appeal on a point of law before the Bundesgerichtshof.

4. Given that the infringement in question must be regarded as an omission on the part of the legislature, since it had not amended the BiStG to accord with Community law, the Bundesgerichtshof points out that compensation for damage is governed in Germany by Paragraph 839 of the Bürgerliches Gesetzbuch (German Civil Code) in conjunction with Article 34 of the Grundgesetz (Basic Law). According to the first paragraph of the latter provision, "If a person infringes, in the exercise of a public office entrusted to him, the obligations incumbent upon him as against a third party, liability therefor shall attach in principle to the State or to the body in whose service he is engaged". The first subparagraph of Paragraph 839 of the Bürgerliches Gesetzbuch provides, in contrast, that if an official wilfully or negligently commits a breach of official duty incumbent upon him as against a third party, he shall compensate the third party for any damage arising therefrom. In the event that he acted negligently, he will be answerable for the damage only if the injured party has no other possibility of obtaining compensation. **[1069]** Apart from the exercise of a public office and a breach of official duty, therefore, the applicability of the rules in question depends on the further requirement that the official duty breached should be "referrable to the third party" (*Drittbezogenheit*), which means that the State is responsible only for breaches of official duties the exercise of which is expressly directed at a third party and therefore has the aim of protecting a right

[2] Law of 14 March 1952 (BGBl I, p. 148) as amended by the Law of 14 December 1976 (BGBl I, p. 3341). Needless to say, Paragraph 10 restricts the use of the description "beer" to beer produced in accordance with the purity requirements compulsorily laid down by Paragraph 9 of the Law.

[3] Case 178/84 *Commission* v. *Germany* [1987] ECR 1227.

of the third party. However, it is precisely that requirement which is normally absent in the case of a legislative wrong, including the illegality in point in this case.[4] As the national court has pointed out, in fact, in the BiStG the legislature imposed burdens concerning the community which do not relate in particular to any individual or class of individual capable of being regarded as third parties for the purposes of the provisions adverted to.[5]

Secondly, the national court observes that neither in this case can there be State liability on account of an unlawful act of the public authority which is capable of being equated with expropriation, a principle developed by the case-law of the Bundesgerichtshof (Federal Court of Justice).[6] The national court considers this to be inevitable in that the principle in question, according to that case-law, does not permit compensation to be granted for loss or damage arising out of laws infringing the Grundgesetz, which is equatable to compensation for loss or damage resulting from infringement of a Community obligation. Moreover and in any event, in this case there was no interference with the appellant's legal interest which may be protected under the law of property.

5. The Bundesgerichtshof, taking the view that German law affords no basis for upholding the appellant's damages claim, has therefore made a reference for a preliminary ruling to the Court in order to establish whether the principle of State liability for loss or damage caused to individuals by infringements of Community law attributable to it, as may be inferred from the judgment in *Francovich*, is applicable to the case pending before it. More specifically, it has asked the Court:

1. Does the principle of Community law according to which Member States are obliged to pay compensation for damage suffered by an individual as a result of breaches of Community law attributable to those States also apply where such a breach consists of a failure to adapt a national parliamentary statute to the higher-ranking rules of Community law (this case concerning a failure to adapt Paragraphs 9 and 10 of the German Biersteuergesetz **[1070]** to Article 30 of the EEC Treaty)?
2. May the national legal system provide that any entitlement to compensation is to be subject to the same limitations as those applying where a national statute breaches higher-ranking national law, for example where an ordinary Federal law breaches the Grundgesetz of the Federal Republic of Germany?

[4] A legislative wrong (*legislatives Unrecht*) is governed by the same rules as liability of the public authorities (*Amtshaftung*). It is precisely because of this that the amenability to compensation of damage arising out of a legislative wrong—still a very controversial subject in Germany—is unquestionably allowed where individual-case laws (*Einzelfallgesetze*) are involved or a legislative measure such as a land development plan (*Bebauungsplan*).

[5] The picture which emerges does not differ much from that which is allegedly peculiar to the Italian system—the distinction between *diritti soggettivi* (individual rights) and *interessi legittimi* (protected interests).

[6] See BGHZ (Reports of Decisions of the Bundesgerichtshof in Civil Matters), 90, p. 17, in particular at p. 29 et seq.

3. May the national legal system provide that entitlement to compensation is to be conditional on fault (intent or negligence) on the part of the organs of the State responsible for the failure to adapt the legislation?
4. If Question 1 is to be answered in the affirmative and Question 2 in the negative:
   (a) May liability to pay compensation under the national legal system be limited to the reparation of damage done to specific individual legal interests, for example property, or does it require full compensation for all financial losses, including lost profits?
   (b) Does the obligation to pay compensation also require reparation of the damage already incurred before it was held in the judgment of the European Court of Justice of 12 March 1987 in Case 178/84 *Commission* v. *Germany* [1987] ECR 1227 that Paragraph 10 of the German Biersteuergesetz infringed higher-ranking Community law?

(b) *Case C-48/93* (Factortame III)

6. The action for damages arising out of the application of the Merchant Shipping Act 1988 brought by the 97 applicants in the main proceedings is the sequel to the well-known *Factortame* affair, of which I shall merely set out the gist.

The law in question provided for a new register for all British fishing vessels and hence also for vessels already registered on the former register. In particular, the new registration system, which became compulsory on 1 April 1989, imposed stricter conditions relating to the nationality, **[1071]** residence and domicile of the natural and legal persons who were the true owners of the vessels. If those requirements were not met, fishing vessels were ineligible to be entered on the new register and consequently were not allowed to fish under the British flag.

The new registration system was challenged in the Divisional Court, which by order of 10 March 1989 suspended the application of the new registration system by interim injunction, which was subsequently overturned by the Court of Appeal.[7] Concurrently, the Divisional Court requested the Court of Justice to give a preliminary ruling on the questions of Community law raised by the applicants, which it did by judgment of 25 July 1991.[8] In that judgment, the Court held that it was contrary to Community law and, in particular, to Article 52 of the EEC Treaty, for a Member State to impose conditions as to the nationality,

[7] In order to give the full picture, it is recalled that following the claimants' appeal to the House of Lords, that court made a reference to the Court of Justice, by judgment of 18 May 1989, for a preliminary ruling on two questions concerning the existence and scope of the jurisdiction of a national court to grant interim relief where rights conferred by Community law were at issue. In its judgment in Case C-213/89 *The Queen* v. *Secretary of State for Transport*, ex parte *Factortame and Others* (*Factortame I*) [1990] ECR I-2433, the Court of Justice ruled that "Community law must be interpreted as meaning that a national court which, in a case before it concerning Community law, considers that the sole obstacle which precludes it from granting interim relief is a rule of national law must set aside that rule". On 11 October 1990, the House of Lords affirmed the interlocutory injunction granted by the Divisional Court pending the determination of the substantive case.

[8] Case C-221/89 *Factortame II* [1991] ECR I-3905.

residence and domicile of owners of fishing vessels such as those laid down by the new registration system in the United Kingdom.

In the meantime, the Commission brought an action against the United Kingdom under Article 169 on the ground of the alleged incompatibility with Community law of the British statute, but only as regards the nationality aspect. The Commission also applied for interim measures requiring the United Kingdom to suspend the application of the statute, which the Court granted by order of 10 October 1989.[9] Following that order, the United Kingdom partially amended the Merchant Shipping Act with effect from 2 November 1989. Subsequently, by judgment of 4 October 1991,[10] the Court of Justice held that, by imposing the conditions as to the nationality of the vessel owners, the United Kingdom had failed to fulfil its obligations under Articles 7, 52 and 221 of the EEC Treaty.

As long ago as 2 October 1991, the Divisional Court made an order giving effect to the judgment of the Court of Justice in Case C-221/89 *Factortame II* in respect of the registration of the fishing vessels of 79 of the applicants, in which it directed that the applicants should give detailed particulars of their claims for damages against the Secretary of State for Transport. Then, by order of 18 November 1992, it gave leave to a number of companies and various other persons to be joined as parties to the proceedings and/or to claim damages and further gave Rawlings (Trawling) Limited, the 37th claimant, leave to amend its statement of claim to include a claim for exemplary damages for unconstitutional behaviour.

[1072] The applicants seek damages under various heads, including, in particular, expenses and losses of profits and income incurred from the entry into force of the new legislation (1 April 1989) until the time at which they were able to resume fishing.[11]

7. In English law, State liability in damages is a creature of case-law. In particular, the same wrongs (individual torts) leading to civil liability have been used in so far as they lend themselves to cover conduct of the public authorities.

First, damages may be awarded where loss or damage is due to a negligent breach committed in the exercise of administrative or legislative

[9] Case 246/89 R *Commission* v. *United Kingdom* [1989] ECR 3125.

[10] Case C-246/89 *Commission* v. *United Kingdom* [1991] ECR I-4585.

[11] Although the national court refers solely to 2 November 1989, the date on which the relevant law was partially repealed, it is pointed out that that repeal related, in accordance with the Court's order in Case 246/86 R *Commission* v. *United Kingdom*, only to those provisions which were discriminatory on grounds of nationality. This means, as the applicants point out in their written observations in these proceedings, that the statute in question ceased to have harmful effects as regards the other conditions held to be discriminatory (residence, domicile) which were the subject of the proceedings in Case C-221/89 *Factortame II* only on 11 October 1990, when the House of Lords, following the Court's judgment in *Factortame I*, affirmed the interlocutory injunction requested. In this connection, see footnote 7.

activity (tort of negligence).[12] Since, however, there must be a "duty of care" on the part of the public authority and the relevant case-law holds that there can be no such duty in the case of pure economic loss,[13] which makes it impossible for damages to be awarded for that type of harm, it would be hard for an infringement of Community law to give rise to liability. The concept and scope of the duty of care are presently being developed in the case-law of the courts of the United Kingdom.[14]

Secondly, liability on the part of the public authorities may be claimed in the event of a breach of statutory duty. In such case, however, the actual chances of obtaining damages are considerably reduced in so far as the prevalent view is that the possibility of obtaining administrative remedies designed to ensure that the law is complied with precludes bringing an action for damages.[15] Admittedly, the existence of liability in damages for infringements of Community law was affirmed in that very context, but only in the case of "ordinary civil actions".[16]

[1073] In contrast, where the breach falls solely within the ambit of public law, liability may be claimed only for misfeasance in public office. This is the only tort which does not cover relations between private persons but specifically the public authorities. However, the requirement for intentional unlawful conduct makes the possibility of obtaining damages a remote one, even where the loss or damage arises out of infringements of Community law. Thus, as the Divisional Court points out in the order for reference, in *Bourgoin*[17] the Court of Appeal held that the State was not required as a matter of English or Community law to compensate the victims of acts which had been found to be contrary to Community law, unless the Minister acted in the knowledge that the act in question was unlawful and with the intention of injuring the claimants. Following the judgment in *Francovich*, however, the House of Lords itself has questioned whether *Bourgoin* was correctly decided.[18]

8. The Divisional Court considers that if English case-law were to be applied, the claimants would have no remedy in damages. Since, in

[12] See, for example, *Rowling* v. *Takaro Properties* [1988] AC 473.

[13] The duty of care is confined to typical sets of circumstances, the upshot being that liability does not attach to every harmful negligent act. However, there are decisions to be found in the less recent case-law in which the duty of care has been identified with the neighbourhood principle, which is essentially equivalent to *neminem laedere*, since liability may be incurred under that principle for harm done to anyone where it was reasonably foreseeable that the victim might be harmed (see, for example, *Donoghue* v. *Stevenson* [1932] AC 562).

[14] See, for example, *Lonhro* v. *Tebbit* [1992] 4 All ER 280.

[15] See, for example, *Thornton* v. *Kirklees MBC* [1979] QB 626.

[16] See *Garden Cottage Foods* v. *Milk Marketing Board* [1984] 1 AC 130 HL, in which the House of Lords essentially accepted, albeit in an *obiter dictum* (the proceedings were concerned with an application for interim measures), the existence of liability in damages to a person who had suffered loss as a result of conduct in breach of Articles 85 and 86 of the Treaty by a private citizen or also by a public authority, but in the event that it acted as a private citizen.

[17] *Bourgoin* v. *Minister of Agriculture, Fisheries and Food* [1986] 1 QB 716 AC.

[18] *Kirklees Metropolitan Borough Council* v. *Wickes Building Supplies* [1992] 3 WLR 170, in particular at 188.

addition, it is uncertain whether the principle of State liability for loss or damage caused to individuals by infringements of Community law attributable to the State, as may be inferred from *Francovich*, applies also to the facts of the case pending before it, it has requested the Court to give a preliminary ruling. Its questions are as follows:

1. In all the circumstances of this case, where:
(a) a Member State's legislation laid down conditions relating to the nationality, domicile and residence of the owners and managers of fishing vessels, and of the shareholders and directors in vessel-owning and managing companies, and
(b) such conditions were held by the Court of Justice in Cases C-221/89 and C-246/89 to infringe Articles 5, 7, 52 and 221 of the EEC Treaty,
are those persons who were owners or managers of such vessels, or directors and/or shareholders in vessel-owning and managing companies, entitled as a matter of Community law to compensation **[1074]** by that Member State for losses which they have suffered as a result of all or any of the above infringements of the EEC Treaty?
2. If Question 1 is answered in the affirmative, what considerations, if any, does Community law require the national court to apply in determining claims for damages and interest relating to:
(a) expenses and/or loss of profit and/or loss of income during the period subsequent to the entry into force of the said conditions, during which the vessels were forced to lay up, to make alternative arrangements for fishing and/or to seek registration elsewhere;
(b) losses consequent on sales at an undervalue of the vessels, or of shares therein, or of shares in vessel-owning companies;
(c) losses consequent on the need to provide bonds, fines and legal expenses for alleged offences connected with the exclusion of vessels from the national register;
(d) losses consequent on the inability of such persons to own and operate further vessels;
(e) loss of management fees;
(f) expenses incurred in an attempt to mitigate the above losses;
(g) exemplary damages as claimed?

Terms of the Problem and Structure of the Opinion

9. The question of State liability for infringements of Community law, which is of considerable importance in terms of both the principles involved and the potential consequences for the Member States were such liability to be affirmed broadly and generally, is complex and by no means free of snares, as witness moreover the susbstantial debate which has taken place in recent years in academic writings.

[1075] In these proceedings, the Court has to establish whether, on what terms and with regard to which classes of injury, there exists an obligation for the State to compensate individuals who have suffered loss or damage as a result of the application of national laws conflicting with Community law.[19]

10. In the first place, it will accordingly be necessary to establish whether liability in damages should be confined to the case, which has already been assessed in *Francovich*, of failure to implement a directive whose provisions, albeit satisfying a number of conditions relating to their special nature, may not be relied on directly by individuals in order to obtain the benefit provided for them by the directive, or whether it should be extended to circumstances, such as those of the cases now before the Court, in which the loss or damage suffered by the individuals arises out of the application of a national law conflicting with Community provisions which may be relied on by individuals directly in the national courts. In order to do so, I consider it useful to set out the terms in which the obligation for Member States to make reparation for infringements of Community law has been affirmed to date, in order, partly by this means, to trace the basis of liability in Community law. In addition, I consider it worthwhile dwelling on the alleged non-liability of the State for acts or omissions of the legislature, which has also been raised (albeit somewhat cautiously) in these proceedings in order to deny, on an abstract level and in principle, the existence of State liability in the circumstances at issue.

Secondly, it will have to be established whether the conditions of liability are those specific to each national legal system—albeit subject to the well-known limits identified in several of the Court's decided cases—or whether, by contrast, it is Community law itself which determines at least the *substantive conditions* which are sufficient in order for the State in breach of its obligations to be required to make reparation for the resulting loss or damage. If the second branch of this alternative prevails, it should obviously be clarified whether any infringement whatsoever which injures an individual is enough or whether something more is needed, as most of the Member States have argued in these proceedings. Then again, can that something more be taken to be the need for fault or are other conditions necessary, for example the very ones which the Court has identified in regard to non-contractual liability on the part of the Community institutions (case-law on Article 215)? In addition, from the point of view of the causal link, it will have to be assessed, for example, whether it is important that the nature of the Community provision infringed was such as to enable the individual to protect his own rights directly so as to eliminate the substantive illegality; furthermore, the time at which the obligation to make reparation arises will have to be assessed in any event. Lastly, there will be a need to dwell on the

[19] For a different case in which the State is claimed to be liable for damage caused by conduct of the administrative authorities contrary to Community law, see pending Case C-5/94 *Lomas*; Advocate General Léger's Opinion of 20 June 1995 in that case also considers some aspects relevant to these proceedings.

procedural requirements governing the right to reparation and on the criteria for quantifying the damage.

[1076] 11. These, therefore, are the aspects which I shall be considering and the questions which I shall be seeking to answer. Accordingly, the analysis set out below will be subdivided into three parts. The first part will deal with the principle of State liability under Community law with a view to identifying its basis and scope, *inter alia* with respect to unlawful acts or omissions on the part of the legislature, and to assessing in particular whether an action for damages is a residual remedy only, in the sense that such an action may be brought only where the individual has no other means of asserting the rights conferred on him by Community law, or whether its ambit is wider.

As for the conditions of liability, I shall say forthwith that the minimum substantive—unlike the procedural—conditions must be common and hence Community conditions. To my mind, this is the only way of avoiding a situation in which the actual possibility of obtaining reparation for a given infringement is not secured equally in the several Member States and in which discrimination consequently arises as between individuals, which a Community based on the rule of law should not tolerate. Accordingly, the second part of my Opinion will deal with the conditions enabling individuals to obtain reparation, that is to say, the Community preconditions for liability, and the limits imposed by Community law on the procedural conditions. In my view, the latter conditions continue—in common with the criteria for determining the quantum of the damages—to be governed by national law.

Lastly, I shall consider the two cases before the Court and reply to the questions which gave rise to these proceedings.

I—*The Principle of State Liability in Community Law: Basis and Scope*

12. The idea of State liability for loss or damage caused by legislative activity does not seem at all surprising. The basic principle of most of the *civil* rules on non-contractual liability is *neminem laedere*, as variously interpreted and limited, under which everyone is bound to make good loss or damage arising as a result of his conduct in breach of a legal duty.[20] It is undeniable that reference is made to that principle by the various rules, mostly created by the courts, governing liability on the part of the public authorities, even though that liability has special features peculiar to itself in view of the activities carried out by those authorities, in particular in the case of legislative activity. Liability of the *public authorities* is also closely, if not indeed necessarily, connected to wrongful damage

[20] Albeit that principle does not have the same general scope in all the legal systems—suffice it to cite the British system, in which there is a limit in terms of the (restricted) scope of the duty of care,—it none the less remains that, inasmuch as it refers to the idea of wrongful damage, it may be regarded as the starting point for any discussion of liability.

by the fact of its having to have been caused by the unlawful conduct; in a manner of speaking, this is the other side of the coin.

[1077] Admittedly, in the case of the public authorities, precisely because of the nature of the activity which they perform and of the consequences which would ensue were there held to be liability and an obligation to compensate generally, the tendency has invariably been to limit the scope of liability in various ways. The extent of that limitation, which may be encapsulated, by way of initial approximation, in the well-known formula according to which the liability in question is "neither general, nor absolute",[21] is consequently related to the need to balance the opposing, competing interests at stake: on the one hand, the injured party's interest in obtaining at least financial restitution for the loss or damage he sustained as the result of an activity—in particular legislative activity—of the State; on the other, the State's interest in not having to answer invariably and in any event for loss or damage caused by the activities of its organs in performing the institutional tasks entrusted to them.

Manifestly, over time significant changes have taken place with regard to the limitation of the scope of responsibility, varying according to the legal system considered. In particular, the emergence of the *State governed by the rule of law* has resulted in an increasing shift of emphasis, at least in the more advanced legal systems, from the conduct of the perpetrator of the damage to the rights of the injured party, as in the case of liability generally. From this point of view, State liability and the resulting obligation to make reparation have ended up by becoming a means of penalizing unlawful and/or, in any event, harmful conduct and thereby of achieving effective protection for individuals' rights.

13. This reasoning prompts an initial, straightforward observation with regard to the principle of State liability for infringements of Community law. The fact that the Member States, even though subject to conditions limiting the scope of liability in different ways, may be called upon to answer for loss or damage caused by legislative activity of the public authorities suggests in itself that it is unreasonable that they should invariably and in any event not be liable for infringements of Community law which have an effect on the financial situation of individuals affected by those infringements.

Consequently, in so far as at least the principle of State liability is part of the tradition of all the legal systems,[22] it must be able to be applied also where the unlawful conduct consists of an infringement of a Community provision.

[21] Judgment of the French Tribunal des Conflits of 8 February 1873 in *Blanco*, D. 1873, II, 20.

[22] For an essential understanding of the relevant rules in the various Member States, see Schockweiler—Wivenes—Godart: "Le régime de la responsabilité extra-contractuelle du fait d'actes juridiques dans la Communauté européenne", in *Revue trimestrielle de droit européen*, 1990, p. 27 et seq., in particular at p. 54.

14. Furthermore, it should be observed straight away that, whilst it is essentially for the State, and hence its institutions, to ensure that Community law is duly implemented and, in particular, to guarantee individuals that the rights conferred on them are effective, it is also unquestionable that, where rights claimed by individuals pursuant to **[1078]** Community provisions are concerned, it falls to the Court to review the degree of adequacy of the protection afforded by the national legal systems. That review has on several occasions extended even so far as to require the Member State concerned to adopt a judicial remedy not available under its legal system.[23]

It would therefore be at odds with the relevant case-law and with the characteristics of the legal system as a whole, in particular the division of tasks between the Community and the Member States, for Community law to disinterest itself completely of compensation for loss or damage, by leaving it, without any review, to each national system.

(a) *The obligation on Member States to make reparation for failures to fulfil obligations as affirmed in the Court's case-law: the* Francovich *judgment and its precursors*

15. The judgment in *Francovich*, which is bound to be the starting point for any discussion of State liability in damages for infringements of Community law, still constitutes the Court's most precise response in this area. The case turned on the non-implementation of the directive on the protection of employees in the event of the insolvency of the employer, which required Member States to set up machinery affording a minimum guarantee in respect of unpaid wage claims. Italian magistrates asked the Court whether, faced with the failure of a Member State to implement that directive, individuals were entitled to rely directly on the Community measure before the national courts in order to obtain its benefits and, in any event, claim damages from the Member State where the directive lacked direct effect. Consequently, the Court was asked, not only about the direct effect of a number of provisions of a directive, but also about compensation for loss or damage resulting from its non-implementation.[24]

Although it found that the relevant provisions of the directive were unconditional and sufficiently precise as regards the determination of the

[23] See sections 43 to 47 below.

[24] I would recall that, as long ago as Case 380/87 *Enichem Base and Others* v. *Comune di Cinisello Balsamo* [1989] ECR 2491, an Italian court asked the Court whether "the administration [is] required under Community law to pay compensation where an unlawful administrative measure taken by it [unlawfully] infringes a right under Community law (*diritto soggettivo comunitario*) which upon its incorporation in the Italian legal system, while retaining its Community character, takes the form of a protected interest (*interesse legittimo*)" (Report for the hearing, loc. cit. at 2494 et seq.). Neither the Advocate General nor the Court answered that question, since it was absorbed into the answers given to other questions. I note, however, that in their observations both the United Kingdom and Italy argued that any right to compensation should be based solely on the substantive and procedural possibilities afforded by national law.

persons entitled to the guarantee and the content of the guarantee itself, the Court held that those provisions could not **[1079]** be relied upon directly before the national court in order to seek the benefit provided for them by the directive. In particular, those provisions did not identify the person liable to provide the guarantee, and the State could not be considered liable on the sole ground that it had failed to take transposition measures within the prescribed period.

16. Turning to whether it was possible for an individual to claim and obtain compensation for any loss or damage sustained, the Court first called to mind the fundamental characteristics of the Community system and, in particular, the tasks conferred on the national courts. It drew the lapidary but incontestable conclusion that "the principle whereby a State must be liable for loss and damage caused to individuals as a result of breaches of Community law for which the State can be held responsible is inherent in the system of the Treaty" (paragraph 35).

More specifically, the Court inferred that principle from two fundamental elements of the Community legal order. First, it pointed out that "the full effectiveness of Community rules would be impaired and the protection of the rights which they grant would be weakened if individuals were unable to obtain redress when their rights are infringed by a breach of Community law for which a Member State can be held responsible" (paragraph 33). The Court also stressed that the possibility of obtaining redress from the Member State is "particularly indispensable where, as in this case, the full effectiveness of Community rules is subject to prior action on the part of the State and where, consequently, in the absence of such action, individuals cannot enforce before the national courts the rights conferred upon them by Community law" (paragraph 34).

Secondly, as it had already done in the judgment in *Humblet*,[25] it derived and inferred that obligation to make reparation from Article 5 of the EC Treaty, "under which the Member States are required to take all appropriate measures, whether general or particular, to ensure fulfilment of their obligations under Community law", which include precisely "the obligation to nullify the unlawful consequences of a breach of Community law" (paragraph 36).

17. What was contemplated, therefore, was the means made available in order to reinforce the effectiveness of Community provisions through the effectiveness of the judicial supervision of the legal interests created by those provisions and likewise in order not to leave Member States' failures to fulfil obligations without—*inter alia*, tangible—consequences.

[1080] Consequently, it is precisely in the light of those objectives that the position of the individual has been used and given its proper

[25] Case 6/60 *Humblet* v. *Belgium* [1960] ECR 559, in particular at 569. In that case, the reference was to Article 86 of the ECSC Treaty, which corresponds to Article 5 of the EC Treaty.

importance. The State's financial liability *vis-à-vis* individuals for loss or damage caused by legislative inaction has been created by the Court in the final analysis as an instrument for securing protection for individuals and thereby also the proper implementation of Community law. From this point of view, it has remote roots, both in terms of specific precedents for the liability and obligation to compensate of the Member States[26] and in the more general setting of the effective protection of rights asserted by individuals under Community provisions.[27]

18. It should not be overlooked that statements relating to the obligation to provide compensation for breaches of Community law of various kinds are to be found in the Court's case-law, if only incidentally, since the early 1960s. I would refer in the first place to the judgment in *Humblet*, which I have already mentioned, where the Court held in particular that if it "rules in a judgment that a legislative or administrative procedure adopted by the authorities of a Member State is contrary to Community law, that Member State is obliged, by virtue of Article 86 of the ECSC Treaty, to rescind the measure in question and to make reparation for any unlawful consequences which may have ensued".[28]

19. In addition, it is on the very assumption that the Member State's failure to fulfil obligations may give rise to a right on the part of an individual to compensation that the Court has, on several occasions, rejected an objection of inadmissibility, despite the fact that the Member State against which infringement proceedings have been brought has fulfilled the relevant obligation in the period between the reasoned opinion and delivery of judgment by the Court.[29]

[26] Suggestions to that effect were also to be found in academic writings: Pescatore, "Responsabilité des Etats membres en cas de manquement aux règles communautaires", in *Foro Padano*, 1972, p. 10 et seq.; Kovar, "Voies de droit ouvertes aux individus devant les instances nationales en cas de violation des normes et décisions du droit communautaire", in *Les recours des individus devant les instances nationales en cas de violation du droit européen*, Brussels, 1978, p. 245 et seq., in particular at p. 272 et seq.; Barav, "Damages in the domestic courts for breaches of Community law by national public authorities", in *Non-contractual Liability of the European Communities*, Europa Instituut, University of Leiden, 1988, p. 149 et seq.

[27] For this aspect, see sections 27 to 32 below.

[28] *Humblet* v. *Belgium*, cited in footnote 25. That case was concerned more specifically with securing the annulment of a measure by the Belgian State and the restitution of sums unduly levied; but the general wording used by the Court—"make reparation for any unlawful consequences"—can sufficiently clearly cover also cases of compensation for any loss or damage sustained.

[29] There is a very clear dictum to this effect that "a judgment by the Court under Articles 169 and 171 of the Treaty may be of substantive interest as establishing the basis of a responsibility that a Member State can incur as a result of its default, as regards other Member States, the Community or private parties" (judgment in Case 39/72 *Commission* v. *Italy* [1973] ECR 101, paragraph 11). The statement that the interest in continuing the proceedings even after the breach at issue has been remedied may consist in "establishing a basis for the liability which a Member State may incur, in particular, towards individuals as a result of the breach of its obligations" is to the same effect (judgment in Case 309/84 *Commission* v. *Italy* [1986] ECR 599, paragraph 18). That dictum appears quite frequently: Case 103/84 *Commission* v. *Italy* [1986] ECR 1759, paragraph 9; Case 154/85 *Commission* v. *Italy* [1987] ECR 2717, paragraph 6; Case C-287/87 *Commission* v. *Greece* [1990] ECR I-125 (summary publication only). The Court has further held that the interest in pursuing the action "may consist [in particular] in establishing the basis for a liability which a

[1081] 20. The affirmation of the obligation on Member States to compensate individuals is even more direct and explicit in *Russo* v. *AIMA*,[30] where the Court held that "If such damage has been caused through an infringement of Community law the State is liable to the injured party for the consequences in the context of the provisions of national law on the liability of the State".

21. It is unquestionably clear from the above dicta, therefore, that a Member State may indeed be called upon to compensate for the damage sustained by individuals consisting in or resulting from an infringement of Community provisions.

However, the case-law makes it clear that liability has to be made out by the national court "in the context of the provisions of national law on the liability of the State".[31] Consequently, it is to the legislation of each Member State that reference is made in principle in order to determine whether the State is obliged to compensate for damage caused by failure to comply with a Community provision.[32]

22. That case-law seems to have been overtaken from this particular point of view by the judgment in *Francovich*, in which the obligation on Member States in breach of their obligations to make reparation is rooted in Community law, even as regards the preconditions for the obligation to make reparation.

Essentially, in *Francovich* the Court did not confine itself to leaving it to national law to draw *all* the legal inferences from the infringement of provisions of Community law, but held that Community law itself imposed on the State an obligation to make reparation *vis-à-vis* individuals by defining, at least as regards the case of liability at issue in *that* case, the "Community" conditions determining liability.

[1082] (b) *The "Community" principle of liability: merely a means of closing a lacuna in the protection of rights or a principle of broader scope?*

23. What must now be considered is precisely whether the approach which can be discerned from the pre-*Francovich* case-law (still) has any

Member State may incur, by reason of its failure to fulfil its obligations, towards those to whom rights accrue as a result of that failure": see the judgments in Case 240/86 *Commission* v. *Greece* [1988] ECR 1835, paragraph 14, Case C-361/88 *Commission* v. *Germany* [1991] ECR I-2567, paragraph 31, and Case C-249/88 *Commission* v. *Belgium* [1991] ECR I-1275, paragraph 41. It is clear that the conferral on individuals of a right to compensation for damage sustained owing to an infringement of the Treaty cannot be inferred from dicta of this type, but only the possibility that, within the limits laid down by national law, the individual may assert his right to compensation in relation to such an infringement.

30 Judgment in Case 60/75 *Russo* v. *AIMA* [1976] ECR 45, paragraph 9.

31 Judgment in *Russo* v. *AIMA*, cited in the preceding footnote, paragraph 9.

32 This stance was further emphasized in the judgment in *Granaria*, where the Court held that "the question of compensation by a national agency for damage caused to private individuals by the agencies and servants of Member States, either by reason of an infringement of Community law or by an act or omission contrary to national law, in the application of Community law does not fall within the second paragraph of Article 215 of the Treaty and must be determined by the national courts in accordance with the national law of the Member State concerned" (judgment in Case 101/78 *Granaria* v. *Hoofdproduktschap voor Akkerbouwprodukten* [1979] ECR 623, paragraph 14).

basis or whether an obligation based on Community law of the Member States to make reparation may and must exist even in cases other than that of failure to implement a directive.

In particular, it has to be determined whether Community law requires a guarantee in terms of compensation even where provisions having direct effect are infringed or whether the fact that in that event an individual may rely directly on the provision in question and therefore ensure that the right claimed is guaranteed by that means rules out that possibility.

24. The German, Netherlands and Irish Governments have argued to that effect in these proceedings. They reason that the Community legislature did not intend to establish a general system of Member State liability for infringements of Community law. This, they maintain, is borne out in particular by the fact that the Member States did not incorporate any provision on this matter in the Maastricht Treaty. The German Government has further argued that it would not be compatible with the system of division of powers between the Community institutions and the Member States as laid down by the Treaty or with the principle of institutional balance for the case-law to flesh out Community law above and beyond cases in which this is justified by a lacuna in the legislation.

In the final analysis, those governments consider that the right to reparation plays merely a residual protective role, in the sense that it comes to the fore only in regard to provisions which could not otherwise be relied on before the national courts. Essentially, the Court used the *Francovich* judgment in order to bridge a lacuna in the system for the protection of rights by imposing a sanction on the Member State in breach in the shape of an obligation to make reparation. Conversely, where an individual is already able to take action directly in order to enforce the provisions of Community law, as in the cases which gave rise to these proceedings, there is no need for the Community system to require damages to be awarded and there is no basis for imposing this. Individuals may be held to have a right to reparation only if and in so far as this is permitted by national law.

25. I do not consider that that view can be accepted. First, it is clear from the Court's case-law itself, which has contemplated on **[1083]** several occasions financial liability on the part of the State for infringements of provisions with direct effect, that the possibility of substantive protection does not indeed preclude financial protection.[33] Whilst it is true that in those cases the Court merely held that it was for the Member State to make reparation, under the rules of national law, for the damage caused

[33] I refer to the judgment in *Russo* v. *AIMA*, which I have already mentioned, relating to a regulation on the common organization of the agricultural markets, and to the judgment in Case C-188/89 *Foster* [1990] ECR I-3313, paragraph 22, in which the Court held that Article 5(1) of Directive 76/207/EEC on equal treatment for men and women "may be relied upon in a claim for damages against a body" responsible for providing a public service. See also, as regards an infringement of Article 30, the judgment in Case 103/84 *Commission* v. *Italy*, cited in footnote 29, paragraph 9.

by it, it is also true that the questions raised by the national courts in those cases were not concerned with the specific subject of the right to compensation. When the subject was specifically tackled in *Francovich*, the Court deliberately specified that the principle of liability is an inherent principle of Community law by a general affirmation of principle which holds good for any situation in which Community law is infringed and not merely where there has been a failure to implement a directive.[34] As far as failure to implement a directive is concerned, the Court merely stated that the right to redress is "particularly indispensable", precisely because otherwise the individual would be deprived of any protection, contrary to the rights conferred on him by the directive. However, this affirmation does not preclude liability in damages for injury caused by breaches of other types, particularly since the Court itself went on to hold that the *conditions under which . . . liability gives rise to a right to reparation depend on the nature of the breach* of Community law giving rise to the loss and damage (paragraph 38).

26. Neither does it seem to me that affirmation of the principle of State liability for breaches of Community provisions having direct effect conflicts in any way with the division of powers, as laid down by the Treaty, between Community institutions and Member States. I would merely observe in this connection that it is the infringement of Community law itself which creates an imbalance in the division of powers freely accepted and subscribed to by the States. Any requirement which may be imposed by Community law to make reparation for loss or damage caused by such an infringement constitutes merely a means of restoring the upset equilibrium.

The State's responsibility for legislative activity (on the part of the legislature proper or of the administrative authorities) constitutes also from that point of view a natural and necessary part of the Community legal system created by the Treaty and by the Member States themselves. I cannot but remind myself that it was the Member States which, completely freely, agreed the contractual rules underlying the system as a whole; **[1084]** and the Member States are still the decisive protagonists in the process for the formulation of Community measures. Consequently, to hold that liability exists for failure to fulfil obligations is tantamount simply to increasing the effectiveness of the system and does not involve any activity supplementing—let alone supplanting—the legislature.

27. This is all the more true when it is borne in mind that the State's financial liability *vis-à-vis* individuals for loss or damage caused by legislative action or inaction has been constructed by the Court, I repeat, as an instrument for ensuring protection of individuals and, thereby, also for the purposes of the proper implementation of Community law in all the Member States.

[34] See, in particular, paragraphs 33, 35 and 37 of the judgment.

In sum, what is contemplated is the same as that contemplated by the—now consolidated—case-law which established direct effect, in the sense that provisions of the Treaty and secondary legislation may be relied upon by individuals directly before national courts, provided of course that they are sufficiently clear and precise and unconditional.

28. By identifying the direct effect of a Treaty provision addressed to the Member States and containing an obligation on them, for instance to remove certain barriers and not to reintroduce them, the individual's right to the elimination of those barriers which is derived therefrom is identified and made relevant, with the further consequence that that right becomes capable of being asserted before the national court with a view to its being duly protected. In this way, therefore, the right arising out of the State's obligation by which the individual would have benefited if the obligation had been implemented properly and precisely is identified and enhanced.

This applies, not only on the substantive, but also on the procedural, level. Suffice it to mention what the Court itself has held: "all direct protection of the individual rights of individuals would be removed" if it were to be held that the guarantees against an infringement of Treaty provisions imposing obligations on the Member States were confined to those afforded under Article 169.[35] In the final analysis, the individual's legal position, which is directly dependent on the Treaty provision, is utilized, even in the absence of an incorrect application of that provision, in order to guarantee full, effective protection of the rights which compliance with the provision in question by the State should secure.

29. The same viewpoint appears—even more clearly—from the case-law which, **[1085]** from a given time, has imposed a sanction for the non-implementation or late implementation of a directive by attributing direct effect to it, obviously where defined preconditions were fulfilled.[36] This confirms the observation that, even in the case of directives, the Community system has found in the position of the individual

[35] Case 26/62 *Van Gend & Loos* [1963] ECR 1, in particular at 13.

[36] So much so that direct effect has been from the outset, and continues to be, what is termed vertical, almost, as it were, in order to reinforce the idea that, rather than an intrinsic quality of the provision, it is a remedy for preventing the States from taking advantage of a failure to fulfil their obligations. It is also significant that the Court's assessment of directives has been progressively refined and broadened. For example, the class of public agencies against which directives can be relied on has widened (see the judgments in Case 103/88 *Fratelli Costanzo* v. *Comune di Milano* [1989] ECR 1839 and Case C-188/89 *Foster*, cited in footnote 33); likewise stress has been placed on the need for courts and administrative authorities in the Member States to interpret national provisions in conformity with the wording and purpose of the directive (see the judgments in Case 14/83 *Von Colson and Kamann* v. *Land Nordrhein-Westfalen* [1984] ECR 1891 and Case C-106/89 *Marleasing* [1990] ECR I-4135, paragraph 8). It is sufficient to observe that the criterion of interpretation in conformity with the wording and purpose of a directive relates to directives as such, irrespective of their possible direct effect and regardless of the entity against which the national provisions are asserted, so much so that, in the ultimate analysis, one is not so far removed from the practical effects which would be achieved by the horizontal effect, pure and simple, of precise and unconditional directives.

an effective lever for securing their implementation where they have not been duly transposed into national law.

30. It is further significant that the Court has reaffirmed the State's obligation to make reparation in the same terms already laid down in *Francovich* in a case involving precisely the possibility of relying, in relations between private individuals, on the direct effect of provisions of a directive which was not implemented within the prescribed period.[37]

Holding that there is an obligation to make reparation where a directive cannot be relied on directly before the national court, either because of the absence of direct effect of all the provisions needed to secure the benefit of the right which it confers on the individual or because of the absence of "horizontal" direct effect of precise and unconditional directives, therefore also constitutes a means of reinforcing the position of the individual by making it possible to offset, at least from the financial point of view, the imbalance created by the State's failure to fulfil its obligations.

31. In the final analysis, the individual's position directly created by a provision with direct effect binding on the State is used in order to guarantee full, effective protection **[1086]** to the rights conferred by that provision. In the same way, the individual's right to compensation is used to guarantee protection of the rights conferred by a provision which does not have direct effect in the sense that it cannot be invoked directly before the national court, yet also places an obligation on the State, in the case of a failure to fulfil an obligation on the part of the State.

Consequently, the concept remains the same: in order to implement a provision putting the State under an obligation, the individual's legal position is used, on the one hand, in terms of its *full*, *substantive content*, on the other, in terms of its *financial content*. Even the result is the same: on the one hand, the failure of the Member State concerned to fulfil its obligations is remedied; on the other, the individual is guaranteed effective protection of rights claimed under Community provisions. The upshot is that the effectiveness of the provision is reinforced and hence that of the system as a whole.

32. The foregoing remarks show sufficiently clearly that, far from being a moment of eccentricity in the case-law of the Court, *Francovich* was completely consistent with and a logical extension of a value which has been upheld on several occasions without question

[37] Judgment in Case C-91/92 *Faccini Dori* v. *Recreb* [1994] ECR I-3325, paragraph 27. After stating that interested parties can enforce an unimplemented directive by relying directly on its provisions having direct effect before a national court or, where that is not possible, by interpreting the relevant provisions of national law, as far as possible, in conformity with the directive, the Court observed that "if the result prescribed by the directive cannot be achieved by way of interpretation, . . . Community law requires the Member States to make good damage caused to individuals through failure to transpose a directive". See, to this effect, also the judgment in Case C-334/92 *Wagner Miret* [1993] ECR I-6911, paragraph 23. In that case, even though a directive (the same as that at issue in *Francovich*) was involved which had already been transposed into national law, the problem arose on account of the failure to take into account in the relevant national provisions a particular category of workers, with respect to whom the directive had not been implemented.

in Luxembourg: effectiveness of Community provisions and hence complete judicial protection.[38]

It is undeniable that this is a fundamental value of any legal system, whether Community or national. It is also undeniable that respecting that value may require guaranteeing individuals, where necessary, the right to compensation for loss or damage sustained by reason of the legislative action or inaction of the public authorities, irrespective of whether or not the individual has other means, in addition to a remedy in damages, of asserting an infringement of the legal position bestowed on him by Community law.

33. Furthermore, the—now uncontested—affirmation of the State's obligation to compensate the individual in cases of failure to implement a directive, hence in cases in which the infringement of the State's obligation (infringement of Articles 189 and 5 of the Treaty) can be linked only indirectly to a breach of a correlative right of the individual, implies—*a fortiori*—that the same protection should be available where provisions are **[1087]** *directly* infringed which guarantee the individual a legal position appertaining to himself and can therefore be relied on directly before the national courts.

In this sense, the argument that it is not possible to "go beyond" liability for failure to implement directives cannot be accepted, not only on the grounds set out above, but also because it ignores that it is the *Francovich* situation itself which represents possibly the furthest which the case-law of the Court can go (and not the nearest port of call). On close inspection, the *Francovich* judgment conferred a remedy (at least a financial one) where the remedy provided for was that laid down in Article 169, which does not afford direct protection for individuals. On the contrary, in cases of infringement of provisions having direct effect, the protection already exists and a remedy may be asserted directly by the individual, with the result that it is necessary only to accompany it by that something less, which is financial protection. Consequently, in this case not even that "small" logical leap has to be made which, in contrast, has to be made in order to move from infringement of Article 189 to a breach of the right potentially conferred on the individual by the directive.

Nor should it be overlooked that, as far as provisions having direct effect are concerned, the Court has consistently held that they "must be

[38] In the sense that "the decision in *Francovich* is undoubtedly consistent with, and a natural and logical extension of, the Court's case-law"; and that, after recognizing direct effect and the obligation upon the Member States to give full effect to Community provisions, "it was but a small step to guarantee their full effect by holding States liable in damages for infringements of those rights for which they were responsible", see Steiner: "From direct effects to *Francovich*: shifting means of enforcement of Community Law", in *European Law Review*, 1993, p. 3 et seq., in particular at p. 9. Notoriously, there is now a substantial body of literature on the judgment in *Francovich*. The most recent contributions include Zenner: "Die Haftung der EG-Mitgliedstaaten für die Anwendung europarechtswidriger Rechtsnormen", Munich, 1995.

fully and uniformly applied in all the Member States from the date of their entry into force and for so long as they continue in force"[39] and that "this consequence also concerns any national court whose task it is as an organ of a Member State to protect, in a case within its jurisdiction, the rights conferred upon individuals by Community law".[40] Consequently, it is quite clear that a Community provision with direct effect confers a legal position appertaining to an individual on the individual as from its entry into force and for as long as it continues in force, irrespective of and even despite any pre-existing or subsequent national provision which may negate that legal position. It therefore follows that the national court is under a duty to provide full, effective judicial protection of the rights conferred on the individual by the relevant Community provision.

34. It is unquestionable that the infringement of a provision gives rise to an imbalance consisting in the reduction or annulment of the legal situation affected, in this case that of an individual; it is also unquestionable that every legal situation appertaining to an individual, every "right", if you prefer, has a substantive content and a financial content, which can generally be quantified. Guaranteeing the effectiveness of judicial protection in the case of an infringement of a provision conferring a legal position on an individual means securing the reinstatement of the content of the right impaired by the **[1088]** infringement of the provision. If that which unlawfully adversely affects the individual's right is an act of a public authority—an administrative measure or a law—it is whoever brought it into being who must reinstate the individual's right or at least its financial content. In the final analysis, reinstating its financial content is something less, a minimum remedy compared with full substantive reinstatement, which remains the optimum means of protection. Annulment of an unlawful measure or setting aside a law which is inconsistent with a superior parameter of legality is necessary in a State governed by the rule of law. At times, however, this is not enough and it may be necessary, in order to render the protection real and effective, to bring back into balance also the financial content of the right which has been impaired and hence to ensure that the damage is made good. Consequently, reinstating financial balance in respect of the right which has been infringed is not something different or something more, even less something novel. Neither does it constitute something *optional* which is sophisticated and remote in a legal system which seeks and needs to be effective.

To sum up, the principle of the State's financial liability must be applied as a remedy which is both alternative and additional to substantive protection; consequently, it must be applied in the event of

[39] See, *inter alia*, the judgments in Case 106/77 *Amministrazione delle Finanze dello Stato* v. *Simmenthal* [1978] ECR 629, paragraph 14, and Case 811/79 *Amministrazione delle Finanze dello Stato* v. *Ariete* [1980] ECR 2545, paragraph 5.

[40] Judgment in *Simmenthal*, cited in the preceding footnote, paragraph 16.

infringements both of provisions without direct effect, in the sense of provisions which may not be directly relied on before the national courts, and of provisions which may be so relied on.

(c) *The obligation of the State to compensate for acts or omissions of the legislature*

35. It does not seem to me that that conclusion may be invalidated by the fact that occasionally or often infringements of Community law are attributable to the legislature.

I would point out in this connection that *Francovich*, with which not even any of the States which have submitted observations in these proceedings have taken issue, makes no distinction depending on whether the loss or damage ensues from an infringement attributable to omissions of the legislature or of the executive. Certainly, that is no reason for considering that a different conclusion should be reached as regards the circumstances under consideration here.

However, as the national courts have shown in their respective orders for reference, they are debarred from awarding damages by their national law, precisely because the infringements at issue of Community law are attributable to the legislature, either because it failed to amend a national law so as to bring it into conformity with Community **[1089]** law (Case C-46/93 *Brasserie du Pêcheur*) or because it passed a national law inconsistent with Community law (Case C-48/93 *Factortame III*). Essentially, therefore, given that it is impossible to bring an action for damages in the event of action or inaction on the part of the legislature, in such cases national law leads to the negation of the very principle of liability.

36. Admittedly, in the past the idea that the State was not liable for acts or omissions of the legislature was a widespread one. Its rationale was that the sovereign could do no wrong or, according to a more modern, democratic version, parliamentary sovereignty. In other words, in so far as it was the highest expression of the sovereign power, the legislature fell in principle outside the general rules governing liability in view, *inter alia*, of its democratic legitimacy.

That view, which took root above all in legal systems in which the law was not reviewed in the light of some higher parameter, should take on a different complexion where there is a higher norm which can be used to verify and, in an appropriate case, deny the legality of the legislature's activity. Yet, also in those legal systems in which there is not only a clear, formal hierarchy as between constitutional rules and legislative rules, but also a mechanism of *ad hoc* supervision as to constant compliance with that hierarchy (Austria, Italy, Germany and Spain, for example), the question as to whether compensation can be awarded for loss or damage ensuing from an unconstitutional law is far from having been incontestably resolved.[41] The fact remains, however, that in such a case

[41] For instance, in Germany such a possibility is not ruled out *per se*, but only to the extent to which the official duty infringed is not referable to a particular third party, which, as I have

it cannot be ruled out that the State will be called upon to answer for the loss or damage caused by laws declared unconstitutional.

37. It is true that when the legislature is bound in carrying out its legislative tasks to comply with particular limits imposed by superior rules, there is no reason in general legal theory for denying that the State may be bound to compensate for the damage caused by laws which exceed those limits. In those circumstances, liability for acts or omissions of the legislature is not conceptually very remote or different from responsibility of the administrative authorities for legislative activity, which is upheld more or less everywhere today without difficulty.

[1090] And that is not all. It is well known that, in most legal systems, compensation is awarded in certain cases for the diminution of assets sustained by individuals on account of a perfectly lawful activity of the legislature, in that it was brought into being without any infringement of any *enabling* law: take, for instance, cases of nationalization and expropriation for purposes of public utility. If, therefore, it is conceded that the sacrifice *lawfully* imposed on the legal and financial situation of individuals for the sake of the public interest must be accompanied by fair compensation, it would be curious, to say the least, not to consider that if such loss or damage is produced by a legislative act which is *unlawful* because it conflicts with a superior rule (constitutional, Community or in any event prevailing over the act) there is no room for compensation.

38. It is scarcely necessary to point out that, in relationships governed by international law, State responsibility for acts or omissions of the legislature is universally and unquestionably acknowledged.[42] Of the many instances, it is worth recalling the principle laid down by the Permanent Court of International Justice to the effect that the obligation to make reparation is the direct consequence of a harmful act contrary to

already mentioned, is true in most cases involving an unlawful act or omission attributable to the legislature; for those very reasons, the possibility in question is unquestionably available in relation to individual-case laws (*Einzelfallgesetze*). However, the prevalent view among academic writers is that an individual should have the right to compensation at least in the event of breaches of fundamental rights (see, for instance, in this connection, Haverkate: "Amtshaftung bei legislativem Unrecht und die Grundrechtsbildung des Gesetzgebers", in NJW, 1973, p. 441). In Italy, in which the question is still the subject of debate, such a possibility has been allowed, for example, in the specific case of presidential expropriating decrees issued pursuant to the agrarian reform which have been declared unconstitutional, where the agrarian reform agency was held liable in damages even though it was not guilty of any unlawful conduct; hence the conviction that in such case the compensation is more in the nature of restitution of undue payments, relating solely to the value of the asset lost (for some more general observations in this connection, see Zagrebelsky in "Processo costituzionale" in *Enciclopedia del Diritto* XXXVI, 1987, p. 639).

[42] In fact, international law contemplates only State liability viewed in the round, that is to say, as a whole: consequently, there is no difference depending on whether the infringement which gave rise to the damage is attributable to the legislature, the judiciary or the executive. Moreover, the same approach can be seen in the Court's case-law on Article 169: the infringement of a Community obligation is imputed to the State in any event, regardless of the entity which was actually responsible for fulfilling the obligation (see, for example, the judgments in Case 77/69 *Commission* v. *Belgium* [1970] ECR 237, paragraph 15, Case 8/70 *Commission* v. *Italy* [1970] ECR 961, paragraph 9, and Case 52/75 *Commission* v. *Italy* [1976] ECR 277, paragraph 14).

international law which is attributable to a State. More specifically, "*It is a principle of international law that the breach of an engagement involves an obligation to make reparation in an adequate form. Reparation therefore is the indispensable complement of a failure to apply a convention and there is no necessity for this to be stated in the convention itself.*"[43]

39. Certainly, I am aware that, in international law, the State's obligation to make reparation for damage arises even where in practice the compensation is aimed at restoring the financial position of individuals *vis-à-vis* one or more States and not, as is sought in the cases now before the Court, directly *vis-à-vis* individuals.

However, it does not seem possible to me to ignore the specific, peculiar features of the Community legal order. That system is based, as far as is relevant for present purposes, on a contractual foundation. The Treaty, in common also with other agreements establishing international organizations, contains a series of obligations on Member States with regard to the achievement of the aims set out therein, which have been freely subscribed to, and to the operation of an institutional structure whose powers are very largely, but not wholly, pre-defined. However, the peculiar, ultimate aim of the contractual basis in the case of the Community is integration and more specifically **[1091]** "lay [ing] the foundations of an ever closer union among the peoples of Europe",[44] *inter alia* through the achievement of the common market. It follows that traditional instruments, those of international law in fact, prepared in order to promote the due, precise fulfilment of obligations on the part of the Member States have resulted and continue to result to a very great extent in giving maximum, direct relevance to the legal position of individuals. The reason for this is that the obligations of the Member States and Community institutions are directed above all, in the system which the Community system has sought and sets out to be, to the creation of rights of individuals. This is the picture drawn by the authors of the Treaty and consolidated by the Community legislature.

40. In case-law, which is only too well known, the Court has simply taken note of that specific intention of the authors of the Treaty and subsequently of the legislature, observing that the EC Treaty set up its own legal order "for the benefit of which the States have limited their sovereign rights, albeit within limited fields".[45] The subjects of that legal order comprise not only the States but also individuals, upon whom Community law confers rights which become part of their legal heritage:

[43] Judgment No 8 of 26 July 1927 *Case concerning the Factory at Chorzów*, CPGI, Series A, p. 21; my emphasis. The same principle was subsequently reaffirmed by the International Court of Justice in the Advisory Opinion of 30 March 1950 on the interpretation of peace treaties with Bulgaria, Hungary and Romania, CGI, 1950, p. 228.

[44] The reference is to the preamble to the EC Treaty.

[45] See, in particular, the judgments in Case 26/62 *Van Gend & Loos*, cited in footnote 35, and in Case 6/64 *Costa* v. *ENEL* [1964] ECR 585.

these rights arise not only where they are expressly granted by the Treaty, but also by reason of the obligations which the Treaty imposes upon individuals, the Member States and the Community institutions.

41. It must therefore be acknowledged that, in relation to the—Community—rules governing the situation of individuals which are recognized as prevailing over domestic rules, a claim that there was a general absence of liability on the part of the national legislature would be without justification. Instead, the very idea of liability of the State *qua* legislator in relation to the obligations imposed by Community law, and hence entered into contractually by the States themselves or brought into being subsequently by procedures laid down for the purpose, is perfectly consistent with—and hence inherent in—the fundamental and typical characteristics of the Community legal order.

42. In the final analysis, even in the light of *Francovich*, but if only in view of the specific nature of the Community legal system considered as a whole, it is completely irrelevant whether the unlawful act or omission is attributable to the legislature or to the executive.

Next, in any event the problem of the liability of the State *qua* legislator is surpassed where the unlawful act or omission is connected with rules having direct effect. The Court's dictum to the effect that "it would be contradictory to rule that an individual may rely upon the provisions of a directive which **[1092]** fulfil the conditions defined above in proceedings before the national courts seeking an order against the administrative authorities, and yet to hold that those authorities are under no obligation to apply the provisions of the directive and refrain from applying provisions of national law which conflict with them"[46] implies in fact that even the administrative authorities are under an obligation to guarantee protection of rights claimed by individuals under Community provisions with direct effect. It follows accordingly that in such a case it is quite possible to enforce the liability of administrative authorities for having adopted prejudicial measures pursuant to a law which is alleged to be incompatible with Community law or, in any event, for having applied such a law.

The French *Conseil d'Etat* (State Council), for example, seems to have taken that approach in inferring State liability from the breach (*faute*[47]) of the administrative authorities, at least where they exercised a discretion

[46] Judgment in Case 103/88 *Fratelli Costanzo* v. *Comune di Milano*, cited in footnote 36, paragraph 31.

[47] It is scarcely necessary to point out that, in relation to legislative activity of the administrative authorities, the term *faute* is used by academic writers and by French administrative case-law (where the concept was evolved) to denote maladministration and hence, even though this may seem odd, does not require fault. Indeed, the rule often referred to is that "toute décision illégale est en principe fautive". In short, in the French system the difference between *responsabilité pour faute* and *responsabilité sans faute* does not correspond so much to that between fault-based liability and strict liability, but, albeit only fairly roughly, to the distinction between liability for unlawful acts and liability for lawful acts.

conferred on them by a domestic law contrary to Community law.[48] Admittedly, in cases of this type the origin of liability is invariably to be found in unlawful conduct attributable to the legislature, that is, in a law incompatible with Community law. However, it is obviously for national law to determine whether attributability to the administrative authorities is an "indispensable" procedural and/or substantive expedient in order to get the legislature to answer or the correct mode of proceeding.

43. What is required by Community law for present purposes is that, in any event, the necessary instruments be made available in order for individuals to be able to seek, and possibly obtain, compensation for loss or damage sustained as a result of infringements of Community law. In this connection, moreover, it should be made very clear that the problem of determining a judicial remedy which is not already known to or permitted by the judicial systems of the Member States is not insuperable or a new problem: this is so on account of the specific factors under consideration in these proceedings, and also because the problem has already been dealt with by the Court in a number of historic, uncontested passages in its case-law.

This is testified to, in particular, by cases such as *Simmenthal*[49] and *Factortame I*,[50] in both of which the Court was asked whether a particular judicial remedy, which the national court held was not available under **[1093]** the national judicial system, could or had to be conferred and implemented by virtue of Community law.

44. What was in question in *Simmenthal* was the Italian court's power itself forthwith to disapply a national provision conflicting with Community law without having first to obtain a prior ruling from the Constitutional Court that it was unconstitutional. By basing on Community law the national court's power/duty to disregard the provision conflicting with Community law, a power/duty unknown to the national system—indeed there was express, repeated case-law of the Constitutional Court to the contrary—, the Court introduced a derogation from the Member States' autonomy in relation to means for the judicial protection of rights conferred on individuals by Community law. Moreover, it is remarkable—also for the present proceedings—that in *Simmenthal* the Court considered intolerable, not the absence of protection, but even a mere delay in protection, thereby giving pre-eminence to that aspect over the advantages in terms of certainty and finality which the system based

[48] Judgment of 28 February 1992 in *Arizona Tobacco Products*, in AJDA, 1992, p. 210. On the other hand, the Cour Administrative d'Appel, Paris, in holding that there was an obligation to pay compensation in respect of an unlawful situation created by the legislature, regard being had to Community law, referred generally to the responsibility of the State in the judgment of 1 July 1992 in *Société Dangeville*, in AJDA, 1992, p. 768, including a critical note by Prétot.

[49] Case 106/77 *Amministrazione delle Finanze dello Stato* v. *Simmenthal* [1978] ECR 629.

[50] Case C-213/89 *The Queen* v. *Secretary of State for Transport*, ex parte *Factortame and Others* [1990] ECR I-2433.

on the assessment of constitutionality as hitherto operated undoubtedly possessed.

In *Factortame I*, the question arose yet again, just as in *Simmenthal*, as to whether where the national court lacked a power under its national judicial system—namely the power to suspend by interim measure a law suspected but not yet found to be incompatible with Community law—such a power could be based on Community law. As in *Simmenthal*, the Court ruled that an obstacle to the effective judicial protection of a right claimed under Community provisions by an individual had to be removed by the national court and that hence any measure providing for that obstacle had to be set aside.

45. In the final analysis, the Member States' autonomy in relation to judicial remedies for the infringement of rights conferred by the Community system, albeit affirmed by the Court,[51] is subject to considerable derogations: in particular, whenever it is essential to derogate in order to ensure the proper implementation of Community law and correct, effective protection of the rights claimed by individuals under Community law.

Accordingly, for example, whereas in *Salgoil* the Court emphasized the obligation on the national courts to ensure direct and immediate **[1094]** protection of individuals' interests, but went on to specify that "it is for the national legal system to determine which court or tribunal has jurisdiction to give this protection and, for this purpose, to decide how the individual position thus protected is to be classified",[52] that ambiguity disappears in *Bozzetti* v. *Invernizzi*. In that judgment, the Court reaffirmed the obligation to ensure that individuals' rights are effectively protected "in each case" and that, within those precise limits only ("subject to that reservation") "it is not for the Court to intervene in order to resolve any questions of jurisdiction which may arise, within the national judicial system, as regards the definition of certain legal situations based on Community law".[53] The qualification "*subject to that reservation*" is manifestly the most relevant key to the interpretation of this passage inasmuch as it marks out the limits to the autonomy of the national systems, and it is no accident, to my mind, that the same qualification is set out in paragraph 42 of *Francovich*.

46. It should not be overlooked that the Community legislature, too, has introduced exceptions to the Member States' autonomy, for example in the field of public contracts governed by Community law, precisely as regards compensation for damage. I refer, obviously, to Council

[51] See the judgment in Case 158/80 *Rewe* v. *Hauptzollamt Kiel* [1981] ECR 1805, paragraph 44, in which the Court held that the Treaty was not intended to create new remedies in the national courts other than those already laid down by national law or to reduce the choice of the courts as to the most effective means of protection. In actual fact, that ruling is much less absolute in scope than would appear at first sight.

[52] Judgment in Case 13/68 *Salgoil* v. *Italy* [1968] ECR 453, in particular at 462 and 463.

[53] Judgment in Case 179/84 *Bozzetti* v. *Invernizzi* [1985] ECR 2301, paragraph 17.

Directive 89/665/EEC of 21 December 1989 on the coordination of the laws, regulations and administrative provisions relating to the application of review procedures to the award of public supply and public works contracts[54] and to the corresponding Directive 92/13/EEC of 25 February 1992 on remedies in relation to the so-called excluded sectors.[55]

Faced with a large variety of solutions in the Member States' legal systems, the Community legislature acted, not only with regard to aspects relating to substantive, hence real, protection, but also by providing for a system—which was certainly novel to a good many national systems—of damages to compensate for the injury caused by unlawfulness of contract award procedures in the event of the absence or insufficiency of real protection.[56]

47. In the final analysis, it can certainly be said that the Member States' autonomy with regard to judicial remedies for the infringement of rights conferred by Community **[1095]** provisions is firmly tied to the result sought by Community law.[57]

Where Community provisions are infringed by Member States, the result which should be attained, as far as is relevant for present purposes, for the proper operation of the Community legal system as a whole is that of ensuring, assuming that specific preconditions are satisfied, that the same legal situation is restored, at least in terms of its financial implications, as would have obtained if the Member State had not failed to fulfil the obligation imposed upon it by Community law.

II—*Conditions for the State's Obligation to Pay Compensation*

48. Consequently, liability attaches to any case in which Community law is infringed, including that in which the loss or damage results from infringements of Treaty provisions having direct effect, regardless of the organ of the State (including the legislature) to which the loss or damage is attributable. It now remains to consider the conditions in which liability exists and, in parallel, the individual's right to compensation.

In the absence of specific Community provisions governing the area, the problem lies in defining the conditions determining State liability and in actually being able to ascertain when they are present. In addition,

[54] OJ 1989 L 395, p. 33.

[55] OJ 1992 L 76, p. 14.

[56] That provision introduced a significant innovation into many Member States' legal systems. For instance, in the Italian system, which, even though it was among those affording the greatest protection and, in any event, one of the few in which it was possible, following the annulment of the unlawful administrative measure, even to have the ensuing contractual situation set aside, provision for compensation for infringement of situations which had traditionally been classed as *interessi legittimi* (protected interests) and not as *diritti soggettivi* (individual rights) constitutes nothing less than a *cultural revolution* (see judgment No 2667 of the Corte di Cassazione of 5 March 1993, in *Il Foro It.*, 1993, I, 3062), albeit confined solely to relationships governed by Community law.

[57] For a somewhat different approach, see Advocate General Jacobs' Opinion of 15 June 1995 in Joined Cases C-430/93 and C-431/93 *Van Schijndel and Van Veen*, [1995] ECR I-4705, I-4707.

careful consideration should be given to the practicality of the possible solutions.

49. Certainly, Community law could very well, as some States have proposed in these proceedings, confine itself to affirming that liability exists in principle and that there is an obligation to compensate, whilst leaving it to national law to determine the preconditions and lay down the detailed substantive and procedural rules.

Such a solution, as I mentioned at the beginning, would however have considerable drawbacks, the first among them being that it would not ensure the result sought by Community law through an affirmation of the principle of liability, that is to say, full, effective protection of the rights claimed by individuals under the Community provision which is assumed to have been infringed. That this is a real risk is shown by the very questions referred by the national courts, **[1096]** which arose precisely because the applicable national law did not allow any compensation to be granted in the cases before them. Again, in any event, it is only too obvious that a mere reference to national law would be in danger of endorsing a discriminatory system, in so far as for a given infringement Community citizens would receive different protection, some none at all.

50. In order for protection in damages to be assured in all the Member States in at least a homogeneous—if not exactly uniform—manner, it is vital that it should be Community law itself which lays down at least the minimum conditions determining the right to compensation, in particular the criteria by which those conditions are established, and the "Community" limits imposed on the "national" conditions relating to compensation, be they procedural or otherwise.

This, moreover, was the solution adopted by the Court in *Francovich*, albeit with some particular features connected with the case at issue. There is no ground for considering that that solution should apply only in the event of failure to implement a directive and not to the infringement of provisions with direct effect.

51. In *Francovich*, I recall, while specifying that it is in the context of the rules of national law that the State is bound to make reparation for the consequences of the damage caused, the Court itself identified and defined the conditions "sufficient to give rise to a right on the part of individuals to obtain reparation, a right founded directly on Community law" (paragraph 41). The Member State to which the failure to implement a directive is attributable is therefore bound in every case to make reparation for the loss or damage sustained by the individual, provided that the conditions laid down by the Court are fulfilled.

However, this must not be taken as meaning that the presence of those conditions is sufficient for the purposes of compensation with respect to any infringement of Community law whatsoever. As the Court itself explained, "Although State liability is thus required by Community law, the conditions under which that liability gives rise to a right to reparation depend on the nature of the breach of Community law giving rise to the loss and damage" (paragraph 38).

52. Consequently, the necessary requirements in order for Member States to be liable are likely to vary from case to case. However, as in *Francovich*, the requirements must be identified and defined by Community law itself.

In other words, it is true that, in the case of infringements of Treaty provisions having **[1097]** direct effect, the conditions set out in *Francovich* may not be necessary and/or sufficient to give rise to a right to reparation. Nevertheless, in such cases too, it will be necessary to identify what conditions are sufficient in order to enable an individual to obtain reparation. It is scarcely necessary to point out that the *sufficient conditions*, as is clear from the *Francovich* judgment itself, relate to the *substantive* preconditions for liability.

53. A rapid appraisal of the rules in force in the national legal systems on liability on the part of public authorities shows that it is commonly accepted at least that the principle should be that the entity to which the event which gave rise to the loss or damage is attributable is answerable for that event, provided that there is causal link between the event and the loss or damage.

The substantive preconditions for liability are more or less the same everywhere: actual damage, a causal link between the damage and conduct on the part of the perpetrator of the damage, and the fact that the conduct was unlawful. In contrast, the differences—which in some cases are important in so far as they affect, for example, even the nature of the individual interests protected[58]—relate to the manner in which those preconditions are defined and the criteria for ascertaining whether they are met.

54. For present purposes, therefore, it is necessary, not so much to identify the general conditions for liability, which in point of fact are practically the same in the various legal systems, but to establish the criteria for determining whether they are met or, if you prefer, those criteria which will enable a common definition to be found of the conditions in question.

To that end, I consider that I should dwell initially on the conditions which the Court considers sufficient in cases of failure to implement a directive in order to give rise to a right on the part of individuals to compensation.

[58] Suffice it to recall the particularities (but see footnote 5) of the Italian system as regards the lack of a remedy in damages for breaches of *interessi legittimi* (protected interests). For the "tormented chapter of the protection in tort of *interessi legittimi*" in Italy, see Ponzanelli: "L'Europa e la responsabilita civile", in *Il Foro It.*, 1992, IV, col. 150. The question raised by the national court in *Enichem Base*, cited in footnote 24, indeed related to the breach of an *interesse legittimo*.

1. *The* Francovich *solution*

55. The obligation on the State to make reparation for legislative omissions was recognized by the Court in cases of failure to implement a directive within the prescribed period, subject to finding that the following three conditions were met: "First, the purpose of the directive must be to grant rights to individuals. Second, it must be possible to identify the content of those rights on the basis of the provisions of the directive. **[1098]** Finally, there must be a causal link between the breach of the State's obligation and the damage suffered."[59] A first question needs to be asked: are those conditions necessary and sufficient also in a case where the loss or damage was caused by infringement of a Treaty provision having direct effect?

56. Leaving aside for the moment the question of the causal link, which is compulsory for tortious liability, I would observe initially that the first condition, to the effect that the result prescribed by the directive should entail the grant of rights to individuals, is concerned with identifying the legal position of the individuals whose infringement may give rise to compensation. Having regard to the relevant case-law, it must be considered that the Court intended by those words to refer generally to all individual legal positions protected by Community law; hence—by definition—this condition is always met in the case of provisions having direct effect. The second condition, which at first blush seems merely to specify the first, emphasizes the need for the right resulting from the directive to have a precise content, that is to say, its subject-matter must be capable of determination, with the result that this condition should again be regarded, in principle, as being satisfied by Treaty provisions with direct effect.[60] It is worth stressing at this juncture that in *Francovich*, as in Joined Cases C-178/94, C-179/94, C-188/94, C-189/94 and C-190/94 *Dillenkofer and Others*, on which I am also delivering an Opinion today, the content of the right conferred on the individuals coincides exactly and precisely with their pecuniary claims asserted by virtue of that same right under the relevant Community provisions and hence with the loss for which damages may be payable.[61] Of course, this does not mean that the condition in question has to be interpreted as meaning that whether damages may be awarded in respect of the damage sustained by the individual is dependent on whether the exact content of the pecuniary loss sustained by the individual is capable of being identified on the basis of the actual provision infringed. In contrast, it is enough for the infringement of the provision in question, which confers on the

[59] However, the three conditions in question, which the Court identified in *Francovich* (paragraph 40), are set out here verbatim in the form in which they were stressed and summarized by the Court in *Faccini Dori* v. *Recreb*, cited in footnote 37, paragraph 27.

[60] For this aspect, see sections 75 and 76 below.

[61] In *Francovich*, I recall, this was the amount owing to the employees following the employer's insolvency; in *Dillenkofer and Others* it is sums paid by purchasers of package holidays for trips never made.

individual a right whose subject-matter can be precisely identified, to have affected the injured party's financial interests. If this were not so, in fact, only claims in cases in which the aim of the provision infringed was precisely to confer a "pecuniary" right on the individual would sound in damages.

57. The above observations lead me to an initial conclusion: in so far as they relate to **[1099]** the legal position which an individual must occupy in order to be able to claim a right to reparation, the conditions laid down by the Court in *Francovich* are manifestly necessary and satisfied even in the case of Treaty provisions having direct effect. What has to be clarified here is whether those conditions are sufficient in every case.

To that end, it is worth examining the reasons which prompted the Court to confine itself to those conditions and not also to specify, for instance, the criteria for holding that the relevant infringement of Community law involves unlawful conduct such as to cause the State to incur liability. In *Francovich*, as I have already said, the Court referred expressly to only one of the classic preconditions for liability: the causal link. In contrast, it provided no further clarification about the unlawfulness of the conduct of the perpetrator of the loss or damage and the actual existence of the loss or damage, the national court not having been asked to carry out any review in that regard.

58. In my view, the choice made by the Court in *Francovich* was due, very simply, to the fact that in that case the existence of the aforementioned two preconditions was obvious at first sight. There could be no doubt as to whether the *omission* on the part of the State was unlawful: the result sought by the directive—in respect of which the State had no margin of discretion, at any rate not in relation to the time within which the directive had to be implemented—was not attained; neither was there any doubt as to whether loss or damage had actually occurred, since it essentially coincided with the amount to which the applicants would have been entitled had the directive been implemented within the prescribed period.

Accordingly, in those circumstances, since the Court had first found that the directive could not be relied on directly by individuals before the national courts, it merely indicated that, for the purposes of the obligation to make reparation of the Member State in breach of its obligations, it must be possible to identify a precise, exact right on the part of the individuals.

59. In sum, it is undeniable that, from the point of view of State liability and the obligation to make reparation, *Francovich* was virtually a textbook case. The fact that the Court did not feel the need to specify the limits of State liability, in particular in so far as it omitted expressly to indicate the *Community* criteria for judging whether the conduct of the State was unlawful, should be seen solely in the light of the particular features of the case before it. It is significant in this regard that different,

even opposite, reactions are to be encountered in academic writings: according to some commentators, **[1100]** the Court intended only to target serious infringements or infringements involving fault;[62] others, in contrast, take the view that it appears from *Francovich* that any infringement of Community law gives rise to liability and an obligation to make reparation.[63]

In the final analysis, the fact that the criteria required by Community law in order for the State to incur liability are not clearly defined in *Francovich* is closely connected with the particularly straightforward nature of that case. The Court's very statement that the conditions under which State liability gives rise to a right to reparation depend "on the nature of the breach of Community law giving rise to the damage" should therefore be construed as meaning not only that the general conditions for liability to be incurred vary according to the type of breach, but also that the particular characteristics of a specific type of breach, such as failure to implement a directive within the prescribed period, may be such as not to require detailed consideration as to whether one or more of the conditions in question are present.

60. To interpret *Francovich* differently would mean that every infringement of Community law affecting the financial interests of an individual occupying a legal position claimed under the provision infringed entailed *per se* and automatically a right to reparation.

It does not seem to me that this was the result intended by the Court or by Community law. Moreover, it would not actually be reasonable, given that, as I have already mentioned, in all the legal traditions liability for legislative activity on the part of the public authorities is limited in various ways. What is more, the Court's own case-law on the non-contractual liability of the Community institutions on account of their legislative activities takes a different line.

2. *The case-law on the second paragraph of Article 215*

61. Although this is not the proper place in which to analyse and discuss this case-law, I consider it necessary at least to point to the need for calm, profound reflection thereon. In these proceedings, the Member States have constantly referred to the case-law in question and asked for the same criteria set **[1101]** forth in that case-law also to be applied in

[62] It shows, among other things, that failure to implement a directive constitutes a conscious breach, consequently a deliberate one and for that very reason one involving fault, Temple Lang: "New Legal Effects Resulting from the Failure of States to Fulfil Obligations under European Community Law. The Francovich Judgment", in *Fordham International Law Journal*, 1992-1993, p. 1 et seq.

[63] In the sense that strict liability is involved in which fault plays no part, see, for example, Caranta: "Governmental Liability after Francovich", in *Cambridge Law Journal*, 1993, p. 272 et seq.; see also Tatham: "Les recours contre les atteintes portées aux normes communautaires par les pouvoirs publics en Angleterre", in *Cahiers de droit européen*, 1993, p. 597 et seq.

respect of liability for infringements of Community law attributable to them.

That point of view does not seem completely baseless, bearing in mind, first, that the second paragraph of Article 215 refers, for the purposes of the reparation of damage caused by Community institutions in the performance of their duties, to the general principles common to the laws of the Member States and, secondly, that consequently that case-law could and should constitute, regard being had to the absence of uniform rules in this field, a useful frame of reference for common rules on State liability.

62. The Court does not seem—or at least not at first sight and unlike that which Advocate General Mischo proposed in his Opinion in *Francovich*—to have intended to make State liability hinge on the same restrictive conditions required by the case-law in order for the Community to incur liability.

Nevertheless, I consider it worth preceding my consideration of each of the general conditions for liability by a few observations designed to assess whether, and to what extent, an infringement of Community law attributable to the State is comparable to an infringement on the part of the Community institutions, and whether, in the final analysis, the criteria set forth in the relevant case-law may or may not constitute a useful frame of reference, at least given similar situations.

63. To that end, I would call to mind as a preliminary point that the Court has consistently held that "the liability of the Community on account of its legislative powers depends on the coincidence of a set of conditions as regards the unlawfulness of the act of the institution, the fact of damage and the existence of a direct link in the chain of causality between the act and the damage complained of".[64] As can be seen, the substantive preconditions are the same—indeed could not be different—also in the case of liability on the part of the Community institutions.

However, the case-law has identified—in particular with regard to the unlawfulness of the conduct imputable to the institutions—conditions which are so restrictive as to make it extremely difficult actually to obtain damages against a Community institution.[65]

64. The limits laid down by the case-law in regard to actions brought under Article 215 of the Treaty are in fact based on the widespread view that, as a matter of principle, **[1102]** compensation may not be recovered for injury caused by the legislature. Moreover, the Court itself has explained its restrictive approach as follows: "the legislative authority, even where the validity of its measures is subject to judicial review, cannot

[64] See, for example, the judgment in Case 50/86 *Grands Moulins de Paris* v. *Council and Commission* [1987] ECR 4833, paragraph 7.

[65] Indeed, to date the number of awards of damages made against Community institutions comes to just eight.

always be hindered in making its decisions by the prospect of applications for damages whenever it has occasion to adopt legislative measures in the public interest which may adversely affect the interests of individuals".[66]

The application of that approach, however, in a good few cases has made for perplexity.

65. The limits of Community liability are relied upon and applied not only in relation to legislative measures which presuppose the existence of a broad discretion on the part of the relevant institution, but also in relation to measures which fall within the ambit of implementing legislation (typically Commission implementing regulations).[67] Essentially, the Court has applied the restrictive criteria formulated in assessing the Community's liability on account of legislative measures of a general nature even where the damage arose out of an individual measure not in fact involving economic policy choices of such scope as to necessitate the fullest possible protection of the institutions' discretionary powers.

Unquestionably, it would be more correct to apply different rules on liability depending on whether the activity in question was more particularly legislative or in the nature of executive activity, given that, in principle, the discretion available to the Community institutions differs significantly in the two cases.[68] More generally, the requirement for virtually arbitrary conduct in order for non-contractual liability on the part of the Commission to arise is justified where the Community has a broad discretion—as in the field of agricultural policy—, but is not justified where, in contrast, the conditions for the exercise of the discretion conferred on the institution are clearly and precisely defined.[69] In the latter

[66] Judgment in Joined Cases 83/76 and 94/76, 4/77, 15/77 and 40/77 *HNL* v. *Council and Commission* [1978] ECR 1209, paragraph 5.

[67] See, for example, the judgment in Joined Cases 194/83 to 206/83 *Asteris* v. *Commission* [1985] ECR 2815, paragraphs 21 and 22, in which the Court held that the Community had incurred no liability for the erroneous fixing by the Commission pursuant to a Council regulation of aid for tomato concentrates. See also the judgment in Case C-152/88 *Sofrimport* v. *Commission* [1990] ECR I-2477, in which the Community was held liable on account of an essentially individual Commission regulation implementing another Commission regulation which in turn implemented a Council regulation, and the rigid criteria used for legislative measures involving choices of economic policy were applied.

[68] See Advocate General Biancarelli's Opinion in Case T-120/89 *Stahlwerke Peine-Salzgitter* v. *Commission* [1991] ECR II-279, at II-340, in which he stated that, as far as liability was concerned, what was important was "—essentially—the margin of appreciation available to the Commission when it adopts its decision and the more or less complex economic context in which the decision is adopted".

[69] This issue was recently raised and discussed before the Court of First Instance in an anti-dumping case in which the applicant argued that the question of Community liability should be assessed differently depending on whether the infringement imputed to the institution was attributable to a breach of the rules inherent in the assessment of complex economic facts or, as in that case, to a breach of procedural rules binding on the institutions. The Court, however, disagreed, confining itself to the lapidary statement that anti-dumping measures constitute legislative action involving choices of economic policy (judgment of 18 September 1995 in Case T-167/94 *Nölle* v. *Council and Commission* [1995] ECR II-2589, paragraphs 44 to 52).

case, the infringement **[1103]** of the relevant provision should in any event be regarded as such as to cause the Community to incur liability.[70]

66. In sum, whilst, according to *Francovich*, loss or damage caused by a provision of national law incompatible with a Community provision must be held to be amenable to an action for damages, it is not easy to understand why damages should be recoverable for the loss or damage ensuing from a Community measure which is *incompatible with the same Community provision* only if the restrictive conditions laid down by the Court (until now) are satisfied.[71] Moreover, in a Community governed by the rule of law, which aims to pay increasing attention and to be increasingly sensitive to the protection of individuals, also from the point of view of compensation, at least equal attention should be paid—as a number of parties have argued—to cases in which the loss or damage suffered by the citizen arises out of an unlawful act or omission attributable to the Community institutions themselves.[72]

From that point of view, it does not seem to me either that it can be validly argued that to transpose to national actions in tort the conditions attaching to actions brought under Article 215 would potentially constitute a step back from the situation existing in some legal systems. From the point of view of the requirements of the protection of the rights conferred on individuals by the Community legal system, it is not acceptable for the judicial protection achievable at Community level to be based on more restrictive and, in the final analysis, less liberal conditions than those obtaining in at least some Member States.[73]

67. In the light of the foregoing, I consider that there is no reason for applying different criteria—naturally in like situations—depending on whether the infringement of Community law in question is attributable to a State or a Community institution. Conversely, different situations can and must lead to different conclusions as regards the criteria employed to find whether the preconditions for liability are satisfied, whether the alleged liability be on the part of the Member States or the Community institutions.

In particular, by way of a first approximation, I take the view that it is absolutely reasonable that State liability—let us be quite clear about this, irrespective of whether or not the provision "breached" has direct effect **[1104]**—should be subject to the same restrictive conditions applying to

[70] To this effect, see also Advocate General Darmon's Opinion in Case C-55/90 *Cato* v. *Commission* [1992] ECR I-2561.

[71] This was the issue raised, *inter alia*, in *Bourgoin* before the Court of Appeal, Civil Division, *Common Market Law Reports* [1986] QB 716, considered in Simon-Barav, "La responsabilité de l'administration nationale en cas de violation du droit communautaire", in RMC, 1987, p. 165, in particular at p. 170 et seq.; Oliver, "Enforcing Community Rights in the English Courts", in *Modern Law Review*, 1987, p. 881, in particular at p. 899 et seq.

[72] To this effect, see, for example, Cartabia: "Omissioni del legislatore, diritti sociali e risarcimento dei danni", in *Giurisprudenza Costituzionale*, 1992, p. 505 et seq.

[73] See, in this connection, the proceedings of the 1992 FIDE Congress: FIDE, "La sanction des infractions au droit communautaire", Volume II, Lisbon, 1992.

the Community institutions whenever they have a margin of discretion or the limits imposed on their action by Community provisions, perhaps in sectors falling (partly) within their sphere of competence, are not clear.

Conversely, Member States should be more readily held liable, as in the case of the Community institutions, wherever the infringement is not coupled with the exercise of a broad discretion.

68. In the final analysis, what should be attained is a system of differentiated liability depending on whether or not the Community institutions (and the national authorities) have a broad discretion. To my mind, this is the most correct and consistent manner of bringing about the essential harmonization of the preconditions for liability, in so far as it would be strange, to say the least, to hold Member States liable, on equivalent facts, for infringements of Community law on different (less strict) conditions than those which the Court applies to liability on the part of the Community institutions.

In a Community governed by the rule of law, in which it is the aim that the acts and conduct of all participants in the system should be amenable to judicial review without privileges for anyone, the requirement for effective protection of the rights claimed by individuals under Community law may not vary—given equal situations—depending on whether a Member State or the Community caused the loss or damage.

69. The appraisal set out below will therefore take into consideration, as the point of reference for determining the obligation on Member States to make reparation, *inter alia* the conditions identified by the Court in its case-law on Article 215. Of course, this will not involve a "blind" transposition of those (restrictive) conditions to the sector under consideration here. I am not overlooking that, in applying Community law, the Member States generally have very limited discretion, with the result that the conditions in question relating to this situation are likely to cause liability more readily to be incurred. At the same time, I consider that it cannot be ruled out that any lack of precision of the obligation on the Member State may be such as to necessitate the application of those same restrictive criteria, even though it does not have a significant margin of discretion in the sector in question.

3. *The "Community" criteria relating to the general conditions for liability*

70. Having said all this, I shall now turn to consider the individual substantive preconditions **[1105]** for incurring liability, starting with the event which gave rise to the damage, that is to say in this case, infringement of Community provisions with direct effect.

(a) *The event which gave rise to the damage: infringement of Community provisions*

71. Defining the limits of liability is primarily and essentially linked with the definition of the unlawful conduct. It is undisputed that the

harmful conduct—here the legislative measure—must conflict with the rules of the system. In order, however, for such unlawfulness to give rise to liability, and at the same time damages, the individual States employ differing concepts,[74] whose meaning does not always correspond exactly and whose practical application may therefore result in different solutions being applied in respect of the infringement of a given provision. This confirms, if confirmation was needed, that it is necessary—particularly as regards the event which gave rise to the damage—to establish the criteria which will enable a common definition to be achieved.

As regards legislative activity of the public authorities, a first attempt has been made by the Council of Europe in a recommendation, Principle I of which states as follows: "Reparation should be ensured for damage caused by an act due to a failure of a public authority to conduct itself in a way which can reasonably be expected from it in law in relation to the injured person. Such a failure is presumed in the case of transgression of an established legal rule."[75] Consequently, mere unlawfulness of the measure is not sufficient under that recommendation in order for the State to incur liability: except where the provision alleged to have been breached is clear, the conduct attributed to the public authorities must also have been "unreasonable".

72. In the Court's case-law on non-contractual liability it has been consistently held that if the damage complained of results from a legislative measure involving choices of economic policy, the fact that the measure in question is invalid is not sufficient to cause the Community to incur liability. In the case of measures of this kind,[76] Community liability cannot arise unless *a sufficiently serious breach of a superior rule of law for the protection of the individual has occurred*.[77]

[1106] Whilst it is true therefore that the prejudicial measure must at least be unlawful in order for non-contractual liability to be incurred, there is the immediate addition of two conditions on which liability for damage caused by measures involving a choice of economic policy depends: the provision infringed must be "a superior rule of law for the protection of the individual" and the breach must be "sufficiently serious" ("grave", "suffisamment caractérisée", "hinreichend qualifiziert").

73. Having said that, I would point out that all the States which submitted observations in these proceedings ruled out an exact match between the reasons for the invalidity of the measure and the preconditions for liability, arguing that not every breach of Community law is

[74] To take just a few systems, suffice it to mention *illecito* in Italian law, the French *faute*, the German *Verschulden* and the English concepts of *breach of a duty of care* or *misfeasance in public office*.

[75] Recommendation R (84) 15 of 18 September 1984.

[76] But, as I have already said, under the case-law in question it is as if all Community legislative measures involved choices of economic policy.

[77] See, in particular, the judgments in *HNL* v. *Council and Commission*, cited in footnote 66, paragraph 4, and in Joined Cases C-104/89 and C-37/90 *Mulder and Others* v. *Council and Commission* [1992] ECR I-3061, paragraph 12.

capable of causing the State to incur liability and, as a result, of giving rise to an obligation in damages in favour of individuals.

Consequently, for the purposes of holding that there is an obligation in damages on the Member State in breach, the emphasis has been placed, on the one hand, on the same criteria formulated by the case-law on Article 215—hence essentially on the concept of a manifest and serious breach—and, on the other, on fault as the element necessary to "characterize" (as serious) the breach of the provision or, in any case, as an indispensable, inherent ingredient of liability.

—Manifest and serious nature of the breach

74. Whilst entering all the caveats and making all the distinctions required as regards Community liability, it must therefore be assessed whether, also for the purposes of liability on the part of the Member States, the breach in question must be manifest and serious and, of course, what is to be understood by the breach having to be manifest and serious.

As I have mentioned, in the relevant case-law that criterion is defined in the following terms: "In the context of Community provisions in which one of the chief features is the exercise of a wide discretion indispensable for the implementation of the common agricultural policy, the Community can incur liability only in exceptional cases, namely where the institution concerned manifestly and gravely disregarded the limits on the exercise of its powers",[78] provided of course that the breach in question was of a superior rule of law for the protection of the individual.

75. The latter requirement seems, for present purposes, to be the least controversial. It is obvious that, in order for an individual to be **[1107]** able to claim a right to compensation, the provision breached must be capable of conferring a legal position upon him as an individual. Moreover, this is the sense in which the first two conditions set out in *Francovich* must be read, conditions which, as I have already stated, are both necessary and satisfied in the case of provisions having direct effect.

In my view, when it comes to Treaty provisions with direct effect, which is what we are concerned with here, some additional specification is needed. In particular, it must be made clear that the fact that such provisions are occasionally or often designed to protect other—*ex hypothesi* general—interests as well cannot be regarded in itself as preventing them from being for the protection of individuals.

76. Next, as regards the requirement that the provision infringed should be a *superior* rule, it is scarcely necessary to point out that if a

[78] *Grands Moulins de Paris* v. *Council and Commission*, cited in footnote 64, paragraph 8. See, in addition, the judgment in Case C-63/89 *Assurances du Crédit* [1991] ECR I-1799, paragraph 12, and, most recently, the judgment of 14 September 1995 in Case T-571/93 *Lefebvre and Others* v. *Commission* [1995] ECR II-2379, paragraph 32.

legislative measure is unlawful, this means—by definition—that it conflicts with a higher-ranking provision. Admittedly, that expression is used in the case-law on Article 215, not to penalize every breach of limits imposed by superior rules, albeit for the protection of individuals, but solely breaches of general principles of the legal system and hence, in the final analysis, to categorize the breach in question as serious.

In this connection, I shall say forthwith that I do not consider it appropriate to propose the same solution also for State liability for infringements of Community law. If it is true that the Member States' obligation in damages is imposed in order to guarantee individuals effective protection of rights claimed under Community provisions, it follows it would not be easy to identify reasons justifying limiting that obligation to the breach of a particular class of rule, albeit one fundamental to the Community system.

77. Indeed, if the standpoint of the injured party is taken, it is only too obvious that any infringement of a Community provision which confers a legal position on him as an individual must be capable of giving rise to compensation. Consequently, infringement of a provision of a regulation cannot result for the individual in consequences differing from those arising out of an infringement of a Treaty provision; it seems to me even less appropriate to draw distinctions between actual provisions of the Treaty by deciding, for example, that only breaches of some of them, that is to say, the fundamental provisions and not the others, are capable of causing the Member State in question to incur liability.[79]

[1108] In the final analysis, I consider it sufficient, from the point of view of the aspect considered so far, that the provision infringed should confer on the individual a right whose content is capable of determination and precise. It is hardly necessary to add that the same should be true of liability on the part of the Community institutions.

78. This having been clarified, it now falls to me to specify the concept of manifest and serious breach as it arises in this context.

It seems to me that, in order to identify the limits of the possibilities for translating unlawfulness into liability, the discretion factor can and must be the decisive element, irrespective of the rank of the provision infringed (Treaty or secondary legislation, at any rate a provision which takes precedence over national law) and of the measure (legislative or executive) which infringes it. The greater or lesser degree of discretion available to the State coincides, moreover,—at least in most cases—with the greater or lesser degree of clarity and precision of the obligation to which it is subject. In fact, it is quite possible to conceive of obligations which

[79] It would still be necessary to specify which provisions also warrant protection in damages on the ground of their scope and in order to secure their effectiveness: is the prohibition of discrimination on grounds of residence, which is indubitably fundamental for the purposes of ensuring effective freedom to supply services, as fundamental as or less fundamental than the prohibition of discrimination on grounds of nationality?

are not at all clear—or better, which are imprecisely demarcated—, even in cases where the States' discretion is small or unimportant. The upshot is that in such cases the limits set to the action of the States are not clearly defined for *that very reason*, with the result that the situation is not very different substantively from that in which the States have a significant margin of discretion.

79. This means that, even in the case of provisions with direct effect, the State may be guilty of breaches which, not by reason only of their having direct effect, must be categorized as *manifest and serious*. I shall explain what I mean using an example based on two provisions having direct effect. The prohibition of discrimination on grounds of nationality (Article 6) identifies precisely and exactly the individual's right, which is—very simply and without any possible alternative—the right not to be discriminated against. The same cannot be said of the provision prohibiting quantitative restrictions and measures having equivalent effect (Article 30) in view of the variety of fact situations conceivable in that area. In that case, the individual's right—which in itself is only too clear—not to be obstructed in his activity by measures contrary to the provision in question may be limited by the provisions of Article 36 or also, in the case of measures applicable without distinction, by imperative requirements relied on by the State with a view to pursuing an objective deemed worthy of protection by Community law itself. The upshot is that the State measure in question, which is in principle incompatible with Community law, may well be taken outside the scope of Article 30 or fall within the exceptions provided for in Article 36. To this end—and it is scarcely necessary to stress this—it may be necessary to obtain a prior determination from the national court and/or from the Community Court.

Furthermore, it is worth pointing out that, for present purposes, it is not decisive in itself whether or not the States have a wide discretion in a given sector, but rather what is decisive is the breadth of the margin of **[1109]** discretion available to them in regard to the individual provision which confers a right on individuals.[80] It is in precisely that way that the discretion ends up by corresponding to the greater or lesser precision of the obligation which it imposes on the States themselves.

80. If the question is seen in those terms, it has to be acknowledged that there will be State liability in principle whenever the State is

[80] I would observe, for example, reiterating what I have already mentioned, that, although Article 30 of the Treaty is certainly not associated with the exercise of a broad discretion on the part of the Member States, it must nevertheless be considered that the limits which it imposes on action by the Member States are not always clear and precise, as clearly emerges, moreover, from the way in which the case-law has evolved. By contrast, the discretion available to the Member States, for instance, under Article 129a of the Treaty (consumer protection), could not in any event be regarded as capable of resulting in the application of more restrictive conditions for liability if, for example, a national provision excluded citizens of other Member States from the benefit of the national provisions.

constrained under Community law to achieve a *precise* result. This is precisely the case, as already held by the Court in *Francovich*, where there is a failure to implement a directive within the prescribed period, provided, of course, that the other conditions set out by the Court are fulfilled. But this is also the case with all other provisions, including those of the Treaty, that are confined to imposing on the Member States precise, clearly identified obligations to refrain from some conduct (suffice it to mention the prohibition on the introduction of new customs duties laid down by Article 12 and, more generally, all the standstill clauses) which concurrently give rise to a right for individuals.

So, in all those sectors and with regard to all those provisions which do not give Member States a significant margin of discretion, in the sense described above, there must be held to be liability and an obligation in damages simply on account of the infringement of a Community provision which confers on individuals a right which is precise and whose subject-matter is determinable; no other factors may be taken into account.

81. Where, in contrast, Member States have a more or less wide discretion or the Community obligations imposed on them are not clearly and precisely defined, the same solution will have to be adopted only where the limits set to their action have been manifestly and gravely disregarded. Obviously, this will be the case where the provision assumedly infringed is clear, perhaps in the way described in *CILFIT*[81] or because it has already been interpreted by the Court with regard to identical or, in any event, similar facts[82] no matter whether the interpretation was given in a preliminary ruling or in a judgment pursuant to Article 169.

As far as the last-mentioned aspect is concerned, it is scarcely necessary to show that, unlike some Member States have argued in **[1110]** these proceedings, there is no reason for making an action for damages dependent upon the Court's having made a prior declaration that the State in question has failed to fulfil its obligations. In this connection, regard must be had to the Commission's discretion in deciding whether or not to initiate infringement proceedings, which would reduce, without any review, the ability of individuals to obtain compensation. Moreover, as the Court itself has held, "the rights accruing to individuals derive, not from that judgment [declaring that the Member State failed to fulfil its obligations], but from the actual provisions of Community law having direct effect in the internal legal order."[83]

[81] Judgment in Case 283/81 *CILFIT* v. *Ministry of Health* [1982] ECR 3415, paragraphs 16 and 17.

[82] See, for a remark to similar effect but regarding the obligation to make a reference pursuant to the third paragraph of Article 177 of the Treaty, the judgment in Joined Cases 28/62, 29/62 and 30/62 *Da Costa en Schaake* v. *Nederlands Belastingsadministratie* [1963] ECR 31.

[83] Judgment in Joined Cases 314/81 to 316/81 and 83/82 *Procureur de la République* v. *Waterkeyn* [1982] ECR 4337, paragraph 16.

82. In contrast, where the Member States have a broad margin of discretion and/or the relevant law is doubtful and has not yet been considered by the Court, even in regard to similar facts, it is impossible for the approach to be different. Simply on an abstract level, it must in fact be considered that in such cases it will be very difficult to find that the limits set to the States' action have been manifestly and gravely disregarded, all the less where this is equated, as in the Article 215 case-law, with *virtually arbitrary* conduct.[84]

Consequently, in such cases the individual continues to have the possibility of relying on the substantive protection of the legal position which may be conferred upon him by the provision in question. Of course, in the event that the Member State does not remedy reasonably quickly the infringement which has been found in the meantime, the injured party may indeed bring an action for damages.

83. Having said that, it certainly cannot be ruled out that the interpretation of the Community rules in question, as made by the national authorities in their legislative activity (or lack of activity), may prove to be *manifestly wrong*, with the result that the Member State in breach of its obligations should be held liable in damages also in such cases.

I would next observe that, from the same perspective, as regards the timely, but incorrect, implementation of a provision of a directive, State liability will exist only where the application of the provision by the Member State in question is manifestly wrong.[85]

[1111] 84. In the final analysis, I consider that, for our purposes, there can be considered to have been a *manifest and serious breach* where:

(a) obligations whose content is clear and precise in every respect have not been complied with;
(b) the Court's case-law has provided sufficient clarification, either by an interpretation given in a preliminary ruling or by means of a judgment pursuant to Article 169, of doubtful legal situations which are identical or, in any event, similar to that at issue;
(c) the national authorities' interpretation of the relevant Community provisions in their legislative activity (or inactivity) is manifestly wrong.

[84] See, for a statement of that concept, the judgment in Joined Cases 116/77 and 124/77 *Amylum* v. *Council and Commission* [1979] ECR 3497, paragraph 19, in which the Court held that, in that case, "these were not errors of such gravity that it may be said that the conduct of the defendant institutions (...) was verging on the arbitrary and was thus of such a kind as to involve the Community in non-contractual liability". To the same effect, see, most recently, the judgment in *Nölle* v. *Council and Commission*, cited in footnote 69.

[85] For a more exact appraisal of this aspect, see the Opinion in Case C-392/93 *British Telecommunications plc* [1996] ECR I-1631, I-1634, also delivered today, in particular paragraphs 33, 34 and 35.

—Fault: an essential ingredient?

85. It remains now to assess whether fault is an essential ingredient in order to hold Member States liable. In this connection, it is appropriate first to clarify that by fault I mean a subjective factor, or, if you prefer, a mental or psychological factor, which characterizes—as being at fault or negligent or in any sense traditionally attributed to the expression fault—the conduct of the entity to which the infringement and, with it, liability is attributed. From this angle, fault is therefore a factor which *is added* to the infringement of the *enabling* provision as a subjective element, by categorizing the conduct which results in the breach, but not directly the breach as such or the legislative measure giving rise to the damage.

Seeking fault in the subjective sense—and, *a fortiori*, wrongful intent—as regards legislative activity raises some considerable difficulties even at the conceptual level, especially since fault as a condition of State liability has always been the subject of profound reflection and conflicting assessments. In particular, attention has been drawn to the difficulties of identifying conduct displaying fault on the part of the public authorities on the basis of the same criteria used for the purposes of civil law, especially since the mechanisms devised for explaining the actions of legal persons by attributing to them the same manner of acting as natural persons are said to prove completely useless or at least inadequate from this point of view. Indeed, even viewed in the abstract, it appears difficult to identify conduct involving fault in the rule-making activity of the legislator or even to conceive of its possibly being aware of the breach. In contrast, it cannot be presumed that the legislator pursues a general interest invariably and in any event.

[1112] 86. Despite this, it must be acknowledged that most national legal systems still refer to fault as the basis for liability,[86] even where, essentially, it is equated precisely with the unlawfulness of the measure. I am thinking, in particular, of the French system, in which the ruling principle is that "toute illégalité constitue par elle-même une faute" (any illegality constitutes fault *per se*)[87] and of the approach of the Italian Corte di Cassazione (Court of Cassation), according to which "as far as unlawful measures are concerned, fault may be found in the infringement *per se* of the provisions which was brought about by the adoption and implementation of the measure".[88]

[86] One exception is certainly the Spanish system, in which liability for legislative measures is strict (see Articles 9(3) and 106(2) of the Constitution and Article 139(1) of the Law of 26 November 1992 on the legal system for the public administration and administrative procedure).

[87] See, for instance, Paillet: "La faute du service public en droit administratif français", 1980, p. 176.

[88] Cassazione Civile, Sezioni Unite, judgment No 5361 of 22 October 1984 (in *Giustizia Civile*, 1985, p. 1419), in which it is also stated that "It cannot be seen . . . how the voluntary enforcement of an administrative measure which is unlawful for contravening the law and which affected an individual right may not embody *per se* the elements of fault, even, possibly, slight fault, especially when referred directly to a public structure, organized and competent to act, which is bound to

In other words, fault, which is at least presumed every time an unlawful legislative act is brought into being, either in view of the unquestionably voluntary nature of measures adopted by the public authorities or on account of infringement of the principles of legality which those authorities are bound to observe, has ended up by losing every subjective connotation.[89]

87. To put it another way, the search for fault has shifted from the perspective of a person to that of the "organization", with the result that even where it does not coincide simply with the unlawfulness of the measure, it is in any event connected with the content of the provision infringed, inasmuch as it attributes relevance to those rules of conduct with which the administration is bound to comply in performing its institutional tasks. In particular, importance attaches to the fact that the action of the administration is constrained by the limits of legality imposed on it.

Whilst, therefore, it is indeed true that liability is still fault-based in most national legal systems, it is also true that the existence of fault is determined, subject to some exceptions,[90] by objective **[1113]** criteria.[91] In sum, in the Member States themselves fault liability ends up being allowed in only by virtue of a series of devices; in any event, it is becoming increasingly objectified, that is to say, it is decreasingly or not at all coupled with a subjective component.

88. I consider that that solution, which is prevalent in the national legal systems and has been adopted by the Court itself in relation to non-contractual liability on the part of the Community institutions,[92] results in liability of Member States for infringements of Community law being strict, no-fault liability.

carry out its activities in accordance with the law". It is also worth citing judgment No 5883 of 24 May 1991 (in *Resp. Civ. Prev.*, 1992, p. 247 et seq.), in which the Corte di Cassazione held that proof of fault on the part of the public administration may consist "either of breach of the rules of common prudence, resulting in negligent or imprudent regulatory activity, or of the infringement of laws and regulations with which the public administration itself is bound to comply, in so far as it has to observe the principles of legality, impartiality and proper procedure laid down by Article 97 of the Constitution".

[89] This is also the case in Belgium, Luxembourg, Greece, Portugal and Denmark.

[90] In the English system, the administrative authorities' liability for legislative activity seems still to be based (and solidly based) on fault as the subjective element of the conduct in question. Thus, an error on the part of the Minister in interpreting the extent of the powers conferred on him may not in itself be regarded as constituting fault (see, for example, *Rowling* v. *Takaro Properties* [1988] 2 WLR, 418 et seq.); likewise, fault, and with it liability, is precluded where the authority in question sought legal advice on the field in which it was called on to act (see *Dunlop* v. *Woollabra Municipal Council* [1981] 2 WLR, 693). Given in addition that damages may not be awarded in the tort of negligence for pure economic loss, it follows that only, or almost only, the unlawful adoption of measures characterized by wrongful intent, namely the tort of misfeasance in public office, constitutes an unlawful act capable of giving rise to liability.

[91] Such a trend can be seen also in the Netherlands and Germany, where fault is equated to conduct in breach of the duties of normal care. In this context, German commentators themselves now refer to the "Objektivierung des Verschuldens" (see Ossenbühl: "Staatshaftungsrecht", 4th ed., Munich, 1991, p. 61).

[92] After some initial wavering, even in the Court's case-law fault is of importance only as a synonym of unlawful conduct.

On the other hand, even if it were to be sought to base such liability on fault, it seems to me, at least as a first approximation, that it could not, for present purposes, not be linked to the provision allegedly infringed or simply identified with its content.

89. To my mind, it is obvious that if the *enabling* provision in question is one intended to achieve a particular result, there is no room for making the emergence of a situation of liability depend on the existence of a subjective connotation of the conduct of the State which may be described as fault in the sense defined earlier. The infringement—the unlawful act—crystallizes at the time at which the State failed to achieve the result sought by the provision. There will then be liability on the part of the State, that is to say, strict or no-fault liability or whatever term one wishes to employ.

Conversely, if the *enabling* provision is a provision relating to conduct, in the sense that it essentially prescribes a duty of care, fault will be an essential component. If so, however, fault is no longer a subjective component characterizing the conduct of the State which brought about the infringement and with it the wrongful damage, but precisely the subject-matter of the infringement. Breach of a duty of care consists precisely in negligent conduct, hence conduct exhibiting fault, with the upshot that fault is the subject-matter of the unlawful act and no longer a subjective component of the conduct.

90. In the final analysis, in order for there to be liability on the part of a Member State which has breached Community obligations to which it is subject, I consider that there is no relevance in inquiring into the existence of fault as a subjective component of the unlawful conduct.

[1114] I would therefore reiterate my conviction, as described earlier, that the conduct of the State in breach of Community law must be assessed in the light of objective factors for the purposes of the obligation to make reparation.

(b) *Existence of the damage*

91. The damage must be real, that is to say, certain and actual. Moreover, those are the requirements generally insisted upon by the national legal systems, and it will be for the national court to find whether they are satisfied in the actual case.

92. Nevertheless, I am minded to dwell, if only briefly, on a number of conditions relating to the nature of the damage which have been prayed in aid or, at any rate, raised during these proceedings, in particular by the French Government, as a criterion for limiting the area of Member State liability following infringements of Community law. I refer, in particular, to the seriousness of the damage, in the sense that the damage should be considerable, and to its special nature, in so far as it should affect a small number of persons.

In my view, those conditions should be regarded as irrelevant for present purposes, even though they have often been applied in the Court's case-law on non-contractual liability.[93]

93. Whilst it is true that under the law of some Member States there are cases in which the right to reparation depends, among other things, on the seriousness of the damage, on its abnormally serious nature and on the special nature of the damage in regard to the injured parties, it is also true and worth stressing that that approach is employed for compensation for damage caused by lawful acts.[94] Accordingly, the terms of the problem are not, and could not be, the same as those arising in this case.

It would indeed be excessive to require of individuals injured by unlawful acts that the damage sustained by them should be abnormal and special, with the result that they would be left to bear, not only consequences of a modest scale, but also those common to a class of individuals which was not of limited **[1115]** size. I consider therefore that the idea of exempting liability for minor loss or damage in this case would be a bad one.

94. In this connection, I would first observe that the argument against accepting the criterion of the seriousness of the financial damage is that an unlawful measure involving a manifest and serious breach contrary to a provision of the system and with the rights of the individual guaranteed thereby, must give rise to compensation in order to restore the balance altered by the unlawful act or omission, irrespective of the scale of the damage. Moreover, if a common approach to liability for unlawful acts or omissions of the public authorities emerges from the laws of the Member States, that approach consists in not making compensation depend on the scale of the damage.

On top of this, State liability does not seem to be able to be confined to cases in which there are specifically determined persons, or groups of persons, and precluded where the legislative act concerns a broad class of persons. Whilst it is true that it could be justifiably argued that public-interest requirements militate in favour of ruling out compensation for damage affecting large classes of persons, *inter alia* in order to avoid heavy financial burdens, it is also true that that approach is based merely on reasons of expediency. It still leaves the question open, given that liability is dependent on a manifest and serious breach of a higher norm which creates rights of the individual, as to the reasons for which the person

[93] See in particular, the judgments in *HNL* v. *Council and Commission*, cited in footnote 66, paragraph 7, Joined Cases 64/76 and 113/76, 167/78 and 239/78, 27/79, 28/79 and 45/79 *Dumortier Frères* v. *Council* [1979] ECR 3091, paragraph 11, and Case 59/83 *Biovilac* v. *EEC* [1984] ECR 4057, paragraphs 27 to 30.

[94] See, for example, the judgment of the Conseil d'Etat of 14 January 1938 in *La Fleurette*, Recueil Lebon, 1938, p. 25 et seq. The German "*Sonderopfer*" (special sacrifice) theory in the field of expropriation, which always relates to financial loss arising out of lawful measures adopted in the public interest, should also be subsumed under this head.

with the right to compensation should be given satisfaction on the basis of the number of other persons with the same right which has been breached.[95]

95. In short, it does not seem possible to me to ignore the fact that liability for unlawful measures and compensation for lawful measures are two radically different creatures. It is certainly not without significance that the condition regarding the seriousness and the special nature of the damage was laid down in the French case-law only for damage arising out of lawful legislative measures.

Moreover, when in the judgment in *Alivar* it depicted State liability for infringements of Community law as *responsabilité sans faute*, seeing that the national measures were justified by the public interest, the Conseil d'Etat itself took the abnormal and special nature of **[1116]** the damage as established;[96] so much so that this has been referred to as *responsabilité sans faute* adjusted by the fact that it is not necessary for the damage to be abnormal and special.[97]

96. In the final analysis, I consider it to be only too obvious that conditions relating to the nature of the damage, which may, moreover, even result in the negation of the actual right to compensation, have no basis and no *raison d'être* where the damage complained of is connected, not with lawful activities, but with unlawful ones.[98] Naturally, this conclusion should also apply to cases of non-contractual liability on the part of the Community.[99]

[95] See Advocate General Capotorti's Opinion in Joined Cases 83/76 and 94/76, 4/77, 15/77 and 40/77 *HNL* v. *Council and Commission* [1978] ECR 1226 et seq., especially at 1234 et seq.

[96] Judgment of 23 March 1984 in *Alivar*, AJDA, 1984, p. 396, including a note by Genevois. This case was concerned with a claim for damages for failure to grant an export licence for potatoes introduced by a general administrative measure, which the Court of Justice subsequently held to be contrary to the prohibition of quantitative restrictions on exports set out in Article 34 of the Treaty. The Conseil d'Etat held that all that there could be in that case was *responsabilité sans faute*, upholding the judgment at first instance, which accepted the damages claim without even inquiring whether the damage was abnormal or special, but found that there was liability on account of an unlawful act (*pour faute*). See, in addition, the Opinion of Commissaire du Gouvernement Laroque in the judgment of the Conseil d'Etat of 28 February 1992 in *Arizona Tobacco Products*, cited in footnote 48, in which it is considered that infringements of Community—and international—provisions give rise to a third system of liability which, unlike *responsabilité sans faute*, does not require the damage to be exceptional in order for a right to compensation to arise.

[97] See on this subject Simon, "Le Conseil d'Etat et les directives communautaires: du gallicanisme à l'orthodoxie?" in *Revue trimestrielle de droit européen*, 1992, p. 265 et seq.

[98] This conclusion is also borne out by the Council of Europe's recommendation of 18 September 1984, to which I have already referred. Principle II(1) of that recommendation expressly covers reparation of damage caused by lawful acts by stating that "reparation should be ensured if it would be manifestly unjust to allow the injured person alone to bear the damage, having regard to the following circumstances: the act is in the general interest, only one person or a limited number of persons have suffered the damage and the act was exceptional or the damage was an exceptional result of the act". For a different view, see Advocate General Léger's Opinion, cited earlier, of 20 June 1995 in Case C-5/94 *Lomas*, judgment of 23 May 1996, ECR I-2553.

[99] Indeed, it would appear from the judgment in *Mulder and Others*, cited in footnote 77, that the Court has already revised, albeit impliedly, its case-law on this point.

(c) *The causal link*

97. The third condition for liability expressly mentioned in *Francovich* relates to the causal link—an obligatory requirement for liability in tort—according to which the damage complained of must be the direct consequence of the harmful event imputed to its perpetrator, hence, in this case, the unlawful legislative measure.

Obviously, it will be for the national court to establish whether this condition is fulfilled. For present purposes, however, I am minded to make a few observations with regard to a break in the chain of causation from two points of view. First, it is worth examining whether it is possible to consider that under Community law the causal chain may be broken by contributory causes or by negligent conduct on the part of the injured party; secondly, this matter raises, albeit under various guises, the question of the ancillary nature of a damages claim in relation to other national judicial remedies.

[1117]—Conduct of the injured party

98. In this connection, it should first be recalled that the Court itself has held that there is "a general principle common to the legal systems of the Member States to the effect that the injured party must show reasonable diligence in limiting the extent of his loss or risk having to bear the damage himself".[100]

Consequently, the injured party is under a duty to act diligently, a duty which consists in taking steps so as to avoid the damage or, at any rate, to reduce its scale.[101]

99. Moreover, this is the purport of the Council of Europe's aforementioned recommendation of 18 September 1984, Principle III of which reads as follows: "*If the victim has, by his own fault or by his failure to use legal remedies, contributed to the damage, the reparation of the damage may be reduced accordingly or disallowed*".

It appears from the wording of that principle that a break in the chain of causation may depend on conduct exhibiting fault on the part of the injured party and that such conduct, in turn, might also consist in his not having made use of the legal remedies available to him.

—Remedies in damages and administrative remedies: independent or ancillary?

100. If the damage could be avoided by the injured party by means of domestic judicial remedies (for example, by contesting the prejudicial measure incompatible with Community law by invoking *vis-à-vis* the

[100] Judgment in *Mulder and Others*, cited in footnote 77, paragraph 33.

[101] For an application of that principle in the case-law on Article 215, see, *inter alia*, the judgment in Joined Cases 5/66, 7/66 and 13/66 to 24/66 *Kampffmeyer* v. *Commission* [1967] ECR 245, in particular at 265 et seq.; see also the judgment in Case 238/78 *Ireks-Arkady* v. *Council and Commission* [1979] ECR 2955, paragraph 14.

public authorities a right conferred by a provision having direct effect embodied in a directive), it is permissible to ask whether failure to have recourse to such remedies does not break the necessary chain of causation between the breach and the damage.

In other words, the question arises as to whether or not failure to use in time remedies challenging the contested measure precludes the possibility of claiming that the State "in breach of its obligations" is liable. In this sense, apart from being a condition for liability, the prior initiation of substantive remedies could well—equally properly—constitute a requirement for the admissibility of the action for damages.

[1118] 101. That problem is resolved in different ways in the various Member States, on the basis of three discernible different approaches. The first consists in making the various possible actions completely autonomous and hence in leaving it to the interested party to choose the one which he deems most appropriate in order to protect his interests.[102] The second makes an action for damages dependent on bringing an action for annulment.[103] The third is more closely connected with the causal link, in so far as it allows the administration not to answer for such damage as the person concerned could have avoided by employing substantive remedies, in particular an action for annulment.[104]

As we know, after initially taking the view that the action for damages was ancillary,[105] subsequently the Court's case-law on non-contractual liability firmly adopted the stance that such actions were autonomous and could be brought irrespective of the availability to the applicant of other judicial remedies. In particular, the Court has held that "the action for damages under Article 178 and the second paragraph of Article 215 of the Treaty was established as an autonomous form of action with a particular purpose to fulfil within the system of actions and the exercise of it is subject to conditions imposed in view of the specific objective thereof".[106]

102. Those dicta show, in particular, that the autonomous nature of the action for damages satisfies needs by way of guarantee, which needs are connected with the various requirements relating to *locus standi* for bringing an action for annulment as opposed to an action for damages. Under the system of protection provided for in the Treaties, individuals

[102] This is, for example, the solution adopted in the French system.

[103] This is the solution in force, for example, in the Italian and British systems.

[104] This intermediary solution is employed in the German system under the third subparagraph of Paragraph 839 of the Civil Code.

[105] I refer to the judgment in Case 25/62 *Plaumann* v. *Commission* [1963] ECR 95.

[106] Judgment in Joined Cases 197/80 to 200/80, 243/80, 245/80 and 247/80 *Ludwigshafener Walzmühle Erling and Others* v. *Council and Commission* [1981] ECR 3211, paragraph 4. In the same judgment, the Court held that that action (for damages) is "different from an action for annulment in that it does not seek the cancellation of a specified measure but compensation for damage caused by the institutions in the exercise of their functions; the conditions for actions for damages are laid down with that objective in mind and accordingly are different from those for an action for annulment".

may not challenge acts of a general nature and it is very difficult for them to obtain a ruling that the Community institutions have failed to act. The fact that the action for damages has been held to be autonomous therefore enables that to be obtained by means of damages which is not obtainable or, in any event, has not been able to be obtained by means of an action for annulment.

That this is the *rationale* of holding that the action for damages is autonomous is borne out by the fact that it is not available in those few cases in which private persons can actually **[1119]** rely on administrative remedies,[107] in particular in the context of Community staff cases.[108]

103. Essentially, the criterion underlying the case-law laying down the rules on actions for non-contractual liability has remained consistent, apart from the formulas adopted from time to time with regard to domestic remedies (preliminary reference on validity in connection with a challenge to the domestic implementing measure) or direct challenges (action for annulment or for failure to act). The aim is to prevent actions for damages from being utilized in order to pursue the same result which could—effectively, of course—have been attained by means of a different action. Hence, an action for damages cannot be the means of neutralizing the effects of a harmful measure where that objective could also be achieved through a normal action for annulment, whether direct or national via a reference for preliminary ruling on validity to the Court. This is subject to the sole reservation that the (in particular, national) judicial remedy must in any case be capable of securing effective protection.

In the final analysis, the fact that actions for non-contractual liability are autonomous favours private individuals, to whom substantive judicial remedies are normally not available, but not also persons who can effectively invoke such remedies.

104. This means, as far as it is relevant to these proceedings, that the Member States cannot reasonably be debarred from making actions for damages dependent on a previous action for annulment having been brought, if and in so far as the aforementioned condition is also prescribed for similar domestic claims.

Moreover, the idea that the action for damages is ancillary in the case of loss or damage caused by infringements of Community law seems—at least at first sight—to have already received the Court's seal of approval. In *Wagner Miret*, the action for damages was portrayed as the individual's

[107] See the judgment in Case 175/84 *Krohn* v. *Commission* [1986] ECR 753, in which the Court held that an application is inadmissible "where an application for compensation is brought for the payment of an amount precisely equal to the duty which the applicant was required to pay under an individual decision, so that the application seeks in fact the withdrawal of that individual decision" (paragraph 33).

[108] See, for instance, the judgments in Case 346/87 *Bossi* v. *Commission* [1989] ECR 303 and in Case T-27/90 *Latham* v. *Commission* [1991] ECR II-35.

last resort, that is to say, the route to take when it is impossible otherwise to attain a worthwhile result, not even through the interpretation of the national provisions in question by the national court in conformity with the relevant Community provisions.[109]

[1120] 4. *The other conditions*

105. As for the *other conditions* relating to compensation for damage, it should first be recalled that, in *Francovich*, after identifying and defining the conditions "sufficient to give rise to a right on the part of individuals to obtain reparation", the Court went on to state that "subject to that reservation, it is on the basis of the rules of national law on liability that the State must make reparation for the consequences of the damage caused" (paragraph 42).

The interpolation "subject to that reservation" manifestly means that, in relation to the rules on the reparation which is due under Community law itself and arises on the conditions laid down by Community law, the relevant rules of national law *are applicable* only in so far as they are necessary in order to govern the *other conditions* relating to the reparation. It is therefore the detailed rules for effectuating the individual's right to reparation which are governed by national law, in particular the procedural conditions.[110]

106. As regards those conditions, the Court also held in *Francovich* that "In the absence of Community legislation, it is for the internal legal order of each Member State to designate the competent courts and lay down the detailed procedural rules for legal proceedings intended fully to safeguard the rights which individuals derive from Community law" (paragraph 42).

In truth, this is no new formula in the Court's case-law, having in fact usually been associated with the Member States' autonomy in procedural matters, an autonomy which, even in that sector, is not however without limits.

107. In that connection, the Court in *Francovich* emphasized a principle which it had already repeatedly expressed in general terms,[111] namely that "the substantive and procedural conditions for reparation of loss and damage laid down by the national law of the Member States concerning reparation of damage must not be less favourable than those relating to

[109] Judgment cited in footnote 37, paragraph 23.

[110] Thus, for example, in Italy an *ad hoc* measure was adopted by Legislative Decree No 80 of 27 January 1992 (GURI, 13 February 1992, p. 246) in order to give effect to the *Francovich* judgment; that measure lays down the rules and the limits as regards reparation for failure to implement the directive on insolvency of employers. The rules provide in particular that the action for damages should be brought against the INPS (Istituto Nazionale di Previdenza Sociale), that the magistrate acting as an employment court is to have jurisdiction and that the limitation period for bringing the action is one year.

[111] See in particular the judgment in Case 33/76 *Rewe* v. *Landwirtschaftskammer Saarland* [1976] ECR 1989 and, most recently, that in Case C-410/92 *Johnson* [1994] ECR I-5483, paragraph 21.

similar domestic claims and must not be so framed as to make it virtually impossible or excessively difficult to obtain reparation" (paragraph 43).

[1121] Consequently, also with regard to reparation of damage, Community law confines the Member States' freedom to laying down procedural and substantive rules on the *other conditions* relating thereto; here again, this is dependent on the requirement to secure individuals real, effective protection.[112]

108. More specifically, the limit to *national treatment*, in the sense that judicial protection must at least be equal to that available for similar legal positions created by national provisions, may at times turn out to be completely worthless. It is sufficient to mention the very cases under consideration in these proceedings, in which national law lays down *no* relevant provision, since the remedy sought is not available in the national legal systems in question. What is doubtless more relevant and determinative, on account of its potential, is the limit consisting in the fact that the national legal system must not be such as to make it *virtually impossible* to exercise the rights which the national courts are bound to protect by virtue of Community law.

At least two consequences flow from that principle: first, judicial protection, in the case of rights claimed by individuals under Community law, must in any event attain a degree of adequacy; secondly, checking that that level has been attained is a matter for the Court.[113] Whilst it is true, therefore, that it is for the Member States to ensure that Community law is implemented properly, also from the point of view of protection in damages, the Court thereby reserves the right to check the level of adequacy of the protection afforded by the national judicial systems.

[112] On this point, see, for example, to cite just one of the authorities, Barav, "Sanction de la non-transposition de la directive CEE relative à l'insolvabilité de l'employeur", in *La Semaine Juridique*, 1992, Nos 2-3, p. 12; see also Kovar, "Voies de droits ouvertes aux individus devant les instances nationales en cas de violation de normes et décisions du droit communautaire", in *Les recours des individus devant les instances nationales en cas de violation du droit européen*, Brussels, 1978, p. 245 et seq.

[113] This emerges, for example, from the judgment in Case 199/82 *Amministrazione delle Finanze* v. *San Giorgio* [1983] ECR 3595, paragraph 14, where the Court held that "any requirement of proof which has the effect of making it virtually impossible or excessively difficult to secure the repayment of charges levied contrary to Community law would be incompatible with Community law". In addition, the adequacy of judicial protection has been linked with providing a statement of reasons on which administrative measures are based, in the sense that the individual must be enabled to decide whether or not to initiate judicial proceedings to protect his rights; hence the need that the choice should be made in full knowledge of the facts (judgment in Case 222/86 *UNECTEF* v. *Heylens* [1987] ECR 4097, paragraph 15). There is also the judgment in *Dekker*, in which the Court stated that, where the sanction chosen by the Member State for infringement of the principle of equal treatment laid down by a directive is contained within the rules governing an employer's civil liability, any breach of the prohibition of discrimination determines the employer's overall liability, "without there being any possibility of invoking the grounds of exemption provided by national law" (Case C-177/88 *Dekker* [1990] ECR I-3941, paragraph 25). Then again, there is the judgment in *Emmott*, in which the Court held that time-limits for bringing proceedings laid down by the national system do not start to run until such time as the directive conferring the rights in question has been properly transposed (Case C-208/90 *Emmott* v. *Minister for Social Welfare and Attorney General* [1991] ECR I-4269, paragraph 24). However, *Emmott* has been attenuated, from the point of view of relevance to these proceedings, by the judgment in *Johnson*, cited in footnote 111.

109. Lastly, and still with regard to the other conditions of the rules on reparation, there was a discussion in these proceedings in particular of the types of damage or loss for which compensation could be granted and of the quantum of damages. In this connection, given that those questions should in principle **[1122]** be left to the law of the Member States, I shall confine myself to some brief observations.

First, it is all too obvious that reparation of damage may not be merely symbolic, but must correspond to the damage suffered. This requirement, which is linked to the very *raison d'être* of the action for damages, consists precisely in ensuring that the financial situation of the injured party is restored. Moreover, the relevant national case-law, the Community case-law on Article 215[114] and the case-law on international relations[115] support this view.

110. Useful indications in this connection may also be found in a number of judgments in which the Court has checked the level of adequacy of the protection afforded by the national legal systems in relation to rights claimed by individuals under Community law. Thus, for example, with regard to the freedom allowed to Member States as respects sanctions for infringements of the prohibition of sex discrimination, the Court stressed that the sanctions in question have to be "such as to guarantee real and effective judicial protection. . . . It follows that where a Member State chooses to penalize the breach of the prohibition of discrimination by the award of compensation, that compensation must in any event be adequate in relation to the damage sustained".[116]

Further, in *Marshall II*, the Court held that, where a Member State elects to impose a sanction for discrimination in the form of compensation, "such compensation must be full and may not be limited a priori in terms of its amount".[117]

111. Next, it is scarcely necessary to add that identifying the types of damage for which compensation may be granted is certainly not likely to involve major difficulties, not even from the point of view of the uniformity of the compensation payable in different Member States for given damage. Despite variations in terminology, all the national systems hold that compensation may be granted in respect of financial damage suffered by the injured party, which damage certainly covers consequential damage and loss of profits and earnings, together with

[114] See the judgment in *Mulder and Others*, cited in footnote 77, in which the Court expressly held that "the amount of compensation payable by the Community should correspond to the damage which it caused" (paragraph 34).

[115] In this connection, it is worth calling to mind judgment No 17 of the Permanent Court of International Justice of 13 September 1928 also in the *Case concerning the Factory at Chorzów*, in which it was held that "reparation must, as far as possible, wipe out all the consequences of the illegal act and re-establish the situation which would, in all probability, have existed if that act had not been committed" (CPGI, Series A, p. 47).

[116] Judgment in *Von Colson and Kamann*, cited in footnote 36, paragraph 23.

[117] Judgment in Case C-271/91 *Marshall* v. *Southampton and South West Hampshire Area Health Authority (Marshall II)* [1993] ECR I-4367, paragraph 34.

interest thereon. As far, more specifically, as the actual quantification of the damage is concerned, it is only too obvious that this is bound to depend on the different economic and social situations peculiar to each Member State and that it will be up to **[1123]** each State to deal with this in accordance with the criteria laid down in this regard in its own national law.

In the final analysis, what is important for Community law is that compensation must be real and effective and hence that the situation which would have obtained if the infringement had not taken place should be restored, at least in terms of its financial content.

5. *The time from which the obligation to make reparation starts to run*

112. As I have already said, the obligation on Member States to pay compensation cannot be made dependent upon the existence of a judgment of the Court finding that there has been a failure to fulfil the relevant obligation. Consequently, such a judgment, even if one has been given, has no major importance for the purposes of determining the time as from which the State is bound to make reparation for the damage caused by an infringement attributable to it.

Moreover, the conditions suggested in regard to the characteristics of a "manifest and serious" breach make it clear that, if the provision infringed confers identifiable, precise rights on individuals, the obligation in damages on the Member State in breach is bound to arise at the time when the harmful event occurred. The same solution must be adopted where the provision infringed had already been clarified by the case-law at the time when the harmful event occurred. In other cases, where a doubtful legal situation is involved, it will not be until after the national court and/or the Community Court has clarified the matter that the State "in breach" can be obliged to make reparation for the damage, naturally in so far as it does not repair the breach reasonably quickly and only in respect of damage arising after the courts have clarified the situation.

113. Lastly, these proposed solutions lead to the conclusion that there is no reason for limiting the right to reparation to injured parties who have already brought a judicial action or lodged an equivalent claim with the national courts.

I consider that the imperative reasons of legal certainty referred to by the German Government are already sufficiently protected by the fact that the right to compensation may be made subject to the condition—if it is already laid down for similar domestic claims—that the injured party should have taken every step available to him in order to avoid the damage or at least reduce its scale. Apart from this, only the limitation and prescription periods laid down by national law, as in the case of actions for damages based on national law, may determine the time within which individuals **[1124]** may rely on the right to reparation for the damage sustained.

III—*Replies to the National Court's Questions*

114. Before making more specific observations on the cases presently before the Court, I think it is worth recalling the conclusions which I have reached so far:

— in order to secure real, effective protection of rights claimed by individuals under Community law, that law requires that reparation be guaranteed to individuals for the loss or damage sustained by them as a result of infringements of Community law attributable to the State;
— it is completely irrelevant that the infringement in question is attributable to the legislature, as a result of which the restrictive conditions imposed by the national legal system for cases of unlawful action or inaction on the part of the legislature are not applicable;
— in order for the right to reparation to arise it is sufficient that the provision assumedly infringed is precise in all respects and unambiguous, which will be the case, for example, where a Member State fails to fulfil a precise obligation to achieve a result or where it fails to take account of established case-law;
— the criteria relating to the quantification of the damage continue to be governed by national law, provided that they are not less favourable than those applying to similar domestic claims and are not such as to make it excessively difficult or virtually impossible to obtain full compensation for the loss or damage arising as a result of the infringement in question;
— the obligation to make reparation arises at the time when the event which gave rise to the damage occurred in the case of a manifest and serious breach as defined above; otherwise it will not arise until there has been a determination by the national court or the Community Court, in the latter case by means of a preliminary ruling or a judgment given pursuant to Article 169.

(a) *Case C-46/93 (Brasserie du Pêcheur)*

115. What is at issue here is an infringement of a Treaty provision having direct effect, **[1125]** namely Article 30, which is attributable to the legislature in so far as it failed to amend the BiStG to accord with that provision. The appellant in the main proceedings is seeking compensation for damage sustained by it between 1981 and 1987, that is to say, from the time at which it was no longer able to export beer of its manufacture to Germany because, it alleges, that beer did not satisfy the requirements of the BiStG, until the date of the judgment in which

the Court held, by judgment pursuant to Article 169, that that law was incompatible with Article 30.

Having regard to my observations so far, it is only too clear that, in order to decide the case pending before it, the national court has to establish whether the obligation conferred on the States by Article 30—whose content, as I have already mentioned, can certainly not be regarded as precise and determinable in every respect—had already been clarified by the relevant case-law at the time when the damage occurred with respect to facts such as those of the case pending before it. In other words, it has to be ascertained whether it was clear already in late 1981 that a law such as the BiStG embodied an unjustified obstacle to activities of traders in the sector and was hence incompatible with Community law.

116. To that end, it should first be recalled that, ever since the well-known "Cassis de Dijon" judgment,[118] hence since February 1979, it has been clear that Article 30 prohibits, not only discriminatory measures, but also measures which are applicable without distinction and unjustified by imperative requirements. On top of this, by judgment of 9 September 1981,[119] which therefore was delivered more or less at the same time as the appellant in the main proceedings was obliged to stop exporting beer to Germany, the Court found that national legislation restricting the designation "vinegar" to wine vinegar was incompatible with Community law. Certainly, there is no ground for considering that a different view had to be taken with regard to the BiStG in so far as it restricted the description "beer" to beer produced using the ingredients mandatorily prescribed by that law.

However, it also transpires from the order for reference that the beer produced by the appellant contained additives, whereas the German law in question laid down an absolute prohibition on marketing beer containing additives in Germany. Whilst it is true that by the judgment of 12 March 1987 in *Commission* v. *Germany* the Court held that the legislation in question was unlawful also from that point of view in so far as it was not justified by the requirement of protecting human health, it is also true that that conclusion could not be regarded as automatic, having regard to the relevant case-law.[120] **[1126]** If the damage complained

[118] Judgment of 20 February 1979 in Case 120/78 *Rewe-Zentral* v. *Bundesmonopol für Branntwein* [1979] ECR 649.

[119] Case 193/80 *Commission* v. *Italy* [1981] ECR 3019, paragraphs 24 to 28.

[120] For example, in the judgment of 6 May 1986 in Case 304/84 *Ministère Public* v. *Muller* [1986] ECR 1511, the Court held that it was for the Member States to "consider, in the context of factual assessments which they must undertake in that regard, whether the marketing of foodstuffs containing additives may present a risk to public health and whether there is a real need for the additives in the particular foodstuffs. In applying those criteria they must take account of the results of international scientific research and in particular of the work of the Community's Scientific Committee for Food viewed *in the light of the eating habits prevailing in the importing Member State*" (paragraph 24, my emphasis). In that judgment, which was delivered a good five years after the harmful event complained of by the appellant in the main proceedings, the Court therefore held

of by the appellant is connected rather with this second aspect of the national legislation in question, a different solution cannot therefore be ruled out.

117. One final observation. I have already mentioned that a Member State is entitled—for the purposes of the right to reparation and provided that it lays down the same conditions for similar domestic claims—to require the injured party to show diligence and hence to set in train such mechanisms as may obviate or at least reduce the damage.

It appears from the documents in the case that it does not seem that the appellant has taken any such steps. Admittedly, as the appellant showed in these proceedings, it stopped exporting because of failure to renew the distribution contract with its (German) sole importer, which meant that it was substantively impossible for it to challenge any measure. Consequently, it is manifestly for the national court to ascertain whether the appellant was actually precluded from being able in any way to rely on Article 30 directly before the national courts.

(b) *Case C-48/93 (Factortame III)*

118. In contrast, in the *Factortame* case the national court has to ascertain whether the infringement which has been found of Articles 7, 52 and 221 of the Treaty and is attributable to the legislature for having passed a national law incompatible with those articles, may be regarded as a manifest and serious breach in the sense defined above.

In other words, it is a question of establishing whether the infringement of provisions conferring clear, precise rights on individuals, such as the right not to be discriminated against on grounds of nationality, is such, despite the discretion available to the Member States in adopting measures relating to the common fisheries policy, as to cause the State to incur liability. In this respect, I consider that a few observations will suffice.

[1127] 119. Whilst it is true, as the United Kingdom has shown, that the Member States have a certain margin of discretion in adopting measures relating to the common fisheries policy, it is also true that that discretion is normally exercised under the constant supervision of the Commission, to which the Member States are obliged to communicate measures adopted by them. In this case, as transpires from the documents in the case, the Commission informed the United Kingdom in good time that the nationality, residence and domicile conditions laid down by the Merchant Shipping Act 1988 for the registration of fishing vessels in the new shipping register had to be regarded as incompatible with Community law.

that Articles 30 and 36 did not preclude national legislation prohibiting the marketing of foodstuffs imported from other Member States, in which they were lawfully sold, which contained particular additives.

What is more, the Court's case-law on the right of establishment is consistent in holding that national measures involving discrimination on grounds of nationality are incompatible with national law; likewise, the Court has held incompatible with Community law the very residence condition imposed on fishing vessels' crews.[121] Lastly, in so far as the legislation in question related to the registration of fishing vessels, its purpose was not to lay down detailed rules on the exploitation of the national fishing quotas and hence could not even be regarded as being justified on that ground.

120. In the final analysis, I do not consider that there can be any doubts as to the manifest and serious nature of the breach in question and hence as to the right to compensation of individuals who suffered damage as a result of it.

Finally, I would observe that, as the Court is well aware, the applicants in the main proceedings have done everything possible in order to avert the damage which eventually occurred. They took steps to that end even before the national provisions subsequently declared incompatible with Community law entered into force, by seeking and obtaining an interlocutory injunction suspending the application of the provisions at issue, the injunction which was set aside by the Court of Appeal and subsequently confirmed by the House of Lords following this Court's judgment of 19 June 1990 in *Factortame I*.

121. As far as the national court's second question is concerned, it is scarcely necessary to recall in the light of my earlier observations that the determination of the types of loss or damage for which damages may be awarded and the quantification of the damages continue to be governed by national law, but must, in any event, be such as to make full reparation for the loss or damage suffered by the injured parties.

[1128] However, the applicants also claim exemplary damages, as provided for by national law for unconstitutional conduct on the part of the administrative authorities, and this warrants separate consideration. Suffice it to observe in this connection that, in accordance with the principle that the conditions imposed by national rules in order to protect legal situations created by Community law may not be less favourable than those applying to similar domestic claims, a Member State is bound to grant that type of damages to the individuals concerned where the preconditions laid down by the relevant national rules are satisfied; this is

[121] Judgment in Case C-3/87 *The Queen* v. *Ministry of Agriculture, Fisheries and Food*, ex parte *Agegate* [1989] ECR I-4459, paragraphs 22 to 26. Whilst, admittedly, that judgment was delivered after the Merchant Shipping Act entered into force, equally it antedated the judgment in *Factortame II*, following which the House of Lords upheld the interim measures requested by the applicants. Moreover, in that case what was involved was a condition imposed so that fishing vessels could count their catches against the national fishing quotas, whereas in the instant case that which is at issue is a measure simply preventing the registration of fishing boats and hence the actual exercise of freedom of establishment.

so, therefore, even where the head of damages in question is completely unknown to the legal systems of the other Member States.

Conclusion

122. In the light of the foregoing considerations, I therefore propose that the Court should reply as follows to the questions raised in the respective cases by the Bundesgerichtshof and the High Court of Justice, Queen's Bench Division, Divisional Court:

(a) *In Case C-46/93 (Brasserie du Pêcheur)*:

1. A Member State is bound to make reparation for the loss or damage occasioned to individuals as a result of infringements of Community law attributable to that State, even where the infringement consists in the fact that the legislature omitted to amend a national law so as to bring it into conformity with Community law, provided that the obligation imposed on the State from which the individual's right is derived is precise in every respect or has been clearly specified by the relevant case-law.
2. A Member State is not entitled to make the right to reparation for infringements of Community law subject to the same restrictions laid down for infringements of national constitutional provisions by the legislature where those restrictions have the effect of making the right to reparation virtually impossible.

[1129] 3. The obligation on the part of the State to make reparation may not be made to depend on finding a subjective component (fault or intention) accompanying the infringement of the provision, if the breach was manifest and serious in the sense explained above.

4. (a) It is for the national legal system to determine the types of injury for which reparation may be awarded and the criteria for quantifying the loss or damage, provided that the requirements laid down to that end are not less favourable than those applying to similar domestic claims and are not such as to make it excessively difficult or virtually impossible for the individual to obtain full reparation for the loss or damage suffered; this would be the case where national law limited the scope of the obligation to legal interests, such as property, yet excluded any possibility of obtaining reparation for lost profits.
   (b) The obligation on the Member State to make reparation for loss or damage occasioned to individuals arises at the time when the event which caused the damage occurred if the provision infringed is clear in the sense specified above or, where the legal situation is doubtful, at the time when it was clarified by Community case-law, either by a preliminary ruling or by a judgment pursuant to Article 169.

(b) *Case C-48/93 (Factortame III)*:

1. A Member State is bound to make reparation for the loss or damage occasioned to individuals as a result of infringements of Community law

attributable to that State, even where the infringement consists in the fact that the legislature passed a national law incompatible with Community law, provided that the obligation imposed on the State from which the individual's right is derived is, as in the case at issue, precise in every respect or has been clearly specified by the relevant case-law.

[1130] 2. It is for the national legal system to determine the types of injury for which reparation may be awarded and the criteria for quantifying the loss or damage, provided that the requirements laid down to that end are not less favourable than those applying to similar domestic claims and are not such as to make it excessively difficult or virtually impossible for the individual to obtain full reparation for the loss or damage suffered. Where the national legal system also provides for the award of exemplary damages, the relevant rules must therefore be applied, without any discrimination, even where rights asserted by individuals under Community law were infringed.

JUDGMENT OF THE COURT

5 March 1996*

[1134] 1. By orders of 28 January 1993 and 18 November 1992, received at the Court on 17 February 1993 and 18 February 1993, respectively, the Bundesgerichtshof (Federal Court of Justice) (Case C-46/93) and the High Court of Justice, Queen's **[1135]** Bench Division, Divisional Court (Case C-48/93) referred to the Court for a preliminary ruling under Article 177 of the EEC Treaty questions concerning the conditions under which a Member State may incur liability for damage caused to individuals by breaches of Community law attributable to that State.

2. The questions were raised in two sets of proceedings between, on the one hand, Brasserie du Pêcheur SA and the Federal Republic of Germany and, on the other, Factortame Ltd and others (hereinafter "Factortame") and the United Kingdom of Great Britain and Northern Ireland.

Case C-46/93

3. Before the national court, Brasserie du Pêcheur, a French company based at Schiltigheim (Alsace), claims that it was forced to discontinue exports of beer to Germany in late 1981 because the competent German authorities considered that the beer it produced did not comply with the Reinheitsgebot (purity requirement) laid down in Paragraphs 9 and 10 of the Biersteuergesetz of 14 March 1952 (Law on Beer Duty, BGBl. I, p. 149), in the version dated 14 December 1976 (BGBl. I, p. 3341, hereinafter "the BStG").

* Languages of the cases: English and German.

4. The Commission took the view that those provisions were contrary to Article 30 of the EEC Treaty and brought infringement proceedings against the Federal Republic of Germany on two grounds, namely the prohibition on marketing under the designation "Bier" (beer) beers lawfully manufactured by different methods in other Member States and the prohibition on importing beers containing additives. By judgment of 12 March 1987 in Case 178/84 *Commission* v. *Germany* [1987] ECR 1227, the Court held that the prohibition on marketing beers imported from other Member States which did not comply with the provisions in question was incompatible with Article 30 of the Treaty.

[1136] 5. Brasserie du Pêcheur consequently brought an action against the Federal Republic of Germany for reparation of the loss suffered by it as a result of that import restriction between 1981 and 1987, seeking damages in the sum of DM 1,800,000, representing a fraction of the loss actually incurred.

6. The Bundesgerichtshof refers to Paragraph 839 of the Bürgerliches Gesetzbuch (German Civil Code, "the BGB") and Article 34 of the Grundgesetz (Basic Law, "the GG"). According to the first sentence of Paragraph 839 of the BGB, "If an official wilfully or negligently commits a breach of official duty incumbent upon him as against a third party, he shall compensate the third party for any damage arising therefrom." Article 34 of the GG provides that "If a person infringes, in the exercise of a public office entrusted to him, the obligations incumbent upon him as against a third party, liability therefor shall attach in principle to the State or to the body in whose service he is engaged."

7. If those provisions are read together, it appears that, in order for the State to be liable, the third party must be capable of being regarded as beneficiary of the obligation breached, which means that the State is liable for breach only of obligations conceived in favour of a third party. However, as the Bundesgerichtshof points out, in the case of the BStG the task assumed by the national legislature concerns only the public at large and is not directed towards any particular person or class of persons who could be regarded as "third parties" within the meaning of the provisions mentioned above.

8. In this context, the Bundesgerichtshof has referred the following questions to the Court for a preliminary ruling:

1. Does the principle of Community law according to which Member States are obliged to pay compensation for damage suffered by an individual as a result of breaches of Community law attributable to those States also apply where such a breach consists of a failure to adapt a national parliamentary statute to the higher-ranking rules of Community law (this case concerning a failure to adapt **[1137]** Paragraphs 9 and 10 of the German Biersteuergesetz to Article 30 of the EEC Treaty)?

2. May the national legal system provide that any entitlement to compensation is to be subject to the same limitations as those applying where a national

statute breaches higher-ranking national law, for example where an ordinary Federal law breaches the Grundgesetz of the Federal Republic of Germany?

3. May the national legal system provide that entitlement to compensation is to be conditional on fault (intent or negligence) on the part of the organs of the State responsible for the failure to adapt the legislation?

4. If Question 1 is to be answered in the affirmative and Question 2 in the negative:

(a) May liability to pay compensation under the national legal system be limited to the reparation of damage done to specific individual legal interests, for example property, or does it require full compensation for all financial losses, including lost profits?

(b) Does the obligation to pay compensation also require reparation of the damage already incurred before it was held in the judgment of the European Court of Justice of 12 March 1987 in Case 178/84 *Commission* v. *Germany* [1987] ECR 1227 that Paragraph 10 of the German Biersteuergesetz infringed higher-ranking Community law?

[1138] *Case C-48/93*

9. On 16 December 1988 Factortame and others, being individuals and companies incorporated under the laws of the United Kingdom, together with the directors and shareholders of those companies, brought an action before the High Court of Justice, Queen's Bench Division, Divisional Court (hereinafter "the Divisional Court"), in which they challenged the compatibility of Part II of the Merchant Shipping Act 1988 with Community law, in particular Article 52 of the EEC Treaty. That act entered into force on 1 December 1988, subject to a transitional period expiring on 31 March 1989. It provided for the introduction of a new register for British fishing boats and made registration of such vessels, including those already registered in the former register, subject to certain conditions relating to the nationality, residence and domicile of the owners. Fishing boats ineligible for registration in the new register were deprived of the right to fish.

10. In answer to questions referred by the Divisional Court, the Court held by judgment of 25 July 1991 in Case C-221/89 *Factortame II* [1991] ECR I-3905 that conditions relating to the nationality, residence and domicile of vessel owners and operators as laid down by the registration system introduced by the United Kingdom were contrary to Community law, but that it was not contrary to Community law to stipulate as a condition for registration that the vessels in question must be managed and their operations directed and controlled from within the United Kingdom.

11. On 4 August 1989 the Commission brought infringement proceedings against the United Kingdom. In parallel, it applied for interim measures ordering the suspension of the abovementioned nationality conditions on the ground that they were contrary to Articles

7, 52 and 221 of the EEC Treaty. By order of 10 October 1989 in Case 246/89 R *Commission* v. *United Kingdom* [1989] ECR 3125, the President of the Court granted that application. Pursuant to that order, the United Kingdom adopted provisions amending the new registration system with effect from 2 November 1989. By judgment of 4 October 1991 in Case C-246/89 *Commission* v. *United Kingdom* [1991] ECR I-4585, the Court confirmed that the registration **[1139]** conditions challenged in the infringement proceedings were contrary to Community law.

12. Meanwhile, on 2 October 1991, the Divisional Court made an order designed to give effect to this Court's judgment of 25 July 1991 in *Factortame II* and, at the same time, directed the claimants to give detailed particulars of their claims for damages. Subsequently, the claimants provided the national court with a detailed statement of their various heads of claim, covering expenses and losses incurred between 1 April 1989, when the legislation at issue entered into force, and 2 November 1989, when it was repealed.

13. Lastly, by order of 18 November 1992, the Divisional Court gave Rawlings (Trawling) Ltd, the 37th claimant in Case C-48/93, leave to amend its claim to include a claim for exemplary damages for unconstitutional behaviour on the part of the public authorities.

14. In that context, the Divisional Court referred the following questions to the Court for a preliminary ruling:

1. In all the circumstances of this case, where:

(a) a Member State's legislation laid down conditions relating to the nationality, domicile and residence of the owners and managers of fishing vessels, and of the shareholders and directors in vessel-owning and managing companies, and

[1140] (b) such conditions were held by the Court of Justice in Cases C-221/89 and C-246/89 to infringe Articles 5, 7, 52 and 221 of the EEC Treaty,

are those persons who were owners or managers of such vessels, or directors and/or shareholders in vessel-owning and managing companies, entitled as a matter of Community law to compensation by that Member State for losses which they have suffered as a result of all or any of the above infringements of the EEC Treaty?

2. If Question 1 is answered in the affirmative, what considerations, if any, does Community law require the national court to apply in determining claims for damages and interest relating to:

(a) expenses and/or loss of profit and/or loss of income during the period subsequent to the entry into force of the said conditions, during which the vessels were forced to lay up, to make alternative arrangements for fishing and/or to seek registration elsewhere;

(b) losses consequent on sales at an undervalue of the vessels, or of shares therein, or of shares in vessel-owning companies;

(c) losses consequent on the need to provide bonds, fines and legal expenses for alleged offences connected with the exclusion of vessels from the national register;

(d) losses consequent on the inability of such persons to own and operate further vessels;
(e) loss of management fees;
[1141] (f) expenses incurred in an attempt to mitigate the above losses;
(g) exemplary damages as claimed?

15. Reference is made to the Report for the Hearing for a fuller account of the facts of the main proceedings, the procedure and the observations submitted to the Court, which are mentioned or discussed hereinafter only in so far as is necessary for the reasoning of the Court.

State Liability for Acts and Omissions of the National Legislature Contrary to Community Law (First Question in both Case C-46/93 and Case C-48/93)

16. By their first questions, each of the two national courts essentially seeks to establish whether the principle that Member States are obliged to make good damage caused to individuals by breaches of Community law attributable to the State is applicable where the national legislature was responsible for the infringement in question.

17. In Joined Cases C-6/90 and C-9/90 *Francovich and Others* [1991] ECR I-5357, paragraph 37, the Court held that it is a principle of Community law that Member States are obliged to make good loss and damage caused to individuals by breaches of Community law for which they can be held responsible.

[1142] 18. The German, Irish and Netherlands Governments contend that Member States are required to make good loss or damage caused to individuals only where the provisions breached are not directly effective: in *Francovich and Others* the Court simply sought to fill a lacuna in the system for safeguarding rights of individuals. In so far as national law affords individuals a right of action enabling them to assert their rights under directly effective provisions of Community law, it is unnecessary, where such provisions are breached, also to grant them a right to reparation founded directly on Community law.

19. That argument cannot be accepted.

20. The Court has consistently held that the right of individuals to rely on the directly effective provisions of the Treaty before national courts is only a minimum guarantee and is not sufficient in itself to ensure the full and complete implementation of the Treaty (see, in particular, Case 168/85 *Commission* v. *Italy* [1986] ECR 2945, paragraph 11, Case C-120/88 *Commission* v. *Italy* [1991] ECR I-621, paragraph 10, and C-119/89 *Commission* v. *Spain* [1991] ECR I-641, paragraph 9). The purpose of that right is to ensure that provisions of Community law prevail over national provisions. It cannot, in every case, secure for individuals the benefit of the rights conferred on them by Community law

and, in particular, avoid their sustaining damage as a result of a breach of Community law attributable to a Member State. As appears from paragraph 33 of the judgment in *Francovich and Others*, the full effectiveness of Community law would be impaired if individuals were unable to obtain redress when their rights were infringed by a breach of Community law.

21. This will be so where an individual who is a victim of the non-transposition of a directive and is precluded from relying on certain of its provisions directly before the national court because they are insufficiently precise and unconditional, brings an action for damages against the defaulting Member State for breach of the third paragraph of Article 189 of the Treaty. In such circumstances, which obtained in the case of *Francovich and Others*, the purpose of reparation is to redress the injurious **[1143]** consequences of a Member State's failure to transpose a directive as far as beneficiaries of that directive are concerned.

22. It is all the more so in the event of infringement of a right directly conferred by a Community provision upon which individuals are entitled to rely before the national courts. In that event, the right to reparation is the necessary corollary of the direct effect of the Community provision whose breach caused the damage sustained.

23. In this case, it is undisputed that the Community provisions at issue, namely Article 30 of the Treaty in Case C-46/93 and Article 52 in Case C-48/93, have direct effect in the sense that they confer on individuals rights upon which they are entitled to rely directly before the national courts. Breach of such provisions may give rise to reparation.

24. The German Government further submits that a general right to reparation for individuals could be created only by legislation and that for such a right to be recognized by judicial decision would be incompatible with the allocation of powers as between the Community institutions and the Member States and with the institutional balance established by the Treaty.

25. It must, however, be stressed that the existence and extent of State liability for damage ensuing as a result of a breach of obligations incumbent on the State by virtue of Community law are questions of Treaty interpretation which fall within the jurisdiction of the Court.

26. In this case, as in *Francovich and Others*, those questions of interpretation have been referred to the Court by national courts pursuant to Article 177 of the Treaty.

[1144] 27. Since the Treaty contains no provision expressly and specifically governing the consequences of breaches of Community law by Member States, it is for the Court, in pursuance of the task conferred on it by Article 164 of the Treaty of ensuring that in the interpretation and application of the Treaty the law is observed, to rule on such a question in accordance with generally accepted methods of interpretation, in particular by reference to the fundamental principles of the Community legal system and, where necessary, general principles common to the legal systems of the Member States.

28. Indeed, it is to the general principles common to the laws of the Member States that the second paragraph of Article 215 of the Treaty refers as the basis of the non-contractual liability of the Community for damage caused by its institutions or by its servants in the performance of their duties.

29. The principle of the non-contractual liability of the Community expressly laid down in Article 215 of the Treaty is simply an expression of the general principle familiar to the legal systems of the Member States that an unlawful act or omission gives rise to an obligation to make good the damage caused. That provision also reflects the obligation on public authorities to make good damage caused in the performance of their duties.

30. In any event, in many national legal systems the essentials of the legal rules governing State liability have been developed by the courts.

31. In view of the foregoing considerations, the Court held in *Francovich and Others*, at paragraph 35, that the principle of State liability for loss and damage caused to individuals as a result of breaches of Community law for which it can be held responsible is inherent in the system of the Treaty.

[1145] 32. It follows that that principle holds good for any case in which a Member State breaches Community law, whatever be the organ of the State whose act or omission was responsible for the breach.

33. In addition, in view of the fundamental requirement of the Community legal order that Community law be uniformly applied (see, in particular, Joined Cases C-143/88 and C-92/89 *Zuckerfabrik Süderdithmarschen and Zuckerfabrik Soest* [1991] ECR I-415, paragraph 26), the obligation to make good damage caused to individuals by breaches of Community law cannot depend on domestic rules as to the division of powers between constitutional authorities.

34. As the Advocate General points out in paragraph 38 of his Opinion, in international law a State whose liability for breach of an international commitment is in issue will be viewed as a single entity, irrespective of whether the breach which gave rise to the damage is attributable to the legislature, the judiciary or the executive. This must apply *a fortiori* in the Community legal order since all State authorities, including the legislature, are bound in performing their tasks to comply with the rules laid down by Community law directly governing the situation of individuals.

35. The fact that, according to national rules, the breach complained of is attributable to the legislature cannot affect the requirements inherent in the protection of the rights of individuals who rely on Community law and, in this instance, the right to obtain redress in the national courts for damage caused by that breach.

36. Consequently, the reply to the national courts must be that the principle that Member States are obliged to make good damage caused to individuals by breaches of Community law attributable to the State is applicable where the national legislature was responsible for the breach in question.

[1146] *Conditions under which the State may Incur Liability for Acts and Omissions of the National Legislature Contrary to Community Law (Second Question in Case C-46/93 and First Question in Case C-48/93)*

37. By these questions, the national courts ask the Court to specify the conditions under which a right to reparation of loss or damage caused to individuals by breaches of Community law attributable to a Member State is, in the particular circumstances, guaranteed by Community law.

38. Although Community law imposes State liability, the conditions under which that liability gives rise to a right to reparation depend on the nature of the breach of Community law giving rise to the loss and damage (*Francovich and Others*, paragraph 38).

39. In order to determine those conditions, account should first be taken of the principles inherent in the Community legal order which form the basis for State liability, namely, first, the full effectiveness of Community rules and the effective protection of the rights which they confer and, second, the obligation to cooperate imposed on Member States by Article 5 of the Treaty (*Francovich and Others*, paragraphs 31 to 36).

40. In addition, as the Commission and the several governments which submitted observations have emphasized, it is pertinent to refer to the Court's case-law on non-contractual liability on the part of the Community.

41. First, the second paragraph of Article 215 of the Treaty refers, as regards the non-contractual liability of the Community, to the general principles common to the **[1147]** laws of the Member States, from which, in the absence of written rules, the Court also draws inspiration in other areas of Community law.

42. Second, the conditions under which the State may incur liability for damage caused to individuals by a breach of Community law cannot, in the absence of particular justification, differ from those governing the liability of the Community in like circumstances. The protection of the rights which individuals derive from Community law cannot vary depending on whether a national authority or a Community authority is responsible for the damage.

43. The system of rules which the Court has worked out with regard to Article 215 of the Treaty, particularly in relation to liability for legislative measures, takes into account, *inter alia*, the complexity of the situations to be regulated, difficulties in the application or interpretation of the texts

and, more particularly, the margin of discretion available to the author of the act in question.

44. Thus, in developing its case-law on the non-contractual liability of the Community, in particular as regards legislative measures involving choices of economic policy, the Court has had regard to the wide discretion available to the institutions in implementing Community policies.

45. The strict approach taken towards the liability of the Community in the exercise of its legislative activities is due to two considerations. First, even where the legality of measures is subject to judicial review, exercise of the legislative function must not be hindered by the prospect of actions for damages whenever the general interest of the Community requires legislative measures to be adopted which may adversely affect individual interests. Second, in a legislative context characterized **[1148]** by the exercise of a wide discretion, which is essential for implementing a Community policy, the Community cannot incur liability unless the institution concerned has manifestly and gravely disregarded the limits on the exercise of its powers (Joined Cases 83/76, 94/76, 4/77, 15/77 and 40/77 *HNL and Others* v. *Council and Commission* [1978] ECR 1209, paragraphs 5 and 6).

46. That said, the national legislature—like the Community institutions—does not systematically have a wide discretion when it acts in a field governed by Community law. Community law may impose upon it obligations to achieve a particular result or obligations to act or refrain from acting which reduce its margin of discretion, sometimes to a considerable degree. This is so, for instance, where, as in the circumstances to which the judgment in *Francovich and Others* relates, Article 189 of the Treaty places the Member State under an obligation to take, within a given period, all the measures needed in order to achieve the result required by a directive. In such a case, the fact that it is for the national legislature to take the necessary measures has no bearing on the Member State's liability for failing to transpose the directive.

47. In contrast, where a Member State acts in a field where it has a wide discretion, comparable to that of the Community institutions in implementing Community policies, the conditions under which it may incur liability must, in principle, be the same as those under which the Community institutions incur liability in a comparable situation.

48. In the case which gave rise to the reference in Case C-46/93, the German legislature had legislated in the field of foodstuffs, specifically beer. In the absence of Community harmonization, the national legislature had a wide discretion in that sphere in laying down rules on the quality of beer put on the market.

[1149] 49. As regards the facts of Case C-48/93, the United Kingdom legislature also had a wide discretion. The legislation at issue was concerned, first, with the registration of vessels, a field which, in view of the state of development of Community law, falls within the jurisdiction of the Member States and, secondly, with regulating fishing, a sector in which implementation of the common fisheries policy leaves a margin of discretion to the Member States.

50. Consequently, in each case the German and United Kingdom legislatures were faced with situations involving choices comparable to those made by the Community institutions when they adopt legislative measures pursuant to a Community policy.

51. In such circumstances, Community law confers a right to reparation where three conditions are met: the rule of law infringed must be intended to confer rights on individuals; the breach must be sufficiently serious; and there must be a direct causal link between the breach of the obligation resting on the State and the damage sustained by the injured parties.

52. Firstly, those conditions satisfy the requirements of the full effectiveness of the rules of Community law and of the effective protection of the rights which those rules confer.

53. Secondly, those conditions correspond in substance to those defined by the Court in relation to Article 215 in its case-law on liability of the Community for damage caused to individuals by unlawful legislative measures adopted by its institutions.

[1150] 54. The first condition is manifestly satisfied in the case of Article 30 of the Treaty, the relevant provision in Case C-46/93, and in the case of Article 52, the relevant provision in Case C-48/93. Whilst Article 30 imposes a prohibition on Member States, it nevertheless gives rise to rights for individuals which the national courts must protect (Case 74/76 *Iannelli & Volpi* v. *Meroni* [1977] ECR 557, paragraph 13). Likewise, the essence of Article 52 is to confer rights on individuals (Case 2/74 *Reyners* [1974] ECR 631, paragraph 25).

55. As to the second condition, as regards both Community liability under Article 215 and Member State liability for breaches of Community law, the decisive test for finding that a breach of Community law is sufficiently serious is whether the Member State or the Community institution concerned manifestly and gravely disregarded the limits on its discretion.

56. The factors which the competent court may take into consideration include the clarity and precision of the rule breached, the measure of discretion left by that rule to the national or Community authorities, whether the infringement and the damage caused was intentional or involuntary, whether any error of law was excusable or inexcusable, the fact that the position taken by a Community institution may have contributed towards the omission, and the adoption or retention of national measures or practices contrary to Community law.

57. On any view, a breach of Community law will clearly be sufficiently serious if it has persisted despite a judgment finding the infringement in question to be established, or a preliminary ruling or settled case-law of the Court on the matter from which it is clear that the conduct in question constituted an infringement.

[1151] 58. While, in the present cases, the Court cannot substitute its assessment for that of the national courts, which have sole jurisdiction to find the facts in the main proceedings and decide how to characterize the breaches of Community law at issue, it will be helpful to indicate a number of circumstances which the national courts might take into account.

59. In Case C-46/93 a distinction should be drawn between the question of the German legislature's having maintained in force provisions of the Biersteuergesetz concerning the purity of beer prohibiting the marketing under the designation "Bier" of beers imported from other Member States which were lawfully produced in conformity with different rules, and the question of the retention of the provisions of that same law prohibiting the import of beers containing additives. As regards the provisions of the German legislation relating to the designation of the product marketed, it would be difficult to regard the breach of Article 30 by that legislation as an excusable error, since the incompatibility of such rules with Article 30 was manifest in the light of earlier decisions of the Court, in particular Case 120/78 *Rewe-Zentral* [1979] ECR 649 ("Cassis de Dijon") and Case 193/80 *Commission* v. *Italy* [1981] ECR 3019 ("vinegar"). In contrast, having regard to the relevant case-law, the criteria available to the national legislature to determine whether the prohibition of the use of additives was contrary to Community law were significantly less conclusive until the Court's judgment of 12 March 1987 in *Commission* v. *Germany*, cited above, in which the Court held that prohibition to be incompatible with Article 30.

60. A number of observations may likewise be made about the national legislation at issue in Case C-48/93.

61. The decision of the United Kingdom legislature to introduce in the Merchant Shipping Act 1988 provisions relating to the conditions for the registration of fishing vessels has to be assessed differently in the case of the provisions making registration subject to a nationality condition, which constitute direct discrimination **[1152]** manifestly contrary to Community law, and in the case of the provisions laying down residence and domicile conditions for vessel owners and operators.

62. The latter conditions are prima facie incompatible with Article 52 of the Treaty in particular, but the United Kingdom sought to justify them in terms of the objectives of the common fisheries policy. In the judgment in *Factortame II*, cited above, the Court rejected that justification.

63. In order to determine whether the breach of Article 52 thus committed by the United Kingdom was sufficiently serious, the national court

might take into account, *inter alia*, the legal disputes relating to particular features of the common fisheries policy, the attitude of the Commission, which made its position known to the United Kingdom in good time, and the assessments as to the state of certainty of Community law made by the national courts in the interim proceedings brought by individuals affected by the Merchant Shipping Act.

64. Lastly, consideration should be given to the assertion made by Rawlings (Trawling) Ltd, the 37th claimant in Case C-48/93, that the United Kingdom failed to adopt immediately the measures needed to comply with the Order of the President of the Court of 10 October 1989 in *Commission* v. *United Kingdom*, cited above, and that this needlessly increased the loss it sustained. If this allegation—which was certainly contested by the United Kingdom at the hearing—should prove correct, it should be regarded by the national court as constituting in itself a manifest and, therefore, sufficiently serious breach of Community law.

65. As for the third condition, it is for the national courts to determine whether there is a direct causal link between the breach of the obligation borne by the State and the damage sustained by the injured parties.

[1153] 66. The aforementioned three conditions are necessary and sufficient to found a right in individuals to obtain redress, although this does not mean that the State cannot incur liability under less strict conditions on the basis of national law.

67. As appears from paragraphs 41, 42 and 43 of *Francovich and Others*, cited above, subject to the right to reparation which flows directly from Community law where the conditions referred to in the preceding paragraph are satisfied, the State must make reparation for the consequences of the loss and damage caused in accordance with the domestic rules on liability, provided that the conditions for reparation of loss and damage laid down by national law must not be less favourable than those relating to similar domestic claims and must not be such as in practice to make it impossible or excessively difficult to obtain reparation (see also Case 199/82 *Amministrazione delle Finanze dello Stato* v. *San Giorgio* [1983] ECR 3595).

68. In that regard, restrictions that exist in domestic legal systems as to the non-contractual liability of the State in the exercise of its legislative function may be such as to make it impossible in practice or excessively difficult for individuals to exercise their right to reparation, as guaranteed by Community law, of loss or damage resulting from the breach of Community law.

69. In Case C-46/93 the national court asks in particular whether national law may subject any right to compensation to the same restrictions as apply where a law is in breach of higher-ranking national provisions, for instance, where an ordinary Federal law infringes the Grundgesetz of the Federal Republic of Germany.

70. While the imposition of such restrictions may be consistent with the requirement that the conditions laid down should not be less favourable than those relating to **[1154]** similar domestic claims, it is still to be considered whether such restrictions are not such as in practice to make it impossible or excessively difficult to obtain reparation.

71. The condition imposed by German law where a law is in breach of higher-ranking national provisions, which makes reparation dependent upon the legislature's act or omission being referable to an individual situation, would in practice make it impossible or extremely difficult to obtain effective reparation for loss or damage resulting from a breach of Community law, since the tasks falling to the national legislature relate, in principle, to the public at large and not to identifiable persons or classes of person.

72. Since such a condition stands in the way of the obligation on national courts to ensure the full effectiveness of Community law by guaranteeing effective protection for the rights of individuals, it must be set aside where an infringement of Community law is attributable to the national legislature.

73. Likewise, any condition that may be imposed by English law on State liability requiring proof of misfeasance in public office, such an abuse of power being inconceivable in the case of the legislature, is also such as in practice to make it impossible or extremely difficult to obtain effective reparation for loss or damage resulting from a breach of Community law where the breach is attributable to the national legislature.

74. Accordingly, the reply to the questions from the national courts must be that, where a breach of Community law by a Member State is attributable to the national legislature acting in a field in which it has a wide discretion to make legislative choices, individuals suffering loss or injury thereby are entitled to reparation where the rule of Community law breached is intended to confer rights upon them, the breach is sufficiently serious and there is a direct causal link between the **[1155]** breach and the damage sustained by the individuals. Subject to that reservation, the State must make good the consequences of the loss or damage caused by the breach of Community law attributable to it, in accordance with its national law on liability. However, the conditions laid down by the applicable national laws must not be less favourable than those relating to similar domestic claims or framed in such a way as in practice to make it impossible or excessively difficult to obtain reparation.

The Possibility of Making Reparation Conditional upon the Existence of Fault (Third Question in Case C-46/93)

75. By its third question, the Bundesgerichtshof essentially seeks to establish whether, pursuant to the national legislation which it applies,

the national court is entitled to make reparation conditional upon the existence of fault (whether intentional or negligent) on the part of the organ of the State to which the infringement is attributable.

76. As is clear from the case-file, the concept of fault does not have the same content in the various legal systems.

77. Next, it follows from the reply to the preceding question that, where a breach of Community law is attributable to a Member State acting in a field in which it has a wide discretion to make legislative choices, a finding of a right to reparation on the basis of Community law will be conditional, *inter alia*, upon the breach having been sufficiently serious.

78. So, certain objective and subjective factors connected with the concept of fault under a national legal system may well be relevant for the purpose of determining **[1156]** whether or not a given breach of Community law is serious (see the factors mentioned in paragraphs 56 and 57 above).

79. The obligation to make reparation for loss or damage caused to individuals cannot, however, depend upon a condition based on any concept of fault going beyond that of a sufficiently serious breach of Community law. Imposition of such a supplementary condition would be tantamount to calling in question the right to reparation founded on the Community legal order.

80. Accordingly, the reply to the question from the national court must be that, pursuant to the national legislation which it applies, reparation of loss or damage cannot be made conditional upon fault (intentional or negligent) on the part of the organ of the State responsible for the breach, going beyond that of a sufficiently serious breach of Community law.

The Actual Extent of the Reparation (Question 4(a) in Case C-46/93 and the Second Question in Case C-48/93)

81. By these questions, the national courts essentially ask the Court to identify the criteria for determination of the extent of the reparation due by the Member State responsible for the breach.

82. Reparation for loss or damage caused to individuals as a result of breaches of Community law must be commensurate with the loss or damage sustained so as to ensure the effective protection for their rights.

[1157] 83. In the absence of relevant Community provisions, it is for the domestic legal system of each Member State to set the criteria for determining the extent of reparation. However, those criteria must not be less favourable than those applying to similar claims based on domestic law and must not be such as in practice to make it impossible or excessively difficult to obtain reparation.

84. In particular, in order to determine the loss or damage for which reparation may be granted, the national court may inquire whether the injured person showed reasonable diligence in order to avoid the loss or damage or limit its extent and whether, in particular, he availed himself in time of all the legal remedies available to him.

85. Indeed, it is a general principle common to the legal systems of the Member States that the injured party must show reasonable diligence in limiting the extent of the loss or damage, or risk having to bear the damage himself (Joined Cases C-104/89 and C-37/90 *Mulder and Others* v. *Council and Commission* [1992] ECR I-3061, paragraph 33).

86. The Bundesgerichtshof asks whether national legislation may generally limit the obligation to make reparation to damage done to certain, specifically protected individual interests, for example property, or whether it should also cover loss of profit by the claimants. It states that the opportunity to market products from other Member States is not regarded in German law as forming part of the protected assets of the undertaking.

87. Total exclusion of loss of profit as a head of damage for which reparation may be awarded in the case of a breach of Community law cannot be accepted. Especially in the context of economic or commercial litigation, such a total exclusion of loss of profit would be such as to make reparation of damage practically impossible.

[1158] 88. As for the various heads of damage referred to in the Divisional Court's second question, Community law imposes no specific criteria. It is for the national court to rule on those heads of damage in accordance with the domestic law which it applies, subject to the requirements set out in paragraph 83 above.

89. As regards in particular the award of exemplary damages, such damages are based under domestic law, as the Divisional Court explains, on the finding that the public authorities concerned acted oppressively, arbitrarily or unconstitutionally. In so far as such conduct may constitute or aggravate a breach of Community law, an award of exemplary damages pursuant to a claim or an action founded on Community law cannot be ruled out if such damages could be awarded pursuant to a similar claim or action founded on domestic law.

90. Accordingly, the reply to the national courts must be that reparation by Member States of loss or damage which they have caused to individuals as a result of breaches of Community law must be commensurate with the loss or damage sustained. In the absence of relevant Community provisions, it is for the domestic legal system of each Member State to set the criteria for determining the extent of reparation. However, those criteria must not be less favourable than those applying to similar claims or actions based on domestic law and must not be such as in practice to make it impossible or excessively difficult to obtain reparation. National legislation which generally limits the damage for

which reparation may be granted to damage done to certain, specifically protected individual interests not including loss of profit by individuals is not compatible with Community law. Moreover, it must be possible to award specific damages, such as the exemplary damages provided for by English law, pursuant to claims or actions founded on Community law, if such damages may be awarded pursuant to similar claims or actions founded on domestic law.

[1159] *Extent of the Period Covered by Reparation (Question 4(b) in Case C-46/93)*

91. By this question, the Bundesgerichtshof asks whether the damage for which reparation may be awarded extends to harm sustained before a judgment is delivered by the Court finding that an infringement has been committed.

92. Following from the reply to the second question, the right to reparation under Community law exists where the conditions set out in paragraph 51 above are satisfied.

93. One of those conditions is that the breach of Community law must have been sufficiently serious. The fact that there is a prior judgment of the Court finding an infringement will certainly be determinative, but it is not essential in order for that condition to be satisfied (see paragraphs 55, 56 and 57 of this judgment).

94. Were the obligation of the Member State concerned to make reparation to be confined to loss or damage sustained after delivery of a judgment of the Court finding the infringement in question, that would amount to calling in question the right to reparation conferred by the Community legal order.

95. In addition, to make the reparation of loss or damage conditional upon the requirement that there must have been a prior finding by the Court of an infringement of Community law attributable to a Member State would be contrary to the principle of the effectiveness of Community law, since it would preclude any right to reparation so long as the presumed infringement had not been the subject of an action brought by the Commission under Article 169 of the Treaty and of a finding of an infringement by the Court. Rights arising for individuals out of Community provisions having direct effect in the domestic legal systems of the Member States cannot depend on the Commission's assessment of the expediency of taking **[1160]** action against a Member State pursuant to Article 169 of the Treaty or on the delivery by the Court of any judgment finding an infringement (see, to this effect, Joined Cases 314/81, 315/81, 316/81 and 83/82 *Waterkeyn and Others* [1982] ECR 4337, paragraph 16).

96. Accordingly, the reply to the national court's question must be that the obligation for Member States to make good loss or damage caused

to individuals by breaches of Community law attributable to the State cannot be limited to damage sustained after the delivery of a judgment of the Court finding the infringement in question.

The Request that the Temporal Effects of the Judgment should be Limited

97. The German Government requests the Court to limit any damage to be made good by the Federal Republic of Germany to loss or damage sustained after delivery of judgment in this case, in so far as the victims did not bring legal proceedings or make an equivalent claim before. It considers that such a temporal limitation of the effects of this judgment is necessary owing to the scale of its financial consequences for the Federal Republic of Germany.

98. It must be borne in mind that, were the national court to find that the conditions for liability of the Federal Republic of Germany are satisfied in this case, the State would have to make good the consequences of the damage caused within the framework of its domestic law on liability. Substantive and procedural conditions laid down by national law on reparation of damage are able to take account of the requirements of the principle of legal certainty.

[1161] 99. However, those conditions may not be less favourable than those relating to similar domestic claims and must not be such as in practice to make it impossible or excessively difficult to obtain reparation (*Francovich and Others*, paragraph 43).

100. In view of the foregoing, there is no need for the Court to limit the temporal effects of this judgment.

Costs

101. The costs incurred by the Danish, German, Greek, Spanish, French, Irish and Netherlands Governments, the United Kingdom and the Commission of the European Communities, which have submitted observations to the Court, are not recoverable. Since these proceedings are, for the parties to the main proceedings, a step in the proceedings pending before the national courts, the decision on costs is a matter for those courts.

On those grounds,

THE COURT,

in answer to the questions referred to it by the Bundesgerichtshof, by order of 28 January 1993, and by the High Court of Justice, Queen's Bench Division, Divisional Court, by order of 18 November 1992, hereby rules:

1. **The principle that Member States are obliged to make good damage caused to individuals by breaches of Community law attributable to the State is [1162] applicable where the national legislature was responsible for the breach in question.**
2. **Where a breach of Community law by a Member State is attributable to the national legislature acting in a field in which it has a wide discretion to make legislative choices, individuals suffering loss or injury thereby are entitled to reparation where the rule of Community law breached is intended to confer rights upon them, the breach is sufficiently serious and there is a direct causal link between the breach and the damage sustained by the individuals. Subject to that reservation, the state must make good the consequences of the loss or damage caused by the breach of Community law attributable to it, in accordance with its national law on liability. However, the conditions laid down by the applicable national laws must not be less favourable than those relating to similar domestic claims or framed in such a way as in practice to make it impossible or excessively difficult to obtain reparation.**
3. **Pursuant to the national legislation which it applies, reparation of loss or damage cannot be made conditional upon fault (intentional or negligent) on the part of the organ of the State responsible for the breach, going beyond that of a sufficiently serious breach of Community law.**
4. **Reparation by Member States of loss or damage which they have caused to individuals as a result of breaches of Community law must be commensurate with the loss or damage sustained. In the absence of relevant Community provisions, it is for the domestic legal system of each Member State to set the criteria for determining the extent of reparation. However, those criteria must not be less favourable than those applying to similar claims or actions based on domestic law and must not be such as in practice to make it impossible or excessively difficult to obtain reparation. National legislation which generally limits the damage for which reparation may be granted to damage done to certain, specifically protected individual interests not [1163] including loss of profit by individuals is not compatible with Community law. Moreover, it must be possible to award specific damages, such as the exemplary damages provided for by English law, pursuant to claims or actions founded on Community law, if such damages may be awarded pursuant to similar claims or actions founded on domestic law.**

5. The obligation for Member States to make good loss or damage caused to individuals by breaches of Community law attributable to the State cannot be limited to damage sustained after the delivery of a judgment of the Court finding the infringement in question.

[Report: [1996] ECR I-1029]

NOTE.—The principles laid down by the Court of Justice have subsequently been the subject of a series of further judgments in which the Court has given rulings on the liability of Member States for other types of acts or omissions involving breaches of Community law:

(a) the incorrect transposition of a Community directive into national law by ministerial regulations. In this case the Court of Justice held that the breach was not sufficiently serious to engage State liability because the United Kingdom had transposed the directive into national law in due time, interpreting it in good faith and in a manner not manifestly contrary to its wording or objective, where no guidance had been given by the Commission or in the case-law of the Court of Justice (Case C-392/93, *Regina* v. *HM Treasury, ex parte British Telecommunications plc*, judgment of 26 March 1996, [1996] ECR I-1631);

(b) an individual decision on the part of a national administration which was in breach of a directly effective Treaty provision (Article 34). The Court found that where, at the time of the infringement, the Member State in question was not called upon to make any legislative choices and had only reduced discretion, or even none, the mere infringement of Community law could be sufficient to establish a sufficiently serious breach (Case C-5/94, *Regina* v. *Ministry of Agriculture, Fisheries and Food, ex parte Hedley Lomas (Ireland) Ltd*, judgment of 23 May 1996, [1996] ECR I-2553);

(c) the non-transposition of a Community directive into national law in due time. The Court held that failure to take any measure to transpose a directive in order to achieve the result it prescribed within the period laid down constituted *per se* a serious breach of Community law and gave rise to a right of reparation for individuals suffering injury (Cases C-178/94 *et al.*, *Dillenkofer and Others* v. *Federal Republic of Germany*, judgment of 8 October 1996, [1996] ECR II-4845).

JUDGMENT OF THE GERMAN FEDERAL SUPREME COURT OF 24 OCTOBER 1996

[975] *Facts*

The plaintiff, a French brewery based in Alsace, exported beer to Germany until 1981 in what it says were considerable quantities. It says that it had to cease making such exports altogether at the end of 1981 because the relevant German authorities objected to the beer it produced on the grounds that it did not comply with the purity requirement of sections 9 and 10 of the Beer Duty Act.[1] Fines were imposed on employees of the plaintiff's domestic German contractual partner, which dealt with the distribution of the beer in Germany, and on buyers acting for grocery chains in which it was sold. The distribution company then stated by a letter to the plaintiff of 4 November 1981 that, because of the frequency of the administrative proceedings which had by then been brought against it as the importer, it found that it would have to suspend importing the plaintiff's beer into Germany forthwith until the definitive clarification of the issues arising on the German purity requirement in the EC. Since the EC Commission took the view that sections 9 and 10 of the Act were contrary to Article 30 EEC, it started proceedings against Germany for breach of the Treaty, which concerned both the prohibition on marketing under the designation "Bier" ["beer"] beers lawfully manufactured in other Member States according to different rules and also the prohibition on the importing of beer containing additives. By its judgment of 12 March 1987[2] the European Court of Justice held *inter alia* that it was incompatible with Article 30 EEC to apply section 10 of the Act, under which the designation "Bier" was reserved for beer brewed in accordance with the purity requirement, to beers lawfully manufactured and put on the market in other Member States. It was also held that Germany was in breach of its obligations under Article 30 inasmuch as it prohibited putting on the domestic market beer lawfully manufactured and marketed in other Member States if it did not comply with sections 9 and 10 of the Act. The plaintiff is now claiming compensation from the defendant, Germany, for damage which it sustained as a result of the restriction on imports during the years from 1981 to 1987, including a partial claim for 1,800,000 DM. The Landgericht and the Oberlandesgericht[3] dismissed the action. With its present appeal on points of law the plaintiff pursues its claim further.

JUDGMENT

The appeal is admissible, but it is unfounded.

The sole factor which can be used to found a liability on the part of Germany is the failure to adapt sections 9 and 10 of the Beer Duty **[976]** Act to the higher-ranking rules of European Community law; in other words, the liability involved is one for a "legislative default". On the other hand, liability on the part of Germany for the individual administrative measures taken on the basis of the said provisions which

[1] Act of 14 March 1952, [1952] I BGBl 149, as amended by Act of 14 December 1976, [1976] I BGBl 3341.

[2] [1987] ECR 1227, [1988] 1 CMLR 780, [1987] NJW 1133 (*EC Commission* v. *Germany*).

[3] [1991] EuZW 574.

infringed Community law is not in issue. According to the plaintiff's own submissions the relevant proceedings, especially those in which fines were imposed, were not brought against the plaintiff itself but against its contractual partner within Germany. In particular, the plaintiff has already referred in its statement of claim to the fact that it was never itself the addressee of the relevant executive acts taken to its disadvantage.

German national law does not offer any basis of claim for the plaintiff's action. This Court has already explained the matter as follows in its decision to order a reference of 28 January 1993:[4]

(a) In particular, no state-liability claim arises as against Germany under section 839(1), first sentence, of the Civil Code in conjunction with Article 34 of the Constitution. The breach of Article 30 EEC for which Germany is responsible consisted in an omission by the Federal Legislature, *i.e.* the failure to adapt the former section 10 of the Beer Duty Act to the higher-ranking rules of Community law. That omission did not, however, result in any breach of official duties directed towards third persons for the purposes of section 839 of the Civil Code in conjunction with Article 34 of the Constitution to the prejudice of the foreign brewery possibly affected by the restriction of imports. Official duties of public bodies are in the first instance for the purpose of the general interest in the proper ordering of public life. In so far as official duties are exclusively concerned with serving that interest, and no special relationships have arisen between those official duties and specific persons or groups of persons, claims for compensation on the part of third parties outside such relationships do not come into question. Official duties of that sort are generally involved in the case of duties imposed upon the responsible bodies in the context of legislative functions. Statutes and regulations always contain general and abstract rules, and the legislature accordingly in general takes responsibility (as regards action and failure to act) exclusively as regards the general public, and such responsibilities are not directed towards specific persons or classes of person. Only in exceptional circumstances (not applicable here) such as Acts implementing specific measures or passed for individual cases, can the position be otherwise or can the interests of specific individuals be directly affected, so that they can be regarded as "third persons" within the meaning of section 839 of the Civil Code.[5] That was not the case with the plaintiff.

(b) In just the same way no liability in respect of an infringement equivalent to expropriation comes into question:

(aa) Compensation for disadvantages brought about directly or indirectly by a formal legislative act contrary to European Community law is something which no longer remains within the boundaries of an established category of liability developed and shaped by judicial decisions in the way that the infringement equivalent to expropriation has been established by the case law of this Court. In German domestic law there is no

[4] [1993] EuZW 226, [1993] NJW 1224 L.

[5] Established case law; see most recently BGH, [1989] NJW 101, BGH Warn 1988 No 208.

adequate legitimation for the introduction and **[977]** development by judicial decision of state liability for the disadvantageous consequences of formal legislation which contravenes higher-ranking European law. The regulation of this matter must continue to be reserved for the legislature.[6]

(bb) In the present case a claim in respect of an infringement equivalent to expropriation must fail in addition for the reason that no infringement of a vested interest of the plaintiff protected as a matter of property was present on the facts. The plaintiff's chances of being able to sell its products on the German market are not classified by the German legal system among the protected assets of the plaintiff's business so long as the core area of property rights is not affected as a result, as was the case here.[7]

I.

The Court has nevertheless had to consider whether the plaintiff can derive a claim directly from European Community law.

The European Court of Justice in its judgment of 19 November 1991 (*Francovich*)[8] affirmed the direct liability of a Member State towards the individual citizen affected by the failure to implement a directive, and in this connection it stressed in particular that the principle of the liability of the State for damage caused to an individual by breaches of Community law for which the State can be held responsible is inherent in the legal system created by the EEC Treaty. It was, therefore, necessary to clarify in the context of the present litigation whether the principles developed in the *Francovich* judgment on the right to claim state liability under Community law in respect of the non-implementation of a directive conferring benefits on individuals, as dealt with by the European Court on that occasion, is also applicable to the case to be decided here of an import restriction contrary to the EEC Treaty itself which is produced by a formal parliamentary law. On this issue, and for the purpose of a more precise formulation and as regards the extent of any state liability, this Court by its order of 28 January 1993[9] referred the following questions to the European Court for a preliminary ruling:

[The preliminary questions were then set out.]

The European Court by its judgment of 5 March 1996[10] answered the questions as follows . . .

[6] See 100 BGHZ 136, at pp. 145 *et seq.*, [1987] NJW 1875, LM Art. 14 [Ba] constitutional provision *re* an unconstitutional parliamentary Act.

[7] See 111 BGHZ 349, [1990] NJW 3260.

[8] [1991] I ECR 5357, [1993] 2 CMLR 66, [1991] EuZW 758, [1992] NJW 165.

[9] BGH, [1993] EuZW 226, [1993] NJW 1224 L.

[10] *Brasserie du Pêcheur* and *Factortame*: [1996] I ECR 1029, [1996] 1 CMLR 889, [1996] EuZW 205, [1996] NJW 1267, [1996] JZ 789, [1996] EuGRZ 144.

II.

The application of those principles to the present case produces the result that the plaintiff also has no claim to compensation under Community law.

[978] The European Court emphasised that State liability for breaches of Community law flows directly from that law itself, and that it is (only) the consequences of the damage caused that have to be remedied in the framework of the domestic law on liability, for which purposes the application of domestic law is subject to the proviso that the conditions which it lays down for reparation may not be less favourable than those for similar domestic claims and may not be so formulated as in practice to make it impossible or excessively difficult to obtain reparation.[11]

The direct derivation of the claim in respect of state liability from Community law is also emphasised in as much as the factual conditions for the State's liability for damage caused to individuals through a breach of Community law may not differ from the conditions applicable to the liability of the Community itself under comparable circumstances unless there is a special reason. The European Court therefore transferred the system which it had developed specifically under Article 215(2) of the European Community Treaty for liability by virtue of Community legislative acts so as to apply to the liability of Member States in issue here in such a way that the factual conditions for the liability of a Member State are congruent with those for the liability of the Community itself. Therefore, if it can be held simply on the basis of those Community-law criteria (as in this case) that no factual condition for liability is satisfied, there is no necessity to refer back to the principles on liability common to the laws of Member States. The subject-matter falling to be considered in this case therefore gives the Court no cause to re-examine its case law on state liability for legislative wrongs in so far as it affects German domestic law. It is not necessary, in particular, to decide whether the factual conditions for official liability for a legislative wrong may have to be changed under an interpretation "in conformity with European law" in such a way that the criterion which grounds and restricts liability—that the infringed official obligation is directed towards a third party—would have to be questioned as regards the sphere of application of the German national legal system.

The system of liability under Community law for defective legislative acts developed by the European Court makes a fundamental distinction in the first place according to whether the acts affect an area already governed by Community law or whether a legal area is concerned where that is not the case. In a legal area already governed by Community law the discretion of the national legislature is correspondingly reduced; in

[11] [1996] EuZW 205, [1996] NJW 1267, para. 67.

an area not so governed the scope of its discretion is substantially wider.[12] The European Court held in the case which falls to be considered here that in the area of foodstuffs, and specifically beer, in the absence of any Community harmonisation, the German legislature possessed a wide discretion in laying down rules on **[979]** the quality of beer put on the market.[13] In the case of a wide discretion of that kind Community law recognises a right to compensation so long as three conditions are satisfied:

1. that the rule of law infringed is intended to confer rights on individuals;
2. that the breach is sufficiently serious;
3. that there is a direct causal link between the breach of the obligation resting on the State and the damage sustained by the injured parties.[14]

The claim to compensation asserted by the plaintiff must fail for the reason that no sufficiently serious breach can be established which could be the direct cause of the damage claimed.

The decisive criterion for answering the question whether a breach of Community law is to be regarded as sufficiently serious lies in the fact that a Member State has manifestly and gravely disregarded the limits imposed on its discretion.[15]

(a) As regards the subject-matter to be appraised here, the European Court points out that the issue of the maintenance in force by the German legislature of the provisions of the Beer Tax Act on the purity of beer, which prohibited the marketing under the designation "Bier" of beers imported from other Member States and lawfully produced under different provisions, has to be distinguished from the retention of the provisions of the same Act prohibiting the import of beers containing additives. The European Court takes the view that, as regards the first aspect, *i.e.* the prohibition of the designation "Bier", it would be difficult to deny that the German legislation was a (sufficiently serious) breach of Article 30 EEC, since the incompatibility of such rules with Article 30 was manifest in the light of decisions of the Court already in existence at the time.[16] By contrast, the criteria available to the national legislature by reference to the relevant case law to determine the other aspect—whether the prohibition on the use of additives was contrary to Community law—were significantly less conclusive until the judgment of 12 March 1987 (*EC Commission* v. *Germany*),[17] in which the Court held that provision to be incompatible with Article 30.

[12] [1996] EuZW 205, [1996] NJW 1267, paras. 45-7.

[13] [1996] EuZW 205, [1996] NJW 1267, para. 48.

[14] [1996] EuZW 205, [1996] NJW 1267, para. 51; see, too, to this effect the later European Court judgments at [1996] I ECR 1631, [1996] 2 CMLR 217, [1996] EuZW 274 (*British Telecommunications*); [1996] 3 CMLR 469, [1996] EuZW 654, [1996] NJW 3141 (*Dillenkofer and Others*—"*Package Tours*").

[15] [1996] EuZW 205, [1996] NJW 1267, para. 55.

[16] [1996] EuZW 205, [1996] NJW 1257, para. 59, with references.

[17] Cited above.

(b) It would not be possible to reach the conclusion from those expositions of the matter, as was done in one of the earliest academic **[980]** opinions on the said judgment,[18] that the first of the two aspects alone was grounds for holding that there had been a sufficiently serious breach of Community law, which as a contributory cause giving rise to consequences for liability could not be subsequently nullified by the fact that the same Member State had added a second causal contribution, which was possibly not sufficiently serious. What was meant, rather, as is shown in particular by the conclusions of Giuseppe Tesauro AG of 21 October 1995,[19] was that an evaluative assessment is required on the question: with which of the two aspects is the damage claimed by the plaintiff connected in a legal sense?

(c) The result of such an assessment in the present case is that the measures taken against the plaintiff on the basis of the legal provisions contravening Community law did not concern the designation of the drink produced by the plaintiff as "Bier". According to the documents entered on the file by the plaintiff itself, the object of the food-inspection controls and administrative-penalty proceedings was, rather, to deal solely with contraventions of the prohibition on using unlawful additives. They therefore concerned an area in which there were not yet any clear Community-law rulings and no unambiguous case law from the European Court. That is also the effect of the plaintiff's submissions in both the statement of claim and the grounds of the first appeal, in as much as it refers expressly to the measures taken by the German authorities against its appointed importers, and argues that "the damage is attributable solely to the restrictive administrative actions of German authorities". But they objected to the beverage produced by the plaintiff only because of the additives it contained. The labelling, too, *viz.*: "Brewed as always in accordance with the German purity requirement" shows that it was of critical importance to the plaintiff to present the *contents* of its product as corresponding with the provisions of the Beer Duty Act and thus to conceal the use of additives. For that reason the requirement of a direct causal connection between the infringing act and the damage is not satisfied as regards the breach of the Treaty relating to the use of the designation "Bier". It is a matter for the national legal systems of the individual Member States to implement the conditions for liability as regards "direct causation" into national law while safeguarding the full effectiveness of Community law.[20] This Court proceeds on the footing that in that respect an evaluative attribution of the consequences as regards liability has to be made by reference to the factual situation relevant to liability, which is comparable to the relationship which in German law is expressed by notions of necessary and sufficient causation. It is not necessary for present purposes to

[18] *Ehlers*, [1996] JZ 776, at p. 780.

[19] See para. 116.

[20] See *Francovich*, cited above, paras. 42 *et seq*.

decide whether, in so doing, the characteristic of directness of causation makes it possible **[981]** to adopt a narrower approach, possibly oriented towards considerations of protective purpose.

(d) As regards the other breach of the Treaty, that is, the prohibition on the import of beers containing additives, the position is as follows:

The Federal Government expressed the opinion in the proceedings instituted by the Commission at the time that, as regards the risk of harm due to the use of additives, the long-term effects of which were not known, and in particular in view of the risks resulting from the accumulation of additives in the organism and their interaction with other substances, such as alcohol, it was necessary to minimise the ingestion of additives as far as possible. Since beer was a foodstuff of which large quantities were consumed in Germany, it was especially important to exclude the use of any additives in its production. That was all the more imperative in as much as the use of additives was not technologically necessary, because it could be avoided if only the ingredients prescribed by the Beer Tax Act were used. Given that factual situation, the prevailing German rules on additives for beer were comprehensively justified by the need to safeguard public health and did not disregard the principle of proportionality.[21] The European Court took that as a cause for investigating whether the prohibition in issue could be justified under Article 36 EEC on grounds of protection of human health. Although in the event it answered the question in the negative, and thus considered the Federal Government's arguments as not being conclusive, there is nothing in the judgment of 12 March 1987 to indicate that the Federal Government's legal position could have been so far removed on this point from the requirements of Community law that it was necessary to hold that there was a manifest and grave transgression of the boundaries placed on the discretion of the national legislature.

(e) In a comprehensive appraisal of the subject-matter set out above this Court—following the rulings of the European Court—regards the breach of the Treaty, in so far as it was the direct cause of the damage, as being in no way sufficiently serious.

(f) The defendant is likewise not liable for the further damage incurred by the plaintiff after the giving of the European Court judgment of 12 March 1987. The defendant submitted without contradiction in both the proceedings below that it caused the judgment to be adhered to immediately following its publication by issuing notices and instructions to the competent authorities. The plaintiff's grounds of appeal, too, concede that the defendant took measures in order to give effect to the judgment of 12 March 1987 as from that date. In so far as the plaintiff had need of a transitional period after the publication of the judgment in order to build up a new distribution organisation, the profits that it lost

[21] *EC Commission* v. *Germany*, cited above, para. 39.

in that period were not attributable to the defendant country; they were late consequences of the defendant's earlier actions, which, as explained, were not a sufficiently serious breach of Community law. The losses were not due to the fact that Germany failed in some way to implement the judgment of 12 March 1987 in good time.

[Report: [1997] 1 CMLR 971]

JUDGMENT OF THE ENGLISH HOUSE OF LORDS OF 28 OCTOBER 1999

[1064] LORD SLYNN OF HADLEY. My Lords, in this important case your Lordships have had the advantage, in addition to formal written cases, of most able and admirably concise oral arguments from counsel on behalf of all parties. Those parties are, as appellant, the Secretary of State for Transport, in effect representing the United Kingdom, and, as the respondents companies (or shareholders or directors of companies) and individuals who owned or managed vessels which were part of the British fishing fleet until they lost their registration on 31 March 1989 as a result of legislation, including delegated legislation, adopted in the United Kingdom. That legislation has been held by the European Court of Justice to constitute a breach of Community law by the United Kingdom and the question on this appeal is whether the appellant's breaches of Community law were sufficiently serious to give rise under Community law to a right to compensatory damages to those who can show that the breach caused them damage. Any question of causation has been left over pending a determination as to the seriousness of the breach for the purpose of Community law.

The Divisional Court and the Court of Appeal unanimously held that the breaches were sufficiently serious for that purpose. A claim for **[1065]** exemplary damages, though originally made, has not been pursued before the Court of Appeal or before your Lordships' House. It is not suggested that there is any need to make a reference to the European Court under article 177 of the Treaty, the assessment of seriousness being for the national court: *Brasserie du Pêcheur SA* v. *Federal Republic of Germany*; *Reg.* v. *Secretary of State for Transport, Ex parte Factortame Ltd* (*No 4*), (Joined Cases C-46/93 and C-48/93) [1996] QB 404, 500, para. 58 ("*Factortame III*").

The Main Facts

The case has a long history both on the facts and in relation to the judicial proceedings before courts in the United Kingdom and before the European Court of Justice. Those facts and proceedings are recited in detail in the judgment of the Divisional Court [1997] EuLR 475 to which I refer. Since with one exception the findings of fact were accepted before the Court of Appeal and before your Lordships' House it is neither necessary nor useful to set them all out again. I therefore confine myself to indicating the important stages of the saga.

From 1970 the European Community established, as part of the common agricultural policy, a fisheries policy, pursuant to article 38 of the EEC Treaty. This arose partly out of concern for the overfishing of stocks in the North Sea and Atlantic Ocean but also out of a desire to ensure equality for the vessels of member states in access to fishing grounds and to exclude the fishermen of non-member states from those grounds other than on terms agreed by the Community. Such an agreement was made by the Community with Spain in 1980 (i.e. before Spain's accession to the Community) giving Spanish vessels the right to fish for particular species in identified waters of the member states.

The adoption of this policy meant that domestic rules as to fisheries had to comply with the rules of the common fisheries policy and the United Kingdom on accession in 1973 became subject to those rules.

The common fisheries policy in fact developed more slowly than the common agricultural policy but in 1980 by Council Declaration of 30 May 1980 on the Common Fisheries Policy (OJ 1980 C 158, p. 2) the Council set out guidelines on which the policy was to be based. These emphasise the importance of having regard to the needs of regions where the local population was dependent on fishing, to traditional fishing activities in those regions and to the fair distribution of catches.

By Council Regulation (EEC) No 170/83 of 25 January 1983 (OJ 1983 L 24, p. 1) the Community set up a system of national quotas for "total allowable catch[es]" based in part on catches for the years 1973-8 and it issued multi-annual guidance programmes dealing with fishing capacity and fleets.

From 1976 Spain had conferred advantages (e.g. as to landing rights) on Spanish fishing, companies which were entered on the register of another state so as to be able to fish in that state's waters, in order that those companies retained their economic links with Spain (Royal Decree 2517/1976). The United Kingdom took the view that Spanish vessels were registered on the British register so as to obtain access to United Kingdom fishing grounds in a way which went beyond what had been agreed between the Community and Spain in 1980 and that to all intents and purposes these were Spanish vessels using up the British quota. The owners of these fishing vessels (and the directors of and shareholders of companies **[1066]** owning vessels) were Spanish; many of the fishermen were Spanish; the catches went to Spain. Local British fishing communities accordingly derived no benefit from these activities which even when carried out on British registered vessels were essentially Spanish.

It is hardly surprising that the British Government wished to do something to protect these British fishing communities and those vessels which were intrinsically, as opposed to merely legally, British and also to protect the British national quotas. There is no doubt that in international law and under domestic law steps could have been taken to control registration on the British register and to regulate the fishing of particular stocks. What could be done was, however, subject to Community law and the British Government sought unsuccessfully to persuade the Commission to take steps to prevent what the United Kingdom was complaining about and which came to be referred to as "quota hopping."

In order to deal with the substantial number of Spanish vessels which had been reregistered on the British register and of British registered boats acquired by Spanish companies and individuals, the United Kingdom enacted in March 1983 the British Fishing Boats Act 1983 and it made the British Fishing Boats Order 1983 (SI 1983 No 482) which required vessels registered on the British register to have a crew of at least 75 per cent EEC nationals before they could fish lawfully in British fishing grounds. That excluded the Spanish fishermen. But when Spain acceded to the Community with effect from 1 January 1986 (and thereby became subject to Community rules) the 1983 legislation ceased to achieve its objective. Pursuant to the Sea Fish (Conservation) Act 1967 new licensing conditions were therefore introduced on 1 January 1986 which required that 75 per cent of the crew must be nationals of EEC States and reside ashore in the United Kingdom. All the crew had to pay United Kingdom social security contributions and the vessels had to show that they operated from British ports either by at least visiting the ports four times a year or by landing and selling 50 per cent by weight of landed fish in the United Kingdom. These conditions as to nationality, residence and social security contributions were held on 14 December 1989 to be contrary to Community law (though the operating condition was held not to be unlawful) by the European Court in *Reg.* v. *Ministry of Agriculture, Fisheries and Food, Ex parte Agegate Ltd* (Case C-3/87) [1990] 2 QB 151. A challenge to the operating condition was made in *Reg.* v. *Ministry of Agriculture, Fisheries and Food, Ex parte Jaderow Ltd* (Case C-216/87) [1990] 2 QB 193. The Spanish-owned vessels agreed to comply with the operating condition and the United Kingdom agreed not to enforce the crew residence and national insurance contribution conditions.

Even before the judgments in the *Agegate* and *Jaderow* cases the Government took the view that the position was getting worse since Spanish controlled vessels were increasing their take from British quotas; British fishing communities accordingly were further disadvantaged. The way to tackle the problem was seen to be to change the rules on registration rather than on licensing. As a result the Merchant Shipping Act 1988 was enacted with effect from 1 December 1988 and the Merchant Shipping (Registration of Fishing Vessels) Regulations 1988 (SI 1988 No 1926) also came into force on the same date.

By section 14 of the Act a vessel could only be entered on the register as a British fishing vessel if it was British owned. To qualify as such the legal owners and not less than 75 per cent, of the beneficial owners had to be qualified persons or companies. In addition the charterer, manager **[1067]** or operator of the fishing vessel had to be a qualified person. The vessel to qualify had to be managed and its operation be directed and controlled from within the United Kingdom. A "qualified person," so far as relevant, meant "(*a*) a person who is a British citizen resident and domiciled in the United Kingdom." A "qualified company" was defined as

> a company which satisfies the following conditions, namely—(*a*) it is incorporated in the United Kingdom and has its principal place of business there; (*b*) at least the relevant percentage of its shares (taken as a whole), and of each class of its shares, is legally and beneficially owned by one or more qualified persons or companies; and (*c*) at least the relevant percentage of its directors are qualified persons.

Section 14 further provided in subsection (4) that where, in the case of any fishing vessel, the Secretary of State was satisfied that the vessel could not be registered as a British fishing vessel because the individuals were not British citizens, but that it would be appropriate to dispense with the requirement of British citizenship in the case of that individual in view of the length of time he had resided in the United Kingdom and been involved in the fishing industry of the United Kingdom, the Secretary of State might dispense with the nationality requirements.

Questions as to the legality under Community law of these conditions were referred to the European Court of Justice under article 177 of the Treaty in March 1989 by the Divisional Court. On 18 May 1989 your Lordships' House referred the further question as to whether under Community law English courts were required to have the power to grant interim protection for rights claimed under Community law, a question answered in the affirmative by the European Court on 19 June 1990 in its judgment in *Reg.* v. *Secretary of State for Transport, Ex parte Factortame Ltd* (Case C-213/89) [1990] ECR I-2433 ("*Factortame I*").

On 7 August 1989 the Commission began proceedings under article 169 of the Treaty against the United Kingdom contending that the nationality condition was in breach of articles 7, 52, 59 and 221 of the Treaty and applying for interim measures to require that condition not to be applied pending the decision in the main proceedings.

On 10 October 1989 the President of the European Court made an order for interim measures in the article 169 proceedings pending judgment in those proceedings. His order was that:

> the United Kingdom shall suspend the application of the nationality requirements laid down in section 14(l)(*a*) and (*c*) of the Merchant Shipping Act 1988 read in conjunction with [subsections] (2) and (7) of that section, as regards the nationals of other member states and in respect of fishing vessels which, until 31 March 1989, were pursuing a fishing activity under the British flag and under a British fishing licence.

This order was given effect to by the Merchant Shipping Act 1988 (Amendment) Order 1989 (SI 1989 No 2006), which came into force on 2 November 1989. This was limited to the nationality condition. In a letter before action of 13 June 1990 pursuant to article 169 the Commission added its objection both to the domicile and to the residence conditions.

In *Reg.* v. *Secretary of State for Transport, Ex parte Factortame Ltd (No 3)* (Case C-221/89) [1992] QB 680 ("*Factortame II*") the European Court on 25 July 1991 held that although member states could determine **[1068]** in accordance with the rules of international law the conditions for the registration of vessels on their register and the right to fly their flag they still had to comply with Community law. The court further held that the requirements of nationality, residence and domicile for legal and beneficial owners, charterers, and managers and operators of fishing vessels registered on a member state's register were contrary to Community law and in particular to article 52 of the Treaty, although articles 5, 7 and 221 thereof were also breached. They held that the power to dispense with the nationality requirement on the grounds of a period of residence did not justify the requirements of nationality, residence or domicile. Nor were such requirements justified by the fact that the common fisheries policy provided for national quotas to be fixed. On the other hand they held that the requirement that the vessel be managed and its operations directed and controlled from within a member state was not contrary to Community law.

That was not, however, sufficient redress for the respondents. They had already claimed that they had suffered financial loss caused directly by the United Kingdom's breach of Community law in adopting and applying the Merchant Shipping Act 1988 on the basis of *Francovich* v. *Italian Republic* (Joined Cases C-6/90 and C-9/90) [1995] ICR 722. Their entitlement to compensation was now the issue. The Divisional Court referred to the European Court first the question whether when the three conditions to which I have referred had been laid down by primary legislation and had been held to infringe articles 5, 7, 52 and 221 of the EC Treaty, the owners or managers of such vessels or directors and shareholders in vessel-owning and managing companies were entitled to compensation as a matter of Community law for the losses suffered as a result of the breaches of the Treaty. Second, the court asked, if they were entitled, what considerations the national court should apply in determining the claims for damage relating to

> (a) expenses and/or loss of profit and/or loss of income during the period subsequent to the entry into force of the said conditions, during which the vessels were forced to lay up to make alternative arrangements for fishing and/or seek registration elsewhere.

In its judgment of 5 March 1996 in *Factortame III* [1996] QB 404, 506 the European Court replied:

(1) The principle that member states are obliged to make good damage caused to individuals by breaches of Community law attributable to the state is applicable where the national legislature was responsible for the breach in question. (2) Where a breach of Community law by a member state is attributable to the national legislature acting in a field in which it has a wide discretion to make legislative choices, individuals suffering loss or injury thereby are entitled to reparation where the rule of Community law breached is intended to confer rights on them, the breach is sufficiently serious and there is a direct causal link between the breach and the damage sustained by the individuals.

It was accepted by the respondent that the relevant rules of Community law were intended to confer rights on individuals and, as I have already said, the question of causation it was agreed should be left over. But it is said that the United Kingdom's breach or breaches were "sufficiently **[1069]** serious" to entitle the respondents to compensation for the damage suffered which it is said is substantial.

The Divisional Court

In addition to the fundamental importance of the principal breach (as held by the European Court of Justice in *Factortame II* [1992] QB 680) the Divisional Court regarded as serious the fact that discrimination on the ground of nationality was the intended effect of the domicile and residence conditions, that the Secretary of State was aware that the imposition of the conditions must necessarily injure the applicants because the conditions were intended to ensure that the applicants would no longer fish against the British quota, that the attitude of the Commission was hostile and that the Government decided to adopt the conditions by primary legislation, the consequence of which was that under domestic law the applicants could not get interim relief. The Divisional Court added [1997] EuLR 475, 518:

In any event, the applicants were deprived of the opportunity of being able to prevent damage being caused to them and it is clear that they did everything possible in order to try to avoid such damage (see para. 120 of the opinion of Advocate General Tesauro in *Factortame III* [1996] QB 404, 489). The situation was aggravated because, at least arguably, the measures adopted infringed the principles of proportionality and legitimate expectation, both of which are superior principles of Community law. Other methods could have been chosen which would have enabled applications for interim relief to be considered on their merits by the national court. The applicants had been carrying on lawful businesses and were forbidden to continue them. In these circumstances, it would be difficult to resist the argument that they should have been afforded a reasonable opportunity to take measures to avoid any serious damage which would otherwise ensue.

The court concluded that the appellants' breaches of Community law including the breach in complying with the President's order of

10 October 1989 were sufficiently serious to give rise to liability for any damage that might subsequently be shown to have been caused by the appellant to the respondents.

The Court of Appeal

The Court of Appeal [1998] EuLR 456, 475 was of the opinion that the seriousness of the breach "has to be judged objectively taking into account all the relevant circumstances [including] the circumstances identified by the European Court of Justice in *Factortame III*." They said, at p. 476:

In a case in which the legislative discretion of a member state is involved, as here, so as to avoid an excessive chilling factor defeating that discretion, a basket or global approach, involving weighing the relevant considerations, is the required approach. None the less, where what is relied on in support of an application for damages is a direct breach of the fundamental principle of the Treaty forbidding discrimination on grounds of nationality that will almost inevitably create a liability for damages. Whether intentional or not, such a breach is inexcusable in a case, such as this, where it is not suggested **[1070]** that the exceptions in article 55 and 56 which apply to the right of establishment granted by article 52 have any relevance . . . Our decision as to the nationality condition means that there is a liability to pay damages during the period from the coming into force of the Act of 1988 until 2 November 1989 when it ceased to have effect for most purposes. For this period we see no cause to distinguish between the three conditions. They are cumulative and it would be artificial to distinguish between them. However, any damage to the applicants was in most cases caused solely by the domicile and nationality conditions. In the course of the hearing before us the Solicitor-General did not seek to disturb the finding of the Divisional Court that the domicile condition is to be equated with the nationality condition. It seems to be implicit in that concession that if, as we find, there ought to be a remedy in damages in relation to the nationality condition while it was in force there ought equally to be a remedy in relation to the domicile condition while it was in force—namely throughout the period ending with the granting of the interim injunction by the House of Lords.

As to the residence condition standing alone (which was relevant to applicants who satisfied the nationality and domicile conditions) the Court of Appeal said, at pp. 476-7:

We have already pointed out that in this case it is artificial to isolate the conditions as to residence for separate treatment because the conditions were cumulative. In addition during the second period, when as a result of the President's decision, nationality was no longer relevant, the Secretary of State is faced with the difficulty that he had not regarded a requirement as to residence by itself as providing the necessary protection. This makes it difficult to justify the more limited requirement of residence by the need to protect the [common fisheries policy]. If the Secretary of State did not regard a condition of residence as capable of combating the problem it can hardly be justifiable as being necessary for that purpose. The Divisional Court pointed out the residence condition was intended to achieve, by an indirect method, the same result as was intended to be achieved by the nationality condition. The Divisional Court stated, "accordingly we can see no difference in principle between a breach of article 52 created by the residence condition and one created by the nationality condition" (at p. 516) . . . Having balanced the conflicting considerations we share the view of the Divisional Court that the indirect discrimination, which the requirement of residence involved, must, at least by 31 March 1989, be regarded as constituting a sufficiently serious breach for the purposes of attracting an entitlement to damages.

Both the Divisional Court and the Court of Appeal expressed concern about the way that the eighty-fourth applicant, Rawlings (Trawling) Ltd (one of whose shareholders and directors, Mr Yllera, was a Spanish national), had been treated on its application for a dispensation under section 14(4) of the Act in view of his integration in the British fishing industry. They also expressed similar concern about the way in which the eighty-fifth to ninety-seventh applicants (Mr and Mrs O'Connor and their companies other than management companies) had been treated. He was an Irish national and his wife a Belgian national. They therefore failed on **[1071]** nationality, but, having been resident in the United Kingdom and having worked with the British fishing fleet since 1978, they applied for but were refused, a dispensation under section 14(4) of the Act of 1988. The Divisional Court thought the policy uncertain and confused and inconsistently applied. The Court of Appeal regarded this treatment as adding to the seriousness of the breach, which was however established sufficiently without reliance on the way they had been treated on their application for a dispensation and the nationality condition.

The Grounds of Appeal

On this appeal the Solicitor-General accepts that since "domicile" in the Act was intended to have its meaning in English law as residence with an intention permanently to reside (and not merely residence with a substantial connection with the United Kingdom), it is to be treated in the same way as the nationality requirement and not in the same way as the residence requirement. He was in my opinion right to take that view since domicile in the intended sense was at least as restrictive and discriminatory as the nationality requirement. He also accepts that the failure to give effect to the President's order of 10 October 1989 until 2 November 1989 was itself a sufficiently serious breach to entitle at any rate the respondents resident here (but not satisfying the nationality test, in particular Rawlings (Trawling) Ltd) to compensation for the period of delay. This was in line with the view of the Divisional Court based in part on the statement by the European Court of Justice in *Factortame III*

[1996] QB 404, 501, para. 64, that if the United Kingdom failed to adopt immediately the measures needed to comply with the President's order of 10 October 1989 this "should be regarded by the national court as constituting in itself a manifest and, therefore, sufficiently serious breach of Community law."

I agree with the Divisional Court that the President's order took immediate effect and that, therefore, to refuse Rawlings' application for registration on the day following the President's order, on the basis that legislation by Order in Council was needed, or at any rate was to be awaited, before the President's order could be put into effect was a breach in itself, and on the basis of the European Court's judgment was a sufficiently serious breach. I consider therefore that the Solicitor-General was right also to accept that result.

The appellant contends, however, that the Divisional Court and the Court of Appeal were wrong in their conclusions that there had been a sufficiently serious breach of Community law. In summary it is said that here the United Kingdom was adopting legislation to deal with a serious economic problem. In deciding what to do it had a wide measure of discretion and damages can only be awarded if there is a manifest and grave disregard of its powers; to impose liability otherwise would be to inhibit legislative action which was necessary. Even where there is a breach of Community law there can be no liability to compensate where the breach was excusable. Here the breach was excusable since the law was not clear until the judgment in *Factortame II* [1992] QB 680 and there were substantial objective grounds to justify what was done when regard is had both to the existence of the common fisheries policy, which is intended to provide national quotas which member states are entitled to protect, and to a state's rights under international law to decide who should be entitled to register a vessel on its register and to fly its national flag. Moreover other member states adopted the same approach as the United Kingdom, **[1072]** the courts here regarded the issue as difficult (as in the judgments preceding *Factortame I* [1990] ECR I-2433 in the European Court) and the Government obtained and relied on independent legal advice that what they proposed to do would be accepted under Community law. Even if the action was discriminatory it could still be in law, and was here, excusable. The United Kingdom was not bound to follow the opinion of the Commission and its action cannot be said to be a sufficiently serious breach merely because the Commission took the view that what was done was a breach of Community law. Moreover the United Kingdom was not deliberately setting out either to breach Community law or to injure the respondents and throughout it acted in good faith even if its clear intention was to prevent foreign owners, and particularly Spanish owners, from using the device of having or registering their vessels on the British register in order to fish against the British quota and thereby to take the fishing away from local British fishing communities and to send the fish to Spain. Even if the breach caused by the nationality condition was sufficiently serious, it is said that the breach consisting of the residence condition was not.

Liability to Compensate—the Principle

My Lords in the *Francovich* case [1995] ICR 722, 772, para. 37, where there had been a failure to implement a directive, the European Court said: "it is a principle of Community law that the member states are obliged to make good loss and damage caused to individuals by breaches of Community law for which they can be held responsible." The court did not indicate what were the conditions for such liability or what if any defences would be available to a member state in breach of Community law obligations, save that in the case of a directive liability was conditional on there being a grant of rights to individuals by the directive, that the contents of those rights were clear, and that the loss suffered was shown to be caused by the state's breach. The further scope of the remedy was left to be worked out in subsequent cases as it has been in *Factortame III*.

The European Court has made it clear that, in deciding whether a state should be held liable, regard should be had to the principles laid down by the Court of Justice in deciding whether the Community itself would be held liable "in accordance with the general principles common to the laws of the member states, [to] make good any damage caused by its institutions" (article 215). In *Factortame III* [1996] QB 404, 497-8, para. 42 the court said:

> the conditions [for state liability] cannot, in the absence of particular justification, differ from those governing the liability of the Community in like circumstances. The protection of the rights which individuals derive from Community law cannot vary depending on whether a national authority or a Community authority is responsible for the damage.

The basic approach is clear. Before a member state can be held liable, a national court must find (i) that the relevant rule of Community law is one which is intended to confer rights on individuals; (ii) the breach must be sufficiently serious; (iii) there must be a direct causal link between the breach and the loss or damage complained of. That condition (i) is satisfied is rightly accepted by the appellants; (iii) is deferred if the respondents succeed on (ii). The question, therefore, is what constitutes being "sufficiently serious" and whether the Divisional Court and the Court of Appeal were right to hold that the breaches here were sufficiently serious. **[1073]** It has in this regard particularly to be borne in mind that what is attacked in the first place here is a state's decision to adopt legislation, though in the second place the respondents complain about the way in which the legislation was applied.

In view of the court's judgment in *Factortame III* it is not necessary to examine in detail the earlier judgments of the Court of Justice under article 215 but reference should be made to *Bayerische HNL Vermehrungsbetriebe GmbH & Co. KG* v. *Council and Commission of the European Communities* (Joined Cases 83 and 94/76 and 4, 15 and 40/77) [1978] ECR 1209, *Ireks-Arkady GmbH* v. *Council and Commission of the European Communities* (Case 238/78) [1979] ECR 2955 and *Mulder* v. *Council and Commission of the European Communities* (Joined Cases C-104/89 and C-37/90) [1992] ECR I-3061.

In the *Bayerische* case, at p. 1224, the court stressed that the fact that Community legislation is null and void does not entitle an individual to compensation where choices of economic policy are involved—it is only where there has been "a sufficiently serious breach of a superior rule of law for the protection of the individual" (para. 4); "public authorities can only exceptionally and in special circumstances incur liability for legislative measures which are the result of choices of economic policy" (para. 5); "the Community does not therefore incur liability unless the institution concerned has manifestly and gravely disregarded the limits on the exercise of its powers" (para. 6).

In the *Ireks-Arkady* case [1979] ECR 2955 the court in adopting what had been said in the *Bayerische* case said, at p. 2973, para. 11, that the prohibition in article 40(3) of the EEC Treaty of discrimination in the common organisation of the agricultural markets "occupies a particularly important place among the rules of Community law intended to protect the interests of the individual." In that case a limited and clearly defined group of commercial operators was affected and the damage alleged "goes beyond the bounds of the economic risks inherent in the activities of the sector concerned." In *Mulder* v. *Council and Commission of the European Communities* [1992] ECR I-3061 the Advocate General analysed the court's approach in the earlier cases. He said, at p. 3103:

> 15. In my view, it appears from this wording—although a clear pronouncement is warranted—that the expression "manifestly and gravely disregarded the limits on the exercise of its powers" qualifies the words "a sufficiently serious breach." It indicates more specifically that in the case of legislative measures carried out pursuant to a broad discretion the public authority is allowed a certain margin of error. Only where the public authority's error is inexcusable, that is to say where it could reasonably not have committed it, have powers been manifestly and gravely disregarded and there therefore has been a sufficiently serious breach (of a superior rule of law for the protection of individuals).
>
> 16. The court's case law fleshes out the criterion "manifest and grave disregard of the limits on powers" and therefore also the requirement for there to have been a "sufficiently serious breach." It appears from the case law that that criterion is made up of two components: on the one hand, a component related to the type and seriousness of the breach, in other words related to unlawfulness; on the other, a component relating to the type of the damage caused thereby.

More specifically, in the judgments of 4 October 1979 in the **[1074]** *Quellmehl*, and [*P. Dumortier Frères SA* v. *Council of the European Communities* (Joined Cases 64 and 113/76, 167 and 239/78, and 27, 28 and 45/79) [1979] ECR 3091], the court invoked the following circumstances in deciding that the Council had manifestly and gravely disregarded the limits on its powers through the exercise of a wide discretionary power essential for the implementation of the common agricultural policy: (i) the particular importance of the principle infringed by the regulation (in those cases, the principle of equality) and hence the (objective) seriousness of the breach; (ii) the fact that the disregard of that principle affected a limited and clearly defined group of commercial operators; (iii) the fact that the damage alleged by the applicants went beyond the bounds of the economic risks inherent in the operators' activities in the sector concerned; (iv) the fact that the principle in question was infringed without sufficient justification (which points to the inexcusable nature of the error made by the authority: see section 15 above).

Accordingly, the circumstances which, according to that line of cases, point to the existence of a manifest, grave disregard of the limits of a discretionary power or of a sufficiently serious breach of a superior rule of law (which means the same thing) include *both* circumstances relating to the serious (i) and unjustifiable or inexcusable (iv) nature of the breach, which are thus concerned more specifically with the unlawful nature of the act, *and* circumstances relating to the group adversely affected (ii) and to whether or not the adverse effect exceeded a normal risk (iii), which therefore are concerned more specifically with the damage caused by the act.

In *Factortame III* [1996] QB 404, the court repeated these principles and said, at p. 498, para. 43:

The system of rules which the court has worked out with regard to article 215 of the Treaty, particularly in relation to liability for legislative measures, takes into account, inter alia, the complexity of the situations to be regulated, difficulties in the application or interpretation of the texts and, more particularly, the margin of discretion available to the author of the act in question.

The strict approach towards the liability of the Community in the exercise of legislative functions was due in part to the need not to hinder legislative action, "whenever the general interests of the Community require legislative measures to be adopted which may adversely affect individual interests".

It was also in part due to the rule that the Community can only be liable where it has gravely and manifestly disregarded the limits on the exercise of its power. A national legislature may be required to achieve a particular result when it does not have a wide discretion but if it does have a wide discretion the same approach must be followed as with Community institutions.

Accordingly, at p. 499:

55. As to the second condition, as regards both Community liability under article 215 and member state liability for breaches of Community law, the

decisive test for finding that a breach of Community law is sufficiently serious is whether the member state or the Community institution concerned manifestly and gravely disregarded the limits on its discretion.

[1075] 56. The factors which the competent court may take into consideration include the clarity and precision of the rule breached; the measure of discretion left by that rule to the national or Community authorities; whether the infringement and the damage caused was intentional or involuntary; whether any error of law was excusable or inexcusable; the fact that the position taken by a Community institution may have contributed towards the omission, and the adoption or retention of national measures or practices contrary to Community law.

More recent cases show the working out of these rules. Thus in *Reg.* v. *HM Treasury, Ex parte British Telecommunications Plc* (Case C-392/93) [1996] QB 615 the court held that, where the interpretation adopted by the United Kingdom was arguable on the basis of an imprecisely worded article of the relevant directive and where there was no case law to give guidance the state was not liable in damages. In *Reg.* v. *Ministry of Agriculture, Fisheries and Food, Ex parte Hedley Lomas (Ireland) Ltd* (Case C-5/94) [1997] QB 139 where there was no or very little room for discretion in granting a licence that could in itself be a sufficiently serious breach. In *Dillenkofer* v. *Federal Republic of Germany* (Case C-178/94) [1997] QB 259 it was held that a failure to implement a directive, where no or little question of legislative choice was involved, the mere infringement may constitute a sufficiently serious breach. In *Denkavit International BV* v. *Bundesamt für Finanzen* (Cases C-283/94) [1996] ECR I-5063 the court held that other member states, after discussion with the Council had adopted the same interpretation of the Directive as Germany and as there was no relevant case law of the court it was held that the breach was not sufficiently serious.

It was also clear from the cases that it is not necessary to establish fault or negligence on the part of the member state going beyond what is relevant to show a sufficiently serious breach.

Application of the Principle in this Case

In the present case the United Kingdom was entitled to consider how it would exercise the margin of discretion left to it under Community law in the application of the common fisheries policy and in particular of the quota system and also, subject to those limits, how it would exercise its rights under international law to provide for registration as a British fishing vessel. Although the three conditions (nationality, domicile, residence) held in *Factortame II* [1992] QB 680 to be a breach of the Treaty taken in conjunction reflect what the British Government was seeking to do, for the purposes of liability to compensate, the conditions have been considered separately. The first question is, therefore, whether in imposing a nationality requirement the United Kingdom committed a sufficiently serious breach in that it had manifestly and gravely disregarded the limits of its discretion.

In the first place it is to be noted that the relevant rule of Community law is not to be found in an ambiguous directive but in a clear and fundamental provision of the Treaty. By article 7 it is provided that "Within the scope of application of this Treaty, and without prejudice to any special provisions contained therein, any discrimination on the grounds of nationality shall be prohibited." The importance of this principle in the present context is underlined in article 40(3) of the EEC Treaty since any common organisation of the market set up under article 39 "shall exclude **[1076]** any discrimination between producers and consumers within the community."

It is obvious that what was done here by the Government was not done inadvertently. It was done after anxious consideration and after taking legal advice. I accept that it was done in good faith and with the intention of protecting British fishing communities rather than with the deliberate intention of harming Spanish fishermen and those non-British citizens with financial stakes in British registered fishing vessels. The inevitable result of the policy adopted, however, was to take away or seriously affect their rights to fish against the British quota.

The nationality condition was obviously discriminatory and in breach of article 52 as *Factortame II* [1992] QB 680 decided. Indeed as far as article 52 was concerned, this was already clear from *Commission of the European Communities* v. *Italian Republic* (Case 63/86) [1988] ECR 29. Although the question whether this was a sufficiently serious breach justifying the award of damages is a matter for the national courts, and therefore for your Lordships, to decide it is to be noted that in *Factortame III* [1996] QB 404, 500, para. 61 the European Court stated bluntly that the nationality condition constituted direct discrimination which was manifestly contrary to Community law.

Can it be said that, even if the Act of 1988 was deliberately adopted, it was an unintentional and "excusable" breach which should prevent what was done being "a sufficiently serious breach" in that it was a manifest and grave disregard of the limits of the United Kingdom's discretion?

The appellant relies on the history of the discussions leading up to the enactment of the Act of 1988 and the making of regulations under it. He explains the problem and the understandable aim of seeking to protect British fishing communities and the British quota. Licensing rules having not been adequate, the only solution they felt was to change the rules on registration by primary legislation (letter Ministry of Agriculture, Fisheries and Food to Foreign Secretary on 14 November 1986). They were, however, aware from the beginning of the legal problems involved.

A memorandum sent to the Law Officers on 2 December 1986 which is set out more fully in the judgment of the Divisional Court [1997] EuLR 475, 490 asks for advice and recognises that "The proposed legislation (and the parallel legislation in other member states) may contravene article 52."

Officials and ministers were clearly aware that there was a risk that if the legislation was adopted it would be held to be contrary to Community law: see letter of Margaret Lind Smith of 17 July 1987 and of Mr Ingram of 6 October 1987. The Secretary of State for Transport wrote to the Attorney-General on 22 October 1987

> Officials have . . . concluded that we should proceed as originally intended. While this does pose a risk to our position on damages, the official view was that the applicant would have to overcome so many obstacles—not least of which would be winning his case in the European Court on the substantive issue on whether our law is compatible with the Treaty—that the risk was worth taking given the drawbacks of the alternatives.

Professor Francis Jacobs QC and other counsel were asked to advise on the basis that a national condition of registration could be challenged before the European Court and that articles 52, 59 and 221 of the Treaty **[1077]** posed a particular difficulty. The Government said that nationality was a more appropriate test than residence:

> Not only may residence be changed more readily than nationality; it is less easy to prove or disprove. In particular, in the case of a shareholder or director of a small fishing company who may spend much of his time on a fishing boat at sea a residence test would be hard to apply.

Counsel advised on 24 February 1987 that

> in our view, any discrimination that arises out of the proposed measures is a natural consequence of the common CFP itself which divides out the available fishing quotas along national lines . . . We consider that rules on the nationality of fishing vessels are the most appropriate way of establishing a genuine link between the member states and the vessel intending to fish for the member state's quota, particularly having regard to possible alternatives.

They recommended, however, that the percentage of shares held legally and beneficially by British nationals resident and domiciled in the United Kingdom should be no more than 75 per cent, that there should be a period of grace before the legislation took effect and they stressed that the dispensation provisions in section 14(4) of the Act of 1988 in respect of nationality where there had been a long period of residence were important. They concluded however:

> In our view the proposed legislation should, if challenged, be held to be compatible with Community law on the basis that such legislation is a necessary consequence of the Common Fisheries Policy.

On 31 March 1987 the Law Officers advised: "that there is a reasonably good prospect that the proposed legislation would be upheld by the European Court."

On 18 November 1988 Mr Advocate General Mischo gave his opinion (a) in *Reg.* v. *Ministry of Agriculture, Fisheries and Food, Ex parte Jaderow Ltd* (Case C-216/87) [1990] 2 QB 193, 208, para. 7 that "Community law does not therefore restrict the power which each member state has under public international law to determine the conditions on which it allows a vessel to fly its flag" and (b) in *Reg.* v. *Ministry of Agriculture, Fisheries and Food, Ex parte Agegate Ltd* (Case C-3/87) [1990] 2 QB 151 that the residence requirement in the crewing condition in the Act of 1983 was compatible with Community law because of the quota system and other features of the fisheries regulation.

On the other hand it is to be remembered that the power of member states in this area is subject to the extensive control exercised by the Community institutions under the common fisheries policy. On 28 March 1988, before the bill received the royal assent the Commission (DG XV) told the United Kingdom Government that the proposed conditions were prima facie contrary to the right of establishment under article 52. The Commission continued to state its opposition to the nationality condition and subsequently to the domicile and residence conditions. The article 169 proceedings against the United Kingdom in respect of the nationality condition, led to the President's order of 10 October 1998 as an interim measure suspending that condition. Moreover it is to be recalled that the Divisional Court had initially suspended all three conditions [1989] **[1078]** 2 CMLR 353 as the House of Lords was to do on 10 July 1989 following *Factortame I*: see [1991] 1 AC 603. The decisions of the European Court in the *Agegate* case [1990] 2 QB 151 and the *Jaderow* case [1990] 2 QB 193 gave the Government no comfort or encouragement.

It was, moreover, obvious as the Divisional Court [1989] 2 CMLR 353 and the Court of Appeal [1989] 2 CMLR 392 thought on the initial hearing in 1988, and as the House of Lords [1990] 2 AC 85 thought on the hearing following *Factortame I* [1990] ECR I-2433, that the damage which would be suffered by the respondents would be serious and immediate.

How far the views of the Commission ought to be taken into account has been much debated in argument. The Divisional Court said [1997] EuLR 475, 519

> Where there is a doubt about the legality of any proposal, a failure by a member state to seek the views of the Commission or, if it receives them, to follow them is likely to lead to any breach being regarded as inexcusable and so manifest.

The Court of Appeal added [1998] EuLR 456, 475:

If a member state [proceeds on its course despite the opinion of the Commission] and it subsequently transpires that this was a course which should not have been followed, the fact that the Commission's advice has not been followed, strengthens the case of those who seek damages for the loss that they have suffered.

The appellant contends that the Court of Appeal and the Divisional Court have overstated the importance of the Commission's role.

It is in my view clear that the views of the Commission are not conclusive (a) as to whether there has been a breach of Community law and (b) as to whether the breach is a sufficiently serious breach to justify an award of damages. The former is as a last resort for the European Court in proceedings under article 169 or on a reference under article 177 and the latter is for the national court. The considered view of the Commission in a case of this kind, where the Community has a substantial role, is however of importance. Indeed in an area so closely subject to Community control as is the common fisheries policy, it is not only wise but often a necessary step to consult the Commission. The Government did here consult the Commission. A member state may choose to ignore the advice given but if it does so, it incurs the risk that, if it proves to be wrong and the Commission to be right, the member state will be found to have gone ahead deliberately, well aware of the Commission's views, and that a court will be more likely to find that the breach has been manifest and grave and thus sufficiently serious. In the present case, the Commission's view was firm, consistent and hostile to the Government.

It seems to me that the appellant can rely on the fact that it took legal advice although that is but one factor in having regard, as I think one must, to all the circumstances. However, the advice of Professor Jacobs QC and others in 1987 was to some extent qualified and was based on the instructions that there would be a dispensing power not just for the residence but also for the nationality and domicile conditions. Moreover as time went on, there was clearly doubt as to whether the Government could really succeed before the European Court and the Commission's letters, to which I have referred, were not it seems the subject matter of any further discussion with counsel. Further, the subsequent opinion of **[1079]** Mr Christopher Bellamy QC, although on a different question, was more qualified as to the overall chances of success.

The shortness of the transitional period, the fact that there was, it seemed, no way in domestic law of challenging the statute, and that the respondents were obliged, not merely to avoid being removed from the old register, but to apply to be put on the new register all emphasise the determination of the Government to press ahead with this scheme despite the strong opposition of the Commission and the doubts of some of its officials. When the judgments in the *Agegate* and *Jaderow* cases [1990] 2 QB 151 and 193 were delivered they gave the Government no encouragement to continue and the view of some government officials (e.g. Mr Timothy Pratt on 14 December 1989 which in retrospect seemed prophetic) and the opinion of Andrew Macnab of counsel on 16 March 1990 made the difficulties more clear. There is indeed, in my view, considerable justification for the Divisional Court's finding that by January 1990 there was really little hope of saving the three conditions.

Accordingly, despite the arguments of the United Kingdom and the advice it received, it seems to me clear that the deliberate adoption of legislation which was clearly discriminatory on the ground of nationality and which inevitably violated article 52 of the Treaty (since it prevented establishment in the United Kingdom) was a manifest breach of fundamental Treaty obligations. It was a grave breach of the Treaty both intrinsically and as regards the consequences it was bound, or at the least was most likely, to have on the respondents. It has not been shown to have been excusable. The Commission opposed it and despite the view of Mr Advocate General Mischo, on the Act of 1983 there was no decision of the European Court to support the Government. What was done, therefore, in regard to nationality plainly constituted a sufficiently serious breach for the purposes of the second condition of liability. Moreover to maintain the legislation in operation after the court's decisions in the cases of *Agegate* and *Jaderow* and to allow such a short transitional period itself constituted a sufficiently serious breach.

It is agreed that "domicile" falls to be treated in the same way as nationality. That condition, therefore, was also a sufficiently serious breach.

As to residence, the European Court said [1996] QB 404, 500:

> 62. The latter conditions are prima facie incompatible with article 52 of the Treaty in particular, but the United Kingdom sought to justify them in terms of the objectives of the common fisheries policy. In the judgment in *Reg.* v. *Secretary of State for Transport, Ex parte Factortame Ltd (No 3)* (Case C-221/89) [1992] QB 680 the court rejected that justification.
>
> 63. In order to determine whether the breach of article 52 thus committed by the United Kingdom was sufficiently serious, the national court might take into account, inter alia, the legal disputes relating to particular features of the common fisheries policy, the attitude of the Commission, which made its position known to the United Kingdom in good time, and the assessments as to the state of certainty of community law made by the national courts in the interim proceedings brought by individuals affected by the Merchant Shipping Act.

I have had some doubt about the condition as to residence. If the aim of protecting the livelihood of British fishing communities, including allied trades such as preparing and processing landed fish, is justified then it is **[1080]** arguable that to require active fishermen to live in these communities might be excusable. The condition here was not however, limited to such fishermen or to such areas. It covered shareholders and directors of companies owning fishing vessels. It allowed the fishermen to live anywhere. It seems to me that this condition cannot be justified where the discrimination is, as it is here, clear. Moreover the British Government all along took the view that the residence condition would not in itself be sufficient to achieve its aims and so taken separately cannot in my view be justified.

It is, moreover, somewhat artificial to separate out the various conditions and in the end I agree with the Court of Appeal that the conditions should be treated as cumulative. Even taken separately, it is clear that discrimination on grounds such as residence can constitute indirect or covert discrimination on the grounds of nationality *Sotgiu* v. *Deutsche Bundespost* (Case 152/73) [1974] ECR 153. I accordingly consider that the residence condition also constituted a serious breach.

I also agree with the Court of Appeal that, if it had been necessary to do so, which it is not, it would have been right to regard the treatment of Mr Yllera and Mr and Mrs O'Connor, under section 14(4) of the Act of 1988 as contributing to the seriousness of the breach.

I, therefore, conclude that the United Kingdom's breach of its Community obligations by imposing and applying the conditions of nationality, domicile and residence in and pursuant to the Merchant Shipping Act 1988 was a sufficiently serious breach so as to entitle the respondents to compensation for damage directly caused by that breach. I consider also that the United Kingdom was in breach of Community law by failing to give effect to the order of the President of the European Court of 10 October 1989 until 2 November 1989 and that this also constituted a serious breach of Community obligations which would, had they not succeeded on the first ground, have entitled Rawlings (Trawling) Ltd to compensation for damage directly caused by that breach.

LORD NICHOLLS OF BIRKENHEAD. My Lords, I have had the advantage of reading a draft of the speeches of my noble and learned friends, Lord Slynn of Hadley and Lord Hope of Craighead. For the reasons they give, I, too, would dismiss this appeal.

LORD HOFFMANN. My Lords, in passing the Merchant Shipping Act 1988 the United Kingdom (acting by its legislature) took a calculated risk. It knew that there was, to put the matter at its lowest, doubt over whether the legislation contravened fundamental principles of Community law. The European Commission had expressed the clear view that it infringed the rights of establishment of citizens of other member states and their right to invest in United Kingdom companies. The UK Government knew that the effect of the legislation would be to cause substantial losses to the owners of boats which they could no longer use for fishing under the British flag. It could have delayed implementation of the legislation until there had been an authoritative ruling on whether it was lawful. Instead, it chose to brook no delay and successfully appealed against a decision of the Divisional Court in March 1989 which would have suspended the operation of the Act until the matter had been determined. In the end, the United Kingdom was held to have been wrong. The judgment of the European Court in July 1991 held unequivocally that the Community rights of the boat owners had been infringed.

[1081] The question is now whether they are entitled to compensation. The Court of Justice [1996] QB 404, 499, para. 55 has ruled that this depends upon whether the breach of Community law was sufficiently serious. It accepts that in principle the area in which the United Kingdom was legislating was one in which it had a wide discretion. In such a case, the breach of Community law will be sufficiently serious only if the legislature "manifestly and gravely disregarded the limits of its discretion."

I agree with my noble and learned friend, Lord Slynn of Hadley, that the actions of the United Kingdom can properly be so described. There is no doubt that in discriminating against non-UK Community nationals on the grounds of their nationality, to which the requirements of domicile and residence were added to tighten the exclusion of non-UK interests, the legislature was prima facie flouting one of the most basic principles of Community law. The responsible Ministers considered, on the basis of the advice they had received, that there was an arguable case for holding that the United Kingdom was entitled to do so. In that sense, the Divisional Court has held that the Government acted bona fide. But they could have been in no doubt that there was a substantial risk that they were wrong. Nevertheless, they saw the political imperatives of the time as justifying immediate action. In these circumstances, I do not think that the United Kingdom, having deliberately decided to run the risk, can say that the losses caused by the legislation should lie where they fell. Justice requires that the wrong should be made good.

The Solicitor-General argued that the breach of Community law was excusable on the grounds that the Government acted upon legal advice. He relied in particular on the written opinion given by Professor Francis Jacobs QC and others in February 1987. I do not think that a member state can rely simply upon the fact that its relevant organ of government acted upon legal advice. It is a basic principle of Community law that in considering the liabilities of a member state, all its various organs of government are treated as a single aggregate entity. It does not matter how their responsibilities are divided under domestic law or what passed between them. Likewise, as it seems to me, the process of advice and consultation undertaken within a member state by its responsible organs of government is irrelevant. Advice received from Community institutions is another matter: as the Court of Justice points out in its judgment on the reference in this case *Brasserie du Pêcheur SA* v. *Federal Republic of Germany; Reg.* v. *Secretary of State for Transport, Ex parte Factortame Ltd (No 4)* (Joined Cases C-46 and 48/93) [1996] QB 404, 499, para. 56), "the fact that the position taken by a Community institution may have contributed towards the omission" is a relevant matter to take into account in deciding whether a breach was sufficiently serious. But the question of whether the error of law was excusable or inexcusable is an objective one and the excuses must be considered on their own merits.

When one comes to consider the strength of the United Kingdom's arguments to justify discrimination against nationals of other member states, it seems to me that there was a fatal divergence between the rhetoric which the Government used to describe the problem and the solution which it adopted. The Act was said to be to ensure that "UK quotas were reserved for UK fishermen." Foreign nationals, mainly Spanish, were said to be "quota hopping," using the British flag to fish against the UK quota. The image conveyed was of disappointed trawlermen from Newquay or Grimsby, returning with empty holds because the fish which were part of the UK quota had been taken by Spanish vessels flying the British flag **[1082]** and landed at Santander. There is a dispute about whether this presented a fair picture of the reality which the Divisional Court found it unnecessary to resolve. Neither do your Lordships, because the provisions of the Act went far beyond anything which was necessary to deal with such a situation. The system of quotas was intended, as stated by a recital to Council Regulation (EEC) No 170/83 of 25 January 1983, to "safeguard the particular needs of regions where local populations are especially dependent on fisheries and related industries." The Court of Justice has always recognised that member states are entitled to take any necessary and appropriate measures to ensure that there is a "real economic link" between operations of vessels fishing against the national quota and the local populations dependent on fishing and related industries: see, for example, the judgment of the Court of Justice in *Reg.* v. *Ministry of Agriculture, Fisheries and Food, Ex parte Jaderow Ltd* (Case C-216/87) [1990] 2 QB 193, 222, para. 27. But the terms of the Act were inappropriate to achieve this object because they were principally concerned, not with the operations of the vessels, but with the nationality, domicile and country of residence of the shareholders in the companies which owned them. One is bound to ask how it could be thought to have made any difference to the interests of the population of an English fishing port whether the shares in a company owning a vessel fishing out of that port were owned by a UK national and domiciliary resident in London or a Spanish national and domiciliary resident in Madrid.

For these reasons, as well as those given by my noble and learned friends, Lord Slynn of Hadley and Lord Hope of Craighead, I would dismiss the appeal.

LORD HOPE OF CRAIGHEAD. My Lords, I have had the advantage of reading in draft the speech which has been prepared by my noble and learned friend, Lord Slynn of Hadley. I agree with it, and for the reasons which he has given I too would dismiss the appeal. I wish merely to add these observations to what he has said.

As the Solicitor-General said at the outset of his argument, the question whether the breach by the United Kingdom of its Community obligations entitles the respondents to damages raises issues of fact as well as issues of law. It seems to me that it is the issues of fact that are determinative of the question which is before us in this case. I am not persuaded that the Divisional Court [1997] EuLR 475 and the Court of Appeal [1998] EuLR 456 were in error in their assessment of these issues.

In *Brasserie du Pêcheur SA* v. *Federal Republic of Germany; Reg.* v. *Secretary of State for Transport, Ex parte Factortame Ltd (No 4)* (Cases C-46/93 and C-48/93) [1996] QB 404, 499, para. 51 ("*Factortame III*") the European Court of Justice set out the conditions for the entitlement to damages in these terms:

> In such circumstances, Community law confers a right to reparation where three conditions are met: the rule of law infringed must be intended to confer rights on individuals; the breach must be sufficiently serious, and there must be a direct causal link between the breach of the obligation resting on the state and the damage sustained by the injured parties.

The first of these three conditions, which raises an issue of law, was held in *Factortame III*, p. 499, para. 54 to have been satisfied. This was on the ground that it was manifest that articles 30 and 52 of the EC Treaty (now **[1083]** articles 28 and 43 EC) were both intended to confer rights on individuals. The third condition, which relates to causation, was held to be a matter for the national courts to determine: p. 501, para. 64. This raises an issue of fact which must be deferred for consideration at a later date. It will have to be considered in the light of the evidence. The dispute at this stage relates to the second condition. Was the breach "sufficiently serious"?

In para. 55 of its decision in *Factortame III* the European Court, following the approach it has taken as to the liability of Community institutions under article 215 of the EC Treaty (now article 288 of the Treaty) in the exercise of their legislative activities, said that the decisive test for finding that a breach of Community law is sufficiently serious is whether the member state "manifestly and gravely" disregarded the limits on its discretion. In the following paragraph, in a list which I would regard as helpful but not exhaustive, six factors were mentioned for consideration by the competent court. Among these are the clarity and precision of the rule breached, whether the infringement was intentional or involuntary and whether any error of law was excusable or inexcusable. In various passages elsewhere in the judgment the court expressed its opinion about the nature of the breach for the consequences of which the respondents are claiming damages. But I would not be inclined to attach much importance to these expressions of opinion, because in para. 58 of the judgment the court made it clear that it was for the national courts to assess the seriousness of the breach. The national courts have the sole jurisdiction to find the facts in the main proceedings. It is for them to decide how to characterise the breaches of Community law which are in issue.

It is a novel task for the courts of this country to have to assess whether a breach is sufficiently serious to entitle a party who has suffered loss as a result of it to damages. The general rule is that where a breach of duty has been established and a causal link between the breach and the loss suffered has been proved the injured party is entitled as of right to damages. In the present context however the rules are different. The facts must be examined in order that the court may determine whether the breach of Community law was of such a kind that damages should be awarded as compensation for the loss. The phrases "sufficiently serious" and "manifestly and gravely" which the European Court has used indicate that a fairly high threshold must be passed before it can be said that the test has been satisfied.

It seems to me that three factors emerge from the facts of this case which justify the conclusion that the breach was sufficiently serious to entitle the respondents to damages. The first relates to the subject matter of the breach. In this regard I agree with the Court of Appeal [1998] EuLR 456, 476 that the three conditions of nationality, domicile and residence in section 14 of the Merchant Shipping Act 1988 must be treated, in the context of the provisions of that Act, as cumulative. It is plain that we are dealing in this case with the adoption and retention in our national law of measures which were contrary to the obligations of the United Kingdom under the EC Treaty relating to nationality and domicile: see article 52, read with articles 5 and 7 (now article 43, read with articles 10 and 14). These are key areas of the Treaty in regard to the free movement of persons and the right of establishment. This is not a case where it can be said that the Treaty obligations were obscure or that they related to matters which were of minor importance. I would not go so far as to say, with the Court of Appeal, at p. 476, that the direct breach of a fundamental **[1084]** principle of the Treaty will almost inevitably create a liability in damages. But the nature of the breach will always be a highly relevant factor in the assessment. The more fundamental the breach, the easier it will be to regard it as sufficiently serious.

The second factor relates to the potential of the breach for causing damage to those who are likely to suffer loss as a result of it. The Divisional Court [1997] EuLR 475, 503 held that the stated and actual purpose of the Government was to protect indigenous British fishing interests, not to injure the respondents, although that might be the effect of the policy. But it was clear that once the law took effect it would almost certainly cause loss to those who were affected by it, and that their loss was likely to be both serious and irremediable. The respondents were to be deprived of their right to fish in United Kingdom waters. They had established themselves here, and for all practical purposes they had nowhere else to go to continue their livelihood. This potential for obvious and immediate damage leads naturally to the conclusion that, even though the Government were acting in good faith, this was a serious breach and that the respondents ought to be entitled to compensation by way of damages if the other two conditions laid down by the European Court are satisfied.

The third factor relates to the methods which were used to achieve the result. The Government chose to resort to primary legislation. This made it impossible for the respondents to obtain interim relief against it under domestic law as it then stood. It then chose to impose a short and inflexible transitional period for bringing the legislation into effect. No interval of time was allowed, in the event of its being challenged, for the issues of principle to be determined by means of a preliminary reference. This was despite the fact that by the time the legislation was introduced the Commission's stance on the matter was well known and the point was by now clearly open for argument. The interests of those who were likely to be affected by the legislation were subordinated to those of the Government. A deliberate decision was taken to proceed in this way, albeit in good faith, in preference to safeguarding the interests of those who were entitled to the protection of the treaty obligations should the legal advice on which the Government was proceeding turn out to be wrong.

This then was more than a trivial or technical breach of the Community obligations. The words "manifest" and "grave" are not easy adjectives to apply in this context. But I have no difficulty at all in seeing what was done here as a breach which was sufficiently serious to entitle the respondents to compensation by way of damages for such losses as they can show flowed directly from the breach. If damages were not to be held to be recoverable in this case, it would be hard to envisage any case, short of one involving bad faith, where damages would be recoverable.

The Solicitor-General laid great stress on the point made by the European Court that one of the factors which could be taken into account in the assessment of seriousness was whether or not the breach was excusable. Much importance was attached by him to the legal advice which had been taken and received. But I was not impressed by this argument. The good faith of the Government is not in question. It is not suggested that it proceeded without taking advice, or that it acted directly contrary to the advice which it received. Nor is it suggested that there was a lack of clarity in the wording of the relevant provisions of the Treaty or that there was some other point which might reasonably have been overlooked. So this case cannot, I think, be described as one which went wrong due to **[1085]** inadvertence, misunderstanding or oversight. The meaning of the relevant articles was never in doubt. The critical issue related to the interaction between these articles and the common fisheries policy. On this matter there was clearly a serious issue to be resolved. Different views had been expressed within government, and the Commission was known to have taken a view contrary to that which the Government decided to adopt.

I do not wish to be taken as suggesting that the Government should have deferred to the views of the Commission on this matter. It was clearly entitled to take a different view and to decide upon its own course. But the Commission's role, while not conclusive, was important. It was seized of the matter, and it had stated its position in terms which were unequivocal. The decision to legislate was taken by the Government in full knowledge of the risks. I find it impossible to describe that decision as having been based on an oversight or an error of law which was excusable.

LORD CLYDE. My Lords, I also agree that this appeal should be dismissed and it is only on account of the importance of the case that I would add some observations of my own.

It was established in *Reg.* v. *Secretary of State for Transport, Ex parte Factortame Ltd* [1992] QB 680 that the requirements for registration of fishing vessels contained in the Merchant Shipping Act 1988 were contrary to the provisions of the treaty and unlawful and invalid in community law. The dispute now concerns the claim for damages which the respondents have brought against the appellant. In circumstances such as the present the European Court of Justice has identified the conditions which require to be met for conferring under Community law a right to reparation against the legislature of a member state following upon a breach by that legislature of Community law. In para. 51 of their judgment in the combined cases of *Brasserie du Pêcheur SA* v. *Federal Republic of Germany; Reg.* v. *Secretary of State for Transport, Ex parte Factortame Ltd (No 4)* (Joined Cases C-46 and 48/93) [1996] QB 404, 499 ("*Factortame III*") the court prescribed three conditions which required to be met. First, the rule of law infringed must be intended to confer rights on individuals; secondly the breach must be "sufficiently serious," and thirdly, there must be a direct causal link between the breach of the obligation and the damage. The first of these is not in dispute and the third is matter to be resolved at a later stage. The only question in the present appeal is whether the breach was "sufficiently serious."

In developing the conditions under which liability may arise the court has looked to its jurisprudence both in relation to article 215 and also in relation to the liability of Community institutions. From this has emerged the recognition of the relevance both of the practical and legal problems involved in particular cases, and also of the extent of the discretion open to the party in breach. In some cases there may be no discretion left to the state, and where there is an absolute duty to act a liability for a failure to act may more readily arise. In other cases there can be a degree of discretion and the wider the discretion the less readily should a claim for damages be available. The rationale for this strict approach, as appears from p. 498, para. 45 of the judgment in *Factortame III*, is the consideration that governments should not be hindered from passing legislation in the general interest of the community which may adversely affect individual interests by the prospects of actions for damages.

It has been recognised by the European Court of Justice that in the circumstances of the present case the United Kingdom legislature had a **[1086]** wide discretion. In p. 499, para. 49 of the judgment the court explains that the legislation was concerned not only with the registration of vessels but also with the regulation of fishing. The former of these falls within the jurisdiction of the member states, and the latter, concerned with the implementation of the common fisheries policy, leaves a margin of discretion to the member states.

Where member states act in a field where there is a wide discretion the situation should be comparable with that of the community institutions in the implementation of community policies. The conditions under which liability may arise should also be comparable.

Where legislative measures are the result of choices of economic policy it is only exceptionally and in special circumstances that liability for those measures should arise. That principle was recognised in the judgment of the court in *Bayerische HNL Vermehrungsbetriebe GmbH & Co. KG* v. *Council and Commission of the European Communities* [1978] ECR 1209, 1224, para. 5. In that case it was held (in para. 6 of the judgment) that the Community does not incur liability "unless the institution concerned has manifestly and gravely disregarded the limits on the exercise of its powers." The language appears to echo a passage in the argument presented by the Council, at p. 1216, that "It must be a breach which is particularly blatant, a particularly clear infringement and a manifest grave violation of the basic content of a principle." In *Factortame III* [1996] QB 404, 499, para. 55 the court stated that "the decisive test for finding that a breach of Community law is sufficiently serious is whether the member state or the Community institution concerned manifestly and gravely disregarded the limits on its discretion."

While the application of the test may not require any too precise analysis, its ingredients may deserve to be identified. That the limits on the discretion have to be disregarded suggests that something more than a mere excess of power is required. More particularly the disregard must be manifest. From p. 500, para. 59 of the judgment in *Factortame III* it is said of one of the provisions in the German legislation in the *Brasserie* case that "it would be difficult to regard the breaches of article 30 by that legislation as an excusable error, since the incompatibility of such rules with article 30 was manifest in the light of earlier decisions of the court . . ." Legislation which is contrary to established case law is thus one example of a manifest breach. It is to be noted that in that passage the court refers to excusability as covering either the case where the breach is not manifest or, which would in such an event follow, where the breach was not sufficiently serious. The Solicitor-General sought to use the concept of excusability as the touchstone for freedom from liability. But it may be preferable to hold to the language of the "decisive test" rather than resort to different expressions which may less exactly reflect the principle, unless the word is clearly used simply as a label to represent the converse of a sufficiently serious breach.

In addition to being manifest the disregard of the limits of the discretion must be grave. This points to some significant and substantial characteristic, as where the breach is of a basic principle of Community law. As can be seen from the judgment in *Factortame III* [1996] QB 404, 499, para. 57, persisting in an infringement despite a judgment finding the infringement to be established would be an example of a sufficiently serious breach. The disregard of the limits of the discretion would be manifest by virtue of the judgment and it would be grave in respect of the persistence in the infringement.

[1087] But it may be too narrow an approach in the practical application of the test to make the distinction between the categorisation of what is manifest and of what is grave. A broader approach is perhaps to be preferred. Moreover the application of the test laid down by the court comes eventually to be a matter of fact and circumstance. In the judgment the court [1996] QB 404, 499, para. 56 lists some of the factors which may be taken into consideration. But that list does not pretend to be complete or exhaustive. It would doubtless be premature to attempt any comprehensive analysis. But it appears to be possible to identify some of the particular considerations which may properly be taken into account, although the relevance in particular cases and the weight to be given to them in particular circumstances may obviously vary from case to case. It is to be noted that liability does not require the establishment of fault as, to use the language of the Advocate General in his opinion [1996] QB 404, 476, para. 90, "a subjective component of the unlawful conduct." It is on the objective factors in the case that the decision on liability requires to be reached. No single factor is necessarily decisive. But one factor by itself might, particularly where there was little or nothing to put into the scales on the other side, be sufficient to justify a conclusion of liability. Some of those factors can be identified as follows.

1. In paragraph 38 of its judgment in *Factortame III*, at p. 497, the court has affirmed that the liability of a member state for damages for a breach of Community law depends on the nature of the breach. This gives rise to consideration of a number of more particular matters, one of the most prominent of which is the importance of the principle which has been breached. Thus in *Mulder* v. *Council and Commission of the European Communities* (Joined Cases C-104/89 and C-37/90) [1992] ECR I-3061

the court founded upon the fact that the breach in question was of a general and superior principle of Community law, namely the protection of legitimate expectations.

2. Another consideration relating to the nature of the breach is the clarity and precision of the rule breached. If the breach is of a provision of Community law which is not framed in clear language and is readily open to construction, then the breach may be the less serious. Questions of the clarity of the rule may require to be associated with questions of the complexity of the factual situation. The application to complex facts even of a rule which is reasonably clear in itself may render the situation open to doubt.

3. Closely related to that last consideration is the degree of excusability of an error of law. That could arise on account of the ambiguity of a Community text. It could also arise out of the uncertainty of the law in some particular area, where there is little or no guidance and evident room for difference of opinion.

4. Another factor relating to the clarity of the law is the existence of any relevant judgment on the point. If there is settled case law, the failure to follow it may add to the seriousness of the breach. On the other hand if the point is novel and is not covered by any guidance then liability should less readily follow.

5. It is also relevant to look at the state of mind of the infringer, and in particular whether the infringer was acting intentionally or involuntarily. A deliberate intention to infringe would obviously weigh heavily in the scales of seriousness. An inadvertent breach might be relatively less serious on that account. Liability may still be established without any intentional infringement. More broadly, the purpose of the infringer should be **[1088]** considered. If the purpose was to advance the interests of the Community a breach committed with that end in view might be seen as less serious than one committed with the purpose of serving merely national interests.

6. The behaviour of the infringer after it has become evident that an infringement has occurred may also be of importance. At the one extreme the immediate taking of steps to undo what has been done and correct any error which has been committed may operate to mitigate the seriousness of the breach. At the other extreme a persistence in the breach, the retention of measures or practices which are contrary to Community law, especially where they are known so to be, will add to the seriousness of what has been done. Indeed, in paragraph 57 of the judgment in *Factortame III*, at p. 499, the court stated that persistence in a breach despite a judgment finding an infringement or clear case law on the point, "will clearly be sufficiently serious."

7. Another aspect relates to the persons affected by the breach. In the *Mulder* case [1992] ECR I-3061 the court also founded upon the fact that there had been a complete failure to take account of the specific situation

of a defined economic group, namely the producers of milk. The fact that the exclusion of the producers from the allocation of a reference quantity was not foreseeable and was beyond the limits of ordinary economic risk made the breach all the more obvious (pp. 3132, 3133, paras. 16-17).

8. A further consideration is the position taken by one of the Community institutions in the matter. It may be that one of the institutions has, to use the language of the court in the judgment in *Factortame III* [1996] QB 404, 500, para. 56 "contributed towards the omission." In the present context this is not to be seen as bearing upon the third of the three necessary conditions for liability which the court has prescribed, namely the existence of a direct causal link between the breach and the damages sustained. Here it is a factor relating to the seriousness of the breach. As phrased in para. 56 it is presented as a mitigating factor and it is wide enough to include various kinds of actions on the part of the institution concerned. But it also includes the giving of information or advice and in that connection the factor could operate in either direction so far as the seriousness of the breach is concerned. Advice from the Commission that the state would not be acting in breach of Community law in taking a particular step would plainly be a mitigating factor. The decision to persist in a proposed step in the face of warnings from the Commission that the state would be in breach of Community law in so doing would add to the seriousness of the state's action.

What then remains is the application of the test to the facts of the case. In para. 58 at p. 500 of the judgment the court records that the national courts have the sole jurisdiction to find the facts and to decide how to characterise the breaches in question. But the court then states that "it will be helpful to indicate a number of circumstances which the national courts might take into account." The first of these appears to be a plain indication that at least the nationality condition was manifestly contrary to Community law. But it is still for the national court alone to determine whether there was a sufficiently serious breach. It may be noted that Advocate General Tesauro expressed himself robustly on the point, at p. 489, para. 120 of his opinion:

> In the final analysis, I do not consider that there can be any doubts as to the manifest and serious nature of the breach in question **[1089]** and hence as to the right to compensation of individuals who suffered damage as a result of it.

Secondly, the court states that the conditions on residence and domicile were prima facie incompatible with the Treaty; that the United Kingdom sought to justify them but that the court rejected that justification in *Factortame II* [1992] QB 680. That leaves open for argument whether at the time the breach was manifest and grave. Thereafter in para. 63 the court details three matters which the national court might take into account in relation to the question whether the breach of article 52 was sufficiently serious. It is not altogether clear whether these are intended to relate to the matter of nationality as well as to the matters of residence and domicile but in the overall appraisal of the case that point may not be critical. The three matters are not intended to be exclusive and they appear to point in divergent directions. The first, a reference to the legal disputes relating to particular features of the common fisheries policy, may indicate a degree of uncertainty in the law which would point in favour of the appellant's case. On the other hand the attitude of the Commission "which made its position known to the United Kingdom in good time" is a factor pointing in favour of the respondents. The third matter, "the assessments as to the state of certainty of Community law made by the national courts in the interim proceedings brought by individuals affected by the Merchant Shipping Act," may be seen as pointing in the appellant's favour. It may be recalled that Bingham LJ observed of the problem of Community law in *Reg.* v. *Secretary of State for Transport, Ex parte Factortame Ltd* [1989] CMLR 353, 399:

> Both judges in the Divisional Court thought this a difficult and important question on which a decision was necessary to enable them to give judgment. I agree, and no criticism has been addressed to that part of their judgments. Like Neill LJ I shall not express even a tentative view on the likely outcome of the reference to the European Court of Justice which the Divisional Court rightly ordered. Both sides accept that the answer is not "acte clair."

There are of course further considerations. For example, account may properly be taken of the fact that the appellant acted in good faith. He took legal advice from a recognised expert in the field. He sought advice from the Commission. He had the serious purpose of seeking to counter what he saw as an abuse of the common fisheries policy. He recognised that the measure would cause loss, but that was not the purpose of it.

The reference to which the European Court responded was made by the Divisional Court on 18 November 1992 and it was to that court that the case was returned to determine the matter in the light of the guidance given. In a detailed and careful judgment that court decided that the breaches by the appellant of Community law were sufficiently serious to give rise to a liability in damages. That decision has been considered and endorsed by the Court of Appeal. I would not propose to open up the whole range of considerations again with a view to forming a fresh assessment of them. I have not been persuaded that there exists any ground for disturbing the conclusion which has already been reached and I consider that the view which has been taken by the Divisional Court and by the Court of Appeal regarding the condition of residence as well as the view taken on the matters of nationality and domicile were sound and correct. On one point only would I venture to express disagreement, and **[1090]** that is only with regard to the matter of the relative weight to be given to the view of the Commission. In the

Divisional Court [1997] EuLR 475, 519 it was stated in relation to the Commission that "a member state which disregards its view does so at its peril." That may be a slight overstatement. The court also stated that a failure to follow the views of the Commission "is likely to lead to any breach being regarded as inexcusable and so manifest." That more moderate formulation was adopted by the Court of Appeal and seems to me to be preferable. But this detail does not touch on the substance of the decision nor the overall assessment. I would dismiss the appeal.

Appeal dismissed with costs.

[Report: [1999] 3 WLR 1062]

Direct effect—Directives—Conditions for direct effect—Whether directive creating rights which may be relied upon by individuals before national courts—Whether content of rights identifiable on the basis of provisions of the directive—Purpose of directive — Relevance of recitals — Council Directive 77/780—Coordination of banking supervision

Enforcement in national courts—Remedies—Claim based alternatively on direct effect and State liability—Whether conditions to establish right to damages essentially the same for both types of claim—Claim against State-controlled body—Breach of Community law for which Member State responsible—Duty of national courts to provide effective remedies for the enforcement of rights of individuals under Community law—Claim brought by individuals in reliance on Council directive

Institutions—Court of Justice—Powers—Jurisdiction under Article 177 of EC Treaty—Scope of duty of national courts to make reference to Court of Justice—Role as final authority for interpretation of Community law — Conditions for making of reference by national courts — Discretion of national courts in deciding whether to make reference—Doctrine of *acte clair*—The law of England

THREE RIVERS DISTRICT COUNCIL AND OTHERS *v.* GOVERNOR AND COMPANY OF THE BANK OF ENGLAND

England, House of Lords. 18 *May* 2000

(Lords Steyn, Hope of Craighead, Hutton, Hobhouse of Woodborough and Millett)

SUMMARY: *The facts*:—Following the collapse in 1991 of BCCI, a bank licensed as a deposit taker in the United Kingdom, some 6,000 former depositors with the United Kingdom branch instituted proceedings against the Bank of England for alleged failures in the fulfilment of its supervisory functions. The depositors argued that the Bank of England was liable to them in damages for the tort of misfeasance in public office and also for breach of its obligations under EC Council Banking Coordination Directive 77/780, on the basis that the Directive had direct effect. The judge at first instance held that neither cause of action was capable of being successful in law and struck out the claim. The Court of Appeal upheld the decision and the depositors appealed to the House of Lords.[1]

[1] The summary and text of the judgment reproduced below deal only with the points of Community law raised in the case.

Held:—The appeal was dismissed in so far as it related to Community law and the case was referred for further argument on the tort under English law of misfeasance in public office.

(1) Community law, as developed by the European Court of Justice, was capable of conferring upon individuals the right to claim damages from a national authority by one or other or both of two distinct routes. The purpose of the right to claim damages was to ensure that provisions of Community law prevailed over national provisions. The full effectiveness of Community law would be impaired if individuals were unable to obtain redress in the national courts of the relevant Member State when their rights were infringed by breach of Community law. The first route by which the right to claim damages against the State or an emanation of the State for the non-implementation or misimplementation of a directive could be asserted was based upon the principle of direct effect (as in the *Becker* case).[2] The second route was based upon the principle of State liability (as in the *Francovich* case).[3] The conditions which the plaintiffs had to satisfy in order to establish a right to damages under each route in a case of the type at issue were so closely analogous as to be essentially the same (pp. 631-5).

(2) The critical questions for determination, in accordance with the case-law of the European Court of Justice, were whether the Directive entailed the grant of rights to individuals and whether the content of those rights was identifiable on the basis of the provisions of the Directive. The question whether the Directive granted rights to individual depositors was to be answered by examining the recitals and articles of the Directive itself without any preconceptions as to its purpose based upon extrinsic materials (pp. 635-41).

(3) The depositors invoked certain recitals and articles of the Directive in order to establish that one of its purposes was to protect depositors and thereby create rights for them. Taken in their context, however, these provisions appeared to be only a first step towards harmonization, through the coordination of the conditions for the supervision of all credit institutions operating within the European Community (pp. 641-5, 653).

(4) So far as the application of the articles of the Directive was concerned, BCCI had already been operating legitimately in the United Kingdom before the Directive came into force, so that the Bank of England had not been obligated by Article 3(1) to require it to obtain authorization as a condition for continuing its activities. Whilst Articles 6 and 7 were concerned with supervision, their purpose was to ensure coordination between the banking supervisory authorities of the Member States and the only duty imposed was one of coordination (pp. 645-51).

(5) Read as a whole, the Directive placed duties of coordination on the Member States but stopped short of prescribing any duties of supervision. Consequently it was not possible to find any provisions entailing the grant of rights to individuals since such rights were not necessary to achieve the intended purposes of the Directive. This interpretation of the Directive was *acte clair* and it was not appropriate to make a reference to the European Court of Justice (pp. 652-4).

[2] Volume 1, p. 103.

[3] Volume 1, p. 188.

The text of the judgments of Lords Steyn, Hutton, Hobhouse and Millett is not reproduced here because the judgments are largely concerned with the requirements for the commission of the tort under English law of misfeasance in public office. The following is the text of the judgment of Lord Hope of Craighead, dealing with the Community law issues, with which the other Lords essentially agreed:

[1236] LORD HOPE OF CRAIGHEAD. My Lords, I have had the advantage of reading in draft the speeches prepared by my noble and learned friends, Lord Steyn and Lord Hutton. As regards the tort of misfeasance in public office, I am in full agreement with what they have said as to the essential elements of the tort and the requirements which must be satisfied. The question with which I wish to deal is whether the plaintiffs have a basis for an action of damages against the Bank in Community law.

Community Law

The appellants' claim that they are entitled to damages for losses caused by breaches of Community law is based upon the following allegations. First, it is alleged that in June 1980 the Bank granted to **[1237]** BCCI SA a full licence to carry on business as a deposit-taker deliberately contrary to the scheme laid down by the First Council Banking Co-ordination Directive (77/780/EEC) of 12 December 1977 on the co-ordination of laws, regulations and administrative provisions relating to the taking up and pursuit of the business of credit institutions ("the Directive of 1977") and the Banking Act 1979 when it knew that the relevant criteria in Schedule 2 to the Act of 1979 were not fulfilled. Then it is alleged that, at all times after the grant of the licence in June 1980 until the eventual closure of BCCI SA, the Bank continued to act contrary to the scheme laid down by the Directive of 1977, the Act of 1979 and the Banking Act 1987 in the respects described in paragraphs 40-4 of the re-amended statement of claim. The essence of this further allegation is that, contrary to the scheme laid down by the Directive of 1977, the Act of 1979 and the Act of 1987, the Bank concluded that it had no discretion or power to revoke the licence to carry on business as a deposit-taker when it knew that BCCI SA had conducted and was conducting its affairs in a way which threatened the interests of its depositors. Furthermore, it permitted BCCI Overseas to carry on a deposit-taking business when it knew that the business of that company was carried on in a manner which might affect the soundness of BCCI SA and place its depositors at risk. It is also alleged that throughout this period the Bank failed to supervise both BCCI SA and BCCI Overseas to the detriment of the depositors.

Shortly put, and based upon these allegations, the plaintiffs' Community law argument proceeds along these lines. Under the EEC Treaty the Directive of 1977 has direct effect in the United Kingdom. The United Kingdom discharged its obligations under the Directive by enacting the Banking Acts of 1979 and 1987. The Bank was at all material times the supervisory authority in the United Kingdom for the purposes of both the Directive of 1977 and the Act of 1979 and the Act of 1987. The Bank as an emanation of the state is liable to the depositors for failing in its functions as supervisory authority to give full effect to the Directive of 1977. National courts are required by Community law to protect the rights which individuals derive from Community law, including those which are derived from a Directive. Accordingly the plaintiffs are entitled, as parties who were intended to benefit from the Directive of 1977, to rely upon its terms against the Bank in order to obtain damages.

The plaintiffs maintain that the Directive of 1977 was intended and designed to protect the savings of depositors. They say that, in order to achieve this purpose, it imposed certain well-defined Community law obligations on the competent authorities of member states in relation to the authorisation and supervision of banks, and that it conferred on depositors and potential depositors corresponding Community law rights against the competent authorities to have these obligations fulfilled. That being so, their Community law rights under the Directive of 1977 must prevail over the requirement in national law to prove bad faith or dishonesty as a prerequisite of the tort of misfeasance in public office under the common law. And they must prevail over the Bank's right to seek exemption from liability under section 1(4) of the Banking Act 1987, which provides:

> Neither the Bank nor any person who is a member of its Court of Directors or who is or is acting as an officer or servant of the **[1238]** Bank shall be liable in damages for anything done or omitted in the discharge or purported discharge of the functions of the Bank under this Act unless it is shown that the act or omission was in bad faith.

The main issue of Community law which arises in this appeal from these allegations is whether the Bank is capable of being liable to the plaintiffs in damages for violations of the Directive of 1977, on the assumption that the facts pleaded in the re-amended statement of claim are true.

The Conditions of Liability

There appeared to be no real dispute between the parties on this point in the course of the argument which was presented to your Lordships, and both the majority judgment in the Court of Appeal [2000] 2 WLR 15, 70-80 and the judgment of Auld LJ, pp. 106-10 have dealt with the whole matter in great detail and with admirable clarity. Nevertheless I think that it is necessary for me to explain at the outset of this chapter the criteria which must be fulfilled before a Directive can be relied upon as a source of rights before a national court.

Community law, as it has been developed by the European Court of Justice, is capable of conferring upon individuals the right to claim damages from a national authority by one or other or both of two distinct routes. The purpose of the right to claim damages is to ensure that provisions of Community law prevail over national provisions. This is because the full effectiveness of Community law would be impaired if individuals were unable to obtain redress in the national courts of the relevant member state when their rights were infringed by a breach of Community law: *Brasserie du Pêcheur SA* v. *Federal Republic of Germany; Reg.* v. *Secretary of State for Transport, Ex parte Factortame Ltd (No 4)* (Joined Cases C-46/93 and C-48/93) [1996] QB 404, 495, para. 20. The first route by which the right to claim damages against the state or an emanation of the state for the non-implementation or misimplementation of a Directive may be asserted is based upon the principle of direct effect. This is the principle which was established in Community law by *NV Algemene Transport- en Expeditie Onderneming van Gend & Loos* v. *Nederlandse administratie der belastingen* (Case 26/62) [1963] ECR 1. The second route is based upon the principle of state liability.

In the *van Gend & Loos* case it was held that article 12 of the EEC Treaty (now article 25 EC) prohibiting customs duties on imports and exports had to be interpreted as producing direct effects and creating individual rights which national courts must protect. The decision in that case has been applied by the European Court in a large number of cases to other articles of the Treaty which the court has construed as having direct effect in member states. Later decisions of the European Court have made it clear, in the light of the provisions of the third paragraph of article 189 of the EEC Treaty (now article 249 EC) which provides that a Directive shall be binding as to the result to be achieved upon each member state, that Directives as well as articles of the Treaty are capable of conferring directly effective rights upon individuals provided certain conditions are satisfied. In *Becker* v. *Finanzamt Münster-Innenstadt* (Case 8/81) [1982] ECR 53, 70-1 the court made the following observations as to the conditions for the application of the direct effect principle to a Directive:

[1239] 22. It would be incompatible with the binding effect which article 189 ascribes to Directives to exclude in principle the possibility of the obligations imposed by them being relied on by persons concerned.

23. Particularly in cases in which the Community authorities have, by means of a Directive, placed member states under a duty to adopt a certain course of action, the effectiveness of such a measure would be diminished if persons were

prevented from relying upon it in proceedings before a court and national courts were prevented from taking it into consideration as an element of Community law.

24. Consequently, a member state which has not adopted the implementing measures required by the Directive within the prescribed period, may not plead, as against individuals, its own failure to perform the obligations which the Directive entails.

25. Thus, wherever the provisions of a Directive appear, as far as their subject matter is concerned, to be unconditional and sufficiently precise, those provisions may, in the absence of implementing measures adopted within the prescribed period, be relied upon as against any national provision which is incompatible with the Directive or in so far as the provisions define rights which individuals are able to assert against the state.

Two things should be noted about the observations which the European Court made in paragraph 25 of its judgment. The first is that in order for there to be liability under this principle, which the Court of Appeal in the judgments in this case has described as *Becker*-type liability, the rights said to have been conferred by the Directive must be "unconditional and sufficiently precise." The second is that a distinction is made between relying upon a Directive to nullify some provision in national law which is incompatible with the Directive in order to give effect to rights under Community law, and relying upon Community law itself to give a right to claim damages in the national courts for breach of an obligation of Community law. The plaintiffs seek to rely on each of these two branches in this case.

In *Francovich* v. *Italian Republic* (Joined Cases C-6/90 and C-9/90) [1995] ICR 722 the European Court established the conditions for state liability, which is described in the judgments in the Court of Appeal as *Francovich*-type liability. The European Court had to deal with two issues in that case. The first concerned the direct effect of the provisions of Council Directive (80/987/EEC) which determined the rights of employees in the event of their employers' insolvency and which Italy had failed to implement: this was *Becker*-type liability. The second concerned the existence and scope of the liability of the state for damage resulting from Italy's breach of its obligations under Community law: this was *Francovich*-type liability. In regard to the direct effect route the court said at p. 768, para. 12 that there were three points to be considered, in order to see whether the provisions of the Directive which determined whether the rights of employees were, in *Becker*-type liability terms, "unconditional and sufficiently precise" to enable them to recover under this route. These were: "the identity of the persons entitled to the guarantee provided [by the Directive], the content of that guarantee and the identity of the person liable to provide the guarantee."

In regard to the conditions for state liability for failure to implement a Directive, the European Court made these observations, at p. 772:

[1240] 39. Where, as in this case, a member state fails to fulfil its obligation under the third paragraph of article 189 of the Treaty to take all the measures necessary to achieve the result prescribed by a Directive, the full effectiveness of that rule of Community law requires that there should be a right to reparation provided that three conditions are fulfilled.

40. The first of these conditions is that the result prescribed by the Directive should entail the grant of rights to individuals. The second condition is that it should be possible to identify the content of those rights on the basis of the provisions of the Directive. Finally, the third condition is the existence of a causal link between the breach of the state's obligation and the loss and damage suffered by the injured parties.

41. Those conditions are sufficient to give rise to a right on the part of individuals to obtain reparation, a right founded directly on Community law.

As Lord Slynn of Hadley said in *Reg.* v. *Secretary of State for Transport, Ex parte Factortame Ltd (No 5)* [1999] 3 WLR 1062, 1072E, state liability is conditional on there being a grant of rights to individuals by the Directive, that the contents of these rights is clear and that the loss suffered is shown to be caused by the state's breach.

In *Dillenkofer* v. *Federal Republic of Germany* (Joined Cases C-178, 179 and 188-190/94) [1997] QB 259 the court restated the conditions for state liability in the light of a number of cases with which it had dealt subsequently to the *Francovich* case. It did so in a manner which, in paragraph 22 of the judgment, applied the tests which *Francovich* had laid down for the direct effect, or *Becker*-type, route to the state liability, or *Francovich*-type, route. The relevant paragraphs are set out in the judgment, at pp. 291-2:

20. The court has held that the principle of state liability for loss and damage caused to individuals as a result of breaches of Community law for which the state can be held responsible is inherent in the system of the Treaty: *Francovich* v. *Italian Republic* (Joined Cases C-6/90 and C-9/90) [1995] ICR 722, 772, para. 35; *Brasserie du Pêcheur SA* v. *Federal Republic of Germany; Reg.* v. *Secretary of State for Transport, Ex parte Factortame Ltd (No 4)* (Joined Cases C-46/93 and C-48/93) [1996] QB 404, 496, para. 31; *Reg.* v. *HM Treasury, Ex parte British Telecommunications Plc* (Case C-392/93) [1996] QB 615, 654, para. 38 and *Reg.* v. *Ministry of Agriculture, Fisheries and Food, Ex parte Hedley Lomas (Ireland) Ltd* (Case C-5/94) [1997] QB 139, 160, para. 24. Furthermore, the court has held that the conditions under which state liability gives rise to a right to reparation depend on the nature of the breach of Community law giving rise to the loss and damage: *Francovich* [1995] ICR 722, 772, para. 38; *Brasserie du Pêcheur* [1996] QB 404, 497, para. 38, and *Hedley Lomas* [1997] QB 139, 160, para. 24.

21. In *Brasserie du Pêcheur*, at p. 499, paras. 50 and 51; *British Telecommunications* [1996] QB 615, 655, paras. 39 and 40, and *Hedley Lomas*, at p. 160, paras. 25 and 26, the court, having regard to the circumstances of the case, held that individuals who have suffered damage have a right to reparation where three conditions are met: the rule of law infringed must have been intended to confer rights on individuals, the breach must have been sufficiently serious, and there

[1241] must be a direct causal link between the breach of the obligation resting on the state and the damage sustained by the injured parties.

22. Moreover, it is clear from the *Francovich* case which, like the present cases, concerned non-transposition of a Directive within the prescribed period, that the full effectiveness of the third paragraph of article 189 of the Treaty requires that there should be a right to reparation where the result prescribed by the Directive entails the grant of rights to individuals, the content of those rights is identifiable on the basis of the provisions of the Directive and a causal link exists between the breach of the state's obligation and the loss and damage suffered by the injured parties.

23. In substance, the conditions laid down in that group of judgments are the same, since the condition that there should be a sufficiently serious breach, although not expressly mentioned in *Francovich*, was nevertheless evident from the circumstances of that case.

In the Court of Appeal it was observed in the majority judgment [2000] 2 WLR 15, 77C that the main difference between the parties, as to the basic principles to be applied, was as to whether a Directive, once it has been transposed into national law, ceases to be the immediate source of rights enforceable by an individual claimant in his national court. For the Bank it was submitted that there is a clear and well-established principle that the Directive is supplanted at that stage by rights under the national law. For the plaintiffs it was submitted that, as the obligation on member states is to ensure that the Directive is applied in practice, a Directive can be the immediate source of enforceable rights under the *Becker*-type principle even if it has been transposed, and correctly transposed, into national law. This is in order to ensure its effectiveness as to the result to be achieved in conformity with the third paragraph of article 249 (ex 189) EC.

The majority in the Court of Appeal [2000] 2 WLR 15, 80A-B found some support in *Norbrook Laboratories Ltd* v. *Ministry of Agriculture, Fisheries and Food* (Case C-127/95) [1998] ECR I-1531 for the view that there may be a category of Directives in relation to which a member state's obligation of proper implementation is not restricted to a once-for-all legislative process, but also requires a continuing administrative process. Auld LJ, who was of the opinion that the plaintiffs were entitled to rely on *Francovich*-type liability, regarded the debate on this point as academic: p. 139E. But, in the course of his development of this point, at pp. 139-42, he gave two further reasons for rejecting the Bank's argument that implementation of the Directive deprived the plaintiffs of recourse to the Directive under the *Becker*-type principle of liability to which, in my view, great weight should be attached. Although the debate on this issue did not receive the same prominence in the arguments which were presented to your Lordships, as Mr Lasok for the Bank addressed the main part of his submissions to the terms of the Directive, I think that Auld LJ's observations are worth recording here in order to set the scene for an examination of the Directive.

The first point which Auld LJ made was that it could be said that the precondition of liability for damages of bad faith on the part of the Bank or its officers in a common law action for misfeasance in public office and as introduced in section 1(4) of the Banking Act 1987, to the extent that they derogate from the Directive (p. 141B) "misimplement" the Directive: p. 139F. His second point was that recent decisions of the European Court, **[1242]** including the *Norbrook* case, indicate that in the main the court is indifferent to the precise route by which it gives effect to a Directive. As he pointed out, at p. 141E-G, neither the Act of 1979 nor the Act of 1987 transposed the Directive of 1977 word for word, and the rights of redress which he found in the Directive were wider than those dependent on proof of bad faith as required by section 1(4) of the Act of 1987 and the common law action of misfeasance in public office. Having noted the differences between the two approaches—one that the United Kingdom legislation properly construed effectively implemented the Directive, the other that it did not fully implement the Directive with the consequence that the United Kingdom courts must have direct recourse to it—he concluded, at pp. 141-2:

As Josephine Steiner observed in "Coming to Terms with EEC Directives" (1990) 106 LQR 144, 146, the question whether a Directive has been correctly implemented can only be assessed by reference to the Directive itself, with the result that it can rarely be disregarded. Clearly, as a result of the court's ready application of the *Francovich* principle, the two approaches can shade into one another. Whichever route is taken, the answer on matters of *Community law* should be the same, with the result that it should prevail over United Kingdom law, including the common law as to misfeasance in public office and Section 1(4) of the Act of 1987, where the latter frustrates it: see *Amministrazione delle Finanze dello Stato* v. *Simmenthal SpA* (Case 106/77) [1978] ECR 629, 643-5, paras. 16-26; the *Brasserie du Pêcheur* case [1996] QB 404, 502, paras. 72-3.

In the result, although the appellants' case under Community law is put in different ways and is based upon both types of liability, the conditions which the plaintiffs must satisfy in order to establish a right to damages against the Bank under each route are so closely analogous that they can be taken to be, at this stage of case, the same. The critical questions in this appeal, following the language of paragraph 22 of the judgment in the *Dillenkofer* case, are whether the Directive of 1977 entails the grant of rights to individual depositors and potential depositors and whether the content of those rights is identifiable on the basis of the provisions of the Directive.

The Legislative Basis and Purpose of the Directive of 1977

Clarke J [1996] 3 All ER 558, 602A held, contrary to the submissions which Mr Stadlen for the Bank had made to him, that an important underlying purpose of the Banking Acts 1979 and 1987 was to protect savers, including both existing savers and future savers, and that the same was true of the Directive of 1977. But he went on to say, at p. 602B, that this was not enough to impose any obligation on the Bank which gave rise to a right in the savers to claim damages for a breach of it. Having examined the terms of the Directive, he held at p. 614J, that it was not intended to confer rights upon savers, even although the underlying purpose of supervision of credit institutions was to be for their benefit. In the Court of Appeal [2000] 2 WLR 15, 82F the majority understood the Bank's position to be that it did not dispute that one of the Directive's purposes was the protection of depositors. Auld LJ, at p. 110, put the matter in this way:

> It is plain that one of the purposes of the Directive was the protection of depositors. The plaintiffs say it was the main purpose. The Bank, to the extent that it recognises it as a purpose of the **[1243]** Directive at all, says it was subsidiary to that of beginning the process of harmonisation. As I have mentioned, the judge regarded it as an important underlying purpose.

It was suggested by the plaintiffs in the course of the hearing before your Lordships that the Bank had changed its position on this point having realised, as Lord Neill put it, that once the concession was made that one of the purposes of the Directive was the protection of depositors it was on a slippery slope from which it now wished to extricate itself. In my view however the position which the Bank has adopted both in its written case and in the oral argument advanced on its behalf by Mr Lasok is based upon a more substantial argument than that which might be thought to have been suggested by that criticism. I am not convinced that there has been, in substance, any change of position on the part of the Bank from its position as Auld LJ understood it to be. There is however a more important point. The plaintiffs still rely, and take as their starting point on this whole issue, on the proposition that one of the purposes of the Directive was to protect depositors. This is a significant step in the argument which they then advance that the Directive also imposed obligations on the Bank which conferred corresponding rights upon which they are entitled to base their claim of damages. The question which the Bank has raised is not only as to the accuracy of the plaintiffs' description of the purpose of the Directive but also as to its relevance as a starting point to an examination of the articles of the Directive in order to discover what rights, if any, they conferred on depositors.

The plaintiffs' submission is that it is evident from the legislative background to the Directive, its terms and cases decided by the European Court that a principal purpose of the Directive of 1977 was the protection of depositors. They rely on article 57(2) of the EEC Treaty with reference to which the Directive of 1977 was enacted, on observations in the opinion of the Economic and Social Committee ("ECOSOC") mentioned in the preamble to the Directive, on recitals and articles set out in the Directive and on several decisions of the European Court of which the most important is *Société Civile Immobilière Parodi* v. *Banque H. Albert de Bary et Cie* (Case C-222/95) [1997] ECR I-3899.

I do not think that the plaintiffs derive any assistance from article 57(2) of the EEC Treaty (now, in a revised form, article 47(2) EC). Its relevance is not in doubt. Article 253 EC (formerly article 190) requires Community instruments such as Directives to state the reasons on which they are based and to refer to any proposals or opinions which were required to be obtained pursuant to the Treaty. The duty to give reasons will normally require specification of the Treaty article on which the measure was based: *Craig and de Búrca, EU Law, text, cases and materials*, 2nd ed. (1998), p. 120. In *Commission of the European Communities* v. *Council of the European Communities* (Case 45/86) [1987] ECR 1493 (the Tariff Preferences case) a Council measure was annulled in part by the European Court because the legal basis of the measure had not been specified. In this case the only article of the Treaty which is referred to by the Directive of 1977 is article 57. This is one of a group of articles which appear in Title III (free movement of persons, services and capital), Chapter 2 (Right of Establishment) of the Treaty. Paragraphs (1) and (2) of article 57, in the terms which were in force in 1977, provided:

[1244] 1. In order to make it easier for persons to take up and pursue activities as self-employed persons, the Council shall, on a proposal from the Commission and after consulting the Assembly, acting unanimously during the first stage and by a qualified majority thereafter, issue Directives for the mutual recognition of diplomas, certificates and other evidence of formal qualifications. 2. For the same purpose, the Council shall, before the end of the transitional period, acting on a proposal from the Commission and after consulting the Assembly, issue Directives for the co-ordination of the provisions laid down by law, regulation or administrative action in member states concerning the taking up and pursuit of activities as self-employed persons. Unanimity shall be required on matters which are the subject of legislation in at least one member state and measures concerned with the protection of savings, in particular the granting of credit and the exercise of the banking profession, and with the conditions governing the exercise of the medical and allied, and pharmaceutical professions in the various member states. In other cases, the Council shall act unanimously during the first stage and by a qualified majority thereafter.

The purpose to which reference is made in the first line of article 57(2) is that of the mutual recognition of qualifications which is the subject of article 57(1). The plaintiffs base their argument that a purpose of the Directive was to protect "savers" on the reference to the protection of "savings" in the second sentence of article 57(2). But this reference appears in provisions which laid down those matters in regard to which proposals were to be dealt with unanimously and those which could be dealt with by qualified majority. The granting of credit and the exercise of the banking profession are taken as two examples of "measures concerned with savings." This seems to me to be no more than a recognition that an ability to protect savings is one of the qualifications which member states will normally require those who wish to grant credit or exercise the banking profession to satisfy. Recognition that this was so, that such measures would need to be co-ordinated throughout member states and the making of provision for the voting formula to be adopted in regard to such matters is one thing. A purpose to direct that provision must be made for the protection of savers and depositors under Community law over and above the protections available under the national law of each member state is quite another. I do not find anything in the wording of the article as a whole to suggest that the protection of individual depositors and potential depositors against loss could be regarded as a purpose for which Directives were to be issued under it.

In *Federal Republic of Germany* v. *European Parliament* (Case C-233/94) [1997] ECR I-2405 the European Court made certain observations about article 57(2) of the Treaty. This was in the context of a challenge to the Deposit Guarantee Scheme Directive (94/19/EEC) by Germany on the ground that, contrary to its preamble, article 57 could not constitute the sole legal basis for the Directive as it did not merely regulate banking operations but was aimed at increasing protection for consumers. The fact that the court rejected this challenge might seem at first sight to provide support for the view that the protection of consumers was a purpose for which Directives could be issued under article 57. But the background to the Directive is important to a proper understanding of the reason why the challenge to its legal base did not succeed. The court had **[1245]** held in earlier cases that member states were entitled in certain circumstances to adopt or maintain measures which were justified on public interest grounds, such as the protection of consumers, which constituted an obstacle to free movement within the Community: p. 2450, paras. 16 and 17. The court said, at p. 2456, para. 41, that article 57(2) of the Treaty authorised the Parliament and the Council to issue Directives with a view to abolishing obstacles of this kind. It was apparent that such an obstacle was to be found in the fundamental differences between the deposit-guarantee systems existing in the various member states, so the laws on those systems were to be harmonised in order to facilitate the activity of credit institutions at Community level. The court held, at p. 2459, para. 48, that there had to be a high level of consumer protection concomitantly with the right of establishment and the freedom to provide services which the Directive aimed to promote. It referred to "the general result" which the Directive sought to achieve, which was a considerable improvement in the protection of depositors within the Community. In that particular context it was legitimate for the Directive to adopt measures which would render the domestic measures for the protection of consumers otiose. The special circumstances which led to that decision are absent in this case.

Consultation with ECOSOC was required by the second paragraph of article 100 of the EEC Treaty (now article 94 EC) prior to the issuing of the Directive. But the observations in its opinion on which the plaintiffs rely do not seem to me to advance their argument. In paragraph 1.1.3 the point was made that

> the lack of harmonisation of member states' legislation, whose main purpose in each country is to provide security for depositors and to protect savings, is liable to create serious disparities with regard to that objective, indeed even certain dangers.

In paragraph 1.4.1 it was stated that the ultimate aim was to harmonise the authorisation requirements for financial institutions in all the member states. The plaintiffs say, under reference to these and other passages in the opinion that the committee recognised that the main purpose of legislation concerning banking regulation was to provide security for depositors and to protect savings. I am willing to accept that this is so. No doubt the committee recognised that the protection of savings is a necessary part of every system at national level for the regulation of credit institutions whose business it is to receive from the public deposits and other forms of repayable funds. But the point to which it was drawing attention in its opinion was the need for the harmonisation of authorisation requirements, without which there would be likely to be serious disparities between the member states. The Community law purpose which was indicated by its observations was that of the harmonisation of regulatory measures affecting the right of establishment with a view to eliminating these disparities. I do not find any indication here that the committee saw the purpose of the Directive as being to confer Community law rights on individual depositors.

In the *Parodi* case [1997] ECR I-3899, 3923, paras. 24-5 the European Court said that the Directive of 1977 was no more than a first step towards the mutual recognition by member states of authorisations issued by each of them to credit institutions, and that it confined itself to imposing a number of minimum conditions on member states. Member states were to be obliged to require authorisation of all credit institutions **[1246]** wishing to commence banking activity within their territory of origin, but this was to be subject to minimum requirements and without prejudice to other conditions of general application laid down by national laws. The question which was raised in that case was whether national legislation requiring authorisation in order to supply banking services was precluded by the Treaty where the bank concerned was already established and authorised in another member state. The court said, at p. 3922, paras. 20-2 that, in view of the special nature of certain provisions of services, specific requirements imposed on the provider that were attributable to the application of rules governing that type of activity could not be regarded as incompatible with the Treaty, and that the banking sector was a particularly sensitive area from the point of view of consumer protection. The following observation was made, at p. 3924, para. 26:

> It must therefore be accepted that, as Community law stood at the time of the facts in the main proceedings, there were within the banking sector imperative reasons relating to the public interest capable of justifying the imposition by the member state of destination of conditions regarding access to the activity of credit institutions and their supervision which could go beyond the minimum conditions required by the first banking Directive and already implemented in the member state of origin.

The conclusion in the *Parodi* case was that member states were entitled to apply their own consumer protection measures in the banking sector, pending the entry into force of the measures in the Second Council Directive 89/646/EEC on the co-ordination of laws, regulations and administrative provisions relating to the taking up and pursuit of the business of credit institutions and amending the Directive of 1977 which rendered the national measures otiose. The plaintiffs rely on the observations in the judgment about the need to protect consumers in the banking sector in support of their argument as to the purpose of the Directive of 1977. But, as I read these observations, they were made, not with reference to the purpose of the Directive of 1977, but in order to justify the application of national measures by a member state during the period prior to the entry into force of the Directive of 1989. The purpose of the Directive of 1977 was to begin the process of harmonisation of national laws so as to remove barriers to the provision of banking services throughout the single market, but without weakening or impairing the protection of depositors. The protection of depositors was seen therefore not as a purpose of the Directive but as a constraint on the provision of banking services to the public which had to be recognised.

In *Criminal Proceedings against Romanelli* (Case C-366/97) [1999] All ER (EC) 473, 479, para. 12, the court said that it was clear from the Directive of 1977 and the Directive of 1989 that the protection of savings constituted one of the objectives of the measures taken to co-ordinate credit institutions. Here again, taken in its context, this observation seems to me to do no more than recognise the point already made in the *Parodi* case [1997] ECR I-3899, 3922, para. 21 that, as a matter of fundamental principle, restrictions on the freedom to provide services under the Treaty must be justified by imperative reasons in the public interest which are objectively necessary to guarantee the protection of the recipient of services and which do not exceed what is necessary to attain these objectives. I do not find in these observations support for the argument **[1247]** that a purpose of the Directive of 1977 was to promote or protect the interests of individual depositors.

In my opinion the question whether the Directive of 1977 granted rights to individual depositors and potential depositors must be answered by examining the recitals and the articles of the Directive itself without any preconception as to its purpose based upon these extrinsic materials.

The Recitals and Articles of the Directive of 1977

The Directive of 1977 contains fifteen recitals and fifteen articles. The plaintiffs rely in particular on the third, fourth, fifth and twelfth recitals and on articles 3, 6, 7 and 8. Article 3 is relevant to their allegation that the Bank acted contrary to the Directive when it granted a full licence to BCCI SA to carry on business as a deposit-taker. Articles 6 and 7 are relevant to their allegation that it failed in its duty under the Directive to supervise BCCI SA and BCCI Overseas. Article 8 is relevant to their allegation that it had a duty under the Directive to revoke the licence which it had granted to BCCI SA. But it is necessary to have regard to some of the other recitals and articles in order to understand the overall effect of the Directive. The question in the case of each of the allegations against the Bank is whether, in terms of the conditions for *Becker*-type liability which were applied to *Francovich*-type liability in paragraph 22 of the *Dillenkofer* case [1997] QB 259, 292:

> the result prescribed by the Directive entails the grant of rights to individuals, the content of those rights is identifiable on the basis of the provisions of the Directive and a causal link exists between the breach of the state's obligation and the loss and damage suffered by the injured parties.

As Lord Neill pointed out, the plaintiffs do not need to show that depositors were the only persons in whose favour obligations were imposed or on whom rights were conferred by the Directive. But in order to satisfy the *Dillenkofer* conditions they must be able to demonstrate that the result to be achieved by the Directive entailed the grant of rights to depositors and potential depositors as well as to the credit institutions operating in several member states whose activities were to be authorised and supervised by the competent authorities. A triangular or tripartite relationship is implied by this argument, between the competent authorities and the credit institutions on the one hand and the competent authorities and the depositors on the other. It is not too difficult to see, as the majority in the Court of Appeal observed [2000] 2 WLR 15, 84G that the Directive conferred rights on the credit institutions which were affected by it. What the plaintiffs have to do is to show that third parties to these arrangements, depositors and potential depositors, were also granted rights by the Directive on the application to its terms of the *Dillenkofer* test.

The first two recitals record the fact that the Treaty prohibited any discriminatory treatment from the end of the transitional period and that, in order to make it easier to take up and pursue the business of credit institutions, it was necessary to eliminate the most obstructive differences between the laws of the member states as to the rules to which these institutions were subject. The third, fourth and fifth recitals are in these terms:

> Whereas, however, given the extent of these differences, the conditions required for a common market for credit institutions **[1248]** cannot be created by means of a single Directive; whereas it is therefore necessary to proceed by successive stages; whereas the result of this process should be to provide for overall supervision of a credit institution operating in several member states by the competent authorities in the member state where it has its head office, in consultation, as appropriate, with the competent authorities of the other member states concerned; Whereas measures to co-ordinate credit institutions must, both in order to protect savings and to create equal conditions of competition between these institutions, apply to all of them; whereas due regard must be had, where applicable, to the objective differences in their statutes and their proper aims as laid down by national law; Whereas the scope of these measures should therefore be as broad as possible, covering all institutions whose business is to receive repayable funds from the public whether in the form of deposits or in other forms such as the continuing issue of bonds and other comparable securities and to grant credits for their own account; whereas exceptions must be provided for in the case of certain credit institutions to which this Directive cannot apply.

The plaintiffs rely upon the reference to the overall supervision of credit institutions in the third recital, upon the phrase "in order to protect savings" in the fourth recital and the reference in the fifth recital to the receipt of repayable funds from the public as indications that it was a purpose of the Directive to protect depositors. Taken in their context however these recitals seem to me to show that the Directive had a quite different purpose. This was, as the first step in a process which would have to proceed by successive stages, to co-ordinate the conditions for the supervision of all institutions of the kind mentioned in the fifth recital operating in several member states, bearing in mind the need for the co-ordinating measures to protect savings on the one hand and for them to create equal conditions of competition on the other.

The sixth to ninth recitals declare that the eventual aim of the harmonisation process was to introduce uniform authorisation requirements throughout the Community for comparable types of credit institution and that, while at the initial stage it was necessary to specify only certain minimum requirements to be imposed by all member states, the eventual aim could be achieved only if the particularly wide discretionary powers which certain supervisory authorities had for authorising credit establishments were progressively reduced. The tenth and eleventh recitals state that the purpose of co-ordination was to achieve a system whereby credit institutions having their head office in one of the member states were exempt from any national authorisation requirement when setting up branches in other member states, but that a measure of flexibility might nonetheless be possible in the initial stage. The twelfth recital, which explains the means by which the gradual approximation of the systems for the monitoring of solvency and liquidity of credit institutions established by the member states was to be brought about, begins with this proposition on which the plaintiffs rely: "Whereas equivalent financial requirements for credit institutions will be necessary to ensure similar safeguards for savers and fair conditions of competition between comparable groups of credit institutions . . ." Here again however the point being made with regard to safeguards for savers and fair conditions of competition between institutions seems to me to be directed to the two requirements which the measures of co-ordination which the **[1249]** Directive was to lay down would have to satisfy, bearing in mind the fact that these measures would to some degree restrict the fundamental principle of freedom of establishment. Nothing turns on the wording of the remaining three recitals.

The first two articles of the Directive are comprised in Title I which deals with definitions and the scope of the Directive. Article 1 contains a number of definitions, including those of the expressions "credit institution" and "branch." It is worth noting that there is no definition of any expression referring to individuals in whose favour rights might be said to have been intended to be created by the Directive. If the result to be achieved was to entail the granting of rights to individuals such as savers or depositors, I would have expected a definition such as that included in article 2 of the Directive (90/314/EEC) concerning package travel, package holidays and package tours which defines the expression "consumer." The meaning and effect of this Directive was considered in the *Dillenkofer* case [1997] QB 259, in *Verein für Konsumenteninformation* v. *Österreichische Kreditversicherungs AG* (Case C-364/96) [1998] ECR I-2949 and in *Rechberger* v. *Republic of Austria* (Case C-140/97) (unreported), 15 June 1999. In each of these cases the European Court held that article 7 of the Directive gave "consumers" a right to be reimbursed or repatriated in the event of the insolvency of the tour operator. The absence of a definition of that kind from the Directive of 1977 suggests that it was not the intention when the Directive was being drafted to grant rights under the Directive in favour of individuals or any group or class of individuals.

In a series of cases, referred to as "the German environmental cases," claims were brought by the Commission against Germany for its failure to implement Directives which laid down various requirements to be observed by member states in relation to water and air quality: e.g. *Commission of the European Communities* v. *Federal Republic of Germany* (Case C-131/88) [1991] ECR I-825; *Commission of the European Communities* v. *Federal Republic of Germany* (Case C-298/95) [1996] ECR I-6747. As Auld LJ [2000] 2 WLR 15, 133A noted, each of these Directives required member states to take specific measures to ensure that water or air was of the quality prescribed by the Directive, but they said nothing about the conferment of rights on individuals. Nevertheless the European Court held that the purpose of certain of the provisions of these Directives was to create rights and obligations for individuals. In Case C-131/88 [1991] ECR I-825, 867 in para. 7 the court said:

> The Directive at issue in the present case seeks to protect the Community's groundwater in an effective manner by laying down specific and detailed provisions requiring the member states to adopt a series of prohibitions, authorisation schemes and monitoring procedures in order to prevent or limit discharges of certain substances. The purpose of those provisions of the Directive is thus to create rights and obligations for individuals.

I agree with the plaintiffs that these cases demonstrate that the potential width of the class of persons granted rights does not militate against the conclusion that the relevant provisions of these Directives were intended to create rights. This does not in itself mean that the persons intended to be granted rights are not sufficiently identifiable. But the cases also demonstrate that the question whether provisions in a Directive create rights and obligations for individuals depends in each case on the subject **[1250]** matter of the Directive, on the context and on the nature and purpose of the provisions which are in issue. The environmental cases were concerned with the protection of human health. This is a matter of concern to everybody, as we all share the environment in which we live. So the absence of a definition of the individuals who were granted rights by the Directives was of no importance. As the court said in Case C-298/95 [1996] ECR I-6747, 6760:

> 15. As the Commission points out, one of the purposes of the Directives at issue is to protect human health through the monitoring of the quality of waters which support, or could support, fish suitable for human consumption . . .
>
> 16. In those circumstances, it is particularly important that Directives should be transposed by measures which are indisputably binding. In all cases where non-implementation of the measures required by a Directive could endanger human health, the persons concerned must be in a position to rely on mandatory rules in order to assert their rights . . .

Article 2 of the Directive of 1977 begins with the proposition that the Directive "shall apply to the taking up and pursuit of the business of credit institutions." It then sets out a number of exceptions and qualifications, but these are not significant for present purposes.

The articles on which the plaintiffs mainly rely are in Title II of the Directive, which bears the headnote "Credit institutions having their head office in a member state and their branches in other member states" and comprises articles 3 to 8. But it is necessary to have regard also to article 10 which is included among the general and transitional provisions in Title IV, as the Bank's contention is that when article 3 is read together with article 10 it is clear that it did not apply to BCCI SA which had already taken up business as a credit institution before the coming into force of the Banking Act 1979. Title III deals with the situation where credit institutions which have their head offices outside the Community have branches in a member state. There is nothing in article 9, which is the only article in Title III, which is relevant to this case.

The first two paragraphs of article 3 provide:

> 1. Member states shall require credit institutions subject to this Directive to obtain authorisation before commencing their activities. They shall lay down the requirements for such authorisation subject to paragraphs 2, 3 and 4 and notify them to both the Commission and the Advisory Committee. 2. Without prejudice to other conditions of general application laid down by national laws, the competent authorities shall grant authorisation only when the following conditions are complied with:—the credit institutions must possess separate own funds—the credit institutions must possess adequate minimum own funds—there shall be at least two persons who effectively direct the business of the credit institution. Moreover, the authorities concerned shall not grant authorisation if the persons referred to in the third indent of the first sub-paragraph are not of sufficiently good repute or lack sufficient experience to perform such duties.

The words "before commencing their activities" in paragraph 1 of article 3 indicate that its function was to deal with the authorisation of credit institutions with their head offices in one member state which were **[1251]** seeking to carry on business in another member state after that member state had implemented the Directive. The plaintiffs claim in their re-amended statement of claim that BCCI SA was incorporated in Luxembourg in 1972, that it carried on business there as a bank under an authorisation issued by the Luxembourg authorities and that it established an office in London in the same year through which it had been carrying on business as a banker and deposit-taker for several years before it was granted a licence under the Banking Act 1979 by the Bank. On these facts it is plain that, as BCCI SA had already commenced its activities as a credit institution in the United Kingdom prior to the implementation of the Directive in domestic legislation by the Banking Act 1979, article 3 did not apply to it. The Bank says that no authorisation procedure was required by the Directive to enable it to continue with its activities. The fact that BCCI SA was granted a licence under the Banking Act 1979 which required all credit institutions to submit to the licensing procedure was a matter of domestic law only, not of Community law.

The Bank submits that this conclusion is confirmed by the first sub-paragraph of paragraph 1 and paragraphs 3 and 4 of article 10, which provide:

> 1. Credit institutions subject to this Directive, which took up their business in accordance with the provisions of the member states in which they have their head offices before the entry into force of the provisions implementing

> this Directive shall be deemed to be authorised. They shall be subject to the provisions of this Directive concerning the carrying on of the business of credit institutions and to the requirements set out in the first and third indents of the first sub-paragraph and in the second sub-paragraph of article 3(2) . . . 3. If a credit institution deemed to be authorised under paragraph 1 has not undergone any authorisation procedure prior to commencing business, a prohibition on the carrying on of its business shall take the place of withdrawal of authorisation. Subject to the first sub-paragraph, article 8 shall apply by analogy. 4. By way of derogation from paragraph 1, credit institutions established in a member state without having undergone an authorisation procedure in that member state prior to commencing business may be required to obtain authorisation from the competent authorities of the member state, concerned in accordance with the provisions implementing this Directive. Such institutions may be required to comply with the requirement in the second indent of article 3(2) and with such other conditions of general application as may be laid down by the member state concerned.

The plaintiffs claim in their reply to this submission that the head office of BCCI SA was in London, not Luxembourg. They point out that there were no authorisation procedures for credit institutions in the United Kingdom prior to the coming into force of the Banking Act 1979. Furthermore all credit institutions were required to undergo the licensing procedure under that Act, irrespective of whether they had previously taken up business in the United Kingdom. The plaintiffs also say that, even if in making that requirement the United Kingdom was exercising its right of derogation under article 10(4), this would not affect the Bank's obligation to grant authorisation only on the conditions permitted by the Directive.

[1252] On the assumption that the facts stated in the re-amended statement of claim are true, there may be some force in the plaintiffs' argument that deemed authorisation under article 10(1) does not apply to BCCI SA as there were no "provisions" regulating the business of credit institutions when it commenced its activities in this country. But on balance it seems to me that this is to construe the word "provisions" too narrowly. An institution which was legitimately carrying on business here under the system of law in force at the time, as BCCI SA was doing because there was no prohibition to the contrary, could be said to be doing so "in accordance with the provisions" of the member state within the meaning of article 10(1). That provision does not stipulate any particular requirements which those provisions had to satisfy. In any event, this still leaves article 10(4), which clearly does apply to BCCI SA as it had not undergone an authorisation procedure in the United Kingdom before commencing business here. The derogation provided by this paragraph, which permits a member state to require credit institutions which are legitimately carrying on business in that state to obtain authorisation on such conditions as may be laid down by that member state, is inconsistent with the view that BCCI SA, which was already legitimately carrying on its activities as a credit institution in the United Kingdom, required to be authorised under article 3(1).

The plaintiffs submit as a general principle that, where a member state voluntarily accepts obligations under Community law, it cannot escape its liabilities by saying that it need not have assumed these obligations in the first place. In support of this proposition they rely on *Wagner Miret* v. *Fondo de garantía salarial* (Case C-334/92) [1993] ECR I-6911, which concerned Directive 80/987 relating to the protection of employees in the event of the employer's insolvency. The Directive permitted member states to exclude certain categories of employee from the scope of the protection, and a list of the excluded categories of employee was set out in an annex to the Directive. Spain requested the exclusion of one category of employee only, and the exclusion of that category was entered in the list. It did not request the exclusion of the category of employee to which Mr Wagner Miret belonged. The European Court held that he was entitled to the protection of the Directive, and that it was no answer to say that Spain could have excluded that category from that protection if it had chosen to exercise the option to do so. It seems to me that that case provides no support for the argument that, in the reverse situation which arises under the Directive of 1977, the United Kingdom was obliged to require an institution which was already legitimately carrying on business here to be authorised. A requirement made under article 10(4) is voluntary, not obligatory. The exercise of the option to make that requirement cannot affect the scope of the obligation under article 3. I think that it is clear, as a matter of principle, that the voluntary incorporation by a member state of a provision in a Directive into national law which it is not obliged to incorporate under Community law does not give rise to a Community law obligation. The scope of that provision is a matter for determination by the national courts as a part of the domestic law of the member state. The European Court may assist the national court in construing the Directive, but it does not follow that the obligation in question is a Community law obligation: see *Leur-Bloem* v. *Inspecteur der Belastingdienst/ Ondernemingen Amsterdam 2* (Case C-28/95) [1998] QB 182, 209, paras. 33-4.

[1253] For these reasons I would hold that the Bank was not obliged by article 3(1) of the Directive to require BCCI SA to obtain authorisation as a condition of continuing to carry on its business in the United Kingdom. But even if it was obliged to do so as a matter of Community law, I do not find a sufficient indication, in the conditions for authorisation of credit institutions which are set out in article 3(2), that the result to be achieved by the Directive entailed the granting of rights to individuals or groups of individuals affected by their activities. The purpose of article 3(1), as indicated by the first, second and eighth recitals, was to take the first step towards the introduction of uniform authorisation requirements for comparable types of credit institution having their head office in one member state and their branches in other member states. The obligations which it imposed were designed to bring to an end, in a manner which was consistent with the nature of the business carried on by credit institutions, any discriminatory treatment as between the laws of member states with regard to establishment and the provision of these services.

Article 6(1) provides:

1. Pending subsequent co-ordination, the competent authorities shall, for the purposes of observation and, if necessary, in addition to such coefficients as may be applied by them, establish ratios between the various assets and/or liabilities of credit institutions with a view to monitoring their solvency and liquidity and the other measures which may serve to ensure that savings are protected. To this end, the Advisory Committee shall decide on the content of the various factors of the observation ratios referred to in the first sub-paragraph and lay down the method to be applied in calculating them. Where appropriate, the Advisory Committee shall be guided by technical consultations between the supervisory authorities of the categories of institutions concerned.

The plaintiffs rely on this article as the basis for their claim that the Bank were under an obligation owed to the depositors to supervise the activities of BCCI SA and BCCI Overseas at all times during the relevant period. Auld LJ said [2000] 2 WLR 15, 113:

Article 6 deals with supervision. In my view, and contrary to that of Clarke J [1996] 3 All ER 558, 616, it imposed on regulators immediate duties of a technical banking nature to "ensure that savings are protected," and it did so in advance of the process and achievement of co-ordination. It is clear from the wording of the article and the context of the Directive as a whole, concerned as it is with "the taking up *and pursuit* of the business of credit institutions" (my emphasis), that the intended purpose of the supervision was to ensure, as a minimum, continuing compliance with the requirements of authorisation under article 3.

In my opinion however article 6, although concerned with supervision, had a more limited purpose in view. As the twelfth recital indicates, it imposed a duty on the supervisory authorities, pending subsequent co-ordination, to formulate structural ratios which would make it possible for the national authorities to co-operate with each other in the setting of standards, or coefficients, to ensure the sound management of credit institutions which in due course would be co-ordinated between member states. The ultimate aim was to set equivalent financial standards which would, in terms of the recital, achieve the twin requirements noted by **[1254]** ECOSOC of ensuring "similar safeguards for savers and fair conditions of competition between comparable groups of credit institutions." It did not impose a duty of supervision. The assumption on which it proceeds is that the competent authorities in each member state would be performing that function under the national law of that member state. No minimum standards of supervision or other criteria are laid down in the article. The whole emphasis is on co-operation between the supervisory authorities, with a view to harmonisation in due course of the means by which the performance of credit institutions carrying on business in more than one member state could be monitored. The protection of savings was assumed to be the purpose of the monitoring system. But it was not necessary in order to establish observation ratios and their co-ordination between member states to impose a Community law duty of supervision or to grant rights in that regard to individuals or groups of individuals.

Article 7 is also concerned with supervision. Here again Auld LJ was of the view that it imposed a duty to supervise: p. 113G. But I think that the duty which it imposed was one of co-operation between the supervisory authorities. Paragraph 1 of the article provides:

> The competent authorities of the member states concerned shall collaborate closely in order to supervise the activities of credit institutions operating, in particular by having established branches there, in one or more member states other than that in which their head offices are situated. They shall supply one another with all information concerning the management and ownership of such credit institutions that is likely to facilitate their supervision and the examination of the conditions for their authorisation and all information likely to facilitate the monitoring of their liquidity and solvency.

As in the case of article 6, article 7 assumed the existence in each member state of a competent authority or competent authorities whose function it was to supervise the activities of credit institutions in that member state.

Prior to the implementation of the Directive of 1977 there were no supervisory authorities in either the United Kingdom or Denmark. So it was necessary, to give effect to the Directive, for authorities to be set up with the function of supervising credit institutions operating in those member states. An obligation to do so is not expressed in article 7. It is to be found in the third paragraph of article 189 of the EEC Treaty (now article 249 EC), which provides that a Directive is to be binding as to the result to be achieved but leaves the choice of form and methods to each member state. Here again however it is necessary to distinguish between the duty under Community law for an authority to be set up under the national law of each member state whose function it was to supervise and the duty under article 7 of the supervisory authorities of each member state to co-operate. I do not think that article 7, which refers to the sharing of information "likely to facilitate" supervision, examination and monitoring, imposed a duty under Community law to supervise. The absence from the article of any prescribed system of supervision, and of any criteria or standards to be applied by the supervisory authority, is an indication to the contrary. It is noteworthy that, although the plaintiffs claim that there was a general duty to supervise, they do not point to the breach by the Bank of any particular duties of supervision imposed by either article 6 or article 7.

[1255] The plaintiffs rely upon the observations of Advocate General Sir Gordon Slynn in *Municipality of Hillegom* v. *Hillenius* (Case 110/84) [1985] ECR 3947, 3948, where he said that article 7 of the Directive of 1977 "provides that the supervisory authorities of the various member states shall collaborate closely in order to supervise credit institutions operating in more than one member state." I do not think that this comment, which simply repeats the wording of paragraph 1 of the article, is in any way inconsistent with the view which I have formed, that the duty under article 7 is a duty to collaborate in order to assist the competent authorities in the performance of their supervisory functions under national law. The observations which the European Court made in its judgment, at p. 3963, paras. 26 and 27, to the effect that the Directive was designed to facilitate the overall monitoring of credit institutions operating in more than one member state by the competent authorities of the member state in which the credit institution has its head office and about the need for the monitoring of banks through supervision within a member state and the exchange of information by the competent authorities to function properly, do not go to the length of suggesting that the court saw the Directive as entailing the grant of rights to individual depositors.

The plaintiffs also rely on *Carbonari* v. *Università degli studi di Bologna* (Case C-131/97) [1999] ECR I-1103. That was a case which was concerned with the direct effect of provisions in two Directives (82/76/EEC amending 75/362/EEC and 75/363/EEC). The first of which related to training periods and remuneration of doctors. Detailed provisions were included about the training requirements, and there was a provision in the Annex to the Directive of 1975 that the posts which specialists were to hold while in full-time training were to be "subject to appropriate remuneration." The European Court, at pp. 1133-4, paras. 44-7 of its judgment applied the first limb of the *Becker* test. The right of the medical students to appropriate remuneration during their training period was in itself unconditional and sufficiently precise. But the Directives were not unconditional as to which institution was to bear the obligation to pay the remuneration. They did not include any Community definition of the remuneration which was to be regarded as appropriate or the methods by which it was to be fixed to enable the national court to determine the body liable to pay it or the level at which it was to be paid. Such definitions were to be a matter for the member states when they were implementing the Directive. In other words, as the Directive did not itself define as a matter of Community law what was appropriate remuneration or lay down a Community law method to fix that amount, the medical students had no Community right which they could enforce to obtain payment.

The plaintiffs say that the *Carbonari* case supports their claim that articles 6 and 7 imposed a duty of supervision notwithstanding that the precise methods or forms of supervision are not specified in the Directive. In my opinion however the case tends to support the Bank's argument. None of the provisions in articles 6 and 7 of the Directive of 1977 define any categories of individual on whom rights were being conferred, nor do they state in obligatory terms that the credit institutions "shall be subject to appropriate supervision" by the competent authorities. Even if such an obligation in general terms could be said to be implied, the absence of even the slightest amount of detail as to the system of supervision required by Community law which was to be adopted and enforced by the national courts would make it impossible to say that, as matter of Community law, **[1256]** the obligation to supervise was unconditional and sufficiently precise to satisfy the *Becker*-type liability test.

The plaintiffs also rely on article 8 which deals with the withdrawal of authorisation. Paragraphs 1 and 2 of this article provide:

> 1. The competent authorities may withdraw the authorisation issued to a credit institution subject to this Directive or to a branch authorised under article 4 only where such an institution or branch: (a) does not make use of the authorisation within 12 months, expressly renounces the authorisation or has ceased to engage in business for more than six months, if the member state concerned has made no provision for the authorisation to lapse in such cases; (b) has obtained the authorisation through false statements or any other irregular means; (c) no longer fulfils the conditions under which authorisation was granted, with the exception of those in respect of own funds; (d) no longer possesses sufficient own funds or can no longer be relied upon to fulfil its obligations towards its creditors, and in particular no longer provides security for the assets entrusted to it; (e) falls within one of the other cases where national law provides for withdrawal of authorisation. 2. In addition, the authorisation issued to a branch under article 4 shall be withdrawn if the competent authority of the country in which the credit institution which established the branch has its head office has withdrawn authorisation from that institution.

In my opinion the key word in paragraph 1 is the word "only" which precedes the list of the various situations in which authorisation may be withdrawn. It seems to me that this is a limiting provision, as indicated by the second recital, with a view to eliminating differences between the laws of member states. The reference in sub-paragraph (e) to cases where "national law provides for withdrawal of authorisation" ensures that the matter is not left to the administrative discretion of the competent authority in that member state.

Auld LJ said [2000] 2 WLR 15, 114G that he recognised the fact that, while paragraph 2 was obligatory, paragraph 1 was in general terms permissive in the various circumstances specified. But his view was that the article should be read as imposing a duty on competent authorities to withdraw authorisation in the circumstances referred to in sub-paragraphs (c) and (d). He added this explanation, at p. 114:

> It is inconceivable that the Directive should be read so as to require banking regulators to insist on certain minimum requirements of authorisation and to supervise to ensure continued satisfaction of them, yet leave them with a discretion, unspecified as to criteria, to permit continuance of trading without check or condition when those requirements are no longer met.

On my reading of the Directive as a whole however, it is to be regarded as laying down a series of provisions with a view to the harmonisation of the criteria to be applied to credit institutions having their head office in a member state and their branches in other member states. That being so, there is nothing surprising in an approach to the withdrawal of authorisation in the circumstances referred to in paragraph 1 which permits withdrawal in these, and only these, circumstances but provides that withdrawal in the situation mentioned in paragraph 2 is to be obligatory. I do not think that there is anything here which entails the **[1257]** grant of rights to individuals to insist upon the withdrawal of authorisation in the circumstances mentioned in paragraph 1. For their part, the credit institutions could hardly object to a decision to withdraw authorisation in the circumstances mentioned in sub-paragraphs (c) and (d) of paragraph 1 which, in order to protect savings, it was obviously necessary to include in the list of circumstances in which the withdrawal of authorisation was to be permissible.

Conclusion

Looking back at the Directive as a whole, the key to a proper understanding of its purpose and effect seems to me to lie in the fact that it was the first step in a process of harmonisation of provisions for the regulation of credit institutions carrying on business within the Community. It was about the removal of barriers to the right of establishment under article 52 of the EEC Treaty (now article 43 EC). It confined itself to imposing a number of minimum conditions and prohibitions on member states as to the authorisation and supervision of credit institutions having their head offices in another member state or having their head offices outside the Community. It was based upon an appreciation of the fact that credit institutions require regulation in order to protect savings. So any measures of harmonisation had to meet the twin requirements of protecting savings on the one hand and creating conditions of equal competition between credit institutions operating in more than one member state on the other. It placed duties of co-operation on the competent authorities where a credit institution was operating in one or more member states other than that in which its head office was situated. But it stopped short of prescribing any duties of supervision to be performed by the competent authority within each member state. It is not possible to discover provisions which entail the granting of rights to individuals, as the granting of rights to individuals was not necessary to achieve the results which were intended to be achieved by the Directive.

For these reasons I am unable, with great respect, to agree with Auld LJ's conclusions [2000] 2 WLR 15, 102H-103A that the Directive of 1977 imposed clearly defined obligations on member states and on their regulatory bodies and that in doing so it gave rise to corresponding Community law rights in depositors to enforce those obligations by an action of damages. I prefer the views of Clarke J [1996] 3 All ER 558, 616, where he said:

> The true position, as it seems to me, is that the Directive was not intended to require the imposition of a duty to supervise upon the supervisory authority because, whatever the underlying purpose of the system of supervision, the immediate purpose of the Directive, rather like that in *Reg.* v. *International Stock Exchange of the UK and the Republic of Ireland Ltd, Ex parte Else (1982) Ltd, Reg.* v. *International Stock Exchange of the UK and the Republic of Ireland Ltd, Ex parte Roberts* [1993] QB 534, was a first step towards harmonisation of the systems in the member states, which were assumed to and no doubt did exist. Its purpose was not to lay down the duty to supervise or radically to alter existing systems, but, even if it was, it was not (as I see it) to confer rights upon either savers or other creditors.

[1258] The majority in the Court of Appeal did not examine the provisions of the Directive in detail. But they said [2000] 2 WLR 15, 84:

> In our judgment it is reasonably clear that the Directive of 1977 does confer enforceable rights on credit institutions which are to be supervised under its provisions. In particular, a credit institution which was refused authorisation for reasons incompatible with article 3, or which had its authorisation withdrawn which for reasons incompatible with article 8, would (in the event of non-transposition of the Directive of 1977) most probably have had a right to challenge the Bank's decision on the basis that the *Becker* conditions [1982] ECR 53 were satisfied. But there is not in our judgment any sufficient clarity or certainty in the position of depositors (or other customers of credit institutions).

Subject to the qualifications that I have substituted the *Francovich* test as applied in *Dillenkofer* for the *Becker* test, on the view that it is more precise and covers both types of liability, and that I do not accept that credit institutions were to be "supervised under" the provisions of the Directive, I agree with the conclusions of the majority on this issue. I would therefore dismiss the appeal on the Community law claim.

In the courts below neither party asked for a preliminary reference under article 234 EC (ex article 177 EEC) on the issues relating to the plaintiffs' claim under Community law. Clarke J said [1996] 3 All ER 558, 625E-F, that he would have referred the matter as to the meaning and effect of the Directive of 1977 had the parties not requested him to give a judgment on the Community law issue without doing so. In the Court of Appeal the majority said, at p. 85D, that they did not regard the question of *Becker*-type liability as acte clair, but that as a matter of discretion the court had decided not to make a reference. The parties' unanimity in asking the court not to make a reference had been a significant factor in that decision. That unanimity was departed from in your Lordships' House. The plaintiffs, having regard to the observations in the courts below, to the fact that there was dissenting judgment in the Court of Appeal and to what they saw as a change of position by the Bank as regards the purpose and intent of the Directive of 1977, have asked for a reference under article 234 EC (ex article 177 EEC) on the question whether the Directive conferred rights, and if so what rights, on depositors which they can exercise against the competent authority designated by the member state for the purpose of carrying out that member state's obligations under the Directive.

I am of the opinion that it would not be appropriate for a reference to be made to the European Court on the critical question in this case, which is whether the Directive of 1977 entailed the granting of rights to individual depositors and potential depositors. I consider that this matter, on which I understand your Lordships to be unanimous and on which we have had the benefit of very full and helpful submissions both orally and in writing from both sides, is acte clair. So I would decline the plaintiffs' request that we should make a reference in this case.

I would make the same order as that proposed by my noble and learned friend, Lord Steyn.

[Report: [2000] 2 WLR 1221]

National constitutions — Constitutional review concerning Community Treaty — United Kingdom — Treaty on European Union, 1992 (Maastricht Treaty) — Protocol and Agreement on Social Policy — Ratification by United Kingdom — Exclusion of applicability to United Kingdom by European Communities (Amendment) Act 1993 — Community expenditure on administrative costs associated with Agreement — Whether any parliamentary authority for indirect contributions to such costs — European Communities Act 1972, Section 2(3)

Powers — Extension by treaty — Financial contributions by Member States — Replacement by Community's own resources — Treaty on European Union, 1992 — Protocol and Agreement on Social Policy — Exemption for United Kingdom — Ratification of treaty by United Kingdom — Whether constituting parliamentary approval for indirect contributions by United Kingdom to administrative costs associated with Agreement, through contribution to Community's own resources — Scope of duty of United Kingdom to contribute to Community budget — The law of Scotland

MONCKTON *v.* LORD ADVOCATE

Scotland, Court of Session (Outer House). 5 *May* 1994

(Lord Milligan)

SUMMARY: *The facts*:—The Protocol on Social Policy to the Treaty on European Union, 1992 provided that the United Kingdom was excluded from the operation of the Agreement on Social Policy annexed to the Treaty, and that any financial consequences entailed by acts adopted thereunder should not apply to the United Kingdom. Section 2(3) of the European Communities Act 1972 provided authority for payment by the United Kingdom of the amounts required to meet Community obligations arising under the Treaties. The 1972 Act was subsequently amended so as to include in "the Treaties" the Council Decision of 28 June 1988 on the Community's system of own resources, which provided that the revenues defined as such resources should be used to meet all expenditure under the Community's budget. The administrative costs associated with the Agreement on Social Policy were therefore payable out of the Community budget. The petitioner, however, sought a declaration that the application of some indeterminate payments, made into the general Community budget by the United Kingdom, to meet the administrative costs of the Agreement on Social Policy, from which the United Kingdom was excluded, would be *ultra vires*.

Held:—The petition was dismissed.

The incorporation of the Decision of 24 June 1988 into "the Treaties", within the meaning of the 1972 Act, provided authority for payment by the United Kingdom of money towards expenditure payable out of the Community budget. Since the administrative costs of the Agreement on Social Policy comprised expenditure properly payable out of the Community budget, the payment by the United Kingdom was lawful.

The following is the text of the judgment of the Court:

[1204] LORD MILLIGAN.—In terms of his petition, the petitioner seeks declarator that "(1) The purported ratification of the Treaty on European Union is ultra vires the Crown." At first hearing of his petition, declarator to this effect is no longer sought. In terms of his petition, the petitioner also seeks declarator that "(2) The Treaty on European Union not having been ratified by the Crown, it has not entered into force." This declarator also is now no longer sought. I was informed by counsel for the petitioner that he now seeks only the third declarator sought in terms of his petition, namely declarator that "(3) The payment of money out of the Consolidated Fund to defray the administrative costs of the Agreement on Social Policy, and the application to those purposes of money already paid out of the Consolidated Fund, is ultra vires the Crown and unlawful."

The respondent to the petition is the Lord Advocate, who has lodged answers.

In the course of the initial stages in particular of the first hearing, the discussion covered issues of competency, and in particular alleged prematurity, and also alleged lack of specification in the remedies sought, these issues being raised in the respondent's answers. However, it was clear throughout the hearing that parties' principal concern was to obtain a decision upon the issue on the merits. In this situation, I propose to turn to that issue at the outset.

The Treaty establishing what was then the European Economic Community was signed at Rome on 25 March 1957. In terms of art. 239 of the Treaty, the Protocols annexed to the Treaty form an integral part thereof. The United Kingdom joined the European Communities, namely the EEC, the European Coal and Steel Community and the European Atomic Energy Community, by Treaty of Accession in 1972. Prior to this, the three Communities mentioned had been sharing the same institutions since the Merger Treaty of 1965. These institutions involved the Commission, the Council of Ministers, the European Parliament and the Court of Justice. The United Kingdom adopted the Community Treaties in terms of the European Communities Act 1972. Originally, there were 12 Protocols annexed to the Treaty of Rome. This Treaty was amended by amendments, including those agreed at Maastricht by the Treaty on European Union on 7 February 1992. The following Protocol was agreed at Maastricht: [his Lordship narrated the terms of the Protocol on Social Policy set out supra and continued:]

The Agreement annexed to this Protocol is in terms which it is unnecessary to quote for present purposes, the United Kingdom not being party to the terms of that Agreement. It is agreed that in terms of this Protocol there is no question of the United Kingdom being liable for any of the substantive costs of the social policy comprised in the Agreement. It is also agreed that the only other costs which could be incurred by the United Kingdom in connection with this Protocol are "administrative costs". It is further agreed that the United Kingdom is, as a matter of fact, paying the same share of those "administrative costs" as it would have been paying had it been a party to the Agreement annexed to the Protocol, namely a full share thereof. There is accordingly no dispute as to what is actually happening. The dispute is as to whether, under United Kingdom law, such payment is ultra vires the Crown. In this connection, Mr Smith for the petitioner submitted that no payment out of the national exchequer may be made without the authority of an Act and then only for the purposes for which the statute has authorised the expenditure (Wade and Bradley on *Constitutional and Administrative Law* (11th ed.), p. 210; *Auckland Harbour Board* v. *R*). The proposition was agreed by Mr Moynihan for the respondent.

A further matter on which there was agreement in the course of the discussion concerns the requirement in some circumstances for authorisation for expenditure by the United Kingdom on Community matters to be by way of Appropriation Act legislation. This arises in any situation in which the expenditure concerned is decided by the Communities to be met other than out of the Community budget. It is accepted for the petitioner that in the event of any of the expenditure in issue falling to be paid other than out of the Community budget, it is the intention of the United Kingdom Government to have such expenditure authorised by appropriate Appropriation Act provision. Senior counsel for the petitioner expressly accepted that in the event of any such requirement, this would be authorised appropriately by such Appropriation Act provision. However, the petitioner contended that the United Kingdom Government was proceeding upon the basis that the expenditure concerned was being met out of the Community **[1205]** budget and the matter fell to be tested upon whether there was United Kingdom statutory authority for payment out of the Consolidated Fund to meet the United Kingdom's share of the expenditure in issue payable out of the Community budget. The Lord Advocate accepted that this was the basis upon which the United Kingdom Government was proceeding and that the matter properly fell to be tested in this way.

It is appropriate now to consider the various United Kingdom statutory and Community provisions founded upon by the respondent as rendering the expenditure in issue properly payable out of the

Consolidated Fund and, accordingly, intra vires the Crown. The respondent's position was explained by Mr Moynihan and, in the final speech, by the Lord Advocate. The Protocol on Social Policy is No 14 of the Protocols annexed to the Treaty of Rome as amended by the Treaty of Union. This was made clear by the terms of art. 239 of the Treaty, as amended, to which reference has already been made. Article 199 of the amended Treaty provides: [his Lordship quoted the terms of art. 199 and continued:]

This provision made it clear, the respondent contended, that the expenditure in issue was envisaged by the Communities as expenditure to be incorporated within the Community budget. The Protocol on Social Policy, in contrast to the Agreement appended thereto, was an agreement between all 12 members of the Community, including the United Kingdom. The penultimate paragraph of the Protocol, which I have already quoted in full, provides that "any financial consequences other than administrative costs entailed for the institutions shall not be applicable to the United Kingdom of Great Britain and Northern Ireland".

Thus, as one of the "High Contracting Parties" agreeing the Protocol itself, although not the Agreement appended thereto, the United Kingdom undertook to contribute the same share of administrative costs as it would have done had it been party also to the Agreement. Accordingly, in terms of art. 199, the United Kingdom agreed that such costs should fall within the Community budget. In particular, no separate provision for such costs was required such as was the case for other expenditure in terms of the second paragraph of art. 199, which I have also already quoted in full. The reason for this was that the Protocol on Social Policy was annexed to and part of the Treaty of Rome. There would be no point in requiring separate provision for the administrative costs in issue when all 12 member states were contributing thereto.

The next stage of the respondent's submission that the expenditure in issue was duly authorised out of the Consolidated Fund, involved the terms of the European Communities Act 1972. The preamble of this Act reads: "An Act to make provision in connection with the enlargement of the European Communities to include the United Kingdom, together with (for certain purposes) the Channel Islands, the Isle of Man and Gibraltar."

The Act was thus to provide the necessary mechanism for giving legal effect domestically to the Community agreements undertaken internationally. Section 2(1) of the 1972 Act provides: [his Lordship quoted the terms of s 2(1) and continued:]

Thus, s 2(1) of the Act made provision regarding directly applicable Treaties. Section 2(2) of the Act makes provision for Treaty provisions which are not directly applicable. In terms of Sched. 1, Pt II, " 'Community obligation' means any obligation created or arising by or under the Treaties, whether an enforceable Community obligation or not". Section 2(3) of the Act provides: "There shall be charged on and issued out of the Consolidated Fund or, if so determined by the Treasury, the National Loans Fund the amounts required to meet any Community obligation to make payments to any of the Communities or Member States".

Section 1(2)(e), as amended, provides that in the 1972 Act "the Treaties" or "the Community Treaties" include "the decision . . . of 24th June 1988, of the Council on the Communities' system of own resources".

Article 1 of the decision of 24 June 1988 provides: [his Lordship quoted the terms of art. 1 and continued:]

Article 2 of the decision defines the revenue which is to constitute "own resources entered in the budget of the Communities". This includes levies and other payments of a specific nature, such as agricultural and customs tariff duty payments and a rate related to VAT, and also application of a rate related to member states' GNP. In terms of art. 6 of the decision, "The revenue referred to in Article 2 shall be used without distinction to finance all expenditure entered in the budget of the Communities".

Accordingly, the United Kingdom required to make payment out of the Consolidated Fund from time to time by way of contribution to expenditure incurred within the Community budget.

In their submissions on behalf of the petitioner, Mr Smith and Mr Brodie agreed that the key issue on the merits was whether or not there was a Community obligation as defined by the 1972 Act to make payment. The question was whether in the provisions founded upon by the respondent there could be found an obligation to make payment to any of the Communities arising by or under the Treaties which comprehended payment to defray the administrative costs of the Social Agreement. The position of the petitioner was that these costs were not covered by the 1988 decision because the Social Agreement fell outwith the ambit of the Community Treaties as recognised by the United Kingdom Parliament. The Social Agreement annexed to the Social Protocol was unique from a Community point of view because it involved the first departure from the principle of **[1206]** implementing common policies. For the first time the question required to be asked: "Is this Community expenditure or is it something different?". The expenditure concerned was not expenditure for the purposes of the 12 members. It was expenditure for the purposes of only 11 of them. The petitioner founded upon the terms of s 1(1) of the European Communities (Amendment) Act 1993 which provides: [his Lordship quoted the terms of s 1(1) and continued:)

This provision demonstrated the manifest intention of Parliament that the Social Protocol was not one of the "Community Treaties". The matter was essentially one of construction of the United Kingdom legislation, namely the 1972 Act, hence the importance of ascertaining which Community provisions were considered by Parliament to be "Treaties" or "Community Treaties" for the purposes of the 1972 Act and, in particular, s 2(1) thereof.

The Lord Advocate submitted that the provisions of the 1993 Act did not avail the petitioner. No qualification of the provisions of s 1(2)(e) of the 1972 Act was introduced by the 1993 Act. Such qualification was necessary before the 1993 Act could have any effect upon the unqualified inclusion of the decision of 24 June 1988 as one of "the Treaties" or "the Community Treaties" for the purposes of the 1972 Act.

The issues between the parties narrowed dramatically at the outset of the hearing with the petitioner's abandonment of his case for the first two declarators originally sought. The case narrowed further in the course of the hearing in respect that potential issues relevant to the outstanding declarator sought turned out to the extent which I have mentioned to be issues not in dispute. In the result, the question in issue on the merits came to be a short one, as was recognised by counsel. Because of the way in which matters developed I have not followed my usual practice of setting out each of counsel's submissions chronologically before adjudicating thereon. Accordingly, no criticism should be implied from my departure from my usual practice with regard to the submissions made, which were clearly presented throughout, however academic in the result some of them came to be. Upon the point left in issue on the merits, I conclude that the submissions of the respondent are correct. In particular, it seems to me clear (1) that in terms of the European Communities Act 1972 payment out of the Consolidated Fund is duly authorised by United Kingdom legislation in respect of any sum payable towards expenditure out of the Community budget in terms of the Council Decision of 24 June 1988; (2) that the administrative costs relating to the Protocol on Social Policy are costs which are to be met by all 12 member states being the "High Contracting Parties" to the Protocol; (3) that those administrative costs comprise expenditure properly entered in the budget of the Communities; and that accordingly (4) the point in issue falls to be decided in favour of the respondent. The matter in issue, so far as the petitioner is concerned, appears to be very much one of the intention of the United Kingdom Parliament. While I accept that this is logically so in that the petitioner's contention is that the necessary authorisation by United Kingdom legislation of contribution to the expenditure in issue is lacking, once authorisation for payment out of the Consolidated Fund for any expenditure out of the Community budget in terms of the Council Decision of 24 June 1988 is established, as I hold it to be, whether the expenditure in issue is properly within that budget or not seems to me to be a matter inevitably of European law. I am not asked by either party to refer that matter to the European Court on that account. This is no doubt logical as no issue arose between the parties in the discussion upon that point of European law. I add only that, had the Community provisions arisen for interpretation domestically, I would have no difficulty in accepting the construction inherent in the respondent's submission.

In coming to the conclusion which I have on the issue on the merits, I have found it unnecessary to take into account a statement made by the Attorney General in the House of Commons on 22 February 1993 in the course of consideration of the European Communities (Amendment) Bill. On that occasion the Attorney General made the following statement: "A number of hon. Members asked about the obligation to share administrative costs of action by the other 11 countries, which is referred to in the social protocol. My view is that the obligation to share those administrative costs is covered by the listing of the own resources decision in section 1(2) of the European Communities Act 1972—I believe that this point is of some interest to the House—assuming that such expenses are included, as seems likely, within the Community budget. If, however, such expenses were not called forward in the Community budget as a whole, in which case there would be the authority that I have just mentioned, expenditure could be made on the authority of votes and on the authority of the annual Appropriation Act alone. In giving authority for that particular expenditure in relation to a treaty obligation, the House will be following exactly the same practice as we follow, for example, in relation to payments to NATO and similar treaties" (HC Debs, Vol. 219, col. 741).

Mr Moynihan for the respondent submitted that it was both competent and appropriate to take account of what the Attorney General said by way of an aid to construction of the 1993 Act, if there otherwise was doubt as to the correct construction of Parliament's intention. Mr Moynihan referred to the case of *Pepper* v. *Hart* and in particular to the speech of Lord Browne-Wilkinson, where he said (at [1993] AC, p. 640) that "the exclusionary rule (as to such statements) should be relaxed so as to permit reference to Parliamentary materials where (a) legislation is ambiguous or obscure, or leads to an absurdity; (b) the material relied upon consists of one or more statements **[1207]** by a Minister or other promoter of the Bill together if necessary with such other Parliamentary material as is necessary to understand such statements and their effect; (c) the statements relied upon are clear. Further than this, I would not at present go".

Mr Moynihan referred to the case of *R* v. *Secretary of State for Foreign and Commonwealth Affairs, ex p. Rees-Mogg*. Lloyd LJ, giving the judgment of the court, said (at [1994] 2 WLR, p. 123B-H):

> If we had thought that the language of section 1(2) of the Act of 1993 was ambiguous, which we do not, Mr Kentridge invited us to look at *Hansard* in order to resolve the ambiguity. The circumstances in which we are permitted to do so were laid down by the House of Lords in *Pepper* v. *Hart* [1993] AC 593. We need not quote from the speech of Lord Browne-Wilkinson in that case. . . .

If there had been any ambiguity, which there is not, we would have regarded this as an appropriate case in which to resort to *Hansard*, in accordance with the principles stated in *Pepper* v. *Hart* [1993] AC 593.

Senior counsel for the petitioner, on this matter, contended that this would not be an appropriate case to seek assistance from what was said in the House of Commons because what was under discussion was a measure amending the original proposed Bill, the amendment was not a Government measure and the minister was not concerned with agreeing with the amendment but advancing objections arising from its acceptance. Albeit that the statement concerned was made in the context referred to by senior counsel, it was nevertheless a ministerial statement which I consider could have been relevant towards construction of the 1993 Act, had such aid been necessary. I do not, however, consider that this is a case where any such aid requires to be invoked. I do not find the legislation concerned either unclear or ambiguous.

As I have indicated, both parties sought a decision upon the merits, although not departing from their positions on preliminary issues. While my decision on the merits in favour of the respondent renders preliminary issues academic, it is appropriate to record what preliminary issues were raised. Mr Moynihan said that the only point on competency being advanced for the respondent was the hypothetical nature of the declarator now sought. He referred to the case of *Macnaughton* v. *Macnaughton's Trs*. In that case Lord Justice Clerk Thomson said (at 1953 SC, p. 392; 1953 SLT, p. 244): "Our Courts have consistently acted on the view that it is their function in the ordinary run of contentious litigation to decide only live, practical questions, that they have no concern with hypothetical, premature or academic questions, nor do they exist to advise litigants as to the policy which they should adopt in the ordering of their affairs. The Courts are neither a debating club nor an advisory bureau. Just what is a live practical question is not always easy to decide and must, in the long run, turn on the circumstances of the particular case. I doubt whether any good purpose is to be served by trying to extract any general rule from the decided cases. Each case as it arises must be considered on its merits, and the Court must make up its mind as to the reality and immediacy of the issue which the case seeks to raise. Unless the Court is satisfied that this is made out, it should sustain the plea of incompetence as it is only with live and practical issues that the Court is concerned."

Mr Moynihan submitted that the present case was hypothetical in respect that it was not known definitely whether the Crown was going to be called upon to meet the expenditure in issue out of Community budget contribution or by separate contribution. In the light of what was said by the Lord Justice Clerk in *Macnaughton's* case the issue raised by the petitioner was accordingly premature and the petition should be dismissed on that account. In anticipation of the submissions for the respondent, Mr Smith referred to an affidavit of the petitioner in which he stated that it was understood that expenditure had been incurred since 1 November 1993. The petitioner had done what he reasonably could to clarify the position about this but it was clear that expenditure had been incurred. Senior counsel on this matter said that he accepted that, if the petitioner succeeded on the issue on the merits, it might be necessary to amend the declarator sought to insert, "unless and until such application is authorised by an Appropriation Act". In the particular circumstances of this particular case, I would not have been disposed to dismiss the petition on the grounds of prematurity but the matter is, of course, academic.

Mr Moynihan next submitted that the petition was irrelevant and lacking in specification. The declarator sought required to be based on sound legal reasons, which were lacking in this case. He referred to Walker on *Civil Remedies* at p. 110 and to *Southern Bowling Club Ltd* v. *Ross* and in particular to what was said by Lord Kincairney at (1902) 4 F, p. 408; (1901) 9 SLT, p. 158. In the present case, the administrative expenses concerned were inextricable from other expenses of Community institutions, the services of which were utilised for many different purposes, only one of which was that to which the present application referred. Senior counsel for the petitioner submitted that mechanical problems of quantification were no sound reason for not granting the declarator sought, if it was otherwise soundly based. Upon the question of relevancy, I sustain the respondent's plea to relevancy in respect of lack of any sound grounds in law for granting the declarator sought, in accordance with my decision on what was treated by parties as the merits of the case. I would not, however, have been inclined to sustain the plea on account of the mechanical difficulty arising in relation to the point mentioned. I also record that, on the matter of specification, the Lord Advocate submitted that the petitioner should state more exactly what was wrong. Had I envisaged this matter as a live issue I would have **[1208]** asked senior counsel for the petitioner to reply to this criticism and in the absence of such reply I do not find it appropriate to comment on this matter.

On the whole matter, I repel the first and second pleas in law for the petitioner of consent and his third plea in law. I sustain the third and eighth pleas in law for the respondent and dismiss the petition.

[Report: Scots Law Times 1995, p. 1201]

INDEX